MW01139568

STUDIES IN BERESHIT (GENESIS)
NEHAMA LEIBOWITZ

עיונים בספר בראשית

בעקבות פרשנינו הראשונים והאחרונים

מאת

נחמה ליבוביץ

מהדורה אנגלית תורגמה ועובדה ע"י אריה ניומן

Studies

in Bereshit (Genesis)

In the Context of Ancient and Modern Jewish
Bible Commentary

by

NEHAMA LEIBOWITZ

Professor of Bible, Tel Aviv University

translated and adapted from the Hebrew

by

ARYEH NEWMAN M.A. Dip. Ling. (Cantab)

Eliner Library

CONTENTS

VAYERA

TOLEDOT

VAYETZE

VAYISHLAH

INTRODUCTION

I. Genesis of the Book

The genesis of the present book can justly be traced to the mimeographed folios of teach-yourself studies in the weekly Jewish Bible readings: *Gilyonot Le-iyyun Befarashat Ha-shavua,* that made their debut on the Eretz Israel and Diaspora scene some thirty years ago. I can recall meeting them for the first time at a Bible study circle held at a religious Zionist youth farm at the height of the Second World War in England intrigued by the questions, particularly, the very difficult ones marked with two asterisks and the promise implied in the legend: "Send your answers to Nehama Leibowitz, Kiryat Moshe, Jerusalem." Originally sponsored by the Mizrachi Women's Organization of America the enterprise was taken over by the Israeli Ministry of Education in 1960. In the autumn of 1971 Nehama announced in a public letter of farewell that the time had come for her to give it up. No better summary of this unusual teacher-student dialogue in Bible study can be given than a reproduction of this letter here. She wrote:

"Many thanks to all my students, near and far, in Israel and overseas, whose questions and replies, perseverance and love of Torah have been a source of strength, pleasure and deepened insight into the profundities of Holy Writ. In the full sense of the phrase, I have learnt more from my students than from anyone else.

"I am especially grateful to those who answered my questions and responded with questions of their own. There were regulars who wrote dutifully week by week, year in year out. Others wrote occasionally, telephoned or even telegraphed, pressing for help in grasping a difficult point ... I wish here to pay tribute to those who contacted me under difficult conditions after a hard day's work, in the burning sun during a break in the field; to the streetsweeper who wrote in the height of a rainstorm after doing his day's stint, to the machinist dropping me a line during the lunch-break amidst the noise of the factory, to the nurse using her precious hours of rest after a back-breaking night shift. There were members of kibbutzim and moshavim who corresponded with me regularly over the years, patiently and affectionately accepting my corrections and reprimands in red ink, the young and not-so-young mothers who found time to study after they had put the children to sleep. There were soldiers who wrote to me under conditions defying description: coastguards, World War II volunteers in the Libyan desert and Jewish Brigade, fighters in the War of Liberation delivering their notes to me personally from a forward position during a chance lull in the Capital's shelling when the postal service was at a standstill, correspondents from the Suez Canal during the War of Attrition, from ambushes in the Golan and from all those guarding the borders of our homeland. To those must be added those distant correspondents in foreign climes (why, oh why do they still remain there!)

"I am enthralled by this vast army of old and young, mothers and girls, teachers male and female, clerks and labourers, veterans and newcomers of all communities, hundreds of thousands (literally!) studying Torah for its own sake. For our joint studies involved no certificates, examinations, marks, prizes; no credits, scholarships, income-tax rebates but simply the joy so deep of the one who studies Torah."

But this of course does not mean the end of Nehama's Bible dialogue. She literally lives Bible. Her students range from the Ministers of State to housewives, generals to privates, and she is equally at home in a village schoolroom as in a university auditorium (she is Professor of Bible at Tel Aviv University) or Kibbutz dining hall. There is scarcely a community or educational institution in Israel that has not felt the impact of her personality and method. Today, through courses she gives to teachers and headmasters, her approach seeps down to grassroot level wherever Bible is taught. In 1956 she was awarded the annual Israel Prize for adult education, by the Ministry of Education in recognition of these services.

Everywhere her goal is the same—to activate the student to teach himself, with the aid of the most famous students of the Bible down the ages, from the Talmudic sages to modern thinkers and commentators of such varied schools as Buber, Kaufman, Hirsch, Dessler and Soloveitchik. In recent years, Nehama has found much in common with contemporary literary criticism, the keynote of which is close reading for different levels of interpretation and nuances of meaning. She is heartily in agreement with those critics who refuse to limit an author's meaning to the one he consciously intended or the one that found most favour with his contemporary audience. But there is all the difference in the world between the scholarly detachment of such modern literary criticism and her deep Jewish religious moral commitment. As one of her students wrote in a recent tribute: "She moulded not only our methods of study but our Jewish outlook, unearthing the religious and ethical message of the Bible for us here and now."

Though the flow of her "Gilyonot" have now ceased, her more popular printed volumes of "Studies in the Weekly Sidra" are still circulating. First produced in English sixteen years ago in response to an invitation from the Torah Education Department of the World Zionist Organization to enable non-Hebrew readers in the far-flung Diasporas to benefit from her method and message, they were translated into French and Spanish and reprinted in the world Jewish press in other languages too, week by week for seven years. Nehama is particularly proud of the use made by rabbis of all persuasions in preparing their pulpit sermons and Bible lessons.

Now she is engaged on what may be termed the "Compleat Nehama Leibowitz"—a carefully pruned and edited version of her Sidra studies throughout the years. The first Hebrew volumes covering Genesis and Exodus respectively have become best sellers in Israel and have run into several editions. The present work is an English version of her *Studies in the Book of Genesis.*

II. The English Edition

At least one of the functions of a translator I feel I have fulfilled. "One should never translate anything one does not admire—a natural affinity should exist between translator and translated".[1] My involvement started with the production of the first weekly leaflets carefully going over my renderings with the author till she considered me capable of carrying out the task unaided. It became even profounder when I used them myself during periods of Bible teaching abroad as Jewish education officer in Australia and New Zealand where I was deeply impressed with the effectiveness of the material.

The latter may be for translation purposes divided into three different strata: first the Bible text proper usually rendered in bold on which I have drawn on three main sources—the Jewish Publication Society's *Hebrew Scriptures* which bases itself stylistically on the *King James* and the *Revised Version,* their new version *The Torah,* and the *New English Bible.* I say "drawn," because in no case have I regarded myself as being bound to any translation. Each quote is determined first by the exigencies of the immediate comment and interpretation. Nowhere have I been consistent in the rendering of terms in the vernacular. My main consideration has been intelligibility, in driving home the interpretation or varieties of interpretation evoked by the text. The use of the archaic singular "thou" and "ye" has been retained, though not consistently in the translation of Biblical texts simply in order to differentiate between singular and plural. It is therefore a case of transference rather than translation,[2] again, in the interests of interpretative intelligibility.

---

[1] E. Nida, *Towards a Science of Translating,* Leiden, 1964, p. 151.
[2] See chapter on "Transference" in Catford, *A Linguistic Theory of Translation,* OUP, 1965, pp. 43–47.

Perhaps the most outstanding example of transference rather than translation in the rendering of the Bible is that of Buber-Rosenzweig who created a kind of special Biblical German dialect in an attempt to reproduce in the vernacular as total a translation as possible. Our aim is far from that. It is on a more amateur and eclectic level—simply to help the reader appreciate the interpretative insights of 'Jewish Bible comment down the ages as presented by the author and see how they spring from the original text. For this purpose we have reproduced the original Hebrew which, after all, is the source, the English being one of the extra veils that must be penetrated by the non-Hebraist before he comes face to face with it.

The second stratum are the earliest classic rabbinic commentators—the Midrashim both legal and homiletic. An attempt here has also been made to reproduce some of the formal aspects of the original and not simply reproduce the sense content.[3] The original has also been appended—since these texts too form part of the Hebrew religious and literary heritage to be studied in their own right. The same applies to Rashi prince of Bible commentators, many of the idioms of modern Hebrew having made their debut in his commentary and to a lesser extent Rambam's monumental code of Judaism. Different is the case of the third stratum: all the other commentaries where the translator has felt entitled and indeed obliged to reproduce a sense or content equivalent, expanding and omitting where necessary in the interests of intelligibility. Whilst use has been made of existing translations of modern Biblical studies and the reference given to extant English versions, the writer has not followed them precisely. I have not deluded myself into imagining that I have avoided the pitfall of an incongruous juxtaposition of modern and archaic. A further difficulty has been the fact that the bulk of the material was translated over a period of seven years in the form of weekly pamphlets. There were

---

[3] Cf.: Bereshit 4 p. 34 my translation of the citation from *Shir-Hashirim Rabbah* where I have tried to preserve the formal correspondence of the Hebrew: נותנים לו אימה, and נותנין עליו אימה by the rendering: "he is given fear" and: "he is given up to fear" respectively.

inevitable changes in style and presentation. In re-editing and revising in the light of the author's own revision and expansion every attempt was made to achieve consistency. But any aspirations to perfection must be disclaimed. The overriding consideration was readability and completion of the book within a reasonable span of time. One challenge we have accepted—that of no untranslatability.[4] We are resigned to a certain loss of information which we have tried to minimalise.[5] The student will compensate for it by his own application.

I am grateful to Providence for what has been for me an extraordinarily fruitful encounter with an outstanding Bible teacher, and to her for the privilege of acting as her interpreter to the English-speaking world. I only hope that I have done her justice and not been guilty of distortion.

---

[4] *Cf*: Roman Jacobson "Linguistic Aspects of Translation" from *On Translation* ed. R. Brower, Harvard, 1954, p. 236.
[5] For a brief summary of the difficulties with particular reference to Bible translation see E. Nida's paper on "Semantic Components in Translation Theory" in *Applications of Linguistics* ed. E. E. Perren et J. L. M. Trim, Cambridge University Press, 1971, pp. 341–348.

III. New and Old Perspectives in Jewish Bible Studies

The uniquely binding and timeless character of the Torah is one of the axioms of Jewish belief. A simple and dogmatic formulation of this is to be found in the prayer book version of Rambam's thirteen principles of faith: "I believe with perfect faith that the message of Moses our teacher ... was true ... that the whole Torah now in our possession is the same that was given to Moses our teacher ... that this Torah will not be changed and that there will never be any other Torah from the Creator blessed be He".[6] Even those thinkers who objected to reducing the whole of Judaism to articles of creed could not dispense with this axiom. Yosef Albo, for instance, discovered three roots or basic principles of Judaism: the existence, providence and revelation of God. In the latter we can again recognise the axiom of *Torah min Hashamayim*—the heavenly or divine origin of Torah. A contemporary Christian summation of this axiom shows its wider impact: "the general conviction has been that the Bible is the religious symbolism par excellence, that through the verbal symbols which make up the total structure of the Bible, the Word of God has been communicated to man." [7]

Torah of course is not synonymous with Bible but refers, in its narrow sense, to the Pentateuch, in the context of a specific Jewish oral and exegetical tradition that too lays claim to

6 Included in many editions of the Jewish prayer book. See *Authorised Daily Prayer Book*, Singer, London p. 89. Rambam's principle is based on the statement in the Mishnah, Sanhedrin Chap. X including "he that says that the Torah is not from heaven" among "those who have no share in the world to come."

7 Dillistone in "Functions of Symbols in Religious Experience," *Metaphor and Symbol*, ed. L. C. Knights and B. Cottle, London, 1960, p. 110.

Sinaitic authority and, in its wider sense, to the whole corpus of Jewish tradition and custom down the ages.

Scientific advances of the 19th century, the decline of faith led to the debunking of the Bible. It was demoted by many from its sacred pedestal and regarded as literature, antiquarial records, a mine of folklore. An ever-latent anti-Judaism catalysed in particular the German schools of Bible Criticism and their documentary theories. Under the impact of archaeological discoveries, the comparisons with the records of other middle east civilizations and in particular the parallels to Biblical themes in Mesopotamean and Canaanite myths and codexes, all sense of reverence for Holy Writ was lost and age-old perspectives recklessly abandoned. The crucial differences between Bible and Babel [8] were overlooked; only the similarities were detected and emphasised. For the Jewish champions of universalism in western Europe all this was so much more oil to grease the wheels of a galloping assimilation. It facilitated their ideology of release from the "medievalist" chains of a Jewish tradition of observance and separation which, in their eyes, remained the only barrier to an age of brotherhood, in which Judaism would take its rightful place as a sublime ethical philosophy, retaining a few, undemanding picturesque reminders of its sectarian past, in particular, those which blended painlessly into the immediate setting. To the early leaders of Reform Judaism the Bible was not a text whose every word was to be deeply studied in the original, in the context of a continuous living tradition. It was a source-book of purple passages useful for adorning a sermon. Apologetics were the order of the day for the ideologically inconvenient texts. Their repudiation of Jewish observance, the Hebrew language and a literal return to Zion and the decanonisation of the Bible were more than a happy coincidence.

Bible perspectives also changed radically in the context of the agonising *kulturkampf* that shook the Talmudist strongholds of

[8] Title of a series of lectures given by Friedrich Delitzsch, anti-semitic German Orientalist in 1902 in which he tried to prove the superiority of Babylonian myth and cult over Judaism. His arguments evoked a flood of protest and rebuttals from many Jewish and Christian scholars.

East Europe from the middle of the nineteenth century onwards. Jewish secular nationalism championed the rebirth of Hebrew, glorified the Biblical period, eagerly drew on Hebrew sources of the past but gave them a secular and humanist colouring. There was a deliberate divorcement from any religious inspiration and an antagonism to what were regarded as rabbinic accretions to the pristine purity of an almost pagan Canaanite-Hebraicism. The Bible was aggrandised at the expense of rabbinic traditions. The written text was idolised, the Oral Tradition neglected or at most carefully pruned to the exclusion of halachic material.[9] The Bible became "the central classic of Jewish culture"[10] no longer: "together with its oral interpretation the word of God ... and book of rules regulating every activity".[11]

In reaction to these two different winds of change—the hard core of those who came to be dubbed as "orthodox" went also back to the written Torah to a deeper study in order to prove

[9] Bialik, the poet laureate of the Hebrew national renaissance (1873–1934) denounced this imbalance and made it the subject of his essay on *Halacha and Aggada* (1916): "the whole world is but Aggada ... of Halacha there is not a trace ... A generation is growing up in an atmosphere of mere phrases and catchwords, and a kind of go-as-you-please Judaism is being created out of the breath of empty words. Our cries are nationalism, revival, literature, creation, Hebrew education, Hebrew thought, Hebrew labour, and these things hang by the gossamer thread of some kind of love—love of the land, love of the language, love of the literature. But what is this love-in-the-air worth? Love? but where is duty? Whence can it come? ... if you wish to build: "make ordinances for you" (Nehemiah 10.1). "That is how our ancestors began to build ... more Halachah than Aggadah" from the translation by Sir Leon Simon, published by Zionist Federation of Great Britain and Ireland 1944, p. 28.

[10] From the introduction to the teaching of Bible in State schools in the official syllabus, issued by the Israeli Ministry of Education and Cultude in 1955, Government Printer, p. 15.

[11] *op. cit. ibid*, from the introduction to teaching of Bible in State *Religious* schools. The contrast between the traditional and secular approach to Bible study is well brought out in these two separate introductions. See Aryeh Newman, "New Curriculum for the Sabra" *Jewish Life*, journal of Orthodox Jewish Congregations of America, vol. XXVI, No. 3 Feb. 1959, pp. 34–40.

its inextricable connection with the Oral Tradition and the impossibility of divorcing it from the corpus of religious observances. Monumental Pentateuch commentaries in Hebrew appeared, straddling the 19th century, starting with *Haketav Vehakabbalah*[12] followed by *Malbim, Haamek Davar* and *Torah Teminah*. These were paralleled in the vernacular by those of Hirsch and Hoffman, first appearing in German but in recent years translated into English and Hebrew. Each in their own way examined every nuance, letter and word of the Biblical text in the light of ancient rabbinic interpretation and commentary. Malbim developed a ·whole system of Biblical linguistics [13]—grammatical, syntactic and semantic usage to account for the findings of rabbinic exegesis. He wished to demonstrate that the latter was no arbitrary system doing violence to the text but arose organically out of a profound feel for the rules of Biblical language, The Netziv in his introduction to the *Haamek Davar* propounded a surprisingly modern definition of the difference between poetry and prose to account for the multiple meaning of Holy Writ. The Pentateuch was by its own definition *shira*. The command at the end of Deuteronomy "Write me down this *shira*" (song) referred to the whole Torah. Surely, Netziv asks, the Torah with a few exceptions was not written in the *form* of poetry! The reference must be to its inner character, to its allusive and metaphorical quality. Poetry, he wrote, is not as explicit as prose is. The meaning must be supplied. No homiletics are involved in this process. On the contrary, the implicit meaning is the heart of poetry. Similarly the so-called hidden implications of the Biblical text are its real meaning. To him the Pentateuch was one grand poem whose meaning must be explicated at different levels,[14] Common to all

---

[12] See index of commentaries for this and other commentators mentioned.

[13] In the treatise *Ayelet Ha-shahar* usually printed together with the first volume of his commentary (Leviticus).

[14] *Cf*.: Owen Barfield in "The Meaning of the word 'Literal' " in *Metaphor and Symbol op. cit.* p. 48: "When we turn to sentences which convey a secondary meaning, whilst still in some measure retaining the primary or literal one we have already crossed the frontier between

was the illumination of the text in the light of rabbinic tradition, a refusal to divorce it from its timeless meaning and contemporary relevance. The issues of emancipation, return to Zion, are writ large in the pages of these commentaries even as those of religious persecution and doctrinal heresy, in those of their medieval precursors. They would probably have heartily endorsed the words of a modern critic when he asserted that "excessive preoccupation with the historical and literal reveals a symbolic and critical deafness".[15]

If however the attacks on the Bible of scientific scholarship on the one hand, and Haskala bibliolatry, on the other, evoked a spate of formidable commentary aimed at harmonising Written and Oral Tradition, they only hardened the opposition of the Yeshivot to modifying their curriculum and alloting time to the study of Torah. Bible study was the hallmark of *maskilim* (the Hebrew secularists) and Christian scholars.

Actually concentration on Talmud to the exclusion of Torah in its narrow sense has a long polemic history behind it, starting with the banning of the Ten Commandments from the daily prayers in the Second Temple times "on account of the arguments of the heretics".[16]

---

prose and poetry." Or Roland Barthes who distinguishes between "transitive" and "intransitive" language. The latter is "capable of sustaining more than one sense. It is enigmatic like an oracle and the critic composes rather than recovers the sense of it with the aid of vital elements in his situation"—from H. M. Davidson's "The Critical Position of Roland Barthes" *Criticism* ed. L. S. Dembo, university of Wisconsin Press, London, 1968, p. 96.

[15] *op. cit.* p. 97.

[16] "That they should not say, Only these were given to Moses on Sinai" (Yerushalmi, Berakhot 1, 5). See Eliner: "History of the Reading of the Ten Commandments" Mayanot, vol. III published by Dept. for Torah Education and Culture in the Diaspora, World Zionist Organization, 1963, pp. 125–30. Also Rabbi R. Katznelbogen (Hebrew), Symposium on Science and Judaism, *Emuna, Dat U-madda* ("Faith, Religion and Science") 11th annual conference on Jewish Thought, published by Israeli Ministry of Education, Torah Culture Dept. Jerusalem, 5726, pp. 11–23.

In those early days it was first the Sadducees, then the Christians followed by the Karaites who respectively took their stand on the written text of the Scripture and repudiated Oral tradition enshrined in Mishnah and Talmud, little realising that what they were doing was to substitute their own interpretation in support of their specific needs and ideology. Thus the Sadduccees "were not inclined to let their devotion to Torah restrict their political interests ... they would not allow the validity of Oral Tradition as an interpretation of the Torah whereby its authority could be extended indefinitely into every department of life." [17] "The Church was faced by this difficulty, that its own position depended largely on the witness of Scripture and according to that Scripture the Jews had been the chosen people of God ... the Church solved this problem by an act of sheer usurpation, boldly declaring that Christians and no longer Jews were the true Israel, that the Scriptures belonged of right to the Christians and not to the Jews and that Christians alone were competent to interpret them ...".[18] Rashi's interpretation of the Talmudic dictum: "don't indulge your children in too much recitation (higayon)" to mean "do not accustom them to too much Bible study because it is distracting" [19] has been a guideline in the laying down of the curriculum and at times a source of controversy and re-interpretation in Jewish religious academies down the centuries. It did not prevent however the flowering of Jewish Biblical scholarship which found expression in the classic commentaries of, to name only a few, Rashi, Ibn Ezra, Redak, Ramban from which Christian scholarship drew inspiration. But the starting point of Jewish Biblical commentary was the supreme authority of Oral Tradition, first officially recorded in the Mishnah.

[17] Travers Herford *The Pharisees*, Allen and Unwin, London, 1924 p. 29. See also chap. III p. 53ff.
[18] *Op. cit.* p. 222.
[19] Berakhot 28b. See Katznelbogen *op. cit.* note 16 and E. Urbach "The Educational Ideal of Judaism" (Hebrew) in vol. 2 of same series, *Hinukh Ha-adam Ve-yi'udo* (Man's Education and Destiny), 1967, Government Printer, Jerusalem 1967 pp. 13–14.

The latter, as Danby points out in the introduction to his translation of the Mishnah [20] "maintains that the authority of those rules, customs and interpretations which had accumulated around the Jewish system of life and religion was equal to the authority of the Written Law itself, even though they found no place in the Written Law. This, again is but an assertion (known also in other religious and legal systems) that side by side with a written code there exists a living tradition with power to interpret the written code, to add to it, and even at times to modify it or ignore it as might be needful in changed circumstances, and to do this authoritatively. Inevitably the inference follows that the living tradition (the Oral Law) is more important than the Written Law, since the 'tradition of the elders', besides claiming an authority and continuity equal to that of the Written Law, claims also to be its authentic and living interpretation and its essential complement."

The impact of the modern return to Zion, the renaissance of Hebrew, the growth of the national Bible-centred school system led to a flowering of Bible study richer in perspective than a purely historical and dryasdust scholarly approach and yet making use of its findings. The student's confrontation with the Biblical military campaigns, for example, was illumined by an encounter with the actual terrain. Above all a newly-awakened national pride, direct contact with the soil of the homeland, re-living of the process of return and redemption spelt out in its pages stimulated a re-reading of the Bible and prompted a drastic re-appraisal of the conclusions of Higher Criticism. The records of antiquity only served to underscore the uniqueness of Israel —its monotheism in a polytheistic world, its ethical message and special destiny unparalleled in the annals of mankind. The data on fertility cults, the codexes, the magic and demonology revealed where Judaism differed, shed light on many a prohibition,[21] uncovered the moral of many a story, explained the

[20] Clarendon Press, Oxford 1933, xvii.
[21] *e.g.* Exodus 23, 19: "You shall not boil a kid in its mother's milk" see Cassuto's *Commentary on the Book of Exodus* p. 305.

point of an omission or apparently superfluous observation.[22] Meeting the Bible critics on their own ground Yehezkel Kaufmann penned his monumental history of the Israelite religion. By dint of an acute analysis of the text and penetrating contrasts with contemporary records he made out a convincing brief for the early Israelite monotheistic revolution described in Scripture as opposed to the picture of later gradual evolution emerging from the patchwork quilt of sources discovered by the Higher Critics.

From an entirely different angle a modern philosophic restatement of Judaism inspired by close reading of the Bible emanated from Franz Rosenzweig and Martin Buber who both collaborated on the unusual Bible translation that we have already referred to. Buber's philosophy of dialogue and ethical Zionism was inextricably connected with constant listening to the Divine message coming through the words of the Bible. Admittedly this new national Israel school of Bible critics no longer subscribed to the doctrinal formulations of the traditionalists. But, on the other hand, they no longer shared the prejudices of their Bible-denigrating iconoclastic predecessors, nor were they oblivious to the value of rabbinic tradition. They had come back to the close-reading approach of their saintly forbears even though they had become estranged from their faith and observance.

A direct demolition of the documentary theories and argument for the unity of the Biblical text together with a verse by verse commentary summarising the trends of modern scholarship, unfortunately uncompleted, was produced by U. Cassutto, late professor of Bible at the Hebrew University, himself an observant Jew, but, as he notes,[23] "It was not my object to defend any particular viewpoint or any particular exegetical method, but only to arrive at a thorough understanding of the Torah's meaning, whatever that might be..." He was well aware that his

---

[22] e.g. Exodus 21, 31 "whether it gores a son . . or a daughter . . ." see Hertz *Pentateuch and Haftorahs*, additional notes F, Soncino, London, 1938 one vol. edition pp. 405–6.

[23] *Commentary on Genesis I*, translated from the- Hebrew by Israel Abrahams, Magnes Press, Hebrew University, Jerusalem, 1961, p. 4.

approach would be suspect by both the scientific and traditional scholar. "There are those, on the one hand, who are accustomed to read the Scriptures in the light of homiletical interpretation and think it wrong to deviate from the explanations that they received from their teachers and from the approach to which they have become used since childhood; and, on the other hand there are those who see in the documentary hypothesis an assured and enduring achievement of science, an impregnable structure... The one group, which is well acquainted with the rabbinic dictum that every verse retains its simple meaning, must admit that the sincere endeavour to comprehend the words of the Torah according to their primary sense, and to fathom the ultimate purport of Scripture, cannot be regarded as something contrary to the spirit of the Bible itself. The other group, which is well aware that science has no dogmas, must grant that there is no scientific theory, however much it may be favoured, which is entitled to permanent acceptance and may not be criticised or replaced by another theory."

The rehabilitation of the Jewish approach to Bible study at academic and scholarly levels was paralleled by a far more promising and radical departure at the grassroots. The fact that the Bible was the central literary and religious text of primary and secondary schools in the renascent Jewish community in Palestine and subsequently the sovereign state of Israel set in motion a new dialogue with Torah dictated by pedagogic considerations. For 12 years, for one to two periods daily the Israeli pupil and teacher grappled with Tenach. In the general a-religious schools national and literary approaches dominated, in the religious, observant ones—these were reinforced and coloured by faith and dominated by the traditional commentaries. Common to both were the insights of Palestinography and archaeology. Outside of these developments the Yeshivot concentrated on Talmud leaving Tenach to the private predilection of students in their spare time and to the weekend reading of the synagogue Bible lessons with commentaries. But it was teachers with this Talmudic background who often found themselves in the modern school system faced with the challenge of Bible teaching.

In this context must be placed the contribution of Nehama Leibowitz. Out of her classroom confrontations and experiments with all ages and outlooks she evolved an approach and teaching technique which in breadth and depth catered to the representatives of almost every nuance of the ideological spectrum. No insight into the text whether it emanated from impeccably traditional sources or theologically suspect ones was disqualified provided, as she herself points out (Vayishlah 4) "it satisfied the primary demand of interpretation: response to the spirit, tone and intention of the narrative."

This universalistic principle is the same that was adopted by Rambam in his commentary to Ethics of the Fathers: "Accept the truth from wherever it may come." What is the truth of a text? Is there one truth or perhaps many? Jewish tradition has always recognised several levels of interpretation of the Torah— primary meaning — *peshat;* secondary — *derash;* allegorical — *remez* and esoteric or mystic — *sod.* They all complement each other and have their specific terms of reference, without of course prejudicing the norms of religious observance or the application of Jewish law (halacha). There are as many readings of the Torah as readers.

Nehama ransacked the whole treasury of Jewish comment down the ages from the earliest Midrashim to contemporary commentators, in the process resurrecting from oblivion many little known works which have been reprinted for the first time for centuries in response to the demand set up by her quotations from them. The purpose was not however dryasdust scholarship but to provide grist for the living dialogue between reader and Torah text. Hitherto close reading of the Bible had been regarded as the privilege of the revivalist, the mystic and fundamentalist. Nehama made it the hallmark of any intelligent and self-respecting Bible study whatever the private views of the reader on God and religious practice. She has illustrated the deep critical insight of the traditional commentators who in the depth of their interpretation and involvement exhausted almost every possible angle of approach to the text. The latter has as it were unlocked its secrets, and revealed the intricacies of its patterning, the meaningfulness of every syllable, word and phrase to those who have had the patience and the dedication to understand it. The concept of *Torah min Hashamayim* is dramatically illustrated for the believer by the seemingly infinite variety of insights that a close study of Holy Writ reveals. The more one probes, with the aid of classic commentary and intelligent unprejudiced but involved application, the more delicate the discovery. For the humanist, the so called non-believer, the sceptic, the exercise is equally justified as part of the discipline of close reading and literary analysis which the study of any classic text calls for. He is also looking for an appropriate and adequate explanation.[24] The results for both will be surprisingly similar.

But one word of warning especially in view of the large part taken by literary analysis of the text in the following pages— a word of warning forcefully formulated by T. S. Eliot:[25] "The 'greatness of' literature cannot be solely determined by literary standards, though we must remember that whether it is literature or not can be determined by only literary standards. The persons who enjoy these writings solely because of their literary merits are essentially parasites ... I could fulminate against men of letters who have gone into ecstasies over 'the Bible as literature' the Bible as 'the noblest monument of English prose' ... the Bible has had a *literary* influence upon English literature not because it has been considered as literature, but because it has been considered as the Word of God. And the fact that men of letters now discuss it as 'literature' probably indicates the *end* of its 'literary' influence." The same could be said of Torah in the Jewish context. The medium is literary, the material is linguistic. As our Sages were wont to say: "The Torah speaks

---

24 *Cf.*: Angus McIntosh et M. K. Halliday, "Some Thoughts on Style" in *Patterns of Language*, Longmans, 1966, p. 86: "I imply by appropriacy that there must always be some explanation (whether we find it or not) of a particular piece of linguistic activity, however. unexpected it may have been in the situation where it so occurred."
25 *Selected Prose*, essay on "Religion and Literature," Penguin 873, pp. 33–34.

in the language of men": "The Creator Who knows the thoughts of man, chose to communicate the highest truth on which His world was built through sublime artistry—omitting all that did not contribute towards His Divine purpose and investing every word and letter with infinite depths of meaning. The Torah according to the traditional view, is no mere literal recording of historical events, a chronicle of facts, scientific or otherwise, but a highly selective manual of moral and religious lessons which are illustrated in the main developments in the universe since its creation seen from the vantage point of its Divine Author. Rabbinic commentary from the Midrashim onward has devoted much labor to uncovering the consummate literary artifice and technique embedded in the sacred text . . . Anomalies in order and phraseology are immediately explained on the grounds of literary technique and the aims and purpose of the narrative." [26]

Of course there are two types of literary criticism "that which laboriously constructs time-and-place bound context of each work" [27] an effort made by Cassutto to which we have already referred, and "that which tacitly or explicitly uses modern canons of language and literary evaluation." [27] To any interpretation exercise there are three elements—the author, the text and reader. The emphasis of each and everyone of these will vary according to person time and place but some account must be taken of all three. When we accept the principle of the inspired nature of Torah and its peculiarly binding relationship on us as Jews as the source of our beliefs, norms of conduct and identity we take account of its Divine authorship. From then on the text reigns supreme illumined by the comment of centuries. From that comment we must separate Torah Sheb'al Peh—the binding Oral Tradition which determines Halacha, the religious code governed by its own internal rules—not subject to the whims of the reader. But its rules, its interpretation do not disqualify the insight of the serious reader who in every genera-

[26] From "The Devout Jew and his Literature" by Aryeh Newman, in *Jewish Life* vol. XXV, 6 Aug. 1958.
[27] Enkvist, Linguistics and Style, OUP, 1964, p. 53.

tion has enriched our understanding of Torah. The reader of course has a duty—to equip himself for the task in the best manner possible in order to be able to develop those insights and make a judicial evaluation which will be "true to the work and not a distorted version of it." [28] Our best precaution against over-subjectivity is "to take everything into account; it must find a place in a system of meaning for every detail." [29] This has been the basic rule observed by all our traditional commentators and underlined in Nehama's *Studies*. But even after all these safeguards, ultimately everything passes through the prism of the reader's mind which will colour any comment of his on the text and reflect his situation and context.

Our classic commentators show their individual approaches and reflect the pressures of private and public experiences. On the one hand, we have Ibn Ezra and Redak who emphasise content rather than form: "we cannot supply a reason for all the additions and omissions (*Hayyei Sara* p. 236) it preserves the sense rather than the wording." But the majority of commentators from the Midrashim through Rashi to modern times have unearthed a fascinating variety and depth ₋of meaning from the principle of accepting no redundancy in Holy Writ. Rashi in his outstanding admission: "I do not know what it teaches us"—his comment to Gen 28.5 s.v. "the mother of Jacob and Esau" (p. 286) only goaded later commentators to supply that lacuna. Nehama herself makes no secret where her sympathies lie "We shall not follow Ibn Ezra or Redak and others . . ." (*Vayiggash* 6 footnote 1 first para). Syntactical anomalies can reveal a wealth of interpretation. Indeed the question arises as to whether there is a real opposition between the literal and homiletic meaning of a text. Very often we find as Nehama writes that "the homiletical explanation is simply another and deeper level of the real meaning of the text." (*Vayeshev* 3). The Torah by its very nature demands multiple interpretation. Anything less does not do justice to its terms of reference and

[28] E. D. Hirsch Jr. in "Literary Valuation as Knowledge" *Criticism op. cit.* p. 56.
[29] *Op. cit.* p. 99.

texture. The surface and deeper meanings correspond to the body and soul of the narrative. They are particularly obvious in the two levels of the Patriarchal stories—their individual lives as the individual Jacob and Esau and the archetypal Israel and Edom.[30]

To sum up we may say with certainty that our relationship with Torah is one of mutuality. Both have an enormous potential. The text is luminous—belongs as far as we are concerned to the sphere of the holiest. But to shine forth, shed its light it requires the application of the reader's mind and heart: both of them. Our reading must not be a matter of the heart only—an undiscriminating untrained display of emotion and fervour nor of the mind only—a dryasdust exercise of the intellect. The more fervent and emotionally involved our intellectual application, the deeper our insight. These are not merely my own sentiments but rather a free English rendering of those expressed by the great Jewish poet, mystic and moralist Moshe Hayyim Luzzato in the opening paragraphs of *Derekh Etz Hayyim*[31] where he writes:

"Once you begin to understand Holy Writ, reading the text again and again, probing deeper and deeper, illumination flashes forth like flames from a coal, assuming many different forms and shades. For infinite are the facets of Torah. Tradition tells us that each individual Jewish soul is rooted in the Torah. Six hundred thousand interpretations corresponding to the grand total of the Jewish people! This is the force of the text (Jeremiah 23.29): "As the hammer shatters the rock.""

ARYEH NEWMAN

Jerusalem, Erev Rosh Hashana 5733

[30] *Cf.*: L. C. Knights, *Metaphor and Symbol op. cit.* in "Idea and Symbol" p. 139: "The sacrifice of Isaac whilst remaining a moving story firmly anchored in the actual, it demands interpretation, demands it by the very manner of its telling, by the kind of claim it makes on the reader and for the sake of the meaning that we sense within it." Knights cites the same passage from *Mimesis* quoted by Nehama in Vayera 6 p. 196.

[31] Included in the Lewin-Epstein edition of *Messilat Yesharim*, Jerusalem, 5720 pp. 75–76.

MAN IN THE IMAGE OF GOD

וַיֹּאמֶר אֱלֹהִים

נַעֲשֶׂה אָדָם בְּצַלְמֵנוּ כִּדְמוּתֵנוּ.

God said:

Let us make man in Our image and likeness

(1, 26)

Man was created on the sixth day and was different from all
that preceded him. Only his creation is recorded in two stages
First God made known His intention to create him and after·
wards the account of his actual creation is recorded.

Man qualified for a special preamble. This separate and
distinctive treatment was, Ramban points out, a measure of his
pre-eminence and his difference in kind from the rest of the
animal world whose creation was announced in the immediately
preceding passage.

In *Rechasim Lebik'a* another and more arresting reason is
advanced for the special preamble: "let us make" accorded to
man. It paralleled the announcement heralding the creation of
woman. There God had said beforehand: "It is not good for
Man to be alone..." These explanatory announcements were
not made in the case of other creatures. Their creation was announced without any such preliminary fanfares. Why? "They
illustrated God's fairness to all His creatures in not intimidating
them by suddenly springing on them a ruler and governor,
without warning. On the contrary, he said to them, 'come let
us make man' like a king about to levy a tax on his people,
announcing: 'Come let us levy a tax on the country in your interest'." [1]

Others have found the source of man's distinction in having been created last, Radak states: that "it was a sign

1

of man's honour and elevated status that he was created last to make known that all mortal creatures were created for his sake and he was made the lord of all them."

Dubnow in the *Biur* elaborates on the same theme: "Man was the crown of creation, a little lower than the angels, possessor of an immortal soul, capable of an intelligent acknowledgement of His creator and ruling the world by dint of his wisdom. Let us make Man, the Creator announced. In other words, after I have created all the foregoing for the sake of man, to supply his needs and enjoyments, let the master enter his palace."

Man's status as the aim of creation and his uniqueness are underlined by the sublime phraseology describing his creation:

וַיִּבְרָא אֱלֹהִים אֶת־הָאָדָם בְּצַלְמוֹ
בְּצֶלֶם אֱלֹהִים בָּרָא אֹתוֹ
זָכָר וּנְקֵבָה בָּרָא אוֹתָם.

So God created man in His own image;
In the image of God created He him;
male and female created He them.   (1, 27)

The style of the verse is poetic and elevated, the fact of man's creation being referred to three times. The chasm separating man from the rest of creation is stressed twice in the statement that he was created in the image of God. Both the duties, responsibilities and glory of man derive from this. In this book *Dat Umadda* (Religion and Science), Prof. Gutmann dwells on the term: "the image of God" (p. 265):

> *Zelem* (image) refers to the personal relationship that can only be found between "persons". The personality of man is placed vis-à-vis the personality of God. For there is a religious approach (not Jewish) that sees the religious ideal in the effacement of man's personality. Man's personality is regarded (according to this approach) as a barrier between him and things . . . but this is not the case with an ethical religion. Only as long as man is a person can he preserve his relationship with God. Man is a

2

world of his own and he is not required to merge himself in nature.

In other words, every individual is equally significant before God, since every man was created in His image.

לפיכך נברא אדם יחידי [דהיינו, הזוג הראשון נברא יחידי], ללמדך, שכל המאבד נפש אחת מעלה עליו הכתוב כאילו איבד עולם מלא וכל המקיים נפש אחת מעלה עליו הכתוב כאילו קיים עולם מלא (סנהדרין לז, ע"א במשנה).

Therefore man was created on his own, to teach you that whoever destroys one soul is regarded by the Torah as if he had destroyed a whole world and whoever saves one soul, is regarded as if he had saved a whole world.   (Mishnah Sanhedrin 37a)

The uniqueness of the individual, a world to himself, unrepeatable is vividly portrayed in the continuation of the same Mishnah:

ולהגיד גדולתו של הקב"ה, שאדם טובע כמה מטבעות בחותם אחד — כולן דומין זה לזה. ומלך מלכי המלכים הקב"ה טבע כל אדם בחותמו של אדם הראשון ואין אחד מהם דומה לחברו (שם).

The greatness of the Holy One blessed be He is thus demonstrated. For whereas when man prints many coins from one die, each one is a replica of the other, the Supreme King of Kings, the Holy One blessed be He stamped every man with the die of Adam and yet no one exactly resembles his fellow.

Man as soon as he was created received a special divine blessing. However, he was not the first creature to be blessed by God, but had been preceded by the fishes. The content of both blessings is similar but a very significant difference can be detected. Compare the blessing accorded the fishes:

— **And God blessed them,** saying,
be fruitful and multiply   (1, 22)
with the blessing received by man —
Then God blessed them and God said unto them,
be fruitful and multiply.   (1, 28)

The fish do not qualify for a special address to them by God. They are merely granted the power to be fruitful and multiply.

3

This is their blessing. Man, however, besides being given the power to be fruitful and multiply, is especially *told by God* to be fruitful and multiply and is conscious of his power to do so. What is merely an impersonal fact with regard to the rest of the animal creation is a conscious fact with regard to man. A similar idea is to be found in the statement in *Pirkei Avot* (3.14).

חביב אדם שנברא בצלם ;
חיבה יתירה — נודעת לו שנברא בצלם.

Beloved is man since he was created in God's image; But it was by a special love that it was made known him that he was created in God's image.

Man who was created in God's image is charged with a special task over and above those applying to the rest of creation .

וַיְבָרֶךְ אֹתָם אֱלֹהִים וַיֹּאמֶר לָהֶם אֱלֹהִים
פְּרוּ וּרְבוּ
וּמִלְאוּ אֶת־הָאָרֶץ וְכִבְשֻׁהָ
וּרְדוּ בִּדְגַת הַיָּם וּבְעוֹף הַשָּׁמַיִם
וּבְכָל־חַיָּה הָרֹמֶשֶׂת עַל הָאָרֶץ.   (1, 28)

And God blessed them, and God said unto them:
Be fruitful, and multiply.
And fill the earth, and subdue it:
And rule over the fish of the sea and over the birds of heaven;
and over every living thing that moveth upon the earth;

The phrase "subdue it" כבשה is rather puzzling at first glance, bearing as it does a bellicose significance which is at variance with the peaceful ideals that our sages considered to be the goal of mankind. Indeed the very origin of man in one single pair was, according to them, activated by the Divine wish to prevent war between mankind. This point is made in the Tosefta cited in the Talmud, *Sanhedrin* 88b:

4

אדם נברא יחידי בעולם, שלא יהו משפחות מתגרות זו בזו. ומה עכשו שנברא יחידי מתגרות זו בזו, אילו נבראו שנים על אחת כמה וכמה!

Man was created alone in the world to prevent inter-family feud. Now if in spite of the fact that he was created alone, strife has developed between them, all the more so if two would have been created!

The Mishnah we have already referred to in Sanhedrin goes further and derives from the creation of the first man and woman the principle of the brotherhood of man and the condemnation of any racial theory.

לפיכך נברא אדם יחידי . . . מפני שלום הבריות, שלא יאמר אדם לחברו : אבא גדול מאביך.

For this reason man was created alone, for the sake of peace between mankind, so that one man should not say to his fellow: My father was greater than yours!

The blessing therefore to "subdue it" cannot refer to man being bidden to make war on his neighbour. Ramban enlightens us on this point. Man he says, was thereby given dominion over the earth to do as his will with the rest of the animal creation, to build, uproot, plant, mine metal from the earth and the like. The phrase, therefore, refers rather to man's conquest of the desert and his constructive and civilising endeavours to build and inhabit the world, harness the forces of nature for his own good and exploit the mineral wealth around him. In the words of Isaiah: "the world was not created to be waste, but to be inhabited" (14,19). It was man's privilege accorded him by his Creator to have dominion over the creation and to rule over the fish of the sea and fowl of the air and over every living thing that moved.

The order of creation also sets man up as the pinnacle of it all, as he comes after the fishes on the fifth day and animals on the sixth. Let us cite once again from the words of Gutmann on this theme:

5

Man is not subservient to the world. The forces of nature are not supernatural ones that are superior to him. But he stands on the side of God against nature.

Man is in our sidra addressed in the second person by God who directs His gaze from above to the earth below. The psalmist in Psalm 8, as he surveys the heavens and their hosts and senses at one and the same time both his insignificance in the whole universe and his honoured position as a ruler on earth, directs his gaze from below to the Above, addressing God in the second person:

כִּי אֶרְאֶה שָׁמֶיךָ מַעֲשֵׂה אֶצְבְּעֹתֶיךָ
יָרֵחַ וְכוֹכָבִים אֲשֶׁר כּוֹנָנְתָּה –
מָה אֱנוֹשׁ כִּי תִזְכְּרֶנּוּ
וּבֶן אָדָם כִּי תִפְקְדֶנּוּ
וַתְּחַסְּרֵהוּ מְּעַט מֵאֱלֹהִים
וְכָבוֹד וְהָדָר תְּעַטְּרֵהוּ.
תַּמְשִׁילֵהוּ בְּמַעֲשֵׂי יָדֶיךָ
כֹּל שַׁתָּה תַחַת רַגְלָיו:
צֹנֶה וַאֲלָפִים כֻּלָּם וְגַם בַּהֲמוֹת שָׂדָי.
צִפּוֹר שָׁמַיִם וּדְגֵי הַיָּם עֹבֵר אָרְחוֹת יַמִּים.

When I consider Thy heavens, the work of Thy fingers, the moon and the stars, which Thou hast ordained; What is man, that Thou art mindful of him? and the son of man, that thou visitest him?

For Thou hast made him a little lower than angels, and hast crowned him glory and honour. Thou madest him to have dominion over the works of Thy hands; Thou hast put all things under his feet: All sheep and oxen, yea, and the beasts of the field; The fowl of the air, and the fish of the sea, and whatsoever passeth through the paths of the seas.

Questions for Further Study

1. בצלמו: בדפוס העשוי לו, שהכל נברא במאמר והוא נברא בידים, שנאמר
(תהלים קל"ט, ה) "ותשת עלי כפכה", נעשה כמטבע העשויה ע"י השם
שקורין קווי"ן בלעז. "בצלם אלהים ברא אותו": פרש לך, שאותו צלם המתוקן
לו – צלם דיוקן יוצרו הוא.

"In his image": in the mould that had been cast for him; for all
else had been created by word, but he by hand, as it is stated
(Psalm 139, 5): "Thou hast laid Thy hand upon me." He was
stamped as a coin is minted. "In the image of God he created
him"—the verse goes on to explain that the same image prepared
for him was indeed the image of his Maker.

(Rashi on Gen. 1, 27)

"ויברא אלהים את האדם בצלמו" – שהוא עתה בעולם.

"So God created man in his image"—the one now in the world.

(Lekah Tov)

Since the phrase "in his image" can be taken to refer to man as
many have imagined, the text proceeds to specify: "in the image
of God" as the sages say: "i.e. such and such a thing." There
are countless examples of this in the Torah and Holy Writ.

(Kaspi)

(a) What is the difference between the above explanations?
(Have we three or only two separate interpretations?)

(b) Which commentator have we followed in our discussion
of the sidra?

2. "in his image" in the image of man. Alternatively: "in the image
of God." Awesomely: "in the image of God He created him."

(Bechor Shor)

What does he mean by "awesomely"? Hebrew: על דרך האיום
—literally: "the terrible or awful approach": Cf.: the phrase:
"great and terrible God" or Blake in *Tiger Tiger*: "thy awful
symmetry."

3. "in the image of God he created him." Cf.: "and at the hand
of man, even at the hand of every man's brother, will I require the
life of man" (Gen. 9, 5) and: "The man who commits adultery

with a man's wife, even if he who commits adultery with his neighbour's wife." (Lev. 20, 10)   (Shadal)

(a) What is common to all three verses?

(b) Which of the explanations in question 1 does Shadal follow?

---

1 The question of the use of the plural in the phrase "let *us* make" that has preoccupied the commentators of all ages is not specifically related to our theme here, namely, the difference between man and the rest of creation. Incidentally, Saadia's explanation in his *Emunot Vedeot* commends itself best of all to us: "we have here a typical Hebrew idiom where the first person plural future is singular in connotation as well. Cf,: Num. 22, 6: "Let us smite him," and Dan. 2, 36: "This is the dream, and we will tell the interpretation thereof to the king." Cf.: the majestic "we" in English which is used with a singular connotation as *we* have done just now!

NOT GOOD FOR MAN TO BE ALONE

Every item specified in the step-by-step account of creation
concludes with the refrain: "God saw that it was good." The
story is rounded off with a similar refrain, but of a more elaborate and finalised nature:

וַיַּרְא אֱלֹהִים אֶת־כָּל־אֲשֶׁר עָשָׂה וְהִנֵּה־טוֹב מְאֹד

And God saw all that He had made
and behold it was very good. (1, 31)

Not only was every part of the whole "good," in its own right,
but of the creation, as a whole, the harmony between its every
part could it justly be said: "and behold it was very good."
Only the creation of man does not evoke the phrase: "And God
saw that it was good." Some commentators have suggested that
the Torah did not wish to repeat the phrase "that it was good"
on the sixth day, since the all-embracing "and behold it was
very good" occurs in that context, thus including man as well.
But this explanation is hardly plausible. The item that is "man"
which did not call forth the phrase "that it was good" is indeed
different from all the other items of creation. Man's "good"
is in his own hands. Only he has free choice. Rambam has
worded this privilege of man for once and for all in his Code
(Teshuva 5):

רשות לכל אדם נתונה, אם רצה להטות עצמו לדרך טובה ולהיות צדיק הרשות
בידו ואם רצה להטות עצמו לדרך רעה ולהיות רשע הרשות בידו ... אין
הבורא גוזר על האדם להיות טוב ולא להיות רע.

Freewill is accorded every man. If he desires to take the good
path and be righteous, he is free to do so; and if he desires to
take the evil one and be wicked he is free to do so ... the Creator
does not preordain man to be good or bad.

Since this is the case, the Torah could not conclude man's creation by observing that "it was good." Accordingly there is likewise no contradiction between the two verses that respectively mark the end of the first epoch of man's history. The reference is to the forthcoming two verses. At the end of the story of creation we find the following passage:

> **And God saw all that He had made and behold it was very good.** (1, 30)

At the end of the sidra we find:

וַיַּרְא יְיָ כִּי רַבָּה רָעַת הָאָדָם בָּאָרֶץ
וְכָל־יֵצֶר מַחְשְׁבוֹת לִבּוֹ רַק רַע כָּל הַיּוֹם.

> **And the Lord saw that great was the wickedness of man on earth and that every imagination of the thoughts of his heart was only evil continually.** (6, 5)

The work of God is contrasted with the works of man and the imagination of his thoughts. This is the answer to the question why the creation of man does not evoke the comment that "it was good." But how could the situation of man call forth the opinion that it was "not good," even before he had begun his life and works? This is what is apparently stated in the verse:

לֹא־טוֹב הֱיוֹת הָאָדָם לְבַדּוֹ.

> **it is not good that man should be alone.** (2, 18)

This verse occurs in the second account of the creation of man before the separation of male and female in chapter two, which is only a more detailed recapitulation of the first,[1] dwelling on the creation of the two sexes.

Cassuto points out that the Hebrew negative לֹא used here has greater force than the word אֵין. The latter merely points out that a thing cannot be considered good without committing the speaker to the opinion that it is absolutely bad. It may merely be neither bad nor good but just middling, whereas לֹא

in Hebrew is emphatic; "not at all," committing the speaker to the opinion that the thing is the opposite of good. What then was "not at all good" about man being alone? Some of our authorities give the phrase a psychological motivation. The loneliness was not good mentally. As the Talmud notes:

השרוי בלא אישה שרוי בלא שמחה, בלא ברכה, בלא טובה. בלא שמחה,
דכתיב (דברים יד, כו): "ושמחת אתה וביתך"; בלא ברכה, דכתיב (יחזקאל
מד, ל): "וראשית עריסותיכם תתנו לכהן להניח ברכה אל ביתך": בלא טובה,
דכתיב: "לא טוב היות האדם לבדו".

A life without a wife is devoid of joy, blessing and wellbeing; devoid of joy, as it is written (Deut. 14, 26): "And thou shalt rejoice thou and thine household"[2] (viz a wife)—of blessing, it is written (Ezek. 44, 30): "And the first of your dough shall ye give unto the priest to cause a blessing to rest on thy house";[3] of wellbeing, as it is written: "it is not good for man to be alone." (Yevamot 62b)

Others see the defect in man's loneliness in the practical field. Man could not easily fend for himself:

במה אשה עוזרתו לאדם? אדם מביא חיטין. חיטין כוסס? (מביא) פשתן.
פשתן לובש? לא נמצאת מאירה עניו ומעמידתו על רגליו?

Wherewith doth woman help man? Man brings wheat. Can he eat it raw? Flax. Can he wear flax? There would be no one to show him the way and put him on his feet. (Yevamot 63a)

In other words, the supply of man's needs calls for a division of labour and partnership. Without a division of labour and partnership no real life can exist. Sforno has a different interpretation:

The end implicit in his likeness and image would not be achieved if he would have to devote himself, all on his own to supplying his daily needs.

Sforno proceeds from an appraisement of man's daily needs to that of his spiritual aspirations as made in the image of God. Without a division of labour and a partner to help him out he would not be able to realise them to the full. What was "not good" in man being alone referred to a defect in his spiritual perfection. Rashi gave an entirely different explanation:

שלא יאמרו שתי רשויות הן : הקב״ה יחיד בעליונים ואין לו זוג וזה יחיד בתחתונים ואין לו זוג.

that it should not be said there are two powers (governing the universe). The Holy One blessed be He is alone in the upper worlds and has no partner and man is alone in the nether worlds and has no partner.

In other words, man was, from the beginning, a dual creation —of dust of the earth and the breath of life inspired in him by his God. Rashi likewise observes:

״ויפח באפיו״: גוף מן התחתונים ונשמה מן העליונים.

"And He breathed in his nostrils" a body from the nether worlds and a soul from the upper worlds.

Nevertheless, he was stamped with the image of God. But had the law of male and female reigning in the animal world not applied to him, the equilibrium of creation would have been violated; he would have made himself into a god. To safeguard his mission and function, to preserve intact the Divine plan in creation, he could not be allowed to remain alone.

Other commentators have been puzzled at Rashi's explanation. What prompted Rashi to reject the more usual explanation of the Rabbis that man's life was not worth living without a wife and adopt instead this theological interpretation? There must have been some special warrant in the text for his preference. The text is not stating a subjective fact that "it is not good for man to be alone"—man's feelings on the subject are not referred to, but rather "it is not good—that man should be alone" an objective statement, that the fact of man being alone is not good—in God's eyes. That was not His purpose. That is how Rashi understood the text in the light of the interpretation that he selected from Talmudic sources.

Since then that it was not God's original purpose to leave man alone, the Torah prefaced its description of the introduction of woman with a statement on the underlying purpose of this development:

אֶעֱשֶׂה־לּוֹ עֵזֶר כְּנֶגְדּוֹ.

I will make a help meet for him.   (2, 18)

We may compare this order with that adopted in the first general account of man's creation which is likewise prefaced by an explanation of the thoughts motivating the Divine deed:

וַיֹּאמֶר אֱלֹהִים נַעֲשֶׂה אָדָם בְּצַלְמֵנוּ.

Then God said, Let us make man in Our Image.   (1, 26)

Cassuto follows his comparison and contrasting of the two accounts of man's creation in this instance too:

> In the first account which belongs to the physical world the text emphasises the sexual aspect of the relationship of the husband to his wife (1, 27) "Male and female He created them"; in this chapter which belongs to the moral world the text emphasises in particular the moral aspect of this relationship—"a help meet for him."

The Midrash which is echoed by Rashi does not regard this phrase עזר כנגדו as expressing a single idea, an idiomatic coupling of two separate words, but rather as being subdivided into two separate phrases:

אמר ר' אלעזר: מאי דכתיב: "אעשה לו עזר כ נ ג ד ו " ? זכה — עוזרתו, לא זכה — כנגדו.

> R. Eliezer stated: "What does the text ... mean? If he is worthy —a help; if he does not show himself worthy—against him.
> (Yevamot 63a)

The Maharal of Prague in his commentary to Rashi, *Gur Aryeh* elaborates on this explanation.

> This explanation contains a profound truth. The male and female respectively represent two opposites. If man is worthy they merge

13

> into a single whole. In all cases two opposites merge to form a single whole when they are worthy i.e., when the Almighty who makes peace between opposites links and joins them. But when they are not worthy the fact that they are opposites causes her to be "against him."

In other words, the good effected by the introduction of woman and the "not good" dissipated by her separate creation is conditional on man's choice of the good. We noted too at the beginning of our *Studies* that the phrase "it was good" was omitted from man's creation because his good was dependent on his own free choice. The fact of man and woman's opposite characteristics is not by itself a guarantee that a combination of both will dispel the "not good" inherent in their isolation from each other. Only if they combine harmoniously in conformity with the will of God will these two opposites merge into a single whole. If they do not show themselves worthy the result will be disharmony—a clash of opposites.[4]

Questions for Further Study

1. His Divine wisdom ensured that the mating of man and woman should not be just sexual on a par with the beasts. He introduced a special personal relationship strengthening their love and social bonds, to help one another in all their affairs with a complete and perfect helpfulness, as is meet for them, that the male and female should not be each for himself as with the beasts around which do not require companionship from each other.

(Akedat Yizḥak)

What verses in our sidra are presumed to contain this idea?

2. This does not imply that God changed His mind but rather to draw our attention to the precious nature of this partnership and to teach us that it is not good for man to be alone. For this reason the Holy One blessed be He willed it that man should be without woman for a brief period and then afterwards introduced her so that she would be dear to him after he had felt something was lacking without her. (Shadal)

What question arising out of reading the sidra prompted the

above observation of Shadal, particularly in view of our comments in the *Studies?*

3. "ויבן ה' אלהים את הצלע" — מלמד שנתן הקב"ה בינה יתירה באשה יותר מבאיש.

"And the Lord made (ויבן) the rib He had taken from man into a woman" (2, 22) teaching that the Holy One blessed be He endowed woman with more understanding (בינה) than man.

On what linguistic and extra-linguistic grounds is this homiletical interpretation based? What quality did our Sages refer to in the phrase "more understanding" בינה יתירה with which they credited woman more than man?

1 General note to the comparison of chaps. 1 and 2 of Genesis (foll. Cassuto *From Adam to Noah* p. 91) : "As for the repetition of the story of man's creation, which is told both in the preceding and present section, it should be noted that such duplications are not at all incongruous to the Semitic way of thinking. When the Torah described man's creation (twice), the one in brief, general outline as an account of the making of *one of the creatures* of the material world and the second at length and in detail, as the story of the creation of the *central being* of the moral world—it had no reason to refrain from duplicating the theme, since such a repetition was consonant with the stylistic principle of presenting first a general statement and thereafter the detailed elaboration, which is commonly found not only in Biblical literature but also in the literary works of the ancient east."

What Cassuto says here in modern scientific language is already contained in the thirteen hermeneutical principles of interpretation *(middot)* enunciated by our Sages that apply to the understanding of the Torah (see Singer's prayer book p. 13). Rashi cites this: "Should you argue that the Torah has already stated that 'God created man in His image . . . male and female, He created them', I have seen in the Baraita of R. Eliezer . . . that here is an illustration of the principle that a general proposition is followed by an enumeration of particulars already comprehended in the general proposition.

"The text 'And God created man in his image . . . male and female He created them' is the general proposition, outlining in general His creation and His actions. Later the text states: 'And the Lord God fashioned man dust from the ground . . . and planted a garden eastward and there He put man . . . and caused a deep sleep to fall upon him' etc. The reader will imagine that we have here another story when it is merely a detailed account of the original story. The text similarly repeats the creation of the animals: 'And the Lord God formed all the beasts of the earth from the ground' in order to explain that 'He brought them to man to call them names'."

2 The text literally means "his household." The wife of a man is however termed "his home." In any case the text cannot mean that he should rejoice with his wife in the partaking of Second Tithe in Jerusalem since a woman is not obliged to make the pilgrimage to Jerusalem ... it must therefore mean that there will be no joy without him having a wife. (Maharsha)

3 It is possible that since this text occurs in *Ezekiel* in connection with the commandment of separating *halla* (the portion of dough), the house is taken to imply "thy wife" since the separation of *halla* is particularly incumbent on her. (Maharsha)

4 When I wrote the above, I had not seen Rabbi Soloveitschik's article: "The Lonely Man of Faith" (*Tradition*, vol. 7 no. 2 Summer 1965 pp. 1–67) which deals in a profound and original fashion with the relationship between chapters one and two and that between Adam and Eve according to those same chapters.

TREE OF KNOWLEDGE

Some of our commentators and authorities reject the allegorising of the Biblical narrative as dangerous, others enthusiastically embrace this approach and there are those who take the middle way. But even those who tend to reject it or reduce their employment of it to the minimum (like Ibn Ezra who devotes a large part of his introduction to his Torah commentary to attacking the allegorists—chiefly aimed at Christian controversialists who wished thereby to justify their repudiation of the law in favour of faith in the articles of their creed) admit that it is the allegorical, hidden meaning of the story of the garden of Eden and tree of knowledge that we must seek.

But the allegorical interpretations given are various. We shall devote our *Studies*, this time, to the approach of Abravanel who dwells at length on this subject.[1] He questions not merely the nature of the tree of knowledge, but the reason for the prohibition:

> For the Divine good will not prevent man from attaining perfection, since God will not withhold the good from those who walk in purity. The knowledge of good and evil is the perfection of man. How then could God have intended to withhold it from him? If it is maintained that the eating of the tree did harm because it involved the knowing of evil, surely it was, at the same time beneficial, in involving the knowledge of good. Why then did He prohibit the good on account of the evil?

The answer, of course, lies in defining the difference between the character of the knowledge of good and evil before the eating and after. Both Rambam and Abravanel agree that it would be inconceivable to explain that the eating of the tree of knowledge implied the achievement of free will and the capacity of intellectual discernment. For man, the product of God's own fashioning, created in His image, could not possibly have lacked this consciousness. Here is how Abravanel presents his case, in taking issue with Ramban:

> As our Sages expounded the text: "Behold it (i.e., Creation) was good"—this refers to the good inclination, "very"—to the evil inclination. In other words, the whole perfection of man lay in his possession of the capacity to choose freely between evil and good. Otherwise he would not have been human and God could not have commanded him: "from all the trees of the garden you may eat but of the tree of the knowledge of good and evil you may not eat thereof"; since a command can only apply to one who possesses a free choice and will.

Accordingly, the knowledge of good and evil achieved by man after his sin could not have been synonymous with free choice or, as Rambam words it, the capacity "to differentiate between good and evil." He states:

> The intelligence with which God has endowed man—that is his ultimate perfection—was his before his rebellion. That was implied in the phrase: "in the image and likeness of God"; on account of this, He spoke with him and commanded him, as it is stated: "And the Lord God commanded to man." A command is not given to animals or to one lacking intelligence. With his intellectual faculty man differentiates between truth and falsehood and this was possessed by him in his pristine perfection and purity.

The knowledge gained by him according to Abravanel, after eating the fruit of the tree was of a much lower order.

> Previously his intellect both practical and theoretical, was perfect but his knowledge of good and evil was, of necessity, intellectual, pure and not applied or prompted by worldly motives.

The knowledge he gained through eating or the tendencies which were then strengthened in him stood, according to Abravanel, in opposition to "nature" and consisted of the conventions and values created and fabricated by man, illusory values, preoccupation with which results in the forfeiting of eternal ones.

Abravanel digresses into a tirade against civilization, human inventions and man's divorcement from the natural path mapped out for him by his Creator:

> The underlying intention of the chapter is to stress that God created man in His intellectual image by which he was prompted to strive to perfect his soul in the acknowledgement of His creator and imitation of His wisdom. For the perfection of the image lies in its closest approximation to the form impressed on it.
>
> God also made available all the things necessary for human existence, food and drink of the fruits of the garden which He planted and the waters of its rivers. All this was in its natural state, requiring no labour or toil or human exertion. All was at his disposal, so that he need not burden himself in satisfying his bodily needs but could concentrate on the perfection of his soul, for which purpose he was created. On this account, God commanded him to rest content with the natural things He had furnished him with and not be attracted to luxuries which require resort to human artifice and worldly things, so that his intellect should not be diverted to the assuring of physical comforts which is the reverse of the spiritual perfection that is the ultimate aim.
>
> The meaning of the decree and command: "Of all the trees of the garden you may certainly eat" was: I do not forbid you the things essential for your bodily sustenance from the trees of the garden and the tree of life. But you may not actually *eat* of the tree of the knowledge of good and evil by which is meant the indulgence in and study of worldly things—what is the good that should be pursued and the evil[2] to be avoided, though you may look upon it and touch it, which is a minimal indulgence, just so much as is absolutely necessary. "Eating" here implies the sustenance of the body from that food and the indulgence in it and that the food ingested becomes identical with the body that absorbs it. From this only spiritual death can ensue; preoccupied with the tree of knowledge you will become divorced from the tree of life, which is synonymous with death. To this the following text (Deut. 30, 15) alludes: "See I have placed before you today, life and good, death and evil; therefore choose life."

Eating is interpreted to symbolise indulgence, the eating from the tree of knowledge of good and evil, the forsaking of the contemplation and acknowledgement of God which is the aim of man, substituting material pursuits, the ambition to change the world by human artifice, the production of luxuries which Abravanel identifies with the pursuit of vanity. Abravanel gives expression to the idea propounded by Jeremiah in his statement that the Jewish people "went after things of nought and became as nought" (Jer. 2) in his illustration of the eating symbol: "Eating implies . . . indulgence and that the food ingested becomes identical with the body that absorbs it, from which only spiritual death can ensure; preoccupied with the tree of knowledge you will become divorced from the tree of life which is synonymous with death."

Nevertheless a minimal preoccupation with bodily needs and a certain deviation from nature is essential for man. Touching the tree was therefore not prohibited. But since man did not rest content with that but ate, the whole order of nature was disrupted. After man had been driven from the garden of Eden, his descendants progressively deteriorated in creating the various branches of man's "accursed" civilisation:

> "Abel was a keeper of sheep and Cain a tiller of the ground" (Gen. 4, 2)—Cain adopted the vocation of tilling the ground because he feared not God and ignored the curse of: "Cursed be the ground for your sake" which was addressed to Adam . . . pursuing material things and the accumulation of possessions— symbolised in his name Cain, which comes from a Hebrew root meaning "acquisition." Abel, however, the proudhearted who pursued illusory honour and lordship became a keeper of sheep . . . for this reason he was called Abel (Hebrew—vanity) since honours and offices are vanity . . .

In the development of our "accursed" civilisation the shepherd retained a certain advantage over the tiller of the ground:

> Abel's offering was no better than Cain's except in the fact that God observed the former's intellectual superiority—since leadership and honour are the product of the intellect. Honour saves man from ignoble qualities. Abel was noble in character, a prince and judge over his work, whereas Cain was a tiller of the ground, akin to the earth which God had cursed, seeking out material labour, becoming a slave to the ground and animal possessions and not a ruler over them. Possessions unaccompanied by honour is the cause of all ignobleness, since he who seeks wealth and

cares not for honour will be led into robbery and other undesirable activities. Abel was superior to Cain in the nature of his occupation. Cain was occupied with artificial pursuits; for the daily ploughing of the farmer to sow, opens up and robs his soil. Abel conducted his life according to nature without artificial labour. Cain was concerned over his wealth, oblivious to prestige; Abel looked upward, and therefore God accepted his offering which was born from the living, according to nature, subjected to no artificial tampering. But He did not favour Cain's offering which was the product of human artifice.

Abel however was not perfect in everything, since he preferred the conventions of political life above spiritual contemplation. It was Seth who realised the true ideal:

"And Adam knew his wife and she bore a son and called his name Seth"—Adam knew that Seth would not emulate the prestige-seeking Abel or the acquisitive Cain, but would be in his image and likeness, attracted to true spiritual perfection. He therefore called him Seth, since he saw the world could be firmly founded (Seth means "foundation") through him.

The teaching that Abravanel outlines here is astonishing. Is this the approach of Judaism, of our prophets and sages to manual labour and human toil, to preoccupation with the material improvement of the world? Is man's use of the intellectual faculties given him by God the result of eating of the tree of knowledge, and the improvement of the land and exploitation of nature to produce plenty for human enjoyment a violation of His trust? Professor Baer[3] places Abravanel's views in the perspective of his experiences as a statesman and leader:

His hatred of civilization and politics is not accidental but firmly entrenched. He found support for this from the rabbinic dictum (Pirkei Avot) "Hate public office and do not be familiar with authority." Man should avoid all forms of public office, failure to do so would involve the holder in violation of all the ten commandments. Let a man rather live in retirement and live on the labour of his hands. Many of our Sages were therefore artisans. How apt are Solomon's words: "Be thou diligent to know the state of thy flocks and look well to thy herds" (Prov. 27, 23), rather than to matters of state. When you want a garment, do not go to the shopkeeper in town to buy from him but make it from the wool of your sheep in your own home. Public office in the town is full of contention, "but the righteous are secure as a young lion" (Prov. 28, 1), dwelling in the country with his sheep," (from Abravanel's commentary to *Pirkei Avot*). The political and social order were established contrary to nature and the will of God. The state and society were products of the evil inclination and the Torah only allowed the Jewish people to lead a political and social existence in deference to human frailty just as in the case of the captive woman (Deut. 21, 10) whom the Israelite was allowed to marry as a lesser evil.

Abravanel's whole life as a politician and statesman in the courts of kings and princes ran counter to his own principles. Perhaps his hankering for a life of tranquility away from the tumult of cities, the intrigues of men and politics was a reaction to his disillusionments, to the ups and downs of his political fortunes, the victim of jealousy and anti-Jewish prejudice. At any rate, his views were not formed by the text of Genesis.

Ramban takes the very opposite view of man's mission on earth. Basing himself on the Divine blessing to man in Genesis (1, 28) to: "subdue the earth," it is to: "lord it over the earth, to do his will with the creatures in it, build, uproot, plant, mine copper from its mountains."

Man must not rest content with nature but improve on it, develop, civilize, conquer the desert, exploit natural resources. Only by so doing could he see the fulfilment of the blessing: "Be fruitful and multiply and fill the earth." We cannot thus accept Abravanel's interpretation of the eating of the tree of knowledge as a divorcement from nature and preoccupation with the artificial products of civilization. This view is foreign to Judaism. As the following Midrash emphasises, Adam's sin was essentially an infringement of discipline, disobedience of God's will. The sin lay not in any consequence of the eating but in the very deviation from the command of God. The eating was wrong simply because God had declared it so:

אמר ר' פנחס בן יאיר: העץ הזה עד שלא אכל ממנו אדם הראשון לא נקרא שמו אלא "עץ" בלבד כשאר כל העצים, אבל משאכל ועבר על גזרתו של הקב"ה, נקרא שמו "עץ הדעת טוב ורע" על שם סופו, כמו שמצינו דברים

רבים שנקרא שמם על שם סופם. ומניין אתה אומר, שלא נקרא העץ כך
מתחילה? מתשובת האשה לנחש. ראה מה השיבה אותו: "ומפרי ה ע ץ אשר
בתוך הגן אמר אלהים לא תאכלו ממנו" ולא אמרה: מפרי ע ץ ה ד ע ת
ט ו ב ו ר ע . ועוד : בשעה שאמר הקב"ה לאדם : למה אתה נחבא ? מה אמר ?
" ה מ ן ה ע ץ אשר צויתיך לבלתי אכל ממנו", ולא אמר : מעץ הדעת. ולמה
קרא שמו "הדעת טוב ורע"? שעל ידי אכילתו ידע האדם רעות, שעד שלא
עבר על הציווי לא נגזר עמל, ולא יגיעה, ולא קור, ולא חום, ולא מכאוב, ולא
כל דבר רע מזיקו, אבל משעבר על חוק גזרתו של מקום, התחילו כל הרעות
נוגעות בו ומצערים מעשיו.
ולמה ציוה אותו הקב"ה שיאכל מכל עץ הגן ומנע ממנו אחד מהם ? כדי שיהא
רואה אותו תמיד, וזוכר את בוראו ומכיר שעול יוצרו עליו ושלא תהא רוחו
גסה עליו.

Said R. Pinḥas ben Yair: Before Adam partook of this tree, it
was called simply "tree," just like all other trees. But as soon
as he partook of it, thereby transgressing the decree of the Holy
One blessed be He, it was called the tree "of the knowledge of
good and evil," alluding to its future destiny, just as we find
many instances where objects are described in terms of their
future destiny. How do you know that the tree was not so named
at the outset? From Eve's reply to the serpent. See what she
replied to him: "And from the fruit of the tree which is in the
midst of the garden God hath said, Thou mayest not eat of it."
She did not say: "Of the fruit of the tree of the knowledge of
good and evil." Moreover, when the Holy One blessed be He said
unto Adam: "Wherefore dost thou hide thyself?" What did he
say? "Hast thou eaten of the tree whereof I commanded thee
thou shouldst not eat?" Why was it then called the tree of the
knowledge of good and evil?—Since through partaking of it
Adam became acquainted with misfortune. Before he transgressed
the command, neither toil nor trouble, neither cold nor heat nor
pain had been ordained, nor had any misfortune hurt him. But
as soon as he transgressed the statutory decree of the Omnipotent,
he was beset by every kind of trouble and dogged by suffering.

Why did the Holy One blessed be He ordain that he might eat
of all the trees of the garden and withhold from him just one
of them?—So that he should continually remember his Creator
and be conscious of the yoke of Him who fashioned him and that
he might not be overweening.   (Midrash Tadsheh)

Benno Jacob in his work on Genesis [4] emphasizes that:

good is love of God and observance of His commands, evil—
disobedience. Man would learn this by accepting the first pre-

23

cept. If he disobeyed, he would learn thereby the nature of evil and know the difference between it and the good that might have been his portion, had he obeyed the first precept given to him. The tree was the touchstone of good and evil, the permissible and forbidden, life and death, irrespective of the content of the precept. On the contrary, by not being influenced by any practical calculations of the benefits of the precept, by directing his will to obeying the author of the command, man would be tested. The command was given man to preclude him imagining he was a god, to make him aware that there was a master over him. The fruit of the tree was not harmful or deadly but, on the contrary, good to eat.

According to the foregoing, the knowledge of good and evil was not an awareness coming in the wake of the punishment, as the Midrash stresses, not the knowledge of good and evil dawning on man in consequence of his sinful deed, but the good and evil in the very commission or omission of the sin. The evil is not the evil of the punishment but the evil in the sin itself, in the deviation of man from the will of God that it involves.

Questions for Further Study

1. "The Lord God commanded (on) man saying, From all the trees of the garden thou mayest freely eat, but from the tree of knowledge of good and evil, thou mayest not eat thereof..." (2, 16–17).

   (a) Why the expression: "commanded on" (ויצו על) and not "commanded the man" (ויצו את)?

   (b) What need was there for prefacing the prohibition with the words: "From all the trees of the garden thou mayest freely eat"? Surely this statement constitutes no obligation?

2. "From the fruit of the tree which is in the midst of the garden hath God said, Thou shalt not eat thereof neither touch it." (3, 3)

   הא הוא דכתיב (משלי ל, ו): "אל תוסף על דבריו פן יוכיח בך ונכזבת".
   תני ר' חייא: שלא תעשה את הגדר יותר מן העיקר, שלא יפול ויקצץ

24

הנטיעות. כך אמר הקב"ה: "כי ביום אכלך ממנו וגו'", והיא לא אמרה כן אלא: "לא תאכלו ולא תגעו".

To this the following text (Prov. 30, 6) refers: "Add not to His words lest He reprove thee and thou be found a liar." R. Ḥiyya expounded: Do not add to the original prohibition; the result will be that he will come a cropper and undermine the very basis. God had said: "On the day thou eatest thereof..." She reported it differently: "Thou shall not eat thereof nor *touch*."

(Midrash, Bereshit Rabba 19, 4)

"ולא תגעו בו": הוסיפה על הציווי, לפיכך באה לידי גרעון, הוא שנאמר (משלי ל, ו): "אל תוסף על דבריו".

"Nor touch it": She added to the prohibition; consequently she was responsible for its diminution. To this the following text refers: "Add not to His words..."   (Rashi)

(a) Do Abravanel's sentiments cited in our *Studies* follow the Midrash?

(b) The commentary *Nimmukei Rashi* asks: "Why did Rashi prefer to cite a supporting text from Proverbs rather than one from the Torah itself, e.g., Deut. 4, 2 or 13, 1?"

3.   On the nature of the tree of knowledge Baḥya in his Torah commentary writes:

The tree of knowledge endowed those who ate of its fruit with desire and choice. This emerges from the use of the Hebrew *da'at* to describe it. In the Talmud the word is used in the sense of "opinion" and "free choice" and in Psalms the phrase: "What is man that Thou art mindful of him" (*va-teda'ehu*) implies: Thou dost desire him. In other words, the tree of knowledge is really the tree of freewill. The Almighty forbade it to man since the latter was destined before the sin, to act like an angel, patterned to be rational in all his ways. But after the sin he achieved freewill and choice and became conscious of his bodily desires. This constitutes a Divine and good quality, in one way, but evil in another.

(a) Does the above follow any of the interpretations we have mentioned or does it strike out on a line of its own?

(b) What objections can be raised to this interpretation?

25

4. "But from the tree of the knowledge of good and evil thou shalt not eat thereof." (2, 17)

What is the point of the word *mimenu* "thereof"? Either it is an idiomatic emphasis as in the construction (Exod. 2, 6): "She opened and saw *him*—the child" or it implies a prohibition of even the slightest taste.
(Ibn Ezra)

The word *mimenu* is added for emphasis just as it is once again repeated in the next phrase.
(Shadal)

The word *mimenu* is obviously anomalous. The prohibition was deliberately worded thus to test man's loyalty and obedience. "Thereof" could be interpreted by man to mean that only the fruit whilst joined to the tree was forbidden. But if the woman were herself to pluck the fruit and give it to her husband this would be permitted. This indeed was Adam's excuse: "The woman gave me of the tree." The text teaches us not to explain away Divine commandments. On account of such behaviour — giving his own twist to the Divine message was the prophet punished in I Kings 13. We should not try to mitigate the force of a Divine command by our own explanations. Man should at least have doubted whether this was indeed the meaning of the command and to have taken the strict explanation to be on the safe side. This was the test: would he resist the temptation to find a loophole in the law?
(Malbim)

(a) What is the difficulty in the text?
(b) Where did Shadal find a further example of such duplication?
(c) In what way does his approach differ from all the others mentioned here?
(d) What is Malbim's proof from Gen. 3, 12?

---

1 Prof. I. Heinemann in his article *Abarbanels Lehre vom Niedergang der Menschheit* MGWJ 1938, S. 381–400 cites a similar question sarcastically asked by the Syrian philosopher Porphyrius (3rd century) in his controversy with the Christians. The question recurs in various forms in anti-Christian polemic and they are referred to, in Heinemann's view, by Rambam in his *Guide*, Part I, chap. 2: "A certain scholar posed me a very difficult question... note the question and our answer. Here is the question: The text would seem to assume that man was originally meant to be just like all other creatures

without intelligence and without mind, unable to differentiate between good and evil. But when he rebelled, his disobedience achieved for him the perfection unique to man—the attainment of that discernment found in us. Is it not very odd that the punishment for disobedience should be the attainment of a perfection which he had never possessed, namely—intelligence?" In Heinemann's view Abravanel understood that Rambam was referring to the same anti-Christian polemic. Rambam however stressed the incompatibility between the punishment and the crime, Abravanel the very incongruity of the prohibition itself. The article explains this difference of approach as it does the difference between the respective replies of Rambam and Abravanel.

2 "Good" and "evil" here have no moral connotations in the sense of obedience to the will of God and its converse—sin. The reference is to a utilitarian good based on pursuit of pleasure and avoidance of pain.

3 "Don Isaac Abravanel and his attitude to the problems of history and the state," Tarbiẓ, vol. 8 Jerusalem 1937 pp. 241–259.

4 Benno Jacob, *Das erste Buch der Tora—Genesis*, Berlin, Schocken Verl. 1930. Extant only in German. His commentary on Exodus is still in MS in the National Library, Jerusalem.

THE SERPENT—THE EVIL IMPULSE

Commenting on chapter 3, verse 7 of our sidra:

וַתִּפָּקַחְנָה עֵינֵי שְׁנֵיהֶם וַיֵּדְעוּ כִּי עֵירֻמִּם הֵם.

**And the eyes of both of them were opened
and they knew that they were naked**

our Sages stated in *Bereshit Rabbah*:

מצוה אחת שהיתה בידם נתערטלו הימנה.

Even of the one precept which they had possessed they had
stripped themselves.

As early as the third chapter of the Torah, immediately after
the completion of the universe, we are confronted by the story
of Adam's first sin. Since the Torah is concerned not with the
behaviour of one individual, but rather with the prototype of
mankind; the workings of sin, the temptation leading thereto,
and consequences proceeding therefrom recorded here, have a
universal, timeless application.

The first *miẓva* given to mankind was a negative one, a
"don't".[1]

מִכֹּל עֵץ־הַגָּן אָכֹל תֹּאכֵל.
וּמֵעֵץ הַדַּעַת טוֹב וָרָע לֹא תֹאכַל מִמֶּנּוּ – –

**Of every tree of the garden thou mayest freely eat.
But of the tree of knowledge of good and evil, thou shalt
not eat ...**   (2, 16, 17)

The area of prohibition and sphere of the permissive is clearly
and explicitly delineated in two separate verses. The range of

objects permitted is wide, comprising the whole expanse of the garden: "Of *every* tree of the garden." The freedom of action granted them is generous: "thou mayest *freely* eat."

The doubling of the verb in Hebrew is a form of emphasis. It is not merely stated: *tokhal* "thou mayest eat" but: *akhol tokhal*—literally rendered: "eating shalt thou eat," and idiomatically: "thou mayest freely eat." (Both renderings are given in the King James' Version.) In other words, here are ample opportunities for exercising one's freedom of choice.

However, on the advent of the serpent (who according to Rabbinic tradition — הוא השטן, הוא היצר הרע — He is the Satan, he is the evil inclination — Baba Batra 16a) with his wily insinuations the prohibition is seen in another light.

The evil inclination magnifies the scope of the prohibition which now seems to loom over the whole of the garden and temptation becomes irresistible:

אַף כִּי־אָמַר אֱלֹהִים: לֹא תֹאכְלוּ מִכֹּל עֵץ הַגָּן.

**Yea, hath God said, ye shall not eat of every
tree of the garden?** (3. 1)

The commentary *Or Haḥayyim* points out that it is the manner of a seducer to indulge in exaggerating the stringency of the prohibition, in order to persuade the victim that all efforts to resist temptation are useless, are going against nature; and that, therefore, he might as well give up the struggle from the first, rather than try to do the impossible.

The phrasing of the serpent's introductory words require deeper study:
Are they merely an expression of questioning curiosity on the part of the serpent as if to say: "Is it really true what I've heard? Has God really prohibited you from eating of all the trees of the garden?" Or perhaps the implication is, as suggested by other commentators, who see in the opening words *af ki* אַף כִּי "Even if" an expression of derision: "Even if God has said such a thing, what of it!"

Although Eve still puts up a resistance to the insinuations of the seducer and strives to correct them, his words have already had some effect. Our Sages expressed this idea as follows: אם אין דבר נכנס כולו נכנס נכנס חציו "If a thing enters not wholly, it enters by half" (if one is not wholly persuaded, one is, at anyrate, half persuaded).

Let us now compare the wording of the prohibition as imparted to Adam by God (2, 16) and subsequently, as phrased by Eve in her reply to the serpent's insinuations:

God	*Eve*
And the Lord God commanded the man saying, Of every tree in the garden thou mayest freely eat.	We may eat of the fruit of the trees of the garden.
But of the tree of the knowledge of good and evil thou shalt not eat of it.	But of the fruit of the tree which is in the midst of the garden, God hath said, Ye shall not eat of it, neither shall ye touch it, lest ye die.
(Gen. 2, 16, 17)	(Gen. 3, 2, 3)

The above comparison clearly demonstrates the way in which the scope of that which was really permitted them has been whittled down and minimised. The generous, qualifying words of "freely" and "every" employed in the original Divine instruction to man have disappeared and we are simply left with the bald phrase: "We may eat of the fruit of the garden."

In contrast to this, to what extent has the original prohibition been magnified and intensified in character, in the eyes of the woman! The tree that stood somewhere, in one corner of the garden, is now described as being in its midst, as if it were the only tree that mattered. It is not called by its title, but simply termed the "tree which is in the midst of the garden." Moreover, to the prohibition of eating has been gratuitously added that of even touching. The most important change however to be noted is the shift from: "God hath said." Eve thereby softened the force of the prohibition from an absolute command, an imperative to a statement.[2]

Let us now compare the consequence of transgressing the prohibition as expressed in the original, Divine instruction with how it appears in the woman's reporting of it to the serpent:

God	Eve
But of the tree of the knowledge of good and evil, thou shalt not eat of it, *for in the day that thou eatest of it, thou shalt surely die.*	But of the fruit of the tree which is in the midst of the garden, God hath said, Ye shall not eat thereof, neither shall ye touch it, *lest ye die.*

Benno Jacob in his work on Genesis aptly comments on the contrast in the phrasing describing the consequences of transgression. What originally constituted in the Almighty's wording, a moral connection between the sin and punishment is transformed by the woman into a mere mechanical link of cause and effect. Such a shift in the significance of the Divine warning offered an ideal breeding ground for doubt and scepticism and even derision. Perhaps the consequences would be delayed, would not follow on immediately! What then would be the value of the prohibition? This same idea underlies the following Midrash:

הדא הוא דכתיב (משלי ל, ו): "אל תוסף על דבריו פן יוכיח בך ונכזבת ...
כך אמר הקב"ה: "ביום אכלך ממנו וכו'", והיא לא אמרה כן אלא: "לא
תאכלו ממנו ולא תגעו בו". כיון שראה [הנחש] אותה עוברת לפני העץ, נטלה
ודחפה עליו, אמר לה: הא לא מתת. כשם שלא באה עליך מיתה בנגיעה כך
אינך מתה באכילה.

Thus it is written: "Add not unto his words lest he reprove thee, and thou be found a liar' (Prov. 30, 6). Thus the Holy One, blessed be He, had said. "For on the day that thou eatest thereof thou shalt surely die" (Gen. 2, 7), whereas she did not say this, but "God hath said, ye shall not eat of it, neither shall ye touch it." When he (the serpent) saw her passing by the tree, he took her and thrust her against it, He said to her: "Behold, thou hast not died! Just as death came not upon thee through touching, so it shall not come upon thee through eating."

(Midrash Rabbah)

The insinuations of the seducer worm their way into the victim's heart and break down all resistance:

לֹא־מוֹת תְּמֻתוּן.

Ye shall not surely die. (3, 4)

This is how the commentary *Ha'amek Davar* interprets the wiles of the serpent:

> Since the woman had changed the wording from: "In the day that thou eatest thereof, thou shalt surely die" to: "lest ye die," the serpent found an opportunity to introduce doubts into her mind and deny the truth of her statement. How was it possible for the Creator to have said "lest" which is an expression of doubt, i.e., you may die but, on the other hand, you may not? Surely the Creator knows, beyond all doubt, what would ensue? The serpent then uses this as an argument, casting doubts on the seriousness of the Divine prohibition. Rather God intended merely to frighten and intimidate them, because He did not want them to eat thereof. This is the characteristic method pursued by the tempter. He insinuates that the punishment threatened will never really come to pass.

After the fear of punishment and the dread of the consequences of sin had been overcome, the most satanic idea yet suggested is then projected by the serpent:

כִּי יֹדֵעַ אֱלֹהִים כִּי בְּיוֹם אֲכָלְכֶם מִמֶּנּוּ וְנִפְקְחוּ עֵינֵיכֶם
וִהְיִיתֶם כֵּאלֹהִים יֹדְעֵי טוֹב וָרָע.

**For God doth know
that in the day ye eat thereof,
then your eyes shall be opened,
and ye shall be as gods,
knowing good and evil.**
(3, 5)

The Divine Lawgiver responsible for the prohibition did not mean it for your benefit but rather to protect Himself from the consequences of your transgression. Apart from the fact that the prohibition itself is without reason, the motives prompting it are neither moral nor pure.

What happened after these insinuations of the serpent was only to be expected:

וַתֵּרֶא הָאִשָּׁה כִּי טוֹב הָעֵץ לְמַאֲכָל
וְכִי תַאֲוָה־הוּא לָעֵינַיִם
וְנֶחְמָד הָעֵץ לְהַשְׂכִּיל.

And when the woman saw
that the tree was good for food
and it was pleasant to the eyes
and a tree to be desired . . .   (3, 6)

At first the woman observed the tree at close quarters. Evidently till then she had been afraid to approach it, just as one keeps far from transgression. Now however the fear had gone and she approached it and began to note all its varied properties.

In the words of the commentary, *Akedat Yizhak:*

Sne already sensed the presence of the tree as she came near to it, to its atmosphere and fragrance.

What we are warned against in another part of the Torah (Num. 5, 39) in connection with the commandment to wear *zizit:* "thou shalt seek not after your own heart and after your own eyes," is exactly with what we are confronted here:

וַתִּקַּח מִפִּרְיוֹ וַתֹּאכַל וַתִּתֵּן גַּם־לְאִישָׁהּ עִמָּהּ וַיֹּאכַל.

And she took of the fruit thereof, and did eat and gave
also to her husband with her; and he did eat.   (3, 6)

No inhibitions stand in their way and the process is a swift one.

The consequences of the sin are not slow in coming. Indeed, they are apparent immediately in verse 7 even before the punishment is meted out to them, namely the curse, the enmity and pain called down on them in verses 15–19. There is a punishment inherent in the *very commission of the sin*, a natural consequence of the deed, even before the statutory Divine punishment becomes effective.

To this our Sages referred, in their comment on the following verse:

**And they heard the voice of the Lord . . .
and Adam and his wife hid themselves
from the presence of the Lord God
amongst the trees of the garden.** (3, 8)

עד שלא יחטא אדם, נותנין לו אימה ויראה והבריות מתפחדין ממנו,
כיון שהוא חוטא, נותנין עליו אימה ויראה ומתפחד הוא מאחרים.
תדע לך, שכן אמר רבי: עד שלא חטא אדם הראשון היה שומע קול הדיבור
[דבר ה׳]. עומד על רגליו ולא היה מתיירא, כיון שחטא — כששמע קול
הדיבור, נתיירא ונתחבא, שנאמר: "את קולך שמעתי ואירא".

Before a man sins, *he is given* (he inspires) fear and awe and creatures are afraid of him. Once he has sinned, he *is given up* to fear and awe and is frightened of others. The proof is that Rabbi (Judah Hanasi) said: "Before Adam sinned, he could listen to the Divine utterance standing upright and without being afraid, but after he had sinned, when he heard the Divine voice he was frightened and hid himself, as it says (Gen. 3, 10): "I heard Thy voice . . . and I was afraid"

(Shir Ha-shirim Rabbah 3, 14)

We can appreciate the workings of sin, its consequences and moral implications by studying carefully not only the nature of the fear prompting man to hide himself and seek a refuge from responsibility or the authority demanding his responsibility, but also by noting the place to which man flees and hides himself.

Cassuto refers to this when pointing out the significance of the recurrence of such motif words as "tree," "midst" and "garden." He writes in his commentary: *From Adam to Noah*:

These words occur often in the chapter, recalling the sin of Adam and his wife. They are not purposeless. Evidently The Torah wishes to allude to the fact that though the sinner strives to forget or erase from human memory his offence, he cannot silence the voice of his conscience and obliterate all vestiges of his deed. At every turn and step he is confronted by things that remind him and others of his sin.

With the *tree which is in the midst of the garden* they sinned and in the *midst of the trees of the garden* they were forced to hide.

Questions for Further Study

1. דחפה עד שנגעה בו; אמר לה: כשם שאין מיתה בנגיעה, כך אין מיתה
באכילה.

"And the serpent said unto the woman, ye shall not surely die"—
he (the serpent) pushed her until she touched it. Said he to her:
Just as no death is incurred through touching, so no death is
incurred through eating. (Rashi on Gen. 3, 4)

Rashi never cites a Midrash unless he has perceived some difficulty in the text which his citation solves. What is the difficulty that Rashi noted in the text which prompted him to cite the above Midrash?

2. "For God doth know." (3, 5)
   (a) What is the implication of the word כי in this verse?
       See Rashi on Gen. 18, 15 on the verse— כי יראה
       כי צחקת for the various meanings of the word.
   (b) Note how the serpent omits one link in the train of
       his argument to win over Eve between verse 3 and
       4. Supply the missing link.
   (c) What is the subterfuge that the tempter resorts to in
       this verse and in what way is it different from the one
       in the previous verse?

3. "And when the woman saw that the tree was good for food"

—the words of the serpent appealed to her and pleased her so
that she believed him. (Rashi on Gen. 3, 6)

35

Explain what prompted Rashi to elaborate on the text here which is so simple and obvious in meaning, and what does his comment add?

4. Compare with our citation from *Shir Ha-shirim Rabbah* the following passage from the *Sifrei* on Num. 5, 3:

ר' שמעון בן יוחאי אומר: בא וראה מה גדול כוחה של עברה שעד שלא פשטו ידיהם בעברה, מה נאמר בהם? (שמות כד, יז) "ומראה כבוד ה' כאש אוכלת בראש ההר לעיני בני ישראל" — לא יראים ולא מזדעזעים. משפשטו ידיהם בעברה, מה נאמר בהם? (שמות לד, ל) "וירא אהרן וכל בני ישראל את משה והנה קרן אור פניו ויראו מגשת אליו".

Rabbi Shimon b. Yohai said: Come and see how dreadful is the effect of transgression. Before they became involved in transgression, what is said of them? (Exod. 24, 17) "The sight of the glory of the Lord like a consuming fire at the top of the mountain in the sight of the children of Israel, they neither feared nor trembled." Once they took to trangsression, what is said of them? (34, 30) "Aaron and all the children of Israel saw Moses and behold the light of his countenance shone and they were afraid to go near him"

Rashi on the latter verse echoes the ancient rabbinic comment:

ומשעשו את העגל, אף מקרני הודו של משה היו מרתיעים ומזדעזעים.

Once they had made the calf they found themselves shaking and trembling at the sight of the majestic glow of Moses' presence.

(a) What idea is common to the foregoing homiletic comment and that quoted from *Shir Hashirim Rabbah* at the end of our *Studies?*

(b) What prompted Rashi to refrain from appending the ancient homiletic exposition of Gen. 3, 8 (from *Shir Ha-shirim Rabbah* on p. 34) to the word "He hid" *(va-yithabe)* and yet to cite a similar rabbinic exposition when commenting on Exod. 34, 4?

---

[1] Apparently there existed an earlier *miẓva*, that of propagating the species: פרו ורבו "Be fruitful and multiply" (1, 28). But the rabbis

stated in the Talmud, *Sanhedrin 59b* that this *mizva* "was derived from that which was said to Noah and his children." Rabbi echoes this in his comment to the second פרו ורבו (9, 7): "The plain meaning is that the first constitutes a blessing, and here a command." On the first he makes no comment, following the Talmud in *Ketubot 5a* that it is a blessing not a commandment. Rambam follows suit in his *Sefer Hamizvot* (commandment 312). *Sefer Hahinukh* takes a different attitude which is supported by the Mishnah in *Yevamot 65b.* But this is not the plain sense of the text.

2 Benno Jacob pointedly contrasts Noah's saintly conduct. He gave a mere saying of God the force of an actual command "God *said* to Noah ... make thee an ark." But Noah is reported to have "done according to all which the Lord had commanded him, so he did."

NEVER TOO LATE TO MEND

וַיֹּאמֶר קַיִן אֶל־הֶבֶל אָחִיו
וַיְהִי בִּהְיוֹתָם בַּשָּׂדֶה
וַיָּקָם קַיִן אֶל הֶבֶל אָחִיו וַיַּהַרְגֵהוּ.

**Cain spoke to Abel his brother,
And when they were in the field, Cain rose up against
Abel his brother, and killed him.** (4, 8)

This happened to the second generation of the human race.
Are we dealing here with a description of what happened in a
particular case, of a quarrel between the two sons of Adam or
rather with an archetypal quarrel between two members of the
human race, between the sons of men? Here is how our Sages
comment on the dread deed:

"ויאמר קין אל הבל אחיו ויהי בהיותם בשדה" — על מה היו מדיינים? אמרו:
בואו ונחלוק את העולם. אחד נטל את הקרקעות ואחד נטל את המטלטלין.
דין אמר: ארעת דאת קאים עליה — דידי [זה אמר: הארץ אשר אתה עומד
עליה שלי היא]. ודין אמר: מה דאת לביש — דידי. [וזה אמר: מה שאתה
לובש שלי הוא]. דין אמר: חלוץ! — דין אמר: פרח! מתוך כך: "ויקם קין
אל הבל אחיו ויהרגהו".
ר' יהושע דסכנין בשם ר' לוי אמר: שניהם נטלו את הקרקעות, ושניהם נטלו
את המטלטלין. ועל מה היו מדיינין? אלא זה אומר: בתחומי בית המקדש
יבנה. וזה אומר: בתחומי בית המקדש יבנה, שנאמר: "ויהי בהיותם בשדה"
ואין "שדה" אלא בית המקדש, דכתיב (מיכה ג, יב): "ציון שדה תחרש".
ומתוך כך: "ויקם קין אל הבל אחיו ויהרגהו".
יהודה בר' אמי אמר: על חוה הראשונה היו מדיינין.

"Cain spoke to Abel his brother. And when they were in the
field"—what were they arguing about? They said: Come let us
divide the world. One took the lands and the other took the
movables. One said: The land on which you are standing is
mine; and the other replied: The clothes you are wearing are

mine. One said: Take them off! the other: Get off! In the course of this Cain rose up against Abel his brother and killed him!

R. Joshua of Sakhnin in the name of R. Levi said: Both took lands and both took movables. But what were they disputing about? One said: In my domain shall the Temple be built. The other said: In my domain shall the Temple be built, as it is stated: "And when they were in the field." The "field" is none other than the Temple, as it is written (Micah 3, 12): "Zion shall be plowed as a field." In the course of this, Cain rose up against Abel his brother and killed him.

Yehuda bar Ami said: They were disputing over Eve.

(Bereshit Rabbah, 22, 16)

It is quite evident from the above citation that the Midrash gives the story of Cain and Abel a universal application. It is concerned not merely with the individual case of Cain and Abel, but with the motives underlying man's desire to quarrel, make war, kill and murder his fellow.

Professor Heinemann in his work *Darkei Aggada*, page 15, notes that our Sages, in contradistinction to the scientific approach, do not generalize the concrete, but on the contrary, express abstractions in concrete terms.

Three answers are given in our Midrash to explain the root causes of bloodshed and murder. According to the first, they are prompted by economic considerations, the quarrel over material possessions. According to the second, bloodshed is prompted by religious and ideological reasons, each side maintaining that the Temple should be built in his domain, that his religion should be accepted. The third view traces the roots of bloodshed and strife to sexual passion—"they were disputing over Eve."

The Midrash is undoubtedly stating a universal truth. But does this emerge from the context? Admittedly, the Rabbis were not concerned here with the individual Cain and Abel— the sons of Man but with men. Since their aim was not explanatory, to clarify the plain sense of the passage but rather to elicit a universal principle from it, they were not bound by the context in their search for an answer to the question: "What were they arguing about?"

וַיָּבֵא קַיִן מִפְּרִי הָאֲדָמָה מִנְחָה לַיָי.
וְהֶבֶל הֵבִיא גַם־הוּא מִבְּכֹרוֹת צֹאנוֹ וּמֵחֶלְבֵהֶן

וַיִּשַׁע יְיָ אֶל הֶבֶל וְאֶל־מִנְחָתוֹ.
וְאֶל קַיִן וְאֶל־מִנְחָתוֹ לֹא שָׁעָה.

**Cain brought of the fruit of the ground
an offering unto the Lord.
And Abel, he also brought of the firstlings of his flock
and of the fat thereof.
And the Lord had regard for Abel and his offering; but
for Cain and his offering He had no regard.** (4, 3–5)

Why did God not accept Cain's gift? Some commentators find
the answer in two allusions buried in the context:

"וַיָּבֵא קין מפרי-האדמה": מן הגרוע.

"Cain brought of the fruit of the ground"—from the inferior.
(Rashi)

Rashi deduces this fact from the subtle differentiation in the
text in its description of the respective offerings of Cain and
Abel. Abel brought "of the firstlings of his flock," implying
of the choicest. But Cain brought simply "of the fruit of the
ground." Moreover, in the case of Abel it is stated: "From the
firstling of *his* flock"—his very own, whilst Cain brought "of
the fruit of the ground." Cain made no individual sacrifice and
did not go out of his way to select the best of his personal
possessions.

What should be the reaction of a man who has done wrong
and senses his fault? He should surely be concerned to remedy
it especially when that is within his power. But Cain did not
follow this path. On the contrary: "Cain was furious." With
whom was he angry? Not with himself:

וַיֹּאמֶר יְיָ אֶל־קָיִן: לָמָּה חָרָה לָךְ
וְלָמָּה נָפְלוּ פָנֶיךָ

The Lord said to Cain:
Why art thou angry?
and why is thy countenance fallen? (4, 6)

Sforno explains the implications of the Divine statement to Cain as follows:

> "Why art thou angry"—why were you jealous of your brother and concerned that I was favourably disposed towards his offering? "And why is thy countenance fallen?"—if a fault can be remedied it is not right to bewail the past, but one should strive to mend matters for the future.

Then come the key words of the Divine message to Cain, in a passage which has been considered to be one of the most difficult in the Torah:

הֲלוֹא אִם־תֵּיטִיב שְׂאֵת
וְאִם לֹא תֵיטִיב
לַפֶּתַח חַטָּאת רֹבֵץ
וְאֵלֶיךָ תְּשׁוּקָתוֹ –
וְאַתָּה תִּמְשָׁל־בּוֹ.

If thou doest well, shall it not be lifted up?
and if thou doest not well,
sin coucheth at the door;
and unto thee is its desire,
but thou mayest rule over it. (4, 7)

Is the word שאת a verb or a noun? Malbim considers it to be a synonym for משאת a word meaning a gift or sacrifice. Here is how he explains our verse.

> He revealed unto him that the Lord took no pleasure in gifts, but only in obedience (Cf. 1 Samuel 15, 22 "to obey is better than sacrifice"). The main thing is that you should better your ways. You did not bring a worthy gift. Improving the gift will

not help matters. For whether you bring a goodly gift or not matters not, since sin lieth at the door to accuse you. The Almighty explained to him three points: (1) that the evil inclination is ever ready and man should study his motives and not allow his baser instincts to get the better of him, since they always lie in wait to poison his behaviour; (2) He further informed him that, on the one hand, his baser passions longed to lead him into sin and demoralize him, and that (3) on the other, it lay within his power to rule over them by exercising the freedom of will given to man. Man was only truly free, if he ruled over the bestial part of his nature, and not if he allowed the latter to rule over him.

According to this interpretation the passage comes to place in its true perspective the role of sacrifices in the scheme of human behaviour. Malbim then regards this passage as containing the same thought that occurs throughout the Scriptures, especially in the Prophetic Writings, that obedience is better than sacrifice. But it is difficult to accept his interpretation of the text, particularly the connotation he ascribes to the Hebrew word of condition אם. Cassuto, in his book *From Adam to Noah* p. 209, states as follows:

It is impossible to explain the verse as if it reads: "whether you do or do not do well." In such a case the text should either have repeated again the whole phrase or simply read "whether you do well or not."
According to the present form of the verse, we have here two contrasting conditions: "If thou doest well;" "if thou doest not well." The word שאת is not part of the "if" clause, but of the main sentence. If you do well—then there will be a lifting up; but if you do not do well—then sin coucheth at the door.

We must then accept the view of the commentators who regard the passage as containing two antithetical sentences of condition. Some, like Onkelos and Rashi, explain the word שאת to connote forgiveness (cf. "forgiving iniquity and transgression" Exod. 134, 7); others (Ibn Ezra, Biur) take it to mean a lifting up in the sense of elation:

"הלא אם תיטיב שאת": כתרגומו פירושו.
[תרגום אונקלוס: הלא אם תיטיב עובדך (מעשיך) ישתבק לך (יסלח לך)]
"לפתח חטאת רובץ": לפתח קברך חטאתך שמור.

"וְאֵלֶיךָ תְּשׁוּקָתוֹ": של חטאת — יצר הרע — תמיד שוקק ומתאוה להכשילך.
"וְאַתָּה תִּמְשָׁל בּוֹ": אם תרצה — תתגבר עליו.

If thou doest well—in accordance with Onkelos: "if you mend your ways He will forgive you."

"Sin coucheth at the door"—at the entrance to your grave is your sin.

"And unto thee is its desire"—the sin's—the evil inclination which continually longs and desires to cause you to stumble.

"But thou mayest rule over it"—if you wish you can overcome it.   (Rashi)

If you do well then your countenance will be lifted up, but if not, "sin coucheth at the door." Sin is ever lying in wait for your soul and continually waiting for you to sin. This is a vivid figure of speech picturing iniquity outside a closed door waiting for an opportunity to enter. But if you wish, you have the power to rule over it, and for this reason I have said that it is within your power to raise yourself out of your dejection. Your anger and fallen spirits are nothing more than wickedness of heart.

(Biur)

The message of the Torah in its opening chapters is therefore one of encouragement to mankind, stressing that man's spiritual salvation lies within himself. There is always an opportunity to repent and mend one's ways. There was therefore no justification for Cain's dejection and despair. This is the force of the Almighty's question:

לָמָּה נָפְלוּ פָנֶיךָ?

Why is thy countenance fallen?   (4, 6)

But Cain was not satisfied with the message contained in the Almighty's words. His reaction is:

Cain spoke to Abel his brother,
And when they were in the field, Cain rose up against
Abel his brother, and killed him.   (4, 8)

Adam the first man committed an offence against his Maker, Cain the second generation of the human race sinned against his brother and murdered him. Such is the beginning of human history.

Questions For Further Study

1. Cassuto outlines the following principles as characterizing the Biblical narrative (in *From Adam to Noah* pp. 184–185):

   The Torah is accustomed to expressing its ideas in concrete form and imparting its lessons through the medium of stories, from which it is possible to draw these lessons. The lessons which the Torah wished to teach us here are not implicit in the incidents described but are contained in the words of God Himself.

   These lessons fall under two headings, (1) those which are obvious even to the superficial reader, (2) those which are apparent after closer study. In the latter category is the protest against the blood feud. The laws of the Torah evince a general tendency to limit the practice of avenging the death of a relative. This tendency is also evident in the story of Cain and Abel.

   Cain, who murdered his brother, is the archetype of the murderer. Since all men are brothers, then the murderer has shed his own brother's blood. The treatment meted out to Cain is then the first example of the laws of homicide. Cain was afraid of vengeance, since every member of the human race, both existing and future ones, were relatives of the victim and potential avengers.

   (a) What are the two obvious lessons of our chapter?
   (b) Where do you find in our chapter evidence of the tendency to counter the practice of the blood feud?
   (c) Where can you find in the legislation of the Torah examples of the tendency to limit the practice of the blood feud?
   (d) What traces did the Torah permit of this custom (the blood feud) to remain within the framework of its legislation?

2.
   וַיֹּאמֶר קַיִן אֶל־הֶבֶל אָחִיו
   וַיְהִי בִּהְיוֹתָם בַּשָּׂדֶה
   וַיָּקָם קַיִן אֶל הֶבֶל אָחִיו וַיַּהַרְגֵהוּ. (4, 8)

   נכנס עמו בדברי ריב ומצה להתעולל עליו להורגו. ויש בזה מדרשי אגדה —
   אך זה יישובו של מקרא.

44

"And Cain said to Abel his brother"—he picked a quarrel with him in order to find cause to kill him. There are Aggadic explanations, but this is the plain meaning of the verse.   (Rashi)

(a) What did Rashi find difficult in our passage?
(b) Rashi in his reference to the Aggadic explanations alluded to the three views outlined in Bereshit Rabbah cited at the beginning of our *Studies*. Can you suggest a reason why Rashi does not cite even one of the three views mentioned there? In what way does his explanation differ in principle from those three views?

3.   "The voice of thy brother's blood crieth unto Me from the ground"—his blood and the blood of his seed.   (Rashi)

דמו ודם זרעיותיו.

(a) What prompted Rashi's comment?
(b) Explain the idea symbolised in these words.

4.   *King James Version*

If thou doest well, shalt thou not be accepted?
And if thou doest not well, sin lieth at the door:
and unto thee shall be his desire
and thou shalt rule over him.   (4, 7)

Buber Rosenzweig:

Ist's nicht so:
meinst du Gutes, trags hoch,
meinst du nicht Gutes aber:
vorm Einlass. Sünde, ein Lagerer,
nach dir sein Begier—
du aber walte ihm ob.

(a) Which of the commentators cited in our *Studies* does each of the above translators follow?
(b) Why has Buber changed the Hebrew word *rovez* from a verbal into a noun form? Cf. also the NEB version. "If you do well, you are accepted; if not, sin is a demon crouching at the door. It shall be eager for you. and you will be mastered by it."

45

MY BROTHERS KEEPER?

הֲלוֹא אִם־תֵּיטִיב שְׂאֵת
וְאִם לֹא תֵיטִיב
לַפֶּתַח חַטָּאת רֹבֵץ
וְאֵלֶיךָ תְּשׁוּקָתוֹ וְאַתָּה תִּמְשָׁל־בּוֹ.

If thou doest well, shall it not be lifted up?
and if thou doest not well,
sin coucheth at the door;
and unto thee is its desire,
but thou mayest rule over it   (4, 7)

In our previous *Studies* (pp. 38–43) we tried to clarify the
obscurities of the above passage. We regarded it as a Divine
warning to Cain prior to his crime, alerting man to the dangers
of sin which ever lies in wait to overwhelm him, and the limits
of the freedom granted him. Man is free to succumb to or overcome temptation. In the second half of the chapter we encounter
Cain, after the deed of fratricide. Cain had made his choice.
succumbing to temptation and again God addressed him:

וַיֹּאמֶר יְיָ אֶל־קַיִן: אֵי הֶבֶל אָחִיךָ?

Then the Lord said to Cain: Where is Abel, thv brother?
                                                    (4, 9)

The late Professor Cassuto in his work *From Adam to Noah*
(p. 217) evokes, in this context, an association with a passage
in Deuteronomy (21, 1) which reads: "If there be found a
corpse on the ground ... fallen in the field; it is not known who
hath smitten him."

To men it is not known, but to God it is. Everything is revealed and foreknown to Him. This is what the Torah meant to teach us here by placing the words "the Lord said" in juxtaposition to "and killed him." God demanded a reckoning from him regarding his deed. (Cassuto)

Obviously the Almighty had asked a rhetorical question and had not requested information. The Divine answer immediately afterwards indicates that it is a rhetorical question resembling the one addressed to Adam after his sin. Rashi notes this in his observation that God had merely wished to engage him in conversation. But there is a difference between the two contexts:

God to Cain 4, 9	*God to Adam* 3, 9
וַיֹּאמֶר יְיָ אֶל־קַיִן: אֵי הֶבֶל אָחִיךָ?	וַיֹּאמֶר לוֹ: אַיֶּכָּה?
להיכנס עמו בדברי נחת, אולי ישיב ויאמר: אני הרגתי וחטאתי לך.	יודע הָיָה היכן הוא, אלא ליכנס עמו בדברים, שלא ירא נבהל להשיב אם יעניֹשֵׁהו פתאום. וכן בקין אמר: "אי הבל אחך?" וכן בבלעם (במדבר כב, ט): "מי האנשים האלה?" — ליכנס עמהם בדברים, וכן בחזקיהו בשלוחי מרודך בלאדן.
Then the Lord said to Cain Where is Abel thy brother?	And He said unto him Where art thou?
Rashi	*Rashi*
Where is Abel thy brother? To soften him with gentle words, perhaps he would repent and say: I have slain a man and sinned against Thee.	God knew where he was but he wished to engage him in conversation, that he should not be deterred from repentance by sudden punishment. Similarly regarding Cain it is stated, "Where is Abel thy brother;" and of Balam (Numbers 22), "Who are these men," in order to engage him in conversation; and with Hezekiah and the messengers of Merodach Baladon.

Rashi's commentators seem to be right in detecting a difference between the two contexts. Adam had already shown signs of remorse by his very act of hiding in the trees of the garden. It was not necessary to soften him with gentle words in order to prompt him to confess his sin. Cain however had shown no signs of remorse after the deed. Rashi therefore explains the question as a last attempt by God to extract from him a confession of his wrongdoing. Cain's answer is also of a different order:

לֹא יָדַעְתִּי, הֲשֹׁמֵר אָחִי אָנֹכִי?

I do not know. Am I my brother's keeper? (4, 9)

This attempt to deaden the voice of his conscience was in vain. It was the voice of the judge responding to the cry of innocent blood that had been shed. Our Sages illustrate the futility of denying sin with two parables:

משל לאחד שנכנס לגינה ולקט תותין ואכל והיה בעל הגינה רץ אחריו,
אמר לו: מה בידך? אמר לו: אין בידי כלום. אמר לו: והרי ידיך מלוכלכות!
כך אמר לו קין להקב"ה: "השומר אחי אנכי"? אמר לו הקב"ה: רשע! "קול
דמי אחיך צועקים אלי".
משל לאחד שנכנס למרעה וחטף גדי אחד והפשילו לאחוריו, והיה בעל
המרעה רץ אחריו, אמר לו: מה בידך? אמר לו: אין בידי כלום! אמר לו:
והרי הוא מפעה אחריך?! כך אמר הקב"ה לקין: "קול דמי אחיד וגו'".

It may be compared to a person who entered a garden and gathered berries and ate them. The owner of the garden ran after him and said to him: What have you in your hand? He said to him. I have nothing. To which the owner replied: But your hands are stained! In like manner did Cain reply to the Holy One blessed be He: "Am I my brother's keeper?" To which the Holy One blessed be He replied: Villain! "The voice of the blood of thy brother crieth unto me."

It may be compared to a person who entered a pasture and snatched a kid and slung it behind him. Whereupon the owner of the field ran after him and said to him: What have you in your hand? To which the latter replied: I have nothing. The owner then retorted: But it is bleating behind you! Similarly the Holy One blessed be He replied to Cain: "The voice of thy brother's blood..." (Gen. Rabbah 22, 9)

Where two parables are cited it is obvious that each has some-thing additional to contribute. What is the difference between the stealer of berries and the kid snatcher? Their attempts, in both cases, to silence the owner were in vain. But the first Midrash tells us: It is no longer possible to deny the sin, since the change in the sinner himself—the stain on his character bears indisputable evidence of the commission of the deed. He is no longer the same person: "But your hands are stained!"

The second Midrash tells us: The sin itself—reality cannot be denied. It is not the same as it was prior to the crime. Its brightness has been clouded, its light dimmed, creation had been darkened and an abyss had opened up: "But it is bleating behind you!"

We noted above that Cain did not react to the Almighty's efforts to prompt him to confess his sin by showing remorse and accepting responsibility. On the contrary, he repudiated responsibility and attempted to shift it elsewhere. This is also illustrated by a parable in the Midrash:

כיון שאמר לו הקב"ה "אי הבל אחיך", אמר לו: "לא ידעתי, השומר אחי
אנכי"? אתה הוא שומר כל הבריות ואתה מבקשו מידי? משל למה הדבר
דומה? לגנב שגנב כלים בלילה ולא נתפש. לבוקר תפשו השוער. אמר לו:
למה גנבת את הכלים? אמר לו: אני גנב ולא הנחתי אומנותי, אבל אתה
אומנותך בשער לשמור, למה הנחת אומנותך? ועכשיו אתה אומר לי כך? —
אף קין כך אמר: אני הרגתי אותו, שבראת בי יצר הרע. אתה שומר הכל ולי
הנחת אותו להרג? אתה הוא שהרגת אותו, שאילו קיבלת קרבני כמותו
לא הייתי מתקנא בו.

As soon as the Holy One blessed be He said unto him: "Where is thy brother Abel?" Cain replied: "I do not know. Am I my brother's keeper?" Thou art the keeper of all creatures; notwith-standing thou dost seek him at my hand? To what may this be compared? To a thief who stole articles by night and got away. In the morning the gatekeeper caught him and asked him: Why did you steal the articles? To which the thief replied: I stole but I did not neglect my job. You however, your job is to keep watch at the gate, why did you neglect your job? Now you talk to me like that? So, too, Cain said: I did slay him because thou didst create in me the evil inclination. Thou art the keeper of all; yet me Thou didst allow to slay him? Thou it was that didst slay him; for hadst Thou accepted my sacrifice the same as his, I would not have been jealous of him.   (Tanhuma)

Cain's exuses are legion. Was I to blame? You were to blame
for creating me with such base instincts, for not saving him
from my clutches, for giving me cause to envy him etc. The
same idea is summed up more incisively and decisively in
another Midrash:

"ויאמר ה' אל קין: אי הבל אחיך? ויאמר: לא ידעתי השומר·אחי אנכי ?"
משל לאיפרכוס [שר הממונה לשמור בני המדינה] שהיה מהלך באמצע פלטיא
[רחוב גדול ברשות הרבים], מצא הרוג ואחד עומד על גביו. אמר לו: מי
הרגו? אמר לו [זה העומד על גבי ההרוג]: אנא בעי ליה גבך ואת בעי ליה
גבי? [אני מבקשו מעמך ואומר שאתה הרגתו, ואתה אומר שאני הרגתיו?
(מתנות כהונה)] אמר לו [האיפרכוס]: לא אמרת כלום.

It may be compared to the prefect who was walking in the
middle of the plaza. He came across a person standing over a
dead body. Whereupon he said: Who killed him? To which the
other answered: That's my question to you; yet you ask me!
The prefect replied: Rubbish! (literally: "you have said nothing").
(Bereshit Rabbah)

The Divine answer is to throw the whole responsibility back
on man. He has been given freewill. "See I have set before thee
today, life and good, death and evil; therefore choose life."
All the arguments, excuses and sophisms attempting to shift
responsibility from man for his own actions are silenced: "You
have said nothing."

Questions for Further Study

1.
ויאמר
מה עשית   קול   דמי אחיך
צועקים אלי   מן האדמה.
ועתה ארור אתה   מן האדמה
אשר פצתה את פיה   לקחת את דמי אחיך
מידך.

And He said,

What have you done? / Hark! your brother's blood
is crying to Me / from the ground.   (verse 10)

And now you are cursed / from the ground,
which has opened its mouth / to receive your brother's
blood from your hand.   (verse 11)

Cassuto observes (From Adam to Noah p. 218):

I have arranged the clauses of verse 11 in such a way as to throw into relief the correspondence between it and the previous verse. The two parts of verse 10 end with the words: "your brother's blood" and "from the ground." In verse 11, the same end phrases recur in reverse order.

What purpose does this correspondence serve?

2.

פרק ג	פרק ד (2)
ויאמר לו:	ויאמר ה׳ אל קין
איכה (ט).	אי הבל אחיך (ט).

And he said unto him	And the Lord said unto Cain
Where art thou איכה	Where is (אי) Abel thy
(3, 9)	brother? (4, 9)

Explain why the Hebrew equivalent *ayeh* is used in both places rather than *efo*? Cf.: Gen. 37, 16; Ruth 2, 19; I Sam. 19, 22; Job 38; 4; where *efo* is used, with: Judges 6, 13; II Kings 38, 34; ibid 2, 14; Jeremiah 20, 28; Gen. 18, 9 where *ayeh* is used.

3.   "A wanderer shall he be in the land"   (Gen. 4, 12)

אין לך רשות לדור במקום אחד.

You are not permitted to settle in one place   (Rashi)
This means that his heart will give him no rest or peace to stay in one place, but he will be an eternal exile ...

(Ramban)

What is the difference between Rashi's and Ramban's approach?

4.   Cf. to the Midrash on p. 50 about the prefect the following Midrash:

אמר ר׳ שמעון בן יוחאי: קשה הדבר לאמרו ואי אפשר לפה לפרשו: לשני אתליטין (יונית: מתגוששים) שהיו עומדים ומתגוששים לפני המלך. אילו רצה המלך — פרשן. ולא רצה המלך לפרשן. נתחזק אחד על חברו והרגו, והיה מצווח ואומר: (= האיש המוכה צווח) "מאן יבעי דיני קדם קדם מלכא" (מתנות

51

כהונה: מי יתבע דיני ודמי מיד המלך, כי דמי בראשו, שאם היה רוצה, היה
מוחה ביד המכה) כך: "קול דמי אחיך צועקים א ל י מן האדמה".

Said R. Shimon B. Yoḥai: The very idea is unutterable and
inexpressible! It may be compared to two athletes who were
wrestling in the presence of the king. If the king had wanted he
could have separated them but he did not want to do so. One
gained the upper hand over the other and killed him. The dying
man cried out: Who will champion my cause and revenge my
death from the King, for he is responsibe; for had he so desired
he could have intervened. That is the force of the text: "The
voice of thy brother's blood cries *unto Me* from the ground."

((Bereshit Rabbah 22, 9)

(a) What is common to this Midrash and the one on the
prefect?

(b) In what way is it different?

(c) How does Rabbi Shimon B. Yoḥai here interpret the
text: "The voice of thy brother's blood ..."?

Bereshit 7

DECLINE OF MAN

וַיַּרְא יְיָ כִּי רַבָּה רָעַת הָאָדָם בָּאָרֶץ
וְכָל־יֵצֶר מַחְשְׁבֹת לִבּוֹ רַק רַע כָּל־הַיּוֹם.

**And the Lord saw that the wickedness of man was great
in the earth,**
**and that every imagination of the thoughts of his heart
was only evil continually.** (6, 5)

In the history of mankind which is gradually unfolded from
its beginnings in this week's sidra "the deeds and habits of man,
his inmost thoughts and secret intrigues and true motives of
his actions," (Rosh Hashana Liturgy) the process of man's repudiation of the sovereignty of God is traced. The decline and
fall of man is recorded in four stages, each of them replete with
symbolism, epitomising the iniquities of each successive epoch
and representing a continuous picture of human fallibility.

Stage One   — Adam's Sin, Chapter 3
Stage Two   — Cain's Sin, Chapter 4
Stage Three — Lemech's Sin, Chapter 4, 17–22
Stage Four — The Collective (not individual) Sin of
              the Sons of God, Chapter 6, 1–4.

We shall endeavour here to probe the significance and symbolism of these stages with the aid of the interpretations offered
by our sages and commentators down the ages. What was
Adam's offence? He was told:

מִכֹּל עֵץ־הַגָּן אָכֹל תֹּאכֵל.
וּמֵעֵץ הַדַּעַת טוֹב וָרָע לֹא תֹאכַל מִמֶּנּוּ – –

53

Of every tree of the Garden thou mayest surely eat but of the tree of the knowledge of good and evil thou mayest not eat thereof. (2, 16–17)

What did this prohibition imply? Here we refer the reader once again to the *Midrash Tadshe* cited on p. 23. The burden of that Midrash may be restated as follows: the tree itself possessed no special properties endowing man with any particular powers. It simply served as a test of man's discipline and the touchstone of his acceptance of the yoke of heaven. Adam's transgression did not spring from any practical need since all the trees of the Garden except this one were at his disposal. His sin was prompted by the desire to do exactly as he chose, as if the world belonged to him and he was master of all. But it was just for this reason that the prohibition had been given in order to teach him the principle, informing numerous precepts of the Torah, that the earth is the Lord's and the fullness thereof, or as is phrased in Ex. 19, 5: "For all the land is mine."

The first transgression of man therefore was not prompted by material considerations.

The second transgression committed by man, the issue of Adam and Eve was murder. The Torah is not explicit about the reasons prompting this crime. This problem we treated in our *Studies* on pp. 38ff.

It is difficult to understand the exact nature of Lemech's crime (4, 17–25). His children were the pioneers of technical advance and civilization and his son Tuval Cain was the forger of brass and iron instruments:

עָדָה וְצִלָּה שְׁמַעַן קוֹלִי
נְשֵׁי לֶמֶךְ הַאֲזֵנָּה אִמְרָתִי
כִּי אִישׁ הָרַגְתִּי לְפִצְעִי
וְיֶלֶד לְחַבֻּרָתִי.
כִּי שִׁבְעָתַיִם יֻקַּם־קָיִן
וְלֶמֶךְ שִׁבְעִים וְשִׁבְעָה.

54

Adah and Zillah, hear my voice;
Ye wives of Lemech, hearken unto my speech;
For I have slain a man for wounding me,
And a young man for bruising me;
If Cain shall be avenged sevenfold,
Truly Lemech seventy and sevenfold!   (4, 23–24)

This poetic outburst is mystifying in content. Is it a song of lament or the boastings of one who is about to display his prowess? The latter opinion sounds more plausible. Indeed this is how Malbim explains it:

> Lemech is here warning people against standing in his way, boasting how he killed a man who had inflicted on him a wound. During the struggle the victim had managed to give him a bruise which is lighter than a wound and in exchange he had killed his children too. There is no one who can stand against me and seek vengeance since there is no way of bringing me to justice because I am too powerful. If you say (Lemech argued) that I shall be punished by heaven then I reply that if in the case of Cain who was the first murderer, God nevertheless ordained that whoever would kill him would be revenged sevenfold, all the more so Lemech who is more powerful than Cain. Whoever slays him will be revenged seven times sevenfold . . .

Cain's crime was that of hot-blooded murder, as a result of a lack of control. Lemech's song is full of the deliberate boastings and braggings of one who has perfected death-dealing weapons enabling him to lord it over his fellows and commit indiscriminate murder.

The fourth sin described in the sidra is not an individual crime but one perpetrated by a whole group of individuals— the sons of God—i.e. the sons of the judges. This is the interpretation followed by most of the commentators, basing themselves on the use of the word *elohim* in Exodus 22: "And the householder shall draw near unto the judges." The stronger enslave the weaker, the classic example of exploitation being the subjugation of the daughters of man—"And they took for themselves wives whomsover they chose." Man thus extended his dominion from the vegetable and animal kingdom to embrace the enslavement of his fellows. The RaDaK (Rabbi David Kimḥi) explains the sins of the sons of God in the same way, pointing out that the word *elohim* and *ish* are used with reference to the nobility, whilst *adam* alludes to the oppressed and weaker classes.

This decline in the moral standards of mankind is accompanied by constant progress in material development and civilization. Both Malbim in the last century and Cassuto in this one have pointed out in their respective commentaries to Genesis that this material development was not activated by any corresponding moral inspiration.

> All the achievements of material civilization are nothing without moral and ethical qualities. (Cassuto)

Our sidra began on a note of promise and light. But we may now appreciate the atmosphere of gloom and foreboding which envelopes its conclusion:

וַיַּרְא יְיָ כִּי רַבָּה רָעַת הָאָדָם בָּאָרֶץ
וְכָל־יֵצֶר מַחְשְׁבֹת לִבּוֹ רַק רַע כָּל הַיּוֹם.
וַיִּנָּחֶם יְיָ כִּי־עָשָׂה אֶת־הָאָדָם בָּאָרֶץ
וַיִּתְעַצֵּב אֶל־לִבּוֹ.

And the Lord saw that the wickedness of man was great in the earth,

and that every imagination of the thoughts of his heart was only evil continually.

And it repented the Lord that He had made man on the earth,

and it grieved Him at His heart. (6, 5–6)

Questions for Further Study

> Lemech's statement to his wives is really a flashback. I have pointed out two similar examples (of the violation of the time sequence: The creation of man is reported in 2, 8–9 before the

planting of trees which of course took place earlier; similarly the prohibition of the tree of knowledge (2, 17–19) before the creation of animal life, though the command was actually issued afterwards.) Cf. also Gen. 24, 22: "Then the man took a gold ring; Exod. 33, 5: "Say to the children of Israel, You are a stubborn people," and Deut. 3, 23: "Then I pleaded with the Lord, at that time, saying."

Our Sages in Bereshit Rabbah 23 explained the reason for Lemech's outburst. Ada and Zillah refused to have children because they were afraid of the curse of Cain which condemned his descendants to an untimely death, starting with the seventh generation removed from him. Lemech reassured them by explaining that he, himself, in fact was, in point of time, the seventh generation and that if anyone, child or adult tried to harm him he would be a dead man. *haragti*—though past in form is future in meaning.[1] Cf. also Gen. 23, 13. If Cain were avengeable seven-fold, then Lemech would be seven times seven since he would have killed in self-defence whereas Cain had been guilty of deliberate murder. In his poetic outbust Lemech was really telling his wives that they had nothing to fear, since the punishment decreed for Cain had come to an end. But of course this was not the case and Lemech's descendants all died in the flood. No trace of Cain remained on account of his violent deed.

(Ibn Ezra on 4, 23)

A certain non-Jewish writer[2] has advanced an attractive explanation. Violence had probably begun to rear its ugly head in those early days. Robber bands hiding in the deserts, in caves and rocky hideouts would descend on settlements, pillage and carry off the womenfolk. The farmers and villagers retaliated by building fortified strongholds and inventing weapons to stave off their attacks. With more sophisticated weapons they could kill without great risk to themselves and the weak armed with a sword or spear could play the mighty man.

Since Tuval Cain the son of Lemech was the master of this skill possibly taught him by his father, as Ramban maintains, Lemech boasts to his wives: I have no further need to fear any man. Should the strongest fight me and succeed in wounding with his fist or a stone, or a child bruise me with his bare hands, I will make mincemeat of him with the new implements at my disposal and take my vengeance sevenfold. The past form *haragti* (lit.: I have killed) implies future: "I shall kill" as Ibn Ezra explains.

(Biur)

1. Point out the similarities and differences between the two approaches outlined above of the Biur and Ibn Ezra respectively.
2. Which of them is closer to the Malbim cited in our *Studies?*
3. Wherein lies the weakness of Ibn Ezra's explanation (pointed out by several commentators)?
4. What is attractive about the explanation offered by the non-Jewish exegete calling forth the praises of Mendelssohn (the author of the Biur to Genesis)?

---

[1] Ibn Ezra would read the text as follows: "For a grown man *(ish)* shall I kill, who wounds me and child who bruises me."

[2] Gottfried Herder, a contemporary of Goethe. The extract is taken from his famous work on the Bible *Vom Geiste der ebräischen Poesie,* 1782.

PROFILE OF NOAH

Noah is the first figure in the Biblical story of mankind to be
awarded special titles of distinction. A witness of a world that
was ridden with corruption and violence, and of the fresh new
world that emerged from the deluge, he is described by the
following epithets:

נֹחַ אִישׁ צַדִּיק תָּמִים הָיָה בְּדֹרֹתָיו.

**Noah was a man, righteous and whole-hearted in his
generations.** (6, 9)

This epithet "whole-hearted" is identical with the one used by
the Almighty in His second message to Abraham:

הִתְהַלֵּךְ לְפָנַי וֶהְיֵה תָמִים.

Walk before Me and be thou whole-hearted. (17, 1)

Many have been puzzled at the Torah's choice of wording here.
According to the text, Noah was evidently endowed with a quality
which Abraham had yet to achieve. Does this then reflect the
true relationship between their respective characters? Our Sages
solved this problem by giving the epithet "whole-hearted" a
much narrower implication in the case of Noah.

מהו "בדורותיו"? יש דורשין לשבח ויש דורשין לגנאי. צדיק בדורותיו ולא
בדורות אחרים. משל למה הדבר דומה: אם יתן אדם סלע של כסף בתוך
סלעים של נחושת, אותה של כסף נראית נאה. כך היה נח נראה צדיק בדור
המבול. יש דורשין אותו לשבח. כיצד? משל לחבית של אפרסמון שהיתה
נתונה בקבר והיה ריחה טוב, אילו היתה בבית על אחת כמה וכמה.

What is meant by "in his generations"? Some interpret it to his
credit and others to his discredit. Righteous in his generations

but not in others. To what may this be compared? If a man places a silver coin among copper coins, then the silver appears attractive. So Noah appeared righteous in the generation of the flood. Others interpret it to his credit. How so? It may be compared to a jar of balsam placed in a grave and it gave off a goodly fragrance. Had it been in the house how much more so!

(Tanḥuma)

Rashi utilises this same Midrash:

"בדורותיו": יש מרבותינו דורשים אותו לשבח, כל שכן שאילו היה בדור של צדיקים היה צדיק יותר.

ויש שדורשים אותו לגנאי: לפי דורו היה צדיק ואילו היה בדורו של אברהם לא היה נחשב לכלום.

"In his generations." Some of our Rabbis interpret it creditably. How much more righteous would Noah have been, had he lived in a righteous generation! Others interpret it discreditably. He was righteous compared with his generation; but had he lived in Abraham's generation he would have been considered as naught.

On this R. Mordekhai Yaffe comments in his gloss to Rashi, *Levush Haora,* as follows:

Know that these two interpretations of Noah's character, one reflecting credit and the other discredit on him, constitute, in actual fact, equal valuations of his righteousness. There is no difference of opinion between the two points of view regarding this. Both maintained that his righteousness bore the stamp of mediocrity. They differed rather on the evaluation of the phrase: "in his generations." One interpreted it to reflect credit, deducing that if Noah had lived in a righteous generation and had had a good example to follow, he would certainly have been a much more righteous man. The other interpreted it discreditably, the phrase implying, according to him, that Noah was righteous in relation to his generation. According to him the text viewed Noah in an unfavourable light. Had he lived in Abraham's generation he would not have been more righteous, for he would not have benefited by the Patriarch's example and would have been considered as naught.

The unfavourable evaluation of Noah's character is further strengthened by the Divine message to Noah, where it is stated:

כִּי־אֹתְךָ רָאִיתִי צַדִּיק לְפָנַי בַּדּוֹר הַזֶּה.

**For thee have I seen righteous before Me
in this generation.**   (7, 1)

The contrast between the character of Noah and that of Abraham
is brought out in their differing reactions to a similar situation.
Both were forewarned of a Divine decree of doom pronounced
on their fellow men (Gen. 6–13 and 18, 20–21).

The Zohar takes note of the contrast between their reactions:

"ויגש אברהם ויאמר: האף תספה צדיק עם רשע" (בראשית יח, כג) — אמר
ר' יהודה: מאן חמא אבא דרחמנותא כאברהם? תא חזי: בנח כתיב (ו,
יג—יד): "ויאמר אלהים לנח: קץ כל בשר בא לפני ... והנני משחיתם את
הארץ. עשה לך תבת עצי גפר ...", ואשתיק ולא אמר לו מידי ולא בעי
רחמי. אבל אברהם, בשעתא דאמר ליה קב"ה: "זעקת סדום ועמרה כי רבה
וחטאתם כי כבדה מאד. ארדה נא ואראה ...". — מיד כתיב: "ויגש אברהם
ויאמר: האף תספה צדיק עם רשע?!". (אמר ר' יהודה: מי ראה אב רחמן
כאברהם. בוא וראה: בנח כתיב: "קץ כל בשר בא לפני ... עשה לך תבת
עצי גפר ...", ושתק [נח] ולא אמר דבר ולא ביקש רחמים. אבל אברהם
בשעה שאמר לו הקב"ה: "זעקת סדום ועמורה כי רבה ... ארדה נא
ואראה...", מיד כתיב: "ויגש אברהם ויאמר: האף תספה צדיק עם
רשע ?!").

"And Abraham drew near and said, wilt Thou also destroy the
righteous with the wicked?" (Genesis 18, 23) — said R. Yehudah:
Who hath seen a father as compassionate as Abraham? Come
and see: Regarding Noah it is stated (6, 13) "and God said to
Noah, the end of all flesh is come before me; ... and behold I
will destroy them from the earth. Make thee an ark of gopher
wood ..." And Noah held his peace and said naught, neither did
he intercede. Whereas Abraham, as soon as the Holy One blessed
be He said to him: "Because the cry of Sodom and Gomorrah is
great, and because their sin is very grievous. I will go down and
see ...". Immediately, as it is stated, "And Abraham drew near
and said: Wilt Thou also destroy the righteous with the wicked?"

Noah was limited in his horizons and belonged to those who
were satisfied to save their own souls. A further point of contrast
we find in the Scriptural description of their respective relationships with the Almighty. Of Noah it is said:

נֹחַ אִישׁ צַדִּיק תָּמִים הָיָה בְּדֹרֹתָיו
אֶת־הָאֱלֹהִים הִתְהַלֶּךְ־נֹחַ.

**Noah was in his generations
a man, righteous and whole-hearted;
Noah walked** with God. (6, 9)

Of Abraham:

הִתְהַלֵּךְ לְפָנַי וֶהְיֵה תָמִים.

Walk before me,
and be thou whole-hearted. (17, 1)

Our Sages who studied carefully every word and phrase in the
Torah pointed out that this variation in phraseology reflects differing levels of closeness to God:

"את האלהים התהלך נח" (בראשית ו, ט) — ר׳ יהודה ור׳ נחמיה: ר׳ יהודה
אמר: משל למלך שהיו לו שני בנים, אחד גדול ואחד קטן. אמר לקטן: הלך
עמי, ואמר לגדול: בוא והלך לפני. כך אברהם שהיה כוחו יפה — "התהלך
לפני והיה תמים". אבל נח שהיה כוחו רע — "את האלהים התהלך נח".
ר׳ נחמיה אמר: משל לאוהבו של מלך שהיה משתקע בטיט עבה, הציץ המלך
וראה אותו. אמר לו: עד שאתה משתקע בטיט — הלך עמי. הדא הוא דכתיב:
"את האלהים התהלך נח". ולמה אברהם דומה: לאוהבו של מלך, שראה את
המלך במבואות האפילים. הציץ אוהבו והתחיל מאיר עליו דרך החלון. הציץ
המלך וראה אותו, אמר לו: עד שאתה מאיר לי דרך החלון — בוא והאיר
לפני.
כך אמר הקב״ה לאברהם: עד שאתה מאיר לי מאספוטמיא ומחברותיה — בוא
והאיר לפני בארץ ישראל!

"Noah walked with God." R. Yehudah said: It may be compared
to a king who had two sons, an older and younger one. He said
to the younger one, walk with me; and to the older: come and
walk before me. Thus to Abraham, whose spiritual powers
were superior, he said: "Walk before Me, and be thou whole-
hearted." But of Noah, whose powers were inferior, it is stated
as follows: "Noah walked with God." R. Nehemiah said: It may
be compared to the king's friend who was sinking in the mire.
The king looked and saw him, and said to him: before you sink
into the mire walk with me. It is therefore written: "Noah walked
with God." To whom may Abraham be compared? To a king's
friend who saw the king walking through a dark alleyway. His
friend seeing him began to show him a light through the window.
When the king looked up and saw him he said to him: before
you give me light through the window come and give light in

front of me. Thus said the Holy One blessed be He: before you give light for Me in Mesopotamia and its neighbours, come and give light before Me in the land of Israel.

(Bereshit Rabbah 30, 10)

Rashi restates the same idea very briefly:

"את האלהים התהלך נח" — ובאברהם הוא אומר: "אשר התהלכתי לפניו".
נח היה צריך סעד לתומכו, אבל אברהם היה מתחזק ומהלך בצדקו מאליו.

Noah needed support but Abraham strengthened himself and walked in his righteousness by himself.

How apt is the parable used by our Sages. One who is sinking in the mire wishes to extricate himself, but cannot on his own. Noah possessed the will to extricate himself from the corruption of his generation. Because he possessed the initial desire to do so the Almighty came to his aid, saying: come and walk with Me. (cf. he who wishes to purify himself is helped from above). But Abraham was in no need of help. On the contrary, to whom may he that walks before the Lord be compared?

To a prince whose progress is heralded by elders.

(ibid. Bereshit Rabbah)

This idea of the Almighty being announced, as it were, and his message spread abroad by His herald who are Abraham and his descendants, is found embodied in Balaam's blessing: "The Lord his God is with him and the shouting for the King is among them."

We constitute the trumpet which heralds and proclaims the progress of the chariot of the King of the Universe at all times and in every place.   (Sar Shalom Adulami: *Mesillot*)

Noah was not charged with the same Divine mission to spread the word of God abroad as Abraham, since he only possessed the capacity to save himself, but not others.

Regarding him it is not stated: "For I have known him" implying Divine choice as in the case of Abraham:

כִּי יְדַעְתִּיו לְמַעַן אֲשֶׁר יְצַוֶּה אֶת־בָּנָיו וְאֶת־בֵּיתוֹ אַחֲרָיו
וְשָׁמְרוּ דֶּרֶךְ יְיָ לַעֲשׂוֹת צְדָקָה וּמִשְׁפָּט.

**For I have known him, to the end that he may command
his children and his household after him,
that they may keep the way of the Lord,
to do righteousness and justice ...** (18, 19)

Noah was singled out for survival, Abraham for a mission.
Buber expresses the difference in his felicitous fashion: "Noah
stays put in nature; a man of the soil is rescued from the
deluge. Abraham is the first to make his way into history as a
proclaimer of God's dominion."[1]

Questions For Further Study

1. Read over the first Rashi cited on p. 60.
    Can you find the reason for Rashi's phrasing which in this
    case, does not reproduce the Talmudic idiom? Why does
    he express the favourable viewpoint as follows: "had he
    lived in a righteous generation," whilst with regard to the
    unfavourable viewpoint he prefers to say: "had he lived
    in Abraham's generation," rather than balancing the first
    by saying: "had he lived in a righteous generation"?

2. The Midrash also contrasts Abraham's conduct with
    Noah's:

אמר ר' סימון: שלוש מציאות מצא הקב"ה: אברהם, דוד וישראל. אברהם,
דכתיב (נחמיה ט, ח): "ומצאת את לבבו נאמן לפניך"; דוד, דכתיב (תהלים
פט, כא): "מצאתי דוד עבדי"; ישראל, דכתיב (הושע ט, י): "כענבים במדבר
מצאתי ישראל". איתיבון חבריא [מקשין חבריו] לר' סימון] והא כתיב
(בראשית ו, ח): "ונח מצא חן בעיני ה'"? [ולמה אם כן לא אמר ר' סימון
ארבע מציאות מצא הקב"ה?] אמר להם: הוא מצא — הקב"ה ל א מצא.

**R. Simon said: the Holy One blessed be He made three finds:
Abraham, David, and Israel. Abraham, as it is stated (Nehemiah
9, 8) and *found*est his heart faithful before Thee. David, as it
is written (Psalm 89, 21) "I have *found* David My servant."
Israel, as it is written (Hosea 9, 10) "I *found* Israel like grapes**

in the wilderness." His colleagues raised an objection to R. Simon: But surely it is written "But Noah *found* grace in the eyes of the Lord"? He answered: he found, but the Holy One blessed be He did not find. (Bereshit Rabbah 29, 3)

Can you explain the meaning of this Midrash, utilising what you have learned in the *Studies*.

3. "And Noah went in... into the ark, before the waters of the flood." (7, 7). We cite here two interpretations:

"מפני מי המבול": אף נח מקטני אמונה היה, מאמין ואינו מאמין שיבוא המבול, ולא נכנס לתיבה עד שדחקוהו המים.

"Before the waters of the flood." Noah too had little faith, only half believing that the flood would come and he did not enter the Ark until the waters drove him. (Rashi)

"And Noah went in." Noah entered the Ark seven days before the deluge. This is the meaning of the phrase "before the waters of the flood"—he entered *before* they came. We do not understand the reason of those who say that Noah had little faith, whereas the text testifies that he was righteous and wholehearted, and did all that the Lord had commanded him. (Radak)

(a) On which word in the text are the two explanations based?

(b) Which of the two attitudes to Noah's conduct fits in with what we have tried to prove in our *Studies*, and which of them is opposed?

4. Cf. the following two comments of Rashi:

אותך ראיתי צדיק: ולא נאמר "צדיק תמים", מכאן שאומרים מקצת שבחו של אדם בפניו וכולו שלא בפניו.
ומפני מה משכן והפרידן ממשה? לפי שאומרים מקצת שבחו של אדם בפניו וכולו שלא בפניו. וכן מצינו בנח: שלא בפניו נאמר: "איש צדיק תמים" ובפניו נאמר: "כי אותך ראיתי צדיק לפני".

"For thee have I seen righteous" (7, 1). The text does not say: "righteous and wholehearted." This is the source for the saying

65

that you sing only part of a man's praises to his face and the whole not to his face.

Why did the Almighty draw them away and separate them from Moses? (Num. 12, 5) Because you sing only a part of a man's praises to his face and the whole not to his face. We find the same with Noah . . .

Give two (educational-ethical) reasons underlying this principle to be sparing of praise to a man's face and to keep them for when he is not present.

[1] From his essay: "Abraham the Seer," p. 35 in *On the Bible* ed. N. Glatzer, Schocken, New York, 1968. Several points in our *Studies* were inspired by the article.

LESSON OF THE FLOOD

Cassuto in his work *From Noah to Abraham* pp. 30–31, comments as follows on the story of the Deluge as related in our sidra:

> The structure of the chapter is carefully worked out down to the last detail. The story is divided into two acts of six paragraphs each. The first part starting at the beginning of the sidra to chapter 7 verse 24 unfolds, stage by stage, the workings of Divine justice, unleashing catastrophe on a world that has become filled with violence. The picture becomes progressively darker, until only one spark of light remains to illuminate the deathly gloom characterising the sixth paragraph (7, 17–24). This is the ark which floated on the awesome waters that had covered everything, and which guarded within its bounds the hope of life in the future:

וַיִּמַח אֶת־כָּל־הַיְקוּם אֲשֶׁר עַל־פְּנֵי הָאֲדָמָה
מֵאָדָם עַד־בְּהֵמָה עַד־רֶמֶשׂ וְעַד־עוֹף הַשָּׁמַיִם
וַיִּמָּחוּ מִן־הָאָרֶץ
וַיִּשָּׁאֶר אַךְ־נֹחַ וַאֲשֶׁר אִתּוֹ בַּתֵּבָה.

And every living substance was destroyed which was upon the face of the ground,

both man, and cattle, and reptile, and the fowl of the heaven;

and they were destroyed from the earth

and no one save Noah remained alive and they that were with him in the ark.   (7, 23)

The second act depicts for us the various successive stages of Divine mercy renewing life on earth. The light that had become reduced to nothing more than a tiny dot in a world of darkness now shines brighter and brighter, till it once again illuminates the whole of our canvas. Now we are shown a tranquil world adorned

with the rainbow, reflecting its spectrum of colour through the
clouds, as a sign and surety of life and peace for the coming
generations.

זֹאת אוֹת־הַבְּרִית אֲשֶׁר הֲקִמֹתִי בֵּינִי
וּבֵין כָּל־בָּשָׂר אֲשֶׁר עַל־הָאָרֶץ.

**This is the token of the covenant which I have established
between me
and all flesh that is upon the earth (9, 17).**

The wrongdoing of the antedeluvians is alluded to in the last
paragraphs of the previous sidra, illustrated in the continuous
moral decline of the human race, from fratricide (Cain and
Abel) to the glorification of battle and the sword, in Lemech's
lyrical outburst, and the deeds of the "sons of God," who "took
themselves wives of all which they chose."

These latter were "strong-arm" men who, in the words of
R. David Kimḥi, "upheld the principle of might is right and
there were none to deliver from their clutches." This picture of
moral disintegration becomes steadily blacker until it is stated
at the end of the last sidra:

וַיַּרְא יְיָ כִּי רַבָּה רָעַת הָאָדָם בָּאָרֶץ
וְכָל־יֵצֶר מַחְשְׁבֹת לִבּוֹ רַק רַע כָּל־הַיּוֹם.

**And God saw
that the wickedness of man was great in the earth,
and that every imagination of the thoughts of his heart
was only evil continually.**   (6, 5)

The moral crime of the generation of the flood is further described
in somewhat different phrasing, in two sentences, at the beginning
of our sidra:

וַתִּשָּׁחֵת הָאָרֶץ לִפְנֵי הָאֱלֹהִים
וַתִּמָּלֵא הָאָרֶץ חָמָס.

**The earth also was corrupt before God
And the earth was filled with violence.**   (6, 11)

68

In the opinion of our Sages cited in Rashi, the first sentence refers to sexual corruption, whilst the second refers to social crimes. חמס *(hamas)* "violence" refers to גזל *(gezel)* "robbery."

In the Divine message to Noah wherein He reveals to him his dread decision to wipe out mankind, only the last type of offence is referred to:

וַיֹּאמֶר אֱלֹהִים לְנֹחַ קֵץ כָּל־בָּשָׂר בָּא לְפָנַי
כִּי־מָלְאָה הָאָרֶץ חָמָס מִפְּנֵיהֶם – – –

And God said to Noah, the end of all flesh is come before me; for the earth is filled with violence (ḥamas) through them. (6, 13)

Our Sages were puzzled by the variation in the description of human behaviour, prior to the Deluge in verse 11 and the naming of the sin that led the Almighty to seal mankind's fate in verse 13.

Here is what our Sages comment on this subject in the Talmud, *Sanhedrin* 108a:

א"ר יוחנן: בוא וראה כמה גדול כוחה של חמס, שהרי דור המבול עברו על הכל ולא נחתם עליהם גזר דינם עד שפשטו ידיהם בגזל, שנאמר: "כי מלאה הארץ חמס מפניהם והנני משחיתם את הארץ".

Said R. Yoḥanan: Come and see how dreadful is the power of violence! For behold the generation of the deluge committed every conceivable transgression, yet their fate was only sealed when they put forth their hands to robbery, as it says: "For the earth is filled with violence through them, and behold I will destroy them from the earth."

The Midrash abounds in descriptions of the wickedness of the generation of the Deluge, of the exhaustive list of iniquities perpetrated by them. Nevertheless it is always stressed that of all their numerous transgressions, only that one specifically named, that of violence, sealed their fate and brought down Divine judgment on them:

כִּי־מָלְאָה הָאָרֶץ חָמָס מִפְּנֵיהֶם.

For the earth was filled with violence.

69

The Midrash aptly sums up the corrupting nature of "violence" which is capable of demoralising all that is good in human nature, and acts as an inexorable barrier between man and his Maker.

וכן איוב אומר (איוב טז, יז): "על לא חמס בכפי ותפילתי זכה".— וכי יש תפילה כעורה ? אלא כל מי שידיו מלוכלכות בגזל, הוא קורא להקב"ה ואינו עונה אותו, למה ? שתפילתו עכורה, שנאמר : "ויאמר אלהים לנח קץ כל בשר בא לפני, כי מלאה הארץ חמס" [גזל], אבל איוב שלא היה בעמלו גזל, היתה תפילתו זכה.

Thus said Job (Job 16, 17) : "Not for any injustice in mine hands: also my prayer is pure." Is there then a prayer that is impure? But he who prays to God with hands soiled by violence is not answered. Why? Because his prayer is impure, as it is said: "And God said, the end of all flesh is come before me; for the earth is filled with violence." But since Job never committed any violence, his prayer was pure.   (Shemot Rabbah)

The words of the *Neila prayer* should still echo in our ears, permeated by its ever-recurrent theme that "we cease from oppression of our hands." An allusion to another concept that is the keynote of the *Neila* prayer is also detected in the sidra by our Sages. This concept is referred to in *Ezekiel* (33, 11), pointing out that God does not desire the death of the wicked but rather their repentance.

The Midrash weaves this theme into the fabric of the story of the building of the ark, and the miraculous deliverance of Noah and his company throught its means.

בוא וראה, למה אמר הקב"ה לנח שיעשה תיבה? כדי שיראו אותו יושב ועוסק ויעשו תשובה. וכי לא יכול היה הקב"ה להצילו בדברו או להעלותו לשמים באמונתו, שאמר לו "עשה לך תיבה עצי גפר", למה כך ? אלא אמר הקב"ה: מתוך שאני אומר לו "עשה לך תיבת עצי גופר" והוא עומד ועוסק בה וכורת ארזים הם מתכנסין אצלו ואומרים לו: נח! מה אתה עושה? והוא אומר: תיבה! שאמר לי הקב"ה שמביא מבול לעולם, ומתוך כך שומעים ועושים תשובה. כך היה הקב"ה מחשב . . . ולא היו משגיחין עליו.

Come and see, why did the Holy One blessed be He command Noah to make the ark? In order that mankind should see him engaged in its construction and repent of their ways. Could not the Holy One blessed be He have saved him by His word or have borne him up to Heaven by his faith that he said to him, "Make for thee an ark of gopher wood"? Wherefore thus? But said the Holy One blessed be He: Since I say to him: "Make for thee an ark of gopher wood," and he becomes engaged in the work and cuts cedar wood, they will gather around him and say to him: Noah! What makest thou? Saith he: An ark!—Because God hath told me that he is bringing a deluge on the earth. As a result of this, they will listen and will repent. So the Holy One blessed be He thought ... but they took no notice.

(Tanḥuma)

Here is another version:

עמד נח ונטע ארזים והיו אומרים לו: ארזים אלה למה? אמר להם: הקב"ה מבקש להביא מבול ואמר לי לעשות תיבה, כדי שאימלט בה אני וביתי. והיו משחקין ממנו ומלעיגין בדבריו. והיה משקה אותן ארזים והן גדלים, והיו אומרים לו: מה אתה עושה? ומשיב להם כעניין הזה. והיו מלעיגים עליו. לסוף ימיו קצצן והיה מנסרן והיו אומרים לו: מה אתה עושה? ואומר להם כך, והיה מתרה בהם. כיון שלא עשו תשובה — — —

Noah went and planted cedars and they asked him: These cedars —what are they for? He said to them: The Holy One blessed be He seeketh to bring a flood and hath told me to build an ark for myself and household to escape in. Whereupon they laughed and mocked at him. Towards the end of his life he cut them down and planed them, whereupon they said to him What art thou doing? He would tell them and give them warning. Since they did not repent ...

This again is the theme of Rashi in the next chapter (7, 12) when the Almighty gave the generation its last chance to repent:

And the rain was upon the earth.   וַיְהִי הַגֶּשֶׁם עַל־הָאָרֶץ.

ולהלן הוא אומר: "ויהי המבול"? אלא כשהורידן, הורידן ברחמים, שאם יחזרו יהיו גשמי ברכה, כשלא חזרו — היו למבול.

"And the *rain* was upon the earth": Further it states: "And the *flood was*... upon the earth" (17)? When He caused it to descend He caused it to descend with mercy, so that in the event of their repenting, the rain would be one of blessing. When they did not repent, it turned into a deluge.

The last warning did not avail and the flood came and wiped them out.

71

1. Read over the story of the flood (6, 9–9, 17) and mark the twelve subdivisions referred to in our quotation at the beginning from Cassuto, in the following manner:

Act I	*Act II*
(1) 6, 9–12	(7)
(2) 6, 13–22	(8)
(3) 7, 1–	(9)
(4)	(10)
(5)	(11)
(6)	(12)

    Pay careful attention to the conclusion of these paragraphs. What is the significance of the similarity in phrasing that you find in the paragraphs concerned?

2. According to Cassuto, the parallels to be observed within these two sections that form the story of the flood are "concentric" in arrangement: the opening of the first section corresponds to the end of the second, the middle of the first to the middle of the second and the end of the first to the beginning of the second.
    Explain what these correspondences in content and phrasing consist of.

3. In the selfsame day entered Noah, and Shem, and
    Ham, and Japhet . . . into the ark.
    They, and every beast after its kind,
    and all the cattle after their kind,
    and every creeping thing that creepeth upon the
        earth after its kind,
    and every fowl after its kind, every bird of every sort.

    (7, 13–14)

    Why does the text diverge from the order of creation (see 1, 20–25) and mention the fowl last?

4. לימדך הכתוב, שהיו בני דורו אומרים: אילו אנו רואים אותו נכנס לתיבה,
אנו שוברין אותה והורגין אותו. אמר הקב"ה: אני מכניסו לעיני כולם
ונראה — דבר מי יקום!

ויסגור ה' בעדו (ז, טז).

רש"י:

הגן עליו שלא ישברוה: הקיף התיבה דובים ואריות והיו הורגים בהם.

"In the selfsame day entered Noah..."—the verse teaches us
that his contemporaries used to say to him: If we were to see
him go into the Ark we would wreck it and slay him. Said the
Holy One blessed be He: I shall install him in the Ark in front
of everyone and we shall see whose words shall prevail!
"And the Lord shut him in..."—protected him from them
wrecking it. He encircled the Ark with bears and lions which
slew them.   (Rashi on Gen. 7, 13–16)

(a) Point out which word or phrase in our text prompted
the above Midrash.

(b) Suggest a psychological explanation for the conduct
of the generation of the deluge to fit the scene depicted
in the Midrash.

(c) Try to explain why the Torah did not include any
description of the conduct of the generation of the
flood when retribution overtook them.

73

AFTERMATH OF THE FLOOD

פְּרוּ וּרְבוּ וּמִלְאוּ אֶת הָאָרֶץ וְכִבְשֻׁהָ
וּרְדוּ בִּדְגַת הַיָּם וּבְעוֹף הַשָּׁמַיִם
וּבְכָל־חַיָּה הָרֹמֶשֶׂת עַל הָאָרֶץ.

Be fruitful and multiply and replenish the earth and the fear of you and the dread of you shall be upon every beast of the earth. (9, 1–2)

The flood had abated. Every living substance upon the face of the earth had been blotted out and only Noah and they that were with him in the Ark survived. The world had been purified from corruption and violence and had been cleansed by the mighty waters. The Almighty swore that he would not bring again a flood on the earth and anticipated the building up of a new world. The new race of mankind, like the original one, would also spring from one progenitor. The reason for this is given by our Sages as follows:

מפני שלום הבריות, שלא יאמר אדם לחברו: אבא גדול מאביך.

In order to promote peace amongst mankind that one man should not say to his fellow, My father was greater than yours.
(Sanhedrin 37a)

שלא יהיו משפחות מתגרות זו בזו.

That families should not engage in feuds with one another.
(Tosefta Sanhedrin 85)

In other words all men were equal by natural descent and there was no room for any racial discrimination, "We all have one father." The first man on earth was a creation of the Almighty Himself and not born of woman. He was certainly perfect and there is no need to sing his praises. Of the second ancestor of mankind, Noah, it is stated:

A man righteous and perfect in his generations.   (6, 9)

The beginnings of mankind both with Noah and Adam were heralded by blessing. Let us compare the text of these blessings:

To Adam	*To Noah*
Be fruitful, and multiply, and replenish the earth, and subdue it; and have dominion over the fish of the sea, and over the fowl of the air, and over every living thing that creepeth upon the earth.	Be fruitful, and multiply, and replenish the earth. And the fear of you and the dread of you shall be upon every beast of the earth, and upon every fowl of the earth, and upon every fowl of the air, and upon all wherewith the ground teemeth, and upon all the fishes of the sea: into your hand are they delivered.
And God said: Behold, I have given you every herb yielding seed, which is upon the face of all the earth, and every tree, in which is the fruit of a tree yielding seed—to you it shall be for food; and to every beast of the earth, and to every fowl of the air, and to every living thing that creepeth upon the earth, wherein there is a living soul, every green herb for food.	Every moving thing that liveth shall be for food for you; as the green herb have I given you all.
(1, 28–30)	(9, 1–3)

There are similarities, but there are also differences. Adam is bidden to subdue the world. But this phrase is omitted in the case of Noah. Let us quote here Ramban's explanation of the phrase "subdue it":

> The Almighty entrusted mankind with power and dominion over the earth to do as it desired with the animal kingdom to build and uproot and plant, to mine copper from the hills and the like.

This process of conquering nature through technical achievements made great strides through the ingenuity shown by the descendants of Cain, as is related, in the building of cities and forging of articles of daily use, including death-dealing weapons and the erecting of gigantic towers for the sake of immortalising human prowess—"making a name." For this reason it was not necessary to repeat this blessing in the case of Noah and his sons since mankind had more than fulfilled the mission entrusted them in this sphere and even abused their trust.

On the other hand the descendants of Noah are seemingly entrusted with wider powers over the animal kingdom than that of their anti-deluvian forbears. Fear and dread succeed the goodwill that was to have reigned between man and his animal subjects in accordance with the blessing of Adam. Adam and the animals were bidden to enjoy equally the fruits of the earth, though man himself was to be lord of creation. But he was to administer and regulate within the framework of a harmonious kingdom rather than dominate and intimidate. In place of this we have in the blessing to Noah the ingredient of fear and dread, the world being divided into two hostile camps in which one intimidates the other. The chief difference therefore between the two blessings is the permission given to Noah's descendants to slaughter animals for food. This difference has been noted by our Sages and our commentators. Some of them regard it as marking the setting up of a complete barrier between animal and man. Man in spite of the enormous difference between him and the animal kingdom, in spite of his being created in the image of God had descended from his pinnacle and narrowed the gap and even intermingled with his brutish fellow creatures. Consequently, the animals were given up to man for food in order that man should know his unique place in creation as separate and above them.

Other commentators suggest different reasons for this dispensation. Here we quote Cassuto in his commentary *From Adam to Noah* (page 58) on Genesis 1, 27:

> You are permitted to use the animals and employ them for work, have dominion over them in order to utilise their services for

your subsistence, but must not hold their life cheap nor slaughter them for food. Your natural diet is vegetarian . . . Apparently the Torah was in principle opposed to the eating of meat. When Noah and his descendants were permitted to eat meat this was a concession conditional on the prohibition of the blood. This prohibition implied respect for the principle of life ("for the blood is the life") and an allusion to the fact that in reality all meat should have been prohibited. This partial prohibition was designed to call to mind the previously total one.

The late Rav Kook explained the implications of the passage under discussion in a somewhat different manner in a work that was written in his youth, entitled *Tallelei Orot* (Dewdrops of Light). Here we shall briefly refer to their content. After the Deluge the descendants of Noah, that is, all mankind was permitted to be carnivorous (Genesis 10). Since the land had become filled with violence and man had given free rein to his worst instincts, man was no longer required to make the supreme moral exertions required to forego the slaughter of animals. It was far more important that he should, at least, utilise what moral fibre he still possessed in refraining from killing his own kind and respecting the life of his neighbour.

It was for this reason, Rav Kook maintained, that mankind has been permitted to slaughter animals for food. He calls this a "transitional tax" or temporary dispensation till a "brighter era" is reached. In the meantime mankind was afforded a controlled outlet for its animal passion. This dispensation is merely a temporary one instituted in deference to mortal frailty, and in force only till the time comes—

וְלֹא יְלַמְּדוּ עוֹד אִישׁ אֶת־רֵעֵהוּ וְאִישׁ אֶת־אָחִיו לֵאמֹר
דְּעוּ אֶת־יְיָ
כִּי כוּלָּם יֵדְעוּ אוֹתִי – לְמִקְטַנָּם וְעַד־גְּדוֹלָם – – –

When they shall teach no more every man his neighbour, and every man his brother, saying, Know the Lord: for they shall all know me, from the least of them unto the greatest of them. (Jeremiah 31, 33)

77

In the latter days when —

לֹא־יִשָּׂא גוֹי אֶל־גּוֹי חֶרֶב
וְלֹא־יִלְמְדוּ עוֹד מִלְחָמָה

**Nation shall not lift up sword against nation neither shall
they learn the arts of war any more —**   (Isaiah 2, 4)

man's compassion will extend to the animal kingdom as well,
and the injustice done to them will be rectified.

PROHIBITION OF MURDER

Our subject this time is the commandment against murder given to Noah after the deluge. This prohibition was not explicitly transmitted to Adam, since the image of God in which he was created provided in itself sufficient warrant for such a prohibition. But after mankind deteriorated and became demoralised to such an extent that the whole earth was filled with violence and was therefore wiped out, this prohibition was explicitly proclaimed and the penalty, too, laid down:

וְאַךְ אֶת־דִּמְכֶם לְנַפְשֹׁתֵיכֶם אֶדְרֹשׁ
מִיַד כָּל־חַיָּה אֶדְרְשֶׁנּוּ.
וּמִיַד הָאָדָם
– מִיַד אִישׁ אָחִיו –
אֶדְרֹשׁ אֶת־נֶפֶשׁ הָאָדָם.

Surely the blood of your lives will I require;
at the hand of every beast will I require it,
and at the hand of man;
by the hand of every man's brother,
I shall require the life of man.   (9, 5)

This verse is long and complex. Evidently the opening clause: "And surely the blood of your lives will I require" is to be taken as a generalisation, with the succeeding clauses specifying the types of bloodshed—that caused by beast and that by man. This is how Ibn Ezra explains the passage:

I permitted you to shed the blood of every living thing except your own blood which I did not permit since you are human. I shall require it: cf.: "for He that maketh inquisition (*doresh*) for blood remembereth them" (Psalm 9, 13). This is a general rule. Subsequently the text explains its detailed application. "By

the hand of man"—if many slay a single person or one individual
another, I shall seek out the blood. I shall also seek it out from
any beast, by commanding another to slay it. For animals are
permitted to you but not you to them.[1]

But this still leaves unexplained the implications of the phrase:
"By the hand of every man's brother." If we accept the approach
that the Torah sometimes repeats for the sake of emphasis,
there is no reason why we should not approve of Luzzatto's
explanation:

> It is in parenthesis adding emphasis to the original injunction,
> that God would seek from man a reckoning for the life of his
> fellow, who is his brother, a human being like himself; and yet
> he had no pity on him.

But our Sages, echoed by Rashi, preferred to elicit something
new from this extra phrase:

"ואך את דמכם": אף על פי שהתרתי לכם נטילת נשמה בבהמה, את דכככם
אדרוש מיד השופך דם עצמו.
"מיד האדם": מיד ההורג במזיד ואין עדים.
"מיד איש אחיו": שהוא אוהב לו כאח והרגו שוגג — אני אדרוש, אם לא יגלה
ויבקש על עוונו לימחל, שאף השוגג צריך כפרה, ואם אין עדים לחייבו גלות
והוא אינו נכנע, הקב"ה דורש ממנו, כמו שדרשו רבותינו במסכת מכות:
"והאלהים אנה לידו" — "הקב"ה מזמנם לפונדק אחד וכו'".

"But the blood of your lives"—Though I permitted you to take
the life of a beast, *your* blood will I seek from the hand of
him who shed the blood . . .
  "By the hand of man"—from the hand of the deliberate murderer, where there were no witnesses to the deed.
"By the hand of every man's brother"—that he loves like a
brother, having slain him inadvertently—I shall seek, if he will
not reveal it and ask forgiveness; since even manslaughter requires
atonement. If there are no witnesses to implicate him and have
him sentenced to exile and he does not surrender himself, the
Holy One blessed be He will seek a reckoning with him, as
our Sages expounded in the Talmud (Makkot 10b) the phrase
"And God directed his hand."[2]

Whichever interpretation we adopt, the poetic or legal, it is
obvious that the penalty referred to in the text is a heavenly

one and that is the force of the word *edrosh*—God will seek
out the offender. On the other hand, the passage which reads:
"Whoso sheddeth the blood of man, by man shall his blood be
shed" refers to human punishment. We may note the chiastic
structure of the passage, stressing that *man* will meet his due
at the hand of *man* and that *blood* will cancel out *blood*. But
most important of all is the reason given:

כִּי בְּצֶלֶם אֱלֹהִים עָשָׂה אֶת־הָאָדָם.

Because in the image of God He made man.   (9, 6)

It is this fact which gives man the warrant to sit in judgement
on his fellow and shed the blood of the murderer. The question
arises which "man" is the text referring to, who was made in
the image of God? Here commentators differ. One view is that
the reference is to the murderer. Man's life is a gift of God
to be used in accordance with His dictates. Instead of building
and becoming a partner of God in creation, he chose to destroy.
Where was then the image of God in him?

> Permission was not given to man to destroy even the most in-
> ferior of his kind, until the Divine command to Noah. A special
> command of God was even required to allow Adam and Eve
> to make use of the plants which are lesser than the animals,
> as it is stated (1, 29): "Behold I have given you all the herbs
> of the field." *Similarly*, the Almighty commanded the shedding
> of a man's blood, if his sin warranted it ... as in the Law of
> Moses, *since he was the first to destroy His image* by violating
> His command.   (Radak)

But Radak too, in line with other commentators explains the
"man" in our text to refer as well to the victim. What justifies
the killing of the murderer? The fact that he had shed the
blood of one created in God's image. Radak continues:

> For man is the highest of God's creatures, created in His image
> and enjoying the gift of intelligence. Other creatures must there-
> fore fear him and one man must not destroy the other, since by
> doing so man destroys the highest work of God, made in His
> image, and *he* went and destroyed it.

81

But others see here a justification of the judge's power to sentence a murderer to death. The judge was created in the image of God and has thereby been vested by God with the task of seeking out the blood of the murderer:

> "For in the image of God He made man"—that there should be justice and a judge for men to fear and not to disparage and curse. (Ḥizkuni)

Questions for Further Study

1. "By the hand of *adam* (men) and by the hand of *ish aḥiv* (every man's brother") (9, 5). The employment of the two different words for man in Hebrew: *ish* and *adam* in conjunction with *aḥiv* suggests to me that we have here two different cases of slaying: (1) with the knowledge of the victim, as vengeance or to rob him and (2) for the good of the victim such as when he is undergoing great suffering and prefers death to life, like Avimelech who said to his servant (Judges 9): "Draw thy sword and slay me," or like Saul to the Amalekite: "Stand, I pray thee, upon me, and slay me" (II Samuel 1). The text speaks of these two kinds of slaying, one against the victim's will and the other which seems even to the closest friend or *brother* of the victim to be a "mercy killing," to spare him further suffering.

(Haketav Vehakabbalah)

  (a) What difficulty does this commentator wish to solve?
  (b) What difference is there between his interpretation and that of Rashi we have cited?

2. Explain the force of the conjunction "similarly" in Radak's first explanation (italicised)? What two parallel themes are here connected?

3. To whom does the pronoun "he" refer at the end of the second Radak citation (italicised)?

4. Which of the explanations cited above (those of Radak and Ḥizkuni) does Malbim follow?

The reason is because God created man in His image, a precious vessel. Whoever touches it will not be held guiltless.

---

[1] The idea of meting out punishment to a manslaying beast appears odd to most of our commentators. A code of right and wrong was

only given to a human being who has free choice. It has therefore been explained that the reference is to the penalty meted out to one who slays his fellow through the instrumentality of beast, taking the words: "by the hand of beast," to mean: 'through the medium of beast'. Maimonides takes this view:

Whoever hires a slayer to slay his fellow or ties him up before a lion and the like and the beast slays him, as well as one who takes his own life—each one of these is a shedder of blood and is guilty of murder and liable to the penalty of death at the hand of heaven; but these crimes do not carry a judicial death sentence. Whence is this the law? Because it is stated: "Whoso sheds the blood of man, by man shall his blood be shed"—this applies to one who carries out the murder himself and not through an agent. "The blood of your lives shall I require"—this is one who takes his own life. "By the hand of any beast will I seek him out"—this refers to one who places his fellow before a wild beast to be torn to pieces. "By the hand of man, by the hand of every man's brother, I shall seek out (require) the life of man"—this refers to one who hires others to slay his fellow. The text explicitly employs the expression *derisha*— "seeking" in all three cases, indicating that their judgment is entrusted to heaven.   (Code, Rotzeaḥ 2)

The idea of punishment being meted out to dumb animals is unheard of in our religion. The Talmudic sages likewise never referred to it. But when some of our more recent authorities heard it from a Moslem sect, it appealed to them and they accepted it.   (Guide)

---

2 "The text speaks of two persons, one of whom had committed premeditated murder and the other manslaughter. In both cases there were no witnesses. The Holy One blessed be He arranges for them to lodge at one inn. The murderer sits under the ladder and the inadvertent slayer descends the ladder falling on him and killing him. The murderer is thus killed and the inadvertent slayer exiled." Thus both providentially get their due.

THE RAINBOW

The lengthy story of the deluge which takes up almost the entire sidra concludes with the Almighty's message to Noah and his sons. This message is divided into three parts—the imparting of commandments, the making of a covenant and the giving of a sign of the covenant (9, 1–17). Each one of these sections is introduced and concluded by parallel phrases which act as a framework.

First we have verse 1 which begins: "And God blessed Noah and his sons and said unto them, *Be fruitful and multiply*" and ends at verse 8 with: "and you, *be ye fruitful and multiply . . .*" Then we have the second section beginning at verse 8 with the words: "And God spoke unto Noah and to his sons with him saying, As for Me, behold, *I establish My covenant with you*" and ends at verse 11: "*And I will establish My covenant* with you. The third action opens with the words (v. 12) "And God said, This is *the token of the covenant* which I make between Me and you . . . and ends at verse 17: "And God said unto Noah, This is *the token of the covenant . .*"

The father of mankind was not given commandments but merely one single commandment:[1] "And the Lord commanded the man . . ." (2, 16). He was confronted with a test of his obedience to God. He was found wanting and failed to pass the test. Mankind was granted a new lease of life after its original ancestors had been wiped off the earth on account of their vicious conduct. But the new human race was charged with explicit commandments as an essential condition for their continued existence on earth—the seven Noachian laws (the seven basic laws of humanity found by our Sages in Gen. 9, 1–7 prohibiting murder, idolatry, theft, incest, meat cut from a living animal, blasphemy and prescribing courts of justice).

The first ancestor of mankind began life with a blessing. Similarly the ancestor of post-deluvian humanity began the second span of human history with a blessing.[2] But Noah was granted a special· gift which was not given to Adam. The Lord made a covenant with him and his sons just as later on in the course of human history He made a covenant with Abraham, the progenitor of the chosen seed, with the ancestor of the Jewish people. The first man to deserve the title of "a man righteous and whole hearted" in the Bible also merited receiving a promise in the form of a covenant from the Lord that "all flesh shall not be cut off any more."

Man is required to show fear and love of his Maker. The Bible and rabbinic writings admonish us to conduct ourselves in this manner and our liturgy expresses this relationship in various forms. An attitude motivated by fear alone savours of idolatry which regards the godhead as a monster desirous of bringing misfortune on man and persecuting him. An attitude which is completely devoid of fear indicates that man fails to regard himself in the appropriately humble light as dust and ashes, fails to appreciate his entire dependence on his Maker and the full burden of responsibility towards Him.

Our sidra in the story of the deluge involving the wiping out of all mankind and ·he making of a covenant with humanity reborn exemplifies the role of the twin attributes of justice and mercy, fear and love. Both aspects are symbolised in the covenant and token of the covenant given to Noah and his descendants.

זֹאת אוֹת־הַבְּרִית אֲשֶׁר־אֲנִי נֹתֵן בֵּינִי

וּבֵינֵיכֶם – – –

אֶת־קַשְׁתִּי נָתַתִּי בֶּעָנָן

וְהָיְתָה לְאוֹת בְּרִית בֵּינִי וּבֵין הָאָרֶץ.

וְהָיָה בְּעַנְנִי עָנָן עַל־הָאָרֶץ

וְנִרְאֲתָה הַקֶּשֶׁת בֶּעָנָן.

זָכַרְתִּי אֶת־בְּרִיתִי – – –

This is the token of the covenant which I make between Me and you.

> I have set My bow in the cloud
> and it shall be for a token of a covenant between Me and
> the earth.
> And when I bring clouds over the earth,
> and the bow is seen in the cloud,
> I will remember My covenant...   (9, 12–15)

Much perplexity has been caused by this link between the bow
and the Divine promise never to wipe out mankind by means
of a flood. Many have searched in the bow, its colour, form
and nature for something which might signify a token. Ramban
offers us some examples of these searchings:

> "This is the token..."—The symbolism of this token, it has
> been said, lies in this. The bow does not reside with its base
> above appearing as if it were being aimed downward at the earth,
> sending His arrows and scattering them on earth. It is shaped the
> opposite way, to show that it is not aiming anything from heaven
> at mankind. Similarly it is the practice of combatants to turn
> their bow the other way to show they are offering peace to their
> adversary. Further the bow has no string by which to shoot the
> arrows.

In other words, the stringless upturned bow symbolises that
retribution and anger (often symbolised in the Bible by arrows.
Cf. Psalm. 144, 6 "cast forth lightning and scatter them, send
out Thine arrows and discomfit them;" Psalm 77; 18: "the
clouds flooded forth waters, the skies sent out a sound, thine
arrows also went abroad," etc.) are being replaced by an era
of love and peace. Ramban himself was not satisfied with this
interpretation and suggests another:

> If you ask the real reason for this token it may be compared to
> Gen. 31, 52 "This heap be witness and the pillar be witness" and
> Gen. 29, 30: "these seven ewe-lambs shalt thou take of my hand
> that it may be a witness unto me." For everything which would
> appear to have been placed before two persons to remind them
> of some vow contracted between them is called 'ot (i.e. a token)
> and every agreement berit (a covenant). Cf. the circumcision,
> where it is said (Gen. 17, 11): "And it shall be a token of a
> covenant between Me and you" on account of the agreement
> that they would circumcise all the seed of Abraham to serve Him..."

86

In other words, we are not to look for and ferret out its symbolism in the form of the bow, its colour or physical characteristics to determine the connection between them and what it represents for us. It is the same as in the case of the *zizit*. We are not to look for its meaning in the number of its knots or threads. The text simply says: "Ye shall behold it and ye shall remember." Similarly the bow will serve as a token or sign because the Almighty has fixed it as a token of His covenant which, in His kindness, He made with mankind that He would never again send a flood to destroy all flesh—not because violence and robbery had disappeared from the world and not because mankind had already been purified of sin, but on account of His mercy and patience. The prophet words this idea as follows:

כִּי־מֵי נֹחַ זֹאת לִי אֲשֶׁר נִשְׁבַּעְתִּי מֵעֲבֹר מֵי־
נֹחַ עוֹד עַל־הָאָרֶץ
כֵּן נִשְׁבַּעְתִּי מִקְּצֹף עָלַיִךְ וּמִגְּעָר־בָּךְ.

For this is as the waters of Noah unto Me; for as I have sworn that the waters of Noah should no more go over the earth,

so have I sworn that I would not be wroth with thee

(Isaiah 54, 9)

On the day of judgement too when we stand before the judge of the universe and beseech His mercy in judgement we recall Noah and the promise given him through the covenant:

וגם את נח באהבה זכרת ותפקדהו בדבר ישועה ורחמים בהביאך את מי המבול לשחת כל בשר מפני רוע מעלליהם. על כן זכרונו בא לפניך ה' אלהינו, להרבות זרעו כעפרות תבל וצאצאיו כחול הים.

Of Noah also Thou wast mindful in Thy love, and didst visit him with a promise of salvation and mercy, when Thou broughtest forth the waters of the flood to destroy all flesh because of their evil deeds. So his remembrance came before Thee, O Lord our God, to increase His seed like the dust of the earth and his offspring like the sand of the sea' (Rosh Hashana, *musaf amida*).

87

The bow in the cloud which accompanies the rain therefore symbolises the message of the prophet Habakkuk (3, 2):

בְּרֹגֶז רַחֵם תִּזְכּוֹר.

In wrath remember compassion

Questions for Further Study

1. Cassuto in his book *From Noah to Abraham*, p. 129 prints the verses we have studied in the following format:

	אל נח ואל בניו אתו	ויאמר אלהים
		לאמר
		ואני —
	א ת כ ם	הנני מקים את בריתי
	אחריכם	ואת זרעכם
	אשר א ת כ ם	ואת כל נפש החיה
א ת כ ם	ובכל חית הארץ	בעוף בבהמה
	לכל חית הארץ	מכל יוצאי התבה
(ט, ח—יא).	א ת כ ם ...	והקימותי את בריתי

8. Then God said / to Noah and his sons with him, saying

9. As for Me—behold, I will establish My covenant / *through you* and your seed / after you,

10. and with every living creature / that is *with you* / the fowl, the cattle and every beast of the earth / *with you*, as many as come out of the ark / even every beast of the earth

11. And I will establish My covenant / *through you*...

He observes in connection with this table that "we have here perhaps a word play in connection with *ve-hitkhem* in verse 2." Explain according to this interpretation the role of the oft-repeated word *itkhem*—"with you" and what can be its connection with the word *hitkhem?*

88

2. On the words "I have set My bow in the cloud" Abravanel comments:

"Regarding the bow given as a sign by God to Noah and his sons as a promise that He would never again bring a flood. What kind of token could it be when the rainbow is a wholly natural phenomenon caused by the refraction of the sun's rays through raindrops to which the prophet refers when he says: "As the appearance of the bow that is in the cloud in the day of rain" (Ezek. 1, 28)?

(a) Explain his question
(b) What contradiction does Abravanel apparently find between our passage and that in Ezekiel 1, 28?
(c) How can his question be disposed of?

3. "And when I bring clouds upon the earth" (9, 14) I shall cause clouding through the media that I have ordained. (Radak)

Explain what difficulty in the passage prompted Radak's comment and how he resolves it.

4. "And I will look upon it, *that I may remember* . . . . the everlasting covenant" (9, 16).

The Torah speaks the language of men since there is no forget-fulness before the throne of His glory. Similarly in Leviticus 26, 42 we read: "then will I remember My covenant with Jacob and also My covenant with Isaac and also My covenant with Abraham will I remember, and I will remember the land." It is all a parable. (Radak)

The verse (9, 16) may also be understood on the basis of Shadal's explanation of Gen. 2, 19:

"He brought (the animals) to the man to see what he would call them": the subject of the infinitive ("to see") is not always identical with the subject of the sentence. Compare also (Psalm 104, 27): "All of them wait for Thee *to give* them their food in due season" implying that Thou (God) giveth them. Similarly: "He placed him in the garden of Eden to till it and look after it"—that he (man) should still and look after it. Similarly in

Proverbs (1, 1–3): "to know wisdom and instruction, to understand"—that he, the reader, should know and understand".

(Shadal)

(a) Explain the difficulty that Radak attempts to solve.
(b) What is the difference between Radak and Shadal's answer?
(c) What is the weakness in Shadal's explanation? In what way do the verses he cites from Gen. and Psalms differ from our verse and fail to support his contention?

Actually there is a difference of opinion in the Talmud Sanhedrin 56b regarding the commandments given to Adam. We have followed the view of Rabbi Yehuda who stated that Adam was given only one commandment, a view that is closest to the wording of the text. See also footnote 1 on p. 36.

[2] In our *Studies* we made a detailed study of the differences between the blessing imparted to Adam (Gen. 1, 28–30) and that addressed to Noah and his sons (9, 1–3).

NIMROD AND BABEL

It should never be thought that the Torah is concerned merely with relating the past of peoples and countries, the annals of the ancient east, for their own sake. Cassuto in his introduction to the tenth chapter of Genesis adds a warning to the modern history-ridden student who approaches the Holy Writ with nothing but archaeological curiosity. Here are his words (p. 174):

> If we try to understand the text properly we shall see that this (ethnology) is not its intention. This chapter does not come to teach us ethnology, just as the first chapter of Genesis is not concerned with teaching us geology or paleontology or other sciences ... the Torah does not offer its readers knowledge for its own sake. The information about peoples is not the main purpose but merely a means of attaining it.

In his view, therefore, this chapter, too, which seems on the surface to proffer information about peoples and their countries is inspired by a moral purpose, worded as follows by him:

> The new race of mankind that emerged after the deluge, was a unity just as much as that which preceded the deluge. It also sprang wholly from one couple and all the peoples were brothers to each other. This outlook serves as the foundation for the prophetic latter-day message that "no nation shall ·lift up sword against nation and neither learn the arts of war any more."

But this new race of mankind betrayed its mission just like its predecessor from Adam to Noah. Equality of all men was replaced by oppression, brotherhood by tyranny. The bearers and symbols of these tendencies were Nimrod and the generation of the builders of the tower of Babel. These tendencies supply the link joining chapter 10 and 11.

This association of ideas is worked out chiefly by Abravanel who follows in his commentary to this sidra his violent antipathy to the products of human artifice. Here are his observations on the text (10, 8): "Cush begat Nimrod; he began to be a mighty man in the land":

> The Torah wished to stress that, hitherto, man had been equal, until Nimrod became mighty and lorded it over his contemporaries. "He began to be a mighty man in the land," in other words, he became a tyrant. Indeed, it is stated further that: "he was a mighty hunter before the Lord." You already know how our Sages interpreted this phrase—that he trapped people by his wiles; but I think that he was literally a great hunter of animals. The text implies that he resorted to two subterfuges to gain ascendancy over his people.
>
> First he made himself a mighty hunter, hunting the wild beasts and conquering them. When people saw how he vanquished the bears and lions with all their strength, they also stood in awe of him and were vanquished. To this the text "he was a mighty hunter before the Lord" refers. Under all heaven there was no hunter mightier than he, till he became a byeword till the time of the writing of the Torah: "wherefore it is said: Like Nimrod a mighty hunter before the Lord." It is also possible that Nimrod offered to the Lord a portion of his venison in order to make an impression of piety and thus win the hearts of the people. This is implied in the words: "a mighty hunter before the Lord."
>
> Second: he built towers and highly fortified cities from which to rule over the whole country, Esconced in a forbidding tower the fear and dread of him inspired all the inhabitants of the plain. This is implied in the text: "And the beginning of his kingdom Babel, and Erech, Accad and Calneh." For he made them there, in the powerful countries where he built the seat of his kingdom.

The regarding of Nimrod as the first monarch, as the founder of the institution of monarchy is not Abravanel's discovery. Others had said so before him.

Radak too shares this view:

> "He began to be a mighty hunter before the Lord"—he began to show his might, to conquer one or more nations and to become

king over them. For till he arose no man had aspired to rule over a people. That is the force of the words "in the land." The text records the boundaries of his kingdom and the cities he conquered, since, till he arose there was no king, and each nation had its own judges and leaders.

"He was a mighty hunter before the Lord." He vanquished the wild beasts and trapped them, till people wondered how he prevailed over them, till he became a proverb. Whenever they saw a person vanquishing wild beasts they would say: Just like Nimrod! "Before the Lord" is a hyperbolic expression. When one wishes to magnify a thing, one says "to God." Cf.: "A great city *unto God*" (Jonah 3, 3), "Thy righteousness like the mountains *of God*" (Psalms 36, 7).

We see that Radak also regards Nimrod as the first monarch. But there is a great difference between Radak and Abravanel. Radak unlike Abravanel does not regard Nimrod as a dictator who, by subterfuge and superior physical force, gained ascendancy over the people. The phrase "he was a mighty man, a hunter before the Lord" is not understood by him in any derogatory sense but simply as a neutral statement, setting down the facts. The institution of monarchy was detested by Abravanel which, according to him, takes the form of tyranny from its very inception, invariably accompanied by the paranoic symptoms of the king who attempts to immortalise himself by huge monuments and edifices, e.g. Pharaoh. Abravanel thus indicates the common denominator between the builders of Babel and Nimrod, a link not dwelt on by other commentators. But the chief innovation introduced by Nimrod was, in this view, his abolition of human equality, the oppression of the weak by the strong. What had begun to take shape in the antedeluvian world with Adam and his sons reached the pinnacle of its development in the generation of Babel.

"And all the land was one speech and few words." The sin of the generation of Babel was similar to that of Adam and Cain and his descendants. With the increase of creature comforts and leisure time, they became dissatisfied with the natural bounty provided by God and became interested in improving human techniques, in building cities, in leaving their agricultural life

93

and becoming urbanized, and developing a highly organised political and social life, imagining this was the goal of mankind, with all the offices, prestige, acquisition of weath, violence, robbery and bloodshed that they, of necessity, involved—a state of affairs that did not obtain when they lived each one for themselves a pastoral existence. As Solomon said: "God created man upright but they have sought out many inventions."

The true implication of the text is that, originally, man shared one universal language and all their possessions were common to them all. No man had any private property. Everything was in common, just like their language. But when they engaged in building the city and tower and the invention of artificial works, they forsook their universal brotherhood and established private property, through barter and monopolisation prompted by their covetousness to take everyone for himself and say, "Mine is mine and yours yours."

Our Rabbis expounded the text "They journeyed from *kedem*" —they divorced themselves from the *first* of the world i.e. from the pristine order of the world, from being content with the essential natural products of the universe and went after vanity, in seeking artificial things to satisfy their craving for luxuries. This diverted all of them from knowing Divine truths. The text was accordingly expounded to imply they journeyed away from the Eternal.

We are familiar with Abravanel's attitude to civilization in his interpretation of Adam and Cain's sins,[2] in their divorcement from nature. In his view, the ideal was communism and private ownership a corruption. There he emphasised his opposition to the divorcement from nature and the development of artificial labours and pursuit of luxury. Here he stresses his disapproval of political organisation, the pursuit of office and prestige instead of the contemplation of things Divine and improvement of the soul. He divides the human occupations that are corruptive into three categories. The first: "those that assist nature to accomplish something like agriculture and medicine." They were punished for this because they wished to help where human help was out of order. God had provided nature with properties which required no further assistance from man. The second category were those processes "foreign to nature since they perform things which nature has no concern with—like those processes concerned with apparel and building houses and ships."

These were worse than the first since they used their skill to overcome the natural life which was the will of God. But the third party was the worst of all, to which Nimrod and the builders of the tower belonged: "the labours opposed to nature such as hurling stones upwards (against the natural force of gravity by mechanical device) and sending fire downward, and the subjecting of men to each other when nature ordained equality."

Why then did not the Torah explicitly prohibit all'these types of labour if they were so sinful? Abravanel answers:

> When God saw that humanity was already sunk in the craving for artificiality and irremediably given over to such activity he did not forbid them His people, but commanded them to purify them, to use them in an upright manner and not to abuse them. It is like the king disapproved of by God. But when He saw that they would, come what may, still elect one, commanded that he should be elected by His prophets and follow certain specific commandments.

We may once again express our astonishment at Abravanel's views, which seem to run counter to the lessons of Judaism. Assisting nature has been praised by our Sages on many occasions: Rabbi Yiẓḥak expounded the text (Gen. 26, 24) "I have blessed him" as encouraging man to work with his own hands and sow his field since "blessing only rests on the work of human hands." Another rabbinic dictum says the same thing, even more explicitly, in its exposition of the text (Deut. 14, 29): "The Lord thy God bless thee in all the work of thine hands which thou shalt perform"—"If a man work, he is blessed; otherwise he is not blessed."—

אם ע ו ש ה אדם — מתברך, ואם לאו — אינו מתברך.

There are numerous dicta praising manual labour, industry and agriculture scattered throughout our literature. With regard to the second category of human endeavour, the processing of the raw material provided by the Creator, we have, in contrast, the statement of the Midrash (Bereshit Rabbah 11, 7):

כל מה שנברא בששת ימי עשייה צריך עשייה.,

Whatever was created during the six days of (God's) handiwork requires working on.

Prof. Y. Heinemann (in an article cited on p. 26) has shown that Abravanel's disapproval of shipbuilding flies in the face of a passage in Psalms (8, 7-9). There man is extolled for his many talents including his capacity for crossing the seas "whatsoever passeth through the paths of the seas".[3]

With regard to the third category, Abravanel regards the very aspiration to organise a political society as evil. But he is not followed to this extremity by his contemporary Isaac Arama (who quotes from Abravanel more liberally than all other commentators):

That generation, being united by one common language and sharing the same ideas become unanimously convinced that the aim of their existence was a political society. Their sin was not in trying to achieve this but in regarding it as an end in itself rather than as a means to a still greater end—spiritual wellbeing.
(Akedat Yizḥak)

In other words, political organization, social life, technical and mechanical achievements were not wicked in themselves. It was not through them that Nimrod and his generation sinned. Human wisdom, skill and power are in themselves not criminal. It was in the abuse of these gifts that they erred. They admittedly found a valley where there were no bricks and they made their own from the clay they found there. But this in itself, though, as Abravanel criticizes, involved a divorcement from nature—was not the reason for their punishment. But they were punished for the purpose to which they put their skills. The things which Abravanel condemned as artificial can, as Rambam[4] has pointed out, be used in the service of God; "for man cannot serve God properly when he suffers hunger or thirst or is sick" (Code Teshuva 9). The same bricks can be used for shelter against the cold and for building a house of study in which to serve God. The sin was not making the bricks but in regarding their manufacture as an end itself.

The Midrash by emphasising *heḥel* ("he began") as a key-word draws attention to a process that began with the generation of Enosh. In the view of our Sages this generation was the first to substitute for the worship of God the worship of the objects of His creation. This process gathered momentum with the generation of the deluge and reached a new peak of intensity with Nimrod and the age of Babel:

(בראשית ד, כו): "אז החל לקרא בשם ה'". אמר ר' סימון: בשלושה מקומות נאמר בלשון הזה לשון מ ר ד : (בראשית ד, כו): "אז ה ו ח ל לקרא בשם ה'"; (בראשית ו, א): "ויהי כי ה ח ל אדם לרב על פני האדמה ובנות יולדו להם"; (שם י, ח): "הוא ה ח ל להיות גבור בארץ".
איתיבון [ומקשים על זה]: והכתיב (יא, ו): "וזה ה.ח י ל ם לעשות"? [אם כן הם ארבעה מקומות ולא שלושה?] קיפח על ראשו של נמרוד: זה המרידן עלי! [מ ת נ ו ת כ ה ו נ ה : קיפח — לשון הכאה; הקב"ה היכה על ראשו של נמרוד; זה החילם והדריכם למרוד בי; ונמרוד כבר חשב בין שלושה המקומות "וזא ה.חל" — ולכן לא חשב ארבעה מקומות].

"Then they began (*huḥal*) to call on the name of the Lord (4, 26). Said R. Simon: In three places the text uses this expression in the sense of rebellion again God: "Then they rebelled to call on the name of the Lord," "And it came to pass when man rebelled (*heḥel*) to multiply over the earth and daughters were born to them" (6, 1); "he rebelled (*heḥel*), to be a mighty man in the land" (10, 8).

But the objection has been raised that we have a fourth text of this kind which states (11, 6): "And this they have rebelled (*heḥelu*) to do." God struck Nimrod's head, exclaiming, It is he who incited them to rebel (thus Nimrod's action is already included in the three passages; the fourth is therefore not counted).

It has been explained that the above Midrash understands the word *huḥal* as related to the word *ḥilul*—desecration or debasement and not to the word *hathala*—beginning, as is usually interpreted and this is the key or motif word connecting the three passages. The first passage refers to the practice of idolatry in the days of Enosh, they profaned or debased the worship of God into idolatry. The second passage refers to the promiscuity of the generation of the deluge—they multiplied in immoral fashion over the earth; the third passage alludes to Nimrod's desecration of physical might turning it in the direction of bloodshed, oppressing the weak and spoiling and killing his opponents.

Questions for Further Study

"אז הוחל": לשון חולין, לקרא את שמות האדם ואת שמות העצבים בשמו של הקב"ה, לעשותן אלילים ולקרותן אלוהות.
"להיות גבור": להמריד כל העולם על הקב"ה בעצת דור הפלגה בעצה שיעץ לבנות את המגדל.
"גבור ציד": צד דעתן של בריות בפיו והטען למרוד במקום.
"לפני ה'": מתכוון להקניטו על פניו.

"To Seth also was born a son and he called his name Enosh; then *huḥal* to call on the name of the Lord" (4, 26). *Huḥal*—an expression of desecration, calling the names of men and idols by the name of the Holy One blessed be He, making them idols and calling them gods.

"And Cush·begat Nimrod; he began to be a mighty man in the land" (10,8) to incite the whole world against the Holy One blessed be He in the advice that he gave to the generation of Babel (to build the tower).

"A mighty hunter" (10, 9). He trapped the minds of people by his wiles and misled them into rebelling against the Omnipotent.

"Before the Lord": Deliberately provoking Him to His face.

(Rashi)

On the above comments of Rashi, *Gur Aryeh* observes:

The plain sense of the text is that he was a powerful monarch. At any rate the allusion to his might before the Lord implies that he provoked rebellion against the Almighty, since *there is no might before the Lord*. He was a mighty man where he should have been humble, alluding to the rebellious character of his power, akin to idol worship. He was called a mighty hunter because the hunter is cunning and he used cunning to incite people against God.

1. Can you explain why Rashi followed the Midrash on the first passage (4, 26) and on ours but not on the second (6, 1)?

98

2. Can you suggest an additional reason to the one offered by *Gur Aryeh* as to what prompted Rashi on our text to cite the Midrash and deviate from the plain meaning?

3. What led the Midrash to the conclusion that it was Nimrod who proposed the project of the tower to his generation?

4. What did Rashi find anomalous in the phrase "before the Lord"?

5. What prompted Rashi to interpret the words "before the Lord" in the sense of: "to His face"? What did he achieve by this?

6. It is accepted that Rashi explains a difficult word, phrase or context in the Torah, the first time it occurs unless there was a special difficulty connected with its second or third appearance. Explain what prompted Rashi here to pass over the phrase "before God" at the beginning of the chapter (6, 11 "And the land was corrupted before God") only to add an explanation, when the same phrase is repeated later (10, 9)?

---

[1] See his interpretation of the Biblical monarchy in his comment to Deut. 17 and in particular to I. Samuel 8. For a detailed analysis of his political philosophy and these passages see E. Urbach—: *Die Staatsauffassung des Isaak Abravanel* MGWJ, 1937, S. 257–270.

[2] See present *Studies* pp. 17–27.

[3] Admittedly some take this phrase to refer to the fish of the sea in the first half of the sentence. But many commentators whom Heinemann follows regard this phrase as referring to the man whom God had made a little less than the angels who had "put all things under his feet"—including the capacity to cross the seas.

[4] See *Studies in Devarim* p. 319.

MAKING OURSELVES A NAME

In our Studies of "Bereshit" (pp. 4–5) we discussed the meaning of the term וכבשה subdue it," in the verse:

מִלְאוּ אֶת־הָאָרֶץ וְכִבְשֻׁהָ.

Fill the earth and subdue it. (1, 28)

and we cited Ramban's explanation of the last phrase:

> Man was hereby given dominion and power over the earth to do his will with the rest of the animal creation, to build, uproot, plant, mine metal . . .

This implies therefore that man was more than permitted to engage in the civilizing task of conquering the forces of nature, he was enjoined and commanded to do so as a positive precept and a blessing. The history of mankind is partly that of the conquest of the earth. We have already read of the beginnings of this conquest, how it was furthered by the son of Cain. His son was "the builder of a city," and one of his descendants was "instructor of every artificer in brass and iron." Immediately afterwards we hear of the first use to which these technical achievements were put.

כִּי אִישׁ הָרַגְתִּי לְפִצְעִי וְיֶלֶד לְחַבֻּרָתִי.

For I have slain a man to my wounding,
And a young man to my hurt. (4, 23)

This account of manslaughter is succeeded by the emergence of class distinction, of oppressed and oppressors, the stealing of women, till the state was reached when—

וַתִּשָּׁחֵת הָאָרֶץ לִפְנֵי הָאֱלֹהִים
וַתִּמָּלֵא הָאָרֶץ חָמָס.

The earth also was corrupt before God,
and the earth was filled with violence. (6, 11)

Then came the end of all flesh and everything was wiped out.

כֹּל אֲשֶׁר נִשְׁמַת־רוּחַ חַיִּים בְּאַפָּיו
מִכֹּל אֲשֶׁר בֶּחָרָבָה מֵתוּ.
וַיִּמַח אֶת־כָּל־הַיְקוּם אֲשֶׁר עַל־פְּנֵי הָאֲדָמָה
מֵאָדָם עַד־בְּהֵמָה עַד־רֶמֶשׂ וְעַד־עוֹף הַשָּׁמַיִם
וַיִּמָּחוּ מִן־הָאָרֶץ
וַיִּשָּׁאֶר אַךְ־נֹחַ וַאֲשֶׁר אִתּוֹ בַּתֵּבָה.

All in whose nostrils was the breath of life,
Of all that was in the dry land, died.
and every living substance was destroyed which was
upon the face of the ground,
Both, man, and cattle, and the creeping things, and the
fowl of the heaven;
And they were destroyed from the earth;
And Noah only remained alive, and they that were with
him in the ark. (7, 22–23)

But what of the new post-deluvian denizens of the earth, the
descendants of Noah? What of their character and deeds? This
is the subject of Chapter 11 in our sidra:

וַיְהִי בְּנָסְעָם מִקֶּדֶם וַיִּמְצְאוּ בִקְעָה בְּאֶרֶץ שִׁנְעָר
וַיֵּשְׁבוּ שָׁם.
וַיֹּאמְרוּ אִישׁ אֶל־רֵעֵהוּ:
הָבָה נִלְבְּנָה לְבֵנִים וְנִשְׂרְפָה לִשְׂרֵפָה
וַתְּהִי לָהֶם הַלְּבֵנָה לְאָבֶן וְהַחֵמָר הָיָה לָהֶם לַחֹמֶר.

And it came to pass, as they journeyed from the east, that
they found a plain in the land of Shinar;
And they dwelt there.
And they said one to another,
Go to, let us make brick, and burn them thoroughly.
And they had brick for stone, and slime had they for
mortar. (2–3)

Benno Jacob in his commentary to Genesis points out that the
Torah demonstrates to us in this verse how technical advances
freed man from the fetters of his natural environment, enabled
him to overcome natural difficulties. Through his inventive genius,
man manages even in a lowland region, in a plain where there
is no natural building material such as stone, to create artificially
the brick made from the clay which is available in the valley,
and turn it into a good strong building material through burning.

By a slight change of the phraseology. the Hebrew original
gives expression to the technical process involved (לבנה — לאבן,
חמר — לחומר) From this time onward man could build houses, for-
tifications, a city, a wall and a tower even in a place devoid of
natural stone or rock.

But demoralization sets in very quickly. This technical mastery gives rise to overweening pride and self-confidence. Does
it say there, "Let us build for ourselves a house as a refuge
from the rain"? Or "Let us build for ourselves cities for our
little ones and folds for our flock"? On the contrary, the
achievements of human skill are transformed from being a
means, to an end in themselves. Man who has the *power* to
reach these technical heights soon imagines that he is *all-power-
ful*. What does the Torah record?

נִבְנֶה־לָּנוּ עִיר וּמִגְדָּל וְרֹאשׁוֹ בַשָּׁמַיִם
וְנַעֲשֶׂה־לָּנוּ שֵׁם!

Let us build us a city and a tower, whose top reach to
heaven;
And let us make us a name. (11, 4)

102

Gigantic buildings, pyramids, marble monuments, impressive squares have always served as the means by which a great dic-. tator has wished to perpetuate and aggrandize his name, likening himself to a god, overcoming through them his feelings of inferiority and through them trying to transcend the inescapable fact of his mortality.

The purpose of these awe-inspiring monuments erected by the technical skill of man is to make man forget his insignificance and transientness, delude him with their greatness and "immortality," in short make for himself a name. The transformation of technical skill from a means to an end, from serving human needs to becoming the purpose and aim itself for its author, is vividly portrayed in the words of the Midrash.

שבע מעלות היו לו למגדל ממזרחו ושבע ממערבו. מעלים את הלבנים מכאן ויורדים מכאן. אם נפל אדם ומת, לא היו שמים לב אליו, ואם נפלה לבנה אחת, היו יושבים ובוכים ואומרים: אוי לנו, אימתי תעלה אחרת תחתיה.

The tower had seven steps from the east and seven from the west. The bricks were hauled up from one side, the descent was on the other. If a man fell down and died, no attention was paid to him, but if one brick fell down, they would sit and weep and say: Woe betide us, when will another one be hauled up in its place?   (Pirkei Derabi Eliezer, 24)

The late Prof. Cassuto in his commentary to Genesis entitled *From Noah to Abraham* p. 227 points out that no story or literary parallel similar to that of the Tower of Babel recorded in our sidra, is to be found in the whole of ancient Babylonian and Near East literature, as far as is known to modern research.

But this lack of parallels to the Biblical account is no cause .for surprise. It was impossible for such parallels to be found among neighbouring peoples since the narrative essentially represents a protest against the outlook and ideas of these people ... The whole theme is diametrically opposed ... and we have here a kind of satire on what appeared to be a thing of beauty and glory in the eyes of the Babylonians ...

In the second section of our chapter (beginning verse five) we are shown how God frustrates their designs ("many are the designs in the heart of man, but the counsel of the Lord, it shall stand"), the turning of the tables on the rebels being mirrored in the very wording of the text, as our commentators note:

"הבה" : מידה כנגד מידה : הם אמרו ה ב ה נבנה
והוא כנגדם מדד ואמר : ה ב ה נרד.

> **Measure for measure.** They said: *"Go to, let us build,"* whilst He paid them back in their own coin and said: *"Go to, let us go down."*
>   (Rashi on verse seven)

A similar point is made in the Midrash *Lekah Tov*:

הם אמרו : " ה ב ה נבנה לנו עיר ומגדל"
והקב"ה אמר : " ה ב ה נרדה ונבלה . . .".
הם אמרו פן נפוץ, והקב"ה הפיצם, דכתיב "ויפץ ה' אותם".

> They said: *"Go to let us build us a city and a tower"*
> And the Holy One blessed be He said: *"Go to let us go down and confound . . ."*
> They said: *"Lest we be scattered abroad."* And the Holy One blessed be He did scatter them as it is written—*"so the Lord scattered them abroad from thence."*

It is no accident that many of our commentators cited Psalm 2 in connection with the story of Babel:

לָמָּה רָגְשׁוּ גוֹיִם
וּלְאֻמִּים יֶהְגּוּ־רִיק,
יִתְיַצְּבוּ מַלְכֵי־אֶרֶץ
וְרוֹזְנִים נוֹסְדוּ־יָחַד׃
עַל־יְיָ וְעַל־מְשִׁיחוֹ׃
נְנַתְּקָה אֶת־מוֹסְרוֹתֵימוֹ
וְנַשְׁלִיכָה מִמֶּנּוּ עֲבֹתֵימוֹ׃
יוֹשֵׁב בַּשָּׁמַיִם יִשְׂחָק –
יְיָ יִלְעַג־לָמוֹ׃

Why do the heathen rage, and the people imagine a vain thing?

The kings of the earth stand up, and the rulers take counsel together,

Against the Lord, and against his anointed, saying,

Let us break their bands asunder, and cast away their cords from us.

He that sitteth in the heavens shall laugh: the Lord shall have them in derision. (1–4)

The story of the building of the Tower of Babel has a timeless application. Not only in ancient times and in one particular generation has man striven to build a tower with its top in heaven, but in every age whenever technical achievements reach new heights of perfection we witness a repetition of that which is depicted in *Pirkei derabi Eliezer*:

If a man fell down and died, no attention was paid to him, but if one brick fell down, they would sit and weep and say: Woe betide us, when will another one be hauled up in its place?

Till when? Until the day that Isaiah the prophet foretold would come:

כִּי יוֹם לַיְיָ צְבָאוֹת
עַל כָּל־גֵּאֶה וָרָם
וְעַל כָּל־נִשָּׂא וְשָׁפֵל.
וְעַל כָּל־אַרְזֵי הַלְּבָנוֹן הָרָמִים וְהַנִּשָּׂאִים
וְעַל כָּל־אַלּוֹנֵי הַבָּשָׁן.
וְעַל כָּל־הֶהָרִים הָרָמִים
וְעַל כָּל־הַגְּבָעוֹת הַנִּשָּׂאוֹת.
וְעַל כָּל־מִגְדָּל גָּבֹהַּ
וְעַל כָּל־חוֹמָה בְצוּרָה.
וְעַל כָּל־אֳנִיּוֹת תַּרְשִׁישׁ
וְעַל כָּל־שְׂכִיּוֹת הַחֶמְדָּה.
וְשַׁח גַּבְהוּת הָאָדָם

וְשָׁפֵל רוּם אֲנָשִׁים
וְנִשְׂגַּב יְיָ לְבַדּוֹ בַּיּוֹם הַהוּא.
וְהָאֱלִילִים כָּלִיל יַחֲלֹף.

For the day of the Lord of hosts
Shall be upon every one that is proud and lofty,
And upon every one that is lifted up; and he shall be
brought low:
And upon all the cedars of Lebanon, that are high and
lifted up,
And upon all the oaks of Bashan,
And upon all the high mountains, and upon all the hills
that are lifted up,
And upon every high tower, and upon every fenced wall,
And upon all the ships of Tarshish, and upon all pleasant
pictures.
And the loftiness of man shall be bowed down,
And the haughtiness of men shall be made low:
And the Lord alone shall be exalted in that day.
And the idols he shall utterly abolish.[1]   (2, 12–18)

Only then when there will be an end of idolatry, that is, man's
pride which takes advantage of the wisdom implanted in him
by God in order to turn himself into a deity and worship the
work of his own hands (cf. Isaiah 2, 8 "they shall bow down
to the work of his hands to that which the fingers have made"),
only when all his greatness, glory and strength have been brought
low, only then shall we reach the day when according to the
Prophet Zephaniah, in alluding to the story of the Babel of
tongues, when no man understood the speech of his neighbour —

כִּי־אָז אֶהְפֹּךְ אֶל־עַמִּים שָׂפָה בְרוּרָה
לִקְרֹא כֻלָּם בְּשֵׁם יְיָ לְעָבְדוֹ שְׁכֶם אֶחָד.

For then will I turn to the people a pure language,
That they may all call upon the name of the Lord,
To serve him with one consent. (3, 9)

Questions for Further Study

1. Cassuto in *From Noah to Abraham* (p. 231) writes:

   In this short episode (11, 1-9) we have a magnificent example
   of Biblical literary art. It comprises two sections (which Cassuto
   correlates with the two arms of the couplet from Proverbs:
   "Many are the plans in the mind of man: but the counsel of
   the Lord alone stands firm") almost identical in size to each
   other and standing in complete contrast to each other in form
   and content.

   (a) What are the two sections?
   (b) Point out the phrases that stand in complete contrast
       to each other in the two sections.

2. נסעו מן מדינחא למיזל למדינחא?! [נסעו ממזרח ללכת למזרח?!]. אמר
   ר׳ אלעזר בר׳ שמעון: הסיעו עצמם מקדמונו של עולם.־אמרו. אי אפשינו
   לא בו ולא באלוהותו.

   "And as they journeyed from the east, they found a plain in the
   land of Shinar and settled there" Did they journey from the east
   to go to the east? Said R. Elazar b. Shimeon: They journeyed away
   from the First (*kedem*-"east" and "first") of the world. They
   said: Neither Him nor His Divinity! (Bereshit Rabbah 38, 7)

   "בנסעם מקדם": שהיו יושבים שם, דכתיב למעלה (י, ל): "ויהי מושבם . . .
   הר הקדם" ונסעו משם לתור להם מקום להחזיק את כולם ולא מצאו אלא
   שנער.

   "As they journed from the east": for there they had lived, as
   borne out by the text above (10, 30): "And their place of settlement ... the mountain of the east." From there they journeyed
   to seek out a place which would support them all. They could
   only find Shinar. (Rashi)

   (a) What is ⋅ the difference between Rashi's and the
       Midrash's explanation of *kedem?*

(b) Why did not Rashi follow the Midrash as he did on Gen. 13, 11?:

"ויסע לוט מקדם". "ומדרש אגדה: הסיע עצמו מקדמונו של עולם אמר: אי אפשי לא באברהם ולא באלוהיו".

"Then Lot journeyed from Kedem." According to the Midrash Aggada he moved himself away from the First (author) of the world saying, Neither Abraham nor his God!

3. "And confound their language that they may not understand one another's speech" (11, 7).
Rashi comments on the words *lo yishmeu* ("that they may not understand") as follows:

"לא ישמעו": זה שואל לבנה וזה מביא טיט וזה עומד עליו ופוצע את מוחו.

When one asked for a brick, the other brought him mortar and the latter retaliated by standing over him and smashing his skull.

(a) What difficulty in the text prompted Rashi's comment?
(b) Why was he not satisfied with the explanation he gave of the same word in Gen. 42, 23: "For Joseph *shome'a*: — understood their language"?
Why did he have to add the vivid description of the consequences of the misunderstanding?

4. "For there the Lord confused the language of the whole earth and from there he scattered them" (11, 9) to the world to come. (Rashi)
What prompted Rashi to offer this explanation?

---

1 The connection between Gen. 11 and Isaiah 2, 12–18 (and ibid., 30, 25) is pointed out by Yeḥezkel Kaufman in his monumental *Toledot Ha-emunah Ha-yisraelit* (*History of the Israelite Religion*) vol. 3, book 1 pp. 202–205: "The generation of Babel marks the beginning of idolatry; the building of the tower inaugurated idolatry, 'when the towers fall' (Isaiah 30, 25) its end will have come." Cf. English edition pp. 221, 294–5, 387, 388 *The Religion of Israel*, translated and abridged by M. Greenberg, Chicago University Press, 1960.

LEAVE YOUR COUNTRY

This is how Rambam in his monumental codification of the Jewish Way of Life, *Mishneh Torah* or *Yad Hahazaka,* traces the decline of monotheism and the growth of idolatry that preceded the advent of Abraham:

> In the days of Enosh the sons of men fell into grave error and the counsels of the wise of that generation became brutish. Enosh himself was one of those who erred and this was their error. They argued: "Since God created these stars and spheres to govern the universe, placing them on high and apportioning them honour as ministers ministering before Him, they were meet to be praised, glorified and paid homage to, and that this was the will of the Almighty to magnify and honour those whom He had exalted and honoured, just as a king desireth to do honour to those standing before him and this is the glory of a king." When they had considered this matter, they began to build temples to the stars and offer them offerings, praising and glorifying them with words and worshipping the Molech, in order to direct the will of the Creator towards them, in their evil intent. This constituted the essence of their worship of the stars. This is the meaning of the statement that originally idol worshippers *were acquainted with its underlying purpose,* since they did not aver that there was no god but this star. To this Jeremiah referred when he said (10, 7): "Who would not fear Thee, O King of the nations? For to Thee doth it appertain: forasmuch as among all the wise men of the nations, in all their kingdoms there is none like unto Thee. But in one thing they are altogether brutish and foolish: The stock (tree) is a doctrine of vanities." In other words, everyone knows that Thou art the only God but the error and foolishness lies in imagining that this vanity is Thy will.
>
> With the passage of time there arose false prophets who contended that God has commanded saying: "Serve such and such a star or all the heavenly bodies, sacrifice to it ... so many sacrifices, build it a temple and make this image for all the people to worship ..." and that He had made known the shape of the image (which the-prophet had really fabricated himself). In

this manner they began to make images in the temples, groves, on the tops of mountains, assembling for worship and telling the people that such an image had the power of doing good or evil and was meet to be feared and served, whilst their priests would advocate particular rites as calculated to have favourable consequences, and would command the people to refrain from other practices . . .

Then other fabricators arose and asserted that the star itself or the angel had instructed them to serve him in a particular manner, prescribing certain rites, and thus it arose that image worship, in various forms, spread throughout the world.

As time went on, the awesome and glorious name of God was forgotten from the mouths of all mankind and from their minds and they recognised Him not. Thus it came about that all the people of the land, women and children were only acquainted with the image of wood and stone, the sanctuary of stones to which they had been reared from childhood to bow down to, to worship and swear by. The wise men they possessed, that is to say, their priests imagined that there was no other God save the stars and spheres represented by these images, whilst there was no one who recognised the Rock of Eternity, no one would acknowledge Him save a few individuals such as Enoch, Methuselah, Noah, Shem and Eber.

In this manner, the world continued on its course till there was born the Pillar of the World—that is the Patriarch Abraham. When this spiritual giant was weaned, whilst yet in his infancy his mind began to rove hither and thither, day and night; he pondered and wondered: "How is it possible for this sphere to revolve continually without a motive force propelling it, since it was impossible for it to revolve itself?" He had neither teacher nor guide, but wallowed in Ur of the Chaldees amongst brutish idolaters, his father and mother and all the people serving the stars, he among them, his mind roving and seeking understanding, till he arrived at the true path and perceived the line of righteousness from his own right reasoning. He perceived that there was one God who governed the spheres and created all, and no other god existed save Him. He perceived that all human beings were at fault and that the cause of their error lay in worship of the heavenly bodies and the images till the truth had eventually become erased from their minds.

Forty years old was Abraham when he acknowledged his Creator. Now that he had been granted perception and knowledge he began to debate and argue with his neighbours protesting that they were not following truth, breaking their idols and publicising

that there was only one God to whom it was meet to serve ...
that all images deserved to be destroyed and broken in pieces
to save the people from error as they therefore imagined there
was no god but them.

Since he began to triumph in his arguments, the king sought
to slay him. A miracle was however wrought for him and he
departed to Haran where he publicly proclaimed the worship of
the true God. He wandered from place to place and kingdom
to kingdom, assembling and addressing the people, till he reached
the land of Canaan. There he proclaimed as it is 'said: "And
called there on the name of the Lord, the everlasting God."

(Laws of Idolatry)

The Torah itself relates nothing of Abraham's inner spiritual
strivings before he arrived at a knowledge of the true God or of
his religious debates with the Chaldeans, his successful arguments and the resultant persecution by the king who sought to
slay him. We know of these biographical details from the stories
retold by our Sages in the Midrash, where, it is recounted, how
Abraham was reared in the house of his father Terach, a pur-
veyor of images, how he would persuade customers not to buy
the images, how he smashed them in pieces and was cast into
the fiery furnace, the first to be thrown to the flames for serving
the true God.

The Torah merely furnishes the bare details of Abraham's
parentage in the last lines of the previous sidra and opens in our
sidra with the verses containing the Divine call to Abraham:

וַיֹּאמֶר יְיָ אֶל־אַבְרָם
לֶךְ־לְךָ מֵאַרְצְךָ וּמִמּוֹלַדְתְּךָ וּמִבֵּית אָבִיךָ אֶל־הָאָרֶץ
אֲשֶׁר אַרְאֶךָּ.
וְאֶעֶשְׂךָ לְגוֹי גָּדוֹל וַאֲבָרֶכְךָ וַאֲגַדְּלָה שְׁמֶךָ וֶהְיֵה בְּרָכָה.
וַאֲבָרְכָה מְבָרְכֶיךָ וּמְקַלֶּלְךָ אָאֹר וְנִבְרְכוּ בְךָ כֹּל מִשְׁפְּחֹת
הָאֲדָמָה.

Now the Lord had said unto Abraham:
Get thee out of thy country and from thy birthplace,
and from thy father's house,
unto a land which I will show thee.

111

And I will make of thee a great nation,
and I will bless **thee,**
and make thy name great,
and thou shalt be a blessing.
And I will bless them **that** bless **thee,**
and curse him that curseth thee;
and in thee shall be blessed **all the families of the earth.**

(12, 1–3)

The opening theme of these three verses, containing the first revelation of the founding father of the Jewish people, is characterised by an extreme particularism, placing a barrier between Abraham and the rest of the world, taking him out of his social surroundings, his family and country. Their closing theme is precisely the opposite—that of a generous universalism: "and in thee shall be blessed all the families of the earth." In other words, Abraham, as he left for the promised land, was to be considered the only glimmer of light wandering through a world of thick darkness, eventually spreading, illuminating the whole of mankind, enveloping the whole world with its glow, "from the shining of the sun to its going down"—"in thee shall be blessed all the families of the earth."

Note how this theme of all-embracing blessings recurs five times in the history of the patriarchs, the founding fathers of the Jewish people. Regarding Abraham it is stated:

וְאַבְרָהָם הָיוֹ יִהְיֶה לְגוֹי גָּדוֹל וְעָצוּם וְנִבְרְכוּ־בוֹ כֹּל גּוֹיֵי הָאָרֶץ.

Seeing that Abraham shall surely become a great and mighty nation, and all the nations of the earth shall be blessed in him.

(18, 18)

Then after the binding of Isaac:

וְהִתְבָּרְכוּ בְזַרְעֲךָ כֹּל גּוֹיֵי הָאָרֶץ –

And in thy seed shall all the nations of the earth be blessed.

(22, 18)

112

To Isaac:

וְהִתְבָּרְכוּ בְזַרְעֲךָ כֹּל גּוֹיֵי הָאָרֶץ.

And in thy seed shall all the nations of the earth be blessed. (26, 4)

And to Jacob in his dream:

וְנִבְרְכוּ בְךָ כָּל־מִשְׁפְּחֹת הָאֲדָמָה – – –

And in thee shall all the families of the earth be blessed. (28, 14

This, however, is looking far ahead into the distant future, to the ultimate goal of human history, the first step toward which we see unfolded in this sidra, with the uprooting and separating of Abraham from all that was near and dear:

> **Get thee out of thy country,**
> **and from thy birthplace, and from thy father's house ...**

Commentators have remarked on the usual order. The verse should have read, in the ordinary way, "from thy father's house, thy birthplace and from thy country." This is the logical sequence, since a person first leaves home, then his birthplace and then his fatherland. The commentary, *Haketav Vehakabbala* penetratingly suggests that there we are referring to a spiritual rather than physical withdrawal, beginning with the periphery and ending with the inner core. The withdrawal from one's birthplace is not such a cruel wrench as the cutting of one's connection with one's family. First, therefore, Abraham was bidden to sever his connections with his country, then his city and finally the most intimate bond, that of home.

Let us once again note the recurrence of parallel phrasing holding together the threads of the narrative. Abraham's first and last trial are prefaced by the words "Get thee out ...":
1. (from the country—12, 1; 2. into the land of Moriah and offer him there for a burnt offering, 22, 2).

In his first trial he is bidden to forgo his past, in the last one, his future.

Let us conclude by citing here the late Benno Jacob's remark on our subject in his work on Genesis.

He notes that the expression of blessing from the root *barekh* ברך occurs five times in the opening verses of the sidra quoted earlier on.

    (1) And I will bless thee
    (2) thou shalt be a blessing
    (3) And I will bless them
    (4) that bless thee
    (5) Shall be blessed

This abundance of blessing corresponds to the fivefold abundance of light created on the first day of Creation (where the word אור "light" occurs five times). Here we have a second world created with the advent of Abraham, a world of blessing given to man by man.

Questions for Further Study

1.   Why did Rambam prefer to cite the verse in *Vayera* (21, 33) "and he called there on the name of the Lord, the everlasting God" rather than any of the others in the previous sidra (12, 8; 13, 4) which make identical statements?

2.   Find a text in the Sidra which would seem to support Rambam's contention that Abraham wandered from place to place proclaiming the worship of the true God.

3.   "Be a Blessing" (2, 12)

והא מבורך.

Be blessed (Onkelos).

הברכות נתונות בידך. עד עכשו הן בידי, ברכתי לאדם ונח, ומעכשו אתה תברך את אשר תחפוץ.

The blessings are placed at your disposal (in your hand). Hitherto they have been in My hand. I blessed Adam and Noah. Henceforth you bless whom you wish. (Rashi)

114

It is the blessing of God that He rejoices in His works. This point is made in the Talmudic story (Berakhot 7a) of the dialogue between God and Rabbi Ishmael. "(The Almighty turned to R. Ishmael and said): Ishmael my son, bless Me! I (R. Ishmael) said to Him: May it be Thy will that Thy mercies be shown to Thy Children." In the light of this the drift of our text is as follows: Be a blessing to Me by thinking deeply and striving to perfect yourself and teaching the people knowledge   (Sforno)

(a) What difficulty do these three commentators find in the text?
(b) Can you find a parallel in the Bible to this turn of phrase?
(c) In what way does Sforno's approach differ from Rashi's. Note the addition of *li* "to me": Be a blessing *to Me*"!

4.   What is the difference between the first revelation to Abraham (12, 1–3) and the second (12, 7)?

CHOICE OF ABRAHAM

Ten generations elapsed between Adam and Noah. The descent of man from Adam's sin to the commission of murder, idolatry and immorality are traced for us till the retribution of the deluge. A further ten generations elapsed between Noah and Abraham. The sins of men increased after the deluge and the deeds of the mighty hunter Nimrod were followed by the dividing of humanity into languages and nations, till the Almighty decided to single out one particular individual from amongst them, and charged him with the mission of founding a kingdom of priests and a holy nation. This Divine act of singling out one human being has the taint of discrimination and unfair privilege. As R. Yehuda Halevi puts into the mouth of the king of the Kazars in his philosophic classic the *Kuzari*, "Would it not have been better had God given His approval to all men alike?" The answer to this question is worked out for us in a Midrash on a verse in Jeremiah (51, 9):

"לך לך" — ר' עזריה פתח: (ירמיה נא, ט): "רפאנו את בבל ולא נרפתה,
עזבוה ונלך איש לארצו". "רפאנו את בבל" — בדור אנוש; "ולא נרפתה" —
בדור המבול; "עזבוה" — בדור הפלגה; "ונלך איש לארצו" — "ויאמר ה'
לאברהם לך לך".

"Get thee out of thy country"—R. Azariah cited in this connection the following verse: "We would have healed Babylon, but she is not healed: forsake her, and let us go every one into his own country." "We would have healed Babylon" refers to the generation of Enosh; "but she is not healed"—to the generation of the flood; "forsake her" in the generation of the dispersion; "and let us go every one into his own country"—"And the Lord said unto Abram: Get thee out of thy country."

(Bereshit Rabbah 39, 5)

This Midrash traces the failures of mankind in three stages. The Healer of all Flesh tried to heal humanity, but it would not be healed. Adam and his descendants failed, A new start was made with Noah and his descendants. After the babel of tongues humanity became divided into nations, and no further efforts could be made to heal it. Mankind would not return to its pristine unity and brotherhood, without a third start, in which one people would be singled out for blessing: "And in thee shall all the families of the earth be blessed," till all the peoples which do not now "understand one another's speech" will become once again one family.

The above Midrash justifies the necessity for selection, since all other men had failed, but it does not explain what justified Abraham's election. The Torah does not relate to us even one detail of Abraham's previous life which would give us reason for understanding the Divine choice. Noah found favour in the eyes of the Lord because, as it is distinctly stated, he was a man righteous and perfect in his generation who walked with God. Even the choice of Moses at the burning bush was preceded by the stories of how he acquitted himself in championing the cause of his persecuted brethren in Egypt, and of the daughters of Jethro in Midian and of his leading his father-in-law's flock. Ramban refers to this difficulty:

> This passage does not clarify all the issues involved. What sense was there in the Almighty ordering him to leave his birthplace and offering him unprecedented rewards, without prefacing that Abraham had deserved it by being loyal to God, or being righteous, or by telling him that by leaving his birthplace and going to another country he would attain a greater nearness to God? It is more usual to find such phrases as "walk before Me and hearken to My voice and I will reward you" as in the case of David and Solomon, or such conditional clauses as "if you walk in My statutes," or "if you hearken to the Lord your God." In the case of Isaac the Almighty blessed him "for My servant Abraham's sake" (26, 24). But surely there is no sense in promising reward and blessing on account of leaving his country.

Admittedly, oral tradition elaborates on Abraham's inner struggle towards recognition of the true God in his youth and his fight against idolatry at home and abroad. We cited on p. 109ff Rambam's reconstruction of his early life based on that tradition. He does not link Abraham's past, his campaign against idol worship with his election. In contrast Ramban explicitly traces the Almighty's choice of Abraham to the latter's meritorious past:

> But the real reason for the Divine promise was the fact that the Chaldeans had persecuted Abraham for his faith in God and he had fled from them in the direction of the land of Canaan and had tarried in Haran. Then God appeared to him and told him to leave and go on further as he had intended to do, in order to serve Him and rally other men to the true God in the chosen land where his name would become great, and the nations there would be blessed through him. Unlike his experience in Chaldea, where he had been despised and reviled for his faith and thrown into the furnace, in the new land He would bless them that blessed him and any individual who would curse him would himself be cursed.

Our Sages are not content with describing Abraham as the iconoclast and fighter for the true faith even as far as martyrdom. They credit him with observing the whole Torah, even before it was given. Our Sages probably wished to emphasise that in Judaism belief in one God and the true faith were impossible without observance of the precepts. Whoever acknowledges one God, must logically carry out His precepts.[1]

If Abraham deserved being chosen by God as a result of what he accomplished in his youth, why did the Torah fail to record his achievements? To this Ramban answers:

> But the Torah did not wish to elaborate on the opinions of the idol worshippers and dwell on the religious issues in Abraham's controversies with the Chaldeans, just the same as the Torah deals very briefly with the generation of Enosh and their innovations in idolatrous belief.

This answer is not very satisfying. Surely the Torah could have found a way of describing Abraham's struggles without giving too prominent a place to idolatrous practices! But another answer has been suggested. Abraham was destined to be tried ten times by the Almighty. The Torah was not interested in Abraham as the son of Terah or the subject of Nimrod, but only in his role as the ancestor of the Jewish people, and as the bearer of the Divine message The very fact that God had chosen him as the object of His trials was in itself evidence that he was worthy to be chosen. This idea is propounded in the Midrash:

א״ר יונתן: היוצר הזה אינו בודק קנקנים מרועעים, שאינו מספיק לקוש עליהם
[להקיש ולהכות] אחת [פעם אחת] עד שהוא שוברם. ובמי הוא בודק? בקנקנים
יפים, שאפילו מקיש עליהם כמה פעמים אינם נשברים. כך אין הקב״ה מנסה
את הרשעים אלא את הצדיקים, שנאמר (תהלים יא, ה): ״ה׳ צדיק יבחן״.

Said R. Jonathan: A potter does not test cracked jars which cannot be struck even once without breaking. What does he test? Good jars which will not break even if struck many times. Similarly, the Holy One blessed be He does not try the wicked but the righteous, as it is said: "The Lord trieth the righteous..."

(Bereshit Rabbah 32)

Henceforth from this first לך לך to the end of *Vayera*—the last לך לך he will go from trial to trial.

Questions for Further Study

1. Cf.:
    Get thee out of thy country, and from thy kindred,
    and from thy father's house,
    unto the land that I will show thee.   (12, 1)
    Take now thy son, thine only son, whom thou lovest,
    even Isaac,
    and get thee into the land of Moriah...
    upon one of the mountains which I will tell thee of.
                                                            (22, 2)

ר׳ לוי בר חמא אמר: אמר לו הקב״ה: לא נסיון הראשון ולא נסיון האחרון,
איני מנסה אותך אלא ב״לך לך״: ״לך לך מארצך״ וכן (כב, ב): ״לך לך אל
ארץ המוריה״.

R. Levi bar Ḥama said: The Holy One blessed be He said to him: In both the first and the last trial I try you with "Get thee out": "Get thee out from thy country" and "Get thee into the land of Moriah."   (Tanḥuma Yashan 4)

119

Modern scholars have proved that the Scripture uses key words and phrases in order to underline the links between the different stories in the Bible or parts of the same story. But our Sages went much further than modern scholarship. They emphasised the identity of expressions in order to connect the incidents concerned and the lessons to be learned from them. Our Sages wove these threads even between precepts and facts and even between one precept and another.[2]

(a) Explain the connection between the two extracts which our Sages wished to emphasise?

(b) What other linguistic evidences do you find linking our passage with chapter 22?

(c) Some commentators query: What does the word *vayakom* (he arose) in 22, 3 add after the text already states *vayashkem* (he arose early)? Cf. a similar insertion in Gen. 43, 15: "Then men took of the gift and the double money they took in their hand and Benjamin too and they *arose* (*vayakumu*) and went down from Egypt" in contrast to: "Joseph's brothers ten went down to buy corn from Egypt".   (42, 3)

(d) Can you explain why the two revelations (of chaps. 12 and 22) do not open with the words "He (the Lord) appeared to him" as in 12, 7; 17, 1 and 18, 1?

2. What is Ramban's view of the miracle of the fiery furnace as emerging from the quotation we have cited?

3. What is the point of Ramban's final thought in our second quotation from him: "he would bless them that blessed him and any individual who would curse him would himself be cursed"? What stylistic anomaly did he explain through this?

4. Which verse in the Sidra of Bereshit did Ramban allude to in his reference "the generation of Enosh and their innovations in idolatrous belief" in our last quotation from him?

---

[1] See: "The Religious Significance of the Halakha" *Erkei Hayahadut*, Efraim Urbach, Mahberot Lesafrut, Tel Aviv 5713.

[2] Quoted from *Darkei Aggada* by Yizhak Heineman p. 66.

ABRAHAM AND LOT

When Abraham left his birthplace at the bidding of God, his nephew Lot went along with him or, to be more exact, was taken by him:

וַיִּקַּח אַבְרָם אֶת־שָׂרַי אִשְׁתּוֹ וְאֶת־לוֹט בֶּן־אָחִיו
וְאֶת־כָּל־רְכוּשָׁם אֲשֶׁר רָכָשׁוּ וְאֶת־הַנֶּפֶשׁ אֲשֶׁר־עָשׂוּ בְחָרָן.

And Abram took Sarai his wife, and Lot his brother's son,
And all their substance that they had gathered,
And the souls that they had gotten in Haran   (12, 5)

We cannot tell here whether Lot went with Abraham of his own free will, and whether he was fully aware of the reasons for this journey to an unknown country which God had promised to "show" Abraham, or whether he had been taken along by his uncle. At any rate, he went, possibly, as a continuation of that journey which Terah had begun:

וַיִּקַּח תֶּרַח אֶת־אַבְרָם בְּנוֹ וְאֶת־לוֹט בֶּן־הָרָן בֶּן־בְּנוֹ וְאֵת
שָׂרַי כַּלָּתוֹ אֵשֶׁת אַבְרָם בְּנוֹ, וַיֵּצְאוּ אִתָּם מֵאוּר כַּשְׂדִּים
לָלֶכֶת אַרְצָה כְּנַעַן וַיָּבֹאוּ עַד־חָרָן וַיֵּשְׁבוּ שָׁם.

And Terah took Abram his son, and Lot the son of Haran
his son's son,
And Sarai his daughter-in-law, his son Abram's wife;
And they went forth with them from Ur of the Chaldees,
To go into the land of Canaan; and they came unto Haran,
and dwelt there.   (11, 31)

We know nothing of the reasons which prompted Terah to make

this journey which, in any case, came to nothing: "And they came unto Haran, and dwelt there."

Lot followed his uncle Abraham on his extensive journeyings, passing through the land of Canaan, accompanying' him on his way to and from Egypt. But his return from Egypt back to the Promised Land differed in some respect from his original journey from Haran to the Holy Land. Let us compare the two verses in question. Regarding the departure from Haran it is stated:

וַיִּקַּח אַבְרָם
אֶת־שָׂרַי אִשְׁתּוֹ
וְאֶת־לוֹט בֶּן־אָחִיו
וְאֶת־כָּל־רְכוּשָׁם.

And Abram took
Sarai his wife, and Lot his brother's son
and all their substance ... (12, 5)

Regarding his return from Egypt to the Holy Land it is stated:

וַיַּעַל אַבְרָם מִמִּצְרַיִם
הוּא וְאִשְׁתּוֹ
וְכָל־אֲשֶׁר־לוֹ
וְלוֹט עִמּוֹ הַנֶּגְבָּה.

And Abram went out of Egypt
He, and his wife   and all that he had,
And Lot with him, into the south. (13, 1)

The order of words in the verse is not accidental. Changes in emphasis, approval and disapproval and shades of meaning are not imparted, in the Torah, through long-winded psychological explanations or verbose analysis, but by a subtle syntactical device or seemingly insignifiant but definitely unusual turn of phrase, combination, order or choice of words.[1]

When they departed from Haran, Lot was an integral part of the family and their substance or property was evidently held in common. When they came back out of Egypt, however, we are confronted with the existence of two separate families. Lot is no longer mentioned immediately after Sarah as part of the family, but as someone who has attached himself to the group and accompanies them in an individual capacity. Further evidence of this is afforded by verse 5 of the same chapter:

וְגַם־לְלוֹט הַהֹלֵךְ אֶת־אַבְרָם
הָיָה צֹאן־וּבָקָר וְאֹהָלִים.

And Lot also, who went with Abram,
Had flocks, and herds, and tents.

Further evidence of the estrangement mirrored in the change in the order of words, placing Lot and his belongings as a separate entity after Abraham, his wife, and property is alluded to explicitly in the next verse:

וְלֹא־נָשָׂא אֹתָם הָאָרֶץ לָשֶׁבֶת יַחְדָּו
כִּי־הָיָה רְכוּשָׁם רָב
וְלֹא יָכְלוּ לָשֶׁבֶת יַחְדָּו.

And the land was not able to bear them,
That they might dwell together:
For their substance was great,
So that they could not dwell together.

What was the cause of their separation? The reason seems to be quite simple: the quarrel over pasturage. Indeed Ramban explains it accordingly:

> The plain meaning of the narrative implies that the quarrel was over the cattle, since the land could not bear them and when Abraham's cattle were feeding in the meadow, Lot's shepherds would come along and feed there. Since both Abraham and Lot were strangers in the country the former was afraid that the Canaanites and the Perizzite, natives of the country, would hear of the large numbers of cattle that were being pastured and would drive them out or smite them with the sword and take away their property and livestock. Residence in the land be-

longed to them at that moment and not to Abraham and this is the implication of the phrase "And the Canaanite and the Perizzite dwelt then in the land." Attention is therefore drawn to the fact that they were dwelling in the midst of numerous native tribes, and that their own cattle were too many for the land to provide for them both.

Ramban's explanation aptly motivates the juxtaposition between the phrase describing the quarrel between the shepherds of Lot and Abraham and the seemingly irrelevant information that "the Canaanite and Perizzite dwelt then in the Land." In other words in those days the time had not yet arrived for the Canaanite and Perizzite to be driven out for their sins and they still dwelt there at the Almighty's pleasure. In these circumstances the land could not provide for Abraham, Lot and the existing tribes who lived there.

Our sages of old, however, did not regard the quarrel between the shepherds referred to here as merely an economic or political one. The Torah devotes space to this quarrel for a deeper reason. Their strife symbolized the opposition between the world of Abraham and between one who wished to be a part of it but did not whole-heartedly share the moral principles and outlook of the Patriarch referred to in the following passage in next week's sidra:

אֲשֶׁר יְצַוֶּה אֶת־בָּנָיו וְאֶת־בֵּיתוֹ אַחֲרָיו
וְשָׁמְרוּ דֶּרֶךְ יְיָ לַעֲשׂוֹת צְדָקָה וּמִשְׁפָּט.

he will command his children and his household after him,
And they shall keep the way of the Lord,
To do justice and judgement;   (18, 19)

Here we shall cite two excerpts on the same theme as elaborated in two different Midrashic works.

ר' ברכיה בשם ר' יהודה בר' סימון אמר: בהמתו של אברהם אבינו היתה
יוצאת זמומה ובהמתו של לוט לא היתה יוצאת זמומה. היו אומרים להם
רועי אברהם: ה ו ת ר ה ג ז ל ? היו אומרים להם רועי לוט: כך אמר הקב"ה
לאברהם: "לזרעך אתן את הארץ הזאת" ואברהם פרדה עקרה ואינו מוליד,
למחר הוא מת ולוט יורשו, ואין אוכלין מדידיהון אינון אכלן [ואף אם אוכלין

בשדות אחרים, משלהם הם אוכלין ואין זה גזל]. אמר להם הקב"ה: כך אמרתי
לו: "לזרעך נתתי" — אימתי? לכשיעקרו שבעת עממים מתוכה. "והכנעני
והפריזי אז יושב בארץ" — עד עכשו מתבקש להם זכות בארץ.

The beast of Abraham our father would go out to pasture
muzzled, whereas that of Lot was not muzzled. The shepherds
of Abraham would thereupon chide them: Robbery has then
been permitted? To which the shepherds of Lot would reply:
Thus did the Holy One blessed be He say to Abraham "to thy
seed shall I give this land," and Abraham is a barren mule
who cannot beget children. Tomorrow he will die and Lot will
inherit him so that even if they (the cattle) eat (violating the
pasture of others), it is ultimately their own that they are eating.

The Holy One blessed be He said unto them: Thus have I said
unto him "To thy seed I give it." When? When the seven nations
will be uprooted therefrom. "And the Canaanite and the Perizzite
dwelt then in the land" so far they still have a title to the land
(that is, their measure of sin is not yet full and the time is not
ripe for their expulsion).   (Midrash Rabbah)

לא מפני רכושם שהיה רב אלא מפני הדינים שהיו בין הרועים, כמו שכתוב
"ויהי ריב בין רועי . . .". ולמה היו מדיינים אלו עם אלו? אלא כשאדם צדיק,
אף בני ביתו כמותו צדיקים . . . וכשאדם רשע, אף בני ביתו כמותו רשעים.
בהמותיו של אברהם היו מוציאים אותם זמומים שלא יגזלו לבריות ובהמותיו
של לוט לא היו הרועים זוממים אותם. התחילו רועים של אברהם מדיינים עם
רועים של לוט ואומרים להם: למה אתם משיאים ללוט שם רע ומוציאים
בהמתו שלא זמומה?! אמרו להם רועים של לוט: אנו הם שאנו צריכים למחות
בידכם, שאתם זוממים את הבהמה, שעל-ידי שאתם יודעים שסוף בהמתו של
אברהם לחזור ללוט מפני שאינו מוליד, אין אתם זנין אותה כראוי! כפני
שאתם יודעים שאין לאברהם בן ולמהר הוא מת ולוט יורשו, אתם עושים
עצמכם צדיקים מבהמותיו של אחר! מה שבהמתו רועה היא גזולה? לא משלה
היא רועה?! לא כך אמר הקב"ה לאברהם: "לזרעך אתן את הארץ הזאת"?
הרי למחר הוא מת ללא בנים ולוט יורשו! ומי לחשך שעל-ידי דברים הללו
היו מדיינים? א"ר יהודה: קרא סופו של פסוק: "והכנעני והפריזי אז יושב
בארץ" — הן שאמרתי לאברהם. שאני נותן לבניו את הארץ — ל ב נ י ו לא
לרשע זה שאתם סבורים; ואפילו מה שאמרתי לאברהם, שאני נותן לבניו
את הארץ — אימתי? כשאגרש את הכנעני ואת הפריזי מתוכה. לאברהם עדיין
לא נתתי בנים, והכנעני והפריזי עד עכשו בעלים עליה ואתם אומרים כן?

... It was not because their substance was large but because of
the strife that existed between the shepherds as it is written: "And
there was strife between the herdmen..." Why did they contend with one another? When a man is righteous the members
of his household are likewise righteous ... and when a man is

wicked the members of his household are wicked like him. The shepherds would lead out Abraham's cattle to pasture muzzled so that they should not rob the public, whereas the shepherds did not muzzle Lot's cattle. Whereupon Abraham's shepherds began to contend with those of Lot, saying to them: "Why do you bring the name of Lot into disrepute by taking out his cattle unmuzzled?" To which Lot's shepherds replied: "On the contrary it is we who ought to protest against you muzzling the beast, forasmuch as you know that Abraham's cattle will ultimately revert to Lot because he cannot beget children, you do not feed them up properly! Forasmuch as you know that Abraham has no son and that tomorrow he will die and Lot will inherit him, you make yourselves out to be righteous at the expense of the cattle of another! Do you think that when the cattle feed they are stealing? Don't they eat of that which rightly belongs to them? Did not the Holy One blessed be He say to Abraham "to thy seed shall I give this land?" Behold tomorrow he will die without children and Lot will inherit him." And how may we deduce that such was the substance of their strife? Said R. Yehudah: Read the end of the verse "And the Canaanite and the Perizzite dwelt then in the land." What is the meaning of this?

But since they were thus contending the Holy One blessed be He said to them: "the Canaanite and the Perizzite dwelt then in the land"—it is true that I promised Abraham to give the land *to his children*, and not to this wicked man, as you imagine. And even the promise that I made to Abraham to give the land to his children—when will that be? When I drive out the Canaanite and the Perizzite from its midst. To Abraham I have still not given children, and the Canaanite and the Perizzite are still rightful owners of the land, and yet you say thus?

(Pesikta Rabbati)

According to both the Midrashic versions quoted, the shepherds quarrelled over the violation of the prohibition against robbery which constituted the chief reason leading God to bring the deluge on mankind.[2.] It was the sin of robbery which separated Lot from Abram both in the physical and moral sense. Lot who had all the time, accompanied Abraham, parted from him when he was called on to refrain from robbery and emulate the moral conduct of his uncle:

וַיִּשָּׂא־לוֹט אֶת־עֵינָיו וַיַּרְא אֶת־כָּל־כִּכַּר הַיַּרְדֵּן
כִּי כֻלָּהּ מַשְׁקֶה – – –
וַיִּבְחַר־לוֹ לוֹט אֵת כָּל־כִּכַּר הַיַּרְדֵּן
וַיִּסַּע לוֹט מִקֶּדֶם
וַיִּפָּרְדוּ אִישׁ מֵעַל אָחִיו.
אַבְרָם יָשַׁב בְּאֶרֶץ־כְּנַעַן
וְלוֹט יָשַׁב בְּעָרֵי הַכִּכָּר
וַיֶּאֱהַל עַד־סְדֹם.
וְאַנְשֵׁי סְדֹם רָעִים וְחַטָּאִים לַיְיָ מְאֹד.

**And Lot lifted up his eyes, and beheld all the plain of
Jordan, that it was well watered every where...
Then Lot chose him all the plain of Jordan;
and Lot journeyed east:
and they separated themselves the one from the other.
Abram dwelt in the land of Canaan,
and Lot dwelt in the cities of the plain,
and pitched his tent toward** Sodom.
But the men of Sodom **were wicked and sinners before the
Lord exceedingly.**   (13, 10–13)

Commenting on the phrase: "And Lot journeyed east"—Rashi
states:

הסיע עצמו מקדמונו של עולם. אמר: אי אפשי לא באברם ולא באלוהיו.

He journeyed away from the Primal Being of the world (a play
on the word קדם which means both "eastward" and "first")
saying: neither Abraham nor his God!

Lot then proceeded to Sodom because "it was well watered every
where" although he knew what went on there and that "the
men of Sodom were wicked and sinners before the Lord exceedingly."

Was it purely accidental that the man who had parted from
Abraham because he preferred to indulge in robbery went from
one extreme to another, from the superlative purity and light
of Abraham's way of life to the evil depths of Sodom, without

pausing to stop midway? Was it accidental or a necessary psychological consequence of his behaviour?

Questions for Further Study

1. "Lot, too, who was going with Abraham, had sheep and cattle and tents" (13, 5)

   "ההולך את אברם": מי גרם שהיה לו זאת? הליכתו עם אברם.

   "Who was going with Abraham": what was the cause of him having this? His going along with Abraham.

   (a) What difficulty in the text prompted Rashi's comment?
   (b) Cf. Rashi's comment here with those on the following verses:

   Gen. 18. 1 *s.v.* ממרא Mamre; Ibid. 14, 12 *s.v.* והוא יושב בסדום "He dwelt in Sodom"; Ibid. 25, 20 *s.v.* בת בתואל הארמי בפדן ארם אחות לבן הארמי "The daughter of Bethuel the Aramean from Padan Aram, the sister of Laban"; Exodus 18, 5 *s.v.* אל המדבר "to the wilderness"; Deut. 1, 4 s.v. סיחון אשר יושב בחשבון "Sihon who dwells in Heshbon."

   What anomaly is common to all the above citations and what approach does Rashi adopt in explaining it?

2. Cf.:
   "There was strife ריב between Abraham's shepherds and Lot's"
   "Let there be no strife (מריבה) between me and you" (13, 8)
   What is the difference in connotation between *riv* and *meriva?*

3. What differences are there in thought and style between the two Midrashic versions cited—that of the Midrash Rabbah and the Pesikta Rabbati?

A particularly instructive example of the way the word order is used to portray character is found in Num. 32, 1: *"Cattle* in plenty had the children of Reuben and Gad, an enormous amount: they took a look at the land of Jazer and Gilead and noted the place was a place for *cattle."* The text opens with cattle *(mikneh)* and ends with cattle. They the cattle-men *anshei mikne* are in the middle emphasising that their whole world and outlook was circumscribed by cattle! Reflected in the very word order of the text is the thought expressed by our Sages that "they were rich and owned much cattle, were fond of their money and settled outside the Holy Land and for this reason were the first to suffer exile" (Bamidbar Rabbah 22).

² See p. 69.

³ The extent the rabbis regarded a man's attitude to robbery as a touch-stone of his character and sterling worth is brought out in the following Midrash: to the text: "Moses used to pasture the flock of Jethro ... and led the flock to the farthest end of the wilderness" (Exodus 3, 1):

ש מ ו ת ר ב ה ב (שמות ג, א) "ומשה היה רועה את צאן יתרו . . . וינהג את
הצאן אחר המדבר . . ." אין הקב"ה נותן גדולה לאדם עד שבודקהו בדבר קטן
ואחר כך מעלהו לגדולה. הרי לך שני גדולי עולם, שבדקן הקב"ה בדבר קטן
ונמצאו נאמנים והעלן לגדולה. בדק לדוד בצאן ולא נהגן אלא במדבר,
להרחיקם מן הגזל, שכן אליאב אומר (שמואל א, יז, כח): "ועל מי נטשת מעט
הצאן ההנה ב מ ד ב ר " . . . וכן במשה הוא אומר (שמות ג, א): "וינהג
את הצאן אחר המדבר" להוציאן מן הגזל. ולקחו הקב"ה לרעות ישראל,
שנאמר (תהילים עז, כא): "נחית כצאן עמך ביד משה ואהרן".

The Holy One blessed be He does not award eminence to man till he has tested him in a small matter. Only then he promotes him to greatness. Examples of this are the two great figures whom the Holy One tested in a small matter and finding them true promoted them to greatness. He tested David with the flock. He only pastured them in the desert to keep them far away from theft. To this Eliav referred when he said: (I Sam. 17, 28) "With whom hast thou left these few sheep in the wilderness?" Similarly regarding Moses it is stated (Exodus 3, 1) "He led the flock to the farthest point of the wilderness"—in order to preclude them trespassing. The Holy One blessed be He took him to shepherd Israel as it is said (Psalms 77, 21): "Thou hast led as the flock Thy people Israel through Moses and Aaron."

THE MELCHIZEDEK INTERLUDE

Melchizedek king of Shalem brought out bread and wine

Puzzling indeed is the encounter between Melchizedek and the
patriarch Abraham on the latter's return from rescuing Lot
and all the men of Sodom. No one knows who he is though
many legends have been woven around him. The Torah does
not even disclose the name of his father and mother. Equally
puzzling is the juncture at which this encounter is introduced.
Prior to it we have:

וַיֵּצֵא מֶלֶךְ־סְדֹם לִקְרָאתוֹ

אַחֲרֵי שׁוּבוֹ מֵהַכּוֹת אֶת־כְּדָרְלָעֹמֶר וְאֶת – – –

אֶל־עֵמֶק שָׁוֵה הוּא עֵמֶק הַמֶּלֶךְ.

And the king of Sodom went forth **to meet him (i.e. Abraham) after he had returned from the slaughter of Chedor-
laomer ... at the vale of Shaveh—the same is the king's
vale.** (14, 17)

After it:

וַיֹּאמֶר מֶלֶךְ־סְדֹם אֶל־אַבְרָם:

תֶּן־לִי הַנֶּפֶשׁ וְהָרְכֻשׁ קַח־לָךְ.

And the king of Sodom said **to Abraham, Give me the persons and take the goods to thyself.** (14, 21)

It would seem that the above two verses follow naturally on,
one from the other, with no room for any interpolation. Abravanel has observed this anomaly:

> In the account of Melchizedek and his blessings—how did it come
> to be interposed in the middle of the story of the kings? The
> text records that the king of Sodom went forth. Before the text

has time to record what it was that the king of Sodom said to Abraham, the subject of Melchizedek is interposed. It would have been more fitting for the text to have finished relating the matter of Abraham and the king of Sodom and afterwards to have told of Melchizedek.

Various answers have been given to this question. Some commentators have regarded this interpolation as a means of throwing light on the character of the king of Sodom. (As is known the Torah does not describe the character of its figures by direct psychological analysis, but only indirectly, through their utterances, actions and even lack of action).

Abravanel explains that the text wished to throw into relief the king of Sodom's cunning. After he had been rescued from defeat and the loss of his kingdom, he would never have been brazen enough to request Abraham to give him anything, since, according to the custom of the time, all that the victor rescued from the enemy was his. But when he saw Abraham's generosity in giving a tenth part to the priest, he immediately took advantage and asked for something.

But closer to the wording of the text is the comment of *Or Haḥayyim*:

The interpolation regarding Melchizedek is introduced to reflect credit on the righteous and show the difference between them and the wicked. The king of Sodom went forth to welcome Abraham empty-handed, though he was *under obligation* to repay him generously. The wicked went empty-handed, whereas Melchizedek the righteous, with *no obligation* behaved generously and welcomed him with bread and wine.

The phrasing of the text supports the above, the action of Melchizedek in producing bread and wine being given a deliberately antithetic formulation. It does not use the normal non-emphatic Hebrew sentence order: Verb with *vav* conversive + subject: *vayoẓi* Melchizedek—"And Melchizedek brought forth," but the reverse order of: subject + verb: *u-Melchiẓedek*

... *hoẕi* "but Melchizedek, (unlike the king of Sodom who brought nothing for the victor) *did* bring—bread and wine." [1]

For the crime of neglecting the elementary duty of giving food to the weary, two peoples—Ammon and Moab—were placed beyond the pale of the Jewish community, forbidden to enter the congregation of the Lord, "because they met you not with bread and water in the way when ye came forth out of Egypt" (23, 5). It is a characteristic example of "pure" wickedness. It characterised the king of Sodom, the seat of wickedness and violence, and it indicated how, in spite of the first catastrophe that befell it as a warning, it had not reformed. We have here a vignette of Sodomite life, that same milieu which is manifested in the next sidra on a large scale. There are others who regard the arrangement of the verses as indicating not the wickedness of the king of Sodom but the righteousness of Abraham:

> The interruption of the account of the King of Sodom's conduct to inform us of Melchizedek's action serves to indicate the truth of Abraham's contention in his reply to the king of Sodom that: "only the young men have eaten" not stating that "we have eaten," but that "the young men have eaten," since he had partaken of Melchizedek's fare.   (Rashbam)

The timing of the introduction of the Melchizedek incident has been interpreted by some commentators as throwing into relief not Abraham's character, but his faith, contrasting, in particular, his faith with Melchizedek's. We have only two verses in the Bible reporting the latter's words and that is all we have to go on regarding his faith:

בָּרוּךְ אַבְרָם לְאֵל עֶלְיוֹן   קֹנֵה שָׁמַיִם וָאָרֶץ.
וּבָרוּךְ אֵל עֶלְיוֹן   אֲשֶׁר־מִגֵּן צָרֶיךָ בְּיָדֶךָ

Blessed be Abram of God Most High, Maker of heaven and earth; and blessed be God the Most High, who hath delivered thine enemies into thy hand.   (14, 19–20)

Was Melchizedek's monotheism as pure as Abraham's, his belief in His unity as absolute and exclusive? Or perhaps he had only attained the level of those polytheists who already acknowledged the supremacy of one Most High over all the rest. The *Or Haḥayyim* takes this view:

> Melchizedek, the text observes, was a priest of God the Most High, because these heathens acknowledged many intermediary deities, but he was a priest to the Most High of all the gods they believed in then.

Admittedly his god was the god of heaven and earth but was he the creator too? Ramban explains the word *koneh* ("Maker") in two different senses. First he cites Rashi who explains *koneh* in the sense of "maker," although, strictly speaking, the word means "acquire" "own"; but we find the word *koneh* in the Bible often used, parallel to "make" e.g. "Is He not thy father that hath *gotten* thee (*konekha*)? Hath He not made thee and established thee?" (Deut. 32, 6). Sometimes we find "make" used in the sense of "gotten" or "acquired" as in Gen. 12: "the souls they had made in Haran" and at others "gotten" in the sense of "make," as in Psalm 139, 13: "for thou hast gotten my reins." Ramban concludes that perhaps the words are interchangeable since making a thing implies the exercise of ownership. By making you become owner.

Thus the English version is correct in rendering *koneh* as "Maker," just as if the text had stated *boré* "Creator." But Ramban is not satisfied with Rashi's view and opposes it with his own. The word *koneh* is only applied to "ownership" and and "acquisition." Flocks are called in Hebrew *mikneh* from the same root, because they are the person's goods. Melchizedek was merely expressing his conviction that God was the owner of the world, its master but not its creator.[3] In contrast to this, Abraham (and the arrangement of the verses enables us to contrast these two outlooks, that of Melchizedek and that of Abraham) expresses his faith in his reply to the king of Sodom by the significant addition of one word:

הֲרִמֹתִי יָדִי אֶל־יְיָ אֵל עֶלְיוֹן   קֹנֵה שָׁמַיִם וָאָרֶץ.

I have lifted up my hand unto the Lord, God Most High, Maker of heaven and earth (14, 22)

This apparently trivial addition of the specific God who had revealed Himself to him, the "Lord God of Abraham," using the Tetragrammaton, indicates Abraham's acknowledgement of the One God, both owner and creator of the universe, the God who blessed him and gave him command.[4] The same formula is used by every Jew in the daily silent prayer—the *Amida*:

> O Lord, the God of Abraham, the God of Isaac and the God of Jacob the Most High God ... the Maker of all.

Questions for Further Study

The Midrash (*Bereshit Rabbah* 43, 8) fills out the text: "Blessed be Abram of God Most High, Maker of Heaven and Earth" with the following picture:

‫... א"ר יצחק: היה מקבל את העוברים ואת השבים ומשהיו אוכלין ושותין‬
‫היה אומר להם: "ברכו!" והם אומרים לו: "מה נאמר?" והוא אומר להם:‬
‫"אמרו: ברוך אל עולם שאכלנו משלו". — אמר לו הקב"ה: אני לא היה שמי‬
‫ניכר לבריותי והכרת אותי בבריותי, מעלה אני עליך כאלו אתה שותף עמי‬
‫בבריתו של עולם, הה"ד: "קונה שמים וארץ".‬

Said R. Isaac: Abraham used to welcome the passers by. When they had dined and wined he would invite them to give thanks. They would turn to him and ask him what they should say. Abraham would answer: "Bless the everlasting God of whose bounty we have partaken." Whereupon the Holy One Blessed be He said to him: My name was unknown to My creatures and you introduced Me to them. I therefore regard you as being a partner with Me in the creation of the world. This is the force of the phrase "Maker of Heaven and earth."

(a) Where does the Midrash differ from other interpretations of the text we cited?

(b) Is it possible to show with the help of verse 22 that the Midrash deviates from the plain sense of the text?

---

[1] This order of the subject+verb with the latter in the ordinary past without the *vav* conversive is often found where the text is contrasting one thing with another: Cf.: "And Laban called it (*vayikra lo Lavan*) Yegar Sahadutha, but Jacob called it (*ve-Ya'acov kara lo*) ..." (Gen.

31, 47); "And Esau returned (*vayashov*) on that day on his way . . . but Jacob journeyed (*ve-Ya'acov nasa'*) to Succoth" (Gen. 33, 16).

² Rashbam here is true to his own exegetical principles. In many places in his commentary, he observes how the Torah introduces a detail apparently out of context, but, in reality, with the intention of preparing the ground, from the beginning, for our understanding of what is to come later on. The example be usually cites in this connection is from Gen. 9, 18: "And Ham is the father of Canaan," *vide* Rashbam *s.v. ba ba-yamim*, Gen. 24, 1.

Attention must also paid to Rashbam's realistic approach (often. overdone). He does not content himself with the emphasis on Abraham's righteousness (implied in the arrangement of the text) on his readiness to forego his own rights but not those of his young men, but asks the question: What did Abraham himself eat, in the meantime?

³ According to Eliezer Ashkenazi in his *Ma'aseh Hashem* chap. 6 *Sha'ar Ma'aseh Avot*, Melchizedek believed in the existence of God but not in the creation of the world in time and Providence till he witnessed the miracle performed for Abraham in his victory over the kings. This is why the text describes him as "a priest of the Most High God" omitting "Maker of heaven and earth."

⁴ According to Dr. Meir Weiss in his article on Psalm 47, Abraham's correction of Melchizedek's formula is alluded to in verse three of the Psalm: "For the Lord is most high, and awe inspiring; a great king over all the earth." This Psalm refers once again to Abraham at the end in describing the gentiles as "the people of the God of Abraham." See M. Weiss, *Perek Ha-teki'ot*, Amana, Ministry of Education, Torah Culture Dept, Erev Rosh Hashana Number, 5716, pp. 13-14.

FEAR NOT

The two words quoted above were addressed by God to all the three patriarchs, but to each one of them the message: "fear not" came in an entirely different context. The circumstances surrounding this utterance in the case of Abraham were particularly puzzling. Abraham had just emerged the victor after a struggle with four mighty kings, had been blessed by the king of Shalem and honoured by the king of Sodom who had offered him great riches. But Abraham declined the honour and the wealth, reposing his confidence in his status as the servant of "the most high God, possessor of heaven and earth" (Gen. 14, 19). It was in such a context that the Divine message came to him:

אַל־תִּירָא אַבְרָם
אָנֹכִי מָגֵן לָךְ
שְׂכָרְךָ הַרְבֵּה מְאֹד.

**Fear not Abram,
I am thy shield, and thy exceeding great reward.** (15, 1)

What had Abram to fear? What protection did he need? Our Sages propounded three answers to this problem, in *Bereshit Rabbah*:

ר' לוי אמר תרתין [שני דרושים] ורבנן אמרו חדא [ורבותינו אמרו דרוש אחד]. ר' לוי אמר: לפי שהיה אבינו אברהם מתפחד ואומר: תאמר, אותן אוכלוסין שהרגתי, שהיה בהם צדיק אחד וירא שמים אחד! משל לאחד, שהיה עובר לפני פרדסו של מלך, ראה חבילה של קוצים ירד ונטלה, הציץ המלך וראה אותו, התחיל מיטמן מפניו, אמר לו המלך: מפני מה אתה מיטמן מפני? פועלים הייתי צריך שיקושו אותה! עכשיו שקשושת אותה, בא וטול שכרך. כך אמר הקב"ה לאברהם: אותן אוכלוסין שהרגת קוצים כסוחים היו! הדא הוא דכתיב (ישעיה לג, יב): "והיו עמים משרפות סיד קוצים כסוחים".

R. Levi said: It was because Abram was apprehensive and said: Perhaps there was among the people I killed one righteous or god-fearing man. This may be compared to a man who was passing by a king's orchard. He saw a bundle of thorns and went down and took them. The king happened to be looking and saw him. Whereupon he hid them behind him. The king said to him: Why are you hiding them from me? I would have needed labourers, in any case, to clear them. Now that you have done so, come and take your due. In like manner, the Holy One blessed be He said to Abram: Those people you slew were like cut up thorns, as it is written: "And the people shall be as the burnings of lime, as thorns cut up, shall they be burned in fire" (Isaiah 33, 12).

ר׳ לוי אמר אוחרי : לפי שהיה אבינו אברהם מתפחד ואומר: תאמרֹ, אותן המלכים שהרגתי שבניהם מכנסין אוכלוסין ובאים ועושים עמי מלחמה! אמר לו הקב״ה: "אל תירא אנכי מגן לך", מה המגן הזה — אפילו כל החרבות באות עליה, היא עומדת כנגדן, כך אתה: אפילו כל אומות העולם מתכנסין עליך, נלחם אני כנגדן!

R. Levi gave another interpretation: It was because Abram was apprehensive and said: Perhaps the sons of those kings I slew will gather together an army and make war against me: Said the Holy One blessed be He to him: "Fear not, I am thy shield." Just as a shield can withstand all the swords that strike it, so even if all the nations of the world gather together against you, I shall fight them.

רבנן אמרי חדא : לפי שהיה אבינו אברהם מתפחד ואומר : ירדתי לכבשן האש וניצלתי, ירדתי למלחמת המלכים וניצלתי, תאמר שקיבלתי שכרי בעולם הזה ואין לי כלום לעתיד לבא ? אמר לו הקב״ה: "אל תירא אנכי מגן לך", כל מה שעשיתי בעולם הזה חינם עשיתי עמך, אבל שכרך מתוקן לעתיד לבוא, "שכרך הרבה מאד", וזה שאמר הכתוב (תהלים לא, כ): "מה רב טובך אשר צפנת ליראיך!"

The Rabbis gave one interpretation: It was because Abram was apprehensive and said: I went into the fiery furnace and was saved; I went to do battle with the kings and was saved. Perhaps I have already used up all my reward in this world, and there will be nothing left for me in the hereafter. Said the Holy One blessed be He to him: "Fear not, I am thy shield." All I did for you in this world, I did gratuitously for you; but your reward is stored up in the hereafter—"thy reward is exceeding great." This idea is contained in the following verse (Psalm 31, 20): "Oh how great is Thy goodness, which Thou hast laid up for them that fear Thee."

According to the first interpretation Abram feared the voice of his conscience. Perhaps he had killed even one innocent man in his punitive expedition against the invading armies to rescue his nephew Lot? The ascribing of such feelings to Abram fits in well with the sentiments he expressed, when he interceded on behalf of Sodom:

אוּלַי יֵשׁ חֲמִשִּׁים צַדִּיקִם בְּתוֹךְ הָעִיר
הַאַף תִּסְפֶּה וְלֹא־תִשָּׂא לַמָּקוֹם – – –
חָלִלָה לְּךָ מֵעֲשֹׂת כַּדָּבָר הַזֶּה
לְהָמִית צַדִּיק עִם־רָשָׁע
וְהָיָה כַצַּדִּיק כָּרָשָׁע
חָלִלָה לָּךְ – הֲשֹׁפֵט כָּל־הָאָרֶץ לֹא יַעֲשֶׂה מִשְׁפָּט?!

Peradventure there be fifty righteous within the city wilt Thou also destroy and not spare the place...
That be far from Thee to do after this manner, to slay the righteous with the wicked... Shall not the Judge of all the earth do right? (18, 24)

We may fittingly presume that what Abram demanded of God, he would, first of all, demand of himself. The second explanation alludes not to his fears regarding the deed itself but the consequences. The Divine message was particularly appropriate after his victory. It was then that danger loomed ahead. Victory is not the end of war. It contains within itself the germs of the next war. "Perhaps the sons of the vanquished kings would engineer a second round." Abram's fears on this score were not out of place. The patriarch Jacob expressed similar apprehension after his two sons, Simeon and Levi, had wreaked their vengeance on Shechem: "And I being few in number, they shall gather themselves together against me, and slay me; and I shall be destroyed, I and my house" (34, 30).

The third and last interpretation propounded by the Rabbis is more difficult to understand. The late Professor Heineman in his monumental study of the Aggada has explained that the picturesque language of ancient rabbinic homily expresses in concrete, figurative form, profound ideas. He explained the interpretation of the Rabbis in this context as follows: Man's sense of justice demands a correlation between his deeds and the destiny meted out to him, between human works and his due. If man sees this equilibrium upset, he appeals to Divine justice to redress the wrong. Why do the righteous suffer and the wicked prosper? In the usual way, man tends to overestimate his good works, what he has contributed to the common weal, whilst he underestimates the benefits he has received. The kindnesses he has received from God are nothing to be compared with his own good deeds and counts his own righteousness as nought. He detects the bounties and wonders of the Creator in everything that befalls him. Like Jacob he says: "I am not worthy of the least of all the mercies, and of all the truth..."

Abram likewise regarded himself as dust and ashes. He was the real righteous man, placing no value on all his good deeds. He was afraid that the abundance of favours he had received at the hand of God had upset the balance between his deeds and the destiny meted out to him, that he had received not less than his due, but more, very much more. His deeds could never hope to catch up with the bounties showered on him from Above: "I went into the fiery furnace and was saved... Perhaps I have used up all my reward in this world and there will be nothing left for me in the hereafter." We would never be able to do sufficient to restore the balance, "for one thousandth or one ten thousandth part of the bounties which Thou hast bestowed on us" (Sabbath prayer *Nishmat*).

The first answer attributes Abram's fear to ethical motives, that perhaps he had violated human relationships, the second, to political, realistic considerations of the dangers ahead from the vengeance of the vanquished. The third answer projects a religious motivation: perhaps the sense of proportion that should inform man's dealing with his Creator had been violated. The verse itself does not specify what Abram's fear consisted of, but merely gives the Almighty's reply of reassurance: "Fear not Abraham, I am thy shield and thy reward is exceeding great."

139

Before we conclude, let us study Rashi's comment on the passage and note the way in which he deviates from the Midrashic explanations we have already cited:

"אחר הדברים האלה": אחר שנעשה לו נס זה שהרג את המלכים והיה דואג ואומר: שמא קיבלתי שכר על צדקותי? לכך אמר לו המקום: "אל תירא אברם! אנכי מגן לך" מן העונש, שלא תיענש על כל אותן נפשות שהרגת, ומה שאתה דואג על קיבול שכרך — "שכרך הרבה מאד".

"After these things . . ." After he had been vouchsafed the miracle of his slaying of the kings, he was worried and said: Perhaps I have, in this way, received my due for all my righteous acts? Because of this, the Omnipotent said to him: "Fear not Abram! I am thy shield" from punishment, ensuring that you will not be punished for all the lives you have taken. As for your concern over your reward—"thy reward shall be exceeding great."

Rashi first deviates from the words of the first interpretation by substituting "all those lives you have taken" for "one righteous man" that he feared he might have slain. According to Rashi, he was concerned not over the one innocent life he might have taken, but over all the lives, both the innocent and the wicked that he had been instrumental in taking. He was not troubled over the isolated cases of injustice dictated by the necessity of war but over the contingency of war itself which necessitated so much bloodshed. Just as we were able to find parallels in other parts of the Torah for the various fears ascribed to Abram in the three views outlined in the Midrash, so we can cite a precedent to support Rashi's approach. In *Chronicles* the views of the Almighty Himself on wars are outlined for us, even wars of self-defence and deliverance countenanced by Him. The Almighty spoke to David on this subject and the latter transmitted the message to his son Solomon:

אֲנִי הָיָה עִם־לְבָבִי לִבְנוֹת בַּיִת לְשֵׁם יְיָ אֱלֹהָי.
וַיְהִי עָלַי דְּבַר־יְיָ לֵאמֹר:
דָּם לָרֹב שָׁפַכְתָּ וּמִלְחָמוֹת גְּדֹלוֹת עָשִׂיתָ,
לֹא־תִבְנֶה בַיִת לִשְׁמִי,
כִּי דָמִים רַבִּים שָׁפַכְתָּ אַרְצָה לְפָנָי.

My son, as for me, it was in my mind to build an house unto the name of the Lord my God. But the word of the Lord came unto Me saying, Thou hast shed blood abundantly, and has made great wars: thou shalt not build an house unto My name, because thou hast shed much blood upon the earth in My sight. (I Chron. 22, 7)

The same sentiments are repeated later on (38, 3):

לֹא־תִבְנֶה בַיִת לִשְׁמִי
כִּי אִישׁ מִלְחָמוֹת אַתָּה וְדָמִים שָׁפָכְתָּ.

But God said unto me: Thou shalt not build an house for My name, because thou hast been a man of war, and hast shed blood.

Questions for Further Study

1. Compare Rashi with the three excerpts from the Midrash. Does Rashi accept only one interpretation or include them all or formulate a new interpretation? Try to explain what prompted Rashi to adopt his mode of explaining the text.

2. "Thy reward is exceeding great"—Not only have your merits not been diminished on account of My saving you, but, in spite of this; there still remains outstanding to your credit, the reward for this your latest good deed, in doing a good turn to your brother and your fellowmen, in delivering the captives from their oppressors.
    (Sforno)

In what way does Sforno deviate from the first Midrash in his view of the reward due to Abram and what prompted it?

3. Compare the following passage from Ramban with the Midrash and Rashi:

    "Fear not"—He was apprehensive of two things: the kings, lest their armies or successors should outnumber him and overwhelm him in a second round, or that he would die without leaving an heir. God therefore promised him that He would shield him from them and he would yet receive an exceeding great reward for walking with Him.

Explain in what way Ramban differs from all the previous quoted commentators and what prompted him to adopt this approach?

THE COVENANT

Seven times did the Lord appear to Abraham. He put him to the test, made demands, held out promises and endowed him with the blessings of land and posterity. At the fourth—the middle one—of these revelations the Lord made a covenant with Abraham. This revelation differs from all those prior to it and those subsequent. It came in the form of "a vision" (15, 1).

Let us try to understand four verses of this vision:

וַיֹּאמַר: יְיָ אֱלֹהִים, בַּמָּה אֵדַע כִּי אִירָשֶׁנָּה?
וַיֹּאמֶר אֵלָיו:
קְחָה לִי עֶגְלָה מְשֻׁלֶּשֶׁת וְעֵז מְשֻׁלֶּשֶׁת וְאַיִל מְשֻׁלָּשׁ
תֹר וְגוֹזָל.
וַיִּקַּח־לוֹ אֶת־כָּל־אֵלֶּה
וַיְבַתֵּר אֹתָם בַּתָּוֶךְ
וַיִּתֵּן אִישׁ־בִּתְרוֹ לִקְרַאת רֵעֵהוּ
וְאֶת הַצִּפֹּר לֹא בָתָר.
וַיֵּרֶד הָעַיִט עַל הַפְּגָרִים
וַיַּשֵּׁב אֹתָם אַבְרָם.

And he said, O Lord God, whereby shall I know that I shall inherit it? And He said unto him, Take Me a heifer of three years old and a she-goat of three years old, a ram of three years old, and a turtle-dove, and a young pigeon.

And he took him all of these and divided them in the midst and laid each half over against the other; but the birds divided he not. And the birds of prey came down upon the carcasses, and Abram drove them away.

(15, 8–11)

What does this vision of carved-up animals and an uncarved bird, of birds of prey coming down on the carcasses signify? The passage is shrouded in mystery. No wonder commentators both ancient and modern have endeavoured to decipher its meaning by resort to allegorical interpretation.[1] We shall first consult Rashi who cites several explanations on Abraham's question:

"במה אדע": לא שאל לו אות, אלא אמר: הודיעני באיזו זכות יתקיימו בה בני. אמר לו הקב"ה: בזכות הקרבנות.

"Whereby shall I know . . . ?"—He did not ask Him for a sign but said: Tell me by what merit shall my children maintain themselves in it (i.e. the land)? The Holy One blessed be He answered him: By the merit of the sacrifices.

Ramban elaborated on Rashi and explained that every promise made by God to the righteous was conditional. If the beneficiary strayed from the path of virtue which had originally entitled him to it, the promise was annulled. This idea is contained in the words of our Sages when they said "Perhaps sin would be the cause of its annulment." Abraham wished to find out for sure that he would really inherit it and that neither his nor his descendants' misconduct would invalidate the promise. In other words, "Whereby shall I know that I and my seed will deserve the non-annulment of the promise on account of their unworthiness?" To this the answer came: "Take Me a heifer of three years old," which Rashi explains to mean that "The Ommipresent showed Abraham the Temple and order of sacrifices." Rashi here bases himself almost word for word on the Midrash:

"במה אדע": ר' חייא ברבי חנינא אמר: לא כקורא תגר, אלא אמר לו: באיזו זכות? אמר לו: בכפרות שאני נותן לבניך.
"קחה לי עגלה משלשת": הראה לו שלושה מיני פרים: פר יום הכיפורים ופר הבא על כל מצוה ועגלה ערופה; ושלושה מיני שעירים: שעירי רגלים, שעיר ראש חדש ושעיר של יחיד . . . ותור וגוזל.

"Whereby shall I know." R. Ḥiyya bar Ḥanina said: Not like a huckster but he asked Him, By what merit? He answered him: By the atonements that I give to Israel. "Take Me a heifer of three years old." He showed him three kinds of bulls—that of

Yom Kippur, that which comes for every precept and the beheaded heifer; and three kinds of goats—that of the festivals, that of the New Moon, that of the individual and a turtle-dove and young pigeon.

2

It is impossible to take the above literally. Rashi's supercommentary *Gur Aryeh* states: "If you take it to mean, by the merit of the actual sacrifices, surely it was not regarding burnt-offering and sacrifice that I commanded your forefathers?" (the reference is to Jer. 7, 22). He explains that the allusion is not just to sacrifices but to the fact that the Almighty would atone for Israel on account of their repentance and prayer for which the sacrifices were a symbol.

Rashi however does not accept the adequacy of his explanation and adds another one in his comment to the words "and divided them"—

"ויבתר אותם": חילק כל אחד לשני חלקים. ו א י ן ה מ ק ר א י ו צ א מ י ד י
פ ש ו ט ו, לפי שהיה כורת ברית עמו לשמור הבטחתו להוריש לבניו את
הארץ, כדכתיב (טו, יח): "ביום ההוא כרת ה' את אברם ברית לאמר: לזרעך
נתתי את הארץ הזאת", ודרך כורתי ברית לחלק בהמה ולעבור בין בתריה,
כמו שנאמר (ירמיה לד, יט): "העוברים בין בתרי העגל", אף כאן: תנור,
עשן ולפיד אש אשר עבר בין הגזרים — הוא שלוחו של שכינה, שהוא אש.

He divided them into two parts. The text must be first understood in its plain sense. He was making a covenant with him that He would keep His promise to bequeath his children the land, as it is written: "In that day the Lord made with Abraham a covenant saying, To thy seed have I given this land" (8, 18). It is the custom of those who make covenants to divide a beast and pass through its pieces, as it is stated (Jer. 34, 19) "Those who pass between the parts of the calf ..." So here the smoking furnace and flaming torch (Gen. 15, 18) which passed between the pieces were the emissaries of the Divine Presence which is fire.

Rashi realised that the allegorical explanation of sacrifices did not do away with the necessity of elucidating the plain sense of the text. If it was alluding to sacrifices only, why did he divide the beasts and lay each half over against the other and why a flaming torch between the pieces? Since these things can be explained with reference to familiar rites of making covenants we must admit that this is the case here, too. A supercommentary on Rashi *Nimukkei Rashi* elaborates as follows:

> Abraham performed a *mortal* act to divide the animals as covenant makers do, whilst God performed a *heavenly* act with a smoking furnace and the emissary of the Divine Presence, a flaming torch passed through the pieces. Abraham did not pass through, because he undertook no obligation in this covenant. Only God made with him a covenant respecting the giving of the land.

But Rashi does not rest here, since the explanation still leaves much to be desired. Why did he not divide the birds? Stranger still is the verse describing the descent of the birds of prey. Surely birds of prey are attracted to carcasses in the normal way. What was unusual in this case warranting a special mention by the text? Accordingly, Rashi reverts to the allegorical explanation. But this time he does not regard the animals as symbolic of the sacrifices but as representing the nations of the world.

"ואת הצפור לא בתר": לפי שהאומות עובדי עבודה זרה נמשלו לפרים ואילים
ושעירים, שנאמר (תהלים כב, יג): "סבבוני פרים רבים . . .", ואומר (דניאל
ח, כ): "האיל אשר ראית בעל הקרנים מלכי מדי ופרס", ואומר (שם, כא):
"והצפיר השעיר מלך יון", וישראל נמשלו לבני יונה, שנאמר (שיר השירים
ב, יד): "יונתי בחגוי הסלע", לפיכך בתר הבהמות, רמז שיהיו האומות כלים
והולכים.
"ואת הצפור לא בתר": רמז שיהיו ישראל קיימין לעולם.

"But the birds divided he not." Because the heathen nations are likened to bulls, rams and he-goats as it is stated: "Many bulls have encompassed me" (Psalm 22, 13) and: "The ram which thou sawest having the horns they are the kings of Medea and Persia" (Daniel 8, 20) and: "and the rough he-goat is the king of Greece" (ibid); whereas Israel are likened to doves as it is stated (Song of Songs 2, 14): "O my dove that art in the clefts of the rock." He therefore divided the beasts symbolising that the heathen nations were destined to be consumed away. Another explanation of the phrase "and the birds divided he not": symbolising that Israel would remain forever.

Radak adopted a similar approach regarding the divided carcasses as symbolic of the nations and the bird as a symbol of

Israel. He, however, appended a lengthy explanation of the vision which is well worth quoting:

> The "heifer" symbolises the first exile that in Egypt, as it is stated (Jer. 46, 20): "Egypt is a very fair heifer"; the goat, the exile of Greece and Rome which we are subjected to today—the fourth kingdom of Daniel, ... the ram is Medea and Persia ...

> "a turtle-dove and a young pigeon"—they are preyed upon but do not prey and the female will not accept another male after the death of her mate. So it is with Israel; in the Exile she is like a widow in exile from the day her husband parted from her with him still very much alive. She served no other gods in exile and though the length of the exile made things seem hopeless, nor "did we forget the name of God or spread out our hands to a strange god?" (after Ps. 44, 21). The pigeon and the dove were symbols of Israel who were a prey to the nations for their transgressions in most ages till the coming of Messiah. Israel is likened to a dove, as is stated in the Song of Songs: "Thine eyes are like doves ..."

> "And he divided them in the middle"—the dividing and leaving whole were done at the bidding of God, though no reference to this fact is made. The symbol here is that all the nations which illtreated Israel would all become divided and cut to pieces, fighting one against the other, divided in their religions and ideologies— thus sowing hatred and envy between them. But this would not be so with Israel whose Torah and faith is not divided In the days of the Messiah they would be united together: "Ephraim will not envy Judah, neither shall Judah distress Ephraim." Accordingly the text states: "The bird divided he not." For though Israel are scattered to the four winds of heavens they are still one people holding fast to their Torah and faith, all of them from east to west share one Torah, have not changed their religion under stress of the exile and the persecution ...

> "And the birds of prey came down on the carcasses" referring to the whole ones—the turtledove and pigeon, he drove them away, symbolising that in every generation the nations attempt to exterminate us but the Holy One blessed be He delivers us from their hands by the merit of Abraham, as it is stated (Lev. 26, 44): "And yet for all that when they are in the land of their enemies, I will not reject them nor destroy them utterly to break My covenant with them" as well as, "But I will remember for their sakes the covenant of their ancestors" (ibid 26, 45)."

147

In other words, the Almighty showed Abraham not only immediate events but the distant future of his people in the Messianic age. He showed him the birds of prey in every generation and also the consolation to come, the eternal loyalty of his descendants to their ancestral faith. Both Rashi and Radak see in the text an allusion to the future loyalty of Israel to God, and in the birds and beasts a reference to the sacrifices. This loyal service would act as the merit on which the fulfilment of God's promise was based. Both commentators accept the symbolism of bird and beast as referring to Israel and the nations respectively too. Thus their symbolic interpretation is multiple.

Ramban, on the other hand, is consistent in his symbolic interpretation:

> The three year old heifer alludes to the three kinds of sacrifices Israel would offer to Him—the burnt-offering, the sin-offering and the peace-offering. The dividing of the carcasses implied that He made with him a covenant to pass through these pieces and all the sacrifices of bird and beast would be from these kinds ...and sacrifices were always cut in pieces. The bird was not divided since regarding the fowl that is offered up; it is stated (Leviticus 1, 17): "he may not divide."
> The swooping down of the birds of prey and Abraham's driving them away symbolised that the heathens would try to abrogate the sacrifices but the seed of Abraham would drive them away.

The difference between Ramban and Rashi is that though the bird of prey is the enemy of Israel, its victim is not Israel itself but the sacrifices they offer up, the divided animals, the service of God which the heathens would try to abrogate. Antiochus and Hadrian forbad the study of Torah, the observance of the religious precepts as have their disciples right down to the present day, knowing full well that if "they abolished the sacrifices" if they suceeded in breaking the link between the nation and its God, if the Torah were forgotten by Israel, there would no future for them. Regarding this ominous future the Almighty promised the ancestor of this people through the medium of a solemn covenant that the birds of prey would not succeed. In this strain, Ramban explains the subsequent passage:

"and, lo, a *dread*, even a *great darkness fell* upon him" (v. 12) alluding to the subjection of the four kingdoms. Four terms are used consecutively: "dread" "darkness" which became "greater" after which he felt as if it was falling upon him like a heavy burden, too heavy for him to bear. The "dread" is Babylon, the "darkness" Medea" which darkened Israel with fast and affliction. "Great" is the kingdom of Antiochus; "fell upon him" is Edom (Rome).

God was telling Abraham in this way, that while He was making a covenant to bequeath the land to his descendants for an eternal possession, nevertheless there was one reservation in His gift. If his children sinned they would be subjected to these four exiles. Afterwards He informed him about another exile—their first one—that of Egypt.

Our Sages regarded the history of mankind, on the basis of the Book of Daniel, as falling into four epochs or kingdoms, the last of which is still reigning today, Babylon, Persia, Greece and Rome, termed Edom by them. The vicissitudes of Jewish history in these four epochs is, according to Ramban, contained in this vision to Abraham.

But can we say that this interpretation exhausts all the possibilities of the text? Benno Jacob, a modern German Jewish commentator in his book on Genesis avers that no reference to the sacrifices is to be found in our text since no utensil or act relating to the sacrificial ritual is remotely alluded to. There is no altar or reference to slaughter in the whole vision. No answer is also found in Ramban's explanation to the reason for the four types of animals, three of which were divided and one which was not. According to Jacob it was not the animals that were suitable for sacrifice which were taken but those nearest to man and under his control.

A further question may be asked. The fact that the Divine message came in the form of a vision suggests that the picture it depicts must represent something which was conveyed to Abraham directly. It is difficult to see any connection between the prophecy about the Egyptian bondage and the vision, whatever interpretation we give it. For this reason Jacob proposed an entirely different explanation, lending special emphasis to the

149

three and fourfold number mentioned. There were four kinds of animals, three of them qualified by a threefold attribute.

The bird according to him symbolises freedom. The same idea is involved in the bird released at the purification of the leper (Lev. 14, 7). The bird which was not divided represents the "fourth generation" which would escape from the Egyptian bondage, after a lapse of four hundred years. The first three kinds of animals are none other than the three generations that would be subjected to servitude, their division symbolising their suffering (Rabbi S.R. Hirsch has a similar explanation). The birds of prey descending on the carcasses (i.e. Israel) represent the persecutor, Pharaoh. But through the merit of Abraham, the Lord would deliver Israel from the Egyptians; "and Abraham drove them away."

We have here selected just a few of the ways in which our commentators tried to solve the mystery of this vision. We do not wish to force any particular interpretation on the student but merely to indicate how susceptible are the words of the Torah to many and even contradictory explanations, a point emphasised by the following quotation from the Talmud:

דבי ר' ישמעאל תנא : (ירמיה כג, כט): "הלא כה דברי כאש נאום ה' וכפטיש
יפוצץ סלע" — מה פטיש זה מתחלק לכמה ניצוצות — אף מקרא אחד יוצא
לכמה טעמים.

The school of R. Ishmael taught: "Are not My words like fire, said the Lord, like the hammer shattering the rock" (Jer 23, 29) — just as the hammer sends the sparks flying so does one text lend itself to many interpretations. (Sanhedrin 34a)

Questions for Further Study

1. What prompted Rashi to apply just to our text the well known principle that "a text must first be explained in its plain sense"?

2. How does Jeremiah help us to understand our chapter?

3. "על הפגרים": על הבתרים.
"וישב": לשון נשיבה והפרחה, רמז שיבוא דוד בן ישי לכלותם ואין מניחים
אותו מן השמים, עד שיבוא מלך המשיח.

150

And the birds of prey descended on the carcasses"—on the pieces; "And Abraham drove them away"—from the Hebrew verb to blow and cause to fly away, symbolising that David the son of Jesse would come to destroy them, but Heaven would not allow him until the King Messiah came.

(a) Explain the difference between Rashi and Ramban with the help of this table.

	The bird of prey	The carcasses	Abraham
Rashi:			
Ramban:			

(b) Which interpretation appears to you more in keeping with the spirit of the chapter as a whole?

(c) What prompted Rashi to qualify the word "carcasses" in the text by adding his comment "on the pieces"? Surely his intention was not to translate the word for us!

(d) Why did Radak take a different view regarding the implication of the word "carcasses" in the text and connect them with the bird? (See Radak ad. loc)?

4. Malbim explains the vision symbolically. Abraham asked by what merit would his descendants keep the land. Malbim followed the Midrash which says, by the merit of the sacrifices which he interprets to mean the complete submission of the worshipper to his Maker which the sacrifice represents:

The various beasts symbolise man's physical powers, all of which have to be brought under the control of the soul. Abraham divided the beasts. He had already brought all his physical instincts under the control of his soul, dedicated them to the service of God, but the bird—his soul had not been divided, had not died within him, but was still living, governing his flesh. The bird of prey— his Divine soul descended on the carcases to revive them with its spiritual vitality. Va-yashev otam Avraham, not Abraham drove them away but he blew into the carcasses a breath of life—he revived them through the bird of prey. The bird of prey (*ayit*) *represents* Abraham's inner spiritual essence, his complete devotion to God by which he killed all his animal instincts and revitalised his soul ...

How does the foregoing explanation differ from all the previous explanations? Point out its flaws and its advantages.

---

[1] Prof. I. Heinemann in his article: *Die wissenschaftliche Allegoristik des jüdischen Mittelalters*, HUCA, XXIII, part 1, Cincinnati, p. 612. 1950–51 asserts: "Both early rabbinic exegesis and medieval Jewish commentators are minimal in their resort to allegorical interpretation. Only where the wording and context call for it do they resort to it. Even then the allegorical exposition merely supplements the immediate plain sense but does not replace it."

SARAH'S TREATMENT OF HAGAR

Prior to chapter 16 Abraham had been promised offspring on three occasions: "And I will make of thee a great nation" (12, 2); "And I will make thy seed as the dust of the earth" (13, 16); "Look now toward heaven, and count the stars, if thou be able to count them . . . so shall thy seed be" (15, 5). To the promise of offspring as numerous as the dust of the earth and the stars of the heaven was added the prospect of descendants that would bring blessing on mankind: "And in thee shall all the families of the earth be blessed" (12, 3).

Subsequently Abraham went through many vicissitudes in Egypt and the land of Canaan. Both he and Sarah became old and still the promise of a son had not been fulfilled. Thereupon Sarah took matters into her own hands—

וַתֹּאמֶר שָׂרַי אֶל־אַבְרָם:
הִנֵּה־נָא עֲצָרַנִי יְיָ מִלֶּדֶת
בֹּא־נָא אֶל־שִׁפְחָתִי אוּלַי אִבָּנֶה מִמֶּנָּה
וַיִּשְׁמַע אַבְרָם לְקוֹל שָׂרָי.
וַתִּקַּח שָׂרַי אֵשֶׁת אַבְרָם
אֶת־הָגָר הַמִּצְרִית שִׁפְחָתָהּ
מִקֵּץ עֶשֶׂר שָׁנִים לְשֶׁבֶת אַבְרָם בְּאֶרֶץ כְּנָעַן
וַתִּתֵּן אֹתָהּ לְאַבְרָם אִישָׁהּ לוֹ לְאִשָּׁה.

Sarai said unto Abram:
Behold now, the Lord hath restrained me from bearing;
go in, I pray thee, unto my handmaid;
it may be that I shall be builded up through her.
Abram listened to Sarai.
And Sarai Abram's wife took
Hagar the Egyptian, her handmaid,

after Abram had dwelt ten years in the land of Canaan, and gave her to Abram her husband to be his wife.

(16, 2, 3)

Sarah's deed would seem to be quite a routine affair in conformity with the spirit and customs of the times. Indeed we find in the Hammurabi Code, that preceded the patriarch Abraham, that a barren woman had the right to give her husband a handmaiden to beget children for her. But the Torah is not interested in noting Abraham's conformity to contemporary custom. On the contrary, it is concerned with drawing attention to the unique contribution and character of the Patriarch. Were merely a contemporary local usage involved why should the Torah dwell at such length on it? Ramban reveals the inner implications of the reference by taking careful account of all the details mentioned in the text. Ramban's observations are made on 16, 2: "Abram listened to Sarai."

> The text does not state that Abraham "did so" but that "he listened to Sarai" implying that although Abraham deeply longed for children he did not take this step without Sarah's permission. Furthermore, even at this stage he had no intention of being "builded up" from Hagar and that the issue should be hers. He only intended to carry out the wishes of Sarai to be "builded up" through her, that she should derive satisfaction from the children of her handmaid, or that she should merit thereby children of her own. Furthermore, it is stated that "Sarai took" implying that Abraham did not rush into the matter until Sarai had herself taken Hagar and given her to him. The text also mentions that Sarai "Abrams wife" took Hagar and gave her to Abraham her husband "to be his wife" implying that Sarai had not given up hope of having children from Abraham and did not keep away from him but they still remained husband and wife. She still wished, however, that Hagar should also have the status of wife and not merely be his concubine. All this underlines Sarah's righteous character and the respect she showed her husband.

These two verses are thus studded with allusions to the peerless character of Abraham and Sarah, their unselfishness and respect for each other. Sarah introduces a rival into her home, making a supreme sacrifice to overcome the natural feelings of jealousy and egotism, whilst Abraham takes no initiative in realising his ambitions for a son, but waits for his wife's agreement, suggestion and action. However, it is difficult for a human being to remain on these lofty heights.

וַתֵּרֶא כִּי הָרָתָה
וַתֵּקַל גְּבִרְתָּהּ בְּעֵינֶיהָ.

And when she (Hagar) saw that she had conceived,
her mistress was despised in her eyes. (16, 4)

The Torah here expresses in this short verse the full force of the suffering caused by the arrogant bearing of the rival drunk with success. What conclusion did Hagar draw from her success?

אמרה הגר: שרה זו אין סתרה כגילויה, מראה עצמה כאילו היא צדקת ואינה צדקת, שלא זכתה להריון כל השנים הללו ואני נתעברתי מביאה ראשונה.

Hagar argued: This Sarah is not what she seems to be. She behaves as if she were a righteous woman when she is not righteous, since she did not merit conception all these years, whilst I became pregnant the first time. **(Rashi)**

Hagar's mockery had a poisoned sting in it. From Sarah's lack of success Hagar drew conclusions regarding her ethical conduct. The effect of this on Sarah is natural—bitterness, protestations, and demands:

אָנֹכִי נָתַתִּי שִׁפְחָתִי בְּחֵיקֶךָ
וַתֵּרֶא כִּי הָרָתָה וָאֵקַל בְּעֵינֶיהָ.

I gave my handmaid into thy bosom;
and when she saw that she had conceived,
I was despised in her eyes. (Verse 5)

Abraham held his peace and Sarah's bitterness soon translated itself into action:

וַתְּעַנֶּהָ שָׂרַי וַתִּבְרַח מִפָּנֶיהָ.

Sarai dealt harshly with her,
and she fled from before her.

155

Sarah's reactions are surely understandable. After selflessly offering Hagar to her husband she sees herself triumphed over by her handmaid. Who would condemn Sarah for her behaviour? Let us, however, cite here some of the views of our commentators on this subject. First Ramban:

> Sarah our mother sinned in dealing harshly with her handmaid and Abraham too by allowing her to do so. God heard her affliction and gave her a son who was destined to be a lawless person who would bring suffering on Abraham and Sarah.

Radak takes a similar attitude and considers that Sarah did not behave in a manner befitting her character. Although Abraham in this matter gave her free rein "do to her that which is good in thine eyes," she should have desisted out of respect to him. She should have been magnanimous and not taken advantage of her power over her handmaid. Thus our commentators find no excuses to condone Sarah's behaviour, look for no psychological explanations in extenuation of her deeds. No appraisal of Sarah's character could condone the sin of "Sarah dealt harshly with her." Perhaps the Torah wished to teach us that before man undertakes a mission that will tax all his moral and spiritual powers he should ask himself first whether he can maintain those same high standards to the bitter end. Otherwise man is liable to descend from the pinnacle of altruism and selflessness into much deeper depths than would ordinarily have been the case. A similar principle is no doubt involved in the disfavour with which our Sages viewed the making of vows and the warnings of the Torah itself against the undertaking of unnecessary obligations. The danger always presents itself that one might fail the test, not honour the obligation and violate the vow. Here we quote Ramban's warning to those who make vows which are beyond their capacity to fulfill:

> Such people possess neither the prudence nor the direction to consider for a moment the possibility that they might not be able to fulfill all these obligations, but they imagine that the good intention which they harboured at the time of the vow would be reckoned in their favour.

Here Ramban denounces those who are over-generous in their pious declarations and noble protestations, who readily announce decisions which are not followed up by practical steps to fulfill them and who experience sudden surges of enthusiasm which are soon extinguished. "A good deed is only credited to the account of the one who completes it." Had Sarah not wished to suppress her instincts and overcome every vestige of jealousy for her rival, had she not dared to scale these unusual heights of selflessness, she would not have fallen victim to the sin of "Sarah dealt harshly with her"—and there may not have been born that individual whose descendants have proved a source of trouble to Israel to this very day. Who knows?

Questions for Further Study

1. Why did Radak and Ramban not direct their severe criticism of Sarah's conduct at her words in 21, 10: "Drive out this handmaid and her son"?

2. Some raise the following objection to Ramban's approach. If Sarah's attitude was not approved of by God then why did His messenger command Hagar to return to her mistress?

3. Compare Ramban's view cited above with his comment to 12,10 in our sidra:

   "There was a famine": Know that Abraham our father committed a grave sin, in error, by placing temptation in the way of his saintly spouse, because he was afraid they might kill him. On the contrary, it was his duty to have trust in God to save him and his wife and all his possessions. For God has the power to help and save. In leaving the Holy Land on account of the famine he committed a similar iniquity. For God would have redeemed him from death by famine. For this deed Isaac was condemned to exile in Egypt by the hand of Pharaoh. Where there is justice there lies wickedness and sin.

   What is the characteristic common to these two comments of Ramban?

THE REVELATION AT MAMRE

וַיֵּרָא אֵלָיו יְיָ בְּאֵלֹנֵי מַמְרֵא
וְהוּא יֹשֵׁב פֶּתַח־הָאֹהֶל כְּחֹם הַיּוֹם.

**And the Lord appeared to him by the terebinths of Mamre
as he sat in the tent door in the heat of the day.** (18, 1)

All our commentators have been puzzled by this opening verse,
especially in view of what follows:

וַיִּשָּׂא עֵינָיו וַיַּרְא וְהִנֵּה שְׁלֹשָׁה אֲנָשִׁים – – –

And he lifted up his eyes and looked, and lo, three men . . .

The story of Abraham's eager reception of his guests is then
related, his meticulous and joyous fulfilment of the rules of
hospitality. But the first verse which describes the Divine revelation to him stands in splendid isolation followed by no explanation of the exact purpose for which God revealed Himself to
the Patriarch. Yet we never find in the Torah another example
of God revealing Himself to His creatures unless it is for the
express purpose of delivering a message, uttering a blessing or
a promise, or issuing a command. The revelation of the Divine
presence is usually followed by the statement "and He said
unto him." What then was the purpose of the Divine revelation
in our sidra? What message, if any, did the Almighty deliver?

The Rashbam, Rambam and others maintain that this opening verse is nothing more than a title to the story that follows,
a general statement, the particulars of which, are elaborated on
in the succeeding narrative. In other words, the succeeding verses
from two onwards do not constitute a detached narrative of new
events but are merely an intensely concrete elaboration of the

cryptic introductory statement in the first verse. This is the
point made by Rashbam in his commentary:

> "And the Lord appeared unto him"—How? Through the arrival
> of three angels in the guise of men.

Some translators accordingly insert between verse one and two
the word "namely" indicating that the latter is not a continuation
but rather an itemisation of the former. In the light of this explanation we are forced to maintain that the Divine messengers
and the Deity Himself Who sent them are synonymous. The
"Lord" referred to in verse 13 must therefore be a synonym
for the angel or messenger who was speaking in His name.[1]
Indeed Rashbam explicitly interprets it to mean "the most
important member" of the angelic triumvirate. Again in verse
22 it is stated:

$$\text{וְאַבְרָהָם עוֹדֶנּוּ עֹמֵד לִפְנֵי יְיָ.}$$

But Abraham stood yet before the Lord.

Rashbam comments "before the *angel* to intercede." Rashbam,
however, points out that whilst in verse 13 the reference to
"the Lord" implies His angelic representative who had been
sent to give the tidings to Abraham and Sarah, the allusion to
the "Lord" in: "is anything too hard for the Lord" is to the
Holy One blessed be He Himself.[2] This explanation may seem
rather far-fetched to some of us. Our Sages, whom Rashi and
Ramban echo, have a different interpretation:

> "וירא אליו": לבקר את החולה. אמר ר' חמא בר חנינא: יום שלישי למילתו
> היה ובא הקב"ה ושאל בשלומו.

> "And the Lord appeared unto him"—to visit the sick. Said R.
> Hama bar Hanina: It was the third day since Abraham had been
> circumcised and the Holy One blessed be He came to inquire
> regarding his health.   (Rashi)

This explanation is certainly not to be taken literally, as it
would constitute a gross anthropomorphism. Rashi echoes

the figurative and symbolic language employed by the Midrash. But Ramban translates it, as his wont, into everyday concepts:

> The Torah narrates that the Lord appeared to Abraham whilst he was still recovering from his circumcision in order to inform us that no prophetic revelation was here involved. Abraham did not fall on his face nor pray. Nevertheless, this vision was vouchsafed him purely as a mark of honour to him. A parallel to this may be found in Leviticus (9, 23) where it is stated that "they went forth and blessed the people, and the glory of the Lord appeared to all the people." The people were rewarded by revelation of the Divine Presence. In both cases this revelation was accompanied by no message nor command but constituted the reward for previous obedience to let them know that God had favourably accepted their deeds, in the sense alluded to in the Psalms (17, 15) "As for me I shall behold Thy face in righteousness; I shall be satisfied, when I awake, with Thy likeness."
> We find a similar revelation in the case of Jacob: "And the angels of God met him" (Genesis 32, 2). No message was delivered on that occasion; Jacob was merely rewarded with a Divine vision and knew that he had found favour. Abraham too was granted this privilege of the Divine revelation. It was accorded as well, so our Sages say, to the Jewish people as a whole at the Red Sea, where "the handmaid at the Red Sea witnessed what the Prophet Ezekiel was not granted to see" (Mekhilta Beshalaḥ). This was a reward for their explicit faith in God and his servant Moses...
> Do not be misled by the chapter separation (between this sidra and the previous). It is all one story and for this reason it is stated "and the Lord appeared unto him" instead of "and the Lord appeared unto Abraham." A new chapter is, however, begun in order to give prominence to the honour accorded Abraham during his circumcision, that the Divine Presence appeared unto him and sent messengers to bring tidings to his wife and save Lot his brother for his sake. This is the implication of the statement of our Sages that God came "to visit the sick." The Almighty delivered no message but came to honour him with His Presence (Bereshit Rabbah 48, 4).

In this connection Ramban quotes another dictum of our Sages:

> "An altar of earth thou shalt make unto Me and shalt sacrifice thereon thy burnt offerings... In every place where I cause My name to be mentioned I will come unto thee and bless thee"

(Exodus 20, 21)—If to him who builds an altar in My name I reveal Myself and bless him, how much more so unto Abraham who circumcised himself for My name!

(Avot Derabbi Nathan)

Accordingly the opening verse of the sidra is not a title giving the main content of the succeeding narrative, but it is rather the conclusion to the previous chapter, the Divine revelation constituting the climax and reward of Abraham's obedience. As Ramban pointed out, the very fact of the verse using the personal pronoun "him" instead of explicitly repeating "Abraham" (as would have been the case if this was the beginning of a completely new narrative with no reference to the preceding) indicates that we have here a continuation of the previous passage:

בְּעֶצֶם הַיּוֹם הַזֶּה נִמּוֹל אַבְרָהָם וְיִשְׁמָעֵאל בְּנוֹ.
וְכָל־אַנְשֵׁי בֵיתוֹ – – – נִמֹּלוּ אִתּוֹ.
וַיֵּרָא אֵלָיו יְיָ.

In the selfsame day was Abraham circumcised, and Ishmael his son.
And all the men of his house ... were circumcised with him— (17, 26–27)

—Then the Lord appeared unto him. (18, 1)

Does not this last verse (18, 1) sound like the grand finale to all that preceded, the reward for all the effort and sacrifice, the crowning touch to the building?

Chapter 18 of our sidra therefore describes two separate "visits"—the privilege and honour of the Divine Presence itself followed by the three messengers with their tidings. Now we may understand more clearly the statement of our Sages that:

גדולה הכנסת אורחים יותר מקבלת פני השכינה.

The deed of hospitality is greater than the welcoming of the Divine Presence.

Hospitality which is the keynote of our sidra constitutes the classic example of love of humanity, altruism and good deeds in general. The welcoming of the Divine Presence symbolises here the mystic enjoyment of direct communion with the Almighty, reserved for the righteous in the Hereafter. In the above dictum of the Sages the view is enunciated that practical good deeds take precedence over any abstract spiritual enjoyment. Under the impress of this revelation of the Divine Presence and the infinite honour paid to him, Abraham rushed, all eagerness, to fulfill the duty of hospitality to the three strangers who stood at the roadside. He did not linger for a moment in the toils of mystic communion with his Creator, but ran to attend to the practical tasks of making welcome some tired and weary wanderers who required food, shelter and rest.

Note how the Torah underlines the eagerness with which Abraham attends to all the wants of his guests in order to serve as an example of true hospitality. The motif words expressing Abraham's haste and eagerness recur over and again.

וַיַּרְא וְהִנֵּה שְׁלֹשָׁה אֲנָשִׁים – – – וַיָּרָץ לִקְרָאתָם – –
וַיְמַהֵר אַבְרָהָם הָאֹהֱלָה אֶל־שָׂרָה וַיֹּאמֶר:
מַהֲרִי – – – לוּשִׁי וַעֲשִׂי עֻגוֹת.
וְאֶל־הַבָּקָר רָץ אַבְרָהָם וַיִּקַּח בֶּן־בָּקָר רַךְ וָטוֹב – –
וַיְמַהֵר לַעֲשׂוֹת אֹתוֹ.

And looked, and, lo, three men ... and when he saw them, he ran **to meet them**
And Abraham hastened **into the tent unto Sarah, and said:**
"Make ready quickly ... **knead it, and make cakes."**
And Abraham ran **unto the herd, and fetched a calf tender and good ...**
and he hastened **to dress it.** (18, 2, 6, 7)

Abraham's example has inspired his descendants down the ages who have always been distinguished for their hospitality, fulfilling to the letter Job's boast that he never left the stranger outside:

> **The stranger did not lodge in the street;**
> **My doors I opened to the roadside.** (Job 31, 32)

In other words, this revelation is different in character from others recorded in the Torah. It is not a means to an end—a method of communicating a particular message but simply a revelation or experience of Divine communion for its own sake, as a mark of grace and honour. Just as a visit between mortals may not always be for a specific practical purpose—to give or extract information but simply social and intimate in character—"the sitting of brothers together," so revelation may be inspired by similar motives; a sign of God's grace, an opportunity for the person so fortunate to be "satisfied, when I awake with Thy likeness."

Questions for Further Study

1.   What is the difficulty presented by Gen. 32, 2, which Ramban removes and what relevance has it to the question discussed by Rashi and Ramban in their comment to our text (18, 1)?

2.   In what sense does Ramban understand the word *be-ẓedek* (the prefix *be* in the *be-ẓedek* translated "in righteousness") in his quotation from Psalm 17? In what way does he deviate from the accepted sense and what forced him to do so?

---

[1] Since this is the first occasion where the text identifies the emissary with the One who sent him Rashbam adds a word of explanation. "There are many occasions when the angel or Divine emissary is identified with the Divine e.g. "For My name is within him" (Exodus 23, 21)—His emissary is like him. Another example is: "The angel of the Lord appeared to him in a flame from the midst of the bush" "Exodus 3, 2) followed by "When the Lord saw that he turned aside to see . . ."

[2] Rashbam had to resort to a similarly inconsistent explanation in the next chapter (19, 24): "The Lord rained down . . . brimstone and fire from the Lord." "The Lord rained down"—the angel Gabriel; "from the Lord"—the actual Divine Presence.

ABRAHAM'S "COMMAND" PERFORMANCE

Chapter 18 (with which our sidra begins) which opens with the words: "And the Lord appeared unto him," and concludes: "And the Lord went His way, as soon as He had left off speaking to Abraham . . ." constitutes, in its entirety, one single grand revelation to Abraham.[1]

But the content of this revelation apparently veers from one extreme to the other in the different parts of the chapter. The content of the first section consists of the message regarding the birth of a son, the last, the pronouncement regarding the destruction of Sodom and Gomorrah and the rest of the cities of the plain. In the first part Abraham is the epitome of hospitality completely at the beck and call of the Divine messengers. He is the one who runs, prostrates, hastens, fetches and carries and stands by them to serve them. In the last section, he is full of fight and defiance, beginning with the "draw near" of verse 23 (Rashi: "We find the expression of "drawing near" used in connection with war . . . peacemaking and prayer and Abraham indulged in all these . . .") till the end. Though the awareness that he is but dust and ashes never leaves him, he nevertheless demands, argues and claims.

Bridging these two sections—the tidings of the birth of a son and the foretelling of the destruction of Sodom—are three verses of supreme importance in the whole book of Genesis.

וַיְיָ אָמָר:
הַמְכַסֶּה אֲנִי מֵאַבְרָהָם
אֲשֶׁר אֲנִי עֹשֶׂה?
וְאַבְרָהָם הָיוֹ יִהְיֶה לְגוֹי גָּדוֹל וְעָצוּם
וְנִבְרְכוּ־בוֹ כֹּל גּוֹיֵי הָאָרֶץ.

כִּי יְדַעְתִּיו
לְמַעַן אֲשֶׁר יְצַוֶּה אֶת־בָּנָיו
וְאֶת־בֵּיתוֹ אַחֲרָיו

וְשָׁמְרוּ דֶּרֶךְ יְיָ
לַעֲשׂוֹת צְדָקָה וּמִשְׁפָּט
לְמַעַן הָבִיא יְיָ עַל־אַבְרָהָם
אֵת אֲשֶׁר־דִּבֶּר עָלָיו.

And the Lord said, Shall I hide from Abraham what I am doing?
seeing that Abraham shall surely become a great nation, and all the nations of the earth shall be blessed in him?
For I have know him to the end that he may command his children and his household after him to keep the way of the Lord, to do righteousness and justice, to the end that the Lord may bring upon Abraham that which He hath spoken to him. (18. 17–19)

At a decisive moment in world history we are allowed to listen in to the considerations which were uppermost, as it were, in the Divine mind, prior to Him proceeding to execute judgement on man and people (see 6, 5–7; 11, 6–7). We overhear, too, the "conversation" of God with Himself, in which one man is chosen to come within the intimate counsels of the Divine. The following description by Amos of the essential character of the prophet is realised in Abraham although he is not explicitly given the title of prophet till later (20, 7): "for he is a prophet":

כִּי לֹא יַעֲשֶׂה אֲדֹנָי אֱלֹהִים דָּבָר
כִּי אִם־גָּלָה סוֹדוֹ
אֶל־עֲבָדָיו הַנְּבִיאִים –

For the Lord God will not do anything until he has revealed His counsel to His servants, the prophets.

165

But the reasons for him qualifying for that title are given us in the verses we are studying, which really act as a bridge between the first half of the chapter—the tidings of the birth of a son—and the second half—the war prosecuted by Abraham in order to rescue Sodom. Let us study the words which constitute the subject of all three parts of the chapter: In the first part (1-15) we are told: "and lo, Sarah thy wife shall have a *son*" (10); "and Sarah shall have a *son*" (14). In the second part that same promised offspring is the subject of the following dictum: "For I have known him to the end that he may command *his children* and his household after him to keep the way of the Lord, to do righteousness and justice." In the third part we overhear the father of these children exclaiming: "Far be it from Thee to do this thing to slay the righteous with the wicked so the righteous should be as the wicked; shall not the Judge of all the earth do justly."

The son who was granted him, through a miracle, at the age of a hundred was reserved for a special purpose. The father was to teach this son and his children after him to observe the "way of the Lord." Buber[2] explains this verse as follows:

> "...to keep the way of the Lord"... is no metaphor. The way of God means the actual movement of God throughout the history of the world. Israel is expected, as the Torah and Prophets repeatedly insist, to follow the Lord's footsteps on this road. The nature of the road is characterised by God, in this passage as doing "justice and righteousness."

This son, the granting of whom to Abraham and Sarah is foretold in the first half of the chapter, this son and his children after him are charged with a mission in the second—to do righteousness and justice. This father who will command his children to do righteousness and justice already himself gives an example of one who demands the doing of justice, even before the birth of the son, and from whom? From the Deity Himself. This is the third part. We may therefore note how these middle verses act as a bridge between the first and third sections linking them to the previous by a theme common to both—"the son."

They are linked to what comes after by the concept of "justice."

Now that we have determined the role of these verses in the chapter, let us subject verse 19 to detailed study. What is the meaning of *yeda'tiv* "I have known him"? Whom didn't He know? Even a superficial reading of the passage indicates that this verb has a special meaning in this context. Here is Rashi's discussion of the problem:

"כי ידעתיו": לשון חיבה, כמו (רות ב, א): "ולנעמי מודע לאישה", (שם ג, ב): "הלא בעז מודעתנו", (שמות לג, יז): "ואדעך בשם". ואמנם עיקר לשון כולם אינו אלא לשון ידיעה, שהמחבב את האדם מקרבו אצלו ויודעו ומכירו. ולמה ידעתיו? — "למען אשר יצווה": לפי שהוא מצוה את בניו עלי לשמור דרכי. ואם תפרשהו כתרגומו: "יודע אני בו שיצוה את בניו" אין "למען" נופל על הלשון.

"For I have known him"—an expression of love as in (Ruth 2, 1): "Naomi had a kinsman (*moda*) of her husband"; (ibid., 3,2) "and now is there not Boaz our kinsman (*moda'tenu*—kinsman or lit.: "one who knows or is acquainted with us"—from the same root as *yada'*—"know," understood by Rashi to denote closeness and intimate knowledge); (Exod. 33, 17) "I know thee by name". Indeed in all these cases the basic idea is knowledge, because he who is fond of a person befriends him and gets to know him intimately. Why have I known him (i.e. become fond of him)? *le-ma'an asher yetzaveh*: because he commands his children to keep to My ways. If you, however follow the Targum which renders it: "I know that he will command his children" the conjunction *lema'an* makes no sense.

Rashi explains that the expressing of knowing here implies not merely cognition, as in many other places in the Bible, but indicates a closeness of relationship to the thing known.[3]

Accordingly, our text contains the fact that Abraham was the chosen of the Lord. We find here for the first time a motivation for this choice:

> To the end (lema'an) **that he may command his children ... to keep the way of the Lord, to do righteousness and justice,** to the end (lema'an) **that the Lord will bring on Abraham what He has spoken.** (18, 19)

There are apparently two goals indicated here—in the repetition of the conjunction *lema'an*. But we shall immediately observe that these two goals are by no means parallel. The first is that of commanding his children to keep to the way of the Lord, and the second, apparently, to receive reward for doing so. Many commentators have noted this anomaly. One of them, *Haketav Vehakabbala* asks:

> How is it conceivable that the Almighty should praise the righteous man of all ages, our Father Abraham, in that he commanded his children to keep the way of the Lord only for the purpose of receiving a reward? Surely he worshipped God out of love (with no thought of reward)?

But a deeper appreciation of Hebrew usage with respect to the word *lema'an* makes the real meaning clear. Ramban explains to us how *lema'an* is capable of two different usages, one of purpose and one of result, in his ·comment to its usage in Deut. 29, 18:

> "that (*lema'an*) the watered be swept away with the dry." *Lema'an* is not in this context an expression of purpose, that I (i.e. the Israelite idolater) shall walk in the stubborness of my heart in order that the watered be swept away with the dry, but that because of this (him walking in the stubbornness of his heart) the result will be that the watered will be swept away with the dry. For every cause followed by an effect or result the word *lema'an* is used, whether the person is the willing instrument as in Deut. 6, 18: "*that* it may be well with you" or whether he is the unconscious instrument. as in: "*that* their hearts may melt (Ezek. 21, 20); "*that* your altars may be desolate" (Ibid 6, 6); "Of their silver and their gold they have made idols *that* they may be cut off" (Hosea 8, 4).

Accordingly the first *lema'an* in our text expresses result deliberately purposed by the subject, and the second, a situation where the man is the unconscious instrument, the result brought about without the deliberate intention of the doer. Abraham did not command his sons because he wished to receive reward but the reward came automatically.

What was, however, the deliberate purpose designed by him?
What was it that "he will command his children"?

וְשָׁמְרוּ דֶּרֶךְ יְיָ.

to keep the way of the Lord (18, 19)

Some commentators identify the way of the Lord with what
Jeremiah terms "knowledge of the Lord." The following two
excerpts from Jeremiah bear out this interpretation. What is
knowledge of the Lord?

אַל־יִתְהַלֵּל חָכָם בְּחָכְמָתוֹ
וְאַל־יִתְהַלֵּל הַגִּבּוֹר בִּגְבוּרָתוֹ
אַל־יִתְהַלֵּל עָשִׁיר בְּעָשְׁרוֹ.
כִּי אִם־בְּזֹאת יִתְהַלֵּל הַמִּתְהַלֵּל
הַשְׂכֵּל וְיָדֹעַ אוֹתִי
כִּי אֲנִי יְיָ עֹשֶׂה חֶסֶד מִשְׁפָּט וּצְדָקָה בָּאָרֶץ
כִּי־בְאֵלֶּה חָפַצְתִּי, נְאֻם יְיָ.

Let not the wise man glory in his wisdom,
neither let the mighty man glory in his might,
let not the rich man glory in his riches;
but let him that glorieth glory in this,
that he understandeth and knoweth Me
That I am the Lord who exercise mercy, justice and
righteousness in the earth,
for in these I delight, said the Lord. (9, 22)

אָבִיךָ הֲלוֹא אָכַל וְשָׁתָה וְעָשָׂה מִשְׁפָּט וּצְדָקָה
אָז טוֹב לוֹ.
דָּן דִּין־עָנִי וְאֶבְיוֹן
אָז טוֹב –
הֲלֹא־הִיא הַדַּעַת אֹתִי, נְאֻם־יְיָ.

Did not thy father eat and drink and do justice and
righteousness? then it was well with him.
He judged the cause of the poor and needy: then it was
well. Is not this to know Me? (22, 15–16)

In both these citations we see that the doing of righteousness
and justice is synonymous with knowing the Lord. In our text
we observe that the keeping of the way of the Lord is synonymous with the doing of justice and righteousness. These two
concepts of righteousness and justice may be taken as hendiadys,
as explained by E. Z. Melamed [4]—"righteous justice".[5] Abraham was chosen therefore to teach his seed to execute just judgement and that constitutes the way of the Lord. We read also in
Amos (where the two constituents of the double-barrelled phrase
"righteousness and justice" are separated and placed in the two
parallel parts of the verse):

וְזִמְרַת נְבָלֶיךָ לֹא אֶשְׁמָע.   הָסֵר מֵעָלַי הֲמוֹן שִׁרֶיךָ
וּצְדָקָה כְּנַחַל אֵיתָן.   וְיִגַּל כַּמַּיִם מִשְׁפָּט

Take thou away from Me the noise of thy songs;
and let Me not hear the melody of thy psalteries.
But let justice well up as waters,
righteousness as a mighty stream. (5, 23)

Questions for .Further Study

1. Abravanel asks:

   "The Lord informed Noah too what He was about to bring to
   pass, namely, the deluge; yet He did not consult Himself nor motivate His reason for revealing the matter to Noah. Why did he
   do so in the case of Abraham?"

2. "For I have known him that he may command" (18, 19).
   Cf.: Rashi (which we cited above with Abravanel's comments on the same text):

The knowledge of the closeness of Providence which I set over Abraham was not for his own sake alone but to serve as a worthy beginning for the nation which would issue from his loins. The text: "for I have known him to the end that he may command his children" implies that My providence cleaves to him so that he may command his children and ensure that they would keep the way of the Lord and do righteousness and justice.

What is the difference between Rashi's explanation and Abravanel's?

3.   "To do righteousness and justice." Explain whether the connotation of *ẓedaka* here is identical with that occurring in Gen. 15, 6 or different from it.

---

1 The problem arising from the first verse of the Sidra as to whether the "appearance" mentioned is synonymous with the arrival of the heavenly messenger or is cut short by their arrival is discussed in the previous Studies on pp. 158–163.

2 From his essay on "Abraham the Seer" p. 40 in: *On the Bible,* 18 Studies, edited by Nahum Glatzer. Schocken books, New York 1968.

3 Buber offers a detailed explanation of the connotation of the Hebrew verb *yada'* in his comment to the last verse of Psalm I: "For the Lord regardeth the way of the righteous but the way of the wicked shall perish." He notes that *yada'* in its usual sense of "know" or "regard" offers no meaningful contrast to the parallel phrase relating to the wicked. We have, he writes, to go back to the elemental connotation of the word in the Bible as opposed to that in Western languages. In the latter it is related to mind and thought, to reflection. But in the former it expressed contact between the person and thing known, immediacy and intimacy—dialogue. This dialogue-relationship between God and His elect, the prophets that He charges with a mission is unique in intensity. "Know" in this context expresses Divine concern and intimate contact with those He has sought out. By His contact with them He separated them from the mass of living objects, in order to communicate with them. See Buber: *Good and Evil:* Two Interpretations, pp. 55–56, Charles Scribner and Sons. New York, 1953.

4 Tarbiẓ 16, vol. 4, pp. 173–198. Jerusalem 5705 (1945).

5 The examples cited here are:

גר ותושב, הסד ואמת, עני ואביון.

171

THE SIN OF SODOM

זַעֲקַת סְדֹם וַעֲמֹרָה כִּי־רָבָּה
וְחַטָּאתָם כִּי כָבְדָה מְאֹד.
אֵרְדָה־נָּא וְאֶרְאֶה הַכְּצַעֲקָתָהּ הַבָּאָה אֵלַי עָשׂוּ.

And the Lord said:

**Because the cry of Sodom and Gomorrah is great
and because their sin is very grievous:
I will go down now, and see
whether they have done altogether according to the cry of it,
which is come unto me ...** (18, 20-21)

Paying attention to the original Hebrew wording, it is not easy to determine to what הכצעקתה "the cry of it" (literally "of her"), refers to. Being feminine, the only previous noun in the feminine gender is Sodom and Gomorrah (i.e. "the city" עיר of Sodom) and this, indeed, is the interpretation followed by most commentators, as constituting the plain sense of the text. However our Sages in the Midrash were not satisfied with this and attributed the feminine reference to the cry of "that young woman" אותה ריבה. Here we shall quote the relevant Midrash (Pirke Derabbi Eliezer, 25) relating her story:

הכריזו בסדום ואמרו : כל מי שהוא מחזיק ידי עני ואביון וגר בפת לחם, ישרף באש! פלוטית בתו של לוט היתה נשואה לאחד מגדולי סדום, ראתה עני אחד מדוקדק ברחוב העיר ועגמה נפשה עליה. מה היתה עושה? בכל יום כשהיתה יוצאת לשאוב מים, היתה נותנת בכד שלה מכל מזון ביתה וכלכלה אותו עני, אמרו אנשי סדום : מאין הוא חי? עד שידעו הדבר הוציאו אותה להישרף. אמרה : אלוהי עולם! עשה משפטי ודיני מאנשי סדום; ועלתה זעקתה לפני כיסא הכבוד. אמר הקב"ה : "ארדה ואראה הכצעקתה הבאה אלי" — אם כצעקת הנערה הזאת עשו אנשי סדום, אהפוך יסודותיה שלה למעלה ופניה למטה.

They issued a proclamation in Sodom, saying: Everyone who strengthens the hand of the poor and the needy with a loaf of bread shall be burnt by fire! Pelotit the daughter of Lot was wedded to one of the magnates of Sodom. She saw a certain very poor man in the street of the city and her soul was grieved on the account. What did she do? Every day when she went out to draw water she put in her pitcher all kinds of provisions from her house and she sustained that poor man. The men of Sodom said: How does this poor man live? When they ascertained the facts they brought her forth to be burnt by fire. She said: Sovereign of all worlds! Maintain my right and my cause at the hands of the men of Sodom! And her cry ascended before the throne of glory. In that hour the Holy One blessed be He said: "I will go down and see whether they have done altogether according to her cry which is come unto me"—and if the men of Sodom have done according to the cry of that young woman, I will turn her foundation upwards and the surface downward . . .

The Midrash wishes to emphasise two points. First, what exactly constituted the wickedness of Sodom? What form had such wickedness to take to warrant the total destruction of the city? The answer given by the Midrash to this question is—social iniquity—even of a passive and not an active form. The prophet Ezekiel describes Sodom's crimes in this very manner when he states:

הִנֵּה־זֶה הָיָה עֲוֹן סְדֹם אֲחוֹתֵךְ:
גָּאוֹן שִׂבְעַת־לֶחֶם וְשַׁלְוַת הַשְׁקֵט הָיָה לָהּ וְלִבְנוֹתֶיהָ
וְיַד־עָנִי וְאֶבְיוֹן לֹא הֶחֱזִיקָה – – –

Behold this was the iniquity of thy sister Sodom:
Pride, fulness of bread, and abundance of idleness
was in her and her daughters,
neither did she strengthen the hand of the poor
and the needy. (16, 49)

But the height of their wickedness lay not in the activities of individual transgressors but in the fact that such iniquitous behaviour was clothed with a cloak of legality, raised to the level of a social norm, as our Midrash seeks to underline:

> *They issued a proclamation* in Sodom saying: Everyone who
> strengthens the hand of the poor and needy with a loaf of bread
> shall be burnt by fire.

Their wickedness was not committed in secret, as something to
be ashamed of, nor was it the product of a spontaneous outburst
of the populace provoked by irresponsible elements. It was rather
the law of the land, and whoever violated this savage law, and
performed a good deed, prompted by his own instincts of pity,
was condemned to be burnt at the stake. There was no remedy
for such a society but total destruction.

...the cry of Sodom is great ... and their sin is very grievous.

The second concept illustrated by the Midrash is that the
catastrophe that overtook Sodom was the direct result of their
encompassing the death of a certain young woman for feeding a
poor man. It was this one deed, this cry that weighted the scales
against them.

In this connection, let us recall Rambam's words in the laws
of *Teshuva* (Repentance):

צריך כל אדם שיראה את עצמו כל השנה כולה כאילו חציו זכאי וחציו חייב,
וכן כל העולם חציו זכאי וחציו חייב. חטא חטא אחד — הרי הכריע עצמו ואת
כל העולם כולו לכף חובה וגרם לו השחתה; עשה מצוה אחת — הרי הכריע
את עצמו ואת כל העולם לכף זכות וגרם לו ולהם תשועה והצלה . . .

> Every man should regard himself, the whole year round, as if
> he were equally balanced between innocence and guilt and, similar-
> ly, that the whole world is equally balanced between innocence
> and guilt. If he commits one sin, behold he has weighted the
> scales to his own detriment and that of the world, and brought
> destruction on it. If he performs one good deed (*mizva*), he has
> weighted the scales in his own favour and that of the world's,
> and brought salvation.

Just as each individual is endowed with his own unique personality and has no exact counterpart, so every deed committed
in the world makes its own particular contribution, positive or
negative to the general welfare, ultimately affecting the fate of

the whole of mankind. Man is no speck of dust or cog in a machine but is created in the image of God, responsible for his every action to himself, society and the world. Every act, however minute, is fraught with consequences for the future, as far as his environment and beyond are concerned.

It was the cry of "that young woman" cruelly put to death which weighted the scales against Sodom and sealed its fate.

Some commentators consider that the first half of chapter 19, describing the savage reception and treatment accorded strangers visiting the city, is meant as a graphic illustration of the wickedness and sin which God had declared in His intention "to go down and see" (18, 21). Let us quote on this point Isaac Arama in his work *Akedat Yizhak*:

> After the Divine probe into the affairs of Sodom had been implemented and it transpired that the whole of Sodom including the sons-in-law of Lot were guilty of the same iniquitous behaviour, the latter not listening to him and mocking him, its fate was sealed for total destruction.

In other words, the sin and wickedness referred to in a general way in chapter 13, 13:

But the men of Sodom were wicked and sinners before the Lord exceedingly

and in chapter 18, 21 are brought to life in chapter 19 and described in detail, and it is this that seals their fate.

What was the reaction of the men of Sodom to the tidings of impending catastrophe? Did they take notice?

Lot is an example of the average man, a study in mediocrity faithfully following in the steps of his master Abraham, until his pocket is affected. As Rashi points out:

> "ויסע לוט מקדם" — הסיע עצמו מקדמונו של עולם, אמר: אי אפשי לא באברהם ולא באלוהיו.

> "And Lot journeyed *east.*" He journeyed away from the Primal Being (a play on the word *kedem* meaning first) of the world. He said: "Neither Abraham nor his God!"

He left Abraham for the fertile fields of Sodom—from one pole to another, from Abraham and his God to Sodom.

וַיִּשָּׂא־לוֹט אֶת־עֵינָיו וַיַּרְא אֶת־כָּל־כִּכַּר
הַיַּרְדֵּן כִּי כֻלָּהּ מַשְׁקֶה
לִפְנֵי שַׁחֵת יְיָ אֶת־סְדֹם וְאֶת־עֲמֹרָה כְּמַ֖־יְיָ
כְּאֶרֶץ מִצְרַיִם – – –
– – – וַיִּסַּע לוֹט מִקֶּדֶם וַיִּפָּרְדוּ אִישׁ מֵעַל אָחִיו.

**And Lot lifted up his eyes, and beheld all the plain of Jordan, that it was well watered everywhere, before the Lord destroyed Sodom and Gomorrah, even as the garden of the Lord, like the land of Egypt ...
And Lot journeyed east ...
and they separated themselves one from the other.**
(13, 10–11)

There is something deeply symbolic in this flight from Abraham to Sodom.

Lot tried to maintain Abraham's way of life even in the heart of Sodom, striving to preserve, at the risk to his life, the elementary obligations of hospitality to strangers, in a city where such behaviour was forbidden by law. Naturally his attempts were doomed to failure, resulting from his inability to choose between Abraham and his environment and Sodom and its environment. His attempt to maintain a kind of underground loyalty to his old way of life, within Sodom leads him to the dilemma resulting in his throwing his daughters to the mercy of the populace, in exchange for his guests. Ramban condemns Lot for this action in permitting his daughters to be thus abused. Rather than be singled out for praise for protecting his guests, Lot demonstrated his condonation of immorality by prostituting his daughters. On this our Rabbis commented:

> In the ordinary way, a man sacrifices his own life to save that of his daughters or wife, whilst this one hands over his daughters to be abused!

If Lot as Abraham's disciple could not maintain his own moral "Abrahamic" integrity in Sodom, much less could he be expected to transmit it to his children. His daughters naturally wedded themselves to the men of Sodom and to them, the magnates of Sodom, as the Midrash reports, Lot brought the news of the impending catastrophe:

וַיֵּצֵא לוֹט וַיְדַבֵּר אֶל־חֲתָנָיו לֹקְחֵי בְנֹתָיו וַיֹּאמֶר
קוּמוּ צְּאוּ מִן־הַמָּקוֹם הַזֶּה כִּי־מַשְׁחִית יְיָ אֶת־הָעִיר – –

And Lot went out and spake unto his sons-in-law which married his daughters, and said, Up, get you out of this place; for the Lord will destroy this city.   (19, 14)

The Torah reports Lot's exact words in direct speech as he addressed his sons-in-law. But their answer is only reported in general terms:

וַיְהִי כִמְצַחֵק בְּעֵינֵי חֲתָנָיו.

But he seemed as one that mocked unto his sons-in-law.
It is left to the Midrash to paint for us an exact picture of their reaction and word for us their reply:

קשה הוא הליצנות, שלא מיהרה פורענות על הסדומיים עד שנתלוצצו בלוט,
שנאמר: "ויהי כמצחק בעיני חתניו". אמרו לו: שוטה שבעולם! נבלים
וכינורות וחלילים בעיר — ואתה אומר: סדום נהפכת?!

Mockery is a grievous matter, since punishment did not overtake the Sodomites till they mocked Lot as it is said: "And he seemed as one that mocked unto his sons-in-law." Said they to him: Fool that you are!' Psalters, harps and flutes in the city and you say: Sodom is to be overthrown!

Apparently the Sodomites, both the original ones and their symbolic heirs (Sodom was destroyed, the archetype no longer exists, but every generation throws up its own "Sodomites") are always punished by blindness. Seeing that they are blessed with prosperity "like the garden of the Lord psalters, harps and flutes in the city" they are blind to the ephemeral nature of it all, are

177

unaware of impending catastrophe and whoever dares to suggest
that everything is not alright, is met with scorn and derision.

Possibly Isaiah referred to this same blindness and complacency
in the following verse:

וְהָיָה כִנּוֹר וָנֶבֶל תֹּף וְחָלִיל וָיַיִן מִשְׁתֵּיהֶם
וְאֵת פֹּעַל יְיָ לֹא יַבִּיטוּ וּמַעֲשֵׂה יָדָיו לֹא רָאוּ.

**And the harp and the viol, the tabret and the pipe
and wine are in their feasts:
But they regard not the work of the Lord,
neither consider the operation of His hands.** (5, 12)

Questions for Further Study

1. Here are three citations from our sources describing the
    sin of the Sodomites:
    First *Ezekiel* from which we have already quoted in our
    Studies:
    As I live, saith the Lord God,
    Sodom thy sister hath not done, she nor her daughters,
    as thou hast done, thou and thy daughters.
    Behold, this was the iniquity of thy sister Sodom:
    pride, fulness of bread, and careless ease was in her and
    in her daughters; neither did she strengthen the hand
    of the poor and needy.
    And they were haughty, and committed abomination
    before Me; therefore I removed them when I saw it.
    (16, 49–50)

Here is the comment of our Sages (Tosefta, Sota 3, Sanhedrin
109a):

אנשי סדום לא נתגאו אלא בשביל טובה שהשפיע להם הקב"ה. ומה כתיב
בהם? (איוב כח, ה-ז): "ארץ ממנה יצא לחם . . . מקום ספיר אבניה ועפרת
זהב לו, נתיב לא ידעו עיט ולא שזפתו עין איה". אמרו [אנשי סדום]: הואיל
וכסף וזהב יוצא מארצנו, למה לנו עוברי דרכים? אין אנו צריכים שיבא

178

אדם אצלנו, שאין באין אלא לחסרנו! בואו ונשכח תורת רגל מארצנו. אמר
להם המקום: בטובה שהשפעתי לכם אתם משכיחים את הרגל מביניכם?! אני
אשכח אתכם מן העולם, שנאמר (איוב כח, ד): "הנשכחים מני רגל – דלו
מאנוש נעו". היא גרמה להם לאשר הביא אלוה בידו. וכן הוא אומר (יחזקאל
טז, מט): "הנה זה היה עון סדום וכו'".

The men of Sodom only became haughty on account of the
bounty with which the Holy One blessed be He had endowed them.
What is written regarding them? "As for the earth, out of it
cometh bread ... The stones thereof are the place of sapphires,
and it hath dust of gold. That path no bird of prey knoweth,
neither hath the falcon's eye seen it" (Job 28, 5–7). They said:
Since gold and silver flows from our land what need have we of
travellers? We do not require any visitors since they only come
to diminish our substance. Come and let us cause the foot of
the traveller to be forgotten from our land. Said the Omnipotent
to them: On account of the bounty with which I endowed you,
do you cause the foot of the traveller to be forgotten from amongst
you? I shall cause you to be forgotten from the world, as it is
said: "They are forgotten of the foot that passeth by" (Job 28, 4).
This was what brought on them the retribution of God. To this
Ezekiel also referred (see above).

Ramban similarly describes their sin:

The Sodomites intended to prevent the entry of all strangers.
They imagined (as our Rabbis maintain) that many people
would come to their land on account of its fertility. They refused
to share their bounty with the less fortunate. They accepted Lot
on account of his wealth or out of respect to Abraham. Ezekiel
similarly testifies that this was the offence: "Behold, this was the
iniquity of this sister Sodom: pride: fulness of bread, and careless
ease was in her hand and in her daughters; neither did she
strengthen the hand of the poor and needy." The reference to
their being "evil and exceeding sinners to the Lord" (Gen. 13, 13)
is to the fact that they rebelled in their prosperity and persecuted
the poor, as Ezekiel states: "And they were haughty, and committed abomination before Me; therefore I removed them when
I saw it." According to our Sages they were notorious for every
kind of evil, but their fate was sealed for their persistence in not
supporting the poor and the needy. They were continually guilty
of this sin, and no other nation could be compared to Sodom for
cruelty.

179

Here is the question propounded by Isaac Arama in his *Akedat Yizhak* on the passage from *Ezekiel*:

> Why did not Ezekiel allude, in the case of Sodom, to the particular sin for which they were singled out in this story (in our sidra), tracing instead their punishment to the fact that they did not remember to perform acts of kindness?

1. What are Ramban's two answers to this question?

2. Can you give a third answer based on the plain sense of the text?

WOULD YOU DESTROY THE RIGHTEOUS
WITH THE WICKED!

The moral stature of the patriarch Abraham was considerably greater than that of Noah, the progenitor of the human race. We quote here the words of the *Zohar* on this point:

"ויגש אברהם ויאמר: האף תספה צדיק עם רשע" (בראשית יח, כג) — אמר
ר' יהודה: מאן חמא אבא דרחמנותא כאברהם? תא חזי: בנח כתיב (ו, יג-יד):
"ויאמר אלהים לנח: קץ כל בשר בא לפני...והנני משחיתם את הארץ.
עשה לך תבת עצי גפר..."; ואשתיק ולא אמר לו מידי ולא בעי רחמי. אבל
אברהם, בשעתא דאמר ליה קב"ה "זעקת סדום ועמרה כי רבה וחטאתם כי
כבדה מאד. ארדה נא ואראה..." — מיד כתיב: "ויגש אברהם ויאמר: האף
תספה צדיק עם רשע?!"

(אמר ר' יהודה: מי ראה אב רחמן כאברהם. בוא וראה: בנח כתוב "קץ כל
בשר בא לפני...עשה לך תבת עצי גפר...". ושתק [נח] ולא אמר דבר
ולא ביקש רחמים. אבל אברהם בשעה שאמר לו הקב"ה: "זעקת סדום ועמורה
כי רבה...ארדה נא ואראה...", מיד כתוב: "ויגש אברהם ויאמר: האף
תספה צדיק עם רשע".)

"And Abraham drew near and said, wilt thou also destroy the righteous with the wicked?" (Genesis 18, 23)—said R. Yehudah: Who hath seen a father as compassionate as Abraham? Come and see: Regarding Noah it is stated (6, 13) "And God said to Noah, the end of all flesh is come before me; ...and behold I will destroy them from the earth. Make thee an ark of gopher wood..." And Noah held his peace and said naught, neither did he intercede. Whereas Abraham, as soon as the Holy One blessed be He said to him: "Because the cry of Sodom and Gomorrah is great and because their sin is very grievous, I will go down now and see..." Immediately, as it is stated, "and Abraham drew near and said: Wilt thou also destroy the righteous with the wicked?"

God indeed afforded Abraham the opportunity for interceding on behalf of the Sodomites, since He said to him—

זַעֲקַת סְדֹם וַעֲמֹרָה כִּי־רָבָּה וְחַטָּאתָם כִּי כָבְדָה מְאֹד
אֵרֲדָה־נָא וְאֶרְאֶה – – –

**Because the cry of Sodom and Gomorrah is great,
And because their sin is very grievous
I will go down and see ...** (18, 20–2)

This passage clearly mirrors the Divine intention to put Abraham
to the test to see whether he would beseech mercy for them. Immediately after this "Abraham drew near." What are the exact
implications of the phrase "drew near" in relation to the Almighty
who fills the whole world with His glory? Rashi explains this to
us, basing himself on ancient Rabbinic sources.

Drawing near to speak harshly (that is to join or draw near to battle, as it were)	הגשה לדבר קשות
Drawing near to appease	הגשה לפיוס
Drawing near to pray	הגשה לתפילה

In other words, Abraham mustered all his inner resource, both
his gentle and hard qualities, love and fear, mildness and boldness, ready to do combat on behalf of Sodom. He argued:

It be far from Thee to do after this manner

and besought:

Oh let not the Lord be angry, and I will speak yet but
this once.

He boldly exclaimed:

Shall not the Judge of all the earth do justice?

and recoiled in awe:

Behold now I have taken upon me to speak unto the Lord,
Which am but dust and ashes.

Let us try to understand the contents of his supplication. On
whose behalf did Abraham intercede? To save the righteous?
Or the wicked as well? Here we quote the first part of his
intercession:

הַאַף תִּסְפֶּה צַדִּיק עִם־רָשָׁע?
אוּלַי יֵשׁ חֲמִשִּׁים צַדִּיקִם בְּתוֹךְ הָעִיר
הַאַף תִּסְפֶּה וְלֹא־תִשָּׂא לַמָּקוֹם
לְמַעַן חֲמִשִּׁים הַצַּדִּיקִם אֲשֶׁר בְּקִרְבָּהּ?
חָלִלָה לְּךָ מֵעֲשֹׂת כַּדָּבָר הַזֶּה

לְהָמִית צַדִּיק עִם־רָשָׁע
וְהָיָה כַצַּדִּיק כָּרָשָׁע,
חָלִלָה לָךְ! הֲשֹׁפֵט כָּל־הָאָרֶץ לֹא יַעֲשֶׂה מִשְׁפָּט?!

**Will thou also destroy the righteous with the wicked?
Peradventure there be fifty righteous within the city:
Will thou also destroy and not spare the place for the
fifty righteous that are therein?
That be far from Thee to do after this manner,
To slay the righteous with the wicked:
And that the righteous should be as the wicked,
Shall not the Judge of all the earth do justice?.**

(18, 23–25)

Our commentators have been puzzled by the seeming contradictions in the above passage. Here we quote the remarks of
Solomon Dubnow in the *Biur*, to Genesis:

First (v. 23) Abraham prayed that God should not slay the
righteous together with the wicked, whereas in the immediately
succeeding verse he besought God to deliver the wicked along
with the righteous, even before his first prayer had been answered.
In the next verse Abraham then reverted to his first plea to
save only the righteous.

Here is a plausible solution as propounded by David ben Samuel
Halevi in his work on Rashi entitled *Divrei David*:

It is only right that you do not destroy the righteous with the
wicked, since that is but justice and requires no prayer. My prayer
is only directed at beseeching You to deliver the whole place
for the sake of the righteous. But if my prayer is of no avail,
then at least, why should You kill the righteous since this is not
a question of seeking a special favour but is only justice!

Two principles are here enunciated, the first, that of righteous
judgment. It is this which emerges in the Torah as the quality
characterising Abraham's conduct and which distinguishes his
spiritual destiny, as worded in the verses preceding his dialogue
with the Almighty:

כִּי יְדַעְתִּיו לְמַעַן אֲשֶׁר יְצַוֶּה אֶת־בָּנָיו וְאֶת־
בֵּיתוֹ אַחֲרָיו
וְשָׁמְרוּ דֶּרֶךְ יְיָ לַעֲשׂוֹת צְדָקָה וּמִשְׁפָּט.

For I know him,
That he will command his children and his household
after him
And they shall keep the way of the Lord,
To do justice **and** judgment. (18, 19)

The phrase: "For I know him" implies that this was the path
that had been marked out for him and his descendants by God.
(cf. Jeremiah 1, "Before I formed thee in the belly *I knew thee*").
But the destiny that had been marked out for Abraham in the
future also fitted the pattern of his conduct in the Biblical narrative. The Patriarch is true to the principles divinely reserved
for his descendants, even before he had yet been granted children. Abraham demands the same standard of conduct, as it
were, from the Judge of the earth:

הֲשֹׁפֵט כָּל־הָאָרֶץ לֹא יַעֲשֶׂה מִשְׁפָּט?

Shall not the Judge of all the earth do justice?!

The second principle that emerges from the dialogue between
Abraham and the Almighty is the responsibility of the righteous
few towards the rest of society, however corrupt, and their capacity to save it from destruction by the sheer force of their own
merit and moral impact. Should there exist in Sodom, the symbol of wickedness and corruption, fifty righteous men, should
not their merit be capable of saving the whole city? Surely even
one light illumines far more than itself and one spark is sufficient to penetrate the thickest darkness! Surely the "place" constitutes but one whole and if its heart is strong and healthy,
should this not result in saving the rest of the body?
   The prophet Jeremiah formulated these same sentiments in a
starker and more extreme manner:

שׁוֹטְטוּ בְּחוּצוֹת יְרוּשָׁלַ͏ִם וּרְאוּ־נָא וּדְעוּ
וּבַקְשׁוּ בִרְחוֹבוֹתֶיהָ
אִם־תִּמְצְאוּ אִישׁ
אִם־יֵשׁ עֹשֶׂה מִשְׁפָּט מְבַקֵּשׁ אֱמוּנָה –
וְאֶסְלַח לָהּ.

Run ye to and fro through the streets of Jerusalem,
And see now, and know,
And seek in the broad places thereof,
If ye can find a man,
If there be any that executeth judgment, that seeketh
the truth;
And I will pardon it.   (Jeremiah 5, 1)

But our sages inserted one important proviso limiting the
power of the few or the individual to save the many through
their merit, finding an allusion to their principle in the Divine
answer to Abraham's first plea in our chapter:

וַיֹּאמֶר יְיָ: אִם־אֶמְצָא בִסְדֹם חֲמִשִּׁים
צַדִּיקִם בְּתוֹךְ הָעִיר
וְנָשָׂאתִי לְכָל־הַמָּקוֹם בַּעֲבוּרָם.

And the Lord said:
If I find in Sodom fifty righteous within the city,
Then I will spare all the place for their sakes.   (18, 26)

It is the repetition implied in the employing of both "in Sodom" and "within the city" that provides our commentators with
the clue. Ibn Ezra briefly but significantly reveals the all-
important implications of this repetition:

> The reason for the words "within the city" implies that they fear
> the Lord *in public*, compare Jeremiah—"run ye to and fro
> through the streets of Jerusalem."

In other words, the few can turn the scales and save the place,
if the righteous individuals concerned are "within the city," play-

ing a prominent part in public life and exerting their influence in its many fields of activity. But if they merely exist, living in retirement and never venturing forth but pursuing their pious conduct unseen and unknown, they will, perhaps, save themselves, but will certainly not possess the spiritual merit capable of protecting the city. The same city which forces the righteous few into retirement so that their scrupulous moral standards should not interfere with the injustice dominating public life, that same city is not entitled to claim salvation by virtue of the handful of righteous men leading a secluded life within it.

Sodom could not boast of fifty, forty, thirty, or even ten righteous men, and if they existed, at any rate, they were not "within the city." Radak, quoting his father, explains Jeremiah's lament referred to above in the same sense, implying that no "man" of any importance could be found "that executeth judgment, that seeketh the truth" in the streets of Jerusalem. Here we cite the Radak on the relevant verse:

> Behold David had said (Psalms 79, 2) "the dead bodies *of thy servants* have they given to be meat unto the beasts of the earth." Behold, then, there *were* in Jerusalem saints and servants of the Lord. How could Jeremiah then say "if there be any that executeth judgment...!" My father, his memory be for a blessing, explained that Jeremiah expressly stated "through *the streets* of Jerusalem" and "in *the broad places* thereof," since the saints who were in Jerusalem hid inside their houses and were not able to show themselves in the streets and public places because of the wicked.

Questions for Further Study

> "Then Abraham drew near and said, Wilt Thou indeed destroy": ...implying that it would be decent and generous of Him to spare the whole population for the sake of the fifty righteous ones. On the other hand, the Almighty would be violating even the letter of the law by destroying both righteous and wicked. This would equate them both, giving an excuse for those who say: "it is vain to serve God" (Malachi 3). How much more would the Judge of the whole earth be violating the quality of mercy. This is the force of the repetition of "far be it from Thee". Ultimately the Holy One blessed be He did agree to spare

the whole place for their sake, treating them with the quality of
mercy.   (Ramban)

"And not spare the place": The text does not read "the people
of the place" since that would mean the guilty ones only, who
would be meeting their just deserts. It was only fair however
not to destroy the place completely so long as there remained fifty
righteous persons within it. The wicked would be destroyed with
the place remaining on the map populated by the surviving
righteous.   (Radak)

(a) What is the difference between these two commenta-
     tors in their approach to the text?
(b) Whom have we followed (see pp. 185–6).

GOD TRIED ABRAHAM

Abravanel prefaces his commentary to this sidra with the following remark:

> This section constitutes the *raison d'être* of Israel in the sight of their Father in Heaven. It forms on this account, a familiar part of our daily devotions and accordingly warrants a deeper and more painstaking study than others.

We shall not, however, tackle the whole section, Abraham's deed and test, but only the three words which form the heading of this chapter.

This expression has been the subject of much discussion among our commentators. Here we quote one wording of the difficulty that it poses:

> The nature of this trial calls for explanation, since there is no doubt that the Almighty does not try a person in order to prove to himself whether he is capable of withstanding the trial since God is allknowing and is in no doubt about anything.
>
> (Rabbenu Nissim)

Here is Rambam's answer given in his *Guide to the Perplexed*:

> ... The sole object of all the trials mentioned in Scripture is to teach man what he ought to do ... so that the event which forms the actual trial is not the end desired; it is but an example for our instruction and guidance. Hence the words "to know (*la-da'at*) whether ye love," etc. (Deuteronomy 13, 4), do not mean that God desires to know whether they loved God; for He already knows it; but *la-da'at*, "to know," has here the same meaning as in the phrase "to know (*la-da'at*) that I am the Lord that sanctifieth you" (Exod. 31, 13), i.e., that all nations shall know ... The account of Abraham our father binding his son, includes two great principles of our faith. First, it shows us the

extent and limit of the fear of God. Abraham is commanded to perform a certain act, which is not equalled by any surrender of property or by any sacrifice of life, for it surpasses everything that that can be done ... He had been without child, and had been longing for a child; he had great riches, and was expecting that a nation should spring from his seed. After all hope of a son had already been given up, a son was born unto him. How great must have been his delight in the child! how intensely must he have loved him! And yet because he feared God, and loved to do what God commanded, he thought little of that beloved child, and set aside all his hopes concerning him, and consented to kill him after a journey of three days. If the act by which he showed his readiness to kill his son had taken place immediately when he received the commandment, it might have been the result of confusion and not of consideration. But the fact that he performed it three days after he had received the commandment, proves the presence of thought, proper consideration, and careful examination of what is due to the Divine command and what is in accordance with the love and fear of God ... For Abraham did not hasten to kill Isaac out of fear that God might slay him or make him poor, but solely because it is man's duty to love and to fear God, even without hope of reward or fear of punishment. The angel, therefore, says to him, "For now I know," etc. (Genesis 22, 12), that is, from this action, for which you deserve to be truly called a God-fearing man, all people shall learn how far we must go in the fear of God. This idea is confirmed in Scripture, where it is distinctly stated that one sole thing, fear of God, is the object of the whole Law with its affirmative and negative precepts, its promises and its historical examples; for it is said, "If thou wilt not observe to do all the words of this Law that are written in this book, that thou mayest fear this glorious and fearful name, the Lord thy God," etc. (Deuteronomy 28, 58). This is one of the two purposes of the *"akedah"* (sacrifice or binding of Isaac) ...

Saadia Gaon referred also to this idea when he stated that the word *nissah* implied that God wished to demonstrate Abraham's righteousness to mankind. Ibn Ezra, who cites this explanation, criticizes it with a remark which must seem to us shortsighted.

Was not the Gaon aware that when Abraham sacrificed his son there was no one present, not even his servant?

But Isaac Arama rebuts this criticism in his *Akedat Yizhak*:

> Since this trial was narrated in the Torah as testimony of the living God, it is as if the trial took place in the presence of every Jew, past, present, and future. No one has failed to witness, through this medium, the greatness of this trial and the steadfastness of Abraham's faith, which became indelibly fixed in the hearts of all members of the human race.

.Abravanel similarly maintains that the trial was designed to promote the welfare of the whole world and teach mankind a lesson:

> This trial was not a test evolved by God to find out what He did not know, but God made a demonstration, the root of the word being from *ness* meaning wonder or sign which Abraham performed at the word of God, as an example and banner to all the peoples for them to follow.

However, his explanation of Abravanel does not take account of the plain sense of the narrative, particularly the implications of the phrase "now I know" (22, 12).

R. Yosef Albo in his *Sefer Haikkarim* takes a different point of view:

> Should you ask, since the Almighty knew whether Abraham would withstand his trial or not, what was the reason for imposing on him these sufferings? The answer is that the reward for potential good is not the same as that for actual good deeds. "Let not him that girdeth on his armour boast himself as he that putteth it off" (1 Kings 20, 11), he who has not performed deeds of valour, who is prepared for battle cannot be compared to the one who has actually fought and performed these deeds and already "putteth off" his armour. For this reason the Holy One blessed be He often inflicts suffering on the righteous in order to habituate it to them so that their outward actions conform to their inner character. The deed will intensify love of God since every action leaves its own indelible mark on the performer. This practice in good actions is termed *nisayon*.

Albo deviates somewhat from the usual connotation of the word, which, according to him, cannot then be rendered by the words "tempt" and "prove" used by the English and other translators. He maintains that the word has the connotation of "experience"—"God gave Abraham experience through this trial." Ramban adheres closer to the ordinary meaning of the term in his explanation:

> This is my idea of what the term *nisayon* implies. Since man is complete master of his own actions, possessing the free will to act or refrain from acting, the term *nisayon* or trial expresses the situation from the point of view of the person himself. On the other hand, God, who confronts him with the trial commands him in order to translate into action the potentialities of his character, and give him the reward of a good deed, in addition to the reward of a good heart.
>
> Know also that the Lord tries the righteous. When he knows that the righteous man will do His will and wishes to show his righteousness, He confronts him with a trial. But he does not try the wicked who will not hearken. All the trials described in the Torah were directed to benefit the recipient.

All the different views we have cited here agree that the trial is not meant to prove anything to the Almighty who is all-knowing. But Ramban and Albo differ from Rambam and those who follow him in that they add the idea that the purpose of the trial, is to improve the character of the subject, and train him in doing positive good and realising to the full his own spiritual potentialities.

Ramban adds, incidentally, some remarks regarding the type of character who deserves to be tried. These remarks afford some solution to the problem of the sufferings of the righteous. In our context we dealt with unusual trials. Ramban discusses also the usual trials that are part and parcel of existence.

> The Master will sometimes try His servant with hard labour to know if he can bear it out of love for him, and sometimes He will grant him good fortune to see whether he will recompense him with good in accordance with the statement of our Sages: "Happy the man who withstands his trial, since there is no creature whom the Holy One blessed be He does not try." The rich man He tries to see if he will be openhanded to the poor, the poor man He tries to see if he can bear suffering without complaint.

Questions for Further Study

1. Which of our commentators does S. Dubnow follow in the passage cited below?

    Sometimes His intention is to strengthen and fortify morally the heart of the subject of the trial. Man's character in the sphere of practical action cannot be perfected merely by a theoretical knowledge of goodness. This must be realised in habitual action so that good deeds become second nature and are performed with joy and without reluctance. This is the meaning of the phrase "God did prove Abraham," implying that He gave him the opportunity to fortify himself in the ways of fearing and serving Him through the awe-inspiring deed He commanded him to perform.
    (Biur)

2. Rashi comments as follows on the verse "fear not; for God is come to prove (*nasot*) you ..." (Exodus 20, 17):

    ״אל תיראו כי לבעבור נסות אתכם בא האלהים״: לגדל אתכם בעולם שייצא
    לכם שם באומות, שהוא בכבודו נגלה עליכם.
    ״נסות״: לשון הרמה וגדולה, כמו (ישעיה סב, י): ״הרימו נס״ (ישעיהו מט,
    כב): ״אריס נסי״ וכן (שם ל, יז): ״וכנס על הגבעה״, שהוא זקוף.

    In order to make you great in the world that your name should be famous among the nations, that He in His glory was revealed to you. *Nasot*, an expression of lifting up and greatness. Cf. (Isaiah 62, 10) "Lift up a *ness* (ensign)," (Isaiah 49, 22) "Set up My *ness*," (Isaiah 30, 17) "And as a *ness* on a hill."

    (a) Which of the extracts we have cited harmonises with Rashi's explanation?

    (b) Why does not Rashi explain in our sidra the term *nissah* as he explained *nassot* in Exodus 20, 17?

3. Cf.:

    Behold, I will cause to rain bread from heaven for you; and the people shall go out and gather a day's portion every day, that I may *prove* them, whether they will walk in My law, or not.
    (Exodus 16, 4)

192

Who fed thee in the wilderness with manna, which thy fathers knew not;

that He might afflict thee, and that He might *prove* thee . . .
(Deut. 8, 16)

Explain in what way the giving of the manna constituted a trial for Israel.

GOD WILL PROVIDE THE LAMB

The story is familiar to us all. We know the nature of the appeal answered by the single, trisyllabic, Hebrew word *hineni* (here-I-am) of Abraham. We are aware of the demand involved and the response which followed the words: "upon one of the mountains which I will tell thee of."—

וַיַּשְׁכֵּם אַבְרָהָם בַּבֹּקֶר
וַיַּחֲבֹשׁ אֶת־חֲמֹרוֹ
וַיִּקַּח אֶת־שְׁנֵי נְעָרָיו אִתּוֹ
וְאֵת יִצְחָק בְּנוֹ
וַיְבַקַּע עֲצֵי עֹלָה
וַיָּקָם וַיֵּלֶךְ אֶל־הַמָּקוֹם אֲשֶׁר־אָמַר־לוֹ הָאֱלֹהִים.

And Abraham rose early in the morning, and saddled his ass, and took two of his young men with him, and clave the wood for a burnt offering, and rose up, and went unto the place of which God had told him (22, 3)

There is no description of Abraham's state of mind or his feelings, no report of any speech or conversation. Without further ado, we find ourselves "on the third day." How are the events of those three days described in the Midrash by our Sages?

"ויקם וילך": קידמו השטן בדרך ונדמה לו בדמות זקן. אמר לו: לאן אתה הולך? אמר לו: להתפלל. אמר לו: ומי שהולך להתפלל למה אש ומאכלת בידו ועצים על כתפו? אמר לו: שמא נשהה יום או יומיים ונשחט ונאפה ונאכל? אמר לו: זקן! לא שם הייתי כשאמר לך הקב"ה "קח את בנך . . ." וזקן כמוך ילך ויאבד בן שניתן לו למאה שנה? (נוסח ה י ל ק ו ט: סבא! אבד לבך! בן שניתן לך למאה שנה — אתה הולך לשחטו?) אמר לו: על מנת כן. ואם מנסה לך יותר מכן, תוכל לעמוד? אמר לו: ויותר. אמר לו: למחר יאמר לך: שופך דם אתה, ששפכת דמו! אמר לו: על מנת כן . . .

"And rose up and went"—The Satan accosted him and appeared to him in the guise of an old man. The latter asked him: Whither goest thou? Abraham replied: To pray. Said the Satan: If a man going to pray, why the fire and the knife in his hand and the wood on his shoulder? Abraham answered: Peradventure we shall tarry a day or two, slaughter, cook and eat. Said he: Old man! Was I not there when the Holy One blessed be He did say to thee: "Take thy son . . ." Notwithstanding an old man the likes of thee will go and put away a son vouchsafed him at the age of a hundred! (*Yalkut*: Gaffer! Thou'rt out of thy mind! Gone to slaughter the son given to thee at an hundred year!) Abraham replied: Just for this. — And if He tries thee more than this, canst thou withstand it? Said he: And more. The Satan retorted: To-morrow He will tell thee, a shedder of blood art thou for shedding his blood! Abraham replied: Just for this.

כיון שראה שלא קיבלו ממנו, הלך ונעשה לפניהם נהר גדול. מיד ירד אברהם לתוך המים והגיעו עד ברכיו. אמר לנעריו: באו אחרי! ירדו אחריו. כיון שהגיעו עד חצי הנהר, הגיעו המים עד צוארו. באותה שעה תלה אברהם עיניו לשמים. אמר לפניו: רבונו של עולם, בחרתני ונגלית לי ואמרת לי אני יחיד ואתה יחיד, על ידך יוודע שמי בעולמי, והעלה יצחק בנך לפני לעולה — ולא עיכבתי והריני עוסק בציוויך, ועכשיו באו מים עד נפש. אם אני או יצחק בני טובע — מי יקיים מאמרך? על מי יתייחד שמך? אמר לו הקב"ה: חייך שעל ידיך יתייחד שמי בעולם! מיד גער הקב"ה במעיין ויבש ועמדו ביבשה.

As soon as he saw that Abraham was not to be moved, he went and assumed the form of a large river. Forthwith Abraham plunged into the waters which reached as far as his knees. He said to his young men, Follow me. They plunged in after him. As soon as they reached midway, the waters came up to his neck. At that moment, Abraham cast his eye heavenward and said before Him: Lord of the Universe, Thou didst chose me, and revealed Thyself to me and said to me: I am one and thou art one. Through thee shall My name become known in My world, so offer up Isaac thy son before Me for a burnt offering. I did not hold back and behold I am engaged in Thy command, but now the waters are endangering life itself. If Isaac or myself doth drown—who will fulfil Thy word? Who will proclaim the unity of Thy name? Said the Holy One blessed be He to him: By thy life! Through thee, shall the unity of My name be proclaimed in the world. The Holy One blessed be He forthwith rebuked the spring and the river dried up and they stood on dry ground.

(Tanḥuma)

195

What is the significance of this dialogue which constitutes, as in many similar cases, a symbolic representation of an internal struggle? The voice of the tempter in the guise of an old man is none other than the promptings of Abraham's own heart during those three momentous days. One by one doubts assail him— the voice of the tempter. First his paternal instinct: "the son given thee at an hundred year?" The voice of conscience: "Tomorrow He will tell thee, A shedder of blood art thou ..." The voice of the one who was familiar with the ways of serving his creator can be detected in the question: "If a man going to pray, why the fire and knife in his hand." In other words, does prayer involve human sacrifice? These are all the promptings of the tempter. As soon as he saw that Abraham was not to be moved he assumed the form of a large river. What does this signify? The objective difficulties that block a person's path. I wanted to do it but I was prevented by circumstances beyond my control. The Sages pictured it as a natural obstacle—a river (in modern parlance: the bus or train was late etc.). Could Abraham have reached mount Moriah if a river stood in his path? But he who really desires to fulfil his duty is deterred by nothing, goes just the same "just for this," and plunges into the river even as far as his neck.

But after we have understood the Midrash, we may well ask what prompted our Sages to fill in the outline of the Biblical text with such picturesque detail? The following excerpt from *Mimesis* [1] a study of the representation of reality in western literature in which the author contrasts the Homeric, Greek style of writing with the Biblical, may help us to understand the problem:

> Even this opening (i.e. Gen. 21, 1: "And it came to pass ..." to end of verse) startles us when we come to it from Homer. Where are the two speakers? We are not told. The reader, however, knows that they are not normally to be found together in one place on earth, that one of them, God, in order to speak to Abraham, must come from somewhere, must enter the earthly realm from some unknown heights or depths. Whence does He come, whence does He call to Abraham? We are not told ... Where is he? We do not know. He says, indeed: Here I am—but

the Hebrew word means only something like "behold me," and in any case is not meant to indicate the actual place where Abraham is, but a moral position in respect to God, who has called to him—Here I am awaiting Thy command. Where he is actually, whether in Beersheba or elsewhere, whether indoors or in the open air is not stated; it does not interest the narrator, the reader is not informed; and what Abraham was doing when God called to him is left in the same obscurity ... and of Abraham too nothing is made perceptible except the words in which he answers God: *Hinne-ni*, Behold me here—with which, to be sure, a most touching gesture expressive of obedience and readiness is suggested, but is left to the reader to visualize ...

After this opening God gives His command, and the story itself begins: everyone knows it; it unrolls with no episodes in few independent sentences whose syntactical connection is of the most rudimentary sort. In this atmosphere it is unthinkable that an implement, a landscape through which the travellers passed, the serving-men, or the ass, should be described, or that their origin or descent or material or appearance or usefulness should be set forth in terms of praise; they do not even admit an adjective: they are serving men, ass, wood, and, knife, and nothing else, without an epithet; they are there to serve an end which God has commanded: what in other respects they were, are, or will be remains in darkness. A journey is made, because God has designated the place where the sacrifice is to be performed; but we are told nothing about the journey except that it took three days, and even that we are told in a mysterious way: Abraham and his followers rose "early in the morning" and "went unto" the place of which God had told him; on the third day he lifted up his eyes and saw the place from afar."

That gesture is the only gesture, is indeed the only occurrence during the whole journey, of which we are told; and though its motivation lies in the fact that the place is elevated, its uniqueness still heightens the impression that the journey took place through a vacuum; it is as if, while he travelled on, Abraham had looked neither to the right nor to the left, had suppressed any sign of life in his followers and himself save only their footfalls.

Thus the journey is like a silent progress through the indeterminate and the contingent, a holding of the breath, a process which has no present, which is inserted, like a blank duration, between what has passed and what lies ahead, and which yet is measured: three days! Three such days positively demand the symbolic interpretation which they later received.

They began "early in the morning." But at what time on the

third day did Abraham lift up his eyes and see his goal? The text says nothing on the subject. Obviously not "late in the evening," for it seems there was still time enough to climb the mountain and make the sacrifice. So "early in the morning" is given not as an indication of time, but for the sake of its ethical significance; it is intended to express the resolution, the promptness, the punctual obedience of the sorely tried Abraham. Bitter to him is the early morning in which he saddles his ass, calls his serving-men and his son Isaac, and sets out; but he obeys, walks on until the third day, then lifts up his eyes and sees the place. Whence he comes, we do not know, but the goal is clearly stated: Jeruel in the land of Moriah. What place this is meant to indicate is not clear ... Just as little as "early in the morning" serves as a temporal indication does "Jeruel in the land of Moriah" serve as a geographical indication; and in both cases alike, the complementary indication is not given, for we know as little of the hour at which Abraham lifted up his eyes as we do of the place from which he set forth—Jeruel is significant not so much as the goal of an earthly journey, in its geographical relation to other places, as through its special election, through its relation to God, who designated it as the scene of the act, and therefore it must be named.

In the narrative itself, a third chief character appears: Isaac. While God and Abraham, the serving-men, the ass, and the implements are simply named, without mention of any qualities, or any other sort of definition, Isaac receives an appositive; God says, "Take Isaac, thine only son, whom thou lovest."

If Auerbach is correct that the Torah deliberately leaves out details and concentrates only on what is essential to the purpose of the narrative, leaving the rest in obscurity, "thoughts and feeling remain unexpressed, are only suggested by the silence and the fragmentary speeches," then we have the answer to our question, why our Sages filled out the stark Biblical story with homiletic embellishments introducing a dialogue between Abraham and the tempter and the latter and Isaac, and Isaac and his father.

As Auerbach states further, the Biblical narrative is multilayer and its characters' feelings which are never completely expressed have "greater depths of time, fate and consciousness" and are "fraught with background." "Doctrine and promise are incarnate" in these stories; for that very reason they are fraught with "background" and mysterious, containing a second, concealed meaning.

In the story of Isaac, it is not only God's intervention at the beginning and at the end, but even the factual and psychological elements which come between, that are mysterious, merely touched upon, fraught with background; therefore they require subtle investigation and interpretation, they demand them.

We may now understand the reason prompting rabbinic interpretation. But we may still ask that if the meaning of the text is so mysterious and elusive, whence did our Sages elicit their data regarding Abraham's internal struggle, the whisperings of the tempter: "Gone to slaughter the son given thee at an hundred year"? We may answer that their description was prompted by the one conversation that is reported to have taken place between father and son recorded for us in the chapter, during the whole of their gloomy and silent three day trek towards their goal:

וַיֹּאמֶר יִצְחָק אֶל־אַבְרָהָם אָבִיו וַיֹּאמֶר: אָבִי!
וַיֹּאמֶר: הִנֶּנִּי, בְּנִי!
וַיֹּאמֶר: הִנֵּה הָאֵשׁ וְהָעֵצִים וְאַיֵּה הַשֶּׂה לְעֹלָה?
וַיֹּאמֶר אַבְרָהָם: אֱלֹהִים יִרְאֶה־לּוֹ הַשֶּׂה לְעֹלָה, בְּנִי.
וַיְהִי אַחַר הַדְּבָרִים הָאֵלֶּה וְהָאֱלֹהִים נִסָּה אֶת־אַבְרָהָם.

And Isaac spoke unto Abraham his father and said, My father:
And he said, Here am I, my son.
And he said: Behold the fire and the wood: but where is the lamb for a burnt offering?
And Abraham said, My son, God will provide Himself a lamb for a burnt offering. (22, 7–8)

In the whole chapter, as in this dialogue, Isaac is addressed by the same term "son." Isaac who had begun to have a premonition of what was ahead grasped hold of his only remaining anchor, his father. Abraham tries to set his fears at rest and then obliquely alludes to the truth. Then follows the phrase which forms a framework into which this dialogue fits. Before it comes the phrase: "and both of them went together." Though their journey is weighed down with silence and gloom, the two making the journey are not yet possessed of equal knowledge. But after their exchange of words, the same phrase recurs, "and both of them went together," this time, *both* of them fully and equally aware of the implications of the situation, in Rashi's words בלב שווה "with equal heart."

---

1 The Representation of Reality in Western Literature by Erich Auerbach, Princeton University Press, 1953, Chap. 1, pp. 8-10.

REMEMBER THE BINDING OF ISAAC

In our *Studies* on p. 194ff. we limited ourselves to a discussion of the three opening words of Abraham's trial—"God tried Abraham," dealing with the well known problem of reconciling God's foreknowledge with His testing of Abraham to see if he was God-fearing. But since the "Binding of Isaac" is a central theme of Judaism "the whole horn and merit of Israel before their Father in Heaven and ever on our lips in our daily prayers" (Abravanel), we have by no means exhausted the subject and shall, on this occasion, discuss the nature of the trial itself and in what way it reflected such eternal credit on Abraham.

The Midrash comments on the significance of the word "after" in the opening phrase:

מאי "אחר"? א"ר יוחנן משום ר' יוסי בן זמרא: אחר דבריו של שטן, דכתיב (בראשית כא, ח): "ויגדל הילד ויגמל ויעש אברהם משתה גדול". אמר שטן לפני הקב"ה: רבונו של עולם! זקן זה חננתו למאה שנה פרי בטן, מכל סעודה שעשה, לא היה לו תור אחד או גוזל אחד להקריב לפניך? אמר לו: כלום עשה אלא בשביל בנו — אם אני אומר לו: זבח את בנך לפני, מיד זובחו, מיד — "והאלהים נסה את אברהם".

"And it came to pass after all these things," After what things? Rabbi Yoḥanan in the name of R. Yose ben Zimra said: After the words of Satan, as it is written: "And the child grew up and was weaned and Abraham made a great banquet." Satan thus addressed the Holy One blessed be He: Lord of the universe! This old man whom you vouchsafed an offspring at a hundred years—couldn't he even spare you one turtle-dove or pigeon from the banquet he made? He answered: Did he not make it only for his son—if I bid him, Sacrifice your son to Me, he will forthwith do so. Wherupon "the Lord tried Abraham."   (Sanhedrin 89b)

Resh Lakish's observation (Bava Batra 16a) that Satan is the evil inclination provides the clue to the above passage. The evil part of man, the evil-mindedness of faultfinders both from Israel and the nations demands to know why Abraham deserved to be the chosen of God. Wherein lay his merits, his devotion and self-sacrifice? R. Yose b. Zimra regarded the story of his sacrifice of Isaac as the Torah's answer to that question. Here we cite two valuations of this act from the many embedded in the classics of Judaism through the ages. First here is Yosef Albo's comment in his philosophic work *The Fundamentals of Judaism* (Sefer Ha-ikkarim):

> Praise or blame cannot be attached to an action that one is forced to do but only of one that is the result of absolutely free choice. For this reason Abraham was to be praised above the rest of mankind for his love of God, till the text called him (Isaiah 47): "Abraham My friend." For no other aim existed in his heart but to do the will of God. No necessity of any sort pressed him to sacrifice his son—not even an express command of God existed obliging him to it. Our Sages expressed this idea in their comment (Bereshit Rabbah 56, 15) on the text: "And Abraham called the name of the place *Adonai Yireh*" (The Lord seeth). Abraham said: Lord of the universe, it is revealed and known to Thee that when Thou didst tell Me to "take I pray thee thy son, thine only son whom thou lovest, even Isaac and offer him to Me as a burnt-offering" I could have said: But surely Thou hast already told me that "in Isaac shall seed be called to thee"; yet I did not say so, but suppressed my compassion and did not question Thy ways. It would appear from the foregoing comment of our Sages that Abraham was not under any obligation, even from the point of view of the command of God, since he could have submitted a justifiable excuse, but he refrained from doing so, suppressing his paternal feelings out of love of God.

> For this reason the active role in the sacrifice of Isaac is attributed to Abraham and not Isaac, although he was 16 years old at the time. Abraham could have excused himself and not performed the sacrifice whereas Isaac had no choice but to do the Divine bidding and surrender himself.

> This is also the reason why Abraham's sacrifice of Isaac calls for greater mention in our prayers than the sacrifice of all the martyrs of Jewish history such as Rabbi Akiva and his disciples. The latter martyred themselves to fulfil the religious duty of "not profaning My holy name that I may be sanctified in the midst of the children of Israel" (Lev. 22, 32). Abraham, on the other

> hand, was obliged by no religious duty and was fully conscious
> of what he was about to do, since three days elapsed from the
> time he was told to take his only beloved son till the sacrifice.

> The criterion of a really free act is whether the person can do the
> opposite without incurring any unpleasant consequences, and yet
> chooses not to do it.

Albo sees Abraham's greatness in this context in the absolute freedom of choice he was offered, prompted by no external necessity, no threats or even just overwhelmed. The Midrash Tanḥuma stresses this same point: "Why does the text tell us that Abraham lifted up his eyes *on the third day?* Why not on the second or first? So that the nations of the world should not say: He was not in his right mind and went and slaughtered his son!"

In other words, Abraham felt no inner compulsion to do what he did. No Divine command existed obliging him. Every moment of those three days he could have excused himself and withdrawn saying: "But surely thou hast already told me that "in Isaac shall seed be called to thee." And he did not. It was this which distinguished him from all the martyrs of Jewish history, since they acted in response to a bounden duty to give their lives, rather than transgress the will of God. Abraham performed his sacrifice because, as Albo points out, "no other aim existed in his heart but to do the will of God."

But there was still opportunity for Satan to accuse and obstruct after the sacrifice just as before. Surely he could argue that the same self sacrifice and devotion displayed by Abraham in sacrificing his son was shared by the heathen idolaters in giving their sons in human sacrifice to Molech. Why was Abraham's act different? It could admittedly be answered that what the idolaters performed out of primitive fear to placate their gods, Abraham did out of love, without any expectation of reward.

But the late Rabbi Kook who detected even in the darkness and abomination of idolatry the signs of the heartsearchings of perplexed souls striving for communion with their Creator gives a different answer. In one of his epistles he dwells on this theme:

203

The absolute self-surrender characteristic of idolatry in which primitive man found his be-all and end-all, till it triumphed over parental pity and made cruelty towards sons and daughters the keynote of Molech worship, springs from an inner hidden conviction that the Divine is more precious than anything else and all that is beloved and admired is as nought before it.

When the Divine light had to shine forth in its purity, it was revealed in the fierceness of its brightness in the trial of Abraham which showed that that passion and self-surrender in a Divine cause, did not have to take the disgusting form of idol worship in which the Divine spark of good has become completely lost but that it could be apprehended in purity (though the primitive imagination cannot be aroused to this height for lack of a material stimulation on a more human plane). It is unnecessary to point out how much this illumines man's path in life, how much it promotes a healthy social life and fortifies the human temperament placing it on a firm basis in respect of its eternal aspirations ...

All these are obvious matters. The distinctive and unusual feature added here is that the self-surrender involved in communion with the Divine on the higher spiritual plane can be no less ecstatic. This was implemented in the decision regarding the test of Abraham's sacrifice of Isaac which remained a natural law for all human time. Even the most refined communion on a plane transcending all the grosser perceptions succeeds in penetrating to the inmost recesses of the heart. Were it not for this, mankind would either have remained sunk in the mire of primitive feeling, though vigorously active in its relationship towards the Divine, or in slightly thawed frigidity lacking the quality of life in depth.

In other words, the purely human brute imagination unrefined by the clear light of a higher religious passion had achieved a self-surrender and spirit of sacrifice of all that was near and dear springing from "an inner hidden conviction that the Divine is more precious than all else." The great question that the world of idolatry could ask Abraham was: Could that that same spirit of sacrifice and longing for communion with the Divine still survive in a world not ruled by primitive material and pictorial conceptions of Divine things? Could true religious ecstasy and devotion exist in the clear, rarified atmosphere of a higher religion or was such enthusiasm the monopoly of savage man in his brutal unsophisticated and physical approach to religion? Could a purely spiritual conviction·of truth bring man to perfect love of God?

Rabbi Kook continued his discussion by referring to the contribution of the great religious personalities of the Bible to the upward progress of the human soul in paving the way for a closer communion with God. On the sacrifice of Isaac he commented:

> "How wonderful is our prayer to remember the merit of the first patriarch who fought against emotional barbarity in the struggle towards the Divine. Its only merit lay in its popular character in plumbing the depth of the heart, that the idolaters claimed human culture could not manage without it because the impression of pure divinity was too lofty and refined to be the feeding ground for a multitude of nations. Came the "father of a multitude of nations" and showed the way. However low humanity would sink, there was always room for the penetration of the pure light. The sacrifice of Isaac is recalled in mercy for his seed for all generations.

Questions for Further Study

הרהורי דברים היו שם. מי הרהר? אברהם. אמר: שמחתי ושימחתי הכל ולא הפרשתי לקב״ה לא פר ולא איל אחד. אמר לו הקב״ה: על מנת שנאמר לך שתקריב את בנך ולא תעכבם.

1. "... after these things." Much cogitation was involved. Who cogitated? Abraham? He said: I have rejoiced and rejoiced everybody but have not separated for the Holy One blessed be He one bull or one ram. Said the Holy One blessed be He to him: So that We should ask you to offer your son and that you should not forbear.
   Cf. the foregoing with R. Yose b. Zimra's statement at the beginning of our *Studies*. What is the difference between the two in their approach to the aim of the trial? Consult the *Studies*: Vayera p. 188ff. and the passages cited there from Rambam and Ramban.

2. Why did Albo resort to the citation from *Bereshit Rabbah* 56? What support did he find there for his approach?

3. In *Midrash Vayosha* (On Moses' song at the Red Sea printed in the Bet Ha-midrash of Jellinek, Tel Aviv as well as in Oẓar Midrashim of Eisenstein New York 1928 p. 147), a further argument is advanced by the Satan to tempt Abraham not mentioned in the Tanḥuma we cited on p. 195.

אמר לו השטן: "לא שם הייתי כשאמר לך המשטין 'קח נא את בנך את יחידך — והעלהו לי לעולה'? וזקן כמותך יאבד בן חמוד כזה ובחור שנתן לך הקב"ה למאה שנה!" אמר לו אברהם: "לא היה המשטין אלא הקב"ה בכבודו ובעצמו; אמר לי: 'קח נא את בנך את יחידך אשר אהבת את יצחק ועשה לפני עולה'".

Said the Satan to him: Was I not present there when the Tempter said to you "Take now thy son, thine only one and offer him up as a burnt-offering"? Should an old man like you destroy this darling son and fine youth which God gave you in your hundredth year! Abraham replied to him: It was no tempter but no less than the Holy One blessed be He Himself. He said to me: "Take now thy son and thine only one, whom thou lovest, even Isaac, and offer before Me a burnt-offering."

What temptation is here proffered by the Satan and how does it differ from the temptations outlined in the Midrash Tanḥuma?

THE CAVE OF MACHPELAH

וּפִגְעוּ־לִי בְּעֶפְרוֹן בֶּן־צֹחַר.
וְיִתֶּן־לִי אֶת־מְעָרַת הַמַּכְפֵּלָה
אֲשֶׁר־לוֹ אֲשֶׁר בִּקְצֵה שָׂדֵהוּ
בְּכֶסֶף מָלֵא יִתְּנֶנָּה לִּי
בְּתוֹכְכֶם לַאֲחֻזַּת־קָבֶר.

**And entreat for me to Ephron the son of Zohar, that he
may give me the cave of Machpelah, which he hath, which
is in the end of his field;
for the full price let him give it to me
in the midst of you for a possession of a burying-place.**

(23, 8–9)

A protracted and wearisome process of negotiation is detailed
at the beginning of this week's sidra, in connection with Abraham's purchase of a burial ground for his family. Researchers
into antiquity have regarded this passage as a source of information on customs and manners in the ancient east, particularly
in the realm of buying and selling. But it would be indeed
strange if the Torah had dwelt on these details, just for the
purpose of the realistic colouring. As a rule, the Torah pays
little attention to the incidentals of human existence, dress and
deportment, domestic manners and the like. Our commentators
have drawn attention to this seemingly strange preoccupation
with the bargaining etiquette of the ancient east:

> What contribution does such a story make to the spiritual message
> and mission of the Torah? (Malbim)

Some have seen it as expressing the initial forging of the Jewish
people's ancient bond with the Holy Land.

207

א״ר יודן ב״ר סימון: זה אחד מג׳ מקומות שאין אומות העולם יכולים להונות
את ישראל לומר: גזולים הן בידכם, ואלו הן: מערת המכפלה ובית המקדש
וקבורתו של יוסף [שכם]. מערת המכפלה, דכתיב (בראשית כג, טז): "וישמע
אברהם אל עפרון וישקל אברהם לעפרון את הכסף"; בית המקדש, דכתיב
(דבהי״א כא, כה): "ויתן דויד לארנן במקום שקלי זהב משקל שש מאות";
וקבורתו של יוסף, שנאמר (בראשית לג, יט): "ויקן את חלקת השדה אשר
נטה שם אהלו מיד בני חמור אבי שכם במאה קשיטה".

> Said R. Yudan bar Simon: This is one of the three places about
> which the nations of the world cannot taunt Israel saying, these
> are stolen lands, and these are they: the Cave of Machpelah, the
> Temple and the burial place of Joseph (Shechem). The Cave of
> Machpelah as it is written: (23, 16) "And Abraham hearkened
> unto Ephron; and Abraham weighed to Ephron the silver"; the
> Temple as it is written: (1 Chronicles 21, 25) "So David gave
> to Ornan for the place six hundred shekels of gold by weight";
> and the burial ground of Joseph as it is written: (Gen. 33, 19)
> "And he bought the parcel of ground, where he had spread his
> tent, at the hand of the children of Hamor, Shechem's father, for
> a hundred pieces of money.   (Bereshit Rabbah, 79, 7)

Ibn Ezra similarly regards this chapter as having been written
"to make known the preeminence of the land of. Israel over
all other lands, both for the living and dead." Oddly enough,
it is Ramban, that rebuilder of the Jewish community in the
Holy Land after the havoc of the crusades, who opposed this
interpretation of Ibn Ezra's: "What praise is this for the Holy
Land? Surely he (Abraham) would not have taken her to
another land to bury her!"

Ibn Ezra suggests another reason for the story of the sale of
the burial plot in this week's sidra:

> To confirm the word of the Lord to Abraham that it would be
> his inheritance.

In this brief explanation he expresses the idea that the chapter
indicates the beginning of the fulfilment of the Divine promises
to Abraham which keep recurring, commencing from the opening words of *Lekh Lekha* "to thy seed will I give this Land,"
through the detailed delineation of the ideal borders of the
country at the Covenant between the pieces (15, 17–18), the

promises of greatness and kingship at the Covenant of Circumcision, and ending with the words "and thy seed shall possess the gate of his enemies" at the story of the sacrifice of Isaac.

Ramban elaborates on this idea:

> This chapter was written in order to dwell on the lovingkindness of God to Abraham, who became a prince in the land to which he had come, as a stranger. Though he had never told anyone that he was a prince or great man they nevertheless addressed him by the title "my lord." Even in his own lifetime the Almighty fulfilled for him the promise of "and make thy name great; and be thou a blessing." His wife died and was buried in the inheritance of the Lord. The Torah also wished to tell us the burial place of our sainted forefathers.

However, a closer look at the story does not give us a picture of Abraham behaving as a prince towards the owners of the land. On the contrary, the chapter is full of Abraham's petitions and prostrations. Hizkuni comments on this as follows:

> "And Abraham rose up, and bowed down to the people of the land" — Abraham needed all of them. Though Ephron had sold him the field, Abraham was not authorised to use it as a burial ground, without the permission of his fellow citizens. He therefore had to rise up in order to bow down to all of them, even to those behind him. But in bowing down to Ephron, who was alone, he had no need to rise up, but simply to make obeisance in front of him.

In the light of this, it is difficult to regard this passage as exemplifying, even in the slightest degree, the promise of sovereignty and majesty which had been promised to Abraham in relation to the land and the inhabitants thereof. It is therefore more plausible to accept the view of our Sages that we have here precisely the opposite. No greater contrast could be imagined than that between "and make thy name great," "Arise, walk through the land ... for unto thee will I give it," "And I will give unto thee, and to thy seed after thee, the land of thy sojournings, all the land of Canaan, for an everlasting possession" and between the story of the humiliation and prostration of the

chosen of the Lord, in this week's sidra, before the Canaanites
—"the lords of the land" in which he begs for four ells of land.
Our Sages regarded his incident as constituting one of the
ten trials to which Abraham was subjected. The greater the
contrast between the promise and the fulfillment, between the
vision and the reality, the greater the challenge. Even Gideon
who had been chosen to save Israel cried out "if the Lord be
with us, why then is all this befallen us?", when confronted by
the contrast between the chosenness and high mission of the
people, and the reality of oppression and humiliation.

The Midrash thus enunciates for us the lesson of the sidra:

בוא וראה ענוותנותו של אברהם אבינו! שהבטיחו הקב"ה לתת לו ולזרעו את
הארץ עד עולם ועכשו לא מצא קבורה אלא בדמים מרובים, ולא הרהר אחר
מידותיו של הקב"ה ולא קרא תגר, ולא עוד אלא שלא דיבר עם יושבי הארץ
אלא בענוה, "שנאמר: "גר ותושב אנכי עמכם" — אמר לו הקב"ה: אתה
השפלת עצמך, חייך שאני אשימך אדון ונשיא עליהם.

Come and see the humility of Abraham our father! The Holy
One blessed be He promised to give him and his seed the land
forever. Yet now he could only find a burial ground by paying
a high price, and yet he did not question the attributes of the
Holy One blessed be He and he did not complain. Moreover,
he addressed the inhabitants of the land with humility, as it is
said: "I am a stranger and a sojourner with you." Said the
Holy One blessed be He to him: Thou didst humiliate thyself;
on thy life I shall make thee a lord and a prince over them.

(Midrash Hagadol)

Even the Accuser, Satan, whose function, as related in the book
of Job, it was to tempt the sons of men and even the most
righteous, had to admit that Abraham was able to withstand
temptation:

(איוב א, ו—ז) "ויהי היום ויבאו בני האלהים להתיצב על ה' ויבא גם השטן
בתוכם. ויאמר ה' אל השטן: מאין תבוא ? . . . ויאמר: משוט בארץ ומתהלך
בה". אמר לפניו: רבונו של עולם, שטתי בכל העולם כולו ולא מצאתי נאמן
כעבדך אברהם, שאמרת לו (בראשית יג, יז): "קום התהלך בארץ לארכה
ולרחבה, כי לך אתננה", ואפילו הכי בשעה שלא מצא מקום לקבור את שרה
לא הרהר אחר מידותיך.
(רש"י: "קום התהלך", היינו דקאמר "ומתהלך בה". מאותו שאמרת לו
"התהלך בארץ" אני בא).

"Now it fell upon a day, that the sons of God came to present themselves before the Lord, and Satan came also among them. And the Lord said unto Satan: Whence comest thou? Then Satan answered the Lord, and said: From going to and fro in the earth, and from walking up and down in it." The Satan said before Him: Lord of the universe, I have traversed the whole world and have found no one as faithful as Thy servant that Thou didst say to him "Arise, walk through the land in the length of it and in the breadth of it; for unto thee will I give it." In spite of this when he could not find a place to bury Sarah, he did not question Thy attributes. (Baba Batra 15b)

Abraham's conduct in this situation is so highly esteemed by our Sages that they placed him, in this context, higher than Moses:

"וארא אל אברהם": אמר לו הקב"ה למשה: חבל על דאבדין ולא משתכחין [אין כמותם בנמצא]. הרבה פעמים נגליתי על אברהם יצחק ויעקב באל שדי ולא הודעתי להם כי שמי ה', כשם שאמרתי לך — ולא הרהרו אחר מ י ד ו ת י . אמרתי לאברהם (בראשית יג, יז): "קום התהלך בארץ לארכה ולרחבה כי לך אתננה"; ביקש לקבור שרה ולא מצא עד שקנה בדמים — ו ל א הרהר אחר מ י ד ו ת י . אמרתי ליצחק (שם, כו, ג): "ויגר בארץ הזאת . . כי לך ולזרעך אתן את כל הארצות האל"; ביקש לשתות מים ולא מצא, אלא (שם, כ): "ויריבו רועי גרר עם רועי יצחק" — ו ל א ה ר ה ר אחר מ י ד ו ת י . אמרתי ליעקב (בראשית כח, יג): "הארץ אשר אתה שוכב עליה לך אתננה ולזרעך"; ביקש מקום לנטות אהלו ולא מצא עד שקנה במאה קשיטא — ולא הרהר אחר מ י ד ו ת י ; ולא שאלני, מה שמי, כשם ששאלת אתה. ואתה תחילת שליחותי אמרת לי: "מה שמו" ולבסוף אמרת (שמות ה, כג): "ומאז באתי . . . לדבר בשמך הרע לעם הזה".

"And I appeared unto Abraham"—Said the Holy One blessed be He to Moses: Alas for those who are gone, never to be replaced! Many times I revealed Myself to Abraham, Isaac and Jacob as God Almighty, but I did not make known to them that My name is the Lord, as I have told thee and they did not question My ways. I said unto Abraham: (13, 17) "Arise, walk through the land in the length of it and in the breadth of it; for unto thee will I give it"—he sought to bury Sarah and did not find where, until he purchased a place with money—yet he did not question My ways. I said to Isaac (26, 3): "Dwell in this land... for to thee and thy seed shall I give all these lands"—he sought to drink water and did not find, "and the shepherds of Gerar strove with the shepherds of Isaac"—yet he did not question My ways. I said unto Jacob (28, 13) "The land which thou liest on, to

211

thee will I give it and unto thy seed"—he sought a place to pitch his tent and did not find, until he acquired it for a hundred kesitah—yet he did not question My ways, and did not ask Me what was My name as thou didst ask. Yet thou at the beginning of My mission didst say unto Me, What is His name? And at the end thou didst say (Exodus 5, 23) "Since I came to speak in Thy name, he hath done evil to this people."

(Bereshit Rabbah, 6, 4)

Questions for Further Study

1. "In the choice of our sepulchres bury thy dead..."—they buried their dead in caves and each family had its own tomb where they buried their dead, each one in its own coffin. The whole cave was called *kever*. They thought that Abraham would ask them for a place in one of their tombs to bury his dead. For this reason they said to him "none of us shall withhold from thee his sepulchre."   (Radak)

    Did the sons of Heth make one or two offers to Abraham from which to choose? Why was not Abraham satisfied with their offer and what did he ask for further?

2. It is difficult to understand why Abraham did not speak directly to Ephron but first applied to the sons of Heth: "Hear me, and entreat for me to Ephron the Hittite."   (Paneaḥ Raza)

    Why Abraham asked the sons of Heth to entreat for him was because the latter was a rich and honoured person. It would not not therefore be fitting for him to sell his ancestral heritage, as in the case of Naboth (1 Kings, 21). Abraham did not therefore go immediately to bargain with Ephron but asked his fellow citizens to arrange a meeting. He uses the expression *"give me,"* "that he may *give* me" in order to emphasise that he regarded it as a *gift*, even though he bought it and paid its full value. He therefore made no mention of the word sale. A similar idea is to be found in the phrases (Deuteronomy 2, 28) "Thou shalt sell me food for money... and *give* me water for money"—i.e. for the gift of water I shall give you money.   (Ramban)

    "Entreat for me to Ephron"—that he should sell, even though it is not fitting for a man of his station to sell his ancestral heritage, as Naboth testifies (1 Kings 21) "The Lord forbid it me, that I should give the inheritance of my fathers unto thee."

(Sforno)

212

(a) What is Ramban's answer to the above question?

(b) Others answer the question by referring us to the passage in Genesis 50, 4. Explain this answer.

(c) Why do the commentators allude to the story in 1 Kings 21?

(d) Can you answer the question of the *Paneaḥ Raza* in another way?

3.   A contemporary scholar Manfred R. Lehman[1] endeavours to illuminate the details of Abraham's purchase of the burial plot by reference to paras 46–47 of the Hittite code (discovered in the present century). It lays down that the services to be rendered to the king by landowners fall only on one who buys a complete plot but not one who purchases only part of a lot. In the latter case these services remain the duty of the original owner. In the light of this, verse 11 connotes not a gift but a complete sale.[2] In Hittite deeds of sale pertaining to lands the exact number of the trees on the area sold is always registered.

Which passages in our chapter are illuminated by this comparison with Hittite laws?

---

[1] Manfred R. Lehman: Abraham's Purchase of Machpelah and Hittite Law (Bulletin of the American Schools of Oriental Research, ed. Albright 1953, February).

[2] §46.. If in a village anyone holds fields under secage as inheritance— if the fields have all been given to him, he shall render the services; if the fields have been given to him only to a small part, he shall not render the services...

§47. If anyone buys all the fields of a craftsman, they shall ask the king, and he shall render those services which the king orders. If there remain fields in the hand of the man from whom he buys, he shall not render the services. (Prichard: Ancient Near Eastern Texts, 1955, Princeton p. 189).

MARRYING OUT

This chapter narrates the last of Abraham's activities. Admittedly the whole chapter depicts the action of God in "causing to chance" before man what he requires. But the action of God here is only in response to the importunings and doings of men. For the Divine blessing rests only on mortal works.[1]

It is Abraham who opens the chapter, who calls to his servant, the elder of his house, it is he who demands, admonishes, prohibits and restricts—adjures. With this he has done his part. When the faithful emissary returns from his journey, we no longer hear Abraham receiving the report of the emissary—but the servant addresses himself to Isaac. To Isaac he relates "all the things which he did." The first patriarchal generation gives way to its successor.

But this mission with which Abraham charged the servant prompts a question. Here are the words of Abraham to the servant:

וְאַשְׁבִּיעֲךָ בַּיָי
אֱלֹהֵי הַשָּׁמַיִם וַאלֹהֵי הָאָרֶץ
אֲשֶׁר לֹא־תִקַּח אִשָּׁה לִבְנִי
מִבְּנוֹת הַכְּנַעֲנִי
אֲשֶׁר אָנֹכִי יוֹשֵׁב בְּקִרְבּוֹ.
כִּי אֶל־אַרְצִי וְאֶל־מוֹלַדְתִּי תֵּלֵךְ
וְלָקַחְתָּ אִשָּׁה לִבְנִי לְיִצְחָק.

And I will make thee swear by the Lord, the God of heaven and the God of the earth, that thou shalt not take a wife for my son from the daughters of the Canaanites, among whom I dwell.

But thou shalt go unto my country, and to my kindred, and take a wife for my son, even for Isaac. (24, 3-4)

Abravanel, among other commentators, asks:

> Why did Abraham command him not to take a wife from the Canaanites? Was it because they were idol worshippers? Surely the inhabitants of Babylon—Aram-Naharaim were no better? What then had he achieved by his command? One can understand why Isaac ordered Jacob not to intermarry with the local womenfolk because of his unfortunate experience with Esau. Abraham had no such experience to justify his avoidance of the Canaanites. Why did he place the daughters of Canaan out of bounds and not the daughters of Nahor and Bethuel? Nahor and Bethuel were just as idolatrous. The question is even harder to answer, when we consider that our Sages interpreted Abraham's prohibition of intermarriage with the people amongst whom he dwelt, to include even the "good" Canaanites such as Aner and Eshkol who were Abraham's intimates. Why did Abraham then forbid intermarriage with them?

Only a few commentators leave the first half of the question, "Why did Abraham command him not take a wife from the Canaanites" and devote themselves to giving an answer to the second half, "why didn't Abraham place the daughters of Bethuel and Nahor out of bounds?" The *Midrash Haggadol* deals with this difficulty:

> "כי אל ארצי ואל מולדתי תלך": והלוא כולם עובדי עבודה זרה, דכתיב (יהושע כד, ב): "בעבר הנהר ישבו אבותיכם תרח אבי אברהם ואבי נחור ויעבדו אלהים אחרים" — ואברהם יצא מהם?! אלא אמר אברהם: הואיל ואני מגייר — אגייר ממשפחתי ומבית אבי, שהן קודם לכל, ולא עוד אלא שהן קרובי תשובה. מכאן אמרו: לעולם תהא דעתו של אדם קרובה לקרוביו, ואם יש לו [קרובים] עושה בטובתן, וכן הוא אומר (ישעיה נח, ז): "ומבשרך אל תתעלם".

"But thou shalt go, unto my country and to my kindred": But surely they were all idol-worshippers, as it is written (Josh 24, 2): "Your fathers dwelt of old time beyond the River, even Terah, the father of Abraham, and the father of Nahor; and they served other gods"—and Abraham left. But this is what Abraham meant: Since I engage in making proselytes, I shall proselytize among my own family and father's house who come first, and what is more they are nearer to repentance. This text prompted the dictum: A man should always give first consideration to his relatives, and if he has relatives promote their welfare. It is similarly stated (Isaiah 58, 7): "From thine own flesh do not hide thyself."

Of course we find in the Torah that charity begins at home, that a person's relative come first in respect of material assistance. But can proselytizing be put in the same category? Futhermore, did the Torah favour the cementing of ties between Abraham and his family? Does not the command to "go forth from your land, birthplace and father's house" indicate that the Almighty favoured the severance of these ties?

Let it not be imagined that Abraham's preference for his own kin sprang from concern for "ethnic purity." No idea is more foreign to our Torah and Judaism. On the contrary, the passage we have just quoted from Joshua within the Midrash insists that Abraham was not the son of any chosen Godfearing line, but the son of Terah and brother of Nahor. It was he himself who acknowledged the true God and became His intimate, whilst his brother and all the descendants of Terah remained idolaters. Abraham was not interested in selecting for Isaac a girl of "pure stock," neither was Abraham the progenitor of any stock, but as Rambam points out:

> The progenitor of upright descendants who walk in his ways and the father of his disciples, namely, every proselyte embracing Judaism. For this reason the proselyte should use the formula in his prayers: "Our God and the God of our fathers, of Abraham, peace be upon him—he is your father.[2]

But there is a much stronger argument against the view of the *Midrash Haggadol*: Did Abraham really command his servant to repair to his family for a wife for Isaac? Surely all that is stated is: "But thou shalt go unto my country and *my kindred* (*molad'ti*) and take a wife for my son Isaac."

The answer to our question depends on the meaning of the word *molad'ti*. Rashi takes it in the usual sense of "birthplace"—"from Ur of the Chaldees." But Ramban cites two possibilities—that of place and family or kindred—which is followed by the English version (though in actual fact "kindred" can likewise be taken in the broader and vaguer sense of blood relationship, common origins, members of the same race and not necessarily family). He does not decide which one is to be preferred, though he does not agree with Rashi's identification of the place with Ur of the Chaldees. But the first and vaguer connotation of birthplace sounds more reasonable, in the light of the servant's subsequent conduct. He was evidently not sent to a particular address but to a locality, and he therefore submitted the daughters of the place, of the local clan to a character test.

The main question is therefore not why Abraham sent his servant to that particular locality but the second half of Abravanel's query: Why did Abraham command him not take a wife from the Canaanites? Shadal (Luzzatto) suggests there were political considerations underlying Abraham's action. If Abraham had intermarried with them, this would have precluded the Israelites at a later date from expelling the Canaanites from their land. They would have been kinsmen and would have come under the same category as the Moabites, Ammonites and Edomites whom God had bidden not to fight or vex.

But this political motivation is far-fetched. The land had been promised to Abraham and his seed by the Almighty and even its border, and the epoch of occupation, ("the fourth generation shall return thither") specified—after the "iniquity of the Amorite was complete." Nothing was said to him about military conquest and when Abraham asked: "How shall I know that I shall possess it" (15, 8) he was not told by what means. Is it conceivable that Abraham, the supreme believer should make such calculations in the face of a Divine promise and Covenant? Furthermore, had he made such political calculations, he might well have deliberately intermarried with the Canaanites and through that subterfuge inherited the land. The Torah however is at pains to emphasise that it was God who granted the land to Abraham and his seed. The reason therefore for this rejection of the Canaanite daughters must be sought elsewhere. That same revulsion against the Canaanite is expressed by Isaac in respect to the marrying of his son Jacob, inspired by a more Abrahamic trend of thought.

Abravanel himself also emphasises that no difference in religious faith between the Canaanites and Babylonians was involved in Abraham's preference. For we have the text in Joshua which explicitly observes that "your fathers dwelt beyond the River, of old, Terah the father of Abraham and father of Nahor and they worshipped other gods." Evidently the difference between the two peoples lay in another sphere. The RaN in his homilies answers our question somewhat differently:

> The commandments and transgressions in the Torah have two aspects: some make an impress on both body and soul, others on the soul alone such as beliefs. Now those that leave an impress on both body and soul will leave a similar impress on the man's descendants, such as hatred, vengeance and cruelty, immorality, slander and the like which affect the soul on account of them being transgressions, and the body, because character traits affect the physiological make-up of man, just as the latter determines, to a certain extent, a man's mental qualities. (The author actually expresses himself according the medieval conceptions of "humours": blood, phlegm, choler, melancholy, whose "complexion" determines temperament—"hot" blood causes irascibility, irascibility heats the blood).

> Mental qualities affect the physical make-up and this is passed on to the children—this was the evil of the men of Canaan. On the other hand, beliefs, however misguided and evil are not hereditary. Therefore, there was no necessity for Laban and Bethuel's idolatrous beliefs to leave an impress on their children. For this reason Abraham chose them and rejected the daughters of the Canaanites.

In other words, it was not the ideas and beliefs of the family of the girl destined to be the mother of the nation that were apt to endanger the whole nation, (either through heredity of example and education) but evil deeds. Now the Torah frequently denounces the inhabitants of Canaan not just as idol worshippers (in which context no other nation was an improvement on them), but as the perpetrators of abominations. With what does the Torah open its chapter forbidding sexual perversions on avoidance of which it conditions our very existence? —

כְּמַעֲשֵׂה אֶרֶץ־מִצְרַיִם אֲשֶׁר יְשַׁבְתֶּם־בָּהּ לֹא תַעֲשׂוּ
וּכְמַעֲשֵׂה אֶרֶץ־כְּנַעַן אֲשֶׁר אֲנִי מֵבִיא אֶתְכֶם שָׁמָּה לֹא תַעֲשׂוּ
וּבְחֻקֹּתֵיהֶם לֹא תֵלֵכוּ.

According to the deeds of the land of Egypt in which you dwelt shall you not do and according to the deeds of the land of Canaan whither I bring you shall you not do and in their statutes shall you not walk.

(Lev. 18, 3)

Rashi comments:

"כמעשה ארץ מצרים": מגיד שמעשיהם של מצריים ושל כנענים מקולקלים מכל האומות.
"אשר אני מביא אתכם שמה": מגיד שאותן עממין שכבשו ישראל מקולקלים מכולם.

This implies that the deeds of the Egyptians and Canaanites were more corrupt than any other nation and that those peoples which the Israelites conquered were more corrupt than any other.

S. R. Hirsch adds a further reason:

"from the daughters of the Canaanite in whose midst I dwell." The influence of a Canaanite girl on my son will be infinitely more potent since I dwell amongst them. Not only the girl but her family, her relatives and friends will all together exert a cumulatively deleterious influence on my son.

In his view, were Isaac to intermarry with the surrounding peoples, he was bound to assimilate, whereas were he to take a wife from a distant country, she was bound to assimilate into the dominant environment of Abraham's household. It was for this reason that Abraham was sent away from his country, kindred and father's house, so that he should have no further contact with them and be a stranger in a foreign clime, he and his seed having nothing at all to do with the inhabitants of the land, with all their respect for him. He did not even want to bury his wife in their burial ground. Similarly, his son must not marry any of their daughters. For this reason he was called Abraham the *Hebrew*, "that all the world was on one side and he on the other" (*ivri* means in Hebrew "a person from the other side" usually taken as a reference to Abraham's origins in Mesopotamia—on the other side of the river).

Questions for Further Study

1.   In Gen. 24 cf.:

Abraham's words to his servant	*His Servants' Report of them to Bethuel*
(4) but unto my country and kindred	(38) unto my father's house and family

"unto my country" this refers to Haran who dwelt there; "to my kindred"—Ur of the Chaldees.   (Ibn Ezra)

"To my country"—and not to those who are not my kinsmen but: "kindred" who are in my country shall you go.   (Rashbam)

The phrase "to my country and kindred" may well be his country and family, since he disapproved of his own country and meant only his actual family. Similarly the passage (7): "And thou shalt take a wife for my son *from there*" alluded to "from my father's house," as the servant said: "thou shalt take a wife for my son from my family and father's house," and again: "when you come to my family"; or perhaps the servant said this to honour them so that they would listen to him.   (Ramban)

The servant lied to them when he said "from my family and my father's house." For Abraham had made no mention at all to father or family, only to his "country" and "kindred." He improved on Abraham's original testament, adding the qualification of "father's house" on his own initiative, to take advantage of the wonderful opportunity that had come his way in the maiden happening to belong to Abraham's immediate family. He took it for granted that Abraham's prohibition of Canaanite girls had been prompted by a wish to be reunited with his own family and father's house. For this reason he consistently substituted the words "family" and "father's house" for the wording of his master: "my country and kindred."   (Akedat Yizḥak)

(a) What is the difference between the various approaches of the commentators? Arrange them in groups. Pay attention to the differing implications of the word *molad'ti*—literally: "my birthplace" but here translated "kindred." It may be noted however that "kindred" can also mean either a close relationship, family, or a more distant vague kinship.

(b) Which of the two interpretations of the word *moledet* is supported by the text in Gen. 43, 7: "The man asked pointedly concerning ourselves and concerning *our kindred*" (*molad'tenu*).

(c) Find some more changes that the servant made in his story "in order to honour them that they should listen to him," just as Ramban explains the change we have referred to here.

2. (a) Cf.: 24, 7: "the Lord God of heaven who took me from my father's house and the land of *my birth* (*molad'ti*); 12, 1: "Go forth from thy country and thy kindred (*molad'tekha*) and from thy father's house." Can you find a reason for the change in order?

(b) Cf.: The Lord God of heaven who *took* me (24, 7)
I am the Lord who *brought thee* out (15, 7).
Can you explain why Abraham used the term "took" rather than "brought"?
Cf.: "Thus saith the Lord of hosts: I *took* thee from the sheepcote, from following the sheep to be a prince over My people, over Israel (II Sam 7, 8);
"The Lord *took* me from following the flock and the Lord said unto me: Go, prophesy unto My people Israel" (Amos 7, 15)

(c) Cf.: Let me, I pray thee, *drink* a little water... (Gen. 24, 17)
Feed me, I pray thee, with that same red pottage (ibid. 25, 30)

Explain the difference between the two italicised terms, paying special attention to the Hebrew words used (*hagmi'-ini, hal'iteni*), Cf.: Proverbs, 13, 25: "The righteous eateth to the satisfying of his soul; but the belly of the wicked shall want."

3. Why is the Torah brief in verse 66: "Then the servant related to Isaac all the things he had seen." Why isn't the whole story related here rather than previously (vv 35–40)?

4. "The Lord blessed Abraham with everything"   (24, 1)
The purpose of the text is to stress that Abraham did not send his servant to seek a wife from his own family abroad because there was a shortage of women in the land of Canaan who were willing to marry him. On the contrary he was blessed with everything. The whole community wished to enter into a marriage alliance with him but he only wanted to intermarry with his own family. This is the force of the servants statement: "The Lord has blessed my master exceedingly and he has become great." That is why it was necessary to insert the preamble: "The Lord blessed Abraham with everything." Cf. 9, 18: "Ham was the father of Canaan."   (Rashbam)

(a) What difficulty in the text prompted Rashbam's comment?
(b) What support does he adduce from Gen. 9, 18?

---

[1] See the Tosefta Berakhot and Bereshit Rabbah quoted in our *Studies* of Noah pp. 95–96.

[2] In a letter to "the righteous proselyte, Obadiah" of Bagdad who inquired whether he could legitimately refer in his prayers to "our God, the God of our fathers" since he was not ethnically a "son of Abraham." The letter is cited in full in our *Studies in Devarim* pp. 265–267.

I'LL WATER THE CAMELS TOO

This sidra features two themes, that of the purchase of the burial plot for Sarah and the bringing of Rebecca to Isaac as his bride—Death and Marriage symbolising the unchanging cycle of mortal existence. One generation departs and another takes its place . , .

At the beginning of the sidra:

וַתָּמָת שָׂרָה בְּקִרְיַת אַרְבַּע הִיא חֶבְרוֹן – –

And Sarah died in Kiryath-Arba; the same is Hebron...
At the end of the sidra: (23, 2)

וַיְבִאֶהָ יִצְחָק הָאֹהֱלָה שָׂרָה אִמּוֹ וַיִּקַּח אֶת־רִבְקָה
וַתְּהִי־לוֹ לְאִשָּׁה וַיֶּאֱהָבֶהָ וַיִּנָּחֵם יִצְחָק אַחֲרֵי אִמּוֹ.

**And Isaac brought her unto his mother Sarah's tent,
and took Rebecca, and she became his wife;
and he loved her:
and Isaac was comforted after his mother's death.**
                                                          (24, 67)

In the previous sidra, Lot settled down in Sodom and inter-married with the local inhabitants. His sons-in-law were Sodom-ites in name and deed. Abraham adjures the "eldest servant of his house":

אֲשֶׁר לֹא־תִקַּח אִשָּׁה לִבְנִי מִבְּנוֹת הַכְּנַעֲנִי אֲשֶׁר אָנֹכִי יוֹשֵׁב.
בְּקִרְבּוֹ

**Thou shalt not take a wife unto my son of the daughters
of the Canaanites, amongst whom I dwell.**   (24, 3)

This command of Abraham's has puzzled the commentators. We dwelt on the motives prompting Abraham's command in the previous *Studies* (pp. 214ff.), regarding as most plausible the approach of those commentators who maintain that the Patriarch did not send his servant to his family specifically, but merely charged him with selecting a suitable spouse for his son. Here we discuss how the emissary went about this selection. What he did when he reached the well at eventime when the water-drawing damsels went forth is familiar. He prayed and gave himself a sign. Our commentators, both ancient and modern have argued over whether Eliezer's mode of selecting a wife constituted sorcery, or a character test. The difference is outlined by Rashi's super-commentary *Gur Aryeh* on verse 13 of our chapter:

> Even total dependence on the sign does not constitute divination since even without it, the test is a reasonable one. The prohibition of divination only applies to a case where divination has no rational basis whatever.

The difference is between one who says—"a deer crossed my path" (see Rashi on Deut. 18, *s.v. menahesh* "diviner") and therefore I cannot set forth on my trip and one who says: "The clouds have gathered" and so I cannot take the trip.

Rambam takes the view that making one's path of action or inaction depend on a sign "if so-and-so happens" "like Eliezer, the servant of Abraham constitutes *nahash*—divination and is forbidden." Raavad strongly objects:

> This is all wrong. On the contrary, it is perfectly allowable... how dare he attribute this sin to such righteous people? (as Eliezer and Jonathan — I Sam 14)

Abravanel maintains that Eliezer resorted to no divination or charm or arbitrary sign but simply applied a character test. Malbim elaborates thus on his comment:

> After selecting the most outwardly attractive of the damsels he required to find out more about her inner qualities and this he did by the "drink and I shall water your camels too" formula.

This would indicate that she was a hospitable, considerate and unassuming person and this on four counts:

(i) "Behold I am stationed by the well" The ordinary reaction of the girl would be: You are standing by the well; help yourself to the water!

(ii) There were plenty of girls going out to fetch water. She could say: Why pick on me when I've already replaced the jug on my shoulder. Pick on another girl who is still holding the water jug in her hand.

(iii) I shall ask her to tilt the jug herself to enable me to drink. This means a special effort for her to let down the brimful water jug in order to give me a drink. She would be justified in being annoyed and saying: Tilt the jar yourself from my shoulder and drink but don't bother me to do it myself.

(iv) Her offer to give my camels a drink too would indicate her thoughtfulness and understanding, showing that she had said to herself: This man is obviously handicapped and cannot draw the water himself from the well and lower the jug. If he can't give himself a drink then he most certainly isn't up to watering the camels too. This would indicate her kindness to animals, not forgetting the thirst of the camels.

To sum up: the servant applied a character test and for this purpose sampled her kindness and generosity.[1]

It was only fitting, therefore, that his future daughter-in-law was singled out for display of his very quality which has distinguished the behaviour of the Jewish household throughout the ages.

It was most apt that Rebecca should be singled out for her hospitality to both man and beast, in furnishing them with the most elementary of human necessities—water.

Let us follow carefully the details of the text. The camel, the "ship of the desert," as is well known, stores up its own water supply for many days, but when, however, it has reached its destination after a long journey, it is quite naturally completely empty and its need for replenishment is considerable. The Torah describes in detail Rebecca's attentions to all Eliezer's camels, and there were ten of them. The text notes no less than twice that the spring was not actually *by* the trough but only in the vicinity and that to draw water she had to go down and come up:

וַתֵּרֶד הָעַיְנָה וַתְּמַלֵּא כַדָּהּ וַתָּעַל.
וַתְּמַהֵר וַתְּעַר כַּדָּהּ אֶל־הַשֹּׁקֶת וַתָּרָץ עוֹד אֶל־הַבְּאֵר
לִשְׁאֹב וַתִּשְׁאָב.

**She went down to the spring, filled her jar and came up
again ...** (24, 16)
**So she quickly emptied her jar into the trough and ran
again to the well to draw and drew ...** (24, 20)

Further, the Torah thrice emphasises that the camels drank until they had done drinking and had their fill:

– – – גַּם לִגְמַלֶּיךָ אֶשְׁאָב עַד אִם־כִּלּוּ לִשְׁתֹּת
– – – וַתִּשְׁאַב לְכָל־גְּמַלָּי.
וַיְהִי כַּאֲשֶׁר כִּלּוּ הַגְּמַלִּים לִשְׁתּוֹת – – –

I will draw water for thy camels also,
until they have done drinking.
And drew for all his camels.
And it came to pass, as the camels had done drinking ...
(24, 19–22)

The lesson of this going into detail is abundantly clear. Rebecca was not satisfied with running once to the well and drawing water. She took the trouble to make a number of journeys to and fro, each time letting down her pitcher filling it and giving them to drink: "Until they had done drinking."
At the sight of all this the man stood "wondering at her" and "held his peace." He and the men that were with him looked on at the way Rebecca discharged her self-appointed task, industriously, unquestioningly and without murmur. "And she drew for all his camels."
Those realists and practical folk who might be drawn to pity

the simplicity of the maiden, who went to all this trouble to quench the thirst of a total stranger and his camels, would do well to remember Akavia ben Mahallel's (Sage distinguished for his "fear of sin" and "wisdom") maxim in the Mishnah:

מוטב לי להיקרא שוטה כל ימי ולא ליעשות שעה אחת רשע לפני המקום.

Better that I should be dubbed a fool for the rest of my days, rather than become a wicked man for one hour before the Omnipotent! (Eduyot 5, 6)

Similarly Rebecca entered into no calculations of profit and loss, when she gave man and beast to drink. It is just such "fools" who have always succeeded in becoming benefactors of mankind.

Questions for Further Study

1. The servant sent by Abraham to bring a wife for Isaac is called by various epithets in Chapter 24 of our sidra. Pay attention to the various epithets and try to explain the reasons for all the variations in referring to him.

> Verse 2. And Abraham said unto his *eldest servant* of his house, that ruled over all that he had.
>
> 5. And the *servant* said unto him, Peradventure the woman will not be willing to follow me.
>
> 9. And the *servant* put his hand under the thigh of Abraham.
>
> 10. And the *servant* took ten camels of his master, and departed; and all the bounty of his master in his hand.
>
> 17. And the *servant* ran to meet her, and said, Let me, I pray thee, drink a little water...
>
> 21. And *the man* wondering at her held his peace, to know whether the Lord had made his journey successful.
>
> 22. And it came to pass, that *the man* took a golden ring...

26. And *the man* bowed down his head, and worshipped the Lord.

29. And Laban ran out unto *the man,* unto the well.

30. And it came to pass, that he came to *the man;* and, behold, he stood by the camels at the well.

32. And *the man* came into the house, and he ungirded his camels.

52. And it came to pass, that when *Abraham's servant* heard their words.

59. And they sent away Rebecca . . . and her nurse, and *Abraham's servant.*

61. And Rebecca arose, and her damsels, and they rode upon the camels and followed *the man;* and *the servant* took Rebecca and went his way.

65. For she had said unto *the servant* . . . and *the servant* had said, it is my master.

2. Why did the servant reverse the order of events when he reported them to Rebecca's parents? Compare:

Narration of the Events	*As Reported by the Servant*
22. And it came to pass, as the camels had done drinking that the man took a golden ring . . . 23. And said: Whose daughter art thou?	47. And I asked her and said, whose daughter art thou? and she said, the daughter of Bethuel . . . And I put the ring in her nose and the bracelets upon her hands.

3. "The Lord, the God of heaven, who took me from my father's house, and from the land of my birth, and who spoke unto me, and who swore unto me, saying: Unto thy seed will I give this land: He will send his angel before thee . . ."   (24, 7)

"ה' אלהי השמים": עד שלא בא אברהם אבינו לעולם, כביכול לא היה הקב"ה
מלך אלא על השמים בלבד, שנאמר: "ה' אלהי השמים אשר לקחני", אבל
משבא אברהם אבינו לעולם, המליכו על השמים ועל הארץ, כעניין שנאמר
(כד, ג): "ואשביעך בה' אלהי השמים ואלהי הארץ".

"The Lord, the God of heaven"—Before Abraham our father
entered the world the Holy One blessed be He was, so to
speak, sovereign only over the heavens alone, as it is said: "the
Lord, God of heaven who took me," but when Abraham our
father came into the world he crowned Him over heaven and
earth, as is indicated by the phrase: "And I will make thee swear
by the Lord, the God of heaven and the God of the earth (24, 3).
(Sifrei: Haazinu)

(a) Elaborate on the significance of this Midrash. Find
support for Rashi's contention that Abraham had initiated humanity into frequent acknowledgment of God.

(b) Where do we find in *Lekh Lekha* an example of this
fact that the name of God was frequently on the lips
of people?

(c) Why did Rashi cite the above Midrash in connection
with verse 7 rather than refer to it in the earlier verse
3, especially since verse 3 forms the scriptural text
for the Midrash?

[1] *Kli Yakar* expands on this theme as follows: Eliezer tested Rebecca's
quality of generosity and kindness only ... Our sages stated "If the
bride has beautiful eyes you don't have to look further." This cannot
be meant literally since it flies in the face of reality. There are plenty
of ugly brides with beautiful eyes. What is more! How could the
Sages call for an examination of external beauty. Surely "False is
charm and vain beauty—a godfearing woman she is to be praised ..."
But what they obviously meant was that one should look for good
deeds to test if she had a "beautiful eye," i.e. a generous and kindly
disposition and kind heart. For if she looked at people with a kindly
and unjaundiced eye then she was undoubtedly endowed with all the
other sterling moral qualities. Our sages learnt from the example of
Eliezer who tested Rebecca for this quality only, since it is the linchpin
of all the others.

TABLE-TALK OF PATRIARCHS' SERVANTS

Our previous study of this sidra was devoted to the significance of the character test to which Rebecca was submitted by Abraham's servant. We noted the qualities of compassion and goodness to all human creatures, reflected in her act of offering to water the camels. This time we shall confine our attention to the activities and words of the servant, and note how admirably he fulfilled the mission with which he was charged.

The Torah relates, with a surprising wealth of detail, every action of the servant in Chapter 24 till verse 26. His experiences are recapitulated (the conversation with Abraham, his prayer at the well, his meeting with Rebecca, her reaction, and the presentation of the bracelets) in the form of his report to Rebecca's family in verses 35 to 48 of the same chapter. This lengthy and seemingly superfluous recapitulation has excited the comment of many of our expositors. In view of the Torah's sparing use of words and avoidance of every unnecessary repetition, even the addition or subtraction of a letter, it is surprising, that we do not meet here with the brief note that the servant related to them all that had occurred, as is, indeed, the case when he returns home—

וַיְסַפֵּר הָעֶבֶד לְיִצְחָק אֵת כָּל־הַדְּבָרִים אֲשֶׁר עָשָׂה.

And the servant told Isaac all the things that he had done. (24, 66)

The Torah must have obviously had a very special reason for recording the servant's recapitulation of his experiences. Our Sages commented on this unsual repetitiveness in the Midrash (Bereshit Rabbah 60, 11) as follows:

אמר ר' אחא: יפה שיחתן של עבדי בתי אבות מתורתן של בנים. פרשתו של
אליעזר — שניים ושלושה דפים הוא אומרה ושונה. והשרץ מגופי תורה ואין
דמו מטמא כבשרו — אלא מריבוי המקרא. [פירושו: לומדים שדמו מטמא
מה"א יתירה. של "וזה לכם הטמא בשרץ" בויקרא יא כט.]

Said R. Aḥa: The table-talk of the servants of the Patriarchs'
households is more notable (literally: "beautiful") than the
Scripture (Torah) of their descendants. Eliezer's story is recorded
and recapitulated, taking up two to three pages, whereas one
of the fundamental rulings of the Torah, to the effect that the
blood of a creeping thing defiles in the same way as its flesh,
is only known to us through the superfluity of one letter in the
Scriptures (i.e. we deduce the principle that the blood of a שרץ
defiles from the superfluous letter "ה" in the verse וזה לכם הטמא
בשרץ literally translated: "these also shall be into you *the* unclean
among the creeping things" (Leviticus 11, 29).

The Story	The Recapitulation
1. And the Lord had blessed Abraham in all things.	35. And the Lord hath blessed ... greatly; and he is become great: and He hath given him flocks, and herds, and silver, and gold, and menservants, and maidservants, and camels, and asses.
3. And I will make thee swear by the Lord, the God of heaven and the God of the earth.	37. And my master made me swear, saying,
3. That thou shalt not take a wife unto my son of the daughters of the Canaanites, among whom I dwell:	Thou shalt not take a wife to my son of the daughters of the Canaanites, in whose land I dwell:

231

4.	But thou shalt go unto my country, and to my birthplace. And take a wife unto my son Isaac.		But thou shalt go unto my father's house, And take a wife unto my son.
5.	Peradventure the woman will not be willing to follow me. unto this land: Must I needs bring thy son again unto the land from whence thou camest?	39.	Peradventure the woman will not be willing to follow me. — — — — — —
7.	The Lord God of heaven, which took me from my father's house, and from the land of my birth, and which spake unto me . . .	40.	The Lord, before Whom I walk,
7.	He shall send His angel before thee, and thou shalt take a wife unto my son from thence.	40.	Will send His angel with thee, And thou shalt take a wife for my son of my kindred, and of my father's house:
8.	Only bring not my son thither again.		— — — — — —
12.	O Lord God of my master Abraham, send me good speed this day, and shew kindness unto my master Abraham.	42.	O Lord God of my master Abraham, if now thou do prosper my way which I go:

14. And she shall say, Drink, and' I will give thy camels drink also: let the same be she that Thou hast appointed for thy servant Isaac: and thereby shall I know that thou hast shewed kindness unto my master.

15. And it came to pass, before he had done speaking.

17. And said, Let me, I pray thee, drink a little water of thy pitcher.

18. And she said, Drink, my lord: and she hasted and let down her pitcher upon her hand, and gave him drink.

19. And when she had done giving him drink, she said, I will draw water for thy camels also, until they have done drinking.

And she hasted, and emptied her pitcher into the trough, and ran again ... to draw water, and drew for all his camels.

44. Both drink thou, and I will also draw for thy camels: let the same be the woman whom the Lord hath appointed out for my master's son.

45. And before I had done speaking in mine heart,

45. And I said unto her, Let me drink, I pray thee.

46. And she made haste, and let down her pitcher from her shoulder, and said, Drink,

And I will give thy camels drink also:

So I drank, and she made the camels drink also.

22. And it came to pass, as the camels had done drinking, that the man took a golden ring . . . and two bracelets for her hands of ten shekels weight of gold.	47. And I asked her, and said; Whose daughter art thou? And she said, The daughter of Bethuel . . .
23. And said, Whose daughter art thou? tell me, I pray thee: is there room in thy father's house for us to lodge in?	And I put the ring upon her nose and the bracelets upon her hands.
26. And the man bowed down his head, and worshipped the Lord. And he said, Blessed be the Lord God of my master Abraham, who hath not left destitute my master of his mercy and his truth: I being in the way, the Lord led me to the house of my master's brethren.	48. And I bowed down my head, and worshipped the Lord, and blessed the Lord God by my master Abraham, which had led me in the right way to take my master's brother's daughter unto his son.

Our classic commentators from Talmudic times onwards, including such great medieval exegetes as Rashi and Ramban, right down to Malbim and the "Netziv" in *Haamek Davar* in the last century made a point of explaining the significance of the variations, both great and small between these two accounts. We have the servant's longer elaboration at the beginning of his report to Rebecca's family in order to emphasise Abraham's wealth, the glossing over of the differences in faith between Abraham and his family in Haran reflected in the omission of phrase "the Lord, the God of heaven, and the God of the God of the earth" which would not be appreciated in Laban's circles (verse 3 and verse 37). We may note the emphasis given to Abraham's command to find a wife for his son from among his "father's house," a sentiment which was not at all uttered by Abraham, (cf. verses 4 and 37, 7 and 40), the omission of the possibility of the suggestion of Isaac having to come to the girl's home (cf. verses 39 and 5), and finally the change in order in regard to the asking of the girl's name and the giving of the presents. This latter change is noted in Rashi on verse 47:

"ואשאל ואשים": שינה הסדר, שהרי הוא תחילה נתן ואחר כך שאל, אלא שלא יתפשוהו בדבריו ויאמרו: היאך נתת לה ועדיין אינך יודע מי היא?

"And I asked and I put"—He changed the order, for in reality, he first gave the presents and afterwards asked, but he did so, so that they should not catch him out and say: How did you give her before you knew who she was?

Isaac Arama in his *Akedat Yitzhak* goes into more detail:

Previously the servant had emphasised that he came on a special mission to Abraham's family, preferring them above all other peoples for his son. If he would have said that he presented the ring to Rebecca before he even knew to which family she belonged, this would have contradicted his previous assertion, since a man will not just give his valuables away to no purpose. Presumably, since he gave them to just any woman, they must have been given as marriage gifts. This is what Rashi referred to when he stated that Eliezer was afraid they would catch him out.

The variations referred to above and many others reveal the wonderful judgment, discretion and devotion of Abraham's servant in carrying out his mission, until he brought it to a successful conclusion. No better evidence of his success can be cited than the very words of his listeners after hearing his persuasive eloquence:

מֵיְיָ יָצָא הַדָּבָר
לֹא נוּכַל דַּבֵּר אֵלֶיךָ רַע אוֹ־טוֹב.
הִנֵּה־רִבְקָה לְפָנֶיךָ קַח וָלֵךְ

וַתְּהִי אִשָּׁה לְבֶן־אֲדֹנֶיךָ –
כַּאֲשֶׁר דִּבֶּר יְיָ.

The matter stems from the Lord:
we cannot speak unto thee bad or good
Behold Rebecca is before thee,
take her, and go,
and let her be thy master's son's wife,
— as the Lord hath spoken.   (24, 50, '51)

Had the Torah rested content with a brief phrase to the effect
that the servant related to Rebecca's family all that had befallen
him, we would not have been apprised of the measure of his
devotion and abilities in carrying out his master's commands. To
this our sages referred when they stated "the table-talk of the
servants of the Patriarchs' households is more notable..."

Questions for Further Study

1. In actual fact he (Eliezer) reported the events as they had hap-
    pened. But we cannot explain the reason for all the additions and
    omissions in his account; for they are legion. He told them all that
    had gone between himself and his master, his transactions with
    Rebecca and that God had providently arranged matters just as
    Abraham had promised. His emphasis on this point was to im-
    press on them that they had no alternative. They could not stop
    the girl from accepting the marriage offer since the matter was
    from God. The recapitulation involves merely a variation in word-
    ing but the sense is the same. This is unavoidable in reported
    speech—it preserves the sense but not the exact wording. (The
    latter sentence is a quotation from Ibn Ezra who repeats it insistent-
    ly).   (Radak on 24, 39)

    (a) In what way does the approach of Radak and Ibn
        Ezra differ from the commentators we have followed?
    (b) List the pros and cons of the two approaches.

2. The Lord God of Heaven who took me from my father's house (24, 7)

ולא אמר "ואלהי הארץ" ולמעלה הוא אומר (ג): "ואשביעך בה' אלהי השמים
ואלהי הארץ". אמר לו: עכשו הוא אלוהי השמים ואלוהי הארץ שהרגלתיו
בפי הבריות, אבל כשלקחני מבית אבי היה אלוהי השמים ולא אלוהי הארץ,
שלא היו באי עולם מכירים בו ושמו לא היה רגיל בארץ.
יפה שיחתן של עבדי בתי אבות מתורתן של בנים.

But he did not say "the God of the earth." Yet above he said: "I
adjured thee by the Lord God of heaven and the God of the
earth." What Abraham meant was: Now He is the God of the
heavens and the God of the earth, since I have accustomed people
to speak of Him; but when He took me from my father's house
He was the God of Heaven, and not the God of earth, since the
peoples of the world did not acknowledge Him, and His name
was not familiar on earth.   (Rashi)

"the God of heaven and the God of earth." The fact that the
text does not say afterwards "the God of heaven" only—presents
no difficulty; for as I have already pointed out to you—explanation is an act of grace and avoidance of it is no crime.

(Ibn Kaspi: Mishneh Kesef)

(a) What does Ibn Kaspi mean by "explanation is an act
of grace and avoidance of it no crime"?

(b) What difference in principle exists between the methods of interpretation represented here by the two
commentators?

(c) Cf. the words of Malchizedek and those of Abraham
vv. 19–22 chap. 14. Which of the two commentators can find support for his approach in those verses?

3.

Akedat Yizhak questions the reason for the four repetitions in the story of Eliezer: "Surely he could have been
idiomatically brief?"

(a) Which four repetitions does he refer to?

(b) Give examples of where the text is "idiomatically
brief".

(c) Try to answer his question why the Torah does not
simply state:

"Then the servant related to Bethuel and Laban all the things he had done" as we find at the end of the chapter when he returns to Isaac.

4. Why is the text brief in verse 66: "Then the servant told Isaac all the things he had done" instead of reporting the whole story verbatim here and not previously in vv, 35–48?

PRAYING TO GOD FOR LUCK

וַיֹּאמַר:

יְיָ אֱלֹהֵי אֲדֹנִי אַבְרָהָם

הַקְרֵה־נָא לְפָנַי הַיּוֹם.

O Lord God of my master Abraham

I pray Thee send me good chance this day . . .   (24, 12)

This plea of Eliezer, Abraham's servant poses a problem. There
is surely a self-contradiction in him praying to God to engineer
a coincidence. This is the literal rendering of his plea which
may be translated as "cause to chance before me today"
Here we quote Abravanel's formulation of the problem raised
by this verse:

> If the servant relied on Divine Providence and for that reason
> prayed to Him, how could he invoke the workings of chance and
> ask him to engineer a coincidence when these are two mutually
> exclusive categories? What happens through the workings of Pro-
> vidence cannot be termed chance or coincidence.

Moreover is it conceivable for one who believed in Divine
Providence to accept the existence of such a thing as "chance"
and even go so far as to request the Almighty Himself to prepare such a situation? In this context we cite here Solomon
Dubnow's explanation of the concept of "chance" in the Torah
in the *Biur* commenting on Ibn Ezra's observation on our verse:

> "Cause it to chance"—in the sense of arranging that it should
> so happen, cf. Gen. 27, 20: "The Lord thy God caused it to
> chance before me."   (Ibn Ezra)

> As a general rule the term "chance" מקרה   is applied by the
> Torah to every situation befalling man not directly brought about

by deliberate intervention and effort. Nevertheless all is ultimately prompted by Divine Providence which mysteriously works in accordance with His hidden purposes. However, that which our moderns term "pure coincidence"—an occurrence which has no cause whatever cannot be found at all in the Bible since such a thing has no existence but in our imagination as a result of our ignorance of the real causes.

Abraham's servant entreated the Almighty as the Prime Mover behind all things to arrange that matters should work out in accordance with his desires. Admittedly the course events would take did appear in the eyes of ordinary mortals blinded to the real cause as pure chance. But since God is the Prime Mover behind all things there can, in the strict sense, be no such thing as chance. Let us compare what is related in I Samuel 6 regarding the attitude of the Philistines to this same problem.

The Philistines had taken the Ark of the Lord captive. They were convinced that by doing so they had taken captive the God of Israel Himself Who was now their vassal. Though Israel's God was able to wreak vengeance on them and plague them, the Philistines maintained that they could readily control the amount of mischief that He could cause them by resorting to simple subterfuges. The Ark could be sent to another city in order to stop the plague in their vicinity. After these efforts were of no avail and a "deadly discomfiture" reigned in all the cities of the Philistines they were faced with no alternative but to send it back home, but they were still doubtful as to whether the Ark was to blame for the troubles that had befallen them. Had not they been visited by plagues before the Ark had arrived and had not the moving of the Ark had no effect on staying the plagues? In order to determine beyond all doubt the source of their discomfiture they arranged, on the advice of their diviners, for the Ark to be placed in a new cart drawn by "two milch kine." The beasts of burden would provide the answer by the road they took. If it be asked how could these kine be relied on as guides and oracles, it may be answered that these beasts of burden were not a whit inferior to the birds whose flight provided kings and princes in ancient times with omens influencing their decisions for peace or war. How were the kine to provide the Philistines with the true answer to their question? —

> Now therefore take and prepare you a new cart, and two milch kine ... and tie the kine to the cart, and bring their calves home from them.

> And take the ark of the Lord, and lay it upon the cart; and put the jewels of gold, which ye return Him for a guilt-offering, in a coffer by the side thereof; and send it away, that it may go.

> And see, if it goeth up by the way of its own border to Beth-shemesh, then He hath done us this great evil; but if not, then we shall know that it is not His hand that smote us; it was a chance that happened to us.

(I Samuel 6, 7-9)

This passage clearly mirrors the spiritual chasm separating the heathen and Jewish outlooks. We have here a typical example of divination and sorcery. Yechezkel Kaufmann in his history of the Israelite Religion (*Toldot Haemunah Hayisraelit* pp. 497-8¹) explains the significance of these enchantments and the Torah's utter rejection of such methods:

Divination constitutes a pseudo-scientific or magical method enabling man to foretell the future and reveal mysteries. It is idolatrous and "an abomination of the Lord" since it is aimed at revealing divine secrets in an ungodly way. The idolater invokes omens and divination is one of the forms of heathen rebellion against God, the fruit of his pride and confidence in his own powers and wisdom, the fruit of his aspiration "to be as God." This path is one of abomination and defilement ... a vain hope since God Himself can bring to nought these idle omens and when the time arrives none of the devices of the diviners can save man from the hands of God. The essence of the mantic idea is the subjection of the Divine to a supra-divine experience. Faith in God which is exclusive and omnipotent cannot be harmonised with such a concept ... there is a radical opposition between these two outlooks.

241

In the Torah even one such as Balaam who came from a
heathen world that lived under the spell of divination and who
wished to blaspheme admitted "that there is no enchantment
in Jacob". What Abraham's servant Eliezer resorted to was not
an enchantment but a psychological test to probe the character
of the woman worthy to be the wife of Isaac and the ancestress
of the nation chosen for its moral calibre.

The heathen and the Jewish approach to the concept of
"chance" is quite different. The Philistines did not say that if
the Ark does not go up by the way of its own border that "we
shall know that it is *Dagon* that smote us," but rather:

$$\text{וְיָדַעְנוּ כִּי לֹא יָדוֹ נָגְעָה בָּנוּ –}$$
$$\text{מִקְרֶה הוּא הָיָה לָנוּ.}$$

**We shall know that it is not His hand that smote us: it
was a chance that happened to us.**　　　　(I Samuel 6, 9)

In their eyes then there existed a power transcending their gods:

> Paganism does not acknowledge the absolute will of a divine
> being ruling all and the prime cause. It admits of a god that is
> supreme over all other gods as well as a creator sustaining the
> order of the universe. But beyond this stands the primeval order
> of existence. Beyond the god there are eternal forces independent
> of it.　　　　　　　　　　　　　　　　　(Kaufmann pp. 298–99 [2])

Since, therefore, heathen gods are not all powerful controlling
all creation, there still exists the possibility of "a chance" which
the Philistine diviners would presume to be responsible if it
transpired that it was not the God of Israel who had "done us
this great evil".

Abraham's servant, however, who "drank from the spiritual
well of his master" (Rashi) was well aware that what seemed
but chance to mortal man was only so because of his blindness.
In reality he knew that every "chance" had been so "directed"
or "engineered" by Divine Providence which was the prime
cause of all things. Hence his paradoxical prayer:

242

Oh Lord, the God of my master Abraham send me, I pray thee, good chance this day.

Worded differently, Joseph gave utterance to the same belief in the workings of Divine Providence which he saw behind all the combinations of circumstance that brought him to Egypt and made him Pharaoh's vice-regent:

לֹא־אַתֶּם שְׁלַחְתֶּם אֹתִי הֵנָּה כִּי הָאֱלֹהִים.

So now it was not you that sent me hither but God.

(Genesis 45, 8)

All the normal factors in his life had conspired to prevent the realisation of his dreams, his father's favouritism, his brothers' hate, Potiphar's wife's jealousy. Yet it was these which had ultimately combined to facilitate their realisation. Both coincidence and chance are in reality engineered by the hidden hand of Providence.

The words of Ramban at the end of *Bo*—explaining the value of those observances commemorating the miracles of the Exodus have a direct bearing on our subject:

> From a recognition of the large-scale historic miracles man is led to acknowledge the hidden ones which constitute the foundation of the whole Torah. For no man has any portion in the law of Moses our teacher until he is convinced that all our affairs and *chance occurrences* and the routine workings of the universe both in the private and public field are miracles and are not to be attributed merely to nature.

---

[1] In Greenberg's English abridgement, *The Israelite Religion*, pp. 90–91.
[2] **op. cit. pp. 21–23.**

THE MATTER STEMS FROM THE LORD

After the servant had recounted, at the home of Bethuel, all
that had befallen him—the oath of Abraham, his prayer at
the well, the sign he had given himseif, the meeting with Rebecca, her conduct in which she realised his hopes to the full,
till his request for her hand in marriage to his master's son—
the father and brother thus responded:

מֵיְיָ יָצָא הַדָּבָר
לֹא נוּכַל דַּבֵּר אֵלֶיךָ רַע אוֹ־טוֹב.
הִנֵּה־רִבְקָה לְפָנֶיךָ קַח וָלֵךְ
וּתְהִי אִשָּׁה לְבֶן־אֲדֹנֶיךָ
כַּאֲשֶׁר דִּבֶּר יְיָ.

**The matter stems from the Lord: we cannot speak
unto thee bad or good. Behold Rebecca is before thee,
take her and go, and let her be thy master's son's wife,
as the Lord hath spoken.** (24, 50)

What did they imply by their answer? The Midrash *Ma'yan
Ganim* wonders what such an expression of faith in God—"the
thing proceedeth from the Lord," was doing on the lips of such
idolaters and heathens as Bethuel and Laban. To solve this problem, we shall have to revert to the lengthy narration of the
servant, about which our Sages observed that "the table-talk
of the servants of the Patriarchs is more valuable than the
teachings of the sons." In our *Studies* on p. 228ff we subjected the
servant's narration to a detailed evaluation, and noted how he
varied, omitted and adjusted his reporting to the audience he
was addressing, all in accordance with the needs of his mission.
But we overlooked one important variation. We shall compare

and contrast the servant's utterances on three different occasions —the outlining of the character test he intended to employ in his prayer to the Almighty, and the answer he expected to receive from Isaac's destined bride; the actual answer given, and his report of the answer to her brother and father:

The Prayer (v. 14)	*The Outcome* (vv. 17–19)	*The Servant's Report* (vv. 45–46)
And let it come to pass, that the damsel to whom I shall say,	And he said,	And I said unto her,
Let down thy pitcher, I pray thee that I may drink	*Let me, I pray thee, drink a little water of thy pitcher*	*Let me drink, I pray thee*
and she shall say,	And she said,	And she made haste, and let down her pitcher from her and said
Drink, and I will give thy camels drink also	*Drink, my lord:*	*Drink, and I will give thy camels drink also*
	and she hasted and let down her pitcher upon her hand and gave him drink. And when she had done giving him drink she said, *I will draw water for thy camels also, until they have done drinking.*	

The damsel did not conduct herself exactly as he had outlined in his prayer. She did not reply: "Drink, and I will give thy camels drink also." But first she briefly indicated her willing fulfillment of his request with the words: "Drink, my lord," then did everything to satisfy his thirst and only afterwards did she proceed to fulfil the second requirement of giving the camels to drink. Did she thereby do more or less than was expected of her? Here we cite three different answers to this question:

This admirable girl meant to go even more out of her way. For had she immediately indicated to him her intention to water his camels, before he had drunk, it would have left an opening for him to lend a hand and lighten her task, since she was still faced with the burden of the camels. But her deferring of her offer to water the camels, till after he had drunk, precluded this happening.

(Or Haḥayyim)

She weighed her every word carefully so as not to give offence to anyone. She did not repeat the same words used by the servant, "Drink, and I will give thy camels drink also," since by this she would be equating him with the camels. She, therefore, stopped short and said, "Drink, my lord." Later on she made her offer to water the camels. (Haketav Vehakabbala)

She stopped him having his fill, because one must be careful not to drink too much cold water after being in the heat and the sun. But in order to prevent him from thinking that she begrudged him the water, she later added, "I will draw water for thy camels, until they have done drinking," i.e. till they had had their fill. In their case she would not withhold from them.

(Ha'amek Davar)

All three commentators agree that Rebecca acquitted herself well and did more than was expected of her. In *Or Haḥayyim* she was concerned for his health and wanted to preclude him hurrying over his drink in order to help with the camels. In *Haketav Vehakabbala* she is pictured as showing the most delicate consideration for the servant's feelings, avoiding mentioning him and the camels in one breath. In *Ha'amek Davar* she considered both his health and his feelings, concerned over the effects of the heat and that he should not misinterpret her withdrawal of the pitcher before he had drunk his fill.

But if her conduct was such as to have exceeded his wildest expectations, why was he so loath to dwell on her consideration, in his report to Laban? Then he contented himself with reporting the matter, in the same brief words he had used in his prayer: "and she said, 'Drink, and I will give thy camels drink also," omitting all mention of her special attention. The answer is to be found in the query of the Midrash *Ma'yan Ganim* referred to, at the beginning of our *Studies*— Surely Bethuel and Laban were heathens, and believers in good and evil omens! The servant did not want to stress that a character test was involved and that the bride-to-be for Abraham's son, one of the matriarchs of the chosen people was required to possess that quality of hospitableness and consideration for others that distinguished its progenitor. Isaac was described as having observed "My charge, My statutes and My laws." This has been interpreted "in its plain sense" by Ramban to mean, "to walk in the paths of the Lord, to be merciful and compassionate and do righteousness and justice." What is said about Him?—"Man and beast Thou savest, O Lord." In the same way, Isaac's prospective bride was expected to emulate these Divine attributes and show consideration to man and beast, quenching their thirst without stint. But would her idolatrous, superstitious family appreciate this? For them it was sufficient to refer to the fulfillment of the omen that the servant was looking for. No further details were necessary. Indeed, the servant's reporting of the bare fact that Rebecca fulfilled the apparently magical conditions set by him was followed by the answer, "the matter stems from the Lord ... let her be thy master's son's wife, as the Lord hath spoken." In Laban's eyes no character test was involved, only the fulfillment of a magical sign. Laban certainly did not appreciate the profounder implication of the words he uttered. The Midrash records some singularly odd comments of our Sages on this verse:

"מה' יצא הדבר" — מהיכן יצא ? ר' יהושע בר' נחמיה: מהר המוריה יצא.
ורבנן אמרי: מהיכן יצא ? — "ותהי אשה לבן אדונך כאשר דבר ה'".

"the matter stemmed from the Lord"—whence did it stem? R. Joshua the son of Nehemiah stated: It stemmed from the mountain of Moriah. The Rabbis stated: Whence did it stem? —"let her be thy master's son's wife, as the Lord hath spoken."
(Bereshit Rabbah)

The question itself is puzzling. Surely the text itself explicitly states that the matter stemmed from God? But we find our Sages often taking this attitude[1] when they were seeking a deeper meaning, going beneath the surface of the words. They meant: How did it happen that this matter went forth from

247

the Lord and how did these heathens come to acknowledge it? R. Joshua maintained that there was no room for any questions, since it was' preordained at mount Moriah when the news about Rebecca's birth reached Abraham, as he was descending therefrom with Isaac after the sacrifice. Rebecca's relatives were unconsciously referring to this inscrutable Divine decree. The Rabbis explained that the allusion was to the Divine plan underlying all that had happened to the servant from the very moment that he had prayed to God "to send him good speed" [2] at the beginning of his mission. His was a story of hidden miracles that brought him to Rebecca, proving that it had proceeded from God. The Lord had spoken through the mysteriously coincidental pattern of events.

Wherever the text reads: "as the Lord hath spoken," Rashi, echoing ancient rabbinic exegesis usually asks the question: "Where had He spoken this?" and answers by giving the source, direct or indirect. But in this case he fails to make any comment at all. But Ramban alludes to our text in his commentary to a similar phrase in Leviticus 10, 3:

> "This is what the Lord spoke . . ." We do not need to connect it with another verse as Rashi does, but to take it in its plain sense to refer to the decrees, intentions and ways of God. The verb "to speak" does for all these things. Similarly we find: "I spoke with my heart," meaning I had this in mind, or, "let her be thy master's son's wife, as the Lord hath spoken."—as He hath decreed or preordained.

There is no need of texts or mysterious Divine voices. The truly perceptive and understanding person catches the word of God in the everyday round of events and the fate of individuals and peoples.

Questions for Further Study

1. Explain in what ways the prayer of Eliezer and the deed of Jonathan (1 Sam. 14) differ from enchantments and divination, as outlined in our *Studies?*

2. Compare the following extract from S. R. Hirsch with the three answers we cited in our *Studies*:

She does't yet mention the camels, as the servant had hoped (v. 14); this too is to her credit. She is not a chatterbox who boasts of her good deeds. Only after he has drunk his fill does she offer to draw water for his camels too and not only to draw water for them but keep on till they had drunk their fill.

Does Hirsch follow any of the three commentators we cited or does he strike out a new path?

3. "She hastened and let down the pitcher from upon her and said: Drink and I shall water thy camels too" (24, 46)

The servant leaves out of his report every nuance of Rebecca's delicacy and refinement. There are some people who on principle suspect anyone who speaks with feeling and enthusiasm. As soon as they see him carried away they begin to doubt his sanity and the reliability of his propositions.   (Hirsch)

In what way is Hirsch's explanation here different from that offered in our *Studies?*

---

1 Cf.: *Studies in Bamidbar* pp. 255ff.: "And the Canaanite, the king of Arad heard that Israel had come" (Numbers 21), on which our Sages commented: "What report did he hear?"; *Mekhilta Yitro*: "And Jethro heard all that . . ."—"What report did he hear that he came?" Also *Studies in Vayikra* p. 239 on the verses "And the son of the Israelite woman went forth"—Whence went he forth?"
2 See *Studies Hayyei Sara*, p. 239ff. on this phrase.

REBELLION OF ADONIJAH

The Haftara pictures king David's palace at the time of his old age. His latter days are not distinguished for their peace and tranquility but are marked by confusion and intrigue. Rabbi I. Jacobson in his book on the Haftarot [1] has aptly described the contrast between the picture of Abraham's old age in our sidra and that of David's in the Haftara:

> An almost idyllic picture of tranquility pervades the tent of Abraham in contrast to the atmosphere of tension at the court of David. We are confronted with the actual contrast between the tent of the patriarchal period and the court of kings. The tent and its future appear to be built on much stronger foundations than the magnificent royal court which already bears the first signs of its decline and decay.

The Haftara relates no less than four times the story of Adonijah's conspiracy at the end of David's reign, recounting who were involved and who opposed it and the chain of events on the day that it was supposed to break out into the open. First the text itself narrates the story, then Nathan the prophet in coming to warn Bathsheba and prompting her what to say to David. The story is once more repeated by Bathsheba and told a fourth time by Nathan the prophet in his audience with the king after Bathsheba had left and in which he followed up her pleas.

The question arises. What prompted Scripture which is always concerned with limiting itself to the absolutely necessary and avoids redundancy to repeat the same account four times? It could surely have rested content with a phrase often used by it: "And he or she told him all these things" without needlessly specifying them? But before we try to answer

our question let us compare side by side the four different accounts of the conspiracy. (See table across pages 252–3).

The differences are striking. Our commentators, Abravanel
in particular, have enlightened us on the reason for each deviation. The text gives a completely objective account of the situation. Such was the division of the parties, these were with
Adonijah, and these were not invited. What transpired there
is likewise related in brief: "And he slew sheep and oxen and
fatlings." Nathan assumes that Bathsheba knows the details
and it was only necessary for him to tell her what to say to
David. In contrast to the dry words of the text which records
that the festivity had been limited to the slaughter of oxen and
fatlings, he said to her "Adonijah doth reign" and emphasises
that she should ask, "why king Adonijah doth reign," that she
should understand that the matter was urgent and no effort
must be spared. When she came to David she followed
Nathan's promptings to emphasise that Adonijah had done
what he had without the king's knowledge. But when she
referred to the oath which David had sworn to her, she
added force and emphasis to her words by saying "thou didst
swear by the Lord thy God",[2] and when she related about the
banquet that Adonijah had made, she added to the text that
"he hath slain oxen and fatlings and sheep *in abundance.*" The
significance of this addition is thus explained by Abravanel:

> He made a luxurious banquet, a most unfitting and unfeeling
> thing to do when his father was approaching death.

When she came to tell him of the participants in the banquet,
those invited and those left out she did not mention that "all
the men of Judah the king's servants" were invited, so that the
aged monarch should not conclude that the situation was hope-
less and despair of doing anything. To impress upon David that
the banquet was not just an innocuous social affair but a serious
attempt to usurp the monarchy, she emphasised that "but Solomon *thy servant* hath he not called," deliberately, because he
is thy servant.

(17) My Lord,	(24) My Lord O king
thou didst swear by the Lord thy	hast thou said
God unto thy handmaid	
Assuredly Solomon thy son shall	*Adonijah shall reign after me,*
reign after me	
and he shall sit upon my throne	and he shall sit upon my throne?
(18) And now, behold Adonijah	
reigneth;	
and thou, my lord the king knowest	
it not!	
	(25) For he is gone down this
	day
(19) And he hath slaughtered	and hath slaughtered
oxen and fatlings and sheep *in*	oxen and fatlings and sheep *in*
abundance	*abundance*
and hath called all the sons of the	and hath called all the king's sons
king,	
	and the captains of the host and
and Abiathar the priest	Abiathar the priest
and Joab the captain of the host	
	and behold they eat and drink be-
	fore him
	and they say Long live king Ado-
	nijah
	But me even thy servant
	Zadok the priest
	and Benayah the son of Jehoyada
but Solomon thy servant hath he	and thy servant Solomon
called not	hath he not called

The story of the text

(7) And he conferred with Joab the son of Zeruyah and with Abiathar the priest; and they following Adonijah helped him.

(8) But Zadok the priest, and Benayah the son of Jehoyada, and Nathan the prophet, and Shimei, and Rei, and the mighty men that belonged to David were not with Adonijah.

Nathan's story to Bathsheba

(11) Hast thou not heard that Adonijah the son of Haggith doth reign and David our lord knoweth it not?

(13) Go and get thee in, unto king David, and say unto him:
Didst not thou, my lord, O king, swear unto the handmaid saying:

Assuredly Solomon thy son shall reign after me
and he shall sit upon my throne?
Why then doth Adonijah reign?

(9) And Adonijah slew
sheep and oxen and fatlings...

and he called all his brethren the king's sons

and all the men of Judah the king's servants

and Nathan the prophet

And Benayah
and the mighty men
and Solomon his brother he called not

The account is different again in the mouth of Nathan. She had assumed that David was entirely ignorant of the whole affair since she knew that the king had sworn that "Solomon thy son shall reign after me" whereas Nathan who could not admit that such an intimate matter between the king and his wife was known to him, pretended that he thought that, perhaps, the whole affair was being conducted in accordance with the king's own wishes, showing no disapproval of Adonijah's actions. Malbim similarly explains the deviations:

> He pretended ignorance of the oath to Bathsheba and asked if the king had said that Adonijah should rule after him, since Adonijah had "gone down" that day ... It was inconceivable that he should act like this in the king's lifetime and invite all the king's sons without the king's knowledge.

The description of the banquet takes even larger proportions in Nathan's account: To the fact that "they slew oxen cattle and fatlings in abundance" he adds "and behold they eat and drink before him" and say "Long live king Adonijah." When he comes to list David's loyalists who were not invited, he places himself at the head: "but me, even me thy servant"; i.e. Adonijah knowing full well that I am thy servant did not invite me.

Malbim sums up his explanation of the principal deviations between the accounts of Bathsheba and Nathan as follows:

> Our Sages have stated that to stimulate a person to action one must arouse all the emotions regarding the subject. Sometimes a man will be worked upon by jealousy and anger and this Bathsheba accomplished in magnifying Adonijah's offence in hiding everything from the king. At others, a man will be worked upon by suspicion and shame and this Nathan did in assuming that David was responsible, arousing the king to activity because he was afraid that he would be suspected of violating the instructions of the prophet and the oath he had made to God.

Let us revert to our original question: What prompted Scripture to elaborate at such length on the details of the story and its recapitulations? Evidently it wished to show us how each one strove with all his might to set at nought Adonijah's designs that the word of the Lord through His prophet should be fulfilled (as recounted in 1 Chronicles 28, 5). Abravanel however still has the following question to ask:

> How came Nathan the prophet to doubt his own prophecy that Solomon would be king that he should feel that all this effort was necessary to further it?

It is very likely that the unusual detail into which the chapter enters was meant to answer the above question, to show that neither the prophet nor those who received his message, relied on miracles, that the prophecy would be fulfilled by itself. They did not regard prophecy as freeing them from action, absolving them of responsibility for their destiny. On the contrary, they accepted the promise of God as obliging them to work and strive to the best of their ability and understanding towards its fulfillment.

Questions for Further Study

1. Explain why David is called in this chapter by the text (and not only by the speakers) "king David" or "the king" and is called at the beginning of chapter 2 just "David"— "And the days of David drew near to die"?

2. Abravanel asks: In verses 13 and 17 it is stated "Didst thou not O lord swear that Solomon thy son shall reign after me and he shall sit upon my throne." Surely it should rather have stated: "that Solomon my son shall reign after *thee* and he shall sit upon *thy* throne"? Why was it not so worded? Try to answer his question.

3. The story of Adonijah's rebellion recurs four times in this chapter. Can you explain the reasons for the variations

255

and discrepancies in the different accounts (in addition to the ones we have noted).

Pay special attention to

(a) Why Bathsheba did not divulge that Adonijah had invited all the men of Judah, the servants of the king, stating instead that she had invited all the "sons of the king and Aviathar and Joab" only?

(b) What prompted Nathan to change Bathsheba's words in verse 17 uttered as a statement of fact into a question in verse 24?

(c) What prompted Bathsheba and Nathan to add to Solomon's name the epithet "thy servant" (in vv. 19, 26) whereas the text calls him "his brother (i.e. Adonijah) Solomon" in verse 9. Study the table.

---

1 *Hazon Ha-mikra* vol. 3, Sinai, Tel Aviv p. 72.

2 Note that Rebecca, too, when striving to arouse Jacob to action transmits to him Isaac's words with a similar addition: Isaac had said (Gen. 27, 4): "... and bring me that I may eat, that my soul may bless thee before I die." Rebecca reports these words as follows: "... and make savoury food that I may eat and bless thee before the *Lord* before my death" (v. 8), to impress upon him that this was not just another paternal blessing, but a specially important one (as Ramban states "that the blessing will come from the Holy Spirit").

A RECLAMATION CONTROVERSY

וַיִּזְרַע יִצְחָק בָּאָרֶץ הַהִיא וַיִּמְצָא בַּשָּׁנָה הַהִיא מֵאָה שְׁעָרִים
וַיְבָרְכֵהוּ יְיָ.
וַיִּגְדַּל הָאִישׁ וַיֵּלֶךְ הָלוֹךְ וְגָדֵל עַד כִּי־גָדַל מְאֹד.
וַיְהִי־לוֹ מִקְנֵה־צֹאן וּמִקְנֵה בָקָר וַעֲבֻדָּה רַבָּה
וַיְקַנְאוּ אֹתוֹ פְּלִשְׁתִּים.
וְכָל־הַבְּאֵרֹת אֲשֶׁר חָפְרוּ עַבְדֵי אָבִיו – – –
סִתְּמוּם פְּלִשְׁתִּים וַיְמַלְאוּם עָפָר.

Then Isaac sowed in that land, and received in the same
year a hundredfold: and the Lord blessed him.

And the man grew richer and richer, until he became
very wealthy:

He had acquired flocks and herds, and a large household
so that the Philistines envied him.

All the wells which his father's servants had dug in the
days of Abraham his father, the Philistines stopped them
up, and filled them with earth.   (26, 12–15ff.)

The Patriarchs dug wells in the Negev and found water. It was
foretold by the prophet Isaiah that the experience of the Patriarchs would be repeated by their descendants in the time
of the redemption—

כִּי־נִבְקְעוּ בַמִּדְבָּר מַיִם
וּנְחָלִים בָּעֲרָבָה.

For in the wilderness shall waters break out,
and streams in the desert.   (Isaiah 35, 6)

257

אֶפְתַּח עַל־שְׁפָיִים נְהָרוֹת
וּבְתוֹךְ בְּקָעוֹת מַעְיָנוֹת
אָשִׂים מִדְבָּר לַאֲגַם־מַיִם
וְאֶרֶץ צִיָּה לְמוֹצָאֵי מָיִם.

I will open rivers in high places,
and fountains in the midst of the valleys:
I will make the wilderness a pool of water,
and the dry land springs of water. (Ibid. 41, 18)

The same promise was made by the Almighty to the Children
of Israel in the Torah:

וַעֲבַדְתֶּם אֵת יְיָ אֱלֹהֵיכָם
וּבֵרַךְ אֶת־לַחְמְךָ וְאֶת־מֵימֶיךָ – – –

And ye shall serve the Lord your God,
And he shall bless·thy bread and thy water.
(Exodus 23, 25)

Water means life for man, land and animal, for the immediate
place and the whole neighborhood. But the Philistines thought
otherwise, as it is stated:

All the wells which his father's servants had dug in the
days of Abraham his father, the Philistines stopped them
up and filled them with earth.

What did they mean by doing this? Surely they were cutting off
their nose to spite their face and withholding benefits from both
themselves and their cattle! But, in addition, to stopping the
wells up, they filled them with earth so that no one would be
able to know that there had been a well at that spot and that
no water should flow again from there. Why did they wish
the land to be desolate? This question has puzzled students of
the Torah throughout the ages. There must be something more
to the matter than what is literally stated. Here we quote an

interesting answer propounded in *Haketav Vehakabala*:

"And he called their names after the names by which his father had called them"—it is conceivable that Isaac's naming of the wells bore affinity to other expressions of calling names—to mark the kindnesses of the Lord such as where it is stated that Abraham called the name of that place: "the Lord will see," "the Lord is my sign," "the well of him that liveth and seeth me." Abraham did the same. thing with regard to the wells which he dug, calling them by the name of the Lord. Since it was his preoccupation to spread abroad the knowledge of the Lord and show the people that idols were valueless, Abraham, thought out a wonderful device to help to bring those who were misled under the wings of the Divine Presence. He called the well by a name that would drive home the lesson of the true existence of the one God. By this he would arouse in them an awareness of the truth by saying, Let us go and draw water from the well of the eternal God! The wells were a public necessity, and in this manner, the people were initiated into a knowledge of the true God. Like the faithful servant of a king who tries to persuade rebellious subjects who had fled, to return to their country, so Abraham strove to turn the hearts of those who denied God. Whilst he was alive—as the prince of God among them, his fear was upon them, and they left the wells intact with their names, but after his death, they reverted to idolatry and n order to erase from their memory the names of these wells, which recalled the very opposite of their false opinions, they stopped up the wells. With the disappearance of the well, the name also disappeared. The Torah then comes to inform us that Isaac followed in his father's footsteps and endeavored to dig out these same wells and resurrect their names in order to restore the crown of the true faith to its former glory.

Our commentator thus considers that the story of the wells must be taken to imply something symbolic. The conduct of the Philistines can only be understood if we take these wells to signify the wells of the true faith which the Patriarchs caused to flow and which the forces of desolation and idolatry stopped up. An ancient Midrash anticipated this explanation stating:

"וכל הבארות אשר חפרו עבדי אביו סתמום פלשתים", אלו שבע מצוות בני נח
שזרום אברהם על עשייתן ושכחו אותם.

259

"All the wells which his father's servants had dug the Philistines stopped them up"—these are the seven commandments of the sons of Noah,[1] the observance of which Abraham had promoted and which they had forgotten.

Today in the age of Jewish renaissance in the homeland where wells are being literally dug in the land of our forefathers fructifying the desert areas of the Negev, we can appreciate the greatness of the Patriarchs who combined their dissemination of the true faith with the practical reclamation of the soil by digging wells and watering the ground. Our sages draw attention, as well, to this side of the Patriarchs' activities:

"וישב יצחק ויחפר את בארות המים" —
גדולין הצדיקים, שהם עוסקים ביישוב העולם.

"And Isaac settled there and dug again the wells of water . . ."—
Great are the righteous, since they occupy themselves with the habitation of the world. (Midrash Ḥefetz)

We know too that the Philistines were not pleased with these wells and did not wish to see the desert made fertile. The Torah itself tells us briefly why this was so—

And the Philistines envied him (v. 14).

And Isaac himself said:

Seeing ye hate me. (v. 27).

Was this reaction characteristic only of the Philistines, three and a half thousand years ago, when Isaac dwelt in his tent and wells were dug with primitive instruments, or can it not be paralleled in every generation, even in our own atomic age? Avimelech's words to Isaac surely strike a familiar note:

וַיֹּאמֶר אֲבִימֶלֶךְ אֶל־יִצְחָק:
לֵךְ מֵעִמָּנוּ כִּי־עָצַמְתָּ מִמֶּנּוּ מְאֹד.

And Avimelech said to Isaac:
Go away from us;
For thou art much mightier than we. (v. 16)

260

The whole history of the Jewish people is marked by expulsions from their homeland, from one exile to another from one town to another, from village to village, from one quarter of a city to another, and this can also be paralleled in the history of the Patriarchs. In our sidra we have, therefore, the first expulsion.

The Midrash offers an alternative interpretation of the phrase "for thou art much mightier than we" based on the two different usages of the letter מ There is the מי of comparison in the sense of "than" (cf. Gen. 39, 9) "there is no one greater in this house—*than me*"— ממני It can also be used in the sense of "from or "of" (cf. "on the day you will eat—of *it*" ממנו — Genesis 2, 2). The obvious meaning of our verse is, as the King James Version has it, and as we have quoted above "for thou art much mightier *than we*" but the Midrash prefers to translate the verse as follows:

"ויאמר אבימלך אל יצחק: לך מעמנו, כי עצמת ממנו". אמר לו: כל אותן
עוצמות שעצמת, לא ממנו היו לך?! לשעבר הוה לך חדא קוקיא [עדר אחד]
וכדון אית לך קוקיא סגין [ועכשיו — עדרים הרבה].

Avimelech said: All the might that thou hast gotten—is it not from us? Formerly you had only one flock and now you have many! (Bereshit Rabbah 64, 6)

The Midrash then reads the verse as follows: For thou hast become mighty *from* us."

In spite of the fact that Isaac sowed the land with his own seed and received the same year an hundredfold and that he himself dug the wells and found water, enriching himself therefore by his own toil and effort and the blessing of the Lord and not by exploiting any other man, in spite of all this, Avimelech accused him of becoming rich and mighty from him and his countrymen

Soon we shall read how the sons of Laban similarly accused Jacob, echoing the Philistine accusation against his father:

And of that which was our father's hath he gotten all this glory. (31, 1)

From then to our own days, the voice of those making this accusation has never been silenced, the history of the forefathers, in this respect, as well, being paralleled in their descendants: מעשה אבות סימן לבנים.

Questions for Further Study

1. "All the wells which his father's servants had dug, the Philistines stopped up and filled them with earth."

    Avimelech was ashamed to tell him to leave, personally. He allowed his people to stop up the wells in the hope that he would take the hint and leave. So long as the king did him no direct harm Isaac kept quiet. Besides he did not want to inform on the servants to their masters. But when Avimelech saw that Isaac was not to be moved by half measures, he took matters into his own hands, spoke personally to him and this is the force of the text: "Then Avimelech said to Isaac: Go away from us." (26. 15)   (Alshikh)

    "He had cattle . . . and the Philistines were jealous of him": those who lived in Gerar the capital city. Presumably they included many wealthy persons who usually reside in the capital. One rich man is jealous of another and particularly if he is a Jew.

    "The Philistines stopped them up" the country-dwellers. He could not complain to the king about them since he lived in Gerar and had no means of knowing who was responsible. The government too turned a blind eye out of animosity.

    "Leave us for you have grown too rich for us" till eventually the king himself said: Leave the town where the ministers of state and magnates live; for you have grown too rich for us and this is like thorns in their eyes. The king cannot tolerate the embarassment caused by his wealthy citizens. I am therefore obliged to violate my treaty with Abraham in which I promised him the right of his descendants to live in his country wherever he desires the same as all the other native inhabitants. The text implies that a similar fate will befall the Jews in the Dispersion whe they will be restricted in their right of domicile (cf. the Pale c Settlement in Russia).   (Ha'amek Davar)

"The Philistines stopped them up" so that his sons should not maintain their hold on them after his death. By this they behaved most unfairly to Isaac since water was very precious in that district and in particular to feed the large numbers of cattle he possessed. Abraham had presented Avimelech with seven ewes in witness of his ownership of the well and Avimelech had given him his word. Now the Philistines in their viciousness stopped up the wells Abraham had dug and which Isaac had reopened.

"Go away from us": The king and his princes were not affected by the jealousy of the people. But Avimelech was afraid that the local inhabitants would, in their jealousy, rebel against the king too who loved Isaac and would cause serious trouble. For his own benefit and for Isaac's too, he quietly suggested to him that it would be better for him to leave town. By making himself scarce he would be doing both of them a good turn. Avimelech only insisted he leave the capital; but permitted him to stay anywhere else in the land of the Philistines. That is why he did not say, "Leave our country" but just: "go away from us."

(Reggio)

(a) What was the attitude of the king to Isaac according to each of the above quoted commentators?
(b) Why did they (particularly *Ha'amek Davar*) maintain that Isaac's enemies were mostly town dwellers?

2. "They dug another well and quarreled over that too and called its name *sitna* (enmity)." Once they saw that they had succeeded in stealing the well by a spurious claim, they continued to steal without any claim at all—just out of sheer enmity.

(Ha'amek Davar)

What difficulty in the text prompted the foregoing comment?

---

[1] The seven basic laws of humanity prohibiting (1) murder (2) idolatry (3) immorality (4) blasphemy (5) theft (6) meat cut from a living animal, and (7) prescribing courts of justice, See Genesis 9, 1-10 and Talmud Sanhedrin 56a-60a.

Toledot 2

YOUR BROTHER CAME WITH DECEIT

The story of Jacob's conduct towards his brother Esau is well
known to us. Our title discloses their father Isaac's appraisal
of the deed committed by Jacob on the promptings of his mother
Rebecca. What is the Torah's view and evaluation of the deed?
As many Bible scholars have noted the Scriptural record rarely
inserts its own verdict on the actions committed by its characters.
One instance of such an evaluation we quote here—regarding
David's conduct in connection with Uriah and Bathsheba:

וַיֵּרַע הַדָּבָר אֲשֶׁר־עָשָׂה דָוִד בְּעֵינֵי יְיָ.

But the thing that David had done displeased the Lord
(II Samuel 11, 27)

But as a rule, Holy Writ allows the events it describes and the
action of its characters to speak for themselves. We may detect
between the lines in our sidra traces of Jacob's reluctance to
play the role of supplanter and deceiver. The commentary *Haketav Vehakabbala* uncovers such traces in the Torah's choice of
words in chapter 27, verse 12.

אוּלַי יְמֻשֵּׁנִי אָבִי – – –
My father peradventure will feel me.

The word פֶּן *lest* implies that the speaker does not wish the
matter to come to pass—it has a negative undertone, cf.: *"lest*
he put forth his hand and take too of the tree of life," (Gen. 3,
22); *"lest* we be scattered abroad upon the face of the earth,"
(ibid. 11, 4); "But Benjamin Joseph's brother, Jacob sent not with
his brethren; for he said, *Lest* harm befall him," (*ibid.* 41,
4). Had Jacob wished to express the hope that his father
would not feel him he should have said "I am afraid *lest* my
father feel me." From here it would seem therefore that Jacob
did not favour this attempt to outwit his father and that he would

rather let matters take their natural course and his father bless whomsoever he thought fit. Jacob hoped that his mother would call off the attempt as a result of his plea. So he said, "peradventure" אולי my father will free me." The word "peradventure" is used when the speaker desires the matter to come to pass, cf. "peradventure he will accept me" (ibid. 32, 21).

Jacob's inner reluctance and distaste for the stratagem is thus revealed in the choice of adverbial prefix to his reply to his mother's importunings. This too is the lesson found in *Haketav Vehakaballah,* driven home by contrasting the description of Jacob's conduct in obtaining the delicacies for his father with that of Abraham in welcoming his guests or Rebecca's in giving the stranger and his camels to drink:

"He went, took and brought": Jacob undoubtedly valued the blessings and when he saw that time was short and very soon Esau was due back from the field he brought the delicacies to his father. Jacob certainly had need to hurry. The text should therefore contain an allusion to this haste. In the case of Abraham the text notes: "he ran to meet them" (Gen. 18, 2). Abraham hurried to the tent of Sarah his wife and said, *quickly* make ready three measures of flour; to the herd Abraham *ran* . . . gave to the lad and *hurried* to prepare it." In the case of· Eliezer: The servant *ran* to meet her. In the case of Rebecca (ibid v. 18). She *hastened* and let down her pitcher . . . and *hastened* and emptied her pitcher into the trough. It should have said of Jacob too that "he *ran* and brought it to his mother" but. it merely says: "He went and took and brought." This indicates that he did not apply himself with any enthusiasm but reluctantly carried out his mother's behest.

Our Sages detected in the text a hint of Jacob's reluctance. In *Bereshit Rabbah* we find the following comment:

"וילך ויקח ויבא לאמו" — אנוס וכפוף ובוכה.

"He went and took and brought to his mother"—under duress, bent and weeping.[1]

The prophet Jeremiah alludes with distaste to Jacob's supplanting of Esau when castigating the sins of his generation:

For every brother will utterly supplant
and every neighbour will walk with slanders

(Jeremiah 9, 3)

But let us revert to our question. What is the attitude of the
Torah to Jacob's conduct? The vicissitudes of Jacob's life teach
us, at every step, how he was repaid—measure for measure—
for taking advantage of his father's blindness. His sons deceived
him when they presented him with Joseph's bloodstained coat
of many colours. Moreover the recurrence of such key or motif
words as "deceit" serve to underline the remorseless workings of
Divine retribution:

כל הלילה היתה עושה עצמה כרחל, כיון שעמד בבוקר "והנה היא לאה",
אמר לה: בת רמאי! למה רמית אותי?! אמרה לו: ואתה למה רמית אביך?!
כשאתה לך (בראשית כז, כא): "האתה זה בני עשו?" אמרת לו: "אנכי עשו
בכורך", ואתה אומר: "למה רימתני"?! ואביך לא אמר עליך: "בא אחיך
במרמה"?!

All that night she (Leah) acted the part of Rachel. As soon as
he arose in the morning, "and behold it was Leah." Said Jacob
to her: Daughter of the deceiver! Wherefore hast thou deceived
me? Said she to him: And thou—wherefore didst thou deceive thy
father?! When he said to thee: "Art thou my very son Esau"?
thou didst say to him: "I am Esau thy firstborn." Yet thou sayest:
"Wherefore then hast thou deceived me!?" Thy father did he not
say of thee: "Thy brother came with deceit?"

(Midrash Tanḥuma, Vayetze 11)

But "deceit" is not the only recurring motif in the pattern of
Jacob's life. Three other motif words are continually encountered: "firstborn right" בכורה "blessing" ברכה and "name" שם[2]:

לֹא־יֵעָשֶׂה כֵן בִּמְקוֹמֵנוּ
לָתֵת הַצְּעִירָה לִפְנֵי הַבְּכִירָה.

And Laban said:
it must not be done so in our country,
to give the younger before the firstborn

(29, 26)

R. Eliezer Ashkenazi in *Ma'aseh Hashem* poses two questions on the above statement of Laban. Why did Laban limit his objection to the fact that it was not the practice *in our country?* Surely such a practice was not followed anywhere! Why did he choose to say "to give the younger before the firstborn" גדולה rather than the younger before the elder בכורה as is indeed stated in verse 16, "the name of the elder was Leah and the name of the younger was Rachel"?

Providence wished Jacob to be reminded of his own supplanting of his brother Esau. Laban's statement contains a veiled allusion to Esau's bitter plaint "he has taken my *firstborn right.*" "In our country it is not done for the younger to usurp the rights of the firstborn as you did." Measure for measure.

Jacob stayed with Laban for twenty years. Thus he referred to his experiences there in retrospect:

וְהֶחֱלִף אֶת־מַשְׂכֻּרְתִּי עֲשֶׂרֶת מֹנִים.

And your father made sport of me
and changed my wages ten times (31, 7)

In the end, Jacob returned to his homeland where he was faced with the task of appeasing his brother. On his way he encountered the mysterious "man" with whom he wrestled. The outcome of the struggle was that the blessing which he had come by through "guile and deceit" was now conferred on him as of "princely" right.

לֹא אֲשַׁלֵּחֲךָ כִּי אִם־בֵּרַכְתָּנִי.
וַיֹּאמֶר אֵלָיו: מַה־שְּׁמֶךָ?
וַיֹּאמֶר: יַעֲקֹב.
וַיֹּאמֶר: לֹא יַעֲקֹב יֵאָמֵר עוֹד שִׁמְךָ כִּי אִם־יִשְׂרָאֵל
כִּי־שָׂרִיתָ עִם־אֱלֹהִים וְעִם־אֲנָשִׁים וַתּוּכָל.

I will not let thee go, except thou bless me.
And he said unto him, What is thy name?
And he said, Jacob (supplanter)

And he said, Thy name shall be no more called Jacob (supplanter), but Israel (a prince of God): for as a prince hast thou power with God and with men, and hast prevailed.
(32, 27–29)

Why did the angelic emissary require to ask him his name? Did he not know it? Some explain that the angel's purpose was to make Jacob admit that he had supplanted his brother and that not for nothing had he been dubbed the supplanter (Jacob). After he had made the admission and uttered his name, the messenger announced the removal of the stain on his character symbolised in the adoption of a new name—Israel. This is indeed Rashi's explanation:

"לא יעקב": לא ייאמר עוד שהברכות באו לך בעוקבה ורמיה, כי אם בשררה
וגילוי פנים, וסופך שהקב"ה נגלה עליך בבית אל ומחליף שמך.

It shall no more be said that the blessings came to thee through guile and deceit but by princely right and publicly. The Holy One blessed be He is destined to appear to thee at Bethel and change thy name.

The angel did not change his name but merely announced and heralded the act of the Almighty Who sent him. Why did not the angel change his name there and then? It may be answered:

עברות שבין אדם לחברו — אין נמחלין לו עד שירצה את חבירו.

Offences committed by man against his fellow—are not remitted him until he makes restitution to him and appeases him.
(Rambam, Teshuva, 2, 9)[3]

Before the name symbolic of his act of supplanting his brother could be dropped, he had to appease his brother. Only after he had said to Esau: "Take, I pray thee, my *blessing*" (33, 11), and after his brother had accepted the *blessing*, could the Almighty reveal Himself to him and announce the fulfilment of the promise made by the angel:

לֹא־יָקָרֵא שִׁמְךָ עוֹד יַעֲקֹב
כִּי אִם־יִשְׂרָאֵל.

Thy name shall be no more called Jacob (supplanter), but Israel (a prince of God):

(35, 10)

Questions for Further Study

1. "She dressed Jacob" (27, 15)

    Jacob let his mother act as his valet to dress him. He did not take the clothes to dress himself. (Haketav Vehakabbala)

    How would you explain this strange behaviour?

2. "Take now my blessing ברכתי which is brought to thee" (33, 11)

    "ברכתי": מנחתי. מנחה זו הבאה על ראיית פנים, כגון (בראשית מו, ז):
    "ויברך יעקב את פרעה"; (מל״ב יח, לא): "עשו אתי ברכה" דסנחריב; וכן
    (שמ״ב ח, י): "לשאול לו לשלום" דתועי מלך חמת, כולן לשון ברכת שלום
    הן, שקורין בלעז שלודא״ר, אף זו "ברכתי" — מו״ן שלו״ד (mon salut).

    "My blessing": in the sense of my offering—a welcome offering cf.: "Jacob blessed Pharaoh" (Gen. 46, 7); "Make your peace (blessing — ברכה) with me" (2 Kings 18, 31) of Senacherib; Toi, king of Hamath's *salute* him" (2 Sam 8, 10)—all are expressions of welcome as in the vernacular (old French) *saludoir*. Similarly my blessing *mon salud* (my salute or welcome greetings). (Rashi)

    Explain (basing yourself on the *Studies*) why the text does not employ the phrase "take my offering" as in "an offering to Esau my brother" (32, 14) preferring the word "blessing"?

3. בא דוד והעמידן (את המצוות כולן) על אחת עשרה דכתיב (תהלים טו) "מי
    יגור באהליך מי ישכון בהר קדשך: הולך תמים ופועל צדק ודובר אמת
    בלבבו: לא רגל על לשונו לא עשה לרעהו רעה...". "הולך תמים" — זה
    אברהם, דכתיב "התהלך לפני והיה תמים", ... "לא רגל על לשונו" — זה
    יעקב, דכתיב "אולי ימושני אבי".

    David came and reduced them (the precepts of Judaism) to eleven as it is written (Ps. 15): "who will sojourn in Thy Tabernacle,

269

who will dwell on Thy holy mount: he that walks uprightly and does good and speaks the truth in his heart: that has no slander on his tongue." "That walks uprightly" refers to Abraham ... "that has no slander on his tongue" to Jacob, as it is written: "perhaps my father will feel me." (Makkot 24a)

This proof text for Jacob's love of truth has puzzled many Bible readers. Can you solve their perplexity with the help of what you have learnt in the *Studies?*

4.   Cf. *Bereshit Rabbah* on the text: "Perhaps the woman will not agree" (24, 5)

אמר (אליעזר): אולי לא תאבה ואתן לו את בתי.
"אלי" כתיב. בת היתה לו לאליעזר והיה מחזר למצוא עילה שיאמר לו אברהם לפנות אליו להשיאו בתו . . .

Eliezer said: Perhaps she will not agree and then I shall offer him my daughter. "Perhaps she will not go along." It is written: "unto me" (like *elai*), Eliezer had a daughter and tried to find an excuse to prompt Abraham to ask her hand for his son.
(Rashi on 24, 39)

The Midrash does not base its exposition on the defective reading of אלי (as if it were: "unto me"). Can you suggest any other basis for the Midrashic interpretation with the help of the *Studies"?*

---

[1] A commentator to the Midrash, Radal suggests the verbal basis for this interpretation is the three prefixes to the Hebrew verbs *vay-vay-vay* connoting onomatopeically 'reluctance and misery.

[2] For details see Buber, *Leitwortstil in der Erzählung des Pentateuchs* appearing in Buber-Rosenzweig's: *Die Schrift und ihre Verdeutschung,* pp. 223–226.

[3] Cf. Mishna Yoma 7, 9; Bava Kamma 92a.

ESAU'S CRY

After the full import of what had happened to him regarding the blessings dawned on Essau:

He cried with a loud and bitter cry.   (27, 34)

The derivation of some special lesson from analogous phrasing recurring in different parts of the Tenach is one of the commonplaces of Rabbinic exegesis. Our Sages connected the above phrase, describing the cry of Esau, with the identical wording that is applied to the cry of Mordecai in the book of Esther, on hearing of Haman's and Ahasuerus' edict to exterminate his people:

He cried with a loud and bitter cry.   (4, 1)

Between the lines they read a lesson of sin and its retribution after a lapse of centuries. Let us quote the Midrash, *Bereshit Rabbah* 67, on this theme:

כל האומר הקב"ה ותרן הוא, יוותרו חייו [רש"י: יופקרו חייו, שמורה לבריות
לחטוא], אלא מאריך אפו וגובה. צעקה אחת הזעיק יעקב לעשו, דכתיב:
"ויצעק צעקה גדולה ומרה", והיכן נפרע לו? בשושן הבירה, שנאמר (אסתר
ד, א): "ויזעק זעקה גדולה ומרה".

Whoever maintains that the Holy One blessed be He is a foregoer (of His just claims), may he forego his life! He is merely long-suffering, but (ultimately) collects His due. Jacob made Esau break out into a cry but once, and where was he punished for it? In Shushan the capital, as it says: "And he cried with a loud and bitter cry."

The punishment for wronging Esau did not follow immediately but remained suspended until the time was ripe.

This same theme recurs in connection with another verse found in Psalm 80, 6. There the phrase דמעות שליש *dema'ot shalish*, taken usually to mean "tears in great measure" is interpreted by Rabbinic exegesis (source unknown) to mean "threefold tears," *shalish* being the Hebrew expression of threefold number (cf. *shelishi*—three), an allusion to the tears shed by Esau.

Here is Rashi's explanation of the verse which reads:

הֶאֱכַלְתָּם לֶחֶם דִּמְעָה וַתַּשְׁקֵמוֹ בִּדְמָעוֹת שָׁלִישׁ.

Thou feedest them with the bread of tears and givest them tears to drink in great measure.

The expression "threefold tears" refers to the three tears shed by Esau as it is said:

And he cried a cry	ויצעק צעקה	implies one	הרי אחת
A loud	גדולה	implies two	הרי שתים
And bitter	ומרה	implies three	הרי שלש

The Almighty, who takes note of our tears, also takes note of those shed by the wicked Esau. They also are noted and cry out for retribution.

Questions for Further Study

1. Compare Isaac's first blessing to Jacob (27, 28–29) with his second one (28, 3–4).

(קהלת ז, ח): "טוב אחרית דבר מראשיתו" — הברכות הראשונות שברך יצחק ליעקב על טללי שמים ועל דגן הארץ, שנאמר: "ויתן לך האלהים מטל השמים". הברכות האחרונות ברכות יסוד עולם ואין בהם הפסק, לא בעולם הזה ולא בעולם הבא, שנאמר: "ואל שדי יברך אותך", ועוד הוסיף לו את ברכת אברהם, שנאמר: "ויתן לך את ברכת אברהם לך ולזרעך אתך" — הוי אומר: "טוב אחרית דבר מראשיתו".

"Better is the end of a thing than the beginning thereof" (Ecclesiastes 7, 8) . . . The first blessings with which Isaac blessed Jacob treated of the dew of heaven and the grain of the earth, as it is stated: 'So God give thee of the dew of heaven...'" The latter blessings, however, were of a permanent and fundamental nature with no interruption, neither in this world nor in the Hereafter, as it is stated: "And God Almighty bless thee." Furthermore, he added for him the blessing of Abraham, as it is stated, "And give thee the blessing of Abraham, to thee and thy seed with thee"—that is to say: "Better is the end of a thing than the beginning thereof".   (Pirkei Derabbi Eliezer)

Explain why Isaac saw fit to bless Jacob a second time with a blessing completely different from the first time.

2.   Compare the Midrash cited above in our *Studies* from *Bereshit Rabbah* with the one cited in Rashi on 33, 16: "so Esau returned that day on his way"

"וישב ביום ההוא עשו לדרכו": עשו לבדו, וארבע מאות איש שהלכו עמו נשמטו מאצלו אחד אחד. והיכן פרע להם הקב"ה? בימי דוד, שנאמר (שמ"א ל, יז): "כי אם ארבע מאות איש נער אשר רכבו על הגמלים וינסו".

Esau returned alone whilst the four hundred men who had accompanied him slipped away from him one by one, and on what occasion did the Holy One blessed be He repay them? In the days of David, as it is stated: "Save four hundred young men, who rode upon camels and fled."   (1 Samuel 30, 17)

What is the idea common to this Midrash and the one quoted previously from *Bereshit Rabbah*?

3.   "And Esau said in his heart: 'Let the days of mourning for my father be at hand...'" (27,41).

(בראשית ח, כא): "ויאמר ה' אל לבו". הרשעים הם ברשות לבם: (תהלים י, א): "אמר נבל בלבו אין אלהים"; (בראשית כז, מא): "ויאמר עשו בלבו: יקרבו ימי אבל אבי ואהרגה את יעקב אחי"; (מל"א יב, כו-כח): "ויאמר ירבעם בלבו: עתה תשוב הממלכה לבית דוד, אם יעלה העם הזה לעשות זבחים בבית ה' בירושלים... ויעש שני עגלי זהב"; (אסתר ו, ו) "ויאמר המן בלבו...". — אבל הצדיקים לבם ברשותם: (שמ"א א, יג): "וחנה היא מדברת על לבה"; (שמ"א כז, א): ויאמר דוד אל לבו"; (דניאל א, ח): "וישם דניאל על לבו", — דומין לבוראם: (בראשית ח, כא): "ויאמר ה' אל לבו".

"And the Lord said unto[1] his heart"—the wicked are in the thrall of their hearts: "The fool hath said in[2] his heart, there is no God" (Psalm 10. 1): "And Esau said in[2] his heart, let the days of mourning for my father be at hand, then will I slay my brother Jacob" (Genesis 27, 41); "And Jeroboam said in his heart: Now will the kingdom return to the house of David. If this people go up to offer sacrifices in the house of the Lord at Jerusalem ... and made two calves of gold" (1 Kings 12, 26, 27, 28). "Now Haman said *in*[2] his heart ..." (Esther 6, 6)—But as for the righteous their hearts are in their thrall: "She spoke *unto*[3] her heart (1 Samuel 1, 13); "And David said *unto*[1] his heart" (1 Samuel 27, 1): "But Daniel purposed *unto*[3] his heart" (Daniel 1, 8)—Just like their Maker: And the Lord said *unto*[1] his heart" (Genesis 8, 21).   (Bereshit Rabbah 34, 11)

(a) Explain the underlying concept of this Midrash. What in the view of our Sages is the meaning of the term: "heart" in these verses?

(b) What is the stylistic[4] basis of this Midrash?

4.   Compare the following verses from chapter 27:
And the words of *Esau her elder son* were told to Rebecca; and she sent and called *Jacob her younger son* ...
And Rebecca took the choicest garments of *Esau her elder son* ...
and put them upon *Jacob her younger son*
I am Esau *thy firstborn*
I am thy son, *thy firstborn*   (42, 15, 19, 32)
Explain why Esau is not given the title "firstborn" rather than "elder" in contrast to the later two verses 19 and 32 where the speaker himself designates himself "firstborn"?

---

[1] *el.*   [2] *be*   [3] *al*

[4] In the English version of the Bible no distinction is made between the Hebrew prepositions *be, el* and *'al*. They are all translated "in". We have, however, preserved the distinction by rendering *el* and *'al* by "unto" and *be* by "in".

THE BLESSINGS

In the second chapter of our *Studies* on this Sidra (p. 264ff.) we devoted our attention to Jacob's conduct and the reason for the "ruse" he employed to achieve his aim. This time we shall endeavour to understand the attitude of his father and mother. Many commentators have been surprised by Isaac's seeming lack of discrimination in his insistence on blessing Esau.

> Why was Isaac so insistent on blessing Esau? Did he not know that Esau was a man of the field and Jacob a simple man? Furthermore, could he not have blessed both equally?   (Malbim)

Indeed there are some commentators who take the view that Isaac did not know what was going on at home and was unaware of the gulf separating Jacob from Esau:

> There is no doubt that Isaac should have given thought to Esau's character, his wickedness and that of his wives, and the likelihood that his children would follow their father's bad example. He should have prayed to God for guidance as to whether he should bless the eldest or the most deserving. Affection, however, ruins one's power of judgement. His affection for Esau blinded him to his faults. That is the implication of the phrase: "When Isaac was old, and his eyes were dim." His powers of judgement grew dim and he was not able to see reality.   (Abravanel)

Abravanel points out Isaac's spiritual blindness basing himself on the opening phrase of the story. But he fails to find a reasonable explanation why Isaac, who had allowed himself to be sacrificed as an "unblemished burnt offering," should have suffered from this blind spot. Our Sages traced this failing of Isaac's to his experience as an offering to God. Here is a Midrash full of anthropomorphic pictures and personifications which may seem to us rather odd:

"ותכהינה עיניו מראות". מראות — מכוח אותה ראייה, שבשעה שעקד אברהם
אבינו את בנו על גבי מזבח בכו מלאכי השרת ונשלו דמעות מעיניהם לתוך
עיניו והיו רשומות בתוך עיניו, וכיון שהזקין — כהו עיניו.
דבר אחר: "מראות" — מכוח אתה ראייה, שבשעה שעקד אברהם אבינו את
יצחק בנו על גבי המזבח, תלה עיניו במרום והביט בשכינה.

"His eyes were dim from seeing"—from that experience (literally
"seeing"). For when Abraham sacrificed his son on the altar the
ministering angels wept and the tears dropped from their eyes
into his eyes and were impressed into his eyes. As soon as he
become old, his eyes therefore became dim. Another explanation:
... When Abraham sacrificed his son Isaac on the altar he sent
his glance on high and beheld the Divine Presence.

(Bereshit Rabbah)

A number of explanations have been suggested for this Midrash.
Some maintain that it symbolises the idea that one who came
so close to the Divine Presence in his aspiration for purity, one
who offered himself up as a sacrifice to Him whose seal is Truth,
is no longer capable of understanding the world of falsehood.

The author of *Hamidrash Vehama'aseh* states that Isaac's deed
was greater than Abraham's, since Abraham had received the
commandment to sacrifice his son direct from the Almighty,
whereas Isaac obeyed it out of faith in his father's words:

Isaac's purity of heart was so far removed from falsehood, that
he was unaware of its existence. It never occurred to him that
it was possible for a person to be hypocritical. Those angelic
tears allude to his otherworldly purity which left an indelible impression on him, dimmed his sight so that he was unable to discern
iniquity in Esau's behaviour. This led, in his old age, to his gulli-
bility and his believing that Esau was more deserving of blessing
than Jacob: "And his eyes were dim so that he could not see,
so he called Esau..."

But this explanation must meet with a serious objection. If
Isaac was really unaware of Esau's behaviour, then the last sentence of the previous sidra, prior to the story of the blessings,
is quite out of place. Before Isaac summoned Esau to bless him,
it is distinctly stated that Esau took Hittite wives, and that
these were "a bitterness of spirit unto *Isaac* and to Rebecca."

276

The Torah then explicitly informs us that Isaac knew only too well of Esau's misconduct, and that, in spite of this, he still thought him more deserving of blessing. R. David Kimḥi and Ibn Atar in his *Or Haḥayim* suggest that Isaac wished to bless him, just because of his weakness and misconduct, in the hope that the paternal invocation of Divine bounty on him, would help him mend his ways.

But the question still remains why should Jacob suffer and not receive the blessing he deserved just because he was not a wicked man? The answer to this may be found by comparing the blessing with which Isaac blessed Jacob unwittingly, thinking he was Esau, i.e. the one that was originally designed for Esau, with the one that the Patriarch blessed Jacob, aware of his true identity, on the eve of his departure for Laban:

Blessing meant for Esau	*For Jacob*
So God give thee of the dew of heaven, And of the fat places of the earth, And plenty of corn and wine. Let peoples serve thee, And nations bow down to thee. Be lord over thy brethren, And let thy mother's sons bow down to thee. Cursed be every one that curseth thee, And blessed be every one that blesseth thee.	And God Almighty bless thee, and make thee fruitful, and multiply thee, that thou mayest be a congregation of peoples; and give thee the blessing of Abraham, to thee, and to thy seed with thee; that thou mayest inherit the land of thy sojournings, which God gave unto Abraham.
(27, 28–29)	(28, 3–4)

We may note the contrast between the two. On the one hand Esau was promised abundance, fatness, power and dominion— material blessings. But the Abrahamic mission, the blessing of seed and the promise of the land were not bequeathed to Esau, since such a spiritual blessing cannot be conferred by succession but only granted to the one who is deserving of it.

> The Almighty promised Abraham that the chosen people who would acknowledge Him as God would come forth from him. His Divine Presence would dwell amongst his descendants, who would inherit the land and be holy to their God. Abraham did not himself deliver this blessing to Isaac, since it lay not in the power of mortal man to bequeath such properties to his sons, since this was a matter, solely dependent on the moral worthiness and holiness of the people concerned. Only after Abraham's death did the Almighty bestow this blessing on Isaac. Similarly, Isaac did not intend handing down Abraham's blessing to his descendants, for he knew too well that this would be of no avail. Only he who was fit and prepared to receive it, would be invested with it by the Almighty. (Malbim)

Esau by his own behaviour, by his intermarriage with the idolatrous inhabitants of the land, forfeited his right to such a blessing. It cannot be argued then that had Jacob not deceived Esau, the former would not have been chosen to become the third Patriarch and ancestor of the Jewish people.

Questions for Further Study

1. Cf.:

Isaac to Esau: *Rebecca to Jacob:*
... that my soul may bless thee   ... and bless thee
before I die   before my death
                          (27, 4)   before the Lord
                                                      (27, 7)

What is the point of Rebecca's addition "before the Lord" to Isaac's instruction to Esau?

2. Esau deferred matrimony till forty—the same age as his father following the example of his father but took two wives from the daughters of Heth in defiance of his grandfather's testament and father's standing.
My grandfather had a question which went like this: How could Isaac favour Esau and give him a better blessing than Jacob after

this rebellion and the notorious disgrace of his? Grandfather answered that Isaac wished to reform Èsau through the blessing, making amends for that one lapse of his, the only one that Isaac was aware of. (Avraham ben Harambam)

(a) How do his views differ from the Midrash?
(b) Explain what he meant by "his grandfather's testament," "his father's standing," "the notorious disgrace."
(c) In what way does Rambam's father's understanding of Isaac's attitude differ from that of most of our commentators, as exemplified by our citation from Abravanel?

JUST WAIT FOR FATHER'S DEATH!

Esau had found out what Jacob had done to him. He gave
vent to "a loud and bitter cry," lifted up his voice and wept.
Isaac's consolatory words had no effect, especially when Isaac,
too, deliberately confirmed his blessing to Jacob with the words:
"I have blessed him—yea, and he shall be blessed." Esau's subsequent reaction is described in the following terms:

וַיִּשְׂטֹם עֵשָׂו אֶת־יַעֲקֹב
עַל־הַבְּרָכָה אֲשֶׁר בֵּרֲכוֹ אָבִיו.
וַיֹּאמֶר עֵשָׂו בְּלִבּוֹ:
יִקְרְבוּ יְמֵי אֵבֶל אָבִי
וְאַהַרְגָה אֶת־יַעֲקֹב אָחִי.

**Now Esau hated Jacob on account of the blessing his
father had given him.
Said Esau in his heart: Just wait for the days of mourning
for my father and I will kill my brother Jacob.** (27, 41)

Rashi comments on the second half of the verse: "Just wait for
the days of mourning of my father":

"יקרבו ימי אבל אבי": כ מ ש מ ע ו , שלא אצער את אבא, ומדרש אגדה
לכמה פנים יש.

in its plain sense, so as not to grieve Father; but the homiletic
explanations are various.

Rashi's comment is puzzling. Why did he require to underline the fact that we are to take the verse in its plain sense?
After all, why not? The verse raises no special problems of

exegesis or interpretation and our traditional commentators have paid no attention to it.

We may take this opportunity to peep into Rashi's laboratory and follow his method of exegesis. If he stated that we are to take a passage whose sense is clear in its plain sense, he must have wished to avoid us taking it in another sense, to exclude another approach, particularly here, where he specifically alludes to that other approach—the homiletic—that of the Midrash Aggada. Here is what the Midrash has to say on this text:

(ויקרא כב, כח): "ושור או שה אותו ואת בנו לא תשחטו ביום אחד". אמר ר' ברכיה בשם ר' לוי: כתיב (משלי יב, י): "יודע צדיק נפש בהמתו ורחמי רשעים אכזרי": "יודע צדיק נפש בהמתו" — זה הקב"ה, שכתוב בתורתו (דברים כב, ו): "לא תקח האם על הבנים"; "ורחמי רשעים אכזרי" — זה סנחריב, שכתוב בו (הושע י, יד): "אם על בנים רוטשה".

ד ב ר   א ח ר : "יודע צדיק" — זה הקב"ה, שכתוב בתורתו (ויקרא כב, כז): "שור או כשב או עז כי יולד והיה שבעת ימים"; "ורחמי רשעים אכזרי" — זה המן הרשע, דכתיב (אסתר ג, יג): "להשמיד להרג ולאבד את כל היהודים מנער ועד זקן טף ונשים ביום אחד".

"You shall not slaughter an ox or a lamb, both it and its young on the same day." R. Berechiah stated in the name of R. Levi: It is written in Proverbs (12): "The righteous knoweth the soul of his beast but the compassion of the wicked is cruel." "The righteous knoweth the soul of his beast": this refers to the Holy One blessed be He in whose Torah is written: "Thou shalt not take the mother with the young"; "and the compassion of the wicked is cruel" refers to Sennacherib, of whom it is written: "the mother was dashed to pieces with the children." Another explanation: "The righteous knoweth"—this refers to the Holy One blessed be He in whose Torah is written: "You shall not slaughter an ox or a lamb, both it and its young on the same day." "And the compassion of the wicked is cruel" refers to Haman the wicked, for it is written: "to destroy, slay, cause to perish all Jews, young and old, little ones and women on one day" (Esther 3).

א מ ר   ר '   ל ו י : אוי להם לרשעים שהם מתעסקים בעצות על ישראל וכל אחד ואחד אומר: עצתי יפה מעצתך. עשו אמר: שוטה היה קין שהרג את אחיו בחיי אביו, ולא היה יודע שאביו פרה ורבה? אני איני עושה כן, אלא (בראשית כז, מא): "י ק ר ב ו   י מ י   א ב ל   א ב י , ואהרגה את יעקב אחי".

פרעה אמר: שוטה היה עשו, שאמר: "י ק ר ב ו   י מ י   א ב ל   א ב י ", ולא

281

היה יודע שאחיו פרה ורבה בחיי אביו? אני איני עושה כן, אלא עד דאינון דקיקין תחות כרסיה דאמהון [קטנים תחת כיסא המשבר של אמם], אנא מחנק יתהון, שנאמר (שמות א, טז): "וראיתם על האבנים כל הבן הילד היאורה תשליכוהו".

המן אמר: שוטה היה פרעה, שאמר: "כל הבן הילוד", ולא היה יודע שהבנות נישאות לאנשים ופרות ורבות מהם? אני איני עושה כן אלא: "להשמיד להרג ולאבד את כל היהודים מנער ועד זקן".

ואף גוג ומגוג לעתיד לבוא עתידין לומר כן: שוטים היו הראשונים שהיו מתעסקים בעצות על ישראל, ולא היו יודעים שיש להן פטרון בשמים? אני איני עושה כן, אלא מתחילה אני מזדווג לפטרון שלהם ואחר להם!! הדא הוא דכתיב (תהלים ב, ב): "יתיצבו מלכי ארץ...על ה'". אמר לו הקב"ה: רשע! לי באת·להזדווג?! חייך שאני עושה עמך מלחמה. הדא הוא דכתיב (ישעיה מב, יג): "ה' כגבור יצא כאיש מלחמות יעיר קנאה", דכתיב (זכריה יד, ג): "ויצא ה' ונלחם בגויים ההם", מה כתיב תמן? ‒ (יד, ט): "והיה ה' למלך על כל הארץ".

R. Levi stated: Woe unto the wicked who are constantly forming designs against Israel, each one saying, My plan is better
than yours! Esau said: Cain was a fool for killing his brother
during his father's lifetime, not taking into consideration that his
father would be fruitful and multiply. I will not make that
mistake but, "just wait for the days of mourning for my father
then will I slay my brother." Pharaoh said: Esau was a fool
in saying, "just wait for the days of mourning for my father,"
not realising that his brother would be fruitful and multiply during his father's lifetime. I will not make that mistake, but when
the Israelites are still tiny, under the birthstools of their mothers,
then will I strangle them. Hence it is written, "You shall look
upon the birthstool, every son that is born shall you cast into
the river."

Haman said: Pharaoh was a fool in ordering every male born
to be cast into the river not realising that the girls would get
married and bear children from them. I will not make that
mistake but will give orders "to destroy, slay all Jews."

Gog and Magog, too in time to come will say the same, namely:
Fools were the ancients for busying themselves with designs against
Israel not realising that they had a Protector in heaven. I will
not make that mistake but will first join issue with their Protector
and then with them. Hence it is written: "The kings of the earth
stand up against the Lord" (Psalm 10, 1):

Said the Holy One blessed be He to him: Villain! Do you come
to join issue with Me? By your life! I will wage war on you.
Hence it was written: "The Lord will go forth like a mighty
man, He will stir up jealousy like a man of war" (Isaiah 42, 13),

and it is written, "Then shall the Lord go forth and fight against the nations" (Zech 14, 3). What is stated thereafter in this connection? "And the Lord shall be king over all earth" (Ibid 9).

(Vayikra Rabbah)

The foregoing Midrash paints a black picture of human progress, conceived in terms of the continuous perfecting of methods of killing other human beings. The greater the intellectual advance, the more devilish and refined are the means of extermination employed by Jew-baiters down the ages. What is more interesting: the moral qualms which prevented the resort to total extermination are viewed by the succeeding generation as the foolishness of their predecessors: "Esau was a fool," "Pharaoh was a fool," "Fools were the ancients." The latest exponent of Jew hatred always promises never to make the mistake of his predecessor, but effect a "final solution." The latest has been the worst. Realising he cannot destroy the bodies, he destroys the Jewish soul, the body automatically falling his victim.

Why did not Rashi cite this prophetic Midrash? Rashi himself supplies the answer. On Gen. 3, 9 Rashi makes one of his rare statements on his methodological principles:

"וישמעו": יש מדרשי אגדה רבים וכבר סדרום רבותינו על מכונם בבראשית רבה ובשאר מדרשות, ואני לא באתי אלא לפשוטו של מקרא ולאגדה המיישבת דברי המקרא דבר דבור אופניו.

There are many homiletic expositions which have been collected by our Rabbis in Bereshit Rabbah and other Midrashim. I am concerned only with the plain sense of Scriptures and the homiletic interpretation which best fits the the wording and context.

Here we have the consideration which governed Rashi in his selection of Midrashic explanations—that which best fits the context, and does least violence to the text. Now in the Midrash we have quoted, Esau's words (the passage with which we headed our *Studies*) are not taken to imply consideration for his father's feelings, but as an expression of fiendish desire to kill his brother at a time when it would be impossible for another to take his place. Why? Because in the Aggada, Esau (like

283

Pharaoh and Haman) is not an individual, a specific historical figure who appeared at a certain time, but a prototype, a symbol, a milestone of Jew-hatred. This is obvious from the presentation of Cain as engaged in forming designs against Israel. A symbol also does not contain both good and bad but it is all of one piece. Esau is the symbol of hate. In the Torah, however, Esau is a human being, the son of Isaac and Rebecca. Rashi is concerned with Esau the man. Like all human beings he has his good and bad sides. His good side was his respect for his parents which is emphasised by the text. Rashi who was concerned with "the plain sense of Scriptures" cannot overlook this creditable side of his, even when Esau was breathing Cain-like vengeance and calling for his brother's blood. Even when he was saying "then will I slay Jacob my brother" the words "just wait for the days of mourning for my father" must be registered to his credit.[1]

The Midrash too emphasises this aspect of Esau's character:

אמר ר' שמעון בן גמליאל: לא כיבד אדם את אבותיו כמו אני את אבותי, ומצאתי שכיבד עשו לאביו יותר ממני.

כיצד? אני הייתי משמש את אבי בכל'ים צואים [מלוכלכים — דרך עבדות!] וכשהייתי הולך לשוק הייתי משליך אותן הכלים ולובש כלים נאים ויוצא בהם. אבל עשו לא היה עושה כן, אלא אותן כלים שהיה לובש ומשמש בהן את אביו — הן מעולים. תדע לך, בשעה שיצא לצוד ולהביא לאביו שיברך אותו, מה עשתה רבקה? נתנה ליעקב מטעמים ואמרה לו: לך אצל אביך וטול הברכות עד שלא יטול אותן אחיך! אמר לה יעקב: אמי, אין את יודעת שעשו אחי איש שעיר ואנכי איש חלק, "אולי ימושני אבי"? אמרה לו: אני מלבשת אותך כלים נאים שאחיך לובש ומשמש בהן את אביך, ואתה נכנס אצלו והוא אוחז בידך, כסבור שאתה עשו ומברך אותך! ומניין? שנאמר (בראשית כז, טו): "ותקח רבקה את בגדי עשו בנה הגדול החמודות אשר אתה בבית ותלבש את יעקב", לפיכך מה יצחק אומר לו? "הקול קול יעקב והידים ידי עשו". ברך אותו ויצא לו ובא עשו. אמר לו: "אני בכורך עשו". כיון ששמע את קולו, ידע שהוא עשו. אמר לו: "בני, בא אחיך במרמה ויקח את ברכתך". באותה שעה התחיל עשו צווח ואומר: בוא וראה מה עשה לי התם הזה! לא רי שצחק לי על שמכרתי לו את בכורתי, והנה עתה לקח ברכתי. הא למדת, שעשו היה זהיר בכבוד אבותיו.

אמר ר' יודן: כיון שבאו ישראל לעשות עמי מלחמה — הראהו הקב"ה למשה אותו הר שהאבות קבורים בו, אמר לו: משה! אמור להם לישראל: אין אתם יכולים להזדווג לי, עד עכשו מתבקש לו שכר הכבוד שכיבד את אלו שקבורין בהר הזה!

Said Rabbi Shimon ben Gamliel: No man respected his parents more than I. Notwithstanding I have found that Esau respected his father more. How so? I ministered to my father in soiled garments and when I went to market changed into my best clothes. Esau, on the other hand, did not behave thus, but ministered to his father in his best clothes. You may know this from the following: when Esau went out to hunt and bring venison to his father that he might bless him, what did Rebecca do? She gave Jacob delicacies and said to him: Go to your father and take the blessings before your brother takes them. Whereupon Jacob replied: Mother, don't you know that my brother Esau is a hairy man and I am a smooth man? "Perhaps my father will feel me?" She replied: I shall clothe you with the fine apparel that your brother wears and in which he ministers to your father. You will go to him and he will hold your hand and imagine you are Esau and bless you. Whence this?—"And Rebecca took Esau's choicest garments which were with her in the house and put them upon Jacob." Whereupon what did Isaac say to him?—"The voice is the voice of Jacob, but the hands are the hands of Esau." He blessed him and he left and then Esau came along. The latter said: "I am Esau your firstborn." As soon as he heard his voice, he knew it was Esau. Isaac said: "My son, your brother came with deceit and took your blessing." That same moment Esau cried out: Come and see what this "simple man" has done to me: It was not enough that he mocked me for selling him my birthright; now he has gone and taken my blessing. From here you may infer that Esau was careful ·in showing respect to his father.

Said Rabbi Yudan: As soon as the Israelites came to do battle with Esau, the Holy One blessed be He showed Moses that same mount where the patriarchs were buried and said to him: Moses, tell the Israelites: You cannot overcome him since the reward due to the honour he paid those buried in this mount is still due to him.   (Devarim Rabbah)

---

[1] See also our *Studies* on Bereshit (5) pp. 38–45 especially question 2 (b) where Rashi refers to a Midrash he does not cite.

MOTHER OF JACOB AND ESAU

We shall consider, on this occasion, Rashi's observation on the following passage, coming near the end of our sidra:

וַיִּשְׁלַח יִצְחָק אֶת־יַעֲקֹב וַיֵּלֶךְ פַּדֶּנָה אֲרָם
אֶל־לָבָן בֶּן־בְּתוּאֵל הָאֲרַמִּי אֲחִי רִבְקָה אֵם
יַעֲקֹב וְעֵשָׂו.

Isaac sent Jacob away: and he went to Padan-aram unto Laban, son of Bethuel the Syrian, the brother of Rebecca, mother of Jacob and Esau. (28, 5)

On the closing phrase (not in bold) Rashi comments:

איני יודע מה מלמדנו.

I do not know what it teaches us.

Many have praised Rashi for this display of humility and his literal fulfillment of one of the seven marks of the wise man outlined in *Pirke Avot* (V, 8): "regarding that which he has not understood he says, I do not understand it." But it behoves us to appreciate what Rashi was driving at, as well as praise his intellectual modesty. The difficulty posed by the text is quite obvious. What prompted the Torah to add the apparently, completely superfluous fact, that Rebecca was the mother of both Jacob and Esau? Surely the whole context of the sidra deals with nothing else but the relations of Rebecca with "Esau her elder son" and "Jacob her younger son." Rashi has taught us, on many other occasions,[1] that any descriptive word or phrase added in apposition to a familiar, and already, fully defined term is not placed there for purely ornamental and rhetorical reasons. It is meant to teach us something new. But Rashi could find no purpose, didactic, informative, or otherwise, in the closing words of our passage, and this is what the prince of commentators says in so many words.

Why did Rashi see fit to proclaim to the world his failure to find a plausible explanation of the superfluous text? Surely the admonition of our Sages to "teach thy tongue to say, I do not know" was meant to apply only in response to an inquiry. But no one was called upon gratuitously to proclaim his ignorance. Surely Rashi has left many passages in the Torah unexplained, and he could very well have passed over our text without comment, since he had none to make. But this presents no difficulty. Rashi left those texts unexplained which were so plain to him, that he presumed they would be clear to any Torah student. If he had remained silent, in our context, he would have been guilty of misrepresentation, allowing scholars to imagine that everything was crystal clear, failing to draw attention to a difficulty in the text. He therefore proclaimed to the world his failure to give an adequate explanation of the final apposition, throwing out a challenge to commentators and scholars to search, probe deeper and labour in their efforts to find their own solution.

Indeed, many of Rashi's commentators were thus goaded to find their own solutions. Rashi's earliest gloss, that penned by Judah ben Eliezer (Riyva) suggested that the Torah wished to explain how it was that Isaac and Rebecca came to have such a wicked son as Esau. The text therefore added the significant allusion connecting Rebecca with her unsavoury kinsmen—"Laban, son of Bethuel, the Syrian, the brother of Rebecca, Jacob's and Esau's mother." R. Obadiah Bertinoro, renowned commentator to the Mishnah, propounds the following explanation:

> This phrase was added, explaining why it was that Rebecca chose to send Jacob away to Laban. The latter was his kinsman to whom he would be able to speak freely about the strife between himself and his brother Esau. He would not have been able to relate such matters to strangers, since it would not be becoming to discuss family quarrels with them.

The author of *Ha'amek Davar* makes a more plausible suggestion:

> Isaac's sending Jacob away did not not look like flight from the vengeance of his brother, since Laban was the uncle of them both.

But we must look for a more satisfactory answer, in the general context, and not limit ourselves to the immediate one. The key to the problem certainly lies in Rebecca's words to Jacob in 27, 45: "Why should I be bereaved of you both in one day?" We shall again cite several interpretations of the text:

לָמָה אֶשְׁכַּל גַּם־שְׁנֵיכֶם יוֹם אֶחָד.

"גם שניכם": אם יקום עליך ואתה תהרגנו, יעמדו בניו ויהרגוך.

> "you both." If he will rise up against thee and thou wilt slay him, his sons will stand forth and slay thee . . .   (Rashi)
> If lhe will slay thee, he will also be slain by the revengers of blood   (Rashbam)
> "you both"—thy father and thyself. Esau had said, "just wait for the days of my father's mourning." This meant that the moment Isaac died, Esau would kill Jacob, so that Rebecca would be bereaved of both of them—her husband and son—in one day.
>   (Ḥizkuni)

Let us examine the foregoing three explanations. Why did Rashi choose to speak of Jacob slaying Esau, when it was the latter who sought to slay his brother, Surely Rebecca feared for Jacob's life.. Why did Rashi have to resort to such a farfetched interpretation, intimating that Jacob would be forced into slaying his brother in self-defence? .Apparently his explanation was dictated by the phrase "you both." If Esau killed Jacob, the latter had no kinsmen to avenge his blood and there would then only be one slaying. Rashi therefore explained that Rebecca was referring to the contingency of Jacob killing Esau in self-defence, in which case, it was most likely that Esau's sons would avenge their father, and slay their uncle. Thus she would be bereaved of *both* in one day. Still the interpretation remains forced.

Rashbam therefore suggested a different explanation, that Rebecca indeed feared for Jacob's life and the subsequent slaying of the murderer by the revengers of the blood. But who was there to avenge Jacob's life? Furthermore, who could say, with certainty, that the wheel would turn full circle, within the space of one day, and that the revengers would accomplish their task with such despatch?

These difficulties led Ḥizkuni to take a different line, and propound his subtler interpretation, identifying the "both" with Jacob and his father. But the objection to this is the use of the expression of "bereave" (*eshkal*) which, at anyrate, is in Hebrew limited to the loss of children. The Hebrew word *almon*— "widowed" is used with respect of loss of husband. Cf. Isaiah 47, 9: "But these two things shall come to thee in a moment in one day, the loss of children (*shekhol*), and widowhood (*almon*)."

After we have absorbed and compared the foregoing three explanations, we shall undoubtedly prefer the one advanced by the Italian Jewish commentator Benamozegh quoted herewith:

> Rebecca said: Whichever of you will be slain I shall be bereaved in one day, since one will be no more, slain, and the murderer of his brother will be detested by me as an enemy and stranger, and will be, in my eyes, as non-existing. I will thus be bereaved of **both of them.**
>
> (Em Lemikra)

This would seem to fit the intention of the verse. At one and the same moment the perpetrator of fratricide and the victim would be no more (one, physically, the other mentally, shut out of her mind) and their mother would have lost two children, as a result of the one deed of murder. Now we can revert to our first question. What prompted the Torah, after Rebecca had connived at Jacob's escape from his brother's vengeance to mention that she was the mother of them both? The interpretation advanced in *Tzeda Laderekh* fits in with the approach that we have now arrived at. The text wished to teach us that Rebecca rescued Jacob from death, not just in her role as the mother of Jacob. She was acting as the mother of Esau, too, in preventing him murdering his brother. Though we have, hitherto, seen her, during the whole story, as acting only in the interests of her younger son Jacob, in this hour of mortal peril, she laid plans, carefully and prudently, as "Jacob's and Esau's mother," so that she should not be bereaved of both of them in one day.

Questions for Further Study

1. Cf.: Now therefore, my son obey my voice and arise, *flee* thou to Laban my brother, to Haran   (Gen. 27, 43)

    Arise, *go* to Padan-aram, to the house of Bethuel, thy mother's brother   (28, 2)

    Abravanel asks why Isaac deviated from the wording of his mother's command telling Jacob to "go ... to Bethuel" rather than "flee ... to Laban," especially, in view of the fact that it is clearly stated that, "Jacob went to Padan-aram, to Laban ..." as his mother had enjoined. Suggest an answer.

2. Flee thou to Laban my brother, to Haran (27, 43)
    Wolf Heidenheim, the renowned Jewish liturgical and grammatical scholar distinguished between the usages of the two Hebrew words for "flee": *nus* and *barah*. The former refers to the flight from immediate, visible danger, from a pursuer, the latter from a place pursued by no one, the action being dictated by a wish to avoid danger in the future.

    (a) Explain, in the light of his distinction, the reason why our text employs *barah* and not *nus*.

    (b) Cite other texts supporting Heidenheim's distinction.

3. Until thy brother's fury turn away;
    Until thy brother's anger turn away from thee
    (27, 44, 45)

Heidenheim observes:

Since man becomes heated during his anger, this is termed in Hebrew *ḥema* from a root meaning hot (*ham*) ... the heat of the person in anger bears a relationship to the subject alone, producing anger or rancour against the object or cause of the provocation. This state of heat precedes the anger taking a definite form against a particular person or object. The fury or heat is then directed towards its object which, as a result, usually becomes known.

Explain how Heidenheim's distinction explains the unusual wording of our text. Study carefully the Hebrew text.

[1] Cf.: Deuteronomy 1, 4: "Sihon, the king of the Amorites who dwelt *in Heshbon*, Og, the king of Bashan, who dwelt at Astaroth." See Rashi *ad loc*. Cf. also: Genesis 25, 20: "When he took Rebecca to wife, the daughter of *Bethuel the Syrian* of *Padan-aram*, the sister to *Laban the Syrian*. See Rashi *ad loc*.

MY NAME IS GREAT AMONG THE NATIONS

The title is taken from the week's Haftara which, like the sidra
is concerned with the struggle between Jacob and Esau. There
are two verses at its beginning alluding to this subject which
present a difficulty:

הֲלוֹא־אָח עֵשָׂו לְיַעֲקֹב – נְאֻם יְיָ
וָאֹהַב אֶת־יַעֲקֹב.
וְאֶת־עֵשָׂו שָׂנֵאתִי
וָאָשִׂים אֶת־הָרָיו שְׁמָמָה
וְאֶת־נַחֲלָתוֹ לְתַנּוֹת מִדְבָּר.

Was not Esau Jacob's brother? said the Lord;
yet I loved Jacob;
but Esau I hated,
and made his mountains a desolation,
and gave his heritage to the jackals of the wilderness.

(Malachi 1, 2–3)

Rashi comments:

"ואהב את יעקב": לתת לו ארץ חמדה, "נחלת צבי צבאות גויים" (כנאמר
בירמיה ג, יט), ארץ שצביון כל צבאות גויים בה.
"ואת עשו שנאתי": לדוחפו אל ארץ שעיר מפני יעקב אחיו.

"He loved Jacob" to give him a pleasant land, "the goodliest
heritage of the nations" (after Jer. 3, 19), a land to which all
the hosts of nations assembled. "But Esau I hated"—to drive him
to the land of Seir from before Jacob his brother . . .

As the verse emphasises, their origins and pedigree were no
different. Why then, in one case did God hate and, in the other,
love? Was partiality involved? Yet this same prophet who
makes this apparent discrimination between the two brothers

proceeds in verse 11 to strike a wholly different and unusual note:

כִּי מִמִּזְרַח־שֶׁמֶשׁ וְעַד־מְבוֹאוֹ
גָּדוֹל שְׁמִי בַּגּוֹיִם
וּבְכָל־מָקוֹם מֻקְטָר מֻגָּשׁ לִשְׁמִי
וּמִנְחָה טְהוֹרָה
כִּי־גָדוֹל שְׁמִי בַּגּוֹיִם
אָמַר יְיָ צְבָאוֹת.

For from the rising of the sun even unto the going down of the same, My name is great among the nations;
and in every place offerings are presented to My name, even pure oblations;
for My name is great among the nations, saith the Lord of hosts.
(Malachi, 1, 11)

The above passage is a unique example in Scripture of generous praise accorded to all mankind, with regard to their acknowledgement of their Creator. Rashi cites two explanations of the passage both echoing the words of our Sages.

"גדול שמי בגוים": אמרו רבותינו (מנחות קי, ע"א): "דקרו ליה אלהא
דאלהיא", אפילו מי שיש לו עבודה זרה, יודע שיש אלוה שהוא על כולם,
ובכל מקום מתנדבים לשמי אף האומות.
ורבותינו פירשו : אלו תלמידי חכמים העוסקים בהלכות עבודה בכל מקום.
וכן [על פי] במדבר רבה יג, ו] כל תפילות ישראל שמתפללים בכל מקום,
הרי הן לי כמנחה טהורה.
וכן תרגם יונתן: "ובכל עידן דאתון עבדין רעותי [ובכל מקום שבו אתם
עושים רצוני] אנא אקבל צלותכון [אני מקבל תפילתכם], ושמי רבא מתקדש
ידיכון, וצלותהכון כקורבן דכי [זכאי] קדמי.
וכן פירש המקרא : ולמה אתם מחללים שמי והלוא גדול הוא בגויים, ואני
אהבתי וחיבתי עליכם, שבכל מקום שאתם מתפללים לפני, ואף בגולה מוקטר
ומיגש הוא לשמי ו"מנחה טהורה" הוא לי, כי על ידכם גדול שמי בגויים.

"My name is great among the nations"—that they call him the God of gods. Even he who worships idols knows that there is a God over all of them and in every place even the gentiles offer willingly to My name. Our Rabbis explained that the passage refers to the Torah scholars who are engaged in the study of the Divine service in every place. Similarly, they interpret that all the prayers of Israel that they pray in every place are to me like a pure oblation. The Targum Jonathan gave a similar explanation: "Wherever you do My will, I accept your prayers and My great name is hallowed through you, and your prayers are like a pure oblation before me." The passage should thus read: Why do you profane My name; surely it is great among the nations and My love and affection is for you; for wherever you pray to Me even in the Exile your offerings are presented to My name, and are a pure oblation before Me, since through you My name is great among the nations.

Two contrasting explanations are cited by Rashi in the name of the Sages. Is His name great among the nations because even the gentiles offer up to His name or is the reference to the Jewish people who are scattered among the nations? Rambam in his *Guide* enlarges on this subject:

You know that no idolater worships his idol in the conviction that there is no other god beside. No man either in the past or future imagines that that the image he made of metal, stone or wood, actually created the heaven and earth and governs them. But they serve it as a symbol mediating between them and the Divine, as the prophet explained when he said "Who would not fear Thee, King of the nations . . ." and: "and in every place offerings are presented to My name, for My name is great among the nations" alluding to the Prime Cause as far as they are concerned. We have already explained this in 'our great compilation.[1] No Torah authority of ours will dispute this fact.

Judah Even Shemuel explains the above passage in his commentary (Tel Aviv 1935) as follows:

Here Rambam unfolds for us the chapter of idolatry and shows it in a new light. It is not a worship of wood and stone but an outlook on the world concerned with communing with the media that stand between us and God; but it is a mistaken outlook and since it relates to the Divine it constitutes a very serious and harmful mistake. Every idolater knows there is only One God in the universe. If he fails to direct his worship to Him, this is only because he sees God as too far above him, too transcendent, whereas the other god is nearer to him But he actually only worships the latter symbolically. The truth is that idolaters do not worship the image except insofar as it serves as a symbol of mediator between man and God. The Baal and Ashtoreth, for instance, serve as symbols of fertility—the angel standing between God and the world presiding over fertility.

"And in every place offerings are presented to My name" alluding to the Prime Cause as far as they are concerned. Even the idolaters accept God as the Prime Cause ... The acknowledgement of God is not the heritage of the children of Israel only, but all mankind have attained it because they are human. It is part of their natural perception to acknowledge the Divine and a realisation of the unity of the source of the whole universe is implicit in their make-up. Rambam's reference to his "great compilation" alludes to chapter one of the laws of idolatry in the Code.[1] "No Torah authority of ours will dispute this fact."—We do not imagine that only we have achieved a recognition of the existence of God and we do not say that members of other faiths repudiate the existence of God.

The views of Rambam expressed here harmonise with those of our Sages cited by Rashi in his first explanation. Ibn Gabirol has expressed these sentiments in his inimitable poetic form in his *Keter Malchut*:

אתה אלוהי האלוהים
וכל הברואים עדיך
ובכבוד זה השם נתחייב כל נברא לעובדך.
אתה אלוה
וכל היצורים עבדיך ועובדיך
ולא יחסר כבודך
בגלל עובדי בלעדיך
כי כוונת כולם להגיע עדיך.

Thou art the God of Gods
and all creatures pay homage to Thee
and every created thing has been obliged to serve Thee with the honour due to Thy name.
Thou art God and all creatures are Thy servants and serve Thee
and Thy glory suffers no diminuiton on account of those who serve others beside Thee,
since the intention of all of them is to achieve communion with Thee.

What connection has the interpretation we have given for our passage from Malachi with the context? Rashi in his first explanation adheres to the plain sense of Scripture. The prophet is rebuking Israel. God has no delight in their worship if they serve him in such a manner that His name is profaned among the nations. God has other worshippers beside Israel; for all that is created He created for His glory and even they intend to pay homage to him. Abravanel elaborates on this theme:

> You should have learnt from the ways of the nations. Though they have not been vouchsafed the light of the Torah ... they magnify and exalt Him and perform the most pure sacrifice that they themselves are capable of doing according to their lights.

Let us now revert to our first question: Why did God then hate Esau? Not because He displayed partiality but because Esau deliberately chose a course of wickedness. Radak explains:

> For their wickedness had become exceeding great before the Lord, in that they dealt treacherously with the sons of Jacob whereas God had commanded Israel, "Thou shalt not abominate an Edomite for he is thy brother." But they dealt evilly with them with the maximum of their spite and rejoiced in their destruction and exile.

The text therefore says of their land that:

They shall be called the border of wickedness

(Malachi 1, 4)

Questions for Further Study

1. Why does Rambam in his *Guide* (cited above) utilise both the passage from Malachi and Jeremiah, whereas in his Code in the laws of idolatry he cites only the passage from Jeremiah and does not mention the other passage from Malachi?

2. In verse ten of Malachi chapter 1, we read: "O that there were among you that would shut the doors, that ye might not kindle fire on Mine altar in vain! I have no pleasure in you, saith the Lord of hosts, neither will I accept an offering at your hand."

296

Rambam quotes the above passage in the Laws of Repentance in his Code:

כמה מעולה מעלת התשובה. אמש היה זה מובדל מה׳ אלוהי ישראל, שנאמר
(ישעיה נט, ב): "עונותיכם היו מבדילים ביניכם לבין אלהיכם", צועק ואינו
נענה, שנאמר (ישעיה א, טו): "גם כי תרבו תפילה אינני שומע", ועושה
מצוות ושורפין אותן בפניו, שנאמר (ישעיה א, יב): "מי בקש זאת מידכם
רמוס חצרי", (מלאכי א, י): "מי גם בכם ויסגור דלתים ולא תאירו מזבחי
הנם אין לי חפץ בכם — ומנחה לא ארצה מידכם". והיום הוא מודבק בשכינה,
שנאמר (דברים ד, ד): "ואתם הדבקים בה׳ אלהיכם", צועק ונענה מיד,
שנאמר (ישעיה סה, כד): "טרם יקראו ואני אענה" ועושה מצוות ומקבלין
אותן בנחת ושמחה, שנאמר (קהלת ט, ז): "כי כבר רצה האלהים את מעשיך",
ולא עוד אלא שמתאוים להם, שנאמר (מלאכי ג, ד): "וערבה לה׳ מנחת
יהודה וירושלים כימי עולם וכשנים קדמוניות".

How powerful is the impact of repentance (*teshuva*)! Yester this man was divorced from the God of Israel, as it is stated: (Isa. 59, 2): "Your iniquities separated between you and your God," crying out to Him and not answered. as it is stated (ibid. 1, 15): "Though you make many prayers I will not hear"; he performs precepts but they are burnt in His presence. as it is stated (ibid. 1. 12): "Who hath required this at your hand. to trample My courts?", "O that there were among you that would shut the doors that ye might not kindle fire on Mine altar in vain!" (Mal. 1. 10). Today he has clung to the Divine Presence as it is stated: And ye that did cling to the Lord . . ." (Deut. 4, 4); he cries and is answered forthwith (Isa.65, 24): "Before they cry I answer," and performs precepts which are accepted with satisfaction and joy, as it is stated (Eccles. 9, 7): "For the Lord hath already accepted thy deeds." Furthermore they are yearned for, as it is stated: "Then shall the offering of Judah and Jerusalem be pleasant unto the Lord, as in the days of old and as in ancient years."

(a) Rambam places the verses from Isaiah chapter I beside our passage. What did he wish to demonstrate through his citation of both of them? What similarity did he find between them,

(b) If we read the verses from Isaiah and then from Malachi. each one within the context of its respective chapter, what difference between them emerges from this linking to their contexts?

---

[1] The reference is to the *Mishneh Torah*. Maimonides' great code of Jewish law in chapter one of the Laws of Idolatry. cited on p. 109.

JACOB'S DREAM

God first reveals himself to Jacob, fleeing from his brother and birthplace, wandering at night in the desert, sleeping in the open with a stone for a pillow, through the medium of a dream.

A modern German Jewish commentator, Benno Jacob, in his work on *Genesis* divides the various dreams occurring in *Genesis* into one of two categories.

The first class comprise those in which God actually speaks to man (20, 3; 31, 24), the second class, those dreams through whose medium, God speaks to man. Examples of the latter are the dreams of Joseph, the chief butler, the chief baker and Pharaoh. The second class are usually in the form of parables, word-pictures which require elucidation.

In Jacob's dream God actually addresses Jacob. Before that, however, comes the picture which calls for our interpretation. Indeed there have been many attempts at such interpretation.

Let us quote the pictorial part of Jacob's dream, the interpretation of which has preoccupied so many expositors, writers and poets down the ages:

וְהִנֵּה סֻלָּם מֻצָּב אַרְצָה וְרֹאשׁוֹ מַגִּיעַ הַשָּׁמָיְמָה
וְהִנֵּה מַלְאֲכֵי אֱלֹהִים עֹלִים וְיֹרְדִים בּוֹ.
וְהִנֵּה יְיָ נִצָּב עָלָיו – – –

And behold a **ladder set upon the earth**
And behold **the angels of God ascending and descending on it**
And behold **the Lord stood above it**   (28, 12, 13)

The following is one of the manifold Midrashic interpretations of the dream, occurring in *Midrash Tanhuma*:

אמר ר' שמואל בר' נחמן: "והנה מלאכי אלהים עולים ויורדים" — אלה שרי
אומות העכו"ם... שהראה לו הקב"ה ליעקב אבינו שר של בבל עולה שבעים
עוקים [שלבים] ויורד, ושל מדי — חמשים ושנים [ויורד], ושל יוון מאה
[שלבים] ויורד, ושל אדום עולה ולא ידע כמה. באותה שעה
נתיירא יעקב אבינו ואמר: שמא לזה אין לו ירידה? אמר לו הקב"ה (ירמיה
ל, י): "ואתה אל תירא עבדי יעקב... ואל תחת ישראל" — כביכול אפילו
רואהו עולה ויושב אצלי — משם אני מורידו! שנאמר (עובדיה א, ד): "אם
תגביה כנשר ואם בין כוכבים שים קנך, משם אורידך נאום ה'".

"And behold the angels of God ascending and descending": These
are the princes of the heathen nations which God showed Jacob
our father. The Prince of Babylon ascended seventy steps and
descended, Media, fifty-two and descended, Greece, one hundred
steps and descended, Edom ascended and no one knows how many!
In that hour, Jacob was afraid and said: 'Peradventure, this one
has no descent?' Said the Holy One blessed be He to him: 'Therefore fear thou not, O my servant Jacob . . . neither be dismayed,
O Israel'. Even if thou seest him, so to speak, ascend and sit by
Me, thence will I bring him down! As it is stated (*Obadiah*, 1, 4):
'Though thou exalt thyself as the eagle, and thou set thy nest
among the stars, thence will I bring thee down, saith the Lord."

This Midrash likewise inspired Sforno's comment on the dream:

"Ascending and descending"—Indeed ultimately, having gained
ascendancy, the gentile princes will go down, and the Almighty
who forever stands above, will not forsake His people as He
promised (Jer. 30,11): For I will make a full end of all the
nations whither I have scattered you, but I will not make a full
end of you.

According to the Midrash, Jacob's dream depicts the rise and
fall of nations and their cultures on the arena of world history.
What has this to do with Jacob's situation, his flight to Padan-
Aram from the wrath of his brother, his mission to choose a wife
and carry on the seed of Abraham and Isaac? In answer, it
may be said, that the Midrash regards the dream, not as referring
merely to Jacob the individual, but Jacob as the symbol of Israel,
the embodiment of the wanderings of the Jewish people, as it is
exiled from one country to another and witnesses the rise and
fall of mighty kingdoms, Egypt, Assyria, Babylon, Persia and
Greece. The author of the Midrash who lived during the period
of the Roman Empire had not yet witnessed its decline and fall.
Rome and the spiritual successors that took its place in Europe

299

afterwards are known in medieval Rabbinic terminology by the name of "Edom." Their downfall is likewise foretold. The Jewish people apprehensive at the apparently never-ending reign of the oppressor, seeing no sign of his impending doom, cries "Peradventure, this one has no descent"—perhaps he is never going Jacob, and the Divine message of reassurance is to be found in the message of Obadiah, the prophet of the ultimate doom of Edom.

> **Though thou exalt thyself as the eagle,**
> **and thou set thy nest among the stars,**
> **thence will I bring thee down, saith the Lord.** (Ob. 1, 4)

Jacob's ladder is taken to imply the ladder of history. The ascent of one nation on it implies the descent of its predecessor. The ladder is not an endless one, but the Lord stands at its top, as the master of history, assuring us that pride and despotism will be brought low, until His sovereignty alone is recognised at the end of days. This "latter-day" vision is described to us by Isaiah (2).

Rashi has however a completely different approach to the text. He sticks to its plain sense. The subject of the narrative is Jacob the Patriarch on his journey to Padan-Aram, in flight from his brother. Rashi has the following question to raise regarding the words: "ascending and descending":

First they ascend and afterwards descend?

Surely, Rashi queries, the angels, the denizens of the Heavens should first have descended; the order should be the reverse. Rashi answers:

‏... מלאכים שליווהו בארץ אין יוצאים חוצה לארץ; ועלו לרקיע, וירדו
‏מלאכי חוצה לארץ ללוותו.

The angels that accompanied him in the Holy Land do not go outside the Holy Land. They therefore ascended to Heaven. Then the angels of outside the Holy Land descended to accompany him.

In other words, man's experiences in his own country are not to be compared with his situation in a strange land. To make his way on foreign soil, he needed different guardians from those that protected him in his own birthplace, amidst familiar landmarks. But wherever he went, Jacob was always furnished with Divine protection.

Rashi's brief remark fits the picture described in the sidra perfectly. The angels of "outside the Holy Land" accompany Jacob throughout his tribulations, from the moment he leaves Beer-sheba (28, 10) to his return to Mahanaim (32, 3), after spending twenty years in exile. There he is again confronted by angels—the guardian angels of the Homeland:

> **And Jacob went on his way, and the angels of God met him.** (33, 2)

These experiences are echoed by the Psalmist in reference not to Jacob the Patriarch, but to the descendants of Jacob:

$$כִּי מַלְאָכָיו יְצַוֶּה־לָּךְ לִשְׁמָרְךָ בְּכָל־דְּרָכֶיךָ.$$
$$עַל־כַּפַּיִם יִשָּׂאוּנְךָ פֶּן־תִּגֹּף בָּאֶבֶן רַגְלֶךָ.$$

> **For He shall give His angels charge over thee,**
> **to keep thee in thy ways.**
> **They shall bear thee up in their hands,**
> **lest thou dash thy foot against a stone.**
>
> (Psalm, 91, 11, 12)

Questions for Further Study

1.   Rambam treats of the parables and allegorical descriptions in the Bible in his introduction to his *Guide*. Here we quote the relevant remarks.

     Know the figures employed by the Prophets are of two kinds: those where every single word in the parable or allegory is significant, and those where it is only that the parable as a whole is significant, the details of the descriptions being only incidental,

301

adding nothing significant to the idea which is being projected. They are merely ornamental or designed to conceal the idea that is being allegorically described.

An example of the first class of prophetic figures is to be found in *Genesis*: "And, behold, a ladder set up on the earth, and the top of it reached to heaven; and, behold, the angels of God ascending and descending on it" (Genesis 28, 12). The word "ladder" refers to one idea; "set up on the earth" to another; "and the top of it reached to heaven" to a third; "angels of God" to a fourth; "ascending" to a fifth; "descending" to a sixth; "the Lord stood above it" (verse 13) to a seventh. Every word in this figure introduces a fresh element into the idea represented by the figure.

An example of the second class of prophetic figures is found in Proverbs (7, 6–23): ' For at the window of my house I looked through my casement, and beheld among the simple ones; I discerned among the youths a young man void of understanding. passing through the street near her corner: and he went the way to her house in the twilight, in the evening, in the black and dark night: and, behold, there met him a woman with the attire of a harlot, and subtil of heart. She is loud and stubborn; her feet abide not in her house ... So she caught him, and kissed him, and with an impudent face said unto him, I have peace offerings with me, this day I paid my vows. Therefore came I forth to meet thee, diligently to seek thy face, and I have found thee. I have decked my bed with coverings of tapestry, with striped cloths of the yarn of Egypt ... Come let us take our fill of love until the morning ... For the goodman is not at home ... he hath taken a bag of money with him, and will come home at the day appointed. With her much fair speech she caused him to yield, with the flattering of her lips she forced him. He goeth after her straightway, as an ox goeth to the slaughter ... as a bird hasteth to the snare, and knoweth not that it is for his life."

The general principle expounded in all these verses is to abstain from excessive indulgence in bodily pleasures ... that man shall not be entirely guided by his animal, or material nature ... An adequate explanation of the figure having been given, and its meaning having been shown, do not imagine that you will find in its application a corresponding element for each part of the figure; you must not ask what is meant by "I have peace offerings with me" (verse 14), ... or what is added to the force of

ings with me" (verse 14); ... or what is added to the force of
the figure by the observation "for the goodman is not at home" ..
For all this is merely to complete the illustration of the metaphor
in its literal meaning.

Which of these two different approaches to Jacob's dream informs
the comments of Midrash Tanḥuma, Rashi and Sforno?

2. And, behold, the Lord stood *alav* ...[1]

(Genesis 28, 13)

On what—Jacob or the ladder? Answer in accordance with
the various points of view formulated by our commentators
regarding the dream as a whole.

3. Compare the following Midrash with the one cited in our
Studies. Both interpret Jacob's ladder:

"ויחלום והנה סלם מצב ארצה וראשו מגיע השמימה והנה מלאכי אלהים
עולים ויורדים בו" — אלו שרי אומות העולם. מלמד שהראה לו הקב"ה
ליעקב שרו של בבל עולה ויורד ושל מדי עולה ויורד ושל יון עולה ויורד
ושל אדום עולה ויורד. אמר הקב"ה ליעקב: יעקב, למה אין אתה עולה?
באותה שעה נתיירא אבינו יעקב ואמר: כשם שיש לאלו ירידה, כך יש לי
ירידה?! אמר לו: אם אתה עולה, אין לך ירידה! לא האמין ולא עלה.
ר"ש בן יוסינה היה דורש: (תהלים עח, עב): "בכל זאת חטאו עוד ולא
האמינו בנפלאותיו". אמר לו הקב"ה: אילו עלית והאמנת [נוסח ויקרא רבה:
"אילו האמנת ועלית" — ושים לב!], לא היתה לך ירידה לעולם, אלא הואיל
ולא האמנת, הרי בניך משתעבדין בהללו ארבע מלכויות בעולם הזה. אמר
לו יעקב: יכול לעולם? אמר לו: "אל תירא עבדי יעקב ואל תחת ישראל,
כי הנני מושיעך מרחוק ואת זרעך מארץ שבים" — מגליא ומאספניא
ומחברותיה. "ושב יעקב" — מבבל, "ושקט" — ממדי, "ושאנן" — מיון, "ואין
מחריד" — מאדום.
"ואותך לא אעשה כלה" — אלא מיסרך ביסורים בשביל לזכותך מעוונותיך
ולצרף אותך.

"... behold the angels of God ascending and descending"—referring to the princes of the nations. The text teaches that the
Holy One blessed be He showed Jacob the prince of Babylon
ascending and descending and that of Medea, Greece and Edom
(Rome) doing likewise. Said the Holy One blessed be He to
Jacob: Jacob, why don't you ascend? At that moment Jacob our
father was afraid. He said: Am I to suffer a descent just the same
as these? He said to him: If you ascend, you shall suffer no
descent. He did not believe and did not ascend.

R. Shimon b. Yosina used to expound the text (Ps. 78. 72): "For all this they sinned still and believed not His wondrous works." Said the Holy One blessed be He to him: Had you ascended and believed (Vayikra Rabbah version: "Had you believed and ascended"—note difference) you would never have experienced a descent. But since you had no faith, your children will be enslaved by these four kingdoms in this world. Said Jacob to him: For ever? He answered: "Fear not My servant Jacob and be not dismayed Israel, for I shall save thee from afar and thy seed from the land of their captivity"—from Gaul from Spain and its neighbours. "Jacob shall return" from Babylon, "and be tranquil" from Medea; "and at ease"—from Greece, "with none to make them afraid" from Edom. "And of thee I shall not completely destroy" but will chastise you with sufferings in order to quit you from your iniquities and refine you.[2]

(Pesikta Derav Cahana)

(a) What is the difference in the approach of the two Midrashim?

(b) What does the ladder symbol (without the angels) in the two?

---

[1] The Hebrew is ambiguous and may be translated "upon him," or: "upon it." The usual translation is: "beside him."

[2] For a penetrating and satisfying explanation of this Midrash see Buber's essay *Herut Ve-yi'ud* Zionist Library, Jerusalem 5720 — pp. 215-217.

JACOB'S VOW

Jacob was vouchsafed in his dream the fulfillment of all that man could desire, and particularly, a man leaving his country and father's house:

וְהִנֵּה אָנֹכִי עִמָּךְ
וּשְׁמַרְתִּיךָ בְּכֹל אֲשֶׁר־תֵּלֵךְ
וַהֲשִׁבֹתִיךָ אֶל־הָאֲדָמָה הַזֹּאת
כִּי לֹא אֶעֱזָבְךָ
עַד אֲשֶׁר אִם־עָשִׂיתִי
אֵת אֲשֶׁר־דִּבַּרְתִּי לָךְ.

Behold I am with thee, and will protect thee wherever thou goest, and will bring thee again into this land; for I will not forsake thee, until I have done that which I have spoken to thee of.   (28, 15)

On awakening in the morning he vowed a vow, the first recorded vow in the Bible:

אִם־יִהְיֶה אֱלֹהִים עִמָּדִי
וּשְׁמָרַנִי בַּדֶּרֶךְ הַזֶּה אֲשֶׁר אָנֹכִי הוֹלֵךְ
וְנָתַן־לִי לֶחֶם לֶאֱכֹל וּבֶגֶד לִלְבֹּשׁ.
וְשַׁבְתִּי בְשָׁלוֹם אֶל־בֵּית אָבִי —
וְהָיָה יְיָ לִי לֵאלֹהִים.
וְהָאֶבֶן הַזֹּאת אֲשֶׁר־שַׂמְתִּי מַצֵּבָה
יִהְיֶה בֵּית אֱלֹהִים
וְכֹל אֲשֶׁר תִּתֶּן־לִי
עַשֵּׂר אֲעַשְּׂרֶנּוּ לָךְ.

If God will be with me, and will protect me on the way that I go, and will give me bread to eat, and raiment to put on;

so that I come again to my father's house in peace; then shall the Lord be my God:

And this stone, which I have set up as a pillar, shall be God's house: and of all that Thou shalt give me I will surely give the tenth unto Thee. (28, 20-22)

The wording of this vow raises a number of problems. Odd indeed is Jacob's reaction to the generous Divine promise to protect him and bring him back to his homeland. Was it right of the patriarch thus to react? Should he have conditioned his loyalty to God and acceptance of His yoke on the receipt of certain material benefits? Here is Abravanel's formulation of the problem:

> How could Jacob act like those who serve upon the condition of receiving a reward, by saying, "If God will be with me and keep me and give me..." so and so, then he would accept Him as his God. Conversely, then, if He would not perform these things for him, He would *not* be his God and he would not serve Him? His grandfather Abraham did not act thus, but was tried many times and withstood temptation.

Various answers have been given to this problem which has been dwelt on by the Sages of old:

> "וידר יעקב נדר...". — וכי עלתה על לב שהיה יעקב אבינו אומר: "אם יהיה אלהים עמדי ושמרני... ונתן לי... ושבתי בשלום... והיה ה' לי לאלהים"? [כביכול — ואם לאו אינו לי לאלוהים?— על פי הילקוט]. מה תלמוד לומר: "והיה ה' לי לאלהים"? — שיחול שמו עלי, שלא תצא ממני פסולת מתחילה ועד סוף.

> "And Jacob vowed a vow." Was it thinkable that Jacob should have uttered these words: "If God will be with me and keep me... and give me... so that I come... in peace, then shall the Lord be my God." Otherwise, so to speak, He is not my God!? But what does the text: "then shall the Lord be my God" really mean?—That His name should be linked with me, that nothing unfit should come forth from me, from the beginning to the end. (Sifrei)

306

Rashi and Rashbam echo this same approach:

„והיה ה׳ לי לאלוהים״: שיסייעני בכל מעשי.

"And the Lord shall be my God"—to help me in all my works.

The abovequoted authorities thus do not regard the phrase: "the Lord shall be my God" as the beginning of the apodosis, marking the consequent and concluding main clause of the conditional sentence as the King James' version has it (by translating the Hebrew conjunctive *vav* by "then"). But they regard it as still part of the protasis, belonging to the conditional half of the sentence. Jacob's promise consisted of two parts only— that he would build God's house on the spot, if it was granted him to return there, and give a tithe of all his worldly goods to Him.

But another objection still remains—one often employed as a weapon against us by malicious critics. How come Jacob to make a commercial "deal" with his Maker, offer something in exchange for favours? We may answer that no "deal" is involved. But if God would not grant him to return to his father's house, how would he be able to erect a temple on the spot? All that Jacob's vow implied was: "Give me the possibility of serving You." It provides the archetype for future formulators of vows which are not meant to be commercial deals with the Almighty but petitions for His help in granting man opportunity to give of himself, his life and soul to God. Hannah's vow falls in the same category: "if Thou wilt indeed take note of the affliction of Thine handmaid and grant unto Thine handmaid a man child, then will I give him unto the Lord" implying, Give me so that I can give to You.

But still another question may be asked regarding Jacob's vow. Why did Jacob have to utter the words: "If God will . . . keep me . . ." after all these things had been explicitly promised him a few moments earlier: "And behold I will be with thee and will protect thee"? Was Jacob doubting the word of God and showing lack of faith in the efficacy of the Divine promise? Our Sages in the Midrash dealt with this point:

ר' אייבו ור' יונתן: חד אמר: מסורסת היא הפרשה]היינו, הדברים קרו
שלא כפי הסדר שנכתבו, תחילה התפלל: "אם יהיה אלהים עמדי" ואחר כך
באו דברי ה' בחלומו: "והנה אנכי עמך"[, וחד אמר: על הסדר נאמרה. מאן
דאמר: מסורסת היא הפרשה, שכבר הבטיחו הקב"ה: "והנה עמך עמך" והוא
אומר: "אם יהיה אלהים עמדי" — אתמהא?! מאן דאמר: על הסדר נאמרה —
מה מקיים: "אם יהיה אלהים עמדי"? אלא כך אמר יעקב: אם יתקיימו בי
התנאים שאמר לי להיות עמדי ולשומרני — אני אקיים את נדרי.

R. Aibu and R. Jonathan. One of them stated: The narrative requires rearranging (chronologically speaking, Jacob's vow was
uttered before the Divine promise to keep him etc.). The other
stated: It requires no rearrangement. The one who said the order
was wrong, said so, because he wondered how it was possible
for Jacob to say, *If* God will be with me, when God had already
promised to be with him? How does the one who maintains that
everything is in the right order understand the words: "If God
will be with me"? But this is what Jacob meant. If the conditions
that God promised me—to be with me and protect me, are fulfilled, then I will keep my vow. (Bereshit Rabbah)

According to the first view, that the order is wrong, Jacob's vow
was not a reaction to the Divine promise but the reverse. Jacob
prayed and petitioned for guardianship and protection and made
his promises and vowed his vow: "If God will be with me," after
which came the dream and the blessings as an answer to his
prayer. According to this Midrash, the Almighty only reveals
Himself after man has approached Him first, in the sense of:
"The Lord is nigh unto all of them that call upon Him, to all
that call on Him in truth." The reason why the first mentioned
authority wished to change the order of the narrative was because
it implied Jacob's lack of faith in the Divine promise. How does
the second mentioned authority meet this objection without changing the order? Surely his answer: "If the conditions that God
promised me are fulfilled" hardly meets the objection. Jacob
is still casting doubts on the certainty of the Divine promise. But
we must understand the Midrash to mean: If I prove worthy of
all those promises. The promises of protection to the righteous
are not absolute and unconditional, but depend on him maintaining his standards of conduct and not deviating to an evil
path. The righteous man cannot assume that he has been granted

an irrevocable title deed to comfort and protection, and he has no longer to stand in awe of his Master but can do as he likes. On the contrary, man stands in judgement at every moment of existence, and at any time, his judgement can change.[1] This point, too, is made in the Midrash:

רב הונא בשם ר' אחא אמר: כתיב: "הנה אנכי עמך" וכתיב: "א ם יהיה אלהים עמדי"? אלא מכאן שאין הבטחה לצדיק בעולם הזה.

R. Huna said in the name of R. Aḥa: It is stated: "And behold I am with thee" and it is also stated: "*If* God will be with me"? But from here we may conclude that there is no promise for the righteous in this world.   (Bereshit Rabba)

Ramban explains that the "reason for the condition, the 'if' qualification, was lest sin should intervene." Jacob then did not, God forbid, cast doubts on the Almighty's word, displayed no lack of faith but impugned his own ability to keep faith with Him. Perhaps, as a result of his long stay at Laban's in alien environment, he might succumb to heathen influences. He doubted his own ability to withstand temptation. He might not ultimately prove worthy of the kindnesses promised him by God. Perhaps sin would soil him. Jacob did not cast doubts on God or His credibility, but on himself and his capacity to withstand temptation.[2]

Questions for Further Study

1.   Compare with the Sifrei and Rashbam quoted at the beginning of our *Studies* the following two views:

"The Lord shall be my God"—this statement includes all the details from "If God will be with me" as far as "to my father's house."
                                                                    (Biur)

The sense of the text supports Ramban that it is the consequent cause, and not Rashi's view. It means that he would not rely on his own might and the power of his hand, but would keep the Lord continually in front of him to lead him. Whilst away from home, with Laban, it was natural for him to place his trust in

309

God and not rely on his own efforts. But it was possible for him to be completely self-reliant at home, in his father's house. Regarding this he made his vow and stated that even there, God would be his guide and support. In actual fact, though the contingency of "the Lord shall be my God" is dependent, in the main, on man himself, on his own will, nevertheless, Divine assistance is necessary. It was necessary for Divine providence to be behind him at every step. Therefore Jacob worded it as consequent condition which he could fulfill, if the Divine promises were realised. The same may be said of Exodus 19, 5: "then ye shall be a peculiar treasure."

(Ha'amek Davar)

(a) Do both of these commentators follow the Rashbam and the Sifrei, or do they adopt a different approach?

(b) What, in the view of *Ha'amek Davar*, is the similarity between our text and the one he cites from Exodus 19; "then ye shall be a peculiar treasure?"

2. Rashi comments on the phrase: "And give me bread to eat" as follows:

"ונתן לי לחם לאכל": כמו שאמר: "כי לא אעזבך". והמבקש לחם הוא נעזב, שנאמר (תהלים לז, כה): "ולא ראיתי צדיק נעזב וזרעו מבקש לחם".

As it is written: "For I will not forsake thee." And he who has to beg for bread is forsaken, as it is stated: "yet have I not seen the righteous forsaken and his seed begging bread" (Psalm 37, 25).

What prompted this explanation of Rashi? What difficulty did he find in our text?

---

[1] Cf. Nineveh, the inhabitants of which, were unequivocally told by the prophet Jonah; "In yet another forty days and Nineveh shall be overthrown." Yet his hearers understood that there was still hope, and the doom foretold would only come to pass, if they did not mend their ways. But if they repented, there was hope and: "who can tell if God will turn and repent, and turn away from His fierce anger, that we perish not" (Jonah 3, 9).

[2] For a development of this theme see p. 382.

310

"JACOB LIFTED HIS FEET"

After Jacob had been vouchsafed his unusual vision of the ladder connecting heaven and earth and had been promised Divine protection and the heritage of the land, he resumed his journey towards Aram Naharaim. But the Torah employs the curious and rare expression quoted above to describe this resumption of his journey. Here are two very different reactions by our Sages to this usage:

"וישא יעקב רגליו" — דרך בני אדם שישאום רגליהם וזה נשא רגליו? מתוך הידבקותו במקום ההוא לא רצה לסור ממנו אלא בטורח גדול ונשיאת רגליו.

In the ordinary way, men are carried along by their feet, whereas this one carried his feet. Out of his longing for that place he was deeply reluctant to leave it and had to force his feet to carry him.   (Midrash Or Ha-afela: Torah Shelemah)

"וישא יעקב רגליו" — לעולם רגליו של אדם נושאין אותו, ויעקב נשא את רגליו? אלא מלמד שנעשה קל מרוב השמחה, שהיה לו, מפני שאמר לו הקב"ה (כח, טו): "והנה אנכי עמך ושמרתיך בכל אשר תלך".

Usually a man's feet carry him along. Why then did Jacob carry his feet? To imply that he became lightfooted from his joy at the Holy One blessed be He's message: "And behold I am with thee and will protect thee whithersoever thou goest" (Genesis 29, 15).
                                                     (Midrash Aggada)

The first Midrash interprets the passage as emphasising Jacob's reluctance to leave the spot. He had been vouchsafed an unusual experience of Divine closeness and protection. What more could he wish for? He had achieved all—the beholding of the Divine Presence.[1] His feet were therefore heavy and he did not want such an ideal situation to pass away.

The second Midrash however regards the vision as a stimulus to Jacob, giving him a foretaste of the good things ahead of him. Armed with the promise of Divine guardianship, he was eager to go ahead towards his destiny and build his home and family.

It is difficult to decide from a study of the verse itself which interpretation is more correct. Sforno however endeavours to do just such a thing.

> We may rightly say that a person carries his feet when we mean that he goes of his own free will. But if a person goes reluctantly, we say rather that his feet carried him. Cf.: Isaiah 47, 9: "Pass ye over to Tarshish; howl ye inhabitants of the coastland. Is this your joyous city whose *feet* in antiquity, in ancient days, *carried her* afar to sojourn?'

A study of the general context, however offers us a more reliable guide to the problem, and would seem to support the second approach. What was Jacob's first reaction on the morrow after awakening from his dream?

> **If God will be with me,**
> **and protect me in this way that I go,**
> **and will give me bread to eat,**
> **and raiment to put on,**
> **so that I come back to my father's house in peace,**
> **... and of all that Thou shalt give me I will**
> **surely give the tenth unto thee** (28, 20–22)

"וישא יעקב רגליו": משנתבשר בשורה טובה שהובטח בשמירה, נשא לבו את רגליו ונעשה קל ללכת.

> After hearing the good tidings of Divine protection, Jacob lifted his feet and the journey became easier. This is the interpretation given in *Bereshit Rabbah.*

In another context Rashi lays down the principle which guided him in his choice of Midrashic interpretation:

"וישמעו": יש מדרשי אגדה רבים וכבר סידרום רבותינו על מכונם בבראשית רבה ובשאר מדרשות, ואני לא באתי אלא לפשוטו של מקרא ולאגדה המיישבת דברי המקרא דבר דבור על אופניו.

There are many homiletic expositions which our Rabbis arranged in *Bereshit Rabbah* and other Midrashim. I have only come to explain the plain sense of Scripture and cite such Aggadic exposition which fits it with the general context.

Further study of the general context bears out Rashi's choice of Midrash. We reproduce here the ensuing dialogue between Jacob and the shepherds at the well when he reached his destination:

וַיֹּאמֶר לָהֶם יַעֲקֹב : אַחַי, מֵאַיִן אַתֶּם?
וַיֹּאמְרוּ: מֵחָרָן אֲנָחְנוּ.
וַיֹּאמֶר לָהֶם: הַיְדַעְתֶּם אֶת־לָבָן בֶּן־נָחוֹר?
וַיֹּאמְרוּ: יָדָעְנוּ.
וַיֹּאמֶר לָהֶם: הֲשָׁלוֹם לוֹ?
וַיֹּאמְרוּ: שָׁלוֹם – וְהִנֵּה רָחֵל בִּתּוֹ בָּאָה עִם־הַצֹּאן.
וַיֹּאמֶר: הֵן עוֹד הַיּוֹם גָּדוֹל לֹא־עֵת הֵאָסֵף הַמִּקְנֶה הַשְׁקוּ הַצֹּאן וּלְכוּ רְעוּ.
וַיֹּאמְרוּ: לֹא נוּכַל עַד אֲשֶׁר יֵאָסְפוּ כָּל־הָעֲדָרִים
וְגָלְלוּ אֶת־הָאֶבֶן מֵעַל פִּי הַבְּאֵר וְהִשְׁקִינוּ הַצֹּאן.

עוֹדֶנּוּ מְדַבֵּר עִמָּם וְרָחֵל בָּאָה עִם־הַצֹּאן אֲשֶׁר לְאָבִיהָ כִּי רֹעָה הִיא.
וַיְהִי כַּאֲשֶׁר רָאָה יַעֲקֹב אֶת־רָחֵל בַּת־לָבָן אֲחִי אִמּוֹ וְאֶת־צֹאן לָבָן אֲחִי אִמּוֹ
וַיִּגַּשׁ יַעֲקֹב וַיָּגֶל אֶת־הָאֶבֶן מֵעַל פִּי הַבְּאֵר וַיַּשְׁקְ אֶת־צֹאן לָבָן אֲחִי אִמּוֹ.

And Jacob said unto them:
My brethren, where are you from?
And they said:
    We are from Haran.
And he said unto them:

Do you know Laban the son of Nahor
And they said:
We know him.
And he said unto them:
Is he well?
And they said:
He is well; and there is, Rachel his daughter coming
with the sheep.
And he said:
Why, it is still broad daylight not time for rounding the
cattle; water the sheep and go and pasture them.
And they said:
We cannot until all the flocks are rounded up and they
roll the stone from the well's mouth; then we water the
sheep.
While he was still speaking with them, Rachel came with
her father's sheep; for she was a shepherdess.
And when Jacob saw Rachel the daughter of Laban his
mother's brother, and the sheep of Laban his mother's
brother, Jacob went up and rolled the stone from the well's
mouth, and watered the flock of Laban his mother's brother.

29, 4–10

The detailed recording of such an everyday, ordinary conversation by the Torah, which is sparing of its every word, is
indeed strange. As we have had cause to note many times, the
Torah does not insert realistic colouring for its own sake, or
to provide background and atmosphere, as in a modern novel.[2]
What was the reason then for this elaboration? Here is Ramban's explanation:

> The story teaches us that they that hope in the Lord are fortified.
> The fear of God gives them renewed vigour. Jacob had come
> straight from his journey, tired and weary. Yet he rolled the
> stone back, all on his own, a task that could not, in the ordinary
> way, be performed by all the shepherds together.

In other words, prophetic inspiration and Divine promise fortify and refresh the person fortunate enough to merit them. Sforno places greater emphasis on the moral impact of the revelation that came to him:

> The righteous man abhors iniquity even when strangers are involved, as it is said: "An unjust man is an abomination to the righteous" (Proverbs 29, 27)

Jacob's communion with his Creator, his beholding of the Divine Presence at Bethel did not turn him into a recluse, contemplating the Heavenly mysteries. Rather his experience spurred him to practical action, to promoting welfare and justice in society. This is the reason, then, for the Torah's lengthy recording of the everyday dialogue between Jacob and the shepherds. Certainly this is the reason why Rashi draws on the second rather than first Midrash.

Questions for Further Study

1. Why is it recorded, on three occasions, in the dialogue cited above, that Jacob spoke *"to them,"* whereas, of the shepherds it is merely stated, that: "they said," without referring to the person they were addressing? The following citations should help with the answer.

"ויאמר להם: השלום לו? ויאמרו: שלום" — ואם לשיחה אתה מבקש, "הנה רחל בתו באה עם הצאן".

"And he said to them: Is he well? And they said: He is well." But if you want to have a talk—"there is Rachel his daughter coming with the sheep." (Avot derabi Nathan)

"ויאמרו שלום" — ואם פטפוטין אתה רוצה "הנה רחל בתו באה עם הצאן" — שהדיבור מצוי בנשים.

"And they said: He is well." But if it is chatter that you are after—"there is Rachel his daughter coming with the flock"; since women are given to chatter. (Bereshit Rabbah)

2. What is the reason for the threefold repetition of the phrase "his mother's brother" in the dialogue quoted in our *Studies?*

3.

לפי שראה אותם רובצים, כסבור שרוצים לאסוף המקנה הביתה ולא ירעו
עוד, אמר להם : "הן עוד היום גדול", כלומר : אם שכירי יום אתם, לא
שילמתם פעולת היום, ואם הבהמות שלכם, אף על פי כן "לא עת האסף
המקנה".

"Why, it is still broad daylight, not time for rounding up the
the cattle"—since he saw them lying down, he thought they wished
to take the cattle home and they did not intend tending them
further. He said to them: "It is still broad daylight"—if you are
hired workers, you have not done a day's work; if the cattle are
yours, in any case, "it is not time for rounding up the cattle."

(Rashi)

What difficulty prompted Rashi's comment here. (Note
this is not the same difficulty that Sforno wished to solve
which was quoted in our *Studies*).

---

1 Malbim elaborates on the theme of "beholding the Divine presence"
as an end in itself in this comment to verse 4 of Psalm 27: "One
thing have I asked from the Lord, that will I seek, my dwelling in
the house of the Lord ... to behold the grace of the Lord." I do not
keep on asking for things as new needs constantly arise—healing, livelihood, rescue from the enemy. I made only one request in the past
and this is the one I am continually seeking after, in the future, namely
—my dwelling in the house of the Lord. The request I made to dwell
in the house of the Lord is identical with what I ultimately seek after.
In other words, David did not make a request which was but a means
to achieve other ends. He did not ask to dwell in the house of the
Lord in order, for instance, to satisfy any of his needs and be saved
from his enemies. Such a request would not be what he was seeking
after (he would be seeking an answer to his needs, not the dwelling
in the house of the Lord). His request is the ultimate end he is seeking—dwelling in the house of the Lord beholding His grace—this the
end in itself; there is no other.

2 See pp. 194–198 in particular the quotation from *Mimesis*.

THE OLDER AND THE YOUNGER

וַיְהִי כִשְׁמֹעַ לָבָן אֶת־שֵׁמַע יַעֲקֹב בֶּן־אֲחֹתוֹ
וַיָּרָץ לִקְרָאתוֹ וַיְחַבֶּק־לוֹ וַיְנַשֶּׁק־לוֹ
וַיְבִיאֵהוּ אֶל־בֵּיתוֹ
וַיְסַפֵּר לְלָבָן אֵת כָּל־הַדְּבָרִים הָאֵלֶּה.

When Laban heard the tidings of Jacob his sister's son,
that he ran to meet him,
and embraced him,
and kissed him,
and brought him to his house.
And he told Laban all these things. (29, 13)

On this occasion, too, it was the daughter of the household,
who was the first to meet the stranger from distant climes of the
family of Abraham, the man who had left his birthplace and
father's house to settle in the land of Canaan. As in the case of
the wooing of Rebecca, so Laban's daughter met the stranger
at the well, and ran home to tell the news, and call her father
to welcome him. This time, however, it was not the servant of
that honoured house who was the guest, but the son of the
Patriarch himself.

Let us recall here what was written about Laban's reception
of Eliezer, a generation earlier:

The damsel ran, and told them of her mother's house these
things.
Rebecca had a brother, whose name was Laban. Laban
ran out to the man, to the well.
And it came to pass, when he saw the nose-ring and bra-
celets upon his sister's hand,

and when he heard the words of Rebecca his sister, saying,
Thus spake the man unto me;
that he came unto the man; and, behold, he stood by the
camels at the well.
And he said, Come in, thou blessed of the Lord;
why dost thou stand outside, when I have made ready
the house, and room for the camels.   (24, 28–31)

We see clearly how the enthusiastic welcome given to the stranger
was excited by the sight of the glittering ornaments and how
the words of greeting "come in, thou blessed of the Lord" were
aroused by the sight of the man standing "by the camels" of
his master, laden with all the good things of his master. Since
we have no grounds for thinking that the host had, in any way,
changed his character since that time, our Sages similarly suspected the genuineness of the warm welcome that he this time
extended to Jacob:

"וירץ לקראתו": כסבור ממון הוא טעון, שהרי עבד הבית בא לכאן בעשרה
גמלים טעונים.

"And he ran meet him"—he imagined that he was laden with
wealth, since the servant of that same household had arrived
there with ten laden camels.   (Rashi)

Similarly, doubt is cast on the sincerity of his embracing and
kissing:

"ויחבק": כשלא ראה עמו כלום, אמר : שמא זהובים הביא והנם בחיקו.
"וינשק לו" : אמר שמא מרגליות הביא והם בפיו.

"And embraced him"—when he saw nothing with him, he said:
peradventure he hath brought gold pieces and they are in his
bosom.
"And kissed him"—he said: peradventure he hath brought pearls
and they are in his mouth.

As soon as he realised, however, that it was a poor relation
who was standing in front of him, destitute (as indeed Jacob
testifies regarding himself twenty years later: "For I passed over
this Jordan with my staff" 32, 11), he took him disappointedly

318

into his house. Characteristic of human nature is this disappointed groan of the one who thought "peradventure he hath brought gold pieces" who finds nothing more rewarding than the good deed of hospitality, a feeling vividly expressed in the Hebrew qualifying word אַךְ (translated "surely") that slips out of Laban's mouth:

וַיֹּאמֶר לוֹ לָבָן: אַךְ עַצְמִי וּבְשָׂרִי אָתָּה.

And Laban said to him,
Surely thou art my bone and my flesh!   (29, 14)

Since the word אַךְ in Hebrew at the beginning of a sentence implies a qualification or opposition to that which has gone previously, and since, in this case, there is no previous conversation of Laban to which it could apply, Rashi supplies us with the undertones, suggesting what Laban felt inside him and left unsaid:

"אַךְ עצמי ובשרי אתה": מעתה אין לי לאוספך הביתה, הואיל ואין בידך
כלום, אלא מפני קורבה אטפל בך חודש ימים. וכן עשה — ואף זו לא לחינם,
שהיה רועה צאני.

"Surely thou art my bone and flesh"—I don't really have to take you in since you are destitute. However, out of kinship I shall look after you for a month. And so he did; But even this was not for nothing, since he pastured Laban's flock.

Should it be asked how Rashi deduces from the context that Jacob was not even Laban's guest for one month, but had to pay for it, the next verse provides the answer:

וַיֹּאמֶר לָבָן לְיַעֲקֹב: הֲכִי־אָחִי אַתָּה וַעֲבַדְתַּנִי חִנָּם?
הַגִּידָה לִּי מַה־מַּשְׂכֻּרְתֶּךָ?

And Laban said unto Jacob:
Just because thou art my brother,
shouldst thou therefore work for me for naught!
Tell me what shall thy wages be.   (29, 15)

The Hebrew *Va-'avadtani* rendered: "shouldst thou work for me" is the past form prefixed by the *vav* conversive which gives it a future meaning. Rashi thus explains it:

וכי בשביל שאחי אתה, תעבדני חינם ?

Just because you are my brother, should you work for me for nothing!

Rashi continues:

"ועבדתני": כמו ותעבדני, וכן כל תיבה שהוא לשון עבר והוסיף ו"ו בראשה
היא הופכת התיבה להבא.

It means the same as the ordinary future "you should work for me." Every verb in the past prefixed by a *vav* changes it into a future meaning.

Hirschenson has aptly expressed for us the astonishment which Rashi's observation has evoked:

How many examples of *vav* conversives abound from: "And He said, "Let there be light" till we reach our verse! Did Rashi have to wait all this time before explaining the principle of *vav* conversive?

But anyone acquainted with Rashi's method knows that he only explains a routine grammatical point when the word is ambiguous and may give rise to misunderstanding. Rashi therefore only remarked on the phenomenon of *vav* conversive here. The *vav* here could equally have been taken for an ordinary conjunctive *vav*, the word implying "you have worked for me" till now— with a past connotation. Rashi wished to rule out this meaning. Laban did not wish to pay him for past services at all but only referred to future ones. What had been was gone and done with. But how do we know that Jacob had at all worked for him? Because he did not discuss the work but only the payment. It is taken for granted that he was already working. Laban had long ago realised that Jacob's services were necessary and worth his while—so much so that he was willing to pay for them.

At this juncture, the conversation between Laban and Jacob is cut short. Between the question "what shall your wages be" and Jacob's answer two and a half verses of narrative intervene:

וּלְלָבָן שְׁתֵּי בָנוֹת: שֵׁם הַגְּדֹלָה לֵאָה וְשֵׁם הַקְּטַנָּה רָחֵל.
וְעֵינֵי לֵאָה רַכּוֹת – וְרָחֵל הָיְתָה יְפַת-תֹּאַר וִיפַת מַרְאֶה.
וַיֶּאֱהַב יַעֲקֹב אֶת-רָחֵל –

Now Laban had two daughters: the name of the elder was Leah and the name of the younger was Rachel. (29, 16)

Leah was tender eyed; but Rachel was shapely and beautiful. (29, 17)

And Jacob loved Rachel; (29, 18)

Only after these two and a half verses, during which the reader is eager to know the answer, is the conversation resumed:

וַיֹּאמֶר: אֶעֱבָדְךָ שֶׁבַע שָׁנִים בְּרָחֵל בִּתְּךָ הַקְּטַנָּה.

And he said, I will serve thee seven years for Rachel thy younger daughter. (29, 18)

Jacob very carefully lays down his condition, identifying the object of his love — רחל בתך הקטנה — by her name — "Rachel," her relations—"thy daughter" and her exact description—"the younger." Rashi queries this point asking:

כל הסימנים הללו למה הם? לפי שהיה יודע בו שהוא רמאי... אמר לו:
אעבדך "ב ר ח ל ". ושמא תאמר: רחל אחרת מן השוק? תלמוד לומר:
"ב ת ך ". ושמא תאמר: אחליף ללאה שמה ואקרא שמה רחל? תלמוד
לומר: "ה ק ט נ ה ". ואף על פי כן לא הועיל, שהרי רימהו.

Wherefore all these marks of identification?—because he knew that Laban was a rogue ... and in spite of all (the precautions), it availed him not; he cheated him just the same.

In direct contrast to Jacob's clear, explicit and unequivocal proposal, came Laban's answer—shifty, vague and ambiguous:

321

**And he said: better that I give her to thee, than give her
to another man.
Stay with me.** (29, 19)

Do these words contain any definite promise or obligation?
It is difficult to give a positive answer. What happened after
that is well known:

וַיְהִי בַבֹּקֶר וְהִנֵּה־הִיא לֵאָה.

Came the morning, behold, it was Leah. (29, 25)

The anguish of one who had served for seven years which
"seemed unto him but a few days for the love he bore her,"
the burning injustice at the base trick played on him, the irre-
parable nature of the deed finds expression in Jacob's cry, the
cry of the weak against the strong, the well-intentioned and
upright against the trickster:

מַה־זֹּאת עָשִׂיתָ לִּי?
הֲלֹא בְרָחֵל עָבַדְתִּי עִמָּךְ
וְלָמָּה רִמִּיתָנִי?!

**What is this thou hast done unto me?
Did not I serve with thee for Rachel?
Wherefore then hast thou tricked me?**

Our Sages whose interpretations we have followed until now,
and who have seemed to take the side of Jacob against Laban
giving the latter no benefit of the doubt, detect the workings of
strict justice which is no respecter of persons, in what had befallen Jacob:

כל הלילה היתה עושה עצמה כרחל, כיון שעמד בבוקר "והנה היא לאה"
אמר לה: בת הרמאי! למה רימית אותי?! אמרה לו: ואתה למה רימית
אביך?! כשאמר לך (בראשית כז, כד): "האתה זה בני עשו"? אמרת לו (שם
שם, יט): "אנכי עשו בכרך", ואתה אומר: "למה רמיתני?! ואביך לא
אמר עליך (שם שם, לה): "בא אחיך ב מ ר מ ה "?

322

All that night she (Leah) acted the part of Rachel. As soon as he rose in the morning "behold it was Leah," he said to her: Daughter of the deceiver! Wherefore hast thou tricked me? Said she to him: And thou, why didst thou deceive thy father? When he said to thee: "Art thou my very son Esau?" Thou didst say to him 'I am Esau thy first born." Yet thou sayest: "Wherefore then hast thou tricked me?!" And thy father did he not say of thee, thy brother came with trickery?   (Midrash Tanḥuma)

Our Rabbis detected in the phrase "wherefore then hast thou tricked me?" an echo of "thy brother came with trickery." This situation then reminded Jacob of the "exceeding bitter cry" of his brother Esau. Our Rabbis went even further and noted the inexorable workings of divine retribution, even in Laban's retort to Jacob:

וַיֹּאמֶר לָבָן: לֹא יֵעָשֶׂה כֵן בִּמְקוֹמֵנוּ
לָתֵת הַצְּעִירָה לִפְנֵי הַבְּכִירָה.

**Laban said: it is not done in our place,
to give away the younger before the firstborn.**   (29, 26)

One of our great 16th Century scholars, R. Eliezer Ashkenazi poses two questions on the above quoted verses, in his work *Ma'aseh Hashem*:

1. Why did Laban who adopted the tactics that attack is the best defence here weaken his own case by saying that "it must not be done so *in our country*"? Surely his argument would have been stronger if he had simply said, this thing is not done anywhere—not because this was the local custom but because such a practice was reprehensible wherever it was followed! Why then did Laban add the qualifying phrase "in our country"?

2. Why did he prefer to say "to give the younger צעירה before the *firstborn* בכירה" rather than "the younger (literally "smaller" קטנה before the elder גדולה" as, indeed, he stated in verse 16 "the name of the elder was Leah and the name of the younger (smaller) was Rachel," and as it is recorded in verse 18 "I will serve thee seven years for Rachel thy younger (smaller) daughter"?

These two questions are answered by one ingenious explanation:

323

It is true in your place perhaps such things are done, that the younger is given precedence over the firstborn, and that his portion is taken away and given to another, and the younger is given the name of "firstborn." But such things are not done "in our country to give the younger before the firstborn."

Laban is seen here then as alluding either consciously or unconsciously to Jacob's dealing with Esau. Whatever the truth of the matter, the moral lesson remains clear—sin and deceit, however justified, bring in their train ultimate punishment. Jacob himself was the victim of deception, married two wives, though he loved only one, the peace of his own family being thereby undermined, his children being divided against each other, the rift between the children of Leah and Rachel persisting for many long years.

Questions for Further Study

1. Cf.: the "running" of two Biblical heroines: Rebecca and Rachel:
   Rebecca: The maiden ran and told her mother's house (24, 28)
   Rachel: She ran and told her father (29, 12)

   לפי שאמה מתה לא היה לה להגיד אלא לו.

   Since her mother had died she could only tell him.   (Rashi)

   Rashi states: "her mother had died" as recorded in Bereshit Rabbah. According to the plain sense she went to tell him the news of a relative's arrival so that he could go and welcome him. For what could her mother do for him? But Rebecca went to her mother to show her the trinkets he had given her as girls normally do.   (Ramban)

   (a) Can you find support for Rashi's contention further on in the continuation of the chapter?
   (b) Which of the two girls behaved "normally" and conventionally, according to Rashi and according to Ramban?

ANATOMY OF LABAN'S APOLOGY

In our *Studies* to this sidra, on page 323 we tried to understand all that transpired between Jacob and Laban as narrated in chapter 29. We dwelt, in particular, on the first verse of Laban's reply, in verse 26, his defence of his action: "It is not done in our place to give the younger before the firstborn." We observed that Laban adopted, according to *Ma'aseh Hashem*, the tactics that attack is the best defence, suggesting to Jacob that the preference of the younger over the firstborn might be acceptable in his locality—an obvious reference to his behaviour to Esau—but "it is not done in our place."

On this occasion we shall deal with the second half of Laban's reply in verse 27—his proposal to make amends:

מַלֵּא שְׁבֻעַ זֹאת
וְנִתְּנָה לְךָ גַּם־אֶת־זֹאת
בַּעֲבֹדָה אֲשֶׁר תַּעֲבֹד עִמָּדִי
עוֹד שֶׁבַע־שָׁנִים אֲחֵרוֹת.

Fulfil the week of this one, and we shall give you the other also for the service you shall serve with me yet another seven years.

The phrase "and we will give you" is the English rendering of an ambiguous Hebrew word *ve-nitnah*. The form of the verb is open to a number of interpretations, and the commentators are not in agreement on this matter.

Onkelos: we shall give you; *Yerushalmi*: and I shall give you.

Rashi: a plural form as in: "let us burn"; "let us go down" (Gen. 11, 3, 7).

Rashbam: And this one too shall be given you, immediately, on account of the service you shall render me after Rachel's marriage,

Radak: The word *venitnah* could be the feminine passive or first person plural active, the plural of majesty.

There are thus two alternatives. *Ve-nitnah* may be the future active, first person, plural, the *vav* being merely conjunctive—"and we shall give you," or the passive, past, third person, singular, the *vav* being conversive—"she shall be given you."

Most of the translators and commentators adopt the first interpretation. Radak does not decide between the two possibilities. Rashbam accepts the second. The difficulty that stands in the way of Rashbam's explanation is the accusative word *et* which always stands before the direc· object. According to Rashbam "the other one" is the subject and not the object of the verb. How then can it be preceded by the accusative symbol of *et*? But if we adopt the first approach and render the text: "we shall give you the other one," *et* is justified and connotes the object. This is presumably what prompted most commentators to choose this explanation.[1] But in that case, why the plural "we." The Yerushalmi meets this difficulty by translating it as. "I" which is unacceptable. Obviously the text did not for nothing employ the plural form. Radak's reference to the majestic plural similarly requires explanation. Why did Laban choose to resort to the majestic plural just here?

Ramban cites Rashi, not taking issue with him but criticising him for not explaining why Laban here uses the plural. As he usually does when he criticises Rashi he offers his own explanation and suggests that we have here the majestic plural, as Radak observes. But like ourselves is not satisfied with leaving it at that. He adds:

> In my view Laban spoke with guile. He told Jacob that things were not done in this way in our place, implying that the community would not let him act like that since it violated their conventions. But fulfil this week and we shall give you, i.e. I and the other members of the community the other one. We shall all agree and honour you and give you a banquet as we did on the first occasion.

Ramban teaches us an important lesson. One of the characteristic signs of a wicked man, standing in the way of reformation, is the flight from personal responsibiliy for the deed he has perpetrated and its placing on someone else's shoulders. But if the deed reflects on the doer and he cannot deny his part in it, man has discovered a good answer to the one who would rebuke him and say to him: What made you go and do this thing? He regards himself as forced into it because the community or some vague body to which he belongs compelled him to act thus.

This dichotomy provides an answer not only to those who would condemn him but, what is more dangerous, to himself and his conscience. In this way man splits himself in two, into his personal "I" who does good and is acceptable and pleasant in the eyes of his friends, and the "I" which is but a cog in the anonymous public machine, be it the state of which he is but a functionary and servant, the army of which he is but one of its nameless soldiers, the party of which he is but one of the rank and file, the enterprise which he does not direct but merely serves. What blame can therefore be attached to him? He personally did not commit this iniquitous offence, but, on the contrary, always does favours to people. As a tiny membrane however in that gigantic anonymous body he is forced to do what is imposed him and he is not responsible.

We might have thought that this dangerous behaviour of shifting responsibility onto an anonymous abstract body (the public, the state the community, organization or movement) by which the individual satisfies both himself and the public at large, and which cannot be brought to justice, thus precluding any possibility of rectifying matters is confined to and characteristic of our days, owing to the growth of bureaucracy and large public organizations. Ramban, however, shows us the timelessness of the subterfuges resorted to by the evil in man. Even in antiquity, in the uncomplex society of Laban and his town, the evil instinct prompted man to hide behind the shoulders of the community and shirk responsibility. "Am I to blame? Was it me who failed to keep my promise? Of course if it

had depended on me ... I am but one man in the community."
"It is not done in our place." "So undertake another seven
year's service and we—I and all my fellowcitizens—shall accede
to your desire."

In contradistinction to this, our Sages have taught us: "There
is no proxy for criminal acts." You are responsible for your own
deeds, not the organization, community or something backing
you or even another part of yourself.

We have seen from Ramban how a decision in a small grammatical point can have such all-important moral implications.
The grammatical question cannot be divorced from that of content and idea. They are all part and parcel of the teaching of
Judaism called Torah, and require study.

Questions for Further Study

1. Compare the words of Rashi and Ramban to our text
    with their comments to verse 15 of our chapter: "Just
    because you are my brother, shall you then work for me
    for nought?"

    Va-avadtani—to be taken in a future sense, a past form con-
    verted to future by the prefix *vav.*   (Rashi)
    The text does not say that Jacob had worked for him previously.
    It is possible, however, that the flock had not left his care ever
    since "he watered the flock of Laban, his mother's brother." On
    seeing Rachel engaged in pasturing the flocks he had taken pity
    on her and out of love for her had taken over the pasturing of
    the flocks.
    We may also suggest that Laban spoke deceitfully to him. He
    told him at first that he was his flesh and blood and that he
    would treat him as considerately as he would himself and closest
    kin. As soon as he observed that Jacob stayed there and supported
    himself from his flocks he said: "Because you are my brother,
    shall you therefore serve me for nought?" for I know that hence-
    forth you will work for me, since you are an honest man and
    will not live off others. I, too, do not want you to work for me
    without pay. Tell me how much you want and I shall give it you.
    Then Jacob divined Laban's real feelings and told him that he

would work for him for seven years for Rachel, work being in the ordinary way sheep pasturing, for that was what they needed and that was the subject of their conversation.   (Ramban)

The difficulty in this verse is similar to the one encountered in our text (27)—an ambiguous form of the verb which allows of both past and present meanings. What is common to Ramban's comment in both cases and characteristic in his treatmen of Rashi?

Compare with Rashi and Ramban's comment cited in question 1 their respective comments to Genesis 41, 38; "Can there be found such a man in whom is the spirit of God"—

. . . If we go and seek it shall we find the likes of him?   (Rashi)
He was a Hebrew and the Hebrews were detested by the Egyptians (they would not dine or associate with them for they regarded them as unclean). He did not wish therefore to appoint him vice-regent without their permission. He accordingly explained to them that it was impossible to find an Egyptian with the same qualifications to do the job since Joseph was endowed with something they hadn't got—the spirit of God. Once they had agreed he said to Joseph: "After the Lord has made known to thee all this . . ."   (Ramban)

(a) What is the difficulty common to נמצא in this verse and נתנה in our *Studies?*
(b) Does Ramban treat Rashi's comment here the same as he does his comment in our *Studies?*

"And Laban said": Do not imagine that I have done this, because I wished to retract and not give you Rachel or that I wanted to force you to marry Leah against your will; on the contrary, I have done this in order to keep my promise to you regarding Rachel. You see things like this are just not done in our place and I cannot give you Rachel till Leah is married, and if I give her to someone else against seven year's service, you will have to wait seven years (for I won't trust anyone else to give him her on credit, to marry Leah and pay later). I am thus doing you a great favour by giving you Leah, since by this you will be able to marry Rachel immediately.

329

"Fulfil this week": Wait over only the seven days of banqueting for this woman—Leah, and then you will be able to marry Rachel in return for the seven years service you have already worked, as we arranged. But know that Leah has been given to you (passive, past) in return for the seven years you are going to work for me in the future, since I trust you and have given you Leah already—on credit... This is for your own good so that you can marry Rachel immediately, to save you having to wait for a long time till Leah gets married.　　　　(Malbim)

In what way does Malbim's interpretation of ve-nitnah differ from that of all the commentators we have cited? What, in your view, is the strength and weakness of this interpretation?

Though we do find et used after a passive verb. See Exodus 10, 8; 21, 28. At anyrate this is an anomalous usage.

CAN I TAKE GOD'S PLACE?

Our Sages were very exacting in their standards where the Patriarchs were concerned. If they found their conduct wanting, they had no qualms about drawing attention to it; they indicated, too, that the righteous man was eventually punished for his fault, emphasing where it was recorded in the narrative and they did not excuse him. Not all our later commentators have shared this approach. Some have tried to seek a justification or, at least, to find an extenuating circumstance. Others have, at least, tried to understand how the righteous man became a victim of such a failing or how he came to deviate, even by a hairsbreadth, from the high standards of conduct that alone befitted him.

In our sidra Rachel appeals in her misery to her husband Jacob:

וַתֵּרֶא רָחֵל כִּי לֹא יָלְדָה לְיַעֲקֹב
וַתְּקַנֵּא רָחֵל בַּאֲחֹתָהּ
וַתֹּאמֶר אֶל־יַעֲקֹב:
הָבָה־לִּי בָנִים וְאִם־אַיִן מֵתָה אָנֹכִי.

**When Rachel saw she had borne no children to Jacob
Rachel became envious of her sister and said to Jacob:
Give me children or else I die.**   (30, 1)

How strange and unfeeling is Jacob's reply:

וַיִּחַר־אַף יַעֲקֹב בְּרָחֵל וַיֹּאמֶר:
הֲתַחַת אֱלֹהִים אָנֹכִי
אֲשֶׁר־מָנַע מִמֵּךְ פְּרִי־בָטֶן.

331

**Jacob's anger was kindled against Rachel and he said:
Can I take the place of God who has denied thee the fruit
of the womb?** (30, 2)

Our commentators, both ancient and modern, have been puzzled
by the patriarch's answer. Did she, on account of her pain and
suffering, deserve such an answer? Didn't Jacob understand that
a person cannot be blamed for what he says out of intense suffering? What fault did he find in her bitter plaint? Ramban
who, of all our commentators probes deepest into the human
heart, seeking in the recesses of the soul for the motive, tries
to understand what prompted Jacob to such an outburst in
reply to the wife he loved most:

> Our commentators explained that Rachel asked to pray for her
> or else she would die (Rashi). For whoever is childless is ac-
> counted dead. This is based on a Midrash of our Sages. But I
> am astonished. In that case why was Jacob so angry? Why did
> he say, Am I in God's stead? The Lord accedes to the wishes of
> the righteous ... Do not the righteous pray on behalf of others?
> Look at Elijah and Elisha who prayed on behalf of foreign wo-
> men! Evidently our Rabbis did indeed find fault with him; for
> they stated in *Bereshit Rabbah*: "Said the Holy One blessed be He,
> Is this the way to answer the troubled?"
>
> According to the plain sense Rachel asked Jacob to give her
> children and in reality she meant to ask him to pray for her
> until she would be granted children, otherwise she would kill
> herself from the suffering. She spoke wrongly out of her envy
> and thought that Jacob out of his love for her would fast and
> put on sackcloth and intercede for her till she was granted child-
> ren so that she should not die on account of her suffering.
>
> Jacob was angry because the prayer of the righteous is not in
> their power that it must automatically and invariably be grant-
> ed ... This was why he told her that he was not in the place
> of God to be able to make fruitful the barren. He was not direct-
> ly concerned since it was from her not him that the fruit of the
> womb was withheld. He spoke thus to chastise and shame her.
>
> Now when the righteous woman saw that she could not rely
> on Jacob's intercession, she betook to praying herself to the
> Answerer of Prayer and this is borne out by the text "And God
> hearkened to her" (5, 22).

> Or perhaps we may take the view of our Sages in the follow-
> ing modified form. It was inconceivable that Jacob had not
> prayed on behalf of his favourite wife because she was barren.
> We must conclude that his prayers had not been answered. Rachel
> however came along and upbraided him for doing nothing, ask-
> ing him, at least, to bring her children through his prayers since
> he was in no whit inferior to his father, Isaac, who had done
> so. Whereupon Jacob became angry and told her that the matter
> lay in God's hand and not in his. As for his father, his prayer
> had been answered because he was a righteous man and was
> destined to have seed; whereas in her case it was from her that
> the fruit of the womb was withheld. This is the true interpreta-
> tion.

In other words, Jacob's anger was not caused by her words or
her adopting the pose of spoilt wives who threaten their hus-
bands with suicide if they cannot have their will. He was concerned with the misleading approach to prayer evident in her
words, her incomprehension of the real relation between man
and God. Herein surely lay the difference between superstition,
idolatrous media of intercession and the pure undefiled prayer
of man to his Maker! The former imagine they can bend the
will of God (whether through the medium of sacrifices, charms,
incantations and other sorts of mumbo jumbo—so long as man's
purpose is to subject the Divine by the potency of his own man-
made media to his own will, he is purely a sorcerer and worshipper of idols [1]) to theirs. The offerer of sincere prayer to the
Deity, however, knows that his prayer cannot force his Maker
to do anything, but that the Lord will do what seemeth good
to Him, and that we must thank Him for misfortune just
as we do for good fortune.

Ramban on another occasion analysed the difference between the acceptable, bona-fide sacrifice and the heathen ones,
in Leviticus, on the words, that man should offer a sacrifice
acceptable to the Lord. There he explains that the worshipper
who sincerely desires to be exalted by his sacrifices wishes to
draw closer to God, whereas the idolater desires to bring down
to his level the supernatural object of his sacrifice, exploiting
it for his own ends. The same applies to the distinction between

true prayer and the prayer that is nothing more than incantation and mumbo-jumbo.

According to Ramban, Rachel was, admittedly, to blame in her desire to mould the will of God through prayer (or, strictly speaking, in her desire that the righteous man should pray for her and cause Him to do her will) and this was the reason for Jacob's anger.

Radak too detects in Rachel's words symptoms of an entirely wrong approach, taking a much more serious view of her sin than Ramban:

> Jacob was angry with her for attributing powers to him rather than God to whom alone is the power and the might even that "the barren might give birth to seven." She had said, Give me children. But if she had merely asked him to intercede for her she would have been justified and he would not have become angry." [2]

Another explanation for Jacob's anger is tendered in the *Akedat Yizhak*, in Genesis, where he speaks of the creation of woman and the names given her:

> The two names "woman" (*isha*) and "Eve" indicate two purposes. The first teaches that woman was taken from man, stressing that like him you may understand and advance in the intellectual and moral field just as did the matriarchs and many righteous women and prophetesses and as the literal meaning of Proverbs 31 about "the woman of worth" (*eshet hayil*) indicates. The second alludes to the power of childbearing and rearing children, as is indicated by the name Eve—the mother of all living. A woman deprived of the power of childbearing will be deprived of the secondary purpose and be left with the ability to do evil or good like the man who is barren. Of both the barren man and woman Isaiah (56,5) states: "I have given them in My house and in My walls a name that is better than sons and daughters," since the offspring of the righteous is certainly good deeds (see Rashi on Gen. 6, 9). Jacob was therefore angry with Rachel when she said, "Give me children or else I die," in order to reprimand her and make her understand this all-important principle that she was not dead as far as their joint purpose in life because she was childless, just the same as it would be, in his case, if he would have been childless.

334

Jacob's anger is here explained as being directed at Rachel's
forgetting the true and chief purpose of her existence which,
according to the *Akedat Yiẓhak* is no different from that of
her partner, the man's. "Like him you may understand and
advance in the intellectual and moral field as did the matriarchs
and many righteous women and prophetesses, as the literal meaning of Proverbs 31 about the woman of worth indicates." She
in her yearnings for a child saw her whole world circumscribed
by the second purpose of woman's existence (according to the
Akedat Yiẓhak "the *secondary* purpose'!) to become a mother.
Without it her life was not worth living. "Or else I die." This
was a treasonable repudiation of her function, a flight from
her destiny and purpose, shirking the duties imposed on her, not
in virtue of her being a woman, but in virtue of her being a
human being.

All three commentators, Ramban, Radak and the author
of *Akedat Yiẓhak* endeavour to extenuate Jacob's conduct, explaining his outburst by magnifying Rachel's guilt and reading
into her words more than an embittered cry of human pain.
Our Sages, on the other hand, condemn his conduct without
in any way trying to extenuate it:

רבנן דדרומאה בשם ר' אלכסנדרי: (איוב טו, ב): "החכם יענה דעת רוח" —
זה אברהם, שנאמר (בראשית טז, ב): "וישמע אברם לקול שרי"; "וימלא
קדים בטנו" (איוב שם, שם) — זה יעקב, שנאמר (בראשית ל, ב): "ויחר
אף יעקב". אמר לו הקב"ה: כך עונין את המעיקות? [לעקרות מצעקות רוח
ומרות נפש] חייך שבניך עתידין לעמוד לפני בנה [יוסף]!

The Rabbis of the South in the name of R. Alexandri applied
the text (Job 15, 2) "Should a wise man make answer with
windy knowledge" to Abraham, as it is stated (Gen. 16, 2): "And
Abraham hearkened to the voice of Sarai" and the text (ibid.)
"and fill his belly with the east wind" to Jacob, as it is stated
(Gen. 30, 2): "And Jacob's anger was kindled." Said the Holy
One blessed be He to him, Is this the way to answer the troubled?
By your life, your sons are destined to stand before hers (i.e.
Joseph)!   (Bereshit Rabbah 71, 10)

Our Sages accused Jacob of giving an unworthy answer to
an appeal from an embittered and troubled soul. Character-

istically our Sages saw a parallel between Jacob's words here and an identical phrase elsewhere.[3] Jacob had said here: "Can I take the place of God." Later Joseph had repeated the same words to his brothers in Egypt (Gen. 50, 19): "Can I take the place of God?"

What is the connection between these two phrases apart from their mere verbal identity? The connection is, as emphasised by the Midrash, a connection, by way of contrast—insulting and hurtful behaviour set against encouraging and consoling words. Jacob had retorted, Can I take the place of God, in response to Rachel's appeal in her trouble for help. He had spurned her request by pointing to the limits of his ability, in the matter. But this belittling of himself was motivated simply by a desire to cover up his unwillingness to help, in order to relieve himself of responsibility. Joseph, on the other hand, had proffered these words to his frightened and dismayed brothers (after their father's death) who had come to ask his forgiveness and pardon for all they had done to him. He had reassuringly answered them with the words: "Fear not, Can I take the place of God?" Joseph likewise recognised his limitations but this belittling of himself had come to prove to his brothers and himself that judgement did not belong to him in his relations with them, but to God.

Questions for Further Study

אָמַר רִ׳ יִצְהָק : כְּתִיב (מִשְׁלֵי כג, יז): "אַל יְקַנֵּא לִבְּךָ בַּחַטָּאִים, כִּי אִם בְּיִרְאַת ה׳ כָּל הַיּוֹם", וְאַתָּה אוֹמֵר: "וַתְּקַנֵּא רָחֵל בַּאֲחוֹתָהּ"? אֶלָּא מְלַמֵּד שֶׁקִּנְּאַתָה בְּמַעֲשֶׂיהָ הַטּוֹבִים. אָמְרָה: אִילוּלֵי שֶׁהִיא צַדֶּקֶת — לֹא הָיְתָה יוֹלֶדֶת.

1. "When Rachel saw that she had borne no children to Jacob, Rachel envied her sister." Said R. Yizḥak: It is written (Prov. 23, 17), "Let not thine heart envy sinners, but be in the fear of the Lord all the day." Yet Thou sayest: "And Rachel envied her sister"? But it teaches that she envied her goods deeds. She said, Had she not been righteous she would not have given birth.
(Bereshit Rabbah)

Rashi cites the same Midrash in his comment on the text.

קינאה במעשיה הטובים. אמרה: אילולי שצדקה ממני, לא זכתה לבנים.

She envied her good deeds. She said, Had she not been more righteous than me she would not have merited children.

Rashi's commentators ask why he chose to cite the Midrash. Surely the verse could have been easily understood in its literal sense. Rashi on Gen. 3, 8 "towards the cool of the day" himself says:

There are many homiletic elaborations on this text which have been arranged by our Rabbis in Midrash Rabbah and other Midrashim. I have only come to explain the plain sense of the Scriptures and cite the homiletic explanation that best fits the sense of the text.

Explain why Rashi had to cite in this case the Midrash, resorting to the homiletic explanation in order to be true to his principle of choosing the explanation best fitting the context?

2.   To Rachel's argument "you should have prayed for me" Jacob retorted: "Is that the reason you demanded I bring you children at all costs? Can I be sure that God will answer my prayer? Perhaps sin will lead to a barrier springing up between me and the Almighty. He will enshroud himsef in a cloud to stop the prayer passing through (cf. Lamentations 3, 44). The one whose prayer is accepted is regarded as if he were standing directly under (*tahat*) God with no barrier intervening between him and God. But where prayer is not accepted there is, as it were a curtain separating the worshipper from God, as it is stated, in Isaiah 59, 2: "Your iniquities separated you from your God."
                                                                  (Kli Yakar)

How does the above explanation differ from all the others we have cited?

[1] See *Studies in Bamidbar* pp. 282 ff.
[2] Cf.: "Why was Rachel punished by dying on the way? Because she equated the creature with its Creator (i.e. Jacob with God)." Midrash *Maayan Ganim* cited by Kasher in *Torah Shelemah*.

[3] Cf. I. Heinemann, *Darkei Aggada* p. 68: Modern scholars have shown that the Bible employs motive words in order to emphasise the link between different narratives and parts of the same narratives and the relations between deed and punishment. Examples cited by modern scholars are already found in the Aggada itself: Cf.: *Bereshit Rabbah* 84, 19: "Said the Holy One blessed be He to Judah: You said to your father "Recognise I pray thee" (Gen. 37, 32). By your life you shall hear: "Recognize I pray thee" (38, 25). In all these homilies the common phraseology indicates a link between the original deed and its consequence.

THESE TWENTY YEARS

After Laban had ransacked all Jacob's belongings and failed to find what he was seeking after, the outraged Patriarch burst out:

מַה־פִּשְׁעִי؟ מַה חַטָּאתִי؟
כִּי דָלַקְתָּ אַחֲרָי.

כִּי־מִשַּׁשְׁתָּ אֶת־כָּל־כֵּלַי,
מַה־מָּצָאתָ מִכֹּל כְּלֵי־בֵיתֶךָ؟
שִׂים כֹּה נֶגֶד אַחַי וְאַחֶיךָ
וְיוֹכִיחוּ בֵּין שְׁנֵינוּ.

זֶה עֶשְׂרִים שָׁנָה אָנֹכִי עִמָּךְ
רְחֵלֶיךָ וְעִזֶּיךָ לֹא שִׁכֵּלוּ
וְאֵילֵי צֹאנְךָ לֹא אָכָלְתִּי.

טְרֵפָה לֹא־הֵבֵאתִי אֵלֶיךָ
אָנֹכִי אֲחַטֶּנָּה מִיָּדִי תְּבַקְשֶׁנָּה
גֻּנְבְתִי יוֹם וּגְנֻבְתִי לָיְלָה.

הָיִיתִי בַיּוֹם אֲכָלַנִי חֹרֶב וְקֶרַח בַּלָּיְלָה
וַתִּדַּד שְׁנָתִי מֵעֵינָי.

זֶה־לִּי עֶשְׂרִים שָׁנָה בְּבֵיתֶךָ
עֲבַדְתִּיךָ אַרְבַּע־עֶשְׂרֵה שָׁנָה בִּשְׁתֵּי בְנֹתֶיךָ
וְשֵׁשׁ שָׁנִים בְּצֹאנֶךָ
וַתַּחֲלֵף אֶת־מַשְׂכֻּרְתִּי עֲשֶׂרֶת מֹנִים.

לוּלֵי אֱלֹהֵי אָבִי אֱלֹהֵי אַבְרָהָם
וּפַחַד יִצְחָק הָיָה לִי
כִּי עַתָּה רֵיקָם שִׁלַּחְתָּנִי
אֶת־עָנְיִי וְאֶת־יְגִיעַ כַּפַּי רָאָה אֱלֹהִים
וַיּוֹכַח אָמֶשׁ.

What is my crime? What is my sin, that thou hast so
hotly pursued after me?

Whereas thou hast rummaged through all my things, what
hast thou found of all thy household objects?
Set it here before my brethren and thy brethren,
that they may judge between us both.

These twenty years have I been with thee: thy ewes and
thy she goats never miscarried, and the rams of thy flock
have I not eaten.

That which was torn by beasts I brought not unto thee:
I bore the loss of it; of my hand didst thou require it,
whether stolen by day, or stolen by night.

Thus I was; in the day the drought consumed me, and
frost by night; and my sleep fled from mine eyes.

Thus have I been twenty years in thy house;
I served thee fourteen years for thy two daughters, and
six years for thy cattle:
and thou hast changed my wages ten times.

Had not the God of my father, the God of Abraham,
and the fear of Isaac been with me,
thou wouldst have sent me away now empty-handed.
But God has seen my flight and the toil of my hands,
and rebuked thee yesternight.   (31, 36–42)

he pent-up feelings of twenty years of Laban's underhand
ealings with him found their outlet in this Jacob's parting

340

outburst. But before that Jacob had held his peace. Only here is it explicitly and significantly stated that "Jacob's anger was kindled." Jacob had taken no umbrage on the occasion of Laban's pursuit after him nor in the wake of his hypocritical admonitions in verses 26–30. Only when Laban ransacked his belongings and found nothing "was Jacob's anger kindled."

The Torah here teaches us an instructive lesson in human conduct and self control. Anger and bitter reproof should be deferred till the last possible moment, till there is no other alternative —only as a last resort. In similar fashion Moses controlled his anger and only rebutted the brazen declarations and denunciations of Korah and his cronies in measured tones, calling Dathan and Abiram for mutual discussion of their grievances. Only after he was apprised of their refusal: "We will not go up . . . wilt thou put out the eyes of these men?" (Numbers 16, 12–14), and was convinced of their unwillingness to be reconciled and listen to reason was his anger kindled. The Almighty Himself is described as acting in a similar manner on hearing Miriam and Aaron's speaking against Moses (Ibid., 12, 1–2). It is not stated that His anger was kindled on hearing their incautious words. First the Almighty explained to them the enormous chasm separating Moses from other prophets and then it is stated:

> **...Wherefore then were you not afraid to speak against my servant, against Moses?**

Only after this gentle chiding was the anger of the Lord kindled against them. (Ibid., 9). On this our commentators observed that only after the Almighty noted that they had not retracted and humbled themselves and admitted their offence declaring "We have sinned" as King David did to Nathan the prophet: "I have sinned against the Lord" (II Samuel 12, 13) did His anger kindle against them.

Jacob's indignant outburst against Laban is characterised by a logical structure. Part 1 of his speech — 36–37 consists of his instinctive reply to Laban's accusations and reference to the current situation. The second part (38–41) is a retrospective survey of his twenty years with Laban which may be subdivided into two sections: (a) 38–39—what Jacob had done for Laban; (b) 40–41—what Laban had given Jacob in return. The third and concluding part (42) comprises a reversion to the present situation and an allusion to what might have happened had . . .

We may note, therefore, how Jacob's twenty years of suffering find their verbal outlet for the first time as a result of the exigencies of the situation. Indeed his outburst contains revelations about Laban's past misdoings. In none of the previous descriptions of Jacob's life in Laban's household do we find any allusion to Jacob's fulfilling of duties over and above those required nor to Laban's changing of his wages except in one instance where Jacob, at the end of the twenty years is talking matters over with his wives:

וַאֲבִיכֶן הֵתֶל בִּי וְהֶחֱלִף אֶת־מַשְׂכֻּרְתִּי עֲשֶׂרֶת מֹנִים.

And your father made sport of me and changed my wages ten times. (31, 7)

This fact has been noted by Ramban in his commentary. He observes:

It was true, though the text had made no reference to it previously.

A similar instance of a revelation deferred till the appropriate moment is to be seen in the statement of Joseph's brethren after they had been hauled before Pharaoh's vice-regent and charged with espionage:

**We are truly guilty in respect of our brother,
in that we saw the anguish of his soul,
when he besought us, and we took no notice;
and that is why this misfortune has befallen us.**

(Genesis 42, 21)

Nowhere previously had there been the slightest allusion to Joseph asking his brothers for mercy when they decided to cast him into the pit and sell him into slavery. Ramban likewise draws attention to this and asks why the text does not refer to this during the account of Joseph's sale. He suggests three answers.

First the narrative of the sale of Joseph is careful not to lay the blame for what happened either on Joseph or on his brethren in any one sided manner. Both sides were equally culpable and the Torah does not cover up their evildoing. Joseph was a talebearer, boastful in his retailing of his dreams to his father and his brothers hated and envied him for it. If the Torah had dwelt, on this occasion, on Joseph's pleas for mercy and the brothers' stony-heartedness it would have upset the balance and undermined the impartiality of the narrative, weighting the odds against them and painting them in too black a light. On this occasion the text therefore did not enlarge on their misconduct. Later on however the allusion to Joseph's pleas for mercy only serves to underline their remorse rather than their cruelty.

Second, the cries and protests were understood and it was not necessary to refer to them. Third, from the point of view of literary technique, repetition is always undesirable and the Torah naturally deals briefly, in one instance, and enlarges, in the other.

It may further be suggested in elaborating on the third reason that the text details, in the later instance, Joseph's pleas for mercy because only then, as a result of the inexorable workings of Divine retribution, had the conscience of the brothers been touched. Only then had they really heard the cries of their brother in their inner heart. When they had cast him into the pit they had been deaf to his cries.

Similarly Jacob had kept quiet during the whole twenty years of mistreatment, convinced that, ultimately, right would triumph and that the Almighty would come to his rescue. Only when the Divine promise was redeemed and his deliverance materialized did he give vent to his feelings, squaring accounts with

Laban and pointing out to him where the debt really lay and how Providence had helped him.

The first six verses of Jacob's speech are typical of the exploited and downtrodden in every age. But the last verse where he points to God as his deliverer from the hands of his oppressor rather than to his own might of hand expresses the authentic voice of the Patriarch Jacob and contains the unique message of Israel.

Questions for Further Study

1. According to Ramban's comment to 31, 7 cited in our *Studies* "it was true..." how could he know that Jacob's tale of woe to his wives ("He changed my wages ten times") was really true? Perhaps he had exaggerated to persuade them to leave home? Can you find any hint in the text that "it was true" and that it should not be explained in the same way as Rashi interpreted the words of Joseph's brothers (Gen. 50, 16 s.v. צוה אביך"Thy father commanded"?)

2. Why did Jacob use a different word for pursue when he denounced Laban (דלק = hotly pursue) from that used to describe Laban's attempt to overtake him (רדף = pursue).

3. "The rams of thy flock have I not eaten": it was the practice of shepherds when they led the flock far afield to find rich pasture, where there was no food to be bought, to take of the rams which were of no use for breeding and eat them.   (Ḥizkuni)

   Why did the statement of Jacob strike Ḥizkuni as strange and how does he solve the difficulty by his interpretation?

4. "that which was torn": by a lion or wolf.   (Rashi)
   What difficulty prompted Rashi's comment? (Do not imagine that he is merely translating the word).
   Or Ḥahayyim questions the use of the verb "brought" in connection with torn by wild beasts. Answer his question.

5. Cf.: These twenty years have I been with thee.   (31, 38)
        Thus have I been twenty years in this house.   (31, 41)

MY LORD ESAU

Jacob is now on his way home to Beersheba, to his father. He had suffered exile for twenty years in Laban's house, in flight from his brother's vengeance. Then Laban had pursued him as he departed secretly with his wife and possessions. After his deliverance from Laban, he continued on his way back home to be met by angels of the Lord (Gen. 32, 5–6).

וַיְצַו אֹתָם לֵאמֹר
כֹּה תֹאמְרוּן לַאדֹנִי לְעֵשָׂו
כֹּה אָמַר עַבְדְּךָ יַעֲקֹב
עִם־לָבָן גַּרְתִּי וָאֵחַר עַד־עָתָּה.
וַיְהִי־לִי שׁוֹר וַחֲמוֹר צֹאן וְעֶבֶד וְשִׁפְחָה
וָאֶשְׁלְחָה לְהַגִּיד לַאדֹנִי לִמְצֹא־חֵן בְּעֵינֶיךָ.

And he commanded them saying Thus shall ye speak unto my Lord Esau; thy servant Jacob saith thus, I stayed with Laban and remained there until now. And I have oxen and asses, flocks, and male and female slaves: and I have sent to tell my lord, that I may find grace in thy sight.

What was the meaning of this delegation to Esau? Did Jacob thereby hope to appease his brother's anger, thinking that his thirst for vengeance had not cooled, after a lapse of twenty years? Was it a peace gesture on the part of Jacob or a display of his strength in order to intimidate him? Various interpretations have been offered by commentators down the ages. Some of our Sages voiced their disapproval of Jacob's behaviour as savouring of unnecessary debasement and appeasement.

Let us quote Rabbi Huna's words on this subject in the Midrash:

"וישלח יעקב מלאכים". רב הונא פתח (משלי כו, יז): "מחזיק באזני כלב עבר מתעבר על ריב לא לו" — — — אמר לו הקב"ה: לדרכו היה מהלך והיית משלח אצלו ואומר לו: "כה אמר עבדך יעקב"?!

"And Jacob sent messengers." Rabbi Huna applied the verse: "He that passeth by and meddleth with strife not his own is like one that taketh a dog by the ears." Said the Holy One blessed be He: He was going his own way, and you despatch a delegation to him saying: "Thus saith thy servant Jacob"?!

(Bereshit Rabbah 75, 2)

In a similar strain Rabbi Judah ben Simon applied the following verse from *Jeremiah*:

(ירמיה יג, כא): "מה תאמרי כי יפקד עליך ואת למדת אותם עליך אלפים לראש" — אמר לו הקב"ה: לדרכו היה מהלך והיית משלח אצלו ואומר לו: "כה אמר עבדך יעקב"?!

"What wilt thou say when he shall punish thee, when thou hast taught them to be captains over thee!" (Hebrew: *alufim*—the title of the leaders of Esau's descendants). Said the Holy One blessed be He: He was going his own way, yet you despatch a delegation to him saying: "Thus saith *thy servant* Jacob"!?

Thus two of our Sages sharply condemn Jacob's behaviour. Such a delegation was entirely superfluous. Worse than that, it was liable to cause untold harm, teaching Esau to lord it over Jacob. This calls to mind another dictum of the Sages:

העושה עצמו שה — הזאב אוכלו.

He who acts like a kid—the wolves devour him.

The following Midrash is even more explicit in condemning Jacob's behaviour:

באותה שעה שקרא יעקב לעשו "אדוני" אמר לו הקב"ה: אתה השפלת עצמך וקראת לעשו "אדוני" שמונה פעמים — חייך, אני מעמיד מבניו שמונה מלכים קודם לבניך, שנאמר (בראשית לו, לא): "ואלה המלכים אשר מלכו בארץ אדום לפני מלך מלך לבני ישראל".

346

> The moment that Jacob called Esau, My Lord (Hebrew: *adoni*),
> the Holy One blessed be He said to him: Thou didst humble
> thyself and called Esau "My Lord" eight times. By thy life! I
> shall raise up from his children eight kings that reigned in the
> land of Edom, before there reigned any king over the children
> of Israel" (36, 31)   (Bereshit Rabbah 75, 11)

The Midrashic preacher utilises the arithmetic correspondence
between the number of times that Jacob employs the title
"Adoni"—"My Lord" and the number of kings that reigned
over Edom. It is taken as a symbol of sin and punishment, the
sin of voluntary self-abasement before the tyrant, punished by
the latter's success in rising to power and ruling over his weaker
antagonist.

Ramban similarly disapproves of Jacob's behaviour. He points
out that Jacob had to pass through Esau's territory in Southern
Palestine to reach home. Afraid of what Esau might do, he sent
messengers to placate him. Ramban then quotes the Midrash
we have first cited and adds his own interpretation of later
history:

> Our fall at the hands of Edom (Rome) was due to the fact
> that the Kings in the Second Temple made advances to the
> Romans.

Ramban sees a parallel between Jacob's behaviour and the behaviour of the Hasmoneans in seeking the good offices of the
Romans. By this, they hastened the downfall of Israel and its
exile.

An opposite point of view is voiced by Rabbi Judah Hanasi,
the famed leader of the Jewish people in the Holy Land in the
second century C.E., editor of the Mishnah and contemporary
and close friend of the Roman Emperor Antoninus. Many
legends are related in the Midrash regarding their association.
Rabbi Judah Hanasi was obliged to maintain good relations
with the Roman authorities in order to protect the interests of
the Jewish population and safeguard the rights the Romans still
allowed them.

The Midrash we shall now quote is a record of a conversation between Rabbi Judah and his private secretary Rabbi Aphes:

רבנו [ר' יהודה הנשיא] אמר לרב אפס : כתוב חד אגרא [מכתב] מן שמי
למרן מלכא אנטונינוס [קיסר רומא]. קם וכתב : מן יהודה נשיאה למרן מלכא
אנטונינוס. לקח רבנו האגרת וקראה וקרעה. אמר לו: כתוב : מן עבדך
יהודה למרן מלכא אנטונינוס. אמר לו [רב אפס] : מפני מה אתה מבזה על
כבודך ? אמר לו : מה אנא טב מן סבי [וכי טוב אני מזקני יעקב], לא כך אמר
יעקב : "כה אמר עבדך" ?

"Thus shall ye speak unto my lord Esau." Rabbi Judah Hanasi said to Rabbi Aphes, Write an epistle from me to His Majesty the Emperor Antoninus. He arose and wrote: "From Judah the Prince (Nasi) to His Majesty the Emperor Antoninus. Rabbi Judah took the letter, read it and tore it up. Said he to him: Write: From thy servant Judah to His Majesty the Emperor Antoninus. Said Rabbi Aphes to him: Wherefore dost thou abase thyself? Rabbi Judah replied: What am I better than my fore-father? Did not Jacob say thus: "Thus saith thy servant Jacob."

Rabbi Judah Hanasi advocates diplomatic discretion in addressing authority, preferring to forego illusive honours in order to achieve practical ends.

The following Midrash defends Jacob's conduct even more forthrightly:

אמר ר' יונתן: כל מי שרוצה לרצות מלך או שלטון ואינו יודע דרכם
וטכסיסיהם — יניח פרשה זו לפניו וילמד הימנה טכסיסי פיוסים וריצויים.

Said Rabbi Jonathan: Whoever wishes to placate a king or authority and is not familiar with their ways and tactics should place this chapter (37 of our sidra) in front of him and learn from it the arts of appeasement and placation.

We shall conclude by referring to Sforno's (Italy, 16th century) treatment of the subject. This commentator maintains that Esau's heart was immediately worked on by Jacob's humble pleadings, comparing his conduct with the parable of the reed that bends before the storm. Sforno contrasts Jacob's prudence with the hot headed behaviour of the Zealots of the Second Temple who led to its destruction and almost prevented Rabbi Yoḥanan ben Zakkai from leaving the besieged city to treat with Vespasian the Roman general, and so save something out of the destruction. "If not for what these zealots did (refusing to treat with the Romans and burning all the stores in Jerusalem) our Temple would not have been destroyed," averred Rabbi Yoḥanan ben Zakkai in the Talmud (Gittin 56b).

The parable of the reed that bends before the storm (found in La Fontaine, Krilov and others, all obviously originating with an ancient common source) is referred to in more detail in the Gemara of *Ta'anit* 20a:

מאי דכתיב (משלי כז, ו): "נאמנים פצעי אוהב ונעתרות נשיקות שונא"? טובה קללה שקילל אחיה השילוני את ישראל מברכה שברכם בלעם הרשע. אחיה השילוני קללם בקנה. אמר להם לישראל (מלכים א' יד, ט): "והכה ה' את ישראל כאשר ינוד הקנה במים". מה קנה זה עומד במקום מים, וגזעו מהליף, ושורשיו מרובין, ואפילו כל הרוחות שבעולם באות ונושבות בו — אין מזיזות אותו ממקומו, אלא הולך ובא עמהן: דממו הרוחות — עמד הקנה במקומו. אבל בלעם הרשע ברכן בארז, שנאמר (במדבר כד, ו): "כארזים". מה ארז זה... אפילו כל רוחות שבעולם נושבים בו אין מזיזין אותו ממקומו כיון שנשבה בו רוח דרומית — עוקרתו והופכתו על פניו.

What is the lesson of the text (Proverbs 27, 6) "Faithful are the wounds of a friend, but the kisses of an enemy are importunate"? Better the curse that Ahiyah the Shilonite cursed Israel than the blessing with which Balaam the wicked blessed them. Ahiyah the Shilonite cursed them with a reed. He said to Israel (I Kings 14, 9): "The Lord will strike Israel as the reed is shaken in the water." Just as a reed stays put in the water: its stock renews itself and its roots are many and not all the winds that blow in the world can make it budge from its place but it bends with them. When the winds subside, the reed stays put. But Balaam the wicked blessed them with a cedar as it is said: "As the cedars" (Num. 24, 6). Just as the cedar: all the winds in the world that blow cannot make it budge; as soon as a south wind springs up it uproots it and turns it upside down.

Now we can appreciate Sforno's comment; he regards Jacob's conduct to be true to the archetypal pattern of Israel's future role among the nations before which she, like the reed always bends and survives, though stronger and mightier nations have disappeared and succumbed—like the oak or cedar which stands firm in the storm and is shattered.

What have we moderns to contribute to this debate between the commentators and expositors of a bygone era?

Questions for Further Study

1. Jacob was faced twice in his lifetime with the problem of placating the anger of an aggressor more powerful than himself. On these two occasions he employed different means of dealing with his opponent. Cf. his preparations for the meeting with Esau with those for the meeting of his children with Zaphenath-Paneah (Gen. 43, 11–14). What differences do you note and by what are they motivated?

2. "גרתי": לא נעשיתי שר וחשוב אלא גר. אינך כדאי לשנוא אותי על ברכת אביך, שברכני (כז, כט): "הוה גביר לאחיך", שהרי לא נתקיימה בי.

   With Laban I stayed, and remained until now"—I did not become a prince and an important personage but merely a sojourner. It is not worth it for you to hate me for your father's blessing with which he blessed me: "be lord over thy brethren" (27, 29), since it has not been fulfilled through me.   (Rashi)

   "שור וחמור": אבא אמר לי (כז, כח): "מטל השמים ומשמני הארץ", זו אינה לא מן השמים ולא מן הארץ.

   "And I have oxen, and asses and flocks, and male and female slaves; and I have sent to tell my lord..."—Father said unto me "Of the dew of heaven and of the fat places of the earth" (27, 28); this is neither of heaven nor of earth.   (Rashi)

   (a) What puzzles Rashi in these two citations?
   (b) What attitude do you think did Rashi adopt regarding Jacob's mission to Esau?

3. Can you explain the subtle distinction between R. Judah bar Simon's statement in *Bereshit Rabbah* 75, 2 and the citation from the same source (75, 11) quoted in our *Studies* above?*

4. To which historical event does Ramban allude in the citation on p. 347 when he refers to the kings in the second Temple making advances to the Romans?

* Note that both condemn Jacob's behaviour, but there is a difference between them.

350

JACOB WAS AFRAID

This week's sidra opens with Jacob's dispatch of emissaries to his brother Esau. In our previous study on this sidra we raised the question whether Jacob acted rightly in his appeal to Esau and his lowering himself to ask for his mercy. We noted that many of our classic commentators differed on this point, some of them approving Jacob's conduct, others disapproving, some praising his discretion and caution, and others condemning him for lack of boldness and drawing a moral lesson for future generations from his weakness:

> For we ourselves initiated our fall at the hands of Edom, since the kings in the Second Temple (Hasmoneans) allied themselves with the Romans, some of them going to Rome, and this was the reason for their overthrow at their hands. This fact is alluded to by our Sages and is publicised in books.   (Ramban)

In this way the history of the Patriarchs as recorded in the Torah serves as the archetype of what future generations might expect. With our own hands we sealed our own fate by lowering ourselves, allowing others to lord it over us. As the prophet Jeremiah (13, 21) words it: "thou has taught them to be captains to be chief over thee." However, this time we shall deal with another point. After Jacob had taken the step alluded to above, the emissaries returned with the following evil tidings:

בָּאנוּ אֶל־אָחִיךָ אֶל־עֵשָׂו
וְגַם הֹלֵךְ לִקְרָאתְךָ וְאַרְבַּע־מֵאוֹת אִישׁ עִמּוֹ.

We came to thy brother, to Esau,
and also he is coming to meet thee, and four hundred
men with him.   (32, 7)

351

What was Jacob's reaction to this news? What were his inner feelings, and what tangible steps did he take to meet the threat? Both these are made clear to us in the Torah. Regarding the state of his inner feelings the Torah explicitly states:

וַיִּירָא יַעֲקֹב מְאֹד
וַיֵּצֶר לוֹ.

Then Jacob was greatly afraid,
and distressed. (32, 8)

All of the commentators express surprise at this. How was it possible that he who had been vouchsafed in his dream the vision of a ladder joining heaven and earth, the angels of God ascending and descending thereon, hearing the word of the Almighty assuring him that He would protect him wherever he went (28, 15): how was it possible that he who had been accompanied by guardian angels, to whom the Almighty had revealed himself in the house of Laban and bade him return to his birthplace, and even warned Laban to beware of harming him—how was it possible that he should doubt the fulfillment of the Divine promise? Surely the Patriarch was at one with the sentiments expressed in the following verses of the Psalms:

For he shall give his angels charge over thee,
to keep thee in all thy ways. (91, 11)

The Lord is on my side
I will not fear:
what can man do unto me? (118, 6)

Our Sages were similarly not unaware of this difficulty and they posed the question in various places and gave their answers:

אדם שהקב"ה הבטיחו — היה ירא ומפחד ?
אלא שאמר יעקב אבינו : אוי לי שמא יגרום החטא!

A man whom the Lord had promised (security), should he fear

and be afraid? But what Jacob meant was: **Woe is me, per-adventure** sin has made me forfeit (Divine protection).

(Mekhilta Beshalaḥ)

A similar idea was expressed by our Sages commenting on Moses' fear of Og (Numbers, 21):

זה שאמר הכתוב (משלי כח, יד): "אשרי אדם מפחד תמיד ומקשה לבו יפול
ברעה". כך היא מידת החסידים, אע"פ שהקב"ה מבטיחן — אינן פורקין יראה.
וכן ביעקב כתיב: "וַיִירא יעקב מאד" למה נתיירא ? אמר: שמא נתקלקלתי
אצל לבן בכלום . . . והניחני הקב"ה !

To this the following verse applies (Proverbs 28, 14): "Happy is the man that feareth alway: but he that hardeneth his heart shall fall into mischief." Such is the character of pious men, though the Holy One blessed be He promises them His protection, they do not throw off fear. So it is written with regard to Jacob: "Then Jacob was greatly afraid." Why was he afraid? He said: Peradventure I strayed in some way whilst with Laban... and the Holy One has consequently left me.

(Tanḥuma, Ḥukkat, 25)

In other words, the righteous man who has been guaranteed Divine protection does not make the mistake of regarding his favourable destiny assured, convinced that no act of his, whether good or bad, will influence his path in the future, since God had already decreed that he would be safe. The genuinely upright man understands that the promise granted him by divine grace is only conditional, depending on him not becoming "soiled by sin" as our Sages phrased it.

On Yom Kippur we read in the book of Jonah how the prophet came to the sinful city and proclaimed its total destruction, with no reservation or condition, on a specific date:

Yet forty days,
and Nineveh shall be overthrown. (Jonah 3, 4)

In spite of the fact that this decree had gone forth from the King of Kings, the men of Nineveh understood that it was possible for man by his own deeds to change his own fate and become a partner with his Creator in deciding his destiny. They did all that was humanly possible to avert the decree, repenting of their deeds and hoping that:

Who can tell, peradventure God will turn and repent, and turn away from his fierce anger. (Ibid. 9)

Conversely, Jacob understood that the promise granted him was no unchangeable decree, or charm (cf. "there is no charm in Jacob," Numbers 23, 23) or bill of debt safely secured in his pocket to be produced to the Creator for honouring, irrespective of circumstances. He knew it was liable to be cancelled, should his deeds and conduct deserve it.

Our Sages pointed this out in their comment [1] on the wording of the original Divine promise to Jacob in the dream:

"אם יהיה אלהים עמדי" (כח, כ) — ר' הונא בשם ר' אחא אמר: "הנה אנכי עמך" — וכתיב: " א ם יהיה ה' עמדי"? אלא מכאן שאין הבטחה לצדיק בעולם הזה.

R. Huna in the name of R. Aḥa said: "And behold I am with thee" (Gen. 28, 15) and it is also written: "If God will be with me" (Ibid, 20). But from here we learn that there is no guarantee for the righteous man in this world. (Bereshit Rabbah 76, 2)

The reason for this is, as given earlier, "peradventure sin has made me forfeit Divine protection."

Jacob's fears, therefore, were not indicative of lack of trust in God, but rather of a lack of confidence in himself, in his own worthiness, righteousness and conduct.[2]

Abravanel offers a psychological rather than theological explanation of Jacob's apprehensions on hearing the news brought by the emissaries:

Jacob's fear of Esau was not due to the weakness of his faith. Indeed he genuinely trusted in God. But his fear was like that of the real hero who going to battle is afraid of death and senses the danger but out of noble motives scorns life and chooses a brave death ... He who enters battle thinking he will not die cannot be called a hero, just the same as he who gives charity to show his scorn of money cannot be called generous, since he does not do this because this is his valued choice, but rather because he despises money. Similarly, the mighty man should be grieved over the possibility of death, nevertheless choosing this because of its nobility... Jacob's fears can be explained in the same way. Had he not been afraid of Esau killing him and his wives and children, his approaches to him would not have indicated trust in God and his destiny, but he would have gone to him thinking that he would behave to him as a brother. But now that he appreciated the measure of Esau's hate toward him and knew it so that his natural fears were aroused, his intelligence which controlled his emotions, as it should be with a man of character, rebuked him for his fear, and he steeled himself for the interview with his brother. Such a man is properly to be called a believer in His prophecy and one who trusts in the destiny of his God.

In other words, Jacob's fear was not of sin or from a sense of unworthiness, but the natural apprehensions that man is heir to, both righteous and wicked, both great and small, assured or not assured of the Almighty's protection. It is the fear which even the bravest of heroes recognises too well: "Like the real hero... who is afraid of death."

Only after overcoming his fears and faintheartedness does the real hero and believer in God emerge. For this reason, the Torah depicts Jacob in his hour of weakness:

וַיִּירָא יַעֲקֹב מְאֹד וַיֵּצֶר לוֹ.

**And Jacob was greatly afraid,
and distressed.**

The Torah perhaps depicts for us too how he strengthened himself as a result of his confidence in God, relying on Him not to forsake him. He took, therefore, the necessary safeguards since it was forbidden for man to rely on a miracle. He prepared three lines of defence: gifts, prayer, and battle דורון, תפילה, מלחמה. We shall discuss the relationship between these three different methods of approach in the next chapter of our *Studies* on this sidra.

Questions for Further Study

1. ### Jacob was greatly afraid and distressed (32, 8)

   "He was greatly afraid and distressed": He was afraid lest he be killed: he was distressed that he might kill others.
   > (Rashi foll. Ber. Rabbah et Tanḥuma)

   Repetition of synonymous phrases to emphasise the degree of his fear.
   > (Radak)

   The fears in his heart promoted his distress, for from them he divined that he was in for trouble.
   > (Ha'amek Davar)

   (a) What difficulty are the foregoing commentators trying to solve?

   (b) What are the differences in approach between the three in their solution to the problem.

2. "The messengers returned to Jacob saying" (32, 7): The messengers carried out their mission but the text does not refer to this because *it was not necessary*. By the report "he is also coming to meet thee" (32, 8) they implied: when you go to meet him he will be already well on his way towards you and you will therefore very soon encounter each other.

   "Jacob was greatly afraid": His fears were prompted by the fact that Esau had left town and was coming to meet him accompanied by as many as four hundred men. He concluded that he had taken them along to attack him. In my opinion the text implies that Esau did not give the emissaries a proper welcome. Perhaps he did not even receive them personally not allowing them to come into his presence and speak to him at all. Otherwise the text would have mentioned that he asked after his brother and sent back greeting to inform him of his impending coming and they would have told Jacob of this. Evidently he still bore Jacob a grudge and was waiting for an opportunity to take his revenge and for this purpose took along his army. The messengers however made their own inquiries and learnt that he was on his way to meet Jacob and this is the force of *gam* "also." For they said: We came to thy brother, to Esau. To us he had nothing to say and for you no message of goodwill and what is more ("also") he is coming to meet you with his strong men. This of course only intensified Jacob's misgivings. The text therefore notes: Jacob was afraid and greatly perturbed. Our rabbis too concluded from the text that the messenger had observed Esau's enmity and this they had expressed in their report when they said: "We came to thy brother, to Esau" you behaved to him as a brother but he still acts like Esau. But in the end when he actually saw Jacob and observed how he humbled himself and prostrated himself seven times from a distance till he reached him, then he was moved and concluded that Jacob now acknowledged his birthright and supremacy, as I have explained elsewhere[3] and was reconciled; for the human heart belongs to God who moulds it in accordance with His wish.   (Ramban)

(a) Point out the various difficulties the Ramban removes in the above comment.
(b) What is the difference between the two explanations of Ramban?
(c) Why does Ramban offer two explanations of the phrase: "He was greatly afraid and distressed"?

Cf. Ramban's remark here: "but the text does not refer to this because it was not necessary" with the following comments of his on other texts:

"The man took a gold ring and two bracelets upon her hands" (Gen. 24, 22). The text omits the verb. It should have read: "The man took the gold ring and *put it* in her nose and the two bracelets *he put* on her hand." But the verb "put" is omitted—a frequent practice.

"Your father mocked me" (ibid. 31, 7) This was true. The fact that the text made no previous mention of this does not matter. Such omissions are frequent in the Torah. In the previous chapter (30, 15-16) there is no mention of Leah's giving of the mandrakes to Rachel.

"Behold I shall rain down this time tomorrow ... and now therefore send hasten in" (Exodus 9, 18-19): These are God's actual words to Moses. Moses went of course and transmitted the Divine message to Pharaoh omitting nothing. But the text does not repeat it verbatim but merely notes that "he that feared the Lord drove his cattle into the houses" in accordance with the instructions Moses had given them.

"Go to Pharaoh" ... Exodus 10, 1-2. The Almighty had obviobviously informed Moses of the impending locust plague and told him here to transmit the news to Pharaoh. Otherwise what was the point of the command "Go to Pharaoh"? The text does not mention the burden of the message he had to tell Pharaoh—which is only reported in the description of Moses's actual audience with Pharaoh—(ibid. vv. 3–6). The text leaves it to be understood and is brief. It similarly leaves it to be understood earlier on with the plague of hail. The Divine message to Moses about it is reported by the text (9, 13) but not Moses' transmission of it to Pharaoh ... Quite simply because the text wishes to be brief, sometimes leaving it to be understood, and at others, being explicit.

What is the difficulty common to all the passages cited and what is Ramban's method of handling the matter?

---

1 See p. 309.

2 Rashbam, however, disapproves of his fear, See p. 367.

3 He is referring to his comment on verse 5: "Thus shall you say to my Lord Esau, thus saith thy servant Jacob": Know that Jacob's paying all his honour to Esau calling him lord and himself servant was prompted by his fear. It was the custom of the younger brother to honour the firstborn as if he was his father. The Torah too takes account of this in the additional *et* in the phrase: כבד את אביך "honour thy father and mother"—added, our Sages observed, to include the eldest brother. Now Jacob had taken away his birthright and blessing for which Esau hated him. He deliberately therefore went out of his way to show him that the sale meant nothing to him and that he was paying him the honour due to a parent in order to eradicate the enmity in his heart.

GIFTS·PRAYER AND BATTLE

As soon as the messengers returned from Esau with the news:
"we came to your brother, to Esau and he is actually on his
way to meet you, accompanied by four hundred men" Jacob
"was afraid and greatly distressed."

This fear of Jacob has been the subject of comment down the
ages, beginning with the Midrash:

ר' פנחס בשם ר' איבו פתח (משלי ג, ה): "בטח אל ה' בכל לבך". שני בני
אדם הבטיחם הקב"ה ונתייראו: בחור שבאבות ובחור שבנביאים. בחור
שבאבות — זה יעקב, דכתיב (תהלים קלה, ד): "כי יעקב בחר לו יה"
והבטיחו הקב"ה, דכתיב (כח, יח): "והנה אנכי עמך ושמרתיך בכל אשר
תלך" — ו נ ת י י ר א , דכתיב (לב, ח): "ויירא יעקב מאד". ובחור
שבנביאים — זה משה, דכתיב (תהלים קו, כג): "לולי משה בחירו", והבטיחו
הקב"ה, דכתיב (שמות ג, יב): "כי אהיה עמך" — ו נ ת י י ר א , שנאמר
(במדבר כא, לד): "אל תירא אותו". למי אומרים "אל תירא" ? — אלא למי
שהוא מתיירא. מכן שאין הבטחה לצדיקים בעולם הזה.

R. Pinḥas in the name of R. Evo opened with the text (Prov.
3, 5): "Trust in the Lord with all your heart." Two men were
given a guarantee by the Holy One blessed be He and were
afraid: the chosen of the Patriarchs and chosen of the prophets.
The chosen of the patriarchs—this refers to Jacob, on the basis
of the text (Ps. 135, 4): "For the Lord has chosen Jacob for
Himself. The Holy One blessed be He gave him a guarantee,
as it is written (Gen. 28, 18): "Behold I am with you and shall
guard you wherever you go." He was afraid, as it is written: "And
Jacob was afraid." The chosen of the prophets was Moses, as it
is written (Ps. 106, 23): 'Were it not for Moses, His chosen
one." The Holy One blessed be He gave him a guarantee, as it is
written (Ex. 3, 12): "For I shall be with you." And he was
afraid, for it is stated (Nu. 21, 34): "Fear him not." Who is told
not to be afraid other than one who is afraid? From here you
may learn that there is no guarantee for the righteous in this
world.   (Bereshit Rabbah 76)

We treated this theme of the righteous man who knows he has no Divine guarantee of wellbeing in this world, and that any such promise given him is always liable to be invalidated by the contingency of sin, in our *Studies* of this sidra on pp. 352 ff. This time we shall study the behaviour that Jacob's fear gave rise to, the three-pronged preparations described by our Sages and heading our *Studies*. Rashi quotes this same dictum in his comment to the passage: "And the camp that is left shall escape" (32, 9):

"והיה המחנה הנשאר לפליטה" (לב, ט): **התקין עצמו לשלושה דברים:** לדורון, לתפילה ולמלחמה. לדורון — (לב, כב): **"ותעבור המנחה על פניו";** לתפילה — (לב, י): "אלהי אבי אברהם"; למלחמה — (לב, ט): "והיה המחנה הנשאר לפליטה".

He prepared himself for three eventualities: gifts, prayer and battle. Gifts—"So the gift went on ahead of him" (32, 22); Prayer—"The God of my father Abraham" (10); Battle—"and the camp that is left shall escape" (9).

Many have been puzzled at this combination of activities, resort to human contrivance, money and force, on the one hand, and appeal for Divine help through prayer, on the other. Here we cite some of Arama's penetrating observations on this subject, in his *Akedat Yizhak* on our sidra:

"Behold the eye of the Lord is towards those that revere Him, to save their soul from death" (Ps. 33, 18–19). Nevertheless, human initiative is still called for, and the lack of it where necessary constitutes a sin. Our Sages emphasised this in their comment to the text (Deut. 2, 7): "For the Lord your God has blessed you in all the work of your hand." Rabbi Eliezer b. Jacob stated: "Blessed you": you might think this is the case even if you sit idle. The text therefore adds: "in all the work of your hand." If he worked, he is blessed, otherwise he is not blessed. What is the meaning of the next phrase: "He hath known your walking"?—your wallowing, your suffering in cking out a livelihood."

Notice that the implication of the verb "know" here is not cognition but approval,[1] identification with the action as if the text read: "I approved your walking, your exertions and struggles." The pun on the word "walking" "wallowing" is meant to suggest that even if man's efforts to satisfy his needs call for labour and toil and even what is considered degrading work, he should not recoil from it.

But Arama is equally well aware that, side by side with this duty of self-help, there exists in Scriptural and Rabbinic writings abundant reference to that of "casting thy burden upon the Lord" (Ps. 55, 23). He endeavours to define the correct balance that is to be preserved between self-help and trust in the Lord, by citing examples from the lives of the patriarchs, prophets and other Biblical heroes:

> The proper way is for man to keep both in mind, to make his own plans, as far as possible, not to shun industry and self-help neither relying on merit (i.e. *zekhut*—Divine reward for his merits) nor giving himself up to depair, but doing as much as is humanly possible in furthering his interests, not trusting however in the success of his own efforts but in the will of God in whose hand is everything. Solomon the wise formulates this idea as follows (Prov. 16, 9) : "A man's heart deviseth his way; but the Lord directeth his steps." Every man is obliged to help himself and not rely on Divine favour. Who can be likened to He who said to Samuel (1 Sam. 16, 2) : "Take a heifer with thee and say, I am come to sacrifice to the Lord"?[2]

This duty of self-help, of man's duty to extricate himself from danger by his own efforts evidently overrides the specific Biblical precept of "Keep far from falsehood." God's advice to Samuel evidently constitutes the most extreme example of the limits to which man himself has to go in extricating himself from a dangerous situation. Samuel, though on a Divine mission, was not told not to be afraid and that those engaged in a holy mission cannot come to harm. On the contrary, he was bidden take all precautions, even to the point of disguising his real intentions, putting on a show. It would seem that Arama needed no more extreme instance of the duty of self-help, but on second thoughts, we are bound to conclude that this is not typical. Samuel did not do this of his own accord but was commanded by God to adopt this line of action. There is therefore no proof here of the duty of self-help in the absence of any explicit Divine instruction to this effect. Arama therefore cites a second example:

361

> Who have we greater and more beloved by God than David? Notwithstanding, he left no stone unturned in helping himself to escape from his enemies and Saul, and did not rely on the Divine promises of his future success, since he knew that these only hold good for those who complement them by human efforts to the limits of mortal capacity. This realisation obliged him to change his behaviour and feign madness, though it involved so much degradation, since it offered a way of escape. After he had done everything in his own power to save himself, he applied to God for help: "I sought the Lord and He answered me and saved me from all my troubles" (Ps. 34, 5), which he would not have deserved, had he not first made every effort to save himself.

> King David himself explained all this in his prayer in the cave (Ps. 142, 5): "Look on my right hand and see, for there is no man that knoweth me; I have no way to flee; no man careth for my soul. I have cried unto Thee O Lord; I have said, Thou art My refuge ... attend unto my cry ... bring my soul out of prison." What he says, in effect, is that he has exhausted all means of self-help. What is left him? His prayer and cry. He says therefore: "attend my cry ... bring my soul out of prison."

This example is much more effective than the previous one. Samuel had received no Divine promise of long life or success in his mission. But David like Jacob had been explicitly promised by God the success of his mission. He knew he had been chosen and anointed king and that He who had chosen him would certain ensure he achieved the kingship. Nevertheless he scorned no subterfuge or effort, however degrading, to extricate himself out of his troubles, only relying on Divine help when all other human avenues were exhausted.

The third example is even more telling—man confronted by a situation from which there is no escape by human effort, however resourceful. Nothing is left but the mercy of heaven: Arama cites the situation facing David in the war waged by Achish king of the Philistines against Saul (1 Sam. 28).[3] He was faced by a terrible dilemma. Achish who summoned him to follow him would have involved him in fighting his own flesh and blood. To refuse would have equally courted mortal danger. It could not be argued that David intended to follow him in the fight against Saul and the people and turn against him acting as a fifth column. "That would have been brazen treachery," notes Arama, who continues:

> But David went along, relying on God somehow to work things out for the best, "for the eyes of the Lord are towards the righteous" and He inspired the servants of Achish to regard him as a traitor and say to their master (1 Sam. 29, 4): "Wherewith should this fellow reconcile himself unto his lord? should it not be with the heads of these men?" The king therefore commanded him to turn back, and though David urged him to allow him to go along, Achish would not accede to his request. In this manner the Lord rescued him from this ticklish situation...
> This is the proper attitude for man to trust in the Lord and rely on His God, when he has done everything possible to help himself. In His providence He will then answer his prayer as He did David when He saved him from sin and treachery.

In the same way, we may understand why the patriarch Jacob both prayed to God and kept his powder dry, as it were. But the order of priority in his preparations is puzzling. First he prepared for battle, then interceded with God and after his prayer, despatched a gift to placate the enemy. On the basis of what we have read in *Akedat Yizhak*, he should first have finished his own human preparations, exhausted all the means of self-help at his disposal, arranged his camp for battle, sent his gifts and only resorted to prayer at the very end. Indeed, this was the order adopted by Jacob himself when he found himself in trouble, on a later occasion, on the eve of his sons' second journey to Egypt. They had been forced to take Benjamin along and Jacob was confronted by the dilemma of courting starvation in Canaan or possible bereavement in Egypt, Joseph and Reuben already gone and now Benjamin having to be risked. He resorted to every human subterfuge: double money, gifts of the choice things of the land and finally: "the Lord send you mercy before the man." As Rashi observes on this text:

"ואל שדי": מעתה אינכם חסרים כלום, אלא תפילה — הריני מתפלל עליכם.

Henceforth you are short of nothing but prayer—so here I pray for you.

Why then did not Jacob adopt this same order in our sidra? Perhaps the Torah has given us leave to peep deep into. Jacob's heart to teach us a lesson in self-improvement. Perhaps the suffering of the twenty years' servitude and exile with Laban, the deceptions practised on him there had not driven home to him the full significance of the deed of "thy brother came with guile." Perhaps he still justified the immoral deed by the justness of the end, given the seal of approval in his father's confirmation of the blessing after the deed: "yea, and he shall be blessed." He had still not experienced even the shadow of a doubt regarding the rightness of his conduct. Only now through his prayer he experienced a re-appraisal of his conduct. He said:

> I am not worthy of all the kindness and of all the truth
> which Thou hast shown to thy servant; for with my staff
> I passed over this Jordan and now I am become two
> camps. (32, 11)

Now he had been brought to realise the greatness of the Creator's kindness to him. Suddenly he realised the greatness of his wealth and at that moment resolved to give it to the one who valued material wealth. Therefore:

> he took of what he had with him, a present for Esau
> his brother, two hundred she-goats and twenty he-goats,
> two hundred ewes, twenty rams, thirty milch-camels and
> their colts, forty kine and ten bulls, twenty she-asses and
> ten foals. (Ibid 14)

The wealth is yours. Take it. This blessing I have not stolen from you. He therefore said to him at the encounter with him: "Take I pray thee, my *blessing* which is brought thee" (33, 11). On this text Rashi comments:

"ברכתי": מנחתי. מנחה זו הבאה על ראיית פנים.

"My blessing"—i.e. my offering, this offering brought to welcome you.

If you should wonder why Jacob uses the word *berakha*—blessing—instead of *minha*—"offering," as in the previous verse, it may be suggested that he deliberately called that abundance of livestock "blessing," to inform Esau that this blessing with which he had been blessed, he would not steal from him, and here it was. It was this type of blessing which he had been interested in.

His prayer had prompted him to see things in their true light.

---

[1] This special meaning of *yada'* is found frequently in the text and is discussed in our *Studies, Vayera* (2) p. 167.

[2] See p. 566.

[3] This chapter merits careful study. It deals with the problem of "dual loyalties" dramatically portraying David's plight. The German Jewish poet Richard Beer-Hofmann made this the subject of his play *Der Junge David*.

A MAN WRESTLED WITH HIM

This is one of the most puzzling chapters in the Torah. Artificial rationalisation of things essentially non-rational will certainly not help us to penetrate this mystery-shrouded narrative. We shall decline to follow that non-Jewish commentator, who endeavoured to trace Jacob's limp, after the wrestling bout with the angel, to an attack of rheumatism, caused by sleeping in the open, all night, in the damp atmosphere of the brook. Such a mechanical approach to supernatural mystical events must be ruled out in favour of the primary demand of interpretation —response to the spirit, tone and intention of the narrative. We shall likewise refrain from entering into the controversy between Rambam and Ramban as to whether this wrestling constituted an external event taking place in the world of the senses, or whether a wholly, inner, prophetic experience in Jacob's soul projected through the medium of a dream. In what way will the authenticity or significance of the event be affected by the question of whether the man was sent to him in a vision of the night, "a prophetic vision," or whether he came to him awake, and wrestled with him "in full possession of his physical senses?" We have merely to try to understand the significance of the struggle, and what the Torah wished to teach us through it.

Who was this man? All the commentators agree that he was no ordinary mortal, no armed brigand waylaying a harmless traveller. The text itself bears ample witness to this. Who introduced him into the intimate counsels of the Almighty, so that he knew what message He intended to transmit to Jacob?—

וַיֹּאמֶר לֹא יַעֲקֹב יֵאָמֵר עוֹד שִׁמְךָ כִּי אִם־יִשְׂרָאֵל.

**No more shall Jacob be called thy name but Israel shall
be thy name.**   (32, 29)

Moreover, Jacob said, after all that had happened to him: "for
I have seen God face to face" (32, 30). Evidently then, the
wrestler was no ordinary man.

Rashbam's view, which we quote herewith, is similarly unacceptable. He states that Jacob wished to flee from Esau his
brother and the Almighty sent the angel—

> from whom he could not flee, that he might see the fulfillment
> of the Almighty's promise that Esau would do him no hurt.
> "When he saw that he could not prevail against him" i.e. the
> angel saw that Jacob wished to extricate himself and flee in spite
> of him—"and the hollow of Jacob's thigh became out of joint."
> Jacob was hurt and lamed, because the Almighty had promised
> him safety and yet he had run away. We find the same thing
> happened to all those who journeyed against the will of the
> Holy One blessed be He or refused to journey, that they were
> punished, as with Moses . . . Jonah . . . Balaam.

Rashbam's approach which is distinguished by a studious avoidance of the allegoric, in favour of the plain, literal sense is
untenable, from the point of view advanced earlier. In any
case, does it sound reasonable to maintain that the phrase "he
could not prevail against him" implies that the angel could
not bring Jacob to obedience to the will of God and trust in
Him and that, consequently the "thou hast prevailed" describing, three verses later, Jacob's victory over the angel implies
that his weakness, his wish to flee from the Lord, his natural
physical fears triumphed over his faith and trust? Such an interpretation is inconceivable. It was as a mark of honour for this
"prevailing," that Jacob was crowned with the name of Israel.
The Midrash seems much closer to the real meaning:

ר׳ חמא חנינא אמר: שרו של עשו היה, דהווה אמר ליה (לג, י): "כי על כן
ראיתי פניך כראות פני אלהים ותרצני".

R. Hama bar Hanina said: It was the prince (tutelary angel) of
Esau, for he said to him: "for therefore I have seen thy face, as

though I had seen the face of God, and thou wast pleased with me"
(Gen. 33, 10).   (Bereshit Rabbah, 77, 3)

This explanation is accepted by Rashi: "Our Sages explained
that he was the prince of Esau." But we still need to understand what the term "prince of Esau" connotes, and what, in
general, the phrase "prince of a nation" (*sar shel uma*) implies.
According to the Midrash, the angels who went up and down the
ladder, beheld by Jacob, in his dream, were the princes of the
nations, whose rise and fall he was symbolically shown. What
is the character of this supernal representative of each nation on
earth? Krochmal in his *Moreh Nevukhei Hazeman* ("Guide of
the Perplexed of This Age") translates the Midrashic imagery
into modern abstract concepts:

> The essence of a nation is not synonymous with its physical ex-
> istence but with its spiritual character... No nation disappears
> completely until the spirit animating it, is destroyed and dis-
> appears. What we call the genius of a people is what is termed
> in the Bible, in the language of the dawn of thought (the figura-
> tive, tangible expressions of the Bible) "the gods of the nation,"
> and by the early visionaries (Daniel) and Talmudic Sages, "the
> prince of the nation." The spiritual essence animating and dist-
> inguishing each people was personified. Just as the king of a na-
> tion represents its visible, external linking and unifying factor,
> so its god represents its unifying and coherent inner essence. This
> helps us to understand the meaning of the following passages:
> "and against all the gods of Egypt I will execute judgment"
> (Exodus 12, 12); "Behold I will punish the multitudes of No,
> and Pharaoh, and Egypt, with their gods" (Jeremiah 46, 25) and:
> "and Chemosh shall go forth in captivity" (ibid. 48, 7). In this
> same sense, we may understand, too, the rabbinic dictum "The
> Holy One blessed be He does not exact retribution from a na-
> tion until He has first exacted retribution from its gods." [1]

If it is true to say that the patriarch Jacob fought with the
"prince of Esau," we may now understand why this particular
spot and hour was chosen. Before Jacob actually encountered
Esau in the flesh, his spirit struggled with that of Esau's, with
his national genius. Only after the prince of Esau had acknowledged his title to the paternal blessing ("And he blessed him

there") was Jacob, injured and limping, able to go forth to meet his brother and become reconciled with him.

If Jacob's opponent was the "prince of Esau," how are we to understand the significance of the struggle, of Jacob's victory and the injury inflicted on his thigh joint by his adversary? Our Sages regarded the whole incident as illustrative of the principle that the "deeds of the patriarchs are a sign to their descendants" (prefiguring similar events in the nation's future history). In his introduction to the sidra, Ramban elaborates on this idea. Midrash *Lekaḥ Tov* explains our text in the light of this symbolic struggle taking place between Jacob and Esau:

"ויאבק איש עמו עד עלות השחר" (לב, כה) — **עד שיעלה שחר לישראל.** ישועת ישראל, שהוא דומה לשחר, כי הגלות דומה ללילה; אומות העולם ומלכות אדום הרשעה הם נאבקים עם ישראל כדי להטעותם מדרך ה', שנאמר (שיר השירים ז, א): "שובי שובי השולמית. שובי שובי ונחזה בך".

"וירא כי לא יכול לו" (שם, כו) — לא יכול להוציא את ישראל מייחודו **של** מקום. "ויגע בכף ירכו" (שם, שם) — זה המילה, וכן גזרה מלכות הרשעה שמד, שלא ימולו את בניהם.

"ותקע כף ירך יעקב בהאבקו עמו" (שם, שם) — **אלה שטמאו בימי השמד.**

"And there wrestled a man with him until the breaking of the day"—until the breaking of the day for Israel, the Salvation of Israel. For the exile is like the night. The nations of the world and the wicked kingdom of Edom wrestle with Israel to lead them astray from the path of the Lord, as it is written (Canticles 7, 1): "Return, return, O Shulamite, that we may look upon thee." "And when he saw that he could not prevail against him"—that he could not dissuade Israel from acknowledging the unity of the Omnipotent, "he touched the hollow of his thigh"—that is the circumcision. Indeed the wicked government instituted religious persecution and forbade the circumcision of their children. "And the hollow of Jacob's thigh was out of joint"—referring to those defiled during the days of persecution.

Ramban alludes to even crueller times, evidently drawn from his own personal experience, as well of those of his predecessors, in interpreting Jacob's wrestling with the angel:

The whole matter represents an allusion to our future history, that there would come a time when the descendants of Esau would overcome Jacob almost to the point of total destruction. This happened during the days of the Sages of the Mishnah in the generation of R. Judah ben Baba and his colleagues, in accordance with their statement: "Said R. Ḥiyya bar Abba: if a man will say to me, Give your life for the sanctification of the name of the Holy One blessed be He, I give it, so long as he will slay me forthwith, but a generation of persecution (*shemad* —forced apostasy), I cannot bear. What did they do in a generation of persecution? They would bring iron balls, make them white hot in the flame and place them under the armpits and drive their souls from them. There were other generations who did such things to us and *worse than this*. But we endured all and it passed us by, as is intimated in the text: "And Jacob came to Shalem" (*Shalem* means "whole" or "perfect" in Hebrew, so that the text may be read, homiletically: "And Jacob came through unscathed").

Both commentators emphasise that Jacob emerged safely out of his ordeal, and that no evil could succeed against him, and both note the heavy price he had to pay for his struggle. The difference between them, lies in the fact that the author of *Lekaḥ Tov* regards the disjointed thigh as a symbol of those myriads, lost to us by their defilement amongst the nations, by their failure to stand the test. Ramban regards the text as alluding to the righteous, the martyrs who sanctified the name of God and were slain, depriving the nation of its most precious manhood. But "we endured all and it passed us by," as intimated in the text: "And Jacob came to Shalem."

But the text promises more than that. Not only will Jacob emerge "whole" from the ordeal. But he will enjoy his adversary's blessing. The breaking of the dawn involves not merely the victory over every adversary, but also his blessing with which he will bless us. The same message of blessing was vouchsafed Abraham, first of the Patriarchs, in the course of the first Divine revelation to him, calling on him to leave his country and kindred and place a barrier between him and the rest of the world. Nevertheless, Abraham was informed:

אדם אומר לבנו : תהא כאברהם.

370

"And all the families of the earth shall be blessed in thee"—A father will say to his son: Be like Abraham!

(Rashi on Gen. 12, 3)

Questions for Further Study

"ברכתני : הודה לי על הברכות שעשו מערער עליהן.

1. "And he said, I will not let thee go, except thou bless me" (Gen. 32, 27)—Acknowledge my title to the blessings which Esau claims.

    (Rashi)

    What warrant can you find in the text for Rashi's interpretation, that the blessing mentioned here did not mean an actual blessing by the angel, but merely recognition of his title to his father's blessing?

2. אמר לו יעקב: כיון שאתה שרו של עשו לא אניחך עד שתמחול לי מן הברכה שברכני אבא! אמר לו : ומי מתרעם עליך ? אמר לו: שאמר לי עשו (כז, לו): "הכי קרא שמו יעקב ויעקבני זה פעמים". "ויברך אותו שם" (לב ל) — וזאת הברכה שברכו, שמחל לו על הברכות.

    "Thy name shall be called no more Jacob, but Israel"—Said Jacob to him: Since you are the prince of Esau, I shall not let you go until you forgive me for the blessing, with which Father blessed me! He replied: Who bears a grievance against thee? Jacob answered: Forasmuch as Esau said to me: "Is he not rightly named Jacob, for he hath supplanted me these two times?" (Gen. 27, 36). "And he blessed him there"—this is the blessing with which he blessed him, that he forgave him for the matter of the blessings.

    (Midrash Aggada)

    (a) In what light according to this Midrash did Jacob himself view his deed in taking away the blessings from Esau, as related in *Toldot?*

    (b) What warrant in the text did the Midrash find for its attitude?

ı Buber supplies an illuminating commentary to this passage from Krochmal in his essay: "The Gods of the Nations and God" in *Israel and the World,* essays in a time of crisis, pp. 195–213, Schocken New York 1963.

HISTORY REPEATS ITSELF

Ramban begins his commentary to the sidra with the following
passage:

> This chapter imparts the message that the Holy One blessed
> be He delivered His servant and redeemed him from the hand
> of the stronger and sent his angel to deliver him. It further teaches
> us that he did not rely on his own righteousness but made every
> effort to help himself. There is an also another message in this
> chapter—all that happened between our ancestor and his brother
> Esau will continually recur in our dealings with the descendants
> of Esau . . .

Ramban followed the line of interpretation adopted by our
Sages who regarded the Patriarchs as models to be emulated
by their descendants and their experiences as the archetype of
what would befall their children. These two ideas were expressed
in the phrase: "The deed of the forefathers is a sign for the
children." [1]

Many parallels in Jewish history have been found by our commentators to the encounter between Esau and Jacob. Just as
Jacob was taken as a symbolic name for the Jewish people, so
Esau was said to represent Rome, the power that destroyed
the Temple and scattered the remnants of Israel.

At the end of the meeting between the two brothers, Esau
urged Jacob to accompany him. The latter however declined
the honour and made various excuses. This is also expounded
in the symbolic sense as prefiguring the course of Jewish history:

> Jacob wished to avoid fraternising with his brother and our
> Sages extracted a message from this: When Rabbi Yannai went
> to meet the authorities, he used to take heed of this chapter and
> did not have the Romans escort him on his way. Once he paid

no heed to this chapter and had the Romans escort him. Where-upon he did not reach Acre till he had sold the coat off his back. (Ramban)

Ramban explains that Rabbinic tradition regarded the story of Esau's encounter with Jacob in our sidra as: "the chapter of exile"—the archetypal pattern of Israel's diaspora existence. When Rabbi Yannai had to go to Rome to treat with the Roman authorities—the "kings of Edom," he would take as his model, his ancestor Jacob's method of dealing with Esau. He therefore refused to accept the offer of the powers-that-be to provide him with an escort since, "they only befriend a man for their own purposes and confiscate his worldly goods."

The historic parallel in our chapter is obvious: Jacob the puny one confronted by the mighty Esau, and attempting to placate him. Let us make a closer study of one remarkable verse in this encounter:

וַיָּרָץ עֵשָׂו לִקְרָאתוֹ וַיְחַבְּקֵהוּ וַיִּפֹּל עַל־
צַוָּארָו וַיִּשָּׁקֵהוּ וַיִּבְכּוּ

And Esau ran to meet him, and embraced him, and fell on his neck and kissed him and they wept (33, 4)

It was not only the vowel points over the phrase "and kissed him," in the Hebrew, that has excited attention but also the unusual display of affection, so uncharacteristic of Esau:

"וישקהו" — נקוד עליו. א"ר שמעון בן אלעזר: בכל מקום שאתה מוצא הכתב רבה על הנקודה [האותיות הבלתי מנוקדות מרובות על המנוקדות] — אתה דורש את הכתב, הנקודה רבה על הכתב — אתה דורש את הנקודה. כאן לא כתב רבה על הנקודה ולא נקודה רבה על הכתב, אלא מלמד שנכמרו רחמיו באותה שעה ונשקו בכל לבו. אמר לו ר' ינאי: אם כן למה נקוד עליו ? אלא מלמד שלא בא לנשקו אלא לנשכו ונעשה צווארו של יעקב אבינו של שיש וקהו שיניו של אותו רשע. ומה תלמוד לומר "ויבכו" ? אלא זה בוכה על צווארו וזה בוכה על שיניו.

Said R. Shimon b. Eliezer: wherever you find that the letters outnumber the vocal points, you expound the letters; where the points outnumber the letters, you expound the points. Here the letters do not outnumber the points, nor the points the letters. This teaches that Esau's compassion was aroused at that moment and he kissed him with all his heart. Said R. Yannai to him. Why then is the word pointed above? But we must understand that he came not to kiss him (*nashko*) but to bite him (*noshkho*). Whereupon the patriarch Jacob's neck turned to marble, setting that wicked man's teeth on edge. What then is the implication of the phrase: "And they wept." This one wept on his neck and the other, on (account of) his teeth.

(Bereshit Rabbah 78, 12)

ביקש עשו לנושכו ונעשה צווארו של שיש, לכך נקוד על "וישקהו", שלא היתה נשיקה של אמת. "ויבכו" — למה בכו? משל למה הדבר דומה? לזאב שבא לחטוף את האיל. התחיל האיל לנגחו, נכנסו שיני הזאב בקרני האיל. זה בוכה וזה בוכה. הזאב בוכה שלא יכול לעשות לו כלום, והאיל בוכה שלא יחזור ויהרגנו. אף כך עשו ויעקב: עשו בוכה על שנעשה צוואר יעקב כשיש ויעקב בוכה שמא יחזור עשו וישכנו. על יעקב הכתוב אומר (שיר השירים ז, ה): "צוארך כמגדל השן". ועל עשו נאמר (תהלים ג, ח): "שיני רשעים שברת".

Esau sought to bite him but his neck turned to marble. This is the reason for the points, indicating that his kiss was not a sincere one. Why did they both weep? To what may this be compared? To a wolf which came to snatch a ram. Whereupon the ram began butting it with his horns, the wolf's teeth becoming entangled in them. Both of them wept; the wolf on account of its impotence and the ram for fear its enemy might try again to kill him. So too here with Esau and Jacob. Esau wept because Jacob's neck had turned to marble and Jacob, for fear that Esau might return to bite him. Regarding Jacob we have the text: "Thy neck is as a tower of marble" (Song of Songs 7, 5); regarding Esau: "Thou hast broken the teeth of the wicked" (Psalm 3, 8).

(Tanḥuma Vayishlaḥ 4)

Two views are expressed regarding Esau's conduct, an optimistic one, that saw a revolutionary change for the better, and a pessimistic one that detected the old Esau behind it. Here are two more citations, expressing opposing views:

כשעבר יעקב לבוא בארץ כנען, בא אליו עשו מהר שעיר בזעף אף זומם להורגו, שנאמר (תהלים לז, יב): "זומם רשע לצדיק וחורק עליו שניו". אמר עשו: איני הורג את יעקב אחי בחצים ובקשת, אלא בפי אני הורגו ומוצץ את דמו, שנאמר: "וירץ עשו לקראתו ויחבקהו ויפל על צואריו וישקהו ויבכו" — אל תקרא "וישקהו" אלא "וישכהו", ונעשה צווארו של יעקב כעצם

השן... כיון שראה עשו שלא עלתה בידו תאוותו, התחיל כועס וחורק
בשיניו, שנאמר (תהלים קיב, י): "רשע יראה וכעס, שניו יחרק ונמס".

When Jacob came to the land of Canaan, Esau came to meet
him from mount Seir full of fury, bent on killing him as it is
written. "The wicked plotteth against the righteous, and gnasheth
at him with his teeth" (Psalm 37, 12). Said Esau: I shall not
slay Jacob with bow and arrows but I shall rather slay him with
my mouth and suck his blood, as it is said: "And Esau ran to
meet him and embraced him and fell on his neck and kissed him
and they wept." Read not: "and *kissed* him" but: "he *bit* him!"
Whereupon Jacob's neck turned to marble ... as soon as Esau
perceived that he had not accomplished his desire, he became
furious and gnashed his teeth, as it is stated: "The wicked shall
see and be vexed; he shall gnash with his teeth and melt away"
(Psalm 112, 10).   (Pirke derabi Eliezer)

"וישקהו" — נקוד. יכול שהיתה נשיקה של אהבה? ר' שמעון בן אלעזר
אומר: והלוא כל מעשיו של עשו עשו בתחילה של שנאה היו?! — חוץ מזו,
שהיא של אהבה.

... Could this have been a kiss of love? R. Shimon b. Eliezer
said: But surely all Esau's deed were motivated by hate—except
this one, which was inspired by love!   (Avot derabi Nathan)

The optimistic view, reflecting perhaps the overtones of nineteenth century emancipation and liberalism is again propounded
by Rabbi S. R. Hirsch:

> The allusion to weeping is a sure sign that what we have here is
> a revelation of genuine humanity. A kiss can be superficial but
> an outburst of tears is a strong presumption in favour of sincerity.
> Esau betrays his Abrahamic origins and shows himself as not
> merely a cruel hunter. Otherwise he could never have reached
> such a leading position in the development of mankind. The
> sword alone, brute force cannot accomplish this. Even Esau gra-
> dually relinquishes his sword and begins to feel the chords of
> human love. It is Jacob who usually provides him with the op-
> portunity for showing his innate humanity. When the strong
> respects the strong, this is discretion. But when the strong, i.e.
> Esau falls on the neck of the weak, of Jacob, and casts his sword
> away, then we know that humanity and justice have prevailed.

375

We shall not quarrel with Hirsch who didn't know what we know today about the "sword" turning into holocaust and not love. Let us cite in contrast a later Jewish sage, one of the first protagonists of the return to the homeland through the Lovers of Zion movement. He detects, in our chapter, a call to leave the diaspora and rebuild the Holy Land:

> Both wept, implying that Jacob's love too was aroused towards Esau. And so it is in all ages. Whenever the seed of Esau is prompted by sincere motives to acknowledge and respect the seed of Israel, then we too, are moved to acknowledge Esau: for he is our brother. As a parallel we may cite the true friendship that existed between Rabbi Judah Hanasi and the Roman emperor Antoninus, and there are many similar instances.
>
> (Ha'amek Davar)

The head of the famed Volozhin yeshiva, author of the foregoing was not impressed by the weeping of Esau but by that of Jacob, who, in spite of all that he had suffered at the hands of his brother, was ready to let bygones be bygones, so long as the smallest gesture of sincerity was forthcoming.

But cannot the text itself provide a clue to the character of Esau's display of affection? Benno Jacob in his commentary to Genesis endeavours to discover such a clue, by carefully comparing all the texts that speak of similar meetings:

Jacob and Rachel:

> And Jacob kissed Rachel and lifted up his voice and wept   (Genesis 29, 11)

Joseph and Benjamin:

> And he (Joseph) fell on the neck of Benjamin his brother and wept   (Ibid 45, 14)

Jacob and Joseph:

> And Joseph harnessed his chariot ... and he presented himself unto him, and fell on his neck, and wept on his neck a good while   (Ibid 46, 29)

376

Moses and Aaron:

> And he (Aaron) went, and met him ... and kissed him.
>
> (Exodus 4, 27)

With the foregoing contrast our passage:

> And Esau ran to meet him, and embraced him and fell on his neck and kissed him and wept.

None of the other encounters are accompanied by such a display of effusiveness. Benno Jacob suggests that this description of Esau's running, embracing, falling, kissing and weeping is suspect. Indeed the patriarch himself does not believe its sincerity and immediately afterwards declines Esau's offer to escoⁱt him. Jacob went his own way, alone. Esau turned to Seir. Jacob's home was elsewhere in the land of Canaan, but the day would come when Esau, and there are many types of Esaus, would come to Jacob to Mount Zion.

Questions for Further Study

1. Why did Jacob drop his first plan of action (32, 8-9): "And he divided the people ... into two camps. And he said: If Esau come to the one camp, and smite it, then the camp which is left shall escape." Our Sages commented (see also Rashi ad loc.) that he prepared to employ three means of combatting Esau: gifts, prayer and battle. Yet we do not find that he made any preparations for battle, nor did he divide the people into two camps. He divided his children according to their handmaids, each mother with her children. What was the reason for this change of plan?

2. What caused Esau's change of heart—the gifts or something else?

3. Cf. Esau's and Jacob's remarks:
   And Esau said: I have enough, my brother ...

And Jacob said: ... because God hath dealt graciously
with me,
and because I have enough. (33, 9–11)

What difference can you detect and what does it teach you
regarding their respective characters?

4. "עד אשר אבוא": היכן חזר לו ? אלא מכאן אמרו: מותר לשנות בדברי
השלום. ר' נתן אומר: מצוה לשנות בדברי השלום, שנאמר (שמ"א טז ב):
"איך אלך ושמע שאול והרגני ?! ויאמר ה': עגלת בקר תקח בידך ואמרת:
לזבח לה' באתי".

"Till I come to my Lord to Seir" (33, 14). When did Jacob ever
come to Seir? But from here we may understand that it is
permissible to modify one's words in the interests of peace.
R. Nathan said: It is *obligatory* to modify one's words in the
interests of peace, as it is stated (I Samuel, 16, 2): "How can I
go? if Saul hear it, he will kill me. And the Lord said: Take a
heifer with thee and say: I am come to sacrifice to the Lord."
(Midrash Haggadol)

Behold Esau offered to escort him till he returned to his father,
in order to pay him honour, on his return home. But Jacob
replied that he would go at his own pace, allowing Esau to repair
to his own city. Jacob, however, intimated that if he returned
home by way of Esau's city, he would be glad of Esau's guard
of honour. But this was no definite promise since Esau did not
really require his presence. (Ramban)

(a) What did the above commentators find difficult in
our text (33, 14)?

(b) What is the exact connotation of the word *leshanot*
in the Midrash which we have rendered "modified"?

(c) Why did R. Nathan prefer to cite in support of his
principle a passage from the Prophets, passing over
appropriate examples that could be adduced from the
Torah (e.g. our context: 33, 14, or 15, or 18, 12–13)?

(d) In what does Ramban's view as expressed above differ
from that of the *Midrash Haggadol?*

מעשה אבות סימן לבנים [1]   Professor Heinemann in his book
Darkei Ha-aggada 4, 2, observes that this interpretation is followed in the text itself: "Often Scripture individualises a group
of people by describing them as a single person. What is
described as happening to the Patriarch really refers to his
descendants." Cf. Genesis 46, 4 the Almighty's message to Jacob: "I shall go down with thee to Egypt and I shall surely
bring *thee* up." Jacob, of course, was not brought out of Egypt.
It could not refer to his bones. But it must certainly allude to
his descendants who are here identified with the Patriarch.

THE STORY OF DINAH

We have here in chapter 34 an account of a massacre of men, women and children, the inhabitants of a whole town. Was such a deed justified? Was it justified as retaliation for the abominable crime referred to in the following rhetorical question of Jacob's two sons Simeon and Levi:

הַכְזוֹנָה יַעֲשֶׂה אֶת־אֲחוֹתֵנוּ?

Should one deal with our sister as with an harlot?
(34, 31)

If the deed was justified why did Jacob angrily reprimand them: "Ye have troubled me . . ."? Admittedly, Jacob advances a purely utilitarian argument in his words of reproof to the two brothers:

עֲכַרְתֶּם אֹתִי לְהַבְאִישֵׁנִי בְּיֹשֵׁב הָאָרֶץ
בַּכְּנַעֲנִי וּבַפְּרִזִּי,
וַאֲנִי מְתֵי מִסְפָּר וְנֶאֶסְפוּ עָלַי וְהִכּוּנִי
וְנִשְׁמַדְתִּי אֲנִי וּבֵיתִי,

You have troubled me to make me odious unto the inhabitants of the land, even unto the Canaanites and the Perizzites;
and, I being few in number, they will gather themselves together against me and smite me;
and I shall be destroyed, I and my house. (34, 30)

But if this does not, on this account, amount to outright condemnation of their action, the same cannot be said of the Patriarch's remarks to them on his deathbed. Then, many years had elapsed since the incident; Jacob dwelt safe and sound in Egypt, in the shelter of Joseph the viceregent of the realm. He had left the Canaanites and Perizzites far behind him. There was nothing to fear from them and no such motives of expediency could be said to motivate his condemnation of the deed which he had evidently not been able to forget:

אָרוּר אַפָּם כִּי עָז
וְעֶבְרָתָם כִּי קָשָׁתָה.

**Cursed be their anger, for it was fierce,
and their wrath, for it was cruel** (49, 7)

Why then, in the first place, did Jacob acquiesce to their stratagem? Why did he not protest during the negotiations with Shechem against their design? The conduct of the Patriarch, the brothers and even the Almighty himself present difficulties. These have been best formulated by Ramban commenting on the verse beginning "And the sons of Jacob answered Shechem . . ." (34, 13):

> . . . there is here a query, since it looks as if they answered in accordance with the will and counsel of their father, since they were in his presence and he knew the implications, that they spoke with guile. Why then did he subsequently become angry? Furthermore, it is inconceivable that he would be a party to marrying his daughter to a Canaanite who had defiled her. Many have wondered how the sons of Jacob could come to committing such a deed as this to shed innocent blood!

Before we approach the answers given to these difficulties let us first consider the conduct of Shechem and Hamor subsequent to the outrage they committed against Dinah.

The prince of the Hivite seemingly approached Jacob with a proposal that was entirely honourable. As if nothing untoward had happened, Hamor suggests an alliance of friendship and marriage between the two tribes:

שְׁכֶם בְּנִי חָשְׁקָה נַפְשׁוֹ בְּבִתְּכֶם
תְּנוּ נָא אֹתָהּ לוֹ לְאִשָּׁה.

381

The soul of my son **Shechem longeth for your** daughter.
I pray you give her unto him to wife (34, 8)

Very different was the tone in which the Hivite notable and his son spoke between themselves on the matter:

קַח־לִי אֶת־הַיַּלְדָּה הַזֹּאת לְאִשָּׁה,

Get me this child **to wife** (34, 4)

To the Patriarch they addressed themselves in dignified terms: "your daughter" "for my son"—as becomes a parent. In the meantime, however, let it not be forgotten that Dinah still remained their captive in their house. Let us further compare the proposal made to Jacob with the way they reported it to their own fellow citizens in Shechem. The character of Hamor and the nature of his proposals will become abundantly clear:

Hamor to Jacob and his sons (verses 9–10)	*Hamor to his fellow-citizens* (21–22–23)
I. (9) and make ye marriages with us; give your daughters unto us; and take our daughters unto you;	II. — — — — — — — — let us take their daughters to us for wives and let us give them our daughters.
II. (10) And ye shall dwell with us; and the land shall be before you; dwell; and trade ye therein; and get you possession therein;	I. (21) These men are peaceable with us; therefore let them dwell in the land. for behold the land is large enough for them. — — — — — — — — and trade therein. — — — — — — — —
— — — — — — — —	III. (23) Shall not their cattle and substance and all their beasts be ours?

382

Hamor's proposal may be divided into two parts involving domestic—intermarriage, and political—settlement considerations. Addressing Jacob he placed the domestic proposals first, since in that lay his main interest. Turning to his fellow citizens he toned down the personal element, giving prominence to the political and commercial advantages. He promised Jacob the twin rights of residence ("dwell") and citizenship ("get you possession"). He omitted the "citizenship" or "possession" clause in his report to the Schechemites. Only after he had dwelt on the commercial advantages of the alliance did he refer to the domestic side and even then he clothed his personal motives in the vestments of public interest. As our Sages have pointed out Jacob was told *"give* your daughters to us" but the Schechemites were promised the prospect of: "let us *take* their daughters."

Rashi makes a similar observation on this verse:

"ואת בנותיכם נקח לנו": אתה מוצא בתנאי שאמר חמור ליעקב ותשובת בני יעקב לחמור, שתלו החשיבות בבני יעקב ליקח בנות שכם את שיבחרו להם, ובנותיהם יתנו להם לפי דעתם, כדכתיב: "ונתנו את בנתינו לכם" (טז) — לפי דעתנו, "ואת בנתיכם נקח לנו" (טז) — בכל אשר נחפוץ. וכשדיברו חמור ושכם בנו אל יושבי עירם הפכו הדברים: "את בנתם נקח לנו לנשים, ואת בנתינו נתן להם" (כא), כדי לרצותם שיאותו למול.

You find that in the proposition made by Hamor to Jacob and the reply of Jacob's sons to Hamor that the stress was laid on the privilege of Jacob's sons to take to wife of the daughters of Schechem, whomsoever they chose, and to give in marriage their own daughters, as they saw fit, as it is stated: "Then we will give our daughters to you" as we see fit: "and we will take your daughters to us" (15)—whomsoever we desire.

And when Hamor and his son Schechem addressed their fellow citizens they changed their tune: "let us take their daughters to us for wives and let us give them our daughters" (21), in order to placate them that they should consent to circumcise themselves.

Hamor thus indicated that they were the initiators, the givers as well as the takers. It was well worth their while. For good measure he added something which his proposal to Jacob contained no hint of:

Shall not their cattle and their substance and all their beasts be ours?

This was how it always ended. The stranger came, toiled and accumulated wealth which ultimately reverted to his hosts. Hamor overcame their resistance and showed them it was worth their pains to accede to the strange condition made by the Israelites.

Let us now consider matters from the vantage point of Jacob and his sons. Jacob himself held his peace and it was his sons who did the talking. Ramban maintains that Jacob was convinced that the Schechemites would not accede to the circumcision proposal. Hence his silence. The way would then be open for the return of Dinah. If however Hamor succeeded for whatever reason in persuading his tribesmen to circumcise themselves, then the brothers would come on the third day whilst they were still convalescing and impotent to resist and take their sister forcibly from Schechem's household:

> This was the design of all the brothers with the permission of their father. Simeon and Levi however wished to avenge themselves of them ... by the avenging sword and slew the king and all the inhabitants of his city; for they were this vassals and he was their liege lord. The covenant by which they had circumcised themselves had no value in their eyes since it had been made to flatter their masters. Jacob reprimanded them here for bringing him into danger: "Ye have troubled me ... the inhabitants of the land ... will smite me; and I shall be destroyed, I and my house." Later (on his deathbed) the Patriarch cursed their anger because they had violated the trust of the Schechemites in declaring to them in his presence: "And we will dwell with you, and we will become one people" (16). They would have chosen them and relied on their word and might perhaps have repented and returned to God. Thus they had slain them without cause for they had done them no evil at all. (Ramban)

Accordingly, neither Jacob nor his sons, with the exception of

Simeon and Levi, ever contemplated putting a whole city to the sword, massacring men, women and children. They were only concerned with rescuing Dinah from the clutches of her captors and violaters. What transpired afterwards was the work of Simeon and Levi alone.

Ramban draws attention to yet another aspect of their crime, commenting on Jacob's denunciation of it, on his deathbed:

> He (Jacob) was further angered that the deed should not be attributed to his counsel, leading to profanation of the Divine Name, that a prophet had committed violence and pillage. This is the implication of the phrase: "Let my soul not come into their council," (49, 6). It disclaims responsibility for their conspiracy when they answered with guile and declares he was not a party to their assembly when they came down on the city and slew them.

There still remains the difficulty of explaining the conduct of the Almighty Himself Who apparently condoned their deed:

> **And a terror of God was upon the cities that were round about them, and they did not pursue the sons of Jacob.**
>
> (35, 5)

In answer it may be pointed out that a miracle constitutes no proof of the truth. The magicians of Egyptian too succeeded in their sorceries; even the false prophet is sometimes capable of producing signs and wonders (cf. Deuteronomy 13): "And if the sign or wonder come to pass ..." History is full of examples of the success of brute force and injustice. The dread inspired by the sword of Simeon and Levi was no proof of the justice of their cause and that God had approved of their action. As a contemporary thinker once phrased it, among all the many names and attributes of God the title "success" cannot be found.

Questions for Further Study

1. Benno Jacob finds in his commentary to Genesis support in the text indicating that Jacob was unaware of Simeon

and Levi's designs and that his sons were unable to consult him on the matter. What is the support in the text for Benno Jacob's assumption?

2. Shechem and Hamor refer to Dinah by different titles depending on the context—whether they are talking to each other or addressing Jacob and his sons. Cf.:
Get me this *child* to wife (34, 4)
The soul of my son Schechem longeth for your *daughter*, I pray thee. Give her unto him to wife (ibid 8).
Give me this *girl* to wife (ibid 12).
Explain the reason for these variations.

3. "His soul did cleave to Dinah, the daughter of Jacob, he loved the girl and spoke comfortingly to the girl" (ibid. 3)

The text indicates that when he first took her he had no intention of marrying her, as was his wont. He simply grabbed her to satisfy his momentary passion. Had he been out to marry her at the very outset he would not have raped her but would have waited till they agreed to give her to him. Only afterwards did his soul cleave to her. There is a difference between emotional love and an intellectual attachment. A prince may be said to fall in love with a girl of low station but there is no meeting of minds —(cleaving of souls) since the difference in backgrounds and culture precludes such a thing, though he may love her. But sometimes two persons of similar levels become intellectually attached to each other. There is a meeting of minds even though no emotional love may exist between them. Here there was both. Then he spoke comfortingly to the girl. Hitherto only animal passion had been involved which did not deserve the name love (had there been true love he would not have inflicted on her that terrible disgrace tantamount to murder) but now true love welled up after the animal passion subsided.
Then he was sorry for having forced her. He spoke to her heart to comfort her from her sorrow and grief.   (Malbim)

(a) What anomaly in the wording of the verse is explained by his comment.

386

(b) Where do we find in the Bible the opposite phenomenon to that described above relating to Schechem,
as outlined by Malbim?

4. "They sacked the city which has defiled their sister."
(34, 27)
"Which had defiled"—this puts paid to any moral objection
since the Lawgiver Himself testifies that they all had a hand in
the crime and He is a reliable enough witness. *The variety of
causes leading up to actions are only too familiar.* Cf.: (Ezekiel
3, 18): "thou givest not warning, nor speakest to warn the wicked
from his wicked way to save his life ... but his blood will I
require at thy hand." Then we have the case of the outcast city
(*'ir hanidahat*—Deut. 13, 13–19) and Jephtah's words of reproof to
the elders of Gilead (Judges 11, 7).[1]

(Ibn Kaspi, Mishneh Kesef)

(a) Which moral objection is referred to?
(b) What is the exact implication of the words italicised?
(c) What is the difference between his approach and that
of Ramban outlined in our *Studies?*
(d) What is the relevance of the citation from Judges?

5. "They came on the city, unawares" (34, 25)
The English translation renders the last word *betah* "unawares" the word itself means "safe". Here are two explanations:

Because they were in pain (Rashi)
They were sitting pretty (safe) and had taken no precautions
against them (the Hebrews). The word *betah* ("unawares" "safe")
is always used to describe those settled in a place, whether it
occurs in the Pentateuch or the Prophets. (Rashbam)

What is the difference between Rashi and Rashbam in
their interpretation of the word *betah?*

[1] Ibn Kaspi here follows Rambam who justifies Simeon and Levi's deed
in putting to the sword not only Shechem but the whole city because
"they saw and knew and did not punish him." Rambam cites this view
and scathingly demolishes it ("it is completely unacceptable in my
eyes").

PILLAR AND ALTAR

Jacob's wanderings had come to an end. His struggles with Laban and Esau were over. He had returned to the land promised
him and his ancestors. Returning like his grandfather to Shechem,
his first stopping-point in the Land, we are told about Jacob
that

וַיַּצֶּב שָׁם־מִזְבֵּחַ
וַיִּקְרָא־לוֹ אֵל אֱלֹהֵי יִשְׂרָאֵל.

**he set up there an altar,
and called it God, the God of Israel**   (33, 20)

The foregoing quotation poses a lexical difficulty besides
other anomalies that call for clarification. The Hebrew word
corresponding to "set up"—*vayazev* is unusual since the usual
term elsewhere in Scripture is "building" or "making." The verb
hazev is more in keeping with an object derived from the same
root—*mazeva* translated "pillar." Indeed in our sidra we find
such a usage in chapter 35 verse 14: "And Jacob set up a pillar
in the place where he spoke with him." Why then does not
the text read: "he *built* (*vayiven*) there an altar"? The Hebrew
collocation is thus anomalous.

Before we proceed to answer this question let us try to solve
another problem somewhat more puzzling. We have noted that
Jacob set up a pillar. At the same time we know that such an act
is strictly prohibited by the Torah: "Thou shalt not raise up
for thee a pillar which the Lord thy God hateth" (Deut. 16,
22). Our Sages answered that pillars were approved in the
days of the patriarchs and hated in the days of their descendants.
Why?

In the first Divine revelation to him Jacob was vouchsafed a vision of a ladder which angels descended and ascended. There as he set up a pillar he made a vow:

וְהָאֶבֶן הַזֹּאת אֲשֶׁר־שַׂמְתִּי מַצֵּבָה יִהְיֶה בֵּית אֱלֹהִים.

The stone which I have set as a pillar shall be a house of God.

(28, 22)

The "house" implied an altar which Jacob did indeed build, on fulfilling his vow, on his return to Bethel: "And he built there an altar" (35, 7). What is the difference between an altar and a pillar? Externally the difference is obvious, and this is how Ramban understood it:

> Our rabbis have explained the difference between "pillar" and "altar," the former being constructed of one stone and the latter of many. It also appears that the pillar was designed for the pouring out of oil and wine libations and not for offerings and sacrifices. When they entered the Land, the erection of pillars was forbidden them because the Canaanites were more addicted to them than altars, though, admittedly, Holy Writ bade them "break down their altars" (Deut. 12, 3). Perhaps, however, God did not wish to forbid them everything outright and left them the altar which was fit for both sacrifice and libation.

But Ramban's explanation is purely a technical distinction and offers us no clarification of the inner significance. Hirsch who took great pains in symbolically interpreting the sacrificial rites likewise explains the respective significance of the altar and pillar.

> The pillar being of one single natural stone, the work of God, fittingly represents a memorial of His kindnesses to man. It was therefore approved in the days of the patriarchs, since their primary role was to acknowledge their Maker and to publicise His name in the world as the author of nature and history. The Torah had not yet been given, and man had not been called upon to devote his whole life, both social and individual to the fulfillment of the will of his Creator. The pillar was therefore an appropriate symbol of the benefits bestowed on man by God, along with the altar as a symbol of the sacrifice of man's personality and works to the will of God.

The pillar consequently served for the pouring out of libations which represent man's gratitude to His benefactor for all the bounty he had received whereas the altar served for sacrifices which express the devotion of all living things to God.

But when the Torah was given the pillar not only receded from view, but disappeared completely and its role was absorbed by the altar. Praise and thanksgiving to the Lord for His miracles and bounty—the pillar—distinct from our devotion and sacrifice and the subjection of our whole lives to His will—the altar— was absolutely forbidden. God no longer desired that we should discern His imprint in His deeds to mankind and in our deeds before Him, or merely acknowledge Him as the presider in majesty over the heaven and earth alone, but rather as the ruler over the deeds of men.

Our lives were no longer to be conditioned exclusively by the impact of external events, but our existence, good and evil, all that befell us were to come forth from our deeds before Him in conformity with His command and wish. This was the reason for the ban on the pillar. It was henceforth the altar that was designed for sacrifice and offering, oblation and libations, signifying: the deeds of man in fulfillment of the will of God as revealed in His Torah would turn the earth into a Mount of God and the fire which would burn on the altar is the Fire of the Law which illumines the earth.

Hirsch would therefore answer that the Torah deliberately used the expression of *vayazev* in our verse indicating that Jacob's action symbolised the changeover from the pre-Torah level of fear of God and human thankfulness to the fear of God inherent in the doing of His will in all the everyday acts of the individual as it emerged from the revelation of His will in the Torah. Jacob prepared the ground for this decisive change, this progress towards a different and higher kind of Godly life by his· act of "setting up an altar."

On this ground will arise the edifice which will elevate the nation in every detail of its public and private life, a monument of stone to the Divine revelation. The Lord and His will will be revealed through the deeds of men. This people will not be content passively to accept all that befalls them, both their joy and sadness from the Lord, with a blessing for both the good and evil alike, but they will subject all events and situations to the implementation of the Divine will as revealed in His Torah.

Rabbi Kook too regarded the approval of the pillar in patriarchal times and its subsequent prohibition as indicating a change in the mode of serving God. Hirsch sees a distinction between passive and active service of God, between thanksgiving and praise and the transformation of every moment of existence into fulfillment of a precept. Rabbi Kook finds a much deeper distinction, a more fundamental one:

Both, he notes, were places of worship, the pillar having fallen into disrepute, the altar remaining in favour. He quotes the Talmud's (Pesaḥim 88a) comment on a verse from Isaiah (2, 3): "Many peoples shall go and say, Come ye and let us go up to the mount of the Lord, to the house of the God of Jacob"— Not like Abraham who called it a mountain (Gen. 22, 14), and not like Isaac who called it a field (24, 63), but like Jacob who called it a house. When Abraham began to worship God he did not practise all the specific rites and order of service associated with Judaism. Before the Torah was given there were no detailed commandments governing every aspect of life. He simply directed the worship of mankind generally to the acknowledgement of the Creator of heaven and earth. Such a form of worship allows of no distinction between one people and another. Every human being can worship in this way and this is the implication of the word *maẓeva*—pillar.

> But such a general approach was purely a transitional stage. The supreme aim was the emergence in the world of the specific mode of worship followed by the chosen people, Israel, to which level not all mankind could equally attain. When Jacob foresaw the specific mode of worship that was destined to emerge from his descendants, he said that "this stone which I have set as a pillar" will not be a centre of generalised free worship, but "a house of God," a special place of worship bounded by walls into which only the worthy can enter. None of the peoples have as yet any concept of the values of this exclusive organized ritual, the minutiae of the Torah and its precepts which distinguish Israel in all their actions.
>
> Though we have not been granted in our time the shining of the light, and the lifegiving power derived from above that informs the specific Torah-governed worship of Jacob has not come into its own and which transcends the indeterminate "call

in the name of the Lord the everlasting God"; in time to come, when all mankind will see what all these rites and judgements, minutiae and fundamental laws have done for this wonderful people which has existed by miracles and flourished in its specific holiness even in the days of direst misfortune, attaining the great light when their righteousness and glory will be made manifest, all shall say:

> Henceforth we realise that the generalized approach to God, the concept of disembodied ("naked") faith which we thought would satisfy all the spiritual functions is not enough for us. But we need to scale the mountain of the Lord which summons to the sacred totality of faith and intimate knowledge of Him, in order to enter the inner sanctum—"the *house* of the everlasting God."

Rabbi Kook finds the superiority of the "house" over the "pillar" which was in favour under the Patriarchs and anathema to their descendants, in the whole complexity of the specific rituals and precepts governing every aspect of human life contrasted with a mere generalized homage to the Supreme Being. It represented th gap between an indeterminate high-minded Deism and a specific worship of a personal God through the medium of an exhaustive series of rites and commandments. The pillar represented the disembodied concept of faith, denuded of the vesture of exact precepts, whereas the House of the Lord symbolized Torah and *mizvot* and good works. The realisation that will dawn on mankind when they see the effect of these precepts on "this wonderful nation" has already been described in the Torah:

> Observe therefore and do them; for this is your wisdom and your understanding in the sight of the peoples that when they hear all these statutes shall say . . .
>
> For what great nation is there that hath God so nigh unto them . . .
>
> And what great nation is there that hath statutes and ordinances so righteous as all this law which I set before you this day. (Deut. 4, 6–8)

392

Rabbi Kook concludes the sentiments he puts in the mouth of the peoples when they realise the effect of the Divine precepts on Israel with their words:

> We shall no longer rest content with generalised acknowledge-ment of God and generalised concepts which we have seen are not sufficient to enkindle the Divine spark in the world and place mankind on firm foundations. We shall return to what we neglected, and the stone we despised must become the corner-stone, comprehending the specific teachings which are the eternal heritage of Jacob. We shall take from them the salve for the wounds of the world and man who is stunted in all his values "that He may instruct us in His ways and that we may walk in His paths."

Questions for Further Study

1.   What is the difference between the approach of Hirsch and Rav Kook in solving the difficulty? Why was the monument beloved of the Patriarchs forbidden to the children?

2.   What is the difference between the two answers given by Ramban?

3.   What is the difficulty in verse 20 ch. 33 which Hirsch tries to remove?

4.   To what does Rav Kook refer when the states: "The stone we despised must become the corner stone" What is the "stone"?

PROVIDENCE'S MYSTERY MAN

This week's sidra marks the beginning of the story of Joseph, the fascinating threads of which constitute the main theme of the remaining chapters of Genesis. Interwoven into the account of mortal doings is the unseen hand of Divine Providence. On the surface, the actors in the story make their own way in life, set in motion their own plans, succeed or fail, start again, all on their own initiative. That is the immediate superficial impression. In fact, however, it transpires that it is Divine Providence which is carrying out, through mankind, its own predestined plan.

Let us deal with the story of the mission with which Joseph was charged by his father:

וַיִּשְׁלָחֵהוּ מֵעֵמֶק חֶבְרוֹן

So he sent him out of the vale of Hebron. (37, 14)

This story ends with the following words of Joseph to his brothers who had been likewise sent after him to Egypt:

לֹא־אַתֶּם שְׁלַחְתֶּם אֹתִי הֵנָּה כִּי הָאֱלֹהִים.

So now it was not you that sent me hither, but God.

(45, 8)

The above verse supplies, as it were, the key to the understanding of the whole story, which unfolds the concept of the two levels on which the actions or missions therein are conducted. First, there is the obvious implication of their acts, the immediate significance of the mission on which Joseph went. Jacob sent his son Joseph from the vale of Hebron to inquire after the welfare of his brothers and their flocks. But underlying that mission, there lay the hidden workings of Providence. God was sending the descendants of Abraham to Egypt, to sojourn in a land not their own.

The Midrash, quoted by Rashi, is aware of the double significance, which it sees implied in the verse we have already quoted:

והלא חברון בהר היא!?... אלא מעצה עמוקה של אותו צדיק הקבור בחברון, לקיים מה שנאמר לאברהם בברית בין הבתרים (בראשית טו, יג): "כי גר יהיה זרעך".

Surely Hebron was in the mountain?... (But the reference is not to the physical Hebron), but to the mysterious advice imparted to that righteous man who was buried in Hebron, in fulfilment of what was said to Abraham at the covenant between the pieces (15, 13): "Thy seed shall be a stranger."   (Rashi)

The homiletical interpretation of the phrase עמק חברון as referring to God's mysterious prophecy to Abraham turns on a play on the word 'emek, literally "deep place."

Since Hebron was in the mountain and not the valley, the apparently superfluous insertion, emek, is taken, figuratively, to imply "deep," in the sense of: "mysterious." Hebron is taken as a figurative expression for the Patriarch Abraham who was buried there. Thus we have an allusion to the "mysterious advice" imparted to Abraham regarding the future of his descendants, that they would sojourn in a land not their own. It was this prophecy that Jacob and Joseph were fulfilling, unwittingly; the father—in sending, and the son—in going to seek his brothers.

Rashi regards the reference to Hebron not merely in the locative-geographical sense, but in the deeper one, of spiritual causation. The Prime Mover of all things was ultimately behind the departure of Joseph, in accordance with the pattern—"the mysterious advice" imparted to Abraham, and who can fathom its mystery?

Ramban notes a similar, double pattern in the incident of the anonymous guide, the man who tells Joseph the way to his brothers. Here again he discovers, on the suggestion of the Midrash, the mortal, plain meaning of the incident and its underlying fitting into a predestined Divine pattern of events.

וַיִּשְׁלָחֵהוּ מֵעֵמֶק חֶבְרוֹן וַיָּבֹא שְׁכֶמָה.
וַיִּמְצָאֵהוּ אִישׁ וְהִנֵּה תֹעֶה בַּשָּׂדֶה וַיִּשְׁאָלֵהוּ הָאִישׁ לֵאמֹר:
מַה־תְּבַקֵּשׁ?
וַיֹּאמֶר אֶת־אַחַי אָנֹכִי מְבַקֵּשׁ, הַגִּידָה־נָּא לִי: אֵיפֹה הֵם
רֹעִים?
וַיֹּאמֶר הָאִישׁ נָסְעוּ מִזֶּה כִּי שָׁמַעְתִּי אֹמְרִים נֵלְכָה דֹּתָיְנָה.
וַיֵּלֶךְ יוֹסֵף אַחַר אֶחָיו וַיִּמְצָאֵם בְּדֹתָן.

So he sent him out of the vale of Hebron and he came
unto Shechem.
And a certain man found him, and behold he was wandering in the field: and the man asked him, saying, what
seekest thou?
And he said: I seek my brethren: tell me, I pray thee,
where they feed their flocks.
And the man said, They are departed hence; for I heard
them say, Let us go to Dothan.
And Joseph went after his brothers, and found them in
Dothan.   (37, 14–17)

This dialogue is inserted between two worlds, between the quiet
and tranquil world of Joseph at home, shielded and spoilt by
his father and the stormy, troubled ruin of a world that was
his, after he met his brothers. Commentators, both ancient and
modern have been puzzled by this insertion. What was the point
of this short dialogue between Joseph and the anonymous passer-
by? The Torah does not usually indulge in such realistic inter-
ludes for the sake of detail. Consequently our Sages endowed
this "man" with a mysterious character. This "man" who opens
the conversation without waiting to be asked, and knows all the
answers, is not a chance passer-by, but an "angel"—a Divine
messenger.

Ramban elaborating on the words of our Sages, maintains
that the Torah inserts the details of Joseph's dialogue with the
"man" to stress the workings of Divine Providence. By all accounts, Joseph should have turned back and not found his

brothers. The Torah points out that Joseph's own diligence availed him not. Only the predestined decree of God working behind the scenes led him to his brothers. God's unwitting instrument was the "man," the chance passer-by who constituted, indeed, a Divine messenger. It was not for nothing, Ramban states, that these verses were included, but to show that "the counsel of the Lord shall be established."

Ramban translated the figurative statement of the Rabbis and Rashi, who state the man was "the angel Gabriel" into the abstract concept of Divine messenger, unwittingly carrying out his mission.

Jacob was not aware where he was sending Joseph, and Joseph did not know where his steps would lead him to. Similarly the "man" did not know what the ultimate results of his instructions would be. Joseph's brothers were not aware of the significance of their own deed.

One thing Joseph knew—that, though he was alone in the world without kith or kinsman, God was with him.

Note carefully the words that Joseph himself utters, during the course of the story. From the time he left his father till he met his brothers, and during his sale and the humiliation he suffered, nothing is recorded, as if he were dumb. He is never recorded as having uttered a word during his abduction to Egypt and sale to Potiphar. It is merely stated that he "had an impressive bearing and good looks." He reached the stage of being appointed overseer over his master's house, and still no word is he mentioned as uttering.

Only during the crisis of his temptation, when he refused the advances of his mistress are his utterances recorded, as he explained to her the reasons for his refusal in terms and conceptions suited to her understanding. His last words there are characteristic and significant.

And sin against God   (39, 9)

His words are again recorded for us by the Torah, when a prisoner, confronted by the request of his distinguished two fellow-prisoners to interpret their dreams. To those who were to prove the instruments of Providence in bringing him before Pharaoh, he said:

Do not interpretations belong to God?
Tell me them I pray you.   (40, 8)

Questions for Further Study

1.   Cf.
      And Joseph dreamed a dream, and he told it to his
      brethren ...   (Gen. 37, 5)
      And he told it to his father, and to his brethren ...
                                                        (ibid. 10)
      Explain why Joseph related his first dream only to his
      brothers, and the second one to his father as well. Why
      did he not relate the first one to this father?

2.   Cf.
      And he dreamed yet another dream, and *told it to his
      brethren ...*   (ibid. 9)
      And he told it to his father, *and to his brethren ...*
                                                        (ibid. 10)
      Explain why after telling his dream to his brothers he went
      and told it again to his father.

3.   Cf.
      ... and they *hated* him yet the more.   (ibid. 5)
      And his brethren *envied* him ...   (ibid. 11)
      Explain why the telling of the first dream resulted in *hate*,
      and the second, in *envy*.

4.   אמר ר' חמא בר חנינא : הדברים הללו היה יעקב אבינו נזכר ומעיו מתחתכין:
      יודע היית שאחיך שונאים אותך והיית אומר לי : "הנני".

      "Israel said to Joseph, Are not thy brothers pasturing in Schechem,
      Come let me send thee to them. Whereupon he said to him,
      Here am I" (37, 13). Said R. Ḥama bar Ḥanina: When Jacob
      recalled these things he winced: You knew your brothers hated
      you and yet you said to me: Here am I.   (Bereshit Rabbah)

(a) On what anomaly in the text is this Midrash based?

(b) What idea is embodied by the Midrash?

5. "A certain man came upon him, and behold he was wandering in the field; and the man asked him, saying, what are you looking for?" The "certain man" according to the plain sense is one of the wayfarers. (Ibn Ezra)

(a) Why did Ibn Ezra preface his comment with the words "according to the plain sense"?

(b) Contrast Ibn Ezra's comment with that of Ramban referred to on p. 397.

Is the latter's comment closer to Rashi's cited at the beginning of our *Studies* on p. 395 or that of Ibn Ezra quoted here, or equally far removed from both?

6. Tell me please where they are pasturing (37, 16)

On the words "where they are pasturing" Ibn Ezra adds "if you know." Why does Ibn Ezra add these words? What difficulty did he wish to remove thereby?

THE SALE OF JOSEPH

וַיַּעַבְרוּ אֲנָשִׁים מִדְיָנִים סֹחֲרִים
וַיִּמְשְׁכוּ וַיַּעֲלוּ אֶת־יוֹסֵף מִן־הַבּוֹר
וַיִּמְכְּרוּ אֶת־יוֹסֵף לַיִּשְׁמְעֵאלִים בְּעֶשְׂרִים כָּסֶף
וַיָּבִיאוּ אֶת־יוֹסֵף מִצְרָיְמָה.

**And there passed by Midianites, merchants; and they
drew and lifted up Joseph out of the pit and sold Joseph
to the Ishmaelites for twenty shekels of silver. And they
brought Joseph to Egypt.** (37, 28)

This chapter constitutes a turning point in the life of Joseph
and the history of the Jewish people; for it marks the descent
of the Israelites into Egypt. The interpretation of the above
verse has been the subject of much dispute.[1] The accepted
explanation is that of Rashi:

"ויעברו אנשים מדינים סוחרים": זו היא שיירה אחרת, והודיעך הכתוב
שנמכר פעמים הרבה.
"וימשכו": ב נ י י ע ק ב א ת י ו ס ף מ ן ה ב ו ר וימכרוהו לישמעאלים
והישמעאלים למדינים והמדיינים למצרים.

This was another caravan, the text informing us that he was sold
many times. "They drew" refers to the sons of Jacob—they took
him out of the pit and sold him to the Ishmaelites and the Ishmaelites to the Midianites and the Midianites to the Egyptians.

Let us try to understand Rashi. The appearance of the Midianite
caravan surprises us. We have hitherto been told:

וַיִּשְׂאוּ עֵינֵיהֶם וַיִּרְאוּ וְהִנֵּה אֹרְחַת יִשְׁמְעֵאלִים.

**They lifted up their eyes and behold a caravan of Ish-
maelites:** (37, 25)

Then we hear Judah's suggestion:

לְכוּ וְנִמְכְּרֶנּוּ לַיִּשְׁמְעֵאלִים.

Come, let us sell him to the Ishmaelites. (37, 27)

Till that point nothing had been mentioned of Midianite merchants. Even in the very verse under study, it is stated: "And they sold Joseph to the Ishmaelites for twenty pieces of silver," evidently according to the suggestion made by Judah which was accepted by the brethren (v. 27: "And his brothers hearkened"). What was the role of the Midianites? where did they fit in? Rashi tried to overcome this difficulty, following Talmudic exegesis, by postulating a threefold sale (the brothers to the Ishmaelites—to the Midianites—to Egypt). Evidently Rashi identifies the Medanites mentioned at the end of the chapter:

וְהַמְּדָנִים מָכְרוּ אֹתוֹ אֶל־מִצְרָיִם
לְפוֹטִיפַר סְרִיס פַּרְעֹה

(37, 36)

and the Medanites sold him into Egypt unto Potiphar ...

with the Midianites.[2] But he provides no explanation for the problem posed by verse 1 Ch. 39:

וַיִּקְנֵהוּ פּוֹטִיפַר סְרִיס פַּרְעֹה שַׂר הַטַּבָּחִים
אִישׁ מִצְרִי מִיַּד הַיִּשְׁמְעֵאלִים

And Potiphar ... bought him from the hand of the Ishmaelites.

Even Mizrahi, Rashi's supercommentary and champion is forced to admit: "I don't know what Rashi makes of this verse."

Rashi's identification of the subject of the second part of the verse with "his brethren" mentioned at the end of the previous verse ("And his brethren hearkened") is followed by a number of commentators, though they propose different solutions to the question of the caravans. Here is Hizkuni:

Whilst the brothers were discussing selling him to the Ishmaelites:
"come, let us sell him to the Ishmaelites," and before the latter
reached them, Midianite merchants passed by, to whom the
brothers sold him, while he was yet in the pit, so that his weeping should not shame them. The Midianites drew him out of
the pit since they had bought him. Whilst they were doing this,
the Ishmaelites came along and the Midianites sold him to the
Ishmaelites, the Ishmaelites to the Medanites and the Medanites
to Pharaoh—a total of four sales. The text states, however, that
Potiphar bought Joseph from the Ishmaelites. Why?—The tribes
had sold him to the Midianites, but this sale was not recorded,
since it was only temporary. The Midianites sold him to the Ishmaelites and the Ishmaelites to the Medanites. This third sale was
likewise not recorded, since it was concluded in haste and secrecy
for fear the Medanites might retract. The Medanites sold him to
Potiphar whose suspicions however were aroused by Joseph's
handsome and commanding appearance. It wasn't usual for
wandering slave traders, for "dark" people, to be selling a "white"
man—it was usually the other way round! He could not therefore be a slave. He asked them for a guarantee that the transaction was *bona fides* and no one would come to reclaim him.
They brought the Ishmaelites who gave the necessary guarantee,
and that is the force of the wording of the text: "He brought
him from the *hand* of the Ishmaelites"—they gave him their
hand or guarantee (cf.: Gen 43, 9: "I shall stand surety, from
my hand shall you require it"—the latter part of Ḥizkuni is
based on *Bereshit Rabbah* 86).

Ḥizkuni's approach is rather complicated but it has two advantages: the many and clandestine sales fit in well with the
atmosphere of dealings in stolen property. The traders realised
that this was no *bona fides* transaction and tried to get rid of
their merchandise. Similarly it disposes of the contradiction between our text (where Joseph is sold finally to the Ishmaelites)
and the last verse of the chapter: "And the Medanites sold
Joseph into Egypt," and the first verse of ch. 39: "And Potiphar
bought from the hand of the Ishmaelites."

The flaw in this explanation is the fact that it presupposes
two sales not recorded in the text. For this reason we cite here
Ramban who suggests another explanation. He regards the two
caravans of Midianite merchants and Ishmaelites as one, in

which the Midianites were the "merchants" and the Ishmaelites the camel-drivers, so that the brothers first caught sight of the Ishmaelite caravan and when they drew near saw Midianite merchants:

> The brothers sold Joseph to the Midianites, the merchants, to trade with him, since the Ishmaelite camel-drivers or hauliers did not engage directly in trade—they merely hired their camels and themselves to traders. The text: "And they sold Joseph to the Ishmaelites" implies that Joseph was handed to the Ishmaelites to be transported to Egypt by them. This is also the implication of the text: "From the hand of the Ishmaelites who had brought him down thither"; but the Midianites were his owners; they traded with him. That is the force of the text: "The Medanites sold him into Egypt."

Ramban then shows that the Torah often attributes a deed, sometimes to its ultimate author and at others to its intermediary or direct commissioner. Thus Moses is sometimes credited, as in (Deut. 34, 12): "the great terror Moses wrought in the eyes of all Israel," and, at others, God, as in (Deut 11, 7): "all the great work God had wrought." Similarly, here, the contradiction between: "the Medanites sold him into Egypt" and "and Potiphar bought him from the hand of the Ishmaelites" is solved by remembering that sometimes a deed is attributed to its immediate and direct cause, and sometimes, to its more remote, indirect one. Ibn Ezra wishes to regard the Midianites and Ishmaelites as identical. But irrespective of the differences between these commentators, they have this in common: The brothers who are not mentioned in our text at all are regarded as the understood subject: "they drew Joseph out of the pit, and they sold Joseph." This interpretation would seem to be borne out by Joseph's words, when he revealed his identity to his brethren: "I am Joseph your brother whom you sold into Egypt."

But this approach raises many difficulties. First, it leaves unexplained how Reuben remained ignorant of the sale, though he no doubt did his best to save Joseph and presumably kept watch on his brothers. Where was he at the time of the sale?

Admittedly, the Midrash states he was engaged otherwise (ministering to his father, subjecting himself to penances for his relations with his father's concubine), but this is forced.[3] Again, it leaves unexplained why the brothers did not answer him when stunned, he said: "the child is not; and as for me, whither shall I go?" Their silence indicates that they were similarly stunned. That the brothers considered him really dead seems to be indicated from a number of texts, besides the fact that otherwise they woud presumably have made every effort to trace him: e.g.: "the one is not" (42, 13 and 32). It is obvious that this phrase implied he was dead. Cf.: 44, 20: "We said unto my lord, we have an old father and a child of his old age; and *his brother is dead.*" Otherwise how would Judah have dared to make such a statement?

When amongst themselves the brothers explicitly indicated their conviction he was dead: "but verily we are guilty . . . did not I tell you, sin not with the child but you did not listen, therefore also his blood is required" (42, 22). Had Rashi's contention been correct that the brothers had sold him to the Egypt-bound caravan, why couldn't the brothers, after they had suffered complete remorse for their act, have hoped to trace him and mend matters? This has led Rashbam and, subsequently, other commentators to seek another way out:

> "And there passed by Midianites, merchants." The brothers sat down to a meal at some distance from the pit, out of qualms of conscience and waited for the Ishmaelites they had seen. But before the latter arrived, others, Midianite traders passed, saw Joseph in the pit and drew him out and sold him to the Ishmaelites, presumably without the knowledge of the brothers. Though the text says, "whom you sold to Egypt," that was meant only in the sense of ultimate responsibility . . . the Midianites passed quite accidentally and they sold him to the Ishmaelites. But even if you wish to say that it was the brothers who sold him to the Ishmaelites, (as his grandfather Rashi learnt), you must say that the brothers had commanded the Midianites to draw Joseph out of the pit, and they sold him afterwards to the Ishmaelites.

Rashbam was forced to find another explanation by the grammatical construction of the text. The only feasible subject of our text is the Midianites, since they are referred to last. He observes therefore that even Rashi's explanation that it was the brothers who drew him out can only be accepted if we take it in the sense that the Midianites did the drawing out, at the brothers' behest. Since this, too, is forced, Rashbam advances the revolutionary but apt explanation that Joseph was sold without their knowledge, thus bearing out Joseph's own contention: "I was surely stolen from the land of the Hebrews" (40, 15). Many commentators have accepted this, including Ḥizkuni (the latter's explanation we cited earlier is an alternative) whose main motivation for adopting it was:

> "when Reuben didn't find him in the pit, they all thought an evil beast had consumed him. They did not lie to their father. Had they really sold him, they would have searched every country in an effort to trace whether he was alive or dead.

Other commentators who follow this approach are Baḥya, Mendelsohn, Hirsch and Malbim. The most exhaustive treatment from this standpoint is Samuel Lali's, in a letter quoted in Luzzatto's commentary to this verse. Here is an extract:

> They moved away from the pit so as not to hear Joseph's cries of mercy ("when we saw the distress of his soul, when he besought us," (42, 21). Whilst they were eating, they caught sight of an Ishmaelite caravan and Judah said: "What profit ... and his brothers listened." They all agreed that as soon as they had finished eating, they would haul Joseph out of the pit and sell him to the Ishmaelites. Whilst they were talking, the Midianites passed by, quite by accident, and took him and sold him to the Ishmaelites for 20 pieces of silver. Reuben, unseen by them, rushed to the pit to haul Joseph out and return him to his father before his brothers would have a chance to sell him. But Reuben was stunned to find the pit empty; rent his garments and was convinced that a bear or lion had dragged him out of the pit alive to devour him in its lair, since there were no traces of bones or blood. He forthwith reported to the brothers what had happened and they believed him. Reuben blamed himself for the tragedy, since it was he who had suggested casting him into the pit ... The brothers thought up the idea of dipping the coat in blood, in order to protect Reuben and convince their father

that Joseph had been devoured by a wild beast. None of them went in search of Joseph, because they were fully convinced that he was no longer alive.

Reuben had kept quiet on hearing Judah's suggestion to sell Joseph because he thought he would be able to rescue Joseph from the pit, unseen by them, before they implemented their design. Now we may understand why the brothers did not react to Reuben's news that "the child is not" by saying "we have sold him," since they knew no more of his whereabouts than Reuben himself. Similarly this explains Joseph's: "I was surely stolen away from the land of Hebrew" ... The discrepancy between the Medanites who sold him and Ishmaelites from whom Potiphar is said to have bought him, may be explained by the fact that Ishmaelite is a generic term for all the descendants of Abraham other than Isaac, or they were the descendants of Medan the son of Abraham (Gen 25, 2). But the Midianites who sold Joseph to the Ishmaelites, though they too were the sons of Abraham, were certainly others who were not in the Ishmaelite caravan. Since the sellers and buyers could not be one and the same, they are termed "merchants" (following Rashbam's explanation).

Joseph's statement: "that you sold me" is no contradiction since, as Benno Jacob points out, "sale" does not cover just the financial side of the transaction but also the more general "disposing of" the object, accompanied by an undertone of bitterness and misfortune. God "sold" Israel into the hands of her enemies. (Ju. 2, 14; 3, 8; 4, 2). Joseph could have meant that his brothers had sold him, in the sense of getting rid or disposing of him, or in the sense of indirect instrumentality.

Jacob finds a more convincing proof that it was not the brothers who sold him. After Judah had suggested selling Joseph to the Ishmaelites, the verse ends with the words: "and the brothers hearkened." Rashi explains this in the sense of their acceptance of his plan. But Jacob argues that it would have to have an object to mean that ("and the brothers hearkened to him or to his voice," cf.: Gen. 23, 16; 30, 22; 34, 24; Ex. 18, 24; Nu. 21, 3).

Vayishme'u by itself implies the contrary, that they "heard him out," but demurred, disapproved. Cf.: Gen. 35, 22: "And

406

Reuben went and lay with Bilhah, his father's concubine, *and Israel heard.*' Thus the last words of verse 27 do not prepare the ground for the brothers' sale of Joseph, but the contrary: that no unanimous decision had been reached, and that in the meantime, the second caravan drew up and hauled Joseph out.

But the main question is how does this new interpretation affect the significance of the story as a whole. To this, Benno Jacob replies: The tribes had not been guilty of the sin of stealing a man and selling him (Ex. 21, 12–18) punishable by death and for which there was no atonement, being tantamount to murder. God had contrived matters that their design was not implemented by them. Joseph was sold by strangers. Had it been by his brothers, it would not have been a permanent sale, since the sale by a Jew, whether to a heathen or another Jew is redeemable. But Joseph was sold by heathens to heathens —into eternal slavery. This is the force of the emphasis in the text that Potiphar, an *Egyptian bought him from the hand* of the Ishmaelites. In spite of all this, the Almighty redeemed him from Egyptian slavery, a foretaste of what was to happen to all Israel, all the tribes of Jacob in Egypt in the house of bondage, from which the Lord would bring them out from slavery to freedom.

Questions for Further Study

1. The following objections have been raised to Rashi's interpretation: What forced Rashi to explain that the brothers sold him to the Ishmaelites and the latter to the Midianites and not that the brothers sold him to the Midianites and the latter to the Ishmaelites, which would fit the text better? Explain which texts this explanation would suit better and why Rashi, in spite of this, preferred his explanation.

2. If we accept the plain sense that it was the brothers who sold Joseph into Egypt, how would you explain Joseph's

words to the chief butler and baker: "For I was surely stolen from the land of the Hebrew"?

3. What did Ramban wish to prove by his quotation from Deut. 11, 7. ("all the great work God has wrought" on p. 403)?

4. Did Joseph contradict himself in stating on one occasion (40, 15): "I was surely stolen from the land of the Hebrews" and on another (44, 4): "whom you sold to Egypt"?

5. The contradiction between "The Medanites sold him to Egypt" (37, 36) and: "Potiphar bought him from the hand of the Ishmaelites" (39, 1) is harmonised quite simply by Benno Jacob, by pointing out that the text reports "they sold him *to Egypt*" and not "*to* the Egyptians" or "*in Egypt*". Explain.

6. "וישמעו אחיו": "וקבילו מיניה". וכל שמיעה שהיא קבלת דברים, כגון זה כגון (בראשית כח, ז): "וישמע יעקב אל אביו" וכגון "נעשה ונשמע" תורגם: נקבל. וכל שהיא שמיעת האוזן, כגון (בראשית ג, ח): "וישמעו . ת קול אלהים מתהלך בתוך הגן", וכגון (בראשית כז, ה): "ורבקה שומעת", (ראשית לה, כב): "וישמע ישראל", כולן מתרגם: "וישמעו", "ושמעת", "שמע".

"His brothers heard": implying they accepted his view. The Hebrew *shema* "hear" wherever it implies agreement, as in Gen. 28, 7 and the phrase *na'aseh ve-nishma'* is translated by Onkelos as "we shall accept." But wherever it implies hearing with the ear as in: Gen. 3, 8; 27, 5; 35, 22 it is translated by Onkelos by the word *shema.*
(Rashi)

Rashi always explains the meaning of a word whether by resort to the Aramaic Targum of Onkelos or to another example in the Bible or by translation into the vernacular (Old French), the first time he comes across it. Why then did Rashi wait till our sidra to explain this connotation of the Hebrew word *shema* instead of in Gen. 28, 7, where it first appears and on which he indeed bases himself?

[1] We have used Benno Jacob's: *Quellenscheidung und Exegese im Pentateuch*, Leipzig 1916 (devoted to a study of *Vayeshev-Miketz- Vayiggash*) an essential aid for anyone wishing to make a close study of the Biblical text and modern insights into it.

[2] Some commentators regard the Midianites and Medanites as two variations of the same name—on the basis of the passage (Gen. 25, 2): "She (Keturah) bore him Zimran, Yoshan, Medan and Midian." Medan, according to B. Jacob is merely an abbreviated form of Midian similar to Dothan which is a shorter variant of Dothin—mentioned in the same chapter as the place where Joseph met his brothers.

[3] Cf. Rashi: "Reuben returned" (37, 29): He was not present at the sale since it was his turn to go and look after his father. Another explanation: He was occupied with his sackcloth and fasting for having cohabited with his fathers' concubine.

The same puzzle is solved by Yosef Bechor Shor in an original and interesting fashion: "They sat down to dine": Shepherds don't usually eat all together but some look after the flocks whilst the others take their meal and then the latter relieve them. Judah was eating with some of the brothers whilst Reuben was tending the sheep with the rest. This was why Reuben was not aware of the sale... Some argue that they took turns in looking after their father and it was Reuben's turn that day. But how was that possible? Surely they were a long way from home and yet Reuben found his way back to the pit!

JOSEPH'S GOOD LOOKS

וְיוֹסֵף הוּרַד מִצְרָיְמָה
וַיִּקְנֵהוּ פּוֹטִיפַר סְרִיס פַּרְעֹה שַׂר הַטַּבָּחִים
אִישׁ מִצְרִי מִיַּד הַיִּשְׁמְעֵאלִים אֲשֶׁר הוֹרִדֻהוּ שָׁמָּה.

**Joseph was taken down to Egypt
and Potiphar, an officer of Pharaoh, the chief steward,
an Egyptian bought him from the Ishmaelites who had
brought him there.** (39, 1)

Divine Providence brought Joseph to no ordinary Egyptian
household but to the residence of a prince and an important man
in Egypt. It was a rich and large household and in it Joseph
advanced from strength to strength:

וַיְהִי יְיָ אֶת־יוֹסֵף
וַיְהִי אִישׁ מַצְלִיחַ.

**The Lord was with Joseph,
and he was a prosperous man;** (39, 2)

Joseph did not begin work as an ordinary slave in the field,
among other slaves, but:

וַיְהִי בְּבֵית אֲדֹנָיו הַמִּצְרִי.

he was in the house of his master the Egyptian.

In other words, he worked near his master and mistress in
functions in which he could distinguish himself. Indeed that
soon became the case, for as we read further:

410

וַיַּרְא אֲדֹנָיו כִּי יְיָ אִתּוֹ
וְכֹל אֲשֶׁר־הוּא עֹשֶׂה יְיָ מַצְלִיחַ בְּיָדוֹ.

And his master saw that the Lord was with him,
and that the Lord made all that he did to prosper in
his hand. (39, 3)

This foregoing information is somewhat astonishing. How could
it happen that his master, an Egyptian idolater, should see
that the Lord was with Joseph? Admittedly, the Torah records
something similar regarding the idolatrous Abimelech, king of
Gerar who said to Isaac:

We saw certainly that the Lord was with thee.
(26, 28)

But in that instance the men of Gerar really saw that God
was with him by the fact that he sowed and reaped a hundredfold and dug wells and found water. But how could Joseph's
master conclude that Joseph's success and the source of all the
plenty in his house came from the one God of his slave? Surely,
whatever Joseph had sown, as it were, and reaped, whatever
success and wealth he had achieved, originated basically from
his master! Some commentators suggest an answer by taking
the pronoun "he" in the phrase "all that he did" (verse 3) to
imply the master and not Joseph:

"All that he (i.e. the master) did, the Lord caused to prosper in his
hand" (i.e. through the hand of Joseph alone). (Kli Yakar)

In other words, Potiphar's transactions only prospered when
they were carried out by Joseph and not through any other servant. However, our Sages interpreted the profound perceptions
of the master in a different fashion. Rashi cites their explanation:

"וירא אדוניו כי ה' אתו": שם שמים שגור בפיו.

"And his Master saw that the Lord was with him"—that the
name of heaven was always on his lips.

411

His master saw and heard Joseph make mention of the name of his God and attribute his success and abilities not to his own powers but to the Almighty. It is quite mistaken to regard this homiletic interpretation of our Sages as in any way doing violence to the plain meaning of the text, and attributing to the Biblical record the conceptions and expressions of a later age such as "God willing" or "please God". Their homiletic explanation is, in actual fact, simply another and a deeper level of the real meaning of the text. In this case, as we shall see, our Sages discharged the proper function of any commentator by carefully examining every facet of the text and analysing all that Joseph is reported as saying whilst in Egypt. His first words in rejecting the advances of the mistress of the household end:

וְחָטָאתִי לֵאלֹהִים.

And sin against God. (39, 9)

Similarly, he does not boast of his own prowess in being able to interpret the dreams of Pharaoh's high officials while in prison but states:

הֲלוֹא לֵאלֹהִים פִּתְרֹנִים.

Do not interpretations belong to God? (40, 8)

His first words to Pharaoh, when his fate hangs in the balance between slavery and freedom, are marked by his publicly proclaimed belief in divine Providence:

בִּלְעָדָי, אֱלֹהִים יַעֲנֶה אֶת־שְׁלוֹם פַּרְעֹה.

God shall give Pharaoh an answer of peace. (41, 16)

Our Sages were, therefore, being true to the spirit of the Biblical record when they interpreted the master's seeing:

That the Lord was with him
and that the Lord **made all that he did to prosper in his hand—** (39, 3)

to imply that the Lord's name was ever on Joseph's lips and his firm faith in the guiding hand of Providence as responsible for his success inspired him at all times.

Joseph continued to advance in his master's household:

> **And he made him overseer of his house**
> **and all that he had, he put into his hand.** (39, 4)

Further we read that:

> **He left all that he had in Joseph's hand;**
> **and he knew not ought he had ...** (39, 6)

Joseph the slave thus became the master of Potiphar's household and estates. But we must remember that he still remained a slave in status. The Romans similarly employed slaves to discharge the most distinguished of functions, to administer their estates, but however distinguished, they were still not free. What was the result of all this advancement on Joseph? Did it go to his head? All that the Torah has to record after its description of Joseph's swift advancement is that:

> **Joseph was a commanding figure**
> **and good-looking** (Ibid)

Surely this does not constitute an appropriate moment for describing Joseph's physical attractiveness! In any case it is unusual for the Torah to go into such details unless at the beginning when the person is first introduced to us. In our case, however, the Torah has long ago described the fortunes of Joseph from his childhood in Canaan to his entering Egypt as a slave, and only now, after he had become promoted to the highest position in the household of an Egyptian dignitary are we told of his physical appearance. Advocates of the plain sense of the text offer the simple explanation that this description is a prelude to the story of his seduction by Potiphar's wife, emphasising that she became infatuated with him

413

just because of his looks. It is simply a case of cause and effect, our verse (6) providing the cause for the episode related in the immediately succeeding verses. Our Sages, however, discovered another significance in it. They found in it an indication of Joseph's reactions to the dramatic changes in his fortunes and environment:

"ויוסף היה יפה תאר": כיון שראה עצמו מושל, התחיל אוכל ושותה ומסלסל בשערו. אמר הקב"ה: אביך מתאבל ואתה מסלסל בשערך ? — אני מגרה בך את הדוב. מיד, "ותשא אשת אדוניו את עיניה אל יוסף".

As soon as he saw himself as a ruler, he began to eat and drink and curl his hair. Said the Holy One blessed be He: Your father is in mourning and yet you curl your hair! I shall incite the bear (Potiphar's wife) against you. Immediately, "his Master's wife cast her eyes upon Joseph." (Rashi)

According to this interpretation then Joseph was enamoured of the new life of luxury that he was living in Egypt, the country of wealth and culture, and his .eyes were blinded to the unreal nature of the power that had been placed in his hands. He forgot his slavery and that he was a stranger amongst them, he forgot the spiritual chasm separating him as a son of Abraham and follower of his way of life from Egypt and its abominations, and began to become more attached to the values of his employer which the Torah describes at a later occasion in the following terms:

> According to the deeds of the land of Egypt wherein ye dwell shall ye not do
> and in her statutes shall ye not walk. (Leviticus 18, 3)

Joseph then "began to eat and drink and curl his hair" and his disgust for idols and the Egyptian regime of slavery and his sense of repulsion for their sexual malpractices began to pall. For this reason our Sages differed regarding the implications of the phrase in verse 11 where it states that:

> Joseph went into the house to do his work

In the words of Rashi:

"לעשות מלאכתו" (יא): רב ושמואל: חד אמר: מלאכתו ממש וחד אמר:
ל ע ש ו ת צ ר כ י ו ע מ ה .

Rav and Samuel disputed regarding the interpretation of this phrase—one said it literally implies his work and the other said, it implied to yield to her.

Joseph then found himself on the brink of spiritual disaster. The plight of the poor and downtrodden exiled from their land and persecuted by hard taskmasters is difficult enough, but doubly dangerous is the plight of one who achieves favour in the eyes of his masters so that they advance him for their own needs to the highest of positions. But here a miracle happened to Joseph. On the brink of the complete eclipse of his spiritual loyalties to the faith and way of life of Abraham and his father Jacob, he was dismissed from his position and lost all that he had acquired during his slavery. Thus he was saved. What stood him in good stead at that time? The Psalmist says "happy is he who hath the God of Jacob as his help". Our Sages tell us that Joseph suddenly saw in front of him the image of his father Jacob and was saved from temptation. He was saved by the fact that he still cherished the memories of the traditions which his father had handed down to him (according to our Sages, Jacob imparted to his favourite son all the hallowed traditions of the Abrahamic line) so that even in the darkness and remoteness of exile the image of his father still hovered in front of him and saved him from temptation. But what of those who have only caught second or third-hand glimpses of their ancient traditions and shadows of the ancestral image during moments of Torah study in their childhood? Do they similarly stand a chance of being saved amidst alien cultures and climes?

Questions for Further Study

1.   In the light of what is narrated in our chapter (39) how would you explain the following from Psalm 105, 22 which

415

briefly recapitulates the story of Joseph:

To bind his princes at his leisure
And teach his elders wisdom

2. "The Lord *was* with Joseph and *he was* a prosperous man and *he was* in the house of his master the Egyptian" (39, 2)

Why does the text repeat the word *vayehi* (and he was) three times?
It would have been sufficient to have read: "The Lord was with Joseph and he prospered in his master's house."   (Abravanel)

Answer Abravanel's question on the basis of our *Studies*.

3. Abravanel asks:

We read (39, 4): "He appointed him over his house and all that he possessed he entrusted to his care." Why then does the text repeat itself. "He left all that he possessed in the care of Joseph" (v. 7)?

Anwer his question and explain the difference between Joseph's station in Potiphar's hourse in verse 4 and that in verse 7.

4. "But he refused and said to his master's wife, Look, my master, with me here, gives no thought to what is in the house ... how then could I commit this grave wrong and sin against God" (39, 8–9).

"and said to his master's wife": The text relates that he refused to do her will though she was his mistress, his master's wife and he feared her. But he feared God more. That is the reason for the inclusion of the phrase "his master's wife." (Ramban).

What anomaly in the wording prompted Ramban's comment?

5. The word "house" recurs three times in verse 5: "appointed him over his *house*"; "the Lord blessed the *house* of the Egyptian"; "in the *house* and the field".
Explain the different connotations of the word "house" in this verse.

SEE, HE BROUGHT US A HEBREW

In our previous *Studies* on this Sidra we discussed Joseph's conduct in the house of the Egyptian and illustrated his overriding loyalty to the God of his forefathers, noting that the first words he is reported as uttering are a reminder of the existence of a Divine Arbiter. To the importunings of Potiphar's wife he answers:

**How then can I do this great wickedness,
and sin** against God?   (39, 9)

Similarly his first words to the imprisoned royal officials in the Egyptian dungeon are:

Do not interpretations belong to God?   (40, 8)

In the same vein, paying no regard to self-advancement he firmly declares to the Egyptian monarch:

It is not in me; God will give Pharaoh an answer of peace.
                                                     (41, 16)

Joseph upholds his belief in the true God before all comers and in all circumstances. Let us on this occasion concentrate our attention on the behaviour of the representatives of the opposite camp, on Egyptian standards of conduct as illustrated in the stratagems employed by Potiphar's wife.

After Joseph's flight she summons the "men of her household." What motive has she in relating to them all that had happened instead of suppressing it in order to cover up her shameful conduct? But it was vengeance and vengeance alone that prompted her. For this she required a favourable "public opinion" to substantiate her story. Let us compare the account of the deed as it is reported by Potiphar's wife to her slaves, and subsequently to her husband, in order to prevail upon him to denounce Joseph:

Biblical Account (v. 12–14)	Potiphar's Wife to the Men of Her Household (v. 14–15)	To Her Husband (v. 17–18)
And he left his garment in her hand,	That he left his garment by me,	That he left his garment by me, and fled out.
and fled, and got him out.	and fled, and got him out.	As I lifted up my voice and cried.
That she called unto the men of her house.	And I cried with a loud voice See, he hath brought in a Hebrew unto us to mock us.	The Hebrew servant ... came in unto me to mock me.

We noted in our *Studies* on *Vayishlah* p. 382 how the slightest variation in phraseology, and addition or omission, may contain a world of significance. We may note how she reported that Joseph left his garment "by me" instead of "in her hand" as had actually happened. Otherwise the real truth would have become immediately self-evident to her hearers. She did not vary her account regarding Joseph's terrified flight in freeing himself from her whilst in her room and his resumption of his normal pace as he left it, for fear that her slaves had, perhaps, seen Joseph leave. But when she repeated the story to her husband she stressed simply that "he fled out" in order to strengthen the impression of his guilt. She emphasises both in the account to her slaves, who heard nothing, and to her husband that she cried out, in order to absolve herself from any suspicion of being an accessory to the deed. (cf. Deuteronomy 22, 24).

Further light is thrown on Potiphar's wife's unscrupulous defaming of Joseph in another subtle differentiation between her phrasing of the account to her slaves and subsequently to her husband. She does not employ the term "slaves" when addressing the slaves themselves. Joseph is called simply a Hebrew (literally: "a Hebrew man"). To her husband however, she says "the Hebrew slave". In order to win over her slaves and gain their sympathies she is at pains not to create any feeling of solidarity among the slaves for Joseph as one of them. After all, it was a common thing for masters to denounce their slaves. They would naturally side with their fellowsufferer. So she subtly changed her tone and stated that it was not one of them but a stranger, a Hebrew, the common enemy of all of them. To strengthen the impression and arouse their hostility for Joseph she does not say that the Hebrew slave came unto me, but rather:

רְאוּ,
הֵבִיא לָנוּ אִישׁ עִבְרִי
לְצַחֶק בָּנוּ.

See, he brought us a Hebrew to mock us.   (39, 14)

In short, the Hebrew has not only wronged me but all of us; he has dishonoured the whole Egyptian nation. How far, however, was that from the truth! In Egypt there were rather two nations, the free men, the Egyptian nobles, and the serfs, the slaves who had no rights at all. In spite of this, Potiphar's wife in her effort to gain sympathy lumps her slaves together with herself as part of one family. The common enemy is the Jew. The immense gap is forgotten, the enormous class distinction between slave and master is overlooked in the cause of temporary self-interest.

This sudden recognition of the brotherhood of man under the pressure of outside circumstances and dictated wholly by self-interest is a common phenomenon. Even our forefathers were guilty of this and aroused the Prophet's ire against them. What did they do during the siege of Jerusalem? First they entered into a solemn covenant—Zedekiah and the people—

to release their Hebrew slaves in accordance with the law of the Torah, only afterwards to enslave them again. Against this violation of their undertaking Jeremiah inveighs:

> **Therefore thus saith the Lord: Ye have not hearkened unto Me, to proclaim liberty, every man to his brother, and every man to his neighbour; behold, I proclaim for you a liberty, saith the Lord, unto the sword, unto the pestilence, and unto the famine; and I will make you a horror unto all the kingdoms of the earth.**
>
> (Jeremiah 34, 17)

The princes of Judah had ignored the regulation promulgated in the Torah to free their Hebrew servants at the end of seven years and had illegally detained them. However, as the Babylonian enemy reached their gates and famine visited the city and they could no longer feed their slaves, but, on the other hand, needed them to help in the battle. They suddenly remembered that were one people and one God had created them, Who had commanded them in His law "that none should make bondmen of them, even of a Jew his brother." Subsequently, however, something happened which changed their whole attitude of human brotherhood and obedience to God:

> **And Pharaoh's army was come forth out of Egypt; and when the Chaldeans that besieged Jerusalem heard tidings of them, they went away from Jerusalem.**
>
> (37, 5)

As soon as the danger subsided there was no further need to regard their fellow-Jews as their brothers:

> **But ye turned and profaned My name, and caused every man his servant, and every man his handmaid, whom ye had let go at your pleasure to return; and ye brought them into subjection, to be unto you for servants and for handmaids.**
>
> (34, 16)

Thus what Potiphar's wife had done in a small way on a purely personal level was done here on a national scale.

Questions for Further Study

1.   "How shall I commit this great wrong and sin against God?" (39, 9)

"והטאתי לאלהים": בני נח נצטוו על העריות.

"And sin against God" the sons of Noah too were commanded regarding adultery.   (Rashi)

"And sin against God" (after citing Rashi above) this is true, but knowing the frivolity of women he first explained to her that what she was asking him constituted treachery to her husband who trusted her. Only afterwards did he add that a sin against God was also involved.
You could also explain that the phrase: "Sin against God" referred to this breach of trust since it would constitute a great wrong for him to have a sin through her before God. For He favours only the loyal of the earth and no betrayer can come before Him. What he said was true enough but he refrained from referring to the prohibition of adultery since he appealed to her female psychology. (Literally: "he spoke to her as the way of women").   (Ramban)

(a) What difficulty did Rashi and Ramban respectively find in the verse?

2.   "See, he brought us a Hebrew man" (39, 14).

The wording: "See he brought us" has a negative overtone. The Hebrews were detested by the Egyptians who could not dine with them; for it was an abomination for them, nor would they go to their homes. She therefore said: Look what a wrong he has done us by bringing into our home a Hebrew and appointing him an overseer. He has every right to mock us as the saying has it in Proverbs (29, 21). "He that delicately bringeth up a servant from a child shall have him become a master at last." This is the force of "thou hast brought us," since his importation into the household was regarded by them as an imposition.

She said: "he hath brought us" referring to her husband in the anonymous third person, out of respect for him or as women do when correcting others *or simply because the referent was understood*. Cf. the book of Job where God is often referred to by the third person pronoun *since the subject was understood*.

Similarly in the case of Abner we read (II Sam 3, 7): "And he said, Why did you come in unto my father's concubine" without mentioning who said, since it was obvious from the context that it was Ishbosheth. (Ramban)

(a) Explain the italicised passages.

(b) Ramban gives three reasons for the anonymity of the subject in our text. The first: "out of respect." The question has been asked: If she failed to mention her husband by name, out of respect for him, why did she not leave him out completely and simply say: "a Hebrew slave came to us" instead of: "he hath brought us"?

(c) What difficulty is common to both our text and that in II Sam. cited by Ramban?

(d) What support can you bring from the Torah for Ramban's point that "the Hebrews were detested by the Egyptians, who could not dine with them"?

(e) Read Chapter 3 of Job and find one of the many examples Ramban refers to of God being referred to in the anonymous third person.

(f) Many have detected in our chapter a clue indicating that Potiphar did not really believe his wife's tale about Joseph, in spite of her histrionic tactics. What is the clue?

THE TRUTH SPEAKS FOR ITSELF

The two ministers who were confined in the same dungeon with the Hebrew slave, Joseph (Gen. 40) did not think him important enough to tell him their dreams. After all, he was not a magician or even remotely connected with the wise men of Egypt that he should be versed in the art of interpreting dreams. But Joseph's statement "Do not interpretations belong to God?" and it is He who apportions of His wisdom to even the smallest creature, therefore come now I, pray you, "tell me" apparently had their effect on the chief cupbearer and he divulged his dream. The chief baker held his peace and said nothing. He waited. Joseph gave his interpretation. Then the chief baker reacted for the first time. The text motivates his reaction:

וַיַּרְא שַׂר־הָאֹפִים כִּי טוֹב פָּתָר.

And when the chief baker saw that he had interpreted well. (40, 16)

But the words of the text are ambiguous. We have rendered the text literally, but the English version reads: "that the interpretation was good." Here are a number of explanations given by our classic commentators:

> He saw in his heart by the hearing of his ears that the interpretation was favourable and imagined therefore that he would give a favourable interpretation. Our Sages said too (Berakhot 55b) "All dreams follow the mouth." Joseph interpreted what he understood in the dream of each one, according to his understanding whether for good or bad. **(Redak)**

> The text recorded that when the chief baker saw that Joseph interpreted the chief butler's dream favourably, he also related

his dream. This shows that the chief baker was worried and afraid to relate it, fearing that its interpretation would be unfavourable, had he not seen that Joseph had favourably interpreted the chief butler's. He believed that their dreams were in reality identical.

(Abravanel)

that he had interpreted it favourably. It was likely therefore that his would also be favourable since dreams follow the mouth (of the interpreter).

(Sforno)

that he had interpreted it favourably.

(Shadal)

All the above four commentators explain the word *tov* "good" in the sense of "favourably." But except for Shadal, all of them are not satisfied with offering the verbal equivalent, but elaborate in an endeavour to answer a further difficulty. Even if we explain the text to imply that Joseph offered a favourable interpretation this does not yet explain why this convinced the chief baker of Joseph's powers. Perhaps the Hebrew lad, the imprisoned slave had fabricated the favourable interpretation in order to flatter and soothe these important personages for the purpose of self-advancement. For this reason the commentators add an explanation clarifying what was at the back of the Egyptian's mind. He believed in the magical powers of the words of the interpreter. If he uttered with his lips a favourable interpretation, the words of his lips would force events to shape themselves favourably. If they were destined to take an evil turn his utterance would deflect them from that unfavourable path. But the word *tov* in the text admits of another explanation, given by Ramban as his first explanation:

> Onkelos explains that "he interpreted it properly" as in Ps. 119,65: "Teach me *good* discernment and knowledge"; as in the text "for they were *fair*" (Gen. 6). This man had looked down on Joseph and thought he would never know how to interpret it and he would not have related to him his dream had he not seen that he had made a good job of interpreting his friend's dream.

The commentary *Haketav Vehakabbala* takes a similar view:

> The word *tov* implies perfection and appropriateness, beauty in

contradistinction to ugliness, justice to injustice and truth to falsehood as in Jer. 1, 12 "Thou hast *well* seen." The text therefore
implies that he had given a true interpretation.

The word *tov* in their view then implies "correct" or "true".
But this raises a serious problem. How could the chief baker
know that the interpretation offered the chief butler by the
Hebrew lad was genuine and not just flattery to curry favour
with him? This question transcends the actual context of our
chapter and the understanding of the chief baker's conduct.
It involves the criteria of truth in general—how they are to be
identified.

But before we answer this question let us first ask another
allied with this subject—not how the chief baker knew the interpretation was the correct one, but how Joseph knew. The question is asked and answered in another commentary *Akedat
Yiẓhak*:

> Both their dreams lent themselves to the same interpretation;
> for the picture of the bird eating the food from off his head was
> similar to that depicted by the chief butler in "I put the cup into
> the hand of Pharaoh," since the king is like a great winged eagle
> (see Ezekiel 17) ... but Joseph was influenced in his interpreta-
> tion by the past case history of the dreamers, their status at
> court and the difference between the crimes for which they were
> sentenced, marking the one for pardon the other for perdition.
> We see therefore that the evaluation of the interpretation is de-
> termined by the appraisal of the dreamer.

On the other hand, Abravanel objects to this explanation:

> If you ask how Joseph knew that they (i.e. the three branches
> or baskets) represented three days and not three months or
> years, I answer you that the Holy Spirit guided Joseph in his
> interpretation not his own imaginative powers alone.

Another answer is given by Benno Jacob in his commentary
to *Genesis*, in which, however, he had been anticipated by the
ancients. The dream itself reflects its character. Our Sages said
that "man's dreams are a reflection of his own thoughts." The

chief cupbearer regarded himself as industrious and active, watching over the wine he was to present to his king from the moment the vine began to bud forth till the cup placed in Pharaoh's hand. His dream therefore reflected his industry, efficiency and sense of responsibility. The chief baker, on the other hand, regarded himself as deprived of active performance—neither reaping nor milling nor refining, nor mixing with water nor kneading nor taking out the oven but staying where he was, the bread being ready in baskets, he even forgetting to cover them. Why should not the birds eat them? He had already borne witness to his own neglect, laziness and to disparagement of his work. The man who is industrious in his work is destined "to stand before kings"; the sluggard, the one who neglects his work in destined for the gibbet.

We have been offered three answers to the question how Joseph knew the interpretation. Perhaps we can learn from them the answer to our first question: how the chief baker knew. The first answer: that the Holy Spirit rested on Joseph cannot help us very much, since that certainly did not apply to the chief baker.

The second answer indicated that Joseph's power of interpretation was based on his knowledge of what went on at the royal court; he knew what was cooking in the diplomatic pot. This answer may perhaps be valid with regard to the chief baker. Perhaps he too was familar with the shifts of favour at court and the varying seriousness of the crimes for which they had been sentenced. But if he really knew then why couldn't he interpret his dream himself?—In the words of the Talmud (*Berakhot* 5):

"The prisoner cannot secure his own liberation from prison." The third answer was a psychological one. Joseph based his interpretation on the details of the dream in accordance with what they taught him about the personality of the dreamer. This answer can well fit our question too. The dreamer surely understands himself. Hadn't he really told him the dream, who he was and what he deserved in judgement. But here we must remember what modern students of dreams have taught us, that the dreamer neither wants nor is able to understand the language of his own dream. Abravanel in the 15th century formulated this idea in words that might have been taken from a contemporary manual of psychology. The dreamer on awakening remembers the empty symbols, the pictures, the parables, but forgets the significance, the illustration, the object of the symbol which is hidden in the folds of his dream pictures like the kernel in the husk. We cannot therefore be satisfied with this answer since the chief baker, if he forgot or repressed the significance of his dream, how did he know, on hearing Joseph's words, that "he had interpreted well"?

The Rashbam's answer appears most plausible to us that "the truth speaks for itself." In other words, the chief butler had no objective proofs, no clues to the detection of the truth of Joseph's interpretation. But he was convinced by the truth because it was the truth. The phrase "the truth speaks for itself" was taken by Rashbam from a passage in the Talmud, *Sota* 9b, discussing the perfidy of Delilah and her seduction of Samson:

"ותרא דלילה כי הגיד לה את כל לבו . . ." (שופטים טז, יח). מנא ידעה?
[רש"י: הלוא כמה כזבים אמר לה קודם לכן ומצאתו שקרן] אמר ר' חנון
א"ר: ניכרין דברי אמת! אביי אמר: ידעה ביה באותו צדיק דלא
מפיק שם שמים לבטלה, כיון שאמר (שם, יז): "נזיר אלהים אני", אמרה:
השתא ודאי קושטא קאמרי [הפעם ודאי דיבר אמת].

"And when Delilah saw that he had told her *all his heart* . . ." (Judges 16, 18). How did she know? (Surely he had told her lies on previous occasions, and she had found him out!). Said Rava: the truth speaks for itself! Said Abaye: She knew that that righteous man would not utter the name of Heaven in vain. As soon as he said (ibid.) "A Nazir *to God* am I", she said: Now I certainly know he is telling the truth.

According to Abaye she was able to detect he was telling the truth by objective signs; according to Rava she had none. But such is the power of truth that it bears its own tell-tale seal. This is its essence and strength which requires no proofs. Often the more important, the more profound the truth, the greater the impossibility of proving it—it bears witness to itself. This is what is implied in the phrase: "the truth speaks for itself."

Questions for Further Study

1. For what purpose do both Redak and Sforno rely on the Talmudic dictum that "dreams go after the mouth"? Explain the dictum. Can it be explained in other than magical terms?

2. What is the additional difficulty in our verse (a linguistic one) which Redak wished to dispose of, at the beginning of his comment?

3. For what reason did Redak add to his explanation the phrase "Joseph interpreted what he understood ... whether for good or bad." Surely this emerges from the reading of the chapter! What was the point of Redak stressing this?

4. What warrant in the Hebrew phraseology of the text did Abravanel find for his view that the chief baker thought that both had dreamt the same dream?

5. According to *Haketav Vehakaballa* the word *tov* applies to other contexts other than the ethical. Which?

6. Rashi appends no explanation to our verse (16): "And when the chief baker saw that he had interpreted well," whereas on verse 5: "And they dreamt a dream, both of them, each man according to the interpretation of his dream, in one night, each man according to the interpretation of his dream," Rashi comments: "they dreamt both of them one dream, this is the plain sense; but the Midrash states that each one dreamt the dream of them both, his own dream and the interpretation of his colleague." What can you learn from Rashi here regarding his explanation of the passage "that he had interpreted well"?

428

7.	Cf.: the words of the two ministers: in Pharaoh's dungeon in reporting their experience to Joseph:
	"We dreamt a dream *and to interpret it there is no one* [1]
	(40, 8)
	With the text from the story of Pharaoh's dream:
	"He sent and called all the magicians of Egypt and her wise men and Pharaoh related to them his dream
	and there is no one to interpret [2] *them* to Pharaoh" (41, 8)
	With Pharaoh's words to Joseph:
	"I have dreamt a dream *and to interpret it there is no one* [1]"
	(41, 15)
	Can you explain the difference in the word-order in terms of difference in context and situation?

8.	Cf.: the comment of *Akedat Yizḥak* with that of Abravanel on p. 425.
	Do they contradict each other or can they be regarded as complementary?

[1] ופותר אין.
[2] ואין פותר.

JOSEPH THE RIGHTEOUS ONE

The Patriarchs were three in number—Abraham, Isaac and Jacob. The title Patriarchs, *"Avot"* ("Fathers") was reserved for them alone. Their children were called not Patriarchs but simply tribes. But one of the tribes, and one only, was awarded the designation of "the righteous one" (*zaddik*). Indeed its holder, Joseph, was the sole Biblical character to qualify for such a title. Why? Do the incidents associated with his early life, described in our sidra warrant such an appellation? He is first introduced in the Torah as:

הָיָה רֹעֶה אֶת־אֶחָיו בַּצֹּאן
וְהוּא נַעַר אֶת־בְּנֵי בִלְהָה וְאֶת־בְּנֵי זִלְפָּה נְשֵׁי אָבִיו
וַיָּבֵא יוֹסֵף אֶת־דִּבָּתָם רָעָה אֶל־אֲבִיהֶם.

feeding the flock with his brethren; and the lad was with the sons of Bilhah, and with the sons of Zilpah, his father's wives: and Joseph brought unto his father their evil report. (37, 2)

What did the last mentioned accusation imply? Rashbam, the literalistic commentator *par excellence* this time accepts the ancient rabbinic homiletic comment:

> An evil report of his brothers (the sons of Leah), according to the explanation of the Midrash Aggada that he said to his father: Thus they abuse the sons of the handmaidens whereas I treat them with respect and am at home with them.

Rashi echoes a Midrash which takes an even harsher view of the implications of the text:

כל מה שהיה יכול לדבר בהם רעה, היה מספר.

Whatever evil he could speak of them, he retailed.

Though the Biblical expression "to bring an evil report" implies that the talebearer says nothing but the truth, it is still regarded as obnoxious and slanderous, since it is inspired with evil intent—to disparage the victim. The one who "brings forth" (*motzi dibba*) an evil report belongs, of course, to a different category, since that expression, in contradistinction to the "bringing of an evil report" [1] actually implies the invention of falsehood. Both however are blameworthy. After the gulf between Joseph and his brethren had widened, to the extent that "they hated him, and could not speak peaceably to him," he came to them to relate his dreams:

And Joseph dreamt a dream, and he told it to his brethren, and they hated him yet the more. (37, 5)

The foregoing verse must be regarded as a general statement summing up Joseph's line of conduct and the consequences which flowed therefrom.[2] The succeeding verses describes them in detail. Was Joseph's dreaming of such dreams in itself reprehensible? Some authorities maintain that this is certainly so since man's dream's are the fruit of his own imaginings, suppressed desires, aspirations and fears. Had he not nursed such ideas of overlordship over his brethren, he would never have been visited by such dreams. Even in his method and tone of retelling Joseph added fuel to the fire and exacerbated matters:

Hear, I pray you **this dream which I have dreamt.**

(37, 6)

Sforno explains that the text wishes to emphasise that Joseph was not content to relate the dream to his brothers. He pointedly emphasised its significance. He urged them to realise its meaning. That is the implication of his "Hear, I pray you" in the sense of "understand." This, of course, aroused their ire the more. They responded: "Shalt thou indeed reign over us?" The results were obvious:

וַיּוֹסִפוּ עוֹד שְׂנֹא אֹתוֹ עַל־חֲלֹמֹתָיו וְעַל דְּבָרָיו.

431

And they hated him yet the more for his dreams, and for his words. (37, 8)

Ramban takes the phrase "for his dreams" to refer to the very fact that he had such a dream (it showed the direction in which his waking ambitions lay), and "for his words" to the fact that he provoked them by telling the dreams. Rashi, however, understands the latter phrase differently:

"ועל דבריו" — על דיבתם רעה שהיה מביא אל אביהם.

> "for his words"—for the evil report of them he brought to his father.

Rashi's supercommentary *Gur Aryeh* meaningfully elaborates:

> The dream fanned their hatred even more, on account of the original cause. This is the nature of hate. Once a new motive for hate appears, additional animosity is engendered against the original cause of it.

But this reaction of the brethren did not deter Joseph from telling them his second dream. Note to whom he relates it, on this occasion:

And he dreamt yet another dream ... and told it to his father, and to his brethren. (37, 9–10)

Our commentators have been puzzled by the fact that Joseph related his second dream, first to his brothers, then to his father, in their presence. The first time, he had contented himself with telling his brothers. It has been suggested that the brothers' reaction, on the first occasion, satisfied him. Their angry response, "Shalt thou indeed reign over us" indicated that they had grasped the true meaning of the dream and acknowledged it. On the second occasion, they had not wanted to give him even that satisfaction. They remained silent. Presumably, their lack of response galled him. He waited and when no reaction was forthcoming brought his dream to his father. He related the dream which, this time, involved his father to the latter in the presence of his brethren, for them to hear their parent's reaction. Though Jacob's reply contained a rebuke, it *ipso facto* interpreted his dream, and the brothers were forced to listen to their father utter sentiments which they themselves had been so loathe to voice:

Shall I and thy mother and thy brethren indeed come to bow down ourselves to thee to the earth? (37, 10)

No wonder their hate turned to jealousy.

We have hitherto studied the narrative background to the dreams. We shall now consider the content of the dreams themselves. Both dreams speak of the act of "obeisance." But there is a difference in the respective contexts. In the first, he and his brothers are down on earth, acting in their customary occupations, on a basis of equality. It is not they who bow to Joseph, but the fruits of their labour that make obeisance to the fruits of his labour. In the second dream, the canvas has widened considerably. It is cosmic with the host of heaven bowing down to him. But he is not in heaven and they on earth. The converse is true. He appears as himself, he is not symbolically represented. He is pictured as a puny mortal to whom heavenly bodies make obeisance:

and, behold, the sun and the moon and the eleven stars made obeisance to me, (37, 9)

Does this not savour of overweening pride and self-importance, remote indeed from the conception of righteousness implicit in the title "Joseph the righteous one"? But we must note that, henceforth, Joseph himself began to change. He had been a young upstart, talebearing on his brothers, taunting them with his dreams, filled with his own sense of importance, going from one success to another in the course of the first 18 verses of our sidra—his father's favourite, the coat of many colours, the first dream and second. But from this juncture, his sufferings begin and his character undergoes a corresponding refining process. This reversal of fortunes and change of character is marked by a brief, very brief, conversation with his father:

וַיֹּאמֶר יִשְׂרָאֵל אֶל־יוֹסֵף: הֲלוֹא אַחֶיךָ רֹעִים בִּשְׁכֶם
לְכָה וְאֶשְׁלָחֲךָ אֲלֵיהֶם.
וַיֹּאמֶר לוֹ: הִנֵּנִי.
וַיֹּאמֶר לוֹ: לֶךְ־נָא רְאֵה אֶת־שְׁלוֹם אַחֶיךָ וְאֶת־שְׁלוֹם הַצֹּאן
וַהֲשִׁבֵנִי דָּבָר.

And Israel said unto Joseph, Do not thy brethren feed the flock in Schechem? come and I will send thee unto them. And he said to him, Here am I. And he said to him, Go I pray thee, see whether it be well with thy brethren and well with the flocks; and bring me word again. (37, 13, 14)

Joseph can utter only one, trisyllabic, Hebrew word *hinneni*— "Here am I"—in response to his father's call. The context of this *hinneni* is different from those of other occasions when this response is given in the Torah. Usually, *hinneni* is the response to the calling of one's name, before the message has itself been transmitted, as if to say, I am here, at your service (cf.: Abraham, Gen. 22, 1 who replied *hinneni* before he knew what God was to demand of him). Joseph however already knew what it was that he had been asked to do. His ready affirmative *hinneni* is, therefore, all the more significant. For this reason, Rashi departs from his usual procedure and comments on the *hinneni* here, despite the fact that he had explained its meaning on another occasion, with respect to Abraham. As a rule, Rashi never explains the same word twice in his commentary, but relies on the student having remembered it from his explanation in the context where it first appeared. But what does Rashi say to our *hinneni* here?

לשון ענוה וזריזות, נזדרז למצות אביו, ואף על פי שהיה יודע שאחיו שונאין אותו.

An expression of humility and readiness, eager to carry out his father's behest, though fully aware of the hatred that his brothers bore him.

Ramban makes a similar comment

"So he sent him out of the vale of Hebron" indicating that Joseph exerted himself out of respect to his father to go after them afar and did not say, How can I go when they hate me so?

His willing and steadfast pursuance of duty persisted even after he failed to find them and had to ask the way:

"And a certain man found him, and behold he had lost his way in the fields . . ." the text dwells on this in order to emphasise that out of respect to his father, Joseph did not turn back, though he had ample occasion to. (Ramban)

Discipline, filial duty, devotion are all evidenced here. But we are not told of any change in Joseph's attitude toward his brethren. From the moment he encountered them, he maintained a complete silence. The text records no justifications, pleadings or arguments of his, but simply reports his summary consignment to the pit. The one who had regarded himself as higher than the host of heaven—cast into the pit! The one who had seen himself king—sold as a slave! Did he learn his lesson? In the six verses of chapter 39 describing Joseph's life as a slave in the Egyptian household, the name of God appears five times:

And the Lord **was with Joseph ... And his master saw that the Lord was with him, and that the** Lord **made all that he did prosper in his hand ... the** Lord **blessed the Egyptian's house for Joseph's sake; and the blessing of the** Lord **was upon all that he had.**

Joseph rose in the Egyptian household, first being separated from the workers in the field and taken into the house as a retainer. Subsequently, he became the master's personal servant.

435

Promotion came even swifter and he soon became the manager of the estate, and, finally, the overseer of everything, without having to render account, even to his master. Was Joseph aware of the hand of Providence behind his mysteriously swift rise? Did he attribute his rising fortunes to the Being that the text itself constantly emphasises as supremely active in the developments of his life? Did he realise that it was not the Egyptians—steeped in idolatry and immorality as they were—who were his benefactors? Verse six opens up a window into Joseph's heart at the time:

And Joseph had an attractive physique and good looks.
(39, 6)

Usually the text describes the external appearance of a character (if allusion is made at all to the subject) the moment he is introduced (cf.: Rachel, Saul, David). It is rather late in the narrative to refer to such a detail. What had been his looks earlier on? Sforno explains the allusion to Joseph's physical attractiveness at this point in objective terms. He had been given by Potiphar a new and more responsible job involving no heavy physical labour as hitherto. This advancement to an easier life resulted in an enhanced physical appearance, no longer weary and work-stained. But as we noted in one of our earlier *Studies* (p. 414) the Midrash regards the allusion to Joseph's appearance as reflecting a subjective change—in his personal conduct:

> As soon as he saw himself a ruler, he began to pamper himself with food and drink and curl his hair. Said the Holy One blessed be He: Thy father mourneth, notwithstanding thou dost curl thine hair ... I shall arouse the bear against thee. Forthwith "his master's wife cast her eyes upon Joseph."

Joseph was attracted by the charms of Egyptian "high life," its wealth, culture and, above all, the power granted him by his master. He forgot his slavery and alien origin, the gulf separating a son of Jacob, bearer of the Abrahamic mission, slave only of the Supreme Master, from the Egyptians. He began to fraternise with them and curry favour with them until the inevitable happened. But at the last moment, at the decisive hour of trial, Joseph's inner strength saved him and, for the first time in Egypt, we hear him speak, and the name of God came naturally to his lips:

how can I do this great wickedness and sin against God?
(39, 9)

But since he had not been completely cured of his love of power and authority, he had to be consigned, a second time, to the pit. Again he rose therefrom. It is interesting to note the resemblances between the verses describing his rise in prison, at the end of the chapter, with those depicting his advancement in the house of Potiphar, at its beginning. Once again, the name of God came naturally to his lips, but he no longer felt himself a ruler. It is significant that the chief cupbearer remembered him as a "young man, a Hebrew, servant to..." (41, 12). Henceforth, he was modest in his self-evaluations. The place in which he found himself is termed "prison" during the whole of chapter 39 as well as in 40, except for one reference. When Joseph recalled the vicissitudes of his past, he said:

For indeed I was stolen away out of the land of the Hebrews; and here also I have done nothing that they should put me in this pit.
(40, 15)

What is the reason for this way of referring to his prison? Had the memory of the first pit into which he had been cast impinged on him? The one who had dreamt of lording it over the host of heaven now realised that his destiny lay in the pit. Evidently Joseph had come to the realisation of his own little worth, and in so doing, had made real progress to the goal of authentic kingship. Joseph however was still puzzled regarding his destiny. He realised that he was, at present, in the pit but was not yet aware of the mysterious purpose underlying his peculiar destiny. At the climax of his career he was able to look back and unravel the mystery of his sufferings. His pride and illusions of grandeur had evaporated.[3] The dreams served no longer as symbols of domination but of responsibility, and duty. Service not dominion had been granted him. Later, he, the vice-regent of the realm would regard himself as a true servant of his father and brothers, as an instrument of Providence, in saving them:

וַיִּשְׁלָחֵנִי אֱלֹהִים לִפְנֵיכֶם
לָשׂוּם לָכֶם שְׁאֵרִית בָּאָרֶץ
וּלְהַחֲיוֹת לָכֶם לִפְלֵיטָה גְדֹלָה.

And God sent me before you to preserve you a posterity in the earth and to save your lives by a great deliverance.
(45, 7)

---

1 See Ramban on Num 13, 32, s.v. ויוציאו את דבת הארץ

2 One of the 32 *middot* or methods of Torah interpretation: "A general statement followed by a narrative, the latter is a particularisation of the former" cited by Rashi on Gen. 2, 8 s.v. *mi-kedem* q.v.

3 Cf. the Psalmist's reading of the Joseph story Ps. 105 vv. 18–19: "the iron entered his soul; until the time his word came true, the word of the Lord refined him." (ed.)

JOSEPH BRINGS GOD INTO PHARAOH'S LIFE

We have already noted, in the previous sidra, how Joseph proudly proclaims his God, during his sojourn in a foreign country, amidst idolaters. He repels the advances of his master's wife ending with the words:

> **How then can I do this great wrong**
> **and sin** against God? (39, 9)

In similar vein he replies to the imprisoned high officials of 'Pharaoh's court who are troubled by their dreams:

> **Do not interpretations belong to God?** (40, 8)

They saw no possibility of finding anyone capable of interpreting their dreams in Pharaoh's dungeon. But the Hebrew prisoner replied that interpretations belonged to God and He chose whom He thought fit, to act as a vehicle for interpreting their dreams.

Again Joseph stands before the court of Pharaoh who had freed him from prison, possibly only temporarily, in order to interpret the dreams that had puzzled the magicians of Egypt. Pharaoh says to Joseph:

> **I have heard say of thee,**
> **that thou canst understand a dream to interpret it.**
> (41, 15)

At this decisive moment in his life, hovering between advancement and reversion to the dungeon, he proudly proclaims the name of his God:

> **And Joseph answered Pharaoh, saying,**
> **It is not in me:**
> **God shall give Pharaoh an answer of peace.**   (41, 16)

Let us read carefully the first section of Joseph's lengthy answer to Pharaoh in which he interprets the dream:

> ... what God is about to do He hath declared **unto Pharaoh.**
>
> ... The seven good kine are seven years; and the seven good ears are seven years;
> the dream is one
>
> ... And the seven lean and illfavoured kine that came up after them are seven years, and also the seven empty ears blasted with the east wind; they shall be years of famine.
>
> ... what God is about to do He hath shown **unto Pharaoh.**
>
> ... Behold, there come seven years of great plenty throughout all the land of Egypt.
>
> ... And there shall arise after them seven years of famine; and all the plenty shall be forgotten in the land of Egypt; and the famine shall consume the land.
>
> ... And the plenty shall not be known in the land by reason of that famine which followeth; for it shall be very severe.
>
> And for that the dream was doubled unto Pharaoh twice, it is because the thing is established by God and God will shortly bring it to pass.
>
> Now therefore let Pharaoh look for a man discerning and wise ...   (41, 25–33)

If we follow carefully the structure of his reply, we shall see that it comprises various stages.

440

First stage: A key to the symbols appearing in the dream, 26–27. The cows=years, the ears of corn=years, the two dreams are one.

Second stage: Explanation of the symbols and the relation between them—plenty and famine following in succession, 29, 31.

Third stage: The rescue proposal of Joseph in detail, following storage by the State of the surplus of the years of plenty with which to maintain the population in the lean years, 33–36.

Here is the speech of Joseph arranged in schematic form:

I. — *Verse* 25, 26–27

II. — *Verse* 28, 29–30–31

III. — *Verse* 32, 33–34–35–36

What function do the verses introducing each stage fulfil? Surely from the point of view of content they add nothing, neither to the explanation of the dream or to the advice how to meet the coming famine. Nevertheless, these three verses repeat something which forms the cornerstone of the whole structure of Joseph's speech to Pharaoh. Joseph in these verses refers to God as the power behind the scenes as the *doer*, the *shower*, the *declarer*, and the *bringer to pass*. The name of God thus occurs in these three verses and is even inserted twice in the last verse against all the rules of syntax, in order to emphasise the central role of Divine Providence.

It is because the thing is established by God
and God **will shortly bring it to pass.** (41, 32)

Here the pronoun "He" would have sufficed, "and He will shortly..." but Joseph proclaims the omnipotence of God at all times, in the midst of an idolatrous world, emphasising *against Whom* man sins, *Who* interprets dreams, *Who* foretells that which is to come and *Who* brings things to pass.

All this Joseph achieves not by a lecture or a discourse but by the rhetoric device of repetition. In the end, even Pharaoh took the hint and thus he answered:

Can we find such one as this,
a man in whom the spirit of God **is?** (41, 38)

441

Instead of approaching Joseph as he did at first, in the light of an "expert" who had been brought out of the dungeon to interpret the royal dream—

> **I have heard say of thee, that thou canst understand a dream to interpret it—**

Pharaoh addresses him as follows:

> **Forasmuch as God hath shown thee all this . . .**
>
> (41, 39)

Pharaoh, king of Egypt defers for the first time to the supreme King of kings.

Questions for Further Study

1. We have emphasised the repeated reference by Joseph to the Deity in chapter 41, verses 25, 28 and 32:
   . . . what God is about to do He hath declared unto Pharaoh
   . . . what God is about to do He hath shown unto Pharaoh
   . . . it is because the thing is established by God, and God will shortly bring it to pass.
   We explained the significance of this repetition. Compare, in the light of this, Exodus 2, 23–25 and Numbers 32, verses 20–28, in particular, where Moses replies to the two and a half tribes. These passages similarly contain an unusual repetition of the name of the Deity. Explain the reason for this in both these passages.

2. Why did not Joseph make mention of the name of God again in his words beginning from verse 32 onwards?

JOSEPH'S ADVICE

In the previous *Studies* of this sidra we demonstrated how Joseph proudly carried the word of God on his lips amidst Egyptian idolatry. From the moment of his entry into Egypt, during his term of employment in Potiphar's house, till his rise to Pharaoh's court, the name of Heaven accompanied his every utterance.[1]

This is particularly evident in his speech to Pharaoh (41, 25–32) in which he invoked the name of God four times and on each occasion in a strategic part of his utterance, whenever he began a new subject:

(25) What *God* is about to do He hath declared to Pharaoh

(28) ... What *God* is about to do He hath shown to Pharaoh

(32) ... it is because the thing is established by *God* and *God* will shortly bring it to pass

It is obvious that this emphasis is deliberate to show the king of Egypt, his wise men and princes, his people and the whole heathen world who is the Doer, the Declarer, the Shower, and the Bringer to Pass.[2]

We shall deal this time with that part of his speech containing no mention of the Deity but concerned with the deeds and role of mortal man:

Now, therefore let Pharaoh look for a man discerning and wise, and set him over the land of Egypt. Let Pharaoh do this, and let him appoint overseers over the land and take up the fifth part of the land of Egypt in the seven years of plenty. And let them gather all the food of these good years that come, and lay up corn under the hand

of Pharaoh for food in the cities and let them keep it. And
the food shall be a store to the land against the seven
years of famine, which shall be in the land of Egypt, that
the land perish not through the famine.   (41, 33–36)

Many of our commentators have wondered how Joseph the
stranger, the slave, summoned from the dungeon, perhaps just
for the moment to answer one question, interpret the dream,
dared to proffer advice, unasked, to Pharaoh, king of Egypt?

There have been commentators who have endeavoured to
explain that not advice is proffered but the continuation of
the interpretation of the dream. So Ramban has explained it,
finding Joseph's plan of the lean years being sustained from
the surplus of the years of plenty as emerging from the passage
describing how the lean ill-favoured cows devoured the fat ones
and the corresponding one about the sheaves.

> Joseph's plan was prompted by the sight of the lean cows devour-
> ing the fat ones, symbolising that the famine years would eat
> of the years of plenty. On the basis of this he advised Pharaoh
> to have all the food of the years of plenty stored for use in the
> famine period. It was not his own advice. Had they commis-
> sioned him to advise the king?[3] It was merely part and parcel of
> the dream's interpretation. "All the plenty shall be forgotten ...
> and the plenty shall not be known" (30), is the interpretation of
> "it could not be known they had eaten them but they were
> still illfavoured" (21). He observed that they did not get well or
> fat but simply managed to subsist (implying that the surplus of
> the years of plenty would not suffice for comfort but merely for
> subsistence in the famine period). This is not according to Rashi
> who states that "all the plenty shall be forgotten" is the inter-
> pretation of the eating up.

The difference between Rashi and Ramban lies chiefly in their
understanding of the metaphorical implications of the term
"eating up" or "devouring". Mizrahi has aptly explained that
eating can imply the destruction of the food and its disappearance. According to Rashi the lean cows devouring of the
fat ones, without any improvement in their state, expresses the
eating in terms of the destruction of the object eaten, and not

444

of the beneficial effect on the eater. Accordingly, the eating and swallowing of the fat cows by the lean ones has to be taken as symbolising the forgetting of the period of plenty in the days of famine. On the other hand, according to Ramban who maintains that Joseph would not have dared to proffer unasked his own advice to Pharaoh, his words were a continuation of the interpretation. The lean eating the fat symbolised the lean years living on the surplus of the fat ones. The eating is conceived in terms of its nutritious effect on the consumer and not of the consumption of the thing eaten. Their different conceptions of the eating were prompted by their divergent views on the character of Joseph's words ("now therefore let Pharaoh see"— 33) whether advice (Rashi) or interpretation (Ramban).

In *Haketav Vehakabbala* the advice theory is not ignored, though Joseph's plan is understood to emerge from the dream. He differs from Ramban in the identification of the source in the dream for this plan:

> Commentators have concluded that Joseph undertook the role of advising the king because he had not been summoned only for the purpose of interpreting the dream. In my opinion this advice was not his own but was also part of the interpretation, prompted by the superfluous phrase "And Pharaoh awoke", at the end of the first dream and again in his retelling: "And I awoke." What difference does it make to us whether he awoke or not? Joseph understood from this that it was Pharaoh's duty to arouse himself, awake to action in order to forestall disaster, by making all the necessary preparations in the period of plenty that would minimise the consequences of the forthcoming calamity.

But the wording of the text and content of the advice would seem to preclude such an interpretation. Joseph's "Now therefore let Pharaoh look for" indicates the beginning of a new theme, as if to say, Now that God has shown you what is going to happen, it is your duty to do your best to meet the emergency.[4] It does not at all sound like the continuation of his interpretation of the dream, as an explanation of a hitherto undeciphered item.

445

Further, according to neither of the commentators (Ramban and *Haketav Vehakabbala*) there is no correspondence between the details of Joseph's plan (the appointment of a responsible person, the overseers, the storage etc.) and the dream, merely a general message, either that of the years of plenty sustaining the lean (Ramban) or the awakening to preventive action (*Haketav Vehakabbala*). Ramban sensed this weakness in his explanation and that Joseph's words contained something more than mere deciphering of the dream symbols. He therefore suggested what is odd and offensive to many commentators, that Joseph was pressing his own suit and suggesting to Pharaoh, in his call for a man, discerning and wise, able to deal with people and versed in the science of food preservation, his own candidature:

> Joseph said all this so that he (Pharaoh) would select him; for the eyes of the wise man are in his head.

Ramban was prompted to this explanation by the strangeness of Joseph's behaviour in arrogating to himself the role of royal adviser. But it is hardly plausible to imagine that the man who was at pains to insist even in the dungeon to the ministers of Pharaoh that he was no magician and that any wisdom he displayed came from God,[5] an attitude he proudly adhered to even before Pharaoh himself, ("It is not in me; God will give Pharaoh an answer") when freedom or reversion to captivity depended on the impression he made, should even so much as hint to Pharaoh: I am that man, discerning and wise who should be entrusted with the affairs of the state.

Pharaoh's own words in reaction to Joseph's are sufficient to dispel this notion. He first turns to his servants and then to Joseph);

> **And Pharaoh said unto his servants: Can we find such a one as this, a man in whom the spirit of God is?**
> **And Pharaoh said unto Joseph: Forasmuch as God has shown thee all this, there is none so discerning and wise as thou. Thou shalt be over my house.** (41, 38–40)

Pharaoh was not prompted by Joseph's hint, as Ramban suggests, but he appreciated Joseph's emphatic fourfold reference to God. Instead of making his starting point Joseph's expertise in clairvoyance after the manner of the Egyptian sorcerers, as he did at first: "I have heard say of thee, that when thou hearest a dream thou canst interpret it" he now recognised in him "a man in whom the spirit of God is",[6] and only now repeats Joseph's words as an indication of acceptance of his proposal: "Forasmuch as God has shown thee all this, there is none so discreet and wise as thou." This was the difference between "the magicians of Egypts and her wise men" and Joseph the discreet and wise who received his wisdom, and accepted that it came—from God.

In further strengthening of the case against Ramban's suggestion that Joseph was hinting at his own eligibility we cite here another explanation, which draws attention to Pharaoh's third statement. Pharaoh once again turned to Joseph:

And Pharaoh said to Joseph: See I have set thee over all the land of Egypt. (41, 41)

This statement is puzzling since Pharaoh had already said as much in the previous verse. The *Midreshei Torah* (Anselm Astruc) gives the following answer:

Possibly Joseph was abashed at the lofty appointment and was not sure whether it was meant seriously, imagining that it was perhaps in mockery of his own statement "Now therefore let Pharaoh seek out a man discerning." For this reason Pharaoh reiterated: "See I have really and truly set thee over all Egypt."[7]

Accordingly, far from Joseph having put himself forward as candidate, he did not even believe his ears when it was first proposed to him.

Reverting to our first question: How could Joseph dare to proffer advice unasked, the best answer would seem to be that advanced by Abravanel.

This advice was prompted from beginning to end by the Holy Spirit. The prophet cannot keep back his prophecy and must unburden himself. Cf.: Jeremiah (20, 9): "there is in my heart as it were a burning fire shut up in my bones, and I weary myself to hold it in but cannot." It is the nature of the Holy Spirit, once it enters the heart of man to force its message out, so that he cannot keep it back.

Joseph's wisdom therefore is that which was accompanied by Divine communion and revelation.

Benno Jacob thus sums up the significance of our chapter in his commentary to *Genesis*:

"Wisdom" was greatly admired in antiquity. Wisdom was a term given to the power of the spirit, science and philosophy, intelligence, experience, wisdom of life as well as artistic gifts and skills. Israel too attached importance to wisdom and the books of the Bible are full of its praise. It implies spirituality, thirst for knowledge, study and research. But the word "wise" appears for the first time in our chapter, since, for the first time, the wise men of the nations, the magicians of Egypt are contrasted with the wise man of Israel, the man in whom the spirit of God is.

Questions for Further Study

1. "They shall be seven years of famine" (41, 27). Regarding the good kine it does not say they symbolise seven years of plenty, one, because Joseph did not immediately grasp the full meaning but came to it gradually, as is the case in most things. Secondly, from the converse one learns its opposite. Aristotle also advises us when we are faced by two unknowns that are opposites, first to try to understand the lesser unknown and then proceed to the more unknown. So it is here. The phenomena of the good kine and ears of corn did not immediately suggest the symbolism of plenty, since they were the norm particularly in a land where all were like that. But the lean and ill-favoured ones were an extraordinary feature that much more easily suggested its own symbolism of evil years, which was not usual in that country, as may be noted from the Scriptures: "And there was a famine in the land and Abram went down to Egypt" (Gen. 12, 10). On account of this, Joseph afterwards became more confident of the interpretation and said: "That is the thing which I spoke to Pharaoh" (41, 28).   (Ibn Caspi)

448

(a) What difficulties in Joseph's interpretation prompted Ibn Caspi's explanation?

(b) Bring examples from Scriptures where the full meaning was not grasped immediately but came gradually.

(c) What did the commentator wish to illustrate by his quotation from Gen. 12, 10?

2. Joseph did not refer to the seven years of plenty, since this itself was not a matter of sufficient note for God to transmit specially to Pharaoh. It would have been just the usual symptom of the wealth and success of the state and would not have made an impression on Pharaoh at that moment. For this reason he did not reveal anything until he had imparted the message of the famine, since that touches on the survival of the world.

(Ha'amek Davar)

(a) What difficulty does he find in the text (41, 26)

(b) What difference is there between his solution and Ibn Caspi's?

3. Arama asks:
What was the reason for Joseph advising Pharaoh to appoint officers? Surely that was the task of the man, discreet and wise to be appointed.

Try to answer, basing yourself on the advice given by Hushi the Archite to Absalom 2 Samuel 17, 1–14.

---

1 Evidently Rashi's comment, echoing the Rabbis, to verse 3, chap. 39: s.v. "when his master saw the Lord was with him:" "implying that the name of God was ever on his lips" was not just a homiletic attempt to solve the difficulty as to how his master. knew the Lord was with him but sprang from close reading of the text itself. See p. 448.

2 To the best of my knowledge the first to detect this underlying meaning in Joseph's speech was Benno Jacob in his commentary to *Miketz*.

3. This expression is taken from II Chronicles 25, 16 uttered by Amaziah in denunciation of the prophet sent to reprove him: "And it came to pass as he talked with him that the king said unto him, Have we commissioned you to advise the King, forbear. why should you get hurt." Here is just one of many examples of Ramban's literary artistry in weaving Biblical passages into the texture of his commentary so

organically that they cannot be felt, in contrast to the artificial flowery neo-Biblicisms of the later Haskala writers.

4 Cf.: with this use of the introductory *ve-'ata* "And now" the sentence: "And now O Israel what doth the Lord thy God require of thee?" Rashi *ad loc*: "Though you have done all this, His compassion still extends to you and in spite of all that you have sinned before Him he requires from you only..." Cf. also Gen. 31, 36; ibid. verse 43 and I Sam. 12, 13 which is immediately followed by the demands Samuel calls on them to fulfil in the light of the new political framework of monarchy.

5 On the text: "Do not interpretations belong to God," Ibn Ezra comments: For the interpretation of dreams is the prerogative of God, for He knows the future and has shown in a dream what will come to pass to whom He wills. Whether I interpret it for good or bad will not affect the issue.

6 See p. 441.

7 Support for this may be found in the wording of the text. Note that the verse begins with the words "Then Pharaoh said to Joseph" even though in the two previous verses (39, 40) the speaker was Pharaoh and he was addressing Joseph. Verse 39 too opens with the preamble "Then Pharaoh said to Joseph". The repetition of this opening, though there is no change of speaker and spoken to, indicates a significant pause between the end of verse 40 and beginning of the next verse in Pharaoh's conversation, as if he were waiting for Joseph's reaction. But no response was forthcoming from Joseph, at least, no verbal response, beyond, possibly, an expression of astonishment and perhaps resistance on the part of Joseph. Cf.: Gen. 15, 2 and 3; ibid. 15, 5; ibid. 30, 27-8; Num. 32, 2-5.

THE THING PLEASED PHARAOH

The thing pleased Pharaoh and all his servants.
And Pharaoh said to his servants: Could we find another
like him in whom is the spirit of God?
So Pharaoh said to Joseph, since God has made all this
known to thee, there is none so discerning and wise as thee.
Thou shalt be over my house and by thy word shall all my
people be ruled.   (41, 37–40)

Isaac Arama in his *Akedat Yizhak* propounds the following
question on this passage:

> Why did Joseph's words ring true in the eyes of Pharaoh and
> his servants? Why did they promote him to high office appoint-
> ing him over all the land of Egypt, before they knew the upshot
> of his forecast?

Abravanel puts the same question even more forcefully adding:

> Even the chief butler did nothing after Joseph had favourably
> interpreted his dream for him. Perhaps his interpretation of
> Pharaoh's dream would not be fulfilled? Why did they then
> exalt him, before it could be tried out and arrange a society
> marriage for him.

The question of principle underlying all the above queries is:
What is the criterion of truth? How is it to be recognised and
detected by the hearers?[1] The point at issue becomes even more
complex, when we take into account the following Midrash,
which maintains that the magicians of Egypt likewise offered
their own rival interpretations of Pharaoh's dreams. But they
did not appeal to the troubled monarch.

ר' יהושע דסכנין בשם ר' לוי : פותרין היו אותו, אלא שלא היה קולן נכנס
באוזניו : שבע הפרות הטובות — שבע בנות אתה מוליד ; שבע הרעות —
שבע בנות אתה קובר. שבע השיבלים הטובות — שבע איפרכיות [מדינות]
אתה כובש ; שבע השיבלים הרעות — שבע איפרכיות מורדות בך.

R. Yehoshua in the name of R. Levi: They interpreted it for
him, but their interpretations failed to convince him. For example
the seven goodly cows signify seven daughters that you will
father; the seven evil looking ones, that you will bury seven
daughters; the seven goodly ears—seven provinces you will conquer; the seven withered ears that seven provinces will rebel
against you.   (Bereshit Rabbah)

There is good warrant in the text itself for the above explanation, where it is not stated that; "there was none to interpret
them" but:

**And Pharaoh told them his dream; but there was none
that could interpret them** unto Pharaoh.   (41, 8)

Interpretations were then offered but none appealed to the
monarch. What was the criterion of truth? A clue to the solution of our problem may perhaps be found in the text itself.
The story of the two dreams ends with the following words:

And Pharaoh awoke, and behold, it was a dream
                                                    (41, 7)

Pharaoh then regarded both dreams as one, as he indeed explicitly says:

**And Pharaoh said unto Joseph: I have dreamt a dream,
and there is none that can interpret** it . . .
**And Pharaoh spoke unto Joseph: In my dream behold
I stood . . .
And I saw in my dream, and behold, seven ears . . .**
                                        (41, 15, 17, 22)

The magicians however regarded Pharaoh's account as contain-

452

ing two separate dreams. Their solutions were therefore far from the truth. Even this is alluded to in the text:

And Pharaoh told them his dream
but there was none that could interpret them **to Pharaoh**

Abravanel comments:

> I think that Pharaoh himself felt that he had experienced one dream, while the magicians imagined there were two, since the king had dreamt them on two separate occasions in time, in different dream pictures, waking in between them both.

But this does not provide us with the criterion of truth, in respect of the dream's interpretation and in the wider field.

S. D. Luzzatto gives the following explanation:

> "... None could interpret them"—no one provided Pharaoh with a satisfying interpretation. He wished them to detect in his dream a message regarding the future of his people, and which it would profit him to know beforehand. He believed that God had not vouchsafed him the dreams for nothing, particularly as they came to him on his birthday. Otherwise what prevented them from offering any interpretation they could think up? According to this, we can appreciate why Joseph offered advice to the king. The latter did not want to know the future but to know what was in store so that he could take preventive steps.

A Midrash would seem to lend support to this explanation of Luzzatto:

> "ובעיני כל עבדיו" — על שנתן עצה להחיות יושבי הארץ, זה שאמר הכתוב
> (משלי טז, ז): "ברצות ה' דרכי איש גם אויביו ישלים אתו", שאפילו שר
> הטבחים והחרטומים הודו לדבריו.

> "... and in the eyes of all his servants" (41, 37)—because he had given advice on sustaining the inhabitants of the land, in accordance with the text: "When a man's ways please the Lord, He maketh even his enemies at peace with him" (Proverbs 16, 7). Even the magicians and chief baker admitted the truth of his words.
> (Midrash Sekhel Tov)

Is the usefulness of a man's word or advice then the real criterion of their truth? Cannot a man's words ring true even when they convey no consolation or good tidings? Conversely do words of flattery sound true to their hearers? The story of Ahab and Jehoshaphat offers us guidance on this very point. King Ahab wanted to do battle and wrest a piece of land from his neighbours. All the prophets, four hundred in all, answered to a man, when asked for their opinion:

> **Go up, and the Lord will deliver into the hand of the King** (I Kings 22, 6)

Nevertheless Jehoshaphat, king of Judah was not satisfied with this response, irrespective of its favourable or unfavourable content. He asked:

> **Is there not here** besides a prophet of the Lord, **that we might inquire of him?** (ibid. 22, 7)

What then is the criterion of truth? Another Midrash gives an answer that appears rather mechanical and external:

> אמר לו יוסף : מי הודיעך שלא פתרוהו כראוי ? אמר לו : כשם שראיתי את החלום, כך ראיתי פתרונו, לכן אינם יכולים [החרטומים על ידי פתרונות שוא] לשחק בי.

> Said Joseph to him: Who told you that they did not interpret the dream rightly? Pharaoh said to him: Just as I saw the dream, so I saw its interpretation. They (the magicians) cannot therefore deceive me. (Midrash Haggadol)

> שנזכר מיד פתרון החלום, כי כמו שפתר לו — כן היה רואה גם הוא, אלא ששכחו ועכשו נזכר.

> He immediately was reminded of the interpretation of the dream, that this was as Joseph had interpreted. He had forgotten it, but now remembered. (Sekhel Tov)

The above explanation would seem to be unsupported both by the text and psychological experience. However Abravanel points a way to understanding the Midrash.

> One who is vouchsafed an authentic dream will look at matters as he has been directed by Divine Providence. But his imaginative

perception will translate this direction into pictures and symbols. As soon as the interpreter discovers their true and accurate meaning, the dreamer will immediately sense that this was what he saw. Memory acts in this manner, particularly where a considerable time has not elapsed since the event. As soon as someone else reminds him he will himself recall that this was what he forgot.[2]

According to this explanation, the dreamer himself detects the meaning behind his dream, its kernel which is concealed inside an outer shell of symbols. The interpreter merely draws attention to what he had subconsciously realised, to the interpretation which he had "forgotten", but had now been "reminded of." His own heart is the witness of its truth.

Question for Further Study

Cf. the narrative version of the dream with Pharaoh's personal account:

The Narrative	*Pharaoh's Version*
And behold he stood by the river	Behold I stood upon the brink of the river
And behold there came up out of the river seven kine, well-favoured and fat-fleshed;	and behold there came up out of the river seven kine, fat-fleshed and well-favoured
And they fed in the reed-grass.	and they fed in the reed-grass
And behold, seven other kine came up after them out of the river	And, behold, seven other kine came up after them, — — — — — — — — —
ill-favoured and lean-fleshed;	poor and very ill-favoured and lean-fleshed
and stood by the other kine upon the brink of the river.	— — — — — — — — —

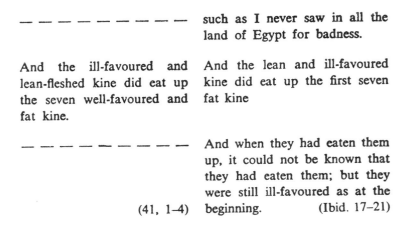

	such as I never saw in all the land of Egypt for badness.
And the ill-favoured and lean-fleshed kine did eat up the seven well-favoured and fat kine.	And the lean and ill-favoured kine did eat up the first seven fat kine
	And when they had eaten them up, it could not be known that they had eaten them; but they were still ill-favoured as at the
(41, 1–4)	beginning. (Ibid. 17–21)

Explain the reason for some of the variations, in particular the omissions (verse 19) and additions (end of verse 19 and verse 21) which Pharaoh was responsible for in his recounting of his dream.

Cf. too the following comments expressing two different approaches to our chapter:

> Pharaoh's report of his dream to Joseph did not tally exactly with his actual experience of the dream ... the text treats some things in detail and others more briefly as the subject demands.
>
> (Abravanel)
>
> The text should not have made any changes in the account of the dream but should simply have read: "Then Pharaoh told Joseph his dream". The fact it did not do so indicates that we must attach special significance to every variation in the wording and these we shall duly explain. (Ha'amek Davar)
>
> We have already noted [3] that in reported speech a person always varies his wording adding or subtracting as he thinks fit but always preserving the essential content. The same is true with the report of the dream which is a faithful one. It is useless to look for any special reason for omissions and addition. These are characteristic of any repetition or paraphrase. The words change but not the content. (Radak)

---

[1] See also Vayeshev 5 "The Truth Speaks for Itself" on pp. 423–9.

[2] See p. 427 for another answer to the same question.

[3] The reference is to the story related by Abraham's servant.

WHY DID JOSEPH CONCEAL HIS IDENTITY?

Joseph recognised his brothers but they did not recognise him.

Then Joseph remembered the dreams which he had dreamed of them and said to them, You are spies!

To see the nakedness of the land have you come.

(42, 8–9)

Joseph's conduct towards his brothers has puzzled our commentators. For what purpose did Joseph falsely denounce them? Abravanel formulates the difficulties in the Biblical account as follows:

> Why did Joseph denounce his brothers? Surely it was criminal of him to take vengeance and bear a grudge like a viper. Though they had meant evil God had turned it to good. What justification then had he for taking vengeance after twenty years? How could he ignore their plight in a strange land and that of their families suffering famine and waiting for them, particularly his aged father gnawed by worry and care? How could he not have pity on him and how could he bear to inflict on him further pain through the imprisonment of Simeon?

Modern non-Jewish Biblical scholars, particulary those moved by animosity to Judaism, have cited this as a proof of the moral superiority of Christianity. They claim that here we have a clear example of vengeance, of unforgiving and even sadistic conduct, apparently approved of by the narrative. Even Joseph's own brothers after the death of his father suspected that he would "hate us and will certainly requite us the evil which we did unto him" (Gen. 40, 15). But let recall here Joseph's reply:

> Fear not: for am I in the place of God?
> But as for you, ye thought evil against me;
> but God meant it unto good . . .
> Now therefore fear ye not.   (50, 19–21)

Joseph could therefore not be accused of being inspired by feelings of vengeance. At any rate when he had a golden opportunity of paying off old scores he not only refrained from doing so but allayed his brothers' fears "comforted them and spoke kindly unto them" (Ibid. 21). Moreover, the tears that he could not hold back and that forced him to clear the room do not support the theory that Joseph was a sadist who enjoyed inflicting pain on his brothers.

A closer study of the text bears out that Joseph is not meant to be depicted as taking vengeance. This is certainly not the plain sense of the Scriptures. Though the exact motive for his denunciation of the brothers is not recorded, the Torah gives us a clue to his mood and the train of thought prompting his conduct. The text does not read "and Joseph remembered all that they (the brothers) had done to him, how they had cast him into the pit . . .", or "how he had entreated them but they had not hearkened". Rather it reads:

> **Then Joseph remembered** the dreams which he had dreamed of them.

From here Ramban and others (including the famous novelist Thomas Mann in his *Joseph and His Brothers*) conclude that Joseph acted in accordance with the path marked out for him by Providence in his dreams. He did not feel himself free to do as he liked, but considered that he was destined to play the part of saviour and leader of his family. This had been the significance of the dream where he had seen:

> **For behold we were binding sheaves in the field and lo my sheaf arose and also stood upright; and behold your sheaves stood round about and made obeisance to my sheaf.**   (37, 7)

458

Here is how Ramban explains the function that Joseph felt he had to perform.

> The text states that when Joseph saw his brothers he remembered his dreams and noted that not one of them had been properly fulfilled on this occasion, since he understood from the first dream "where *we* were binding sheaves," that *all* his brothers had first to bow down to him. The second dream alluded to a second occasion on which the "sun, moon and eleven stars," i.e. his parents and brothers would bow down to him. Noting that Benjamin was absent at this first meeting, he schemed to bring Benjamin along and thus effect the realisation of the first dream, where just the brothers—all eleven of them would bow down to him. Consequently he did not reveal his identity to them and ask them to bring his father along as he did later, for then his father would have undoubtedly come immediately. After the first dream had been fulfilled and Benjamin joined them to make the brotherly circle complete, he revealed his identity in order to effect the realisation of the second dream.
>
> Otherwise we would have to conclude (i.e. if this were not the real explanation of Joseph's conduct) that Joseph committed a grave sin inflicting pain on his father and allowing him to suffer an unnecessarily prolonged bereavement for him and Simeon. For even if we agree that he wished to make his brothers suffer, he should, at least, have had pity on his father's old age. But Joseph carried out everything in the appropriate manner in order to fulfill the dreams knowing that they would really come true.

This explanation of Ramban was strenuously opposed by later commentators including R. Isaac Arama in his Akedat Yizhak:

> I am astonished at Ramban' explanation that Joseph did what he did in order to make his dreams come true. What did this benefit him? And even if it profited him he should not have sinned against his father. As for the dreams, leave it to Him Who sends them to make them come true. It seems infinitely foolish for a man to strive to fulfill his dreams which are matters beyond his control.

We may certainly repudiate Arama's suggestion to leave it to Providence to fulfill the dreams that He communicates to man. Gideon (Judges 7, 13–14) did not leave it to Providence to fulfill the dream that foretold that he would deliver Midian

459

into the hands of Israel. Rather he immediately made practical preparations to further the success of Israel's armies. Similarly, though Jeremiah foretold that God would restore the Jewish people to their land after seventy years of exile in Babylonia, the leaders of the Babylonian exile did not wait for it to come to pass. But before the seventy years were up Zerubabel and Jeshua the son of Jozadak (their leaders) went up to the land "with forty-two thousand three hundred and three score" (Ezra 2) of their fellow Jews. But there is another objection to Ramban's explanation. Could not Joseph have accomplished the realisation of his dreams without making his brothers and his father suffer?

For this reason another explanation is to be preferred. It is also alluded to by Ramban himself as well as other commentators. The house of Jacob was guilty of a serious iniquity in the wrong that had been done to Joseph. How could this iniquity be atoned for and the unity and spiritual honour of the Chosen Seed be restored? In this connection let us cite Rambam's prescription for genuine repentance, basing himself on the Talmud, Yoma 86b:

אי זו היא תשובה גמורה? זה שבא לידו דבר שעבר בו יאפשר בידו לעשותו, ופרש ולא עשה מפני התשובה, לא מיראה ולא מכשלון כוח.

כיצד? הרי שבא על אשה בעבירה ולאחר זמן נתיחד עמה, והוא עומד באהבתו בה ובכוח גופו ובמדינה שעבר, ופרש [ממנה] ולא עבר — זהו בעל תשובה גמורה.

What constitutes complete repentance?—He who was confronted by the identical thing wherein he transgressed and it lies within his power to commit the transgression but he nevertheless abstained and did not succumb out of repentance, and not out of fear or weakness. How so? If he had relations with a woman forbidden to him and he was subsequently alone with her, still in the full possession of his passion for her and his virility unabated and in the country where the transgression took place; if he abstained and did not sin, this is a true penitent.

(Code, Teshuva 2, 1)

In other words, a man must be confronted by the same temptation to which he had previously succumbed. If he stands the test and resists, he has proved his mettle. How could this be effected in the case of Joseph and his brothers? Whatever affection they might show to their brother in Egypt now, would be no indication of their true remorse. With Joseph as the vice-regent of Egypt they could, in any case, do him no hurt and whatever they would do would constitute a reform prompted by "fear and weakness." How could Joseph test them and give them the possibility of achieving true repentance? Indeed, Joseph arranged everything appropriately, as Ramban has observed.

He had to arrange for his other brother, Benjamin, the son of his mother Rachel, and like him, the beloved of his father to be brought into a similar situation. This time the brothers would find themselves really faced by a valid excuse for leaving their brother to his fate. For how could they fight the whole Egyptian empire? If, in spite of that, they would refuse to go back to their father without Benjamin and would be willing to sacrifice their lives as indeed Judah indicated when he said:

> **Now, therefore, I pray thee let thy servant abide instead of the lad, a bondman to my lord; and let the lad go up with his brethren—** (44, 33)

Only then could the brothers be considered true penitents and Joseph would be able to make himself known to his brothers and the game would be over. How Joseph, by his concealment of his true identity, his stratagems (accusation of spying, return of the money and the cup) succeeded in rousing them to a true sense of remorse for what they had done will be the subject of the next chapter of our *Studies* on this Sidra.

461

WE ARE TRULY GUILTY

Joseph's brethren went down to Egypt to buy corn at the bidding of their father. Let us study the first six verses of chapter 42 which starts from this point:

– – – וַיֹּאמֶר יַעֲקֹב לְבָנָיו : לָמָה תִּתְרָאוּ.
וַיֵּרְדוּ אֲחֵי־יוֹסֵף עֲשָׂרָה לִשְׁבֹּר בָּר מִמִּצְרָיִם.
וְאֶת־בִּנְיָמִין אֲחִי יוֹסֵף לֹא־שָׁלַח יַעֲקֹב אֶת־אֶחָיו –
וַיָּבֹאוּ בְּנֵי יִשְׂרָאֵל לִשְׁבֹּר בְּתוֹךְ הַבָּאִים – – –
– – – וַיָּבֹאוּ אֲחֵי יוֹסֵף וַיִּשְׁתַּחֲווּ־לוֹ אַפַּיִם אָרְצָה.

Jacob said unto his sons, Why do ye look one upon another?

And Joseph's ten brethren went down to buy corn in Egypt.

But Benjamin, Joseph's brother, Jacob sent not with his brethren.

And the sons of Israel came to buy corn amongst those that came.

And Joseph's brethren came, and bowed down themselves before him with their faces to the earth.

We may note here that the identical subject in each of the above quoted verses (the ten brothers) is referred to under differing epithets. They are referred to as "the sons of Jacob", "Joseph's brethren", "the sons of Israel". Our commentators remarked on the significance of these variations. Jacob first addresses *his sons*, dispatches them to Egypt, but as soon as we reach the subject of "Egypt" the Biblical record prepares us

and them for the meeting with Joseph. This is explained to us
as follows by Rashi:

"וירדו אחי יוסף": ולא כתב בני יעקב — מלמד שהיו מתחרטין בגנבתו ונתנו
לבם להתנהג עמו באחוה.

"Joseph's brethren:" It is not written: "the sons of Jacob," alluding
to the fact that they repented of their stealing him and under-
took to conduct themselves towards him as *brothers*.

Benjamin was not sent along with "his brothers" (not with "the
sons of Jacob") underlining the fact that though they were his
brothers, Jacob was again guilty of favouritism and discriminated
between the brothers, It is the whole *tribe* which arrives in Egypt
and, as far as the Egyptians were concerned, the group who
arrived from the land of Canaan were neither Joseph's brothers
nor the sons of Jacob, but merely the "sons of Israel". As they
stood before the Egyptian prince, who, as Providence would
have it, was also their long-lost brother, the dramatic irony of
the epithet, "Joseph's brethren", as they bow down to Joseph
and thereby fulfill the dream, becomes apparent. Joseph, however, does not reveal his true identity to his brothers immediately, but speaks to them harshly. Many reasons have been advanced and these were the subject of our previous *Studies*.
Ramban apparently quite justifiably explains, that all the suffering that he inflicted on them from that moment until he revealed himself to them, was intended for their benefit, in the
sense implied in the following phrase occurring in the Psalms
(119) "It is good for me that I have been afflicted; that I might
relate of thy statutes." This implies that the aim of all this
was to refine them and purify them, as it were, and put them
to the test.[1] In the course of our further study of this point
we shall understand this more clearly.

On three occasions the feeling of guilt and consciousness of
their wrondoing emerges and wells up from the words uttered
by the brothers. The first occasion occurs during their conversation, after Joseph had released them from prison where they
had been placed for three days:

וַיֹּאמְרוּ אִישׁ אֶל־אָחִיו:
אֲבָל אֲשֵׁמִים אֲנַחְנוּ עַל־אָחִינוּ
אֲשֶׁר רָאִינוּ צָרַת נַפְשׁוֹ בְּהִתְחַנְנוֹ אֵלֵינוּ
וְלֹא שָׁמָעְנוּ;
עַל־כֵּן בָּאָה אֵלֵינוּ הַצָּרָה הַזֹּאת.

And they said to one another,
We are truly guilty concerning our brother,
in that we saw the anguish of his soul,
when he besought us,
and we paid no heed;
therefore is this distress come upon us. (42, 21)

Ramban was the first to note how the information regarding Joseph's supplication for the mercy of his brothers reaches us, indirectly, through the remorseful reminiscing of the brothers, rather than in its true chronological context,[2] when Joseph was standing at the pit before his brothers. There is no mention before this chapter that Joseph had begged them for mercy.

Here is the comment of Meir Weiss in an article on the narrative artistry of the Bible[3] devoted to the "flashback" technique, one example of which is the passage we have quoted:

> The recalling of this long buried episode here, at this juncture, represents the awakening of the brothers' conscience. Joseph's heartrending pleas for mercy more than they emanate from the pit now well up from the depths of their own hearts. This constitutes the underlying intention of the narrative in citing this detail here. It is meant to reveal what was going on in the consciousness of the brothers at the moment indicating their remorse.

Only now do the brothers recall that painful memory:

> When he besought *us* and we paid no heed;
> therefore is this distress come upon *us*.

Our commentators discussed, at length, why these feelings of guilt and remorse are only awakened, after the brothers had

464

suffered three days imprisonment, and after the Egyptian governor had relented and agreed to send them home, keeping back only one of them. Why did they not recall the sale of their brother during the three long days in prison, when they lived in fear of what destiny awaited them and were apprehensive that they would not return home. Surely such incarceration is particularly appropriate for stimulating feelings of remorse.

In the light of this, the *Akedat Yizhak* (15th century) provides us with an illuminating explanation. This commentary suggests that only when they were faced with the prospect of returning home to their father, one brother short, did the memory of Joseph arise in their minds, by association:

Our brother, in that we saw the anguish of his soul.

Measure for measure the sin and its punishment were mirrored clearly before their eyes:

Therefore is this distress come upon us.

On the second occasion, they sense this retribution and their guilt even more intensely, in the inn:

And he said unto his brethren,
My money is restored; and, look, it is even in my sack:
and their heart failed them, and they were afraid,
saying one to another,
What is this that God hath done unto us?

There are commentators, including Rashi who maintain that the last exclamation of the brothers did not represent an admission of guilt but rather their resentment at being placed in such a situation. But the objection to this approach found in *Haketav Vehakaballa* seems to be more acceptable:

Rashi comments on the words "What is this the Lord has done to us"—to bring us to this false accusation; for the money was only returned to us to incriminate us. This would, then show the brothers as questioning God's justice. Surprising! Had they so quickly forgotten their confession of "verily we are guilty"?

It seems to me that we have to split the sentence into two parts as indicated by the cantillation. The *tevir* under *zot* indicates a pause. The sentence reads: What is this? Here they simply register their astonishment at the discovery of the money and their sorrow at the provocation. But immediately they sensed that this was no mere coincidence but the intervention of Divine justice repaying them measure for measure. Just as previously they had accepted their deserts by saying verily we are guilty, so now they felt that they were being justly punished by being suspected of spying and cast into the pit just as they had done to Joseph. Simon who had played the major role in the sale of Joseph remained under arrest in the prison. Now too the money was found in Levi's sack who also prominently figured in the sale. They realised this was retribution from God and accepted it exclaiming: "The Lord has done this to us." It is no accident but the workings of Divine justice.

Whether we accept his splitting of the sentence into two parts—into an exclamation followed by a statement or not we must agree it most plausible to regard the brothers' exclamation as an expression of their concern and guilt.

Here we note the great progress that had been achieved in their sense of sin, in comparison with the first occasion. Then too they realised the connection between their conduct towards Joseph in the past, and what they were suffering now. But the source of that retribution, who it was who was responsible for linking these two events had not received explicit recognition. Here at the inn "their heart failed them" (literally—"went forth") the source had been discovered:

What is this that God hath done unto us?

An even more intense realisation of their guilt and more profound sense of remorse overcomes them on the third occasion, when the cup is discovered. Here are Judah's words:

מַה־נֹּאמַר לַאדֹנִי – – –

מַה־נְּדַבֵּר וּמַה־נִּצְטַדָּק

הָאֱלֹהִים מָצָא אֶת־עֲוֹן עֲבָדֶיךָ

הִנֶּנּוּ עֲבָדִים לַאדֹנִי
גַּם־אֲנַחְנוּ – גַּם אֲשֶׁר־נִמְצָא הַגָּבִיעַ בְּיָדוֹ.

What shall we say unto my lord?
what shall we speak?
or how shall we clear ourselves?
God hath found out the iniquity of thy servants:
behold, we are my lord's servants,
both we, and he also with whom the cup is found.

(44, 16)

Judah surely knew that they had not stolen the cup, neither they nor the man with whom it had been found. He was quite aware that they were being wrongly accused,[4] but he was not confessing to this crime, though this was how it was meant to be understood by the Egyptian governor. But he was confessing to the iniquity, not which the Egyptian had "found" in him but that: "God hath found out the iniquity of thy servants".

For this reason he and his brothers accepted any punishment and any fate, realising that they deserved it. This ambivalency in Judah's words is referred to in the following Midrash.

"מה נאמר לאדני" – בכסף ראשון, "מה נדבר" – בכסף שני, "ומה נצטדק"
– בגביע. "מה נאמר לאדני" – במעשה תמר, "מה נדבר" – במעשה ראובן,
"ומה נצטדק" – במעשה שכם.
"מה נאמר לאדני" – מה נאמר לאבא שבארץ כנען ביוסף, "מה נדבר" –
בשמעון, "ומה נצטדק" בבנימין.

"What shall we say unto my Lord?"—referring to the first money (in Benjamin's sack). "What shall we speak?"—referring to the second money (in Benjamin's sack), "or how shall we clear ourselves?"—with the cup.

"What shall we say unto my Lord?"—referring to the incident of Tamar, "What shall we speak?"—referring to the deed of Reuben (see Genesis 35, 22), "Or how shall we clear ourselves?"—referring to the deed of Shechem (see Genesis 34).

"What shall we say unto my Lord?"—what shall we say to Father in the land of Canaan regarding Joseph? "What shall we speak?"—with reference to Simeon, "Or how shall we clear ourselves?"—regarding Benjamin.
(Midrash Rabbah)

467

The Midrash sees a triple implication in the above verse, explaining the words "my lord" אדוני in three different ways: (1) as the Egyptian governor standing in front of them, (2) as the Lord of the Universe who knows their guilt, (3) as their aged father in Canaan against whom they had sinned.

The Midrash unearths for us the nine different sins recalled by the text, showing us how the brothers repented not merely of one wrongdoing but emulated the true *baal teshuva* (penitent) who sees his guilt and sin in every step and turn, a thought which is expressed instructively in the following phrase occuring in the Psalms (51):

And my sin is ever before me.

After his brothers had reached this level of penitence, remorse, and sense of sin, Joseph can then make himself known to them.

---

1 The same view is expressed in *Akedat Yiẓhak*:—"Evidently Joseph's intention had from the outset been to test them to see whether they still hated him or regretted their deed. He saw no other way of doing it except through his brother Benjamın, to observe how they would react when they saw him in distress and danger. To that end he thought up on, the spur of the moment, the stratagem of the cup. But since Benjamin was not with them he had to abuse them and trick them into bringing him."

2 See p. 342 for a treatment of this phenomenon and Ramban's various answers to the question why the text did not report Joseph's pleadings in their chronological sequence.

3 *Melekhet sippur ha-mikra*, Molad, Tishre 5723 — pp. 402–406.

4 Some commentators take the view that this was precisely the reason why Joseph returned them their money the first time, that they should not suspect, on the second occasion, when they found the cup that Benjamin had really stolen it. Here is Abravanel's comment:

"In spite of all the feelers that Joseph had put out through accusing his brothers of being spies he still could not be sure whether they loved Benjamin or still nursed hatred for the children of Rachel his mother. He particularly wanted to put Benjamin to the test by the cup to see if they would try to save him. At the same time, he was concerned that perhaps his brothers might imagine that Benjamin had indeed stolen the cup just as Rachel stole the teraphim from her father. Perhaps on account of this they would say: The soul that sinneth shall die. and would not make every effort to plead for his life, not because they hated him but because of their shame for what he had done. Joseph with this in mind ordered the corn and their money to be placed together with the silver cup. They would then be bound to understand that it had nothing to do with Benjamin but was a provocation of the ruler. Knowing this, if they really had compassion on him they would try to save him. He would then know that they loved him and he would be right in regarding them as sincere repentants and would reveal himself to them and look after their welfare, as he actually did . . ."

THEN LET ME BEAR THE BLAME FOR EVER

Joseph's brothers had returned home without Simeon. Ten of them had set forth, nine returned, just as, on a previous occasion, eleven had set forth and ten returned. This was not all. They had been bidden to take along to Egypt with them, the next time, the tenth brother who was still at home—the son of Rachel and of his father's old age. Without him they would not be able to return to Egypt to buy provender. All this, and all that had befallen them on the way, all that the man had demanded of them had to be related to Jacob. The Torah does not content itself with the general statement:

And they came unto Jacob their father unto the land fo Canaan, and told him all that had befallen them.

(42, 29)

It records for us exactly what they related to Jacob, how they phrased their report. Let us note what they said and what they left unsaid, what they toned down and what they added:

The conversation between Joseph and his brothers (vv. 9–20)	*As reported by the brothers to Jacob* (vv. 30–34)
And Joseph said unto them, Ye are spies; to see the nakedness of the land ye are come.	The man who is the lord of the land, spoke roughly to us, and took us for spies of the country.
And they said, Thy servants are twelve brethren, the sons of one man in the land of Canaan	We be twelve brethren, sons of our father

and behold the youngest is this day with our father, and the one is not.	one is not, and the youngest is this day with our father, in the land of Canaan.
that is that I spoke to you, saying, Ye are spies Hereby ye shall be proved: By the life of Pharaoh *ye shall not go forth hence,* except your youngest brother come hither. Send one of *you,* and let him fetch your brother and *ye* shall be kept in prison.	— — — — — — — — — — - - — — — — — — — — — — — — — — — — — —
If ye be true men, let one of your brethren be bound	Hereby shall I know that ye are true men; leave one of your brethren here with me.
in the house of your prison. go ye, carry corn for the famine of your houses	— — — — — — — — — — and take food for the famine of your houses.
But bring your youngest brother unto me; so shall your words be verified and ye shall not die	And bring your youngest brother unto me, then shall I know that ye are no spies, but that ye are true men.
— — — — — — — — — —	so will I deliver your brother, and ye shall trade in the land.

Jacob's sons could not very well hide from him the charge of spying, since they had to explain Simeon's absence. But Joseph's original design to keep *them all* in Egypt and send only one of them back home, they did not divulge. If the Egyptian had foregone his original design, what point was there in frightening their father? They likewise did not tell

471

him about the three days they spent in prison. Simeon's imprisonment they turned unto a prolonged visit at the regent's home. Instead of "one of your brethren be bound" they told their father, "leave one of your brethren here with me," completely omitting all reference to the threat of death. Joseph had ended his words with the ominous words:

> **But bring your youngest brother unto me; so shall your words be verified,** and ye shall not die.

Whereas they "deviated from the original wording, for the sake of peace, so that their father would acquiesce in sending Benjamin", as Ramban observes. Moreover, they added to Joseph's words, when they attributed to him the offer "to bring merchandise, as much as you desire, with which to trade for corn and I shall not take away your merchandise in order to to requite you for your shame" (Ramban). This is the implication of the passage:

> **And bring your youngest brother unto me, then ˙ shall I know that ye are no spies, but that ye are true men,** **so will I deliver your brother** and ye may trade in the land.

But all these careful approaches did not avail them. Jacob adamantly refused to let Benjamin go. Then Reuben submitted his proposal:

> **Kill my two sons, if I bring him not unto thee; deliver him into my hand, and I will bring him to thee again.**
>
> (42, 37)

But his offer did not even qualify for a reply. Jacob neither remonstrated with him nor discussed the matter with him in any shape or form, but persisted in his refusal to all of them:

> **My son shall not go down with you; for his brother is dead and he is left alone: if mischief befall him by the way in which ye go, then shall ye bring down my gray heirs with sorrow to the grave.** (42, 38)

No reply is forthcoming from them, since they had nothing to say. In the meantime, the days were passing. The Torah bridges the time that elapsed between Jacob's first conversation with his sons and subsequent refusal, and his second conversation that ended with his acquiescence, in three Hebrew words:

And-the-famine   was-sore   in-the-land   והרעב כבד בארץ

Jacob again persisted in his refusal and voiced his misgivings until Judah made his offer:

וַיֹּאמֶר יְהוּדָה אֶל־יִשְׂרָאֵל אָבִיו:
שִׁלְחָה הַנַּעַר אִתִּי וְנָקוּמָה וְנֵלֵכָה
וְנִחְיֶה וְלֹא נָמוּת
גַּם־אֲנַחְנוּ גַם־אַתָּה גַם־טַפֵּנוּ.
אָנֹכִי אֶעֶרְבֶנּוּ מִיָּדִי תְּבַקְשֶׁנּוּ
אִם־לֹא הֲבִיאֹתִיו וְהִצַּגְתִּיו לְפָנֶיךָ
וְחָטָאתִי לְךָ כָּל־הַיָּמִים.

And Judah said unto Israel his father, Send the lad with me, and we will arise and go, that we may live and not die, both we, and thou, and also our little ones. I will be surety for him; of my hand shalt thou require him: if I bring him not unto thee, and set him before thee, then let me bear the blame forever.   (43, 8–9)

At this point, Jacob relented and acquiesced. What influenced him and overcame his refusal? What elicited from him those decisive words: "Take also your brother, and arise, go again unto the man"? The *Midrash Hagadol* propounds an answer to this question:

"ואת אחיכם קחו": מעשה בשני חסידים שפרשו בים הגדול לדבר מצוה,
עמד עליהם נחשול בים וביקש לטובעם. אמר חד מינהון [אחד מהם]: לית
ביש מן דא [אין רע מזה]. אמר לו חברו: אית [יש] ביש רב מן דא! אמר לו:
אנו על שערי מיתה, ואית לך בישא מן הדא?! [ויש רע מזה?!] אמר לו:
הן! אמר לו: ואיזה? — זה היום שבנו אומר לו: תן לי פת ואין לו מה יתן
לו. תדע לך, הרי יעקב אבינו, כל זמן שהיתה קופה מלאה פת היה לועס

473

ואומר: "לא ירד בני עמכם", כיון דחסלת אמר: "ואת אחיכם קחו". והתחיל
מתפלל עליהם: "ואל שדי יתן לכם רחמים".

"Take also your brother." A story is told of two pious men
who went on a sea journey on a sacred mission. A huge wave
threatened to sink their ship. One of them said: This is the
worst! His friend replied: It could still be much worse! Said he:
We are at the gates of death; can there be anything worse? Said
the other: Yes, there could. Said he: And what may that be?
—The day when your son says to you: Give me a morsel of
bread and you have'nt got it to give him. You may know this
from Jacob our father. As long as the bin was full of bread, he
chewed and said: "My son shall not go with you." As soon as
his stock was exhausted, he said: "Take also your brother." And
he began to pray for them "And God Almighty give you mercy."

Simeon's plight imprisoned in foreign parts, awaiting release,
moved him not, neither did his son's entreaties nor Reuben's
appeal. The hunger of the little ones finally broke his resistance.
Judah meaningfully ended the first sentence of his appeal, with
the words: "and also our little ones."

But Judah's words contain something more significant. Both
Judah and Reuben wished to convince their father and inspire
him with confidence in their ability to bring Benjamin back
again. Both invoked the direst of punishments on themselves,
if they failed to restore the beloved son of his old age. Let us
compare the two passages concerned:
First Reuben:

Slay my two sons, if I bring him not unto thee.

(42, 37)

Then Judah:

**If I bring him not unto thee ... then let me bear the
blame forever.** (43, 9)

וְחָטָאתִי לְךָ כָּל הַיָּמִים.

What did Judah imply by these last words: "let me bear the
blame forever"? The Italian Jewish commentator, Benamozegh
derives a profoundly significant message from it:

474

This figure of speech contains a valuable lesson, teaching us something not otherwise explicitly alluded to, in the Torah: that there is no punishment outside of the sin. Sin itself is its own punishment in the Divine scheme of judgement and serves the purpose of reward and punishment. This is the meaning of: "then shall I bear the blame to my father forever" (44, 32).

(Em Lamikra)

Questions for Further Study

"So will I deliver to you your brother and trade in the land" (42, 34)

תסובבו — וכל לשון סוחרים וסחורה על שם שמחזרים וסובבים אחר הפרקמטיא.

Wherever you have the expressions *soḥarim* and *seḥora* the reference is to the seeking and wandering around after merchandise.

(Rashi)

(a) Rashi usually explains a difficult word the first time it appears in the Torah unless there is a special reason for commenting on it in a context later on.

(b) Why did not Rashi apply to the word *tisḥaru* in our verse the same connotation given to it by Ramban: "that you bring merchandise of your choice herewith to buy corn"? (see p. 472).

DID JACOB BELIEVE JOSEPH DEAD?

We are used to reading quickly and superficially with the eye, but there is another kind of reading, slow and deliberate, taking in every word, phrase and nuance. It is surely this kind which our Torah deserves. Rambam in his *Guide* denounced those "who would understand this book, our guide throughout the ages by glancing through it in the little spare time left us after we have taken our pleasure as if it were just another story book."

This week's sidra forms part of a larger narrative that extends over three sidrot: *vayeshev-mikez-vayiggash.* We noted in the first chapter of our *Studies* on this Sidra how the narrative develops on two planes, how the natural doings of men are subtly fitted into a Divine master plan.[1] We also noted that the key or motif word of the narrative is "mission" or "sending".[2] Here again the sending is of two kinds—a human and a Divine one. The human one set in motion by Jacob:

לְכָה וְאֶשְׁלָחֲךָ אֲלֵיהֶם.

Come I will send you to them   (37, 13)

is paralleled by the Providential one:

כִּי לְמִחְיָה שְׁלָחַנִי אֱלֹהִים.

For God did send me to preserve life   (45, 5)

We shall choose here for close reading chapters 42–43. They too—begin with a statement of mission. Three times did Jacob send his sons away from him and, on each occasion, the reactions of those sent were different. On the first, Jacob sent Joseph to his brethren, (unaware that by so doing he was sending the Jewish people into Egypt). Here is what Jacob says: "Are not your brothers pasturing in Schechem, come and let me send you to them". On the second occasion he sent his sons (without Benjamin) to Egypt to buy corn. On the third, he sent them, having no alternative, with Benjamin to "the man" who so insistently demanded him. But we hear the reaction of the person sent only on the first occasion: "And he (Joseph) said to him, Here am I" (37, 13).

This "Here am I" recalls another mission much more difficult than this one—the one involved in Abraham's sacrifice of Isaac: "And he said to him, Abraham. And he said, Here am I. And He said, Take now thy son, thine only one . . ." (Gen. 22, 1–2) But Joseph's "Here am I" is different from all the others in Scripture. In other words, the "Here am I" was not an expression announcing merely his presence but his readiness to sacrifice himself, devotion to duty, since it came not before, but after becoming aware of what was required of him.[3] But there was no reaction to the second mission:

> **When Jacob saw there was corn in Egypt, then said Jacob to his sons:**
> **Why do ye look one upon the other? And he said, Behold I have heard that there is corn in Egypt. Get you down thither and buy from us from thence, that we may live and not die.** (42, 1–2)

There was no reply but forthwith—

> **Joseph's [4] ten brethren went down to buy corn from Egypt.** (42, 3)

Where no obstacle existed, where no inhibitions had to be overcome both with regard to the sender and the sent, no reply was called for, not even that of assent. No parting words of godspeed were even necessary since they were understood. How very different was the parting on the third occasion when Jacob sent his sons off with Benjamin whom he had hitherto refused to allow accompany them, only acquiescing when all else was lost!—

**The famine was severe in the land.
And when they had eaten up the corn which they had
brought out of Egypt their father said to them, Go again
buy us a little food.** (43, 1–2)

How earnestly he still hoped for a miracle to happen rendering
it unnecessary for them to take Benjamin—though deep in his
heart he knew full well he would have to let him go—emerges
from the addition of one tiny word. Let us compare with each
other the first two missions on which the sons of Jacob were,
sent by their father:

The first mission	*The second mission*
Get you down thither and buy for us from thence (42, 2)	Go again, buy us a *little food* (43, 2)

What is the significance of the qualification "a little". Surely
"the famine was severe in the land"! A little would not suffice!
   Maybe Jacob thought that if they lowered their demands
they stood more chance of obtaining their desire without having to comply with that cruel condition. Does not this qualification of Jacob reflect this clutching at a straw? We shall see further indications of Jacob's inner agonies in his reply to Judah.
Judah confronted him with the situation in all its grim reality
without attempting to sugar the pill:

**The man did earnestly forewarn us, saying,
You shall not see my face unless your brother is with
you. If thou wilt send our brother with us, we will go
down and buy thee food; but if thou wilt not send him,
we will not go down for the man said unto us: You shall
not see my face, unless your brother is with you.**

(43, 3–5)

Such a reply left no room for avoidance of the issue. There
was only one alternative. Should he refuse it and die of hunger
or accept it and send Benjamin? He still struggled within him.

478

> **Why did you serve me so ill as to tell the man whether you had a brother?** (43, 6)

What is this? Recriminations? What avail were they at that moment? It had a momentary benefit in deferring the dread decision for a few more seconds or minutes whilst the arguments and counter-arguments went on. But even this moment passed by. Jacob had his say; his sons theirs, Judah his[5] and the patriarch was broken. But this time, as we have noted he did not summarily dismiss them, as on the previous occasion. Jacob prefaced his parting message with the words: "If it be so now, do this?" Do we not detect here how he agonisingly wrenches himself away from Benjamin, Joseph, Rachel and all that was dear to him? Now for his last words, the last he uttered till the good tidings arrived that his son Joseph was still alive:

> **Take of the choice fruits of the land ... and take double money in your hand—** (43, 11-12)

advice and ruses, presents to soften the man, restoration of the money, of course, and, once again, the hope and wish that "peradventure it was an oversight", knowing full well that there was no oversight but only a deliberate plot to entrap them. Still the heart clings to hope. Then comes the most difficult decision of all:

> וְאֶת־אֲחִיכֶם קָחוּ וְקוּמוּ שׁוּבוּ אֶל־הָאִישׁ.

> **Take also your brother and arise and go again to the man.** (43, 13)

Once again—one wrench after another: take-arise-go again. Unlike the previous occasion Jacob ended his parting message with a lengthy addition, each word of which is charged with significance:

> **And God Almighty give you mercy before the man that he may release unto you your other brother and Benjamin.** (43, 14)

479

Rashi observes:

"וְאֵל שַׁדַּי": מֵעַתָּה אֵינְכֶם חֲסֵרִים כְּלוּם אֶלָּא תְּפִלָּה — הֲרֵינִי מִתְפַּלֵּל עֲלֵיכֶם.

Henceforth you are wanting nothing but prayer—behold I hereby pray for you.

The additional sentence prefixed by the significant *vav* conjunctive is attended to indicate that his words hitherto had referred to mortal actions. Now the rest was up to the Almighty. This contrast is emphasised by the Hebrew order of the words — subject — God Almighty — verb — give — object — you; whereas the non-emphatic normal Hebrew usage is as in the blessing of Isaac (27, 28): "So give thee God": verb — object — subject.

There is one other anomaly in the text, not a matter of an extra letter or change of order but the omission of a letter. Let us translate it literally: "that he may release to you your brother another (*aḥer*) and Benjamin". It should have read *'aḥikhem ha'aḥer*—"your other brother" and not "your brother another". This has been explained by our Sages as follows:

יַעֲקֹב נִתְנַבֵּא וְלֹא יָדַע מַה נִּתְנַבֵּא, שֶׁנֶּאֱמַר: "וִישַׁלַּח לָכֶם אֶת אֲחִיכֶם אַחֵר וְאֶת בִּנְיָמִין", "אֲחִיכֶם" — זֶה שִׁמְעוֹן, "אַחֵר" — זֶה יוֹסֵף, "וְאֶת בִּנְיָמִין" — זֶה בִּנְיָמִין כְּמַשְׁמָעוֹ.

Jacob prophesied but knew not what he was prophesying ... "your brother"—refers to Benjamin; "another"—refers to Joseph; "and Benjamin"—Benjamin, as its plain sense indicates!

(Avot d'rabbi Natan)

Similarly Rashi observes:

"אֶת אֲחִיכֶם": זֶה שִׁמְעוֹן. "אַחֵר": רוּחַ הַקֹּדֶשׁ נִזְרְקָה בּוֹ: לְרַבּוֹת יוֹסֵף.

The Holy Spirit prompted him to include Joseph.

Ramban explains:

Apparently the text in its plain sense reflects the fact that Simeon was not in his fathers good graces on account of the incident at Schechem. He therefore did not say: "Simeon my son and Benjamin." He made no mention of him by name during the whole time they had left him in Egypt. Had it not been for the

480

complete dearth of food at home he would not have let Benjamin go but would have left him (i.e. Simeon to his fate) in Egypt. Rashi observes that the Holy Spirit sparked him to include Joseph as in the Midrash ... This is true, for he directed his prayers also to the other one—perhaps he was still alive.

The omission of the Hebrew letter *heh* reveals Jacob's state of mind, aware that his son had been torn by wild beasts yet refusing to accept it, reflecting his hope in his despair, his fortifying himself in his prayers to make an oblique allusion to what he dared not make public reference to:

וְשִׁלַּח לָכֶם אֶת־אֲחִיכֶם אַחֵר וְאֶת־בִּנְיָמִין.

**and he may release unto you your brother
another one
and Benjamin**

Questions for Further Study

1. Cf. 42, 3 with 43, 15, the first descent to Egypt with the second.

    Why is the number of the brothers "Joseph's ten brethren" specified on the first and not the second?

2. Cf. carefully the story the brothers told their father on their return from Egypt in 42, 34 with their account to their father on the eve of their departure, a second time in 43, 3, 7. Give reasons for the variations in the wording of their respective accounts. Was their report in 43, 7 true or false?

3. 43, 11: "And Israel their father said to them, if it be so now do this ... "Why does the text add "their father"? Surely it is obvious that he was their father? Suggest a reason fitting the context."

481

4. "That he may release unto you your brother the other one, Benjamin, *and as for me*, if I am bereaved I am bereaved."

(43, 14)

Abravanel asks:

Why does the text add the phrase: "and as for me" (*ve-ani*)? Let it simply read: "if I am bereaved, I am bereaved," in the same way as Esther said: "if I perish, I perish"

Try to answer his question.

---

[1] See p. 395.

[2] The role of the Hebrew root שלח "send" as the key word in Moses' mission is pointed out by Benno Jacob in his commentary to Exodus (still in MS in the H.U. National Library). Cf.: the revelation at the burning bush Exodus 3, 10 where the text echoes the very words used by Jacob when he sent Joseph on his mission to the brothers. Also vv. 12, 14, 15 Moses' activity in connection with the ten plagues are similarly initiated by the use of the word "send" in 7, 16. In Num. 16, 28 the motif word "send" is employed by Moses in his dispute with the mutineers. At the close of his mission, at the end of the Torah, his career is summed up with the words: "that the Lord *sent* him to perform in the Land of Egypt."

[3] The force of the word *hineni* is underlined by our Sages in *Bereshit Rabbah* 84, 12: "Said R. Hama b. Hanina: Whenever Jacob our father recalled these matters (Joseph's cryptic *hineni*) he winced, saying to himself: though you were aware your brothers hated you yet you said to me *hineni*."

[4] Regarding the variations in the way the brothers are described: "sons of Jacob", "brothers of Joseph", "Brothers of Benjamin", "children of Israel" etc. see p. 462.

[5] Regarding Judah's words and their convincing impact see our previous *Studies*.

JUDAH DREW NEAR

Our sidra opens with Judah's impassioned plea on behalf of his brother Benjamin:

וַיִּגַּשׁ אֵלָיו יְהוּדָה וַיֹּאמֶר

Then Judah came near unto him and said...

(G   (44, 18)

What, in effect, could he say. The cup *was* found in Benjamin's sack. Everything now depended on Judah's eloquence, on the effect it would have on the apparently tyrannical Egyptian governor.

Judah's address which is the longest oration recorded in Genesis can be divided into three sections:

(1) Verses 18–29: a recapitulation of the past
(2) Verses 30–32: a description of the consequences in the present
(3) Verses 33–34: a proposal and a plea.

The first section of the speech merely recapitulates what had happened till that moment, all reported in direct speech—"And we said", "And thou saidst" etc., as if Judah were reading out the minutes of the proceedings. Judah was presenting the facts of the case, neither adding his own embellishments nor glossing over anything.

Though the first verse opens on a seemingly supplicatory note:

Oh my lord, I pray thee, let thy servant speak a word in my lord's ears—and let not thine anger burn against thy servant— (44, 18) yet the immediately succeeding verses impart merely factual information, recapitulating the chapter of Joseph's relations with them until then:

> My lord asked his servants, saying,
> Have you a father, or a brother?
> And we said unto my lord,
> we have a father, an old man,
> and a child of his old age, a little one; and his brother
> is dead and he alone is left of his mother,
> and his father loveth him.
> And thou didst say unto thy servants:
> Bring him down unto me that I may set eyes on him.
>
> (44, 19–21)

What was the point of repeating to Joseph what was already well known to him? Between the lines however can be detected a note of pathos and grievance. This, indeed, is how our Sages interpreted the passage:

> ״אדוני שאל את עבדיו״ — מתחילה בעלילה באת עלינו. מכמה מדינות ירדו
> למצרים לשבור אוכל ולא שאלת אחד מהן. שמא בתך באנו לקחת או אחותנו
> אתה סבור לישא? אף על פי כך לא כיסינו ממך דבר.

> "My lord asked his servants"—from the beginning didst thou come upon us with a pretext. From many countries did they come down to Egypt to buy corn, and thou didst not question anyone of them. Peradventure came we to take the hand of thy daughter? Or thou art of a mind to wed our sister? Even so, we hid nothing from thee.   (Tanḥuma)

Note also the constant repetition of the word "father" with all its emotional undertones. This word which occurs fourteen times in Judah's oration is calculated to arouse compassion in the hardest of hearts, appealing to the most elemental of affections—parental love. Judah emphasised that the father advanced in years could not live without his son that he deeply loved. In spite of all this, ignoring all these humane considerations:

> Thou didst say unto thy servants,
> Bring him down to me ...

484

Here may be noted a departure from the actual words spoken by Joseph in Judah's report of the conversation. Judah added the phrase:

... that I may set my eyes upon him.

What was the implication of Judah's insertion? Again this underlines the emotional undertones of Judah's apparently objective recapitulation of the facts. Let us quote the Midrash on this point:

זוהי השמת עין שאמרת לנו ז!

Is this then the setting eyes upon him that thou didst imply!?
(Bereshit Rabbah)

חשבנו, שאתה מלך ואתה עומד בדיבורך.

We thought you were a king, who stood by his word.
(Lekaḥ Tov)

Judah wished to emphasise the injustice of the treatment meted out to them. He dwelt on the callousness of the Egyptian governor who had ignored their explanations that the father was likely to die if parted from his son:

Thou didst say unto thy servants,
Unless your youngest brother comes down with you,
you shall see my face no more.   (44, 23)

Judah then proceeded to recapitulate what had happened at home between them and their father:

And our father said, Go back, and buy us a little food.
And we said, We cannot go down: if our youngest brother
be with us, then will we go down: for we may not see the
man's face, unless our youngest brother is with us.
And thy servant my father said unto us, you know
that my wife bore me two sons.
And the one went out from me, and I said,

Surely he is torn to pieces; and I have not seen him since. And if you take this one from me too, and mischief befall him, you shall bring down my grey hairs with sorrow to the grave. (44, 25–29)

Judah here reported a conversation between his father and his ten children that we have no record of in the Torah. Moreover, it is inconceivable that Jacob should have uttered, in the presence of his ten sons the children of Leah, Zilpah and Bilhah such words as these: *"You know that my wife bore me two sons"*. How could Jacob have described Rachel to the children of his other wives, as his wife? Had he not been punished enough for showing favouritism to his son Joseph? Presumably, therefore, Jacob had not uttered these words. Judah had added them for effect in order to arouse the compassion of the Egyptian governor. He was taking the *only* son left by the only woman Jacob regarded as his wife. Even if Jacob had not uttered these words, Judah was giving a faithful picture of his father's feelings.

Now Judah reached the real point of his oration, after finishing his account of the past:

וְעַתָּה כְּבֹאִי אֶל־עַבְדְּךָ אָבִי וְהַנַּעַר אֵינֶנּוּ אִתָּנוּ
– וְנַפְשׁוֹ קְשׁוּרָה בְנַפְשׁוֹ –
וְהָיָה כִּרְאוֹתוֹ כִּי־אֵין הַנַּעַר – וָמֵת!
וְהוֹרִידוּ עֲבָדֶיךָ אֶת־שֵׂיבַת עַבְדְּךָ אָבִינוּ בְּיָגוֹן שְׁאֹלָה.

Now, therefore when I come to thy servant my father, and the lad is not with us; seeing that his life is bound up in the lad's life —
And it shall come to pass, when he sees that the lad is not with us—he will die,
And thy servants shall bring down the grey hairs of thy servant our father with sorrow to the grave.

(44, 30–31)

Pay attention to the syntactical construction of the above verses. The verse divisions in *Genesis* usually correspond to the gram-

486

matical construction of a complete sentence, the modern punctuation of a full stop corresponding to the ancient notation denoting the verse-ending (*sof pasuk*). In the above quoted verse (30), according to the grammatical construction, we have only a subordinate clause. The verse ends in the middle of the sentence before we reach the main clause. The next verse (31) continues with a further subordinate clause:

And it shall come to pass when he sees...

the suspense being intensified until the climax is reached and the main clause, for which we have waited for so long, follows and comprises (in Hebrew) the single word *vamet* "he will die", driving home the stark, pitiless consequence of the tyrant's callousness. Judah, as it were, had hesitated to utter the dread word, delaying it by adding qualification to qualification.

Now, however, after Judah had outlined what might happen if he persisted in holding Benjamin, he proposed an alternative, practical suggestion:

**Now, therefore, I pray thee, let thy servant remain
instead of the lad a bondman to my lord;
and let the lad go up with his brethren.** (44, 33)

The word *eved*, slave or bondman, occurs thirteen times in the oration, and twice in the above verse, underlining their humble posture in front of the mighty ruler.

Finally, Judah concluded, after he had exhausted all his reasonings and considered arguments, with an impassioned rhetorical question:

כִּי־אֵיךְ אֶעֱלֶה אֶל־אָבִי וְהַנַּעַר אֵינֶנּוּ אִתִּי
פֶּן אֶרְאֶה בָרָע אֲשֶׁר יִמְצָא אֶת־אָבִי.

**For how can I go back to my father, when the lad
is not with me?
Lest I see the evil that shall come
on my father.** (44, 34)

The word *avi*, the keyword of Judah's speech occurs twice in the foregoing verse. Joseph's parting words were: "Go back in peace to *your father*", striking a note of bitter irony for Judah. Peace for whom? what kind of going back to their father without Benjamin! Judah echoes Joseph's parting words but in a note of desperation: "Lest I see the evil that will come upon my father". "My father" are his last words.

Questions for Further Study

1.   Why did Judah omit in his speech to Joseph the latter's accusation of spying?
    Abravanel answers this question as follows:
    He did not allude to the allegation of spying so as not to give Joseph an opportunity to condemn him and refer to that subject again.

    Try to give another answer to this question.

2.   "For thou art even as Pharaoh"   (Gen. 44, 18)
    What was the point of this additional phrase "for thou art even as Pharaoh"? Some commentators maintain that the Hebrew כי means "although", as in Exodus 34, 9 "though it is a stiffnecked people"; and Psalms 41, 5 "Heal my soul; though[1] I have sinned against thee". But this is not the real meaning of the word. כי is an expression of cause, as is evident from the very verses we have just quoted.
    Answer Abravanel's question, taking *ki* in the sense of "because" or "for".

3.   "If I bring him not unto thee,
    then I shall bear the blame to my father for ever."
                                    (Gen. 44, 32)

    The phrase here used by Judah teaches us a lesson that is not expressly mentioned in the Torah. It teaches us that sin brings its own punishment. The sin itself constitutes the punishment and is in place of the meting out of reward and punishment

This is the meaning of Judah's statement that "then shall I bear the blame to my father for ever". This alone was sufficient shame and discomfiture.   (Benamozegh)

(a) Explain what puzzles this commentator in our verse and how he answers it.

(b) Cite other verses in the Torah where you can find an allusion to the same idea.

(c) Do you know of a Talmudic epigram containing this idea?

4.   Why did not Judah conclude his speech with verse 33 which contains his proposal and request? What prompted him to add verse 34 and end with it?

5.   Cf: "if he leaves his father *he will die*" (44, 22)
      "that the lad is not with us—*he will die*" (44, 31)
      To whom does the word ומת refer to in verse 22 and to whom in verse 31?

6.   "Let thy servant speak I pray thee a word in the ears of my lord". (44, 18)
      Rashi comments: "Let my words enter your ears".

יכנסו דברי באזנך.

(a) What difficulty did Rashi find in the above text?

(b) Rashi's commentators ask: "why did not Rashi explain the text in its plain sense that he wished to speak to him privately?" Try to justify Rashi's explanation and find support for it from the text.

---

¹ In actual fact the authorized version and NEB read also here "for".

489

"THE ROPE HAS FOLLOWED THE BUCKET"

We analysed in the previous chapter of our *Studies* on this sidra
Judah's moving speech which marks the climax of the story
of Joseph and his brethren. Judah uttered it at the most critical
juncture. The brothers, who had once been strangers to the feeling of brotherhood, who had, deaf to his entreaties sold him
into slavery were now put to the test. Would they leave the
other brother, a son of Rachel too, in bondage and return to
their aged father, once again, a brother-by-Rachel-short or would
they fight to rescue him even at the cost of their own freedom?

Judah, as we have noted, resorted, in his speech, to every
psychological and rhetorical device to stir the feelings of the
Egyptian. Our sages, however, turned this speech into a duel
of words, a tussle between Joseph and Judah. Here is an excerpt
from this lengthy verbal duel:

"אדוני שאל את עבדיו היש לכם אב או אח" — מתחילה בעלילה באת עלינו.
מכמה מדינות ירדו למצרים לשבור אוכל ולא שאלת אחד מהן. שמא בתך
באנו ליקח או אחותנו אתה סבור לישא, אף על פי כן לא כיסינו ממך דבר.
אמר לו יוסף: יהודה! למה אתה דברן מכל אחיך? ואני רואה בגביע שיש
באחיך גדולים ממך!
אמר לו (יהודה): כל זאת רואה בשביל הערבות שערבתי אותו.
אמר לו (יוסף): מפני מה לא ערבת את אחיך כשמכרתם אותו לישמעאלים
בעשרים כסף וציערת את אביך הזקן ואמרת לו: "טרף טרף יוסף", והוא לא
חטא לך! אבל זה שחטא וגנב הגביע — אמור לאביך: ה ל ך ה ח ב ל א ח ר
ה ד ל י.
כיון ששמע יהודה כך, צעק ובכה בקול גדול ואמר: "כי איך אעלה אל אבי
והנער איננו אתי?"
אמר לו יוסף: בוא ונתווכח שנינו. אמור מליץ וסדור דיניך. מיד אמר יהודה
לנפתלי: לך וראה כמה שווקים יש במצרים! קפץ וחזר ואמר לו: שנים
עשר.
אמר יהודה לאחיו: אני אחריב מהן שלושה וטלו כל אחד — אחד ולא נשאיר
בהם איש. אמרו לו אחיו: יהודה, מצרים אינה כשכם, אם אתה מחריב
מצרים, תחריב את העולם כולו.

"My lord asked his servants, saying: Have ye a father, or a brother?" (44, 19)—From the outset thou didst come upon us with a pretext. From many provinces did they come down to Egypt to buy victuals; yet thou didst not interrogate any of them. Peradventure we came for thy daughter's hand, or our sister's hand didst thou seek? Even so, we hid nothing from thee.

Joseph replied to him: Judah! Wherefore art thou the spokesman of all your brethren, whereas I see in my divining goblet that thou hast brothers older than thyself? Answered Judah: All that thou seest is due to the bond that I stood for him.

To which Joseph replied: Why didst thou not stand surety for thy brother when ye sold him to the Ishmaelites for twenty pieces of silver and grieved thine old father, when thou didst say unto him: "Joseph has been torn by a wild beast", when he did thee no wrong? Regarding this one who did wrong and stole the goblet, tell thy father: The rope has followed the bucket.

As soon as Judah heard this, he cried out bitterly: How can I go up to my father when the lad is not with me? Joseph then said to him: Come let us debate the matter. Have thy say and arrange thine arguments. Whereupon Judah immediately called to his brother Naphtali: Go and see how many markets there are in Egypt. Whereupon he leapt forth, returned and told him; Twelve. Said Judah: I shall lay waste three of them; the rest of you, take each one a market and spare no one. His brethren answered him: Judah, Egypt is not Shechem; Shouldst thou destroy Egypt, thou destroyest the whole world. (Tanḥuma)

מיד כעס יהודה ושאג בקול גדול והלך קולו ת' פרסה עד ששמע חושים בן דן וקפץ מארץ כנען ובא אצל יהודה ושאגו שניהם וביקשה ארץ מצרים ליהפך.

...Judah immediately became furious and raged at the top of his voice, so that the sound travelled four hundred parasangs till Hushim the son of Dan heard it and leapt to his side from the Land of Canaan. Both of them raged and sought to overthrow the land of Egypt. (Bereshit Rabbah)

אמר לו יהודה ליוסף : תדע לך שמתחלה לא באת עלינו אלא בעלילות. בתחילה אמרת לנו : מרגלים אתם ! שנית אמרת : לראות ערות הארץ באתם ! שלישית : גביע גנבתם : אתה נשבעת בחיי פרעה הרשע, ואני נשבע בחיי אבי הצדיק. אם אוציא חרבי מנרתיקה, אמלא כל מצרים הרוגים.
אמר לו יוסף: אם תוצא חרבך מנרתיקו, אני כורכו על צוארך.
אמר לו יהודה: אם אפתח את פי אבלע אותך.
אמר לו יוסף: אם תפתח פיך, אני סותמו באבן.

אמר יהודה ליוסף: מה נאמר לאבא?

אמר לו יוסף: כבר אמרתי לך: אמור לאביך: הלך החבל אחר
הדלי.

אמר לו יהודה: דין שקר אתה דנת אותנו!

אמר לו יוסף: שקר — לשקרנים. אין לך דין שקר כמכירת אחיכם.

אמר לו יהודה: אש של שכם דולקת בלבי!

אמר לו יוסף: אש של תמר כלתך היא — אני אכבנה.

אמר לו יהודה: עכשו אצא ואצבע כל שוקים שבמצרים בדם.

אמר לו יוסף: צבעים הייתם מימיכם, שצבעתם כתונת אחיכם בדם ואמרתם
לאביכם: "טרֹף טֹרף!"

אמר להם יוסף: לא כך אמרתם, שאחיו של זה מת? אני קניתיו, אקראנו
ויבוא אצלכם. התחיל קורא: יוסף יוסף בן יעקב, בוא אצלי! יוסף בן יעקב
בוא אצלי, ודבר עם אחיך שמכרוך! והיו נושאין עיניהם בארבע פינות הבית.
אמר להם יוסף: למה אתם מסתכלים לכאן ולכאן? אני יוסף אחיכם! מיד
פרחה נשמתם ולא יכלו לענות אותו. א"ר יוחנן: וי לנו מיום הדין! וי לנו
מיום התוכחה! ומה יוסף כשאמר לאחיו: "אני יוסף אחיכם" — פרחה נשמתן,
כשעומד הקב"ה לדין, דכתיב (מלאכי ג, ב): "ומי מכלכל את יום בואו" —
על אחת כמה וכמה? ומה זה — נבהלו אחיו מפניו, כשיבוא הקב"ה לתבוע
עלבון המצוה ופשעה של תורה — על אחת כמה וכמה? עשה הקב"ה להם נס
וחזרה נשמתן.

Judah said unto Joseph: Knowest thou, that from the beginning
thou didst only seek a pretext. Thou didst first say unto us: Ye
are spies. Then didst thou add: To see the nakedness of the land,
ye have come, and then: Ye have stolen a goblet. *Thou* didst
swear by the life of Pharaoh the *wicked;* whereas *I* swear by the
life of my father, the *righteous one.* If I unsheathe my sword, I
shall fill all Egypt with corpses. Said Joseph to him: If thou
wilt unsheathe thy sword, I shall bind it round thy neck. Judah:
If I open my mouth I shall swallow thee up. Said Joseph: If
thou wilt but open thy mouth, I shall stop it up with a stone.
Said Judah: *What shall we say to Father?* Said Joseph: I have
already told thee. Tell him: The rope has followed the bucket.
Said Judah: Thou dost mete out a perverse judgement on us.
Said Joseph: Perverseness for the perverters. No greater perver-
sion of justice could be imagined than the sale of your brother!
Said Judah: The fire of Shechem doth burn within me. Said Jo-
seph: the fire of thy daughter-in-law Tamar it is—I shall douse it.
Said Judah: Now I shall go forth and dye all the markets of
Egypt in blood. Said Joseph: Ye were dyers aforetimes when ye
dyed your brother's coat in blood and said to your father: He
is torn to pieces.

Said Joseph: Did ye not say thus, that the brother of this one
is dead? I purchased him. I am going to call him and he will come
to you. He began to call: Joseph the son of Jacob, come to me!

492

> Joseph the son of Jacob come unto me! Speak with thy brethren who sold thee. Whereupon they looked to the four corners of the house. Said Joseph to them: Wherefore do ye look hither and thither? I am Joseph your brother! whereupon their souls flew out and they could not answer him. Said R. Yoḥanan: Woe to us on account of the day of Judgement! Woe to us on account of the day of retribution! If in the case of Joseph who said unto his brethren: "I am Joseph your brother", their souls souls flew out, all the more so, when the Holy One Blessed be He stands in judgement, as it is written: "Who may abide the day of His coming?" (Malachi 3, 2). And if, in this case, his brethren were affrighted at his presence, all the more so, when the Holy One blessed be He comes to judge us for neglect of His commands and the violation of the Torah!
>
> The Holy One blessed be He performed a miracle for them and their souls returned. (Tanḥuma)

What was the reason for this fanciful interpretation of Judah's moving speech, this transformation of a skilfully-woven emotional appeal and monologue into a bitter denunciatory dialogue?

But the fanciful embroidery of our Sages is also skilfully built up into a dialogue which moves, stage by stage, into a climax. There is, however, a difference. Judah, in the original Biblical petition only hints at injustice, indirectly. In the Midrash, he beseeches, threatens and denounces, whilst Joseph aggressively answers him back in mocking and ironic tone: "The rope has followed the bucket." The more Judah rages, the more "Joseph" angers and wounds him, recalling his treatment of their younger brother in the past. Joseph of course could not have said these words. Who then is the "Joseph" in the Midrash, who plays the role of the accuser? Our Sages wished to personify Judah's conscience, the inner voice of remorse which plagued him at this turning of the tables.[1]

The more Judah denounces the injustice of the regent's conduct, the more his conscience reminds him of the injustice he inflicted on Joseph.

> Thou dost mete out a perverse judgement on us. Perverseness for perverters.
> No greater perversion of justice could be imagined than the sale of your brother!

When Judah's natural indignation at injustice knows no bounds he threatens to envelop a whole empire with catastrophe for the slander of innocent people in peril of starvation:

> Now shall I go forth and dye all the markets of Egypt with blood.

But his conscience cooled his raging fury with the words:

> Ye were dyers aforetimes when ye dyed your brother's coat in blood and told your father: He is torn to pieces by wild beasts.

Perhaps the picture of Judah's ragings are meant to depict the effort to drown the voice of conscience which taunted him:

> Wherefore didst thou not stand surety for your brother, when ye sold him for twenty pieces of silver?

The Midrash contrasts their situation in Egypt, the justice meted out to them, with their conduct towards their brother, on the advice of Judah, in the past. This idea is also expressed in the text itself, in the last words of Judah's speech:

> **Now therefore let thy servant, I pray thee, abide instead of the lad a bondmen to my lord;**
> **and let the lad go up with his brethren . . .**
>
> (44, 33)

Once Judah, who here represents all the brothers, had reached the stage of not being able to return to his father without Benjamin, being prepared to give his life for him, the wrong they had all originally perpetrated against their other brother was atoned for and Joseph could reveal his identity to them.

---

[1] Similar personifications abound in the Midrash. Cf.: Satan who in the guise of an old man appeared to Abraham, on his way to the sacrifice of his son, Isaac. The old man asks him: 'The son He granted thee at a hundred—him thou goest to slaughter?" or: "If He putteth thee to the proof yet more, canst thou withstand it?" "Tomorrow He will denounce thee as a shedder of blood, in that thou didst shed the blood of thy son." The struggle that went on in the mind of Abraham is here personified.

NOT YOU SENT ME BUT GOD

After the brothers had shown their genuine and complete remorse for what they had done, giving practical evidence of their
change of heart by their willingness to sacrific themselves for
Benjamin, Joseph revealed his identity. Let us study Joseph's
opening words:

אֲנִי יוֹסֵף אֲחִיכֶם

אֲשֶׁר־מְכַרְתֶּם אֹתִי מִצְרָיְמָה.

וְעַתָּה, אַל־תֵּעָצְבוּ וְאַל־יִחַר בְּעֵינֵיכֶם

כִּי־מְכַרְתֶּם אֹתִי הֵנָּה

כִּי לְמִחְיָה שְׁלָחַנִי אֱלֹהִים לִפְנֵיכֶם.

וַיִּשְׁלָחֵנִי אֱלֹהִים לִפְנֵיכֶם לָשׂוֹם לָכֶם שְׁאֵרִית בָּאָרֶץ

וּלְהַחֲיוֹת לָכֶם לִפְלֵיטָה גְדֹלָה.

וְעַתָּה, לֹא־אַתֶּם שְׁלַחְתֶּם אֹתִי הֵנָּה

כִּי הָאֱלֹהִים . . .

I am Joseph your brother
whom you sold into Egypt.
Now be not grieved or angry with yourselves
because you sold me hither;
it was to save life God sent me ahead of you.
God has sent me ahead of you to ensure your survival on
earth and to save your lives by a great deliverance.

(G (45, 4–5; 7)

Note the change-over from the verb מכר (sell) to the verb שלח
(send). First Joseph identifies himself as the brother whom they
had sold to Egypt, a fact which could not be denied. In the
final resort it was the brothers who were responsible for his
sale, whether we accept Rashi's interpretation that it was they
who took him out of the pit and sold him to the Ishmaelites,
or whether we accept Rashbam who maintained that it was

the Midianites who heard his cries and took him out of the pit, selling him to the Ishmaelites, whilst the brothers were waiting for the Ishmaelite caravan and were unaware of his sale. Joseph therefore reminds them of their ultimate responsibility for this iniquity. But Joseph immediately proceeds to appease them:

Now be not grieved,
nor angry with yourselves, because you sold me hither.

In this case the verb מכר appears in the subordinate and not the main clause, referring to the train of thought of the brothers. "You are experiencing remorse at the thought that you sold me; but that is only according to how you see it. In reality, however, this was not the case.

To save life God sent me ahead of you.

Consequently there was no sale at all here but rather a providential mission. The two different facets of the deed are placed side by side—the deed as it appeared superficially, and its deeper implications. On the surface, to the eye, it appeared a sale. But on deeper insight, a mission was revealed. As if this explanation were inadequate, the verse continues to elaborate on this point:

God has sent me ahead of you
to ensure your survival on earth,
and to save your lives by a great deliverance.

Two clauses of purpose, setting forth the aims of divine Providence occur here, one after the other. First the minimum purpose of saving life from starvation "to ensure your survival", followed by the second, but greater and more sublime aim, alluding to the future, historic destiny of the people: "to save your lives by a great deliverance".

Joseph's address to his brothers now reaches a climax, as one by one, the purely surface implications of events and developments as grasped by the senses are peeled away, as it were, to reveal the true inner core and significance:

וְעַתָּה, לֹא־אַתֶּם שְׁלַחְתֶּם אֹתִי הֵנָּה
כִּי הָאֱלֹהִים...

**So it was not you who sent me here.
but God.** (45, 8)

The verb מכר (sale) appears no more and is forgotten. What had originally appeared as a criminal deed of kidnapping now stands revealed in its true perspective, as part of a providential scheme for saving life and furthering the national destiny. But this time it is God and not the brothers who is the initiator and the contrast is now between these two parties "not you ... but God."

In order to gain a clearer understanding of the principle enunciated here, we shall cite the words of Rambam, in his *Guide to the Perplexed* (II, 48). They have a direct bearing on the subject we have just discussed:

It is clear that everything produced must have an immediate cause which produced it; that cause again a cause, and so on, till the First Cause, viz., the will and decree of God is reached. The prophets therefore sometimes omit the intermediate causes, and ascribe the production of an individual thing directly to God, saying that God has made it. This device is well known, and we, as well as others who seek the truth, have explained it; it is the belief of our co-religionists. After having heard this remark, listen to what I will explain in this chapter; direct your special attention to it... It is this: As regards the immediate causes of things produced, it makes no difference whether these causes consist in substances, physical properties, freewill, or chance... The prophets omit them and ascribe the production directly to God and use such phrases as, God has done it, commanded it, or said it.

In all such cases the verbs "to say", "to speak", "to command", "to call", and "to send" are employed. What I desired to state in this chapter is this: ... I will give you instances, and they will guide you in the interpretation of passages which I do not mention. As regards phenomena produced regularly by natural causes

497

such as the melting of the snow when the atmosphere becomes warm, the roaring of the sea when a storm rages, I quote the following passages. "He sendeth his word and melteth them" (Ps. 147, 18); "And he saith, and a storm-wind riseth, and lieth up its waves" (ibid. 107, 25). In reference to the rain we read: "I will command the clouds that they shall not rain", etc. (Isa. 5, 6). Events caused by man's freewill, such as war, the dominion of one nation over another, the attempt of one person to hurt another, or to insult him, are ascribed to God, as e.g., in reference to the dominion of Nebuchadnezzar and his host, "I have commanded my holy ones, also I have called my heroes for my anger" (Isa. 13, 3); and "I will send him against a hypocrite nation" (ibid. 10, 6); in reference to Shimei, son of Gera, "For God said to him, Curse David" (II Sam. 16, 10); in reference to the deliverance of Joseph, the righteous, from prison, "He sent an angel and loosed him" (Ps. 105, 20); in reference to the providing of food to Elijah, "I have commanded there a woman, a widow, to maintain thee" (I Kings 17, 9); and Joseph, the righteous, says: "Not you sent me here but God".

In other words, each one sees the immediate implications and motivations of his own deeds. We imagine that we are carrying out our own set purpose, without realising the workings of divine Providence, leading each person towards his destiny. Our story begins with:

And he sent him from the vale of Hebron (37, 14)

Jacob imagined that he was only sending Joseph away for a number of days from Hebron to Shechem to his brothers, and did not know that this sending formed part of the Divine scheme for bringing the Children of Israel to Egypt, in fulfillment of the decree:

That thy seed shall be a stranger in a land that is not theirs, and shall serve them; and they shall afflict them four hundred years, and also that nation, whom they shall serve, will I judge. (15, 13–14)

This is in line with Rashi's interpretation of the verse quoted above:

498

"Vale (*emek*) of Hebron"—from the deep counsel of the righteous man buried in Hebron (Abraham), as it is said: "Thy seed shall be a stranger . . ."

Here we have a play on the word *emek*, meaning a "vale" or a "deep place", taken here as an allusion to the deep or mysterious information imparted by God to Abraham, regarding the future exile of his children to Egypt. Our story began with the plain, factual statement regarding Jacob: "So he sent him out of the vale of Hebron" and ends with the words that are an explanation, a solution to all that had happened: ."So it was not you who sent me now, but God. Fortunate is he to whom it is granted to detect in the metamorphoses of his daily existence and the vicissitudes of his personal affairs, the workings of Providence—a mission on which he has been sent by God.

Questions for Further Study

Read the Rambam extract again and explain:

(a) What are the "intermediate causes" that Joseph omitted in his words?
(b) How does our verse: "So it was not you who sent me here, but God" differ from all the verses in Samuel, Kings, Isaiah and Psalms cited by Rambam?
(c) Do Rambam's words provide an answer to Abravanel's question:

How come Joseph to say: "So it was not you who sent me here but God"? Surely they deliberately and knowingly sold him to harm him. The fact that by a fluke the sale turned out well, did not mitigate their offence. A person is not judged by the accidental results of his deeds but by his intent. The accidental results are irrelevant to the moral dimension.

FEAR NOT TO GO DOWN TO EGYPT

This exhortation "fear not" was uttered by the Almighty on various occasions to each one of the patriarchs and to Moses too. There is no previous indication given in the text that Jacob or any of the Patriarchs were afraid of anything. It is as if the Torah wished to teach us that nothing is hidden from God. The fear of the mighty and the confident that lies deep down in their hearts stands revealed to the all-knowing·God. The question may here be asked what had Jacob to be afraid of? He was going to see his long-lost favourite son for whom he had mourned for twenty years. In Egypt he would live under the protection of his son who was vice-regent of the realm. Abravanel formulates the question as follows:

> What need was there for the Almighty to say to Jacob "fear not to go down into Egypt"? Jacob had evinced no trepidation regarding this step and prior to the Divine revelation explicitly stated "I will go and see him before I die", and he had indeed already "taken his journey with all that he had". (Gen. 46, 1)

It has been suggested that the answer to this question lies in the same verse that has just been quoted where it is stated further that Jacob offered sacrifices "unto the God of his father Isaac". This link with Isaac is further followed up in the Divine revelation to Jacob:

> **I am God, the God of thy father;**
> **fear not to go down to Egypt.** (46, 3)

In this connection it will be recalled that Isaac was explicitly forbidden to leave the Holy Land:

Go not down into Egypt;
dwell in the land which I shall tell thee of. (26, 2)

Presumably then this was what Jacob was afraid of—that he
would be violating an explicit Divine command issued to his
father Isaac. This explanation, however, does not completely
meet the objection referred to by Abravanel. Evidently the fear
alluded to here is not connected with Jacob's personal feelings.
It is part of the symbolic or archetypal dread of the founder
of the nation of the spiritual consequences of leaving the homeland and going into Egypt. Ḥizkuni follows this line of thought
in his commentary echoing a Midrash that has not come down
to us:

> The expression "fear not" is only directed to one who is afraid.
> Jacob was afraid and said: Now that I am about to go down
> to Egypt the days are at hanu foretold my forefathers regard-
> ing the decree of bondage and affliction on my seed in a land
> not their own. Thereupon the Holy One blessed be He set his
> mind at rest, saying: "fear not to go down into Egypt". Notwith-
> standing that I warned thy father I have come to promise thee
> that though the days of bondage and affliction are at hand, so
> too is the blessing wherewith I blessed thy grandfather, "that I
> shall make thee a great nation . . .".

Jacob was concerned for the future of the nation as a whole,
the future of his children in the Egyptian exile and the bondage
to come. Though he knew full well that he was going to a land
of plenty and to live in comfort, who would guarantee that his
descendants would want to leave Egypt and return to the land
of Canaan which alone had been promised tc his forefathers?
Perhaps his children would forget their destiny as they wallowed
in the plenty of Egypt and would not want to leave. To these
misgivings and doubts did the Divine message allude.
Rashi states quite simply that Jacob—

"אל תירא מרדה מריצמה": לפי שהיה מיצר על שנזקק לצאת לחוצה לארץ.

was distressed because he had been obliged to leave the homeland.

Our study of the above problem may help us to decide another problem that arises a little later on in the same chapter where the dramatic moment where father and son meet after an absence of twenty-two years is described:

וַיֶּאְסֹר יוֹסֵף מֶרְכַּבְתּוֹ וַיַּעַל לִקְרַאת־יִשְׂרָאֵל אָבִיו גֹּשְׁנָה
וַיֵּרָא אֵלָיו
וַיִּפֹּל עַל־צַוָּארָיו
וַיֵּבְךְּ עַל־צַוָּארָיו עוֹד.

And Joseph made ready his chariot,
and went up to meet Israel his father, to Goshen;
and he appeared unto him
and [he] fell on his neck,
and [he] wept on his neck a good while.   (46, 29)

It is not clear who is described as doing the weeping. Only one thing is clear that unlike the description of the meeting of Jacob and Esau (33, 4) where both of them wept, here the singular form "and he wept" is used. But to whom does this refer? To the subject of the verse, Joseph, or to the antecedent of the pronoun "his father Israel"? Here we give the views of two commentators:

"וירא אליו": יוסף נראה אל אביו.
"ויבך על צואריו עוד": לשון הרבות בכיה, וכן (איוב לד, כג): "כי לא על
איש ישים עוד", לשון ריבוי הוא, אינו שם עליו עילות נוספות על חטאיו;
אף כאן הירבה והוסיף בבכי יותר על הרגיל; אבל יעקב לא נפל על צוארי
יוסף ולא נשקו, ואמרו רבותינו, שהיה קורא את שמע.

It was Joseph who appeared unto his father and wept on his neck ... But Jacob did not fall on Joseph's neck and did not kiss him. Our Rabbis state that he was reciting the Shema.

(Rashi)
I do not understand the implication of the phrase "and he appeared unto him"; for it was obvious that they saw each other as soon as he fell on his neck. Moreover, it was not befitting for Joseph to fall on his father's neck, but he should rather have bowed down to him or kissed his hands.
    Cf.: "Joseph removed them from between his knees and bowed

low with his face to the ground" (48, 12). Here too bowing low would have better suited the occasion. Further the implication of the Hebrew word עוֹד is "more"—an addition to something already there, rather than "much" or a lot. Cf.: Job. 34, 23 "He will not impose on man more" (עוֹד) where Elihu chiding Job for questioning Divine justice insists that God will not impose on man more than his due punishment on account of his sins.[1]

But the true explanation is, in my opinion, that Israel's eyes were already dim with age or that Joseph came in his chariot with his face covered by the turban as is the custom of Egyptian kings and was not recognised by his father ... Therefore the text reminds us that as soon as he appeared unto his father and he was able to look at him closely his father recognised him and fell on his neck and wept for him more, in continuance of the constant weeping for him till this day, during all the time that he had not seen him. After that Jacob said: Now I can die having seen thy face." It is a wellknown phenomenon. By whom are tears more easily shed? By the aged parent who finds his long-lost son alive after despairing and mourning for him or the young son who rules?

Take no account of the fact that the next verse (46, 30) opens with the words "Then Israel said". This does not imply that hitherto we have been dealing with a different subject, but, on the contrary the text often specifies a subject already understood. Cf.: "Then *he* gathered all the food of seven years that had accumulated in the land of Egypt and distributed food in all the cities" (41, 48) followed by "then *Joseph* stored corn ..." Cf.: 46, 50 and elsewhere.   (Ramban)

We have here apparently a familiar grammatical problem, one that often divides commentators: Who is the subject?[2] Have we here a multiple sentence with Joseph as the subject all the way through? It was Joseph who harnessed his chariot, appeared, fell and wept. Or perhaps the object of the first sentence which is indeed the antecedent of the pronominal subject of the second and succeeding ones, i.e. Jacob becomes the subject and it is Jacob who appears, falls and weeps?

Grammatically speaking there is little to choose between the two alternatives.[3] The strongest argument in favour of Ramban's interpretation that it was Jacob who wept is to be found in the word "more", alluding to the fact that Jacob had been constantly weeping throughout the twenty two years of Joseph's absence.

In actual fact, Rashi too, felt that the phrase: "he wept on his neck yet more" was an apter description of Jacob. He therefore cited a text from Job indicating that not every עוד meant "more" but could be taken as "much", offering no indication therefore that Jacob not Joseph wept.

Rashi's explanation can be traced to a rabbinic Midrash which maintained that weeping was not the kind of thing Jacob would have been guilty of at this happiest moment of his life. One of Rashi's most recent supercommentaries *Beer Yiẓhak* thus fills in the picture:

> Love, however intense must never make one forget the supreme object of all love—The Creator blessed be He. Absolute love must be reserved for God alone. The ecstatic love and joy experienced by Jacob at his reunion with his long-lost favourite son Joseph almost enveloped him to the exclusion of all else. From this Jacob recoiled realising that such overriding love must be reserved exclusively for the Creator and Cause of all.
>
> He therefore diverted the wellsprings of love to their true source. This is what our Sages meant when they observed that at the moment of their reunion Jacob recited the Shema. By a deliberate effort of mind he directed his intense love to the Creator.

The wording of the text would seem to support Rashi:

וַיֹּאמֶר יִשְׂרָאֵל אֶל־יוֹסֵף:
אָמוּתָה הַפָּעַם אַחֲרֵי רְאוֹתִי – –

Then Israel said: Now I can die having seen thy face
(46, 30)

Since the subject is mentioned: "Israel" we are entitled to infer that hitherto it was not Israel. At any rate this affords no conclusive indication, as Ramban pointed out: "Take no account of the fact that the next verse opens with the words: 'Then Israel said'." He cites other texts where the subject is specified without there being any change in its identity. To sum up: there is no conclusive indication from the text itself as to who is the subject—Jacob or Joseph neither from the use of the word עוד or the context. Ramban's strongest card is a psychological one: who was more likely to weep:

> It is a well known phenomenon. By whom are tears more easily shed? By the aged parent who finds his long lost son alive after despairing and mourning for him or the young son who rules?

Ramban's interpretation may also be said to fit in better with the thread of the narrative and the undertones that we have referred to previously. At the beginning we noted that Jacob was concerned for the spiritual future of his children in Egypt. He was afraid that the descent into exile might constitute the signal for a corresponding moral decline and repudiation of their national destiny. We may, therefore, assume that Jacob's tears were prompted not only by feelings of joy, but also by those of concern for the future. This was evidently the motivation behind Joseph's earnest wish that his brothers should not catch the attentions of Pharaoh and should not remain within the royal orbit. He wished them to remain segregated from the Egyptian community, undistinguished as shepherds, in a special corner of the land reserved for them. This would help them to retain their national identity in preparation for their eventual departure from Egypt. These issues underly the audience of the five brothers with Pharaoh and Joseph's previous promptings as to how they should conduct themselves, briefing them as to what they should say, and what they should keep back. This will form the subject of one of our next *Studies*.

Questions for Further Study

Here is Hirsch's comment on 46, 27:

> Joseph not Jacob wept. Joseph wept liberally, but Jacob's tears had long since dried up. Joseph continued to weep even after Jacob had already begun conversing with him. These little touches mirror the true situation. Jacob had lived lonely and isolated and his whole life had been centred on mourning for Joseph. Joseph

had experienced many changes of fortune. These had not let him dwell on his homesickness. But the encounter with his father as he fell on his neck aroused in him nostalgic memories of home twenty years earlier and all these pent-up feelings surged out in his tears.

(a)   What is the difference both in interpretation and approach between Hirsch and Ramban?

(b)   Which appears to you closer to the plain sense of the text?

1 "But will repay him his just deserts and not make him suffer more than his iniquity" (Ramban in his commentary to Job).

2 Cf.: Gen. 15, 6: "He accounted it to him for righteousness." Who accounted to whom? See Rashi and Ramban *ad loc.*, see also: *Gilyonot Le-iyyun be-farashat ha-shavua, Lekh Lekha* 5717. Cf.: also I Sam. 15, 27: "He grasped hold of the edge of his garment"—Who grasped hold? See Rashi and Redak *ad loc.*, also *Studies in Vayikra* p. 317 (Haftarat Shabbat Zachor) question 4.

3 Cf.: 2 Kings 8.14: "He left Elisha and came to his master and he said to him, What did Elisha tell you?" Here it is quite obvious that the referent of the first two hes is quite different from the last one, although the same pronoun is still used. See *Gilyonot Ki Tissa*, 5718.

4 Where the wording and grammar accords no decisive clue, Ramban often settles for a particular interpretation on psychological grounds. Cf.: Gen. 29, 12 s.v. ותגד לאביה and ibid. 29, 27; s.v. ונתנה לך; ibid. 29, 30 s.v. ויאהב גם את רחל Exodus 32, 16 s.v. והלוחות; ibid 32, 21 s.v. מה עשה לך העם הזה etc.

EXILE AND RETURN UNDER GOD

The Almighty appeared to Jacob, on the eve of his departure to Egypt. This was the last Divine revelation to him and to the patriarchs, as a whole. In the previous *Studies* we tried to understand the meaning of the word "fear" in the message: "Fear not to go down to Egypt." We found it difficult to understand what Jacob had to fear, on the eve of his departure to Egypt. He was going to meet his favorite son who was the viceregent of the country, the son whom he had not seen for twenty two years, and for whom he had mourned and remained inconsolable. We cited the words of Hizkuni, which endeavoured to penetrate beneath the surface of the patriarch's soul and reveal the mainsprings of the fear and apprehension that troubled him. We noted too that Jacob was not merely concerned over the physical bondage in store for his children when he accompanied them in their trek from the land of penury and privation to the country of huge granaries, civilization and wealth where their brother occupied the post of vice regent. He was haunted by another fear: perhaps, once the famine or even the bondage was over, they would no longer be eager to leave this country of plenty to return to claim the land of Canaan, which alone had been promised them from the days of the Patriarchs.

The *Ha'amek Davar* gives the following interpretation of this fear:

> Jacob was afraid that his seed would be absorbed by the Egyptian nation. Only in the land of Israel could the unique Jewish spark be preserved down the ages. It was on this score the Almighty reassured him: "Fear not, for there I shall make of thee a great nation." Our Sages interpreted the phrase "great nation" to imply that the Jews would preserve their national identity, and not be absorbed into Egypt.

We shall study the Almighty's subsequent promise to Jacob, cited at the beginning:

אָנֹכִי אֵרֵד עִמְּךָ מִצְרַיְמָה
וְאָנֹכִי אַעַלְךָ גַם־עָלֹה – – –

I will go down with thee into Egypt; and I will also surely bring thee up again. (46, 4)

We know that Jacob did not return to Canaan and died in exile. To what then did the Divine promise refer? Rashi explains that the reference is to his burial in the Holy Land. But it is difficult to accept that the Almighty came to promise him no more than that, especially if we assume that Jacob was principally concerned about the fate, spiritual and otherwise, of his sons and descendants.

We must look elsewhere for a solution. The passage no doubt exemplifies a feature found quite often in the Torah. The father is the prototype of the nation. Professor Heinemann has referred to the rabbinic technique of interpreting the saga of the patriarchs and the biblical narrative, as a whole, as affording an archetypal pattern of Jewish history, and has noted that this can be traced to the Torah itself. The *Mekhilta* interprets our passage in this vein too:

וחכמים אומרים: "ואנוהו" – אלווני עד שאבוא עמו לבית מקדשו. משל למלך שהלך בנו למדינת הים, ויצא אחריו ועמד עליו, הלך למדינה אחרת, ויצא אחריו ועמד עליו, כך ישראל: כשירדו למצרים – שכינה עמהם, שנאמר: "אנכי ארד עמך מצרימה", עלו – שכינה עמהם, שנאמר: "ואנכי אעלך גם עלה", ירדו לים – שכינה עמהם, שנאמר (יד, יט): "ויסע מלאך אלהים ההולך לפני מחנה ישראל וילך מאחריהם", יצאו למדבר – שכינה עמהם, שנאמר (שמות יג, כא): "וה' הולך לפניהם יומם בעמוד ענן לנחותם הדרך".

Our Sages said: "And I shall glorify him" [1]—I shall accompany Him until I come with Him to His temple. This may be compared to a king whose son left him for foreign parts. Wherever his son went the king went too. So it was with Israel. When they went down into Egypt, the Divine presence accompanied them, as it is stated: "I will go down with thee into Egypt." When they left, the Divine presence accompanied them, as it is stated:

"and I will surely bring thee up again." They went forth into
the sea, the Divine presence accompanied them, as it is stated:
"And the angel of God, who went before the camp of Israel,
accompanied them from behind." They went forth into the wilderness, the Divine presence accompanied them, as it is said: "And
the Lord went before them in a pillar of cloud by day to show
them the way."

A similar feature may be observed in *Shemot Rabbah*, in its
comment to the Almighty's words to Moses at the burning
bush:

אמר הקב"ה למשה: אני אמרתי ליעקב אביהם, "אנכי ארד עמך מצרים
ואנכי אעלך גם עלה" ועתה ירדתי לכאן להעלות בניו כמו שאמרתי ליעקב
ולהיכן אני מעלך? — אל המקום אשר הוצאתיך משם, אל הארץ אשר
נשבעתי לאבותם, הדא הוא דכתיב (שמות ג, ח): "ולהעלותו מן הארץ
ההיא".

Said the Holy One blessed be He to Moses: I said to their father
Jacob: "I will go down with thee into Egypt; and I will surely
bring thee up again." Now I have come down here to bring out
his descendants, in accordance with My promise to their fore-
father, Jacob. Where will take them to? To the place from
whence they came forth, to the land which I swore to their
fathers, as it is written: "To bring them up out of that land"
(Ex. 3, 8).

Buber emphasises in his book *Kingship of God*[2] that the
God of the Patriarchs and Israel is not bound to a particular
holy place, land or sanctuary, but He is pictured as a king
who accompanies His people everywhere, leading and com-
forting them, bringing them out and taking them in. The Almighty
reassures Jacob, in our passage, that He will take his bones out of
Egypt and have them buried in Canaan. But He implies, too,
that the great nation being formed in Egypt would also be
brought home by Him.

The Almighty is thus not referring to Jacob, alone, as an
individual, but speaking of the nation, as a whole. The phrase
"For there I will make of thee a great nation" must also be taken
in this sense. The Egyptian bondage would be a blessing to the
Israelites, in schooling them for nationhood. The *Ha'amek Davar*

suggests such an interpretation. The Hebrew word *goy*, he says, implies a nation with its own homeland and government. In Egypt they received the training and experience necessary for attaining these goals. In the light of this, the verse, with which the one who subdivided the Pentateuch into *sidrot* chose to end, is highly significant; underlining the blessing, of their stay in Egypt:

> **And Israel settled in the land of Egypt, in the land of Goshen; they acquired holdings therein, and were fruitful, and increased greatly in numbers.** (47, 27)

The comfort and affliction, their experiences both pleasant and unpleasant in Egypt were meant purely as means to attain their goal—their restoration to the homeland. The reassurance that God would be with them wherever they went, even in the darkest exile was prompted by the Divine wish to safeguard the spark of Jewishness in his people, in all situations, until they returned home. The "Divine presence was exiled with them"[3] for this purpose. The author of the *Ha'amek Davar*, Rabbi Naphtali Zvi Judah Berlin, a staunch lover of Zion, detected an allusion to the darkness of the exile in the timing of the Divine vision that came to Jacob.

> "And God spoke unto Israel *in the visions of the night*"—In the daytime itself, He appeared unto him in the visions of the night, to make him understand that the time had come to shoulder the yoke of exile, that is termed "night." The world is then darkened and deprived of the holy spirit, which manifests only for brief periods, according to need, just as the lightning flashes punctuate the night.

Ramban detected an allusion to the exile in the very name the Almighty used in calling to the patriarch.

> After the Almighty had told him that "his name should no more be called Jacob, but Israel shall be thy name," it was only right that He should address him by this honoured title. The Almighty's employment of his old name "Jacob," on this occasion, implies

that henceforth he would not strive with God and men and prevail, but remain in the house of bondage until He would bring him out. The exile was beginning. This too is the reason for the use of "Jacob" in the passage: "And these are the names of the children of Israel who came to Egypt, Jacob and his sons." They entered Egypt as the children of Israel, alluding to the fact that the children would be fruitful and multiply and become honoured and renowned. But at the present moment, it was just Jacob.

This final revelation to Jacob is shrouded in the darkness of impending exile, weighted down by the fears of physical and spiritual bondage, "in the visions of the night." The sole ray of light is the Divine promise:

וְאָנֹכִי אַעַלְךָ גַם־עָלֹה.

I will also surely bring thee up again

Questions for Further Study

1. Compare the following citation from *Meshekh Ḥokhma* of R. Meir Simḥa of Dvinsk with our last excerpt from *Ha'amek Davar*:

We find that it was only in the case of Jacob, and not of Abraham and Isaac, that God appeared in "visions of the night." This was because he was prepared to go and live outside the Holy Land. The Divine revelation came to him, at night, to show him that the Divine presence rests on Israel even in the night, in the darkness of the exile, as they stated: "Wherever Israel was exiled, the Divine presence accompanied them. They were exiled to Egypt, the Divine presence accompanied them ... to Babylon, the Divine Presence accompanied them." Regarding this, Psalm 20 observes: "The Lord answer thee in the day of trouble; the name of the God of Jacob set thee up on high." Whilst they are in trouble and in the darkness of the night, the God of Jacob who was revealed to him at night, will set thee up on high.

According to both authorities, the revelation came to Jacob in the visions of the night, in allusion to the character of the exile. What is the difference in their respective approaches to and evaluation of the exile?

2.   God said to Jacob in our sidra: "Fear not to go down to Egypt." To Abraham, the Almighty said: *"Fear not Abraham, I am thy shield;"* to Isaac: "I am the God of Abraham thy father, *fear not*, for I am with thee," to Moses: "And the Lord said unto Moses, *Fear him not"* (Num. 21, 34). Why was this Divine admonition not to be afraid not preceded by the information that Abraham, Isaac and Moses were, in the first instance, afraid?

3.   "I am the Lord God of thy father"—I am He who said to thy father (26, 2) "Go not down into Egypt." I am He who saith unto thee: 'Fear not to go down to Egypt" now, "for I shall make of thee a great nation there." For had your children remained in this land (i.e. the Holy Land) they would have intermarried with the Canaanites and assimilated, whereas this will not happen in Egypt, since the Egyptians cannot dine together with the Hebrews. They will thus be a nation set apart, as our Sages stated (Sifrei Deut. cited also in the Pesaḥ Haggada): "And they became there a nation"—this teaches you that the Israelites were distinguished there (prominent and set apart).   **(Sforno)**

Where can you find in *Genesis* support for Sforno's contention that Jacob's sons might be tempted to intermarry with the Canaanites and associate with them, had they remained there?

---

1 Exodus 15, 2: The song at the Red Sea.
2 Harper and Row New York 1967 pp. 99–101.
3 Megillah 29a:

בכל מקום שגלו ישראל שכינה עמהם, גלו למצרים שכינה עמהם, גלו לבבל שכינה עמהם . . .

"Wherever Israel were exiled to, the *Shekhinah* accompanied them; they were exiled to Egypt, the *Shekhinah* accompanied them, to Babylon the *Shekhinah* accompanied them."

GOSHEN: THE GHETTO OF CHOICE

Wherever we find in the Torah a detailed recapitulation of a story that has already been narrated in full, and there are many examples of his, it behoves us to make a careful comparison between the two, verse by verse, and word for word, looking for the reasons for every addition or omission or variation in the phraseology. The choice of every word is deliberate and there is nothing accidental or coincidental in it but the imparting of some specific lesson.[1]

It does not matter what kind of recapitulation. It may be the story of one of the actors himself who relates to his hearers what happened to him and what we have already been told (in the previous chapter), as for example the story of Abraham's servant who recapitulates all that had befallen him after the text had already related it;[2] or the story of Potiphar's wife who gives her version of what transpired between Joseph and herself after the text had already described the incident. She actually tells the story twice over, to the members of her household and then her husband.[3] It may, on the other hand, consist of the implementation of a command or piece of advice after the original instruction has already been outlined in detail, as for example, Jacob's last testament to Joseph[4] or the ordainment of Joshua by Moses.[5] Then we have the record of a conversation where one person outlines a proposal to another and his colleague recapitulates the proposal in detail as in Moses' talks with the two and a half tribes and the proposals made by them to bear arms first in helping their brethren. Moses recapitulated their proposal in his own version.[6] Sometimes we encounter a dialogue in which a proposal is made by one of the speakers who then repeats it to another audience as in the case of Hamor the father of Schechem who proposes an alliance both marital and commercial to Jacob and his children and then gives his own deliberate colouring to that proposal when he recapitulates it to his fellow-citizens.[7]

In our sidra we encounter this phenomenon twice: first, when Joseph revealed his plans in his discussions with his brethren and subsequently on coming to Pharaoh to implement them, second, when Joseph instructed his brothers what to say to Pharaoh and their words when they actually came before Pharaoh.

Here we compare them:

Joseph to his brothers (46, 31–32)	*Joseph to Pharaoh* (47, 1)
I will go up and tell Pharaoh ... My brethren and my father's house who were in the land of Canaan have come unto me. And the men are shepherds, for they have been keepers of cattle; and they have brought their flocks and their herds and all that they have.	My father and my brethren and their flocks and their herds, and all that they have, have come out of the land of Canaan. And behold they are in the land of Goshen.
Joseph instructs his brothers what to say to Pharaoh (46 33–34)	*Joseph's brothers speak to Pharaoh* (47, 2–4)
And it shall come to pass when Pharaoh shall call you and say: What is your occupation? that you shall say:	And from among his brethren he took five men and presented them to Pharaoh. And Pharaoh said unto his brethren: What is your occupation? And they said unto Pharaoh:
Thy servants have been keepers of cattle from our youth	Thy servants are shepherds both we and our fathers.

514

| even until now, both we and our fathers. | And they said unto Pharaoh: To sojourn in the land have we come; for there is no pasture for thy servants' flocks, for the famine is sore in the land of Canaan. Now therefore we pray thee let thy servants dwell in the and of Goshen. |

This is how Abravanel explains the differences in the first case:

> After Joseph had seen his family, he told them: "I will go up and tell Pharaoh"—it is better for me to go now and tell Pharaoh of your arrival—that he should hear from me rather than anyone else. Joseph did not tell this to his father but to his brethren and father's household. He did not want his father to fear that their settlement in Goshen was still a matter of doubt, but he told his brothers and promised them he would speak to Pharaoh in such a way that he would offer it of his own accord.
>
> Note that though Joseph told his brothers he would tell Pharaoh: "My brethren and fathers house have come *unto me*", when he came to Pharaoh he omitted the words "unto me", lest Pharaoh should suspect that they had come to be supported from the royal treasury. But Joseph emphasised that they had come from the land of Canaan and said: "and their flocks and their herds and all that they have, have come" indicating to him that they were wealthy and in no need of support. Joseph thus changed the wording according to need, from what he told his brothers he wanted to say to Pharaoh, and what he actually said.

He added in his audience with Pharaoh the information that they were already in the land of Goshen in order to prompt Pharaoh in the right direction. This is pointed out in *Or Ha-ḥayyim*.

> "And behold they are in the land of Goshen", as you (Pharaoh) commanded them to do in your statement (45, 18): "And I shall give you the best of the land of Egypt", the land of Goshen possessing the best pasture land of the country.

In comparing Joseph's instructions with the way the brother's carried them through, we shall see that the latter did not show the same self-respect and self-confidence that Joseph had expected of them. Had not they bowed to the ground even before Pharaoh's viceregent (whereas Jacob in audience with Pharaoh the greatest potentate on earth, at the time, had not prostrated himself). They had not shown themselves capable of giving Pharaoh brief answer but they abased themselves, besought his favour, dwelt on their misfortunes.

Ramban points out another significant variation. Joseph had told them to point out that they were shepherds, "for they have been keepers of cattle" (*anshei mikne*—implies owners of their own cattle) who did not work for others but owned their own flocks. But the brothers omitted this and said simply: "Thy servants are shepherds" to arouse his compassion for their plight. Similarly they did not observe Joseph's advice to wait for Pharaoh to offer them Goshen, on his own initiative, but they rushed to suggest it themselves.

Joseph's intention had been to ensure: "that ye may dwell in the land of Goshen; for every shepherd is an abomination unto the Egyptians". But why did Joseph emphasise this negative aspect of their presence in Egypt, championing, as it were, the Egyptian point of view?

Rashi comments on the passage: "that ye may dwell in the land of Goshen:

"בעבור תשבו בארץ גשן": והיא צריכה לכם, שהיא מרעה, וכשתאמרו לו,,
שאין אתם בקיאים במלאכה אחרת, ירחיקכם מעליו ויושיבכם שם.
"כי תועבת מצרים כל רועה צאן": לפי שהם להם אלוהות.

it needs you since it is a land of pasture and when you say that you are not versed in any other work, he will send you far away from himself and settle you there.
"for all shepherds are an abomination to the Egyptians"—since they worship sheep.

Isaac Arama observes:

He chose for them what is good and upright and hated public office. For there is no doubt that if he had wanted he could have appointed them to high positions but he wanted them to say that they had been shepherds from their youth, both they and

516

their fathers, till that vocation had been theirs from time imme-
morial and they could not leave it. The idea was to segregate them
from the Egyptians; the shepherds were an abomination to them.
This would lead to their being settled in Goshen. This was Rashi's
meaning, when he said: "when you say you are not versed in any
other work he will send you far from himself" you will settle in
Goshen, that he would prompt the Egyptians to have them segregated, the choice of Goshen being accidental.

Actually it is Arama and not Rashi who explains the motives
for Joseph's advice. Arama, one of the refugees from the Span-
nish Expulsion knew only too well the intrigues and tensions
of court life and corruptions of office and regarded the divorcement from this as Joseph's aim (Abravanel too shares his general attitude).[8] But the Netziv sees it in another light, in his commentary *Ha'amek Davar*:

"For it is an abomination of the Egyptians": He will not therefore want to settle you in the main centres. It was in this way
that Joseph contrived matters to achieve the goal that they
would dwell apart, though it involved degrading his family in
the eyes of Pharaoh. Everything was worth sacrificing in order
to ensure the preservation of Israel's sanctity.

No negative aim was involved—that of excluding them from
a court career and its tensions, but a positive one—to preserve
the sanctity of Israel.

The Netziv was one of the few and first leading rabbinic scholars to join the Zionist movement (i.e. the pre-Herzlian movement of the Lovers of Zion; the religious Kibbutz En Hanetziv
is called after him). The national ideology left its impact on
his commentaries. Even in those places where he acknowledges
our universalistic mission to be a light to the nations, his fight
against the desire to assimilate amidst the surrounding peoples
finds its expression in his insistence that such a mission can
only be realised if the Jewish people dwells alone in its own
land. We have his comment, for instance, on the text, Gen. 17,
6–7: "And I will give thee to nations (usual translation: "I
will make nations of thee") ... and I will give unto thee and
thy seed after thee the land of thy sojournings, all the land

517

of Canaan". "I will give thee to nations" implying that you will teach the nations as in Jer. 1: "I have set thee a prophet to the nations" that you should make the nations wise and upright. "I will give thee ... the land of thy sojournings" that Abraham should not imagine that the sole purpose of Israel was to wander among the nations and make them wise and that they did not have any territorial mission in the world to live the life of an independent kingdom. The text therefore adds that "I will give thee all the land of Canaan".

We must understand his explanation here too in this light. Nevertheless, in spite of all Joseph's endeavours to prevent them settling down permanently in the land and ascending the social ladder, they forgot the temporary nature of their sojourn in Egypt and the last verse of our sidra alludes to the dangers of assimilation:

> **And Israel settled in the land of Egypt and in the land of Goshen; they acquired them holdings therein, and were fruitful and increased greatly in numbers.** (47, 27)

It was nececessary for both Jacob and Joseph, before their deaths, to divert the attention of the "settlers" in the land of Egypt in Goshen to their place of origin, the land which the Lord had sworn to Abraham Isaac and Jacob.

Questions for Further Study

1.   "When Pharaoh will ask you: What is your occupation". In the view of Benno Jacob this question has to be interpreted like others in Genesis (3, 9, 11; 4, 9; 33. 5). Explain the significance of the question here in the light of the other citations. What prompted him to interpret the question: "What is your occupation?" in this manner?

2.   Explain the reason for the difference in the choice of verbs in the following texts (47, 2; 47, 7)

ומקצה אחיו ל ק ח . . . ו י צ י ג ם לפני פרעה (מז, ב).

ו י ב א יוסף את יעקב אביו ו י ע מ י ד ה ו לפני פרעה (מז, ז).

Note that while both verbs are synonymous one is from a root meaning "to present" the other from "to stand". Remember the meaning of the noun in modern Hebrew derived from the first verb.

3. "The men are shepherds; for they were men of cattle"
(46, 32)

He told his brothers the purpose of offering this information to Pharaoh. Their occupation was obnoxious in the eyes of the Egyptians. Pharaoh would of his own accord demand they live in Goshen far away from the native centres of population.

"For they were men of cattle"—they had been, in times past. *Mikneh* "cattle" included all livestock, horses, asses and camels too. Breeders of the latter were not despised like shepherds ... Joseph wanted to mitigate as far as possible the bad impression their mean occupation would make on Pharaoh. He therefore said they had originally been cattle-men but had fallen on bad times and been reduced to shepherds.   (Ha'amek Davar)

(a) What textual difficulty prompted the foregoing comment?

(b) What is the difference between the above explanation and that proffered by Ramban cited on p. 516?

(c) What proof can you find in our sidra that *mikneh* included all livestock and not just sheep?

---

[1] We shall not follow Ibn Ezra, Redak and others who maintain that these variations have no specific significance but are merely stylistic because people usually repeat the content rather than the exact wording. Though these commentators are adherents of the plain sense, in our opinion by overlooking these variations in the wording they miss a great deal of the total meaning. See our citations from Radak p. 236 and Ibn Caspi p. 237.

[2] See Hayyei Sara pp. 230ff.

[3] Supra Vayeshev pp. 417ff.

[4] Infra Vayehi pp. 530ff.

[5] Studies in Bamidbar pp. 343ff.

[6] *op.cit.* pp. 382ff.

[7] Vayishlah pp. 380ff.

[8] For Abravanel's opposition to political life see Bereshit on pp. 17ff and in particular the citation from Prof. Baer.

PRIESTS IN EGYPT AND ISRAEL

At the end of chapter 41 in *Mikez* the Torah devotes six verses to Joseph's economic activity in preparing the country for the impending calamity of seven lean years. In our Sidra, 14 verses are devoted to a description of the implementation of Joseph's austerity programme (47, 13–26).

We shall make a careful study of this programme and observe how our Sages in the Midrash understood it. For those who have experienced one and even two world wars, Joseph's rationing operations are no novelty, but for previous generations they were, and we may presume that they constituted something entirely revolutionary in his own time. What was his programme? First of all, public storage of all foodstuffs. Private storage of food would not save the population, as a whole. In any case there was the problem of preserving from rot, theft and vermin. Joseph alluded to this problem in his interpretation of Pharaoh's dream:

וְיִקְבְּצוּ אֶת־כָּל־אֹכֶל הַשָּׁנִים הַטֹּבוֹת הַבָּאֹת הָאֵלֶּה
וְיִצְבְּרוּ־בָר תַּחַת יַד־פַּרְעֹה
אֹכֶל בֶּעָרִים וְשָׁמָרוּ.

Let them gather all the food of the good years to come and let them store up corn under the hand of Pharaoh for food in the cities and let them take good care of it.

(41, 35)

Some commentators (Rashbam and others) observe that "gather" (*veyikbezu*) refers to taking the crop from the owners of the fields, whilst "store up" (*veyizberu*) refers to placing it in store by the officials in charge of the public granaries. The Midrash observes that they stored the corn in damp red soil which preserves the produce from rot. The text emphasises that all foodstuffs not merely corn or grain (*bar*) were stored by Joseph.

Ramban comments:

> He stored everything and doled it out to them in annual rations. The references in the text (verses 38, 48, 49) to both grain and foodstuffs in general indicates that even figs and raisins were included.[1] He may have bought it from them at the lowest market price with money from the king's treasury and sold it back to them in the famine years as it is written: "And Joseph gathered all the money that was in Egypt" ... or perhaps the king requisitioned it since it is stated: "I kept it" (otherwise they would have let it go waste).

Joseph's stocking programme was so well organised and successful that he was able to supply the needs of other countries which, though they experienced no years of plenty, yet suffered the famine, as can be detected in the text itself. The *Or Ha-ḥayyim* has pointed this out, noting the employment of the term "land of Egypt" with respect to the years of plenty and the general reference to "the land" or "the whole land" when it speaks of the famine:

> **Behold seven years are coming (of) great plenty** in all the land of Egypt.
> **And there shall arise seven years of famine after them and there will be forgotten all the plenty in** the land of Egypt
> **and the famine will ravage** the land   (41, 29–30)
> **Came to an end the seven years of plenty which had reigned in** the land of Egypt   (ibid. 53)
> **And the famine reigned over** the whole land   (ibid. 56)

Here are the comments of the *Or Ha-ḥayyim*:

> The text is careful to refer to "all the land of Egypt" twice (*vv.* 29 and 30) not stating merely "the land"—i.e. the whole region including both Egypt and the surrounding countries, as is the

case with the famine, "which was over the whole land". On the other hand, regarding the plenty it is stated: "Came to an end the seven years of plenty which had reigned *in the land of Egypt*, indicating that the plenty was confined to Egypt.

Nevertheless we note further that Joseph supplied the needs of the neighbouring countries:

> **And all the world came to Egypt to buy grain from Joseph since the famine had become severe in the whole land.**
>
> (41, 57)

Some commentators (Malbim) even assert that Jacob's decision to send his sons to Egypt was prompted by the actual sight of merchants bringing corn back from there (and not as Ibn Ezra maintains, that the expression "Jacob saw" implied that he merely heard). According to Ramban whom we cited earlier on, the rationing began in the years of plenty so as to conserve the produce of those years.

We may also note that Joseph solved the problem of transporting the produce from farm to granary, not by concentrating it all in the capital, but by gathering all the food of the good years and storing it for food in the cities. The Midrash, by way of illustration, states that he decentralised the storage facilities in the various cities of Egypt to serve as distribution centres or, as the Sages word it: "He placed in the area of Tiberias that which belonged to Tiberias..." The question may be asked: If everything was so well organised and successful why does the text note that "the people cried to Pharaoh for bread" (41, 55). *Or Ha-ḥayyim* explains that the cry was prompted more by psychological reasons than actual physical want:

> Since one who has bread in his basket cannot be compared to one who has not. He therefore meant to satisfy the psychological feeling of want by opening the granaries for them to see the plenty garnered there and rest secure.

The Midrash even pictures for us the detailed administrative measures employed by Joseph to forestall profiteering:

522

שלא ייכנס אדם בשני חמורים, ושלא יוליכו חמרים תבואה ממקום למקום,
ושלא ייכנס אדם שלא יכתוב שמו ושם אביו ושם זקנו.

It was prohibited for one man to enter the country with two
asses and for asses to transport the produce from one place to
another, and no one was permitted to enter the country without
registering his name, that of his father and grandfather.

(Bereshit Rabbah 91, 4)

The reason for these measures is abundantly clear. No man was
permitted to take more than the needs of his household—the
burden of one ass. The burden of two asses would mean he
intended to profiteer in the rest. Similarly, inside the country
it was forbidden for the corn to be moved outside its area,
again preventing unfair distribution and profiteering. The third
measure calling for passports was also designed to stop illicit
dealing in corn.

Even Joseph himself strictly adhered to the rationing regulations he himself had designed in regard to his own family—his
brothers and father.

He took no mean advantage but "Joseph sustained his father
and his brethren, and all his father's household with bread according to the *want of their little ones*". Sforno observes that
though he could have given them more than their ration, he
merely supplied their needs, following the Talmudic dictum
(*Ta'anit* 11a): "When the public experiences calamity, let no
man say, I shall betake myself to eat and drink and couldn't
care less."

It is unnecessary to emphasise that he did not exploit his position for personal advantage. The text states that Joseph collected
all the money that was to be found in the land of Egypt and
the land of Canaan, in exchange for the corn they bought, and
Joseph brought the money to the house of Pharaoh. Ramban
understands this text to demonstrate Joseph's personal honesty.
He did not build up his own secret hoard in Egypt or conceal
it in the land of Canaan but gave it all to the king who had
placed his trust in him.

After the famine became more acute, Joseph instituted even
more severe measures. The Egyptians submitted a proposal in

no way astonishing when we bear in mind that Egypt was a house of bondage:

> **Buy us and our land for bread, and we and our land will be bondmen to Pharaoh.** (47, 19)

What was Joseph's answer? —

> **So Joseph bought all the land of Egypt for Pharaoh; for the Egyptians sold every man his field.** (47, 20)

Deeply rooted is man's instinct to shirk responsibility for himself and his livelihood and that of his family. He would much rather saddle his superior with the burden of providing for him, let him do all his thinking for him, give him orders, lead him and support him, "that we and our land will be bondmen to Pharaoh."

The Torah bids us humiliate the Hebrew slave who loves his master, to drill his ear "since the children of Israel are my servants" and this one went and acquired for himself a master. In the same way, Joseph refrained from turning free men into bondmen, sold body and soul to their sovereign. Ramban understands the text in the same way:

> The Egyptians offered their bodies to Pharaoh. Joseph likewise said: "Behold I have bought you this day and your land for Pharaoh". Yet earlier it is stated that: "Joseph bought all the land of Egypt for Pharaoh" (47, 20); in other words, only their land! The reason is that they offered themselves as bondmen for the king to use them as he thought fit. But Joseph only wished to buy their land stipulating that they should be perpetual leaseholders or tenants of Pharaoh. The meaning of verse 20 is that, "Behold I have bought you this day with your land" not as bondmen, as you offered, but as tenants. By rights, the king as lord of the land is entitled to four-fifths and you as tenants to one-fifth. But I will treat you generously and give you the landowner's share and Pharaoh the tenant's. But you will be bound to the land and not permitted to leave it. That is the force of "let us find favour in the sight of my lord", that you

generously allowed us four fifths that we may be able to eke a livelihood out of them and "be bondmen to Pharaoh" as we vowed . . .

We have here the first example of land nationalisation or as a contemporary writer expresses it ("State Communism," Dr. Israel Eldad: *Hegyonot Ha-mikra* p. 71), control, centralisation of food supply, and equal distribution accompanied by the nationalisation of private property, first of money, then cattle, and finally, land. Henceforth all the lessees of Pharaoh's lands pay him "the state" ground rent, and live on the residue.

This nationalisation of the land necessitated also changes in the distribution of the population, the direction of labour and its resettlement:

וְאֶת־הָעָם הֶעֱבִיר אֹתוֹ לֶעָרִים
מִקְצֵה גְבוּל־מִצְרַיִם וְעַד־קָצֵהוּ.

And as for the people, he removed them city by city, from one end of the border of Egypt to the other (21).

The English version here quite rightly does not render *"le-arim"* "to the cities". Obviously, Pharaoh did not divert the population from the country to the town, since that would have defeated his purpose. He wished them to remain farmers and cultivate the land. Rashbam indeed wishes to compare Pharaoh's action to Sennacherib's (2 Kings 18, 32) in transferring the population so as to alienate them from their ancestral lands. To be preferred is Luzzatto's explanation that Pharaoh moved them "city by city", did not split them into heterogenous groups but preserved their social groupings, resettled them according to their families and neighbourhood ties.

How great the danger of demoralisation, disintegration of traditional patterns when man is divorced from his friends and relations is evidenced by the situation in countries of mass immigration. To avoid this happening Joseph resettled the people "according to their cities", "so that they should not lose touch with their social group" (*Ha'amek Davar*). Herzl's plan in his

525

Judenstaat envisaged the same preservation of social and lands-manschaft groupings in his plan of mass settlement of Israel.

One question still remains to be answered, one asked in the *Akedat Yizhak*. What is the message of this detailed story of Joseph's nationalisation of the land, his freeing of the priests from the confiscation? Surely its place was in the ancient historical records of Egypt, rather than in the words of the Living God, in his Torah! The answer may perhaps lie in that very measure alluded to in our question and in the title to our *Studies* which we have as yet failed to discuss—the privileged position of the priests:

רַק אַדְמַת הַכֹּהֲנִים לֹא קָנָה

כִּי חֹק לַכֹּהֲנִים מֵאֵת פַּרְעֹה

וְאָכְלוּ אֶת־חֻקָּם

אֲשֶׁר נָתַן לָהֶם פַּרְעֹה

עַל־כֵּן לֹא מָכְרוּ אֶת־אַדְמָתָם.

Only the land of the priests bought he not, for the priests had a portion from Pharaoh, and did eat their portion which Pharaoh gave them; wherefore **they sold not their land".** (47, 22)

Can we not detect here the Torah's pilloring of the so-called justice and equity of Egyptian custom which left individuals sure of their livelihood, subsidised by Pharaoh with their land intact. These who had were given more. Or perhaps the Torah recorded it as a contrast to the priestly regulations in Judaism, to enable us the better to appreciate its disinheritance of our priests. Perhaps it is meant to show us that He who delivered us from Egypt forbad us such institutions and abhorred them. The land is not Pharaoh's but

וְהָאָרֶץ לֹא תִמָּכֵר לִצְמִתֻת

כִּי־לִי הָאָרֶץ

כִּי־גֵרִים וְתוֹשָׁבִים אַתֶּם עִמָּדִי.

the land shall not be sold in perpetuity, for Mine is the
land,
since strangers and settlers are ye with Me ...

כִּי־עֲבָדַי הֵם אֲשֶׁר־הוֹצֵאתִי אֹתָם מֵאֶרֶץ מִצְרָיִם
לֹא יִמָּכְרוּ מִמְכֶּרֶת עָבֶד.
כִּי־לִי בְנֵי־יִשְׂרָאֵל עֲבָדִים
עֲבָדַי הֵם אֲשֶׁר־הוֹצֵאתִי אוֹתָם מֵאֶרֶץ מִצְרָיִם – – –

For My servants are they, whom I brought out of the land
of Egypt;
they shall not be sold the sale of bondmen ...
for to Me are the children of Israel bondmen,
My bondmen are they, whom I brought out of the land
of Egypt (Lev. 25: 23, 42, 55)

What is the Jewish law regarding the priests? —

וּבְתוֹךְ בְּנֵי יִשְׂרָאֵל לֹא יִנְחֲלוּ נַחֲלָה.
כִּי אֶת־מַעְשַׂר בְּנֵי־יִשְׂרָאֵל אֲשֶׁר יָרִימוּ לַיְיָ תְּרוּמָה
נָתַתִּי לַלְוִיִּם לְנַחֲלָה
עַל־כֵּן אָמַרְתִּי לָהֶם
בְּתוֹךְ בְּנֵי יִשְׂרָאֵל לֹא יִנְחֲלוּ נַחֲלָה.

In the midst of the children of Israel they shall not inherit
an inheritance,
For the tithe of the children of Israel which they set apart
as a gift unto the Lord
have I given to the Levites as an inheritance;
wherefore I have said unto them:
Among the children of Israel they shall have no inheritance
(Num. 18, 23–24)

It would appear that the "wherefore" motivating the reason
why the Egyptian priests, who in any case had all they needed
sold not their land, a "wherefore" full of irony is echoed in
the Divine "wherefore" in Leviticus supplying the reason why

527

the Levites were given no inheritance, because their needs had been supplied from another source.

The Levites had not been chosen in order to enable them accumulate wealth and exploit their flock but:

בָּעֵת הַהִיא הִבְדִּיל יְיָ אֶת־שֵׁבֶט הַלֵּוִי לָשֵׂאת אֶת־אֲרוֹן בְּרִית־יְיָ

לַעֲמֹד לִפְנֵי יְיָ לְשָׁרְתוֹ וּלְבָרֵךְ בִּשְׁמוֹ עַד הַיּוֹם הַזֶּה.

עַל־כֵּן לֹא־הָיָה לְלֵוִי חֵלֶק וְנַחֲלָה עִם־אֶחָיו

יְיָ הוּא נַחֲלָתוֹ – – –

at that time the Lord separated the tribe of Levi to bear the ark of the covenant of the Lord
to stand before the Lord, to minister to Him and bless in His name to this day;
wherefore Levi hath no portion nor inheritance with his brethren,
the Lord is his inheritance (Deut. 10, 8–9)

Questions for Further Study

1. "There was no bread in the whole of the country.".
(47, 13)

Ordinary bread was not baked but it was mixed with bran and this is not termed bread (cf.: Mishnah Ḥallah 2, 6)
(Ha'amek Davar)

What prompted him to proffer this explanation?

2. Cf.: "Why should we die in front of thee?" (47, 15)
"Why should we die in *front of thine eyes*." (47, 19)
What is the reason for the change in wording?

---

1 A lengthy article detailing Joseph's economic activities in Egypt based on Midrashic and later commentaries in particular *Or Ha-ḥayyim* and

Malbim was penned by the late S. Fraenkel who during the first world war headed the planning authority for the rationing of textiles in Germany. See: Sigmund Fraenkel, *Die Sieben aegyptlschen Hungerjahre, eine wirtschaftliche Studie*, Jeschurun, Wohlgemuth, Berlin 1925 pp. 228–245; 309, 321; 412–428. We have made use of his findings in these *Studies*.

² Though Onkelos translates the Hebrew *okhel* ("food") and *bar* ("corn") by the same word *avur* ("corn"). (Cf.: Joshua 5, 10: "They ate of the *avur* (corn) of the land"). Ramban's view that Joseph's policy of stockpiling was not confined to grains is to be preferred.

JACOB'S TESTAMENT

Before his death, the Patriarch imparted a last wish to his favourite son Joseph. This wish Joseph divulged to Pharaoh, after Jacob's death. Let us compare Jacob's wording of his own dying wish to Joseph, and the latter's reporting of it to Pharaoh:

Jacob's testament to Joseph	*As reported to Pharaoh by Joseph*
If now I have found grace in thy sight,	— — — — — — — — —
put, I pray thee, thy hand under my thigh	My father made me swear, saying,
and deal kindly and truly with me;	— — — — — — — — —
bury me not in Egypt, I pray thee:	— — — — — — — — —
But I will lie with my fathers,	Lo I die
And thou shalt carry me out of Egypt,	
And bury me in their burying-place.	In my grave which I have digged for me in the land of Canaan, there thou shalt bury me.
(Genesis 47, 29–30)	(Gen. 50, 5)

The reason for the variations are abundantly clear. Joseph is cautious in his approach to Pharaoh. As a foreigner in Egypt he did not want to offend the susceptibilities of his host. Jacob, however, as the sturdy opponent of the idolatrous world and Egyptian abominations did not want to be buried in Egypt and said so quite bluntly to Joseph:

אַל־נָא תִקְבְּרֵנִי בְּמִצְרָיִם..
וּנְשָׂאתַנִי מִמִּצְרַיִם.

Bury me not, I pray thee, in Egypt,
Thou shalt carry me out of Egypt...

These statements are not, of course, reproduced by Joseph, in reporting his father's wish to Pharaoh. Let us now follow Jacob's request and the form of oath with which he adjures Joseph:

אִם־נָא מָצָאתִי חֵן בְּעֵינֶיךָ
שִׂים־נָא יָדְךָ תַּחַת יְרֵכִי
וְעָשִׂיתָ עִמָּדִי חֶסֶד וֶאֱמֶת –

If now, I have found grace in thy sight
Put, I pray thee, thy hand under my thigh
And deal kindly and truly with me...

The above sentiments were naturally not meant for foreign consumption and were addressed privately to Joseph. He therefore omitted them in his interview with Pharaoh. On the other hand, Joseph understood how to influence the king and persuade him to give the necessary permission for burying such an important personage outside the country, and allow the vice-regent of the realm accompany the cortege.

Joseph substituted the following wording for what Jacob had actually said:

בְּקִבְרִי אֲשֶׁר כָּרִיתִי לִי בְּאֶרֶץ כְּנַעַן שָׁמָּה תִּקְבְּרֵנִי.

In my grave which I have digged for me in the land of
Canaan, there thou shalt bury me.

The reference here is, of course, to the cave of Machpelah which Jacob had not himself dug. Joseph, however, was well acquainted with Egyptian custom. An Egyptian nobleman always prepared in his lifetime his own grave, and only there would he be buried. Pharaoh would therefore appreciate the force of Joseph's request.

It is quite clear, therefore, that the variations, the omissions and insertions made by Joseph were not accidental.

Another point worth examining is the conversation between Jacob and Joseph regarding the taking of an oath. Jacob opened with a request that Joseph take an oath to carry out his last wish:

> **If now I have found grace in thy sight,**
> **Put, I pray thee, thy hand under my thigh.**

Joseph had not immediately acceded to his father's request by taking the oath but answered in a general way:
> **And he said, I will do as thou hast said.**

Our commentators express surprise at the fact that Joseph did not immediately take the oath as requested by his father, and only did so after being pressed a second time:

> **And he said, Swear unto me. And he swore unto him.**

His behaviour contrasted with that of Abraham's servant who was similarly asked by his master to swear, which he readily did:
> **And Abraham said to his eldest servant,**
> **Put, I pray thee, thy hand under my thigh.**
> **And I will make thee swear by the Lord, God of heaven ...**
> (24, 2)

Forthwith, the servant acceded to his master's request:

> **And the servant put his hand under the thigh of Abraham**
> **his master ...** (ibid. 9)

The Midrash aptly explains the difference between Joseph's behaviour and that of Abraham's servant:

אמר ר' יצחק: העבד עשה כעבדותו ובן חורין עשה כחירותו. **העבד עשה** כעבדותו, שנאמר (בראשית כד, ט): "וישם העבד את ידו . . ."; ובן חורין עשה כחירותו: "ויאמר: אנכי אעשה כדברך".

Said Rabbi Isaac: The servant acted servilely and the freeman as a free agent. The servant acted servilely, as it is said: "And the servant put his hand..." Whilst the freeman acted as a free agent: "And he said, I will do as thou hast said".

(Bereshit Rabbah 96)

A servant has to do the behest of others. Since he is not a free agent, he must be bound on oath or otherwise compelled, to make sure that he carries out his obligations. It does not matter whether the force applied is moral or physical. A free agent however is only bound by his conscience, and chooses his own actions in accordance with his own freely arrived-at decisions.

Malbim makes a similar distinction. Joseph, Malbim explains, replied to his father that it was better for him not to swear but rather to carry out his obligations as part of his filial duty. It was better for him to do it out of his own free will, rather than be bound on oath. In the latter instance, he could not take the credit for fulfilling his obligations freely.

This explanation may help us understand Biblical and Rabbinic disapproval of vows. Man should rather conduct himself as a free agent rather than be bound by external artificial bonds. Nevertheless, Jacob insisted on Joseph taking an oath:

הִשָּׁבְעָה לִי

And he said, Swear unto me.

The reason for this is quite clear when we recall what we said at the beginning about Joseph's need to placate Pharaoh and approach him diplomatically. On oath: "My father made me swear", Joseph's request would carry greater force in Pharaoh's eyes. Pharaoh's answer indicates the effect Joseph's words had on him:

עֲלֵה וּקְבֹר אֶת אָבִיךָ כַּאֲשֶׁר הִשְׁבִּיעֶךָ.

Go up and bury thy father as he made thee swear.

(50, 6)

Questions for Further Study

1. Compare Abraham's words to his servant with Jacob's to Joseph in the following excerpt:

    "And I (Abraham) will make thee swear by the Lord God of heaven ..." (24, 3)

    Contrast the above with Jacob's simpler form of adjuration (47, 31):

    "Swear unto me"
    What is the reason for the difference?

2. הרי כל שבחו של יוסף, שהיה מפליג על כבוד אביו — ולא נכנס אצלו בכל
    שעה?! שאלולי שבאו אחרים ואמרו לו: אבא חולה, לא היה יודע? אלא
    להודיעך צדקו, כלא רצה להתייחד עם אביו, שלא יאמר לו: היאך עשו בך
    אחיך ? — ומקללם . . . לפיכך לא היה הולך אצל אביו כל שעה.

    "... One told Joseph, behold thy father is sick" (48, 1). Behold all Joseph's praiseworthiness consisted of the great respect he paid to his father, yet he did not go in to see him every hour!? For were it not for the fact that others came to tell him, "Father is sick", wouldn't he have known? The purpose of this, however, is to make known unto you his righteousness, that he did not want to be alone with his father that he should not say to him: What did your brothers do to you? and he (Jacob) would be prompted to curse them. For this reason he did not visit his father at frequent intervals. (Pesikta Rabbati)

    (a) Can you find in our sidra support for the view that Jacob never knew what the tribes had done to Joseph?

    (b) Cannot the verses 15–16–17 in chapter 50 be considered a contradiction of the opinion of the above-quoted Midrash on this point?

534

3.   Cf. Rashi on Genesis 49, 9 with the *Pesikta* quoted above:

"Judah is a lion's whelp; From the prey, my son, thou art gone up."

"He stooped down, he couched as a lion, and as a lioness; who shall rouse him up?"

"מטרף": ממה שחשדתיך (לז, לג) ב"טרף טרף יוסף, חיה רעה אכלתהו" — וזה יהודה שנמשל לאריה.

"עלית": סילקת את עצמך ואמרת (לז, כו): "מה בצע כי נהרג את אחינו".

"From the prey"—regarding that which I suspected you (Genesis 37, 33) in respect of: "Joseph is without doubt rent in pieces"; "an evil beast hath devoured him"—alluding to Judah who is likened to a lion.   (Rashi)

"Thou art gone up"—thou didst disassociate thyself and say "what profit is it if we slay our brother ..." (Genesis 37, 26)
                                                                (Rashi)

Can you explain this verse differently from Rashi in such a way that it will contain no contradiction to the view expressed in the *Pesikta?*

4.   "Then Joseph spoke to the house of Pharaoh saying: if I find favour in your eyes, kindly speak in the ears of Pharaoh ..."   (50, 4)

On this Sforno comments:

For one must not enter the king's gate dressed in sackcloth.

Can you suggest an alternative to Sforno's answer? Why did Joseph say to Pharaoh: "My father made me swear", rather than: "I swore to my father"?

535

RACHEL DIED UNTO ME

In our *Studies* of Vayigash (p. 500) we dealt with the entry of Jacob and his sons into Egypt. "With seventy souls did our fathers go down into Egypt". In this sidra we find ourselves on the eve of Jacob's death seventeen years after his arrival in Egypt. What was the situation of those seventy souls who had arrived there as immigrants? This is indicated to us in the last verse of Vayigash:

> **And Israel settled in the land of Egypt,**
> **in the land of Goshen;**
> **and they acquired holdings therein, and were fruitful, and**
> **greatly increased in numbers.** (46, 3)

Evidently then their situation was very rosy. They had settled in the land, grown rich and become thoroughly acclimatised, but it was just this that did not appeal to Jacob. It was this that he had been afraid of on the eve of his departure for Egypt when the Almighty had appeared to him and calmed his fears:

> **I am the Lord God of thy father fear not.** (47, 3)

He was not afraid of the persecution and the bondage that had been foretold to his forefather Abraham (15, 13) but rather of the wealth and prosperity that might turn their heads and cause them to repudiate their historic national destiny to leave Egypt for the Promised Land. That this was Jacob's chief concern is indicated quite clearly from his last words to his favourite son Joseph. He insisted that Joseph should bury his remains in the Holy Land as a perpetual reminder to his descen-

dants of their true homeland which they should always aspire
to reach. Let us compare the Divine message to Jacob at Beth-
El with the Patriarch's transmission of it to Joseph on his
deathbed.

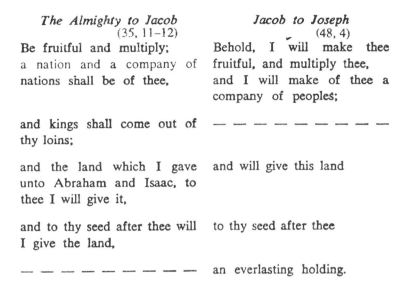

The Almighty to Jacob (35, 11–12)	*Jacob to Joseph* (48, 4)
Be fruitful and multiply; a nation and a company of nations shall be of thee,	Behold, I will make thee fruitful, and multiply thee, and I will make of thee a company of peoples;
and kings shall come out of thy loins;	— — — — — — — — —
and the land which I gave unto Abraham and Isaac, to thee I will give it,	and will give this land
and to thy seed after thee will I give the land,	to thy seed after thee
— — — — — — — — —	an everlasting holding.

The omission of the allusion to "the kings" who would come
forth from his loins is immediately conspicuous. According to
our commentators this was deliberately omitted since these kings
were destined to come from the tribe of Judah and therefore
had no place in Jacob's blessing to Joseph. But we may perhaps also suggest that Jacob left it out because such a promise
was not the one that he wanted to stress to Joseph and his sons
who had attained almost royal status in Egypt. His allusion
might therefore have been misinterpreted by them. On the contrary, the Patriarch emphasised the promise of the Holy Land
and the fact that it had been entrusted by the Almighty to his
descendants. The land of Canaan had been promised by God as
"an everlasting holding". These last two words were added by
Jacob as a significant antidote to his children's acclimatisation

and acquiring holdings in the land of Egypt. This was as if to
say that the foothold they had acquired in Egypt was illusory;
their permanent holding was the land promised them by God.

Jacob followed up his transmission of the Abrahamic blessing
to Joseph with the following words:

וַאֲנִי בְּבֹאִי מִפַּדָּן מֵתָה עָלַי רָחֵל
בְּאֶרֶץ כְּנַעַן בַּדֶּרֶךְ בְּעוֹד כִּבְרַת־אֶרֶץ לָבֹא אֶפְרָתָה
וָאֶקְבְּרֶהָ שָּׁם בְּדֶרֶךְ אֶפְרָת הִיא בֵּית לָחֶם.

**And as for me, when I came from Padan, Rachel died
unto me in the land of Canaan in the way, when there
was still some way to come unto Ephrath; and I buried
her there in the way to Ephrath—the same is Bethlehem.**
(48, 7)

At first sight this reminiscing of Jacob regarding the burial of
Rachel seems to have no connection with the context. Why
did Jacob find it necessary to remind Joseph that he had not
buried his mother in the Patriarchal tomb at Machpelah whilst
he was requesting him to bury his remains there? Our commentators put forward various explanations regarding the passage.
Most of them consider that Jacob was here excusing himself
before his son who may have thought that he had not paid the
full honour due to his mother in not bringing her remains to
Machpelah. Ramban explains the implication of Jacob's remarks as follows:

> The plain explanation is that Jacob spoke in an apologetic tone
> pleading with Joseph not to be angry with him for this last re-
> quest to bury him in the Cave of Machpelah on the grounds that
> he had not buried his mother there, though he had buried Leah
> there. For this reason he said to him that she had died in the
> land of Canaan and that she had not been buried outside the
> Holy Land as would be the case with Jacob if his remains were
> left in Egypt. Rachel, he explained, had died on the journey sud-
> denly and he had not been able to bury her in the family tomb.
> For how could he have left his children and cattle on the way
> and have gone quickly to the Cave of Machpelah? Where were

the embalmers and medicaments to embalm her? This is the implication of the word עלי ('unto me" or "upon me"). Though
the Cave of Machpelah was not more than half a day's journey from where Rachel died, Jacob was heavily burdened with
cattle and members of his household and would only have been
able to reach there in a number of days. Indeed it took him many
days until he reached his father's home.

Sforno, the Italian Jewish commentator who was a physician and
lived in the times of the Renaissance, suggests a psychological
motive for this neglect on Jacob's part. Commenting on this
verse he puts these words in Jacob's mouth:

> I was so overcome by my grief that I could not collect myself
> to take her to the ancestral tomb at Hebron, but there is no
> doubt that since then there has been a void in my heart.

The depth of Jacob's grief for Rachel is indeed expressed in
the phrase "Rachel died unto me" in accordance with the point
made by our Sages:

ואין אשה מתה אלא לבעלה שנאמר: "ואני בבאי מפדן מתה ע ל י רחל".

> A wife only dies for her husband (i.e. only a husband feels the
> full depth of grief), as it is stated: and as for me, when I came
> from Padan, Rachel died *unto me*.   (Sanhedrin 22b)

Ibn Ezra makes a similar point:

> Rachel died suddenly and I could not bury her in the Cave as I
> buried Leah. He mentioned this to Joseph that he should not be
> angry for asking him for something which he had not done on
> behalf of his mother.

But our Sages were not content with regarding Jacob as the
bereaved husband of Rachel. But to them he was the prototype
of the nation itself which was destined to go forth into exile
and suffer persecution and massacre. They concerned themselves
not with the immediate causes prompting Jacob's action but with

its ultimate purpose.[1] This symbolic interpretation is alluded to in Rashi on our verse:

"ואני": ואף על פי שאני מטריח עליך להוליכני להיקבר בארץ כנען ולא כך עשיתי לאמך, שהרי מתה סמוך לבית לחם.

"ואקברה שם": ולא הולכתיה אפילו לבית לחם להכניסה לארץ וידעתי שיש בלבך עלי, אבל דע לך שעל פי הדיבור קברתיה שם שתהא לעזרה לבניה כשיגלה אותם נבוזראדן והיו עוברים דרך שם יצאת רחל על קברה ובוכה ומבקשת עליהם רחמים, שנאמר (ירמיה לא, יד): "קול ברמה נשמע נהי בכי תמרורים רחל מבכה על־בניה מאנה להנחם על־בניה כי איננו", והקב"ה משיבה (ירמיה שם, טו—טז): "מנעי קולך מבכי ועיניך מדמעה כי יש שכר לפעולתך נאום־ה' ושבו מארץ אויב, ויש־תקוה לאחריתך נאם־ה' ושבו בנים לגבולם".

"And as for me"—though I trouble you to bring my remains to the land of Canaan, a thing which I did not do for your mother who died at Bethlehem—"And I buried her there"—and I did not even bear her remains to Bethlehem to bring her into the Holy land and I know that you have a grievance against me for this. But let it be known to you that I buried her there in accordance with the Divine command that she should be of assistance to her children in time to come. When Nebuzaradan will exile them they will pass by in that vicinity and Rachel will go forth on her grave and weep and intercede for them, as it is stated (Jeremiah 31. 15): "A voice is heard in Ramah, lamentation and bitter weeping. Rachel weeping for her children; she refuseth to be comforted for her children for they are not". The Holy One blessed be He will reply: "Refrain thy voice from weeping, and thine eyes from tears; thy work shall be rewarded, saith the Lord; and they shall come back from the land of the enemy. And there is hope for thy future, saith the Lord; and thy children shall return to their own border" (ibid).

Ramban too finds an allusion to this symbolic meaning in the verse, and after quoting Rashi adds:

At any rate there should be some allusion in the text to this idea. Perhaps to this the text alludes when it repeats "Rachel died unto me in the way ... and I buried her there in the way" implying in the way that her children were destined to pass did she die and there she was buried in their interests, since she had not actually died "in the way" but at 'Ramah" which is a town in the land of Benjamin and there she was buried, but what the

540

text meant to suggest was that she was buried at a spot where her descendants were destined to pass, when they were *on the way* going into exile. The text does not, however, explicitly refer to future events, but merely alludes to them.

Rachel then is pictured as the symbol of the Matriarch of Israel standing by to protect her descendants on their way into exile and interceding on their behalf for their eventual return to the homeland. The Patriarch himself did not want to be buried in Egypt in order to preclude his children settling for good there. The Matriarch was buried by him on the path destined to be followed by the Babylonian exiles so that she could intercede on their behalf for their return. Eretz Israel was always situated between two fires with enemies to the north and to the south. Allusions then to these dangers can be found in the sidra expressing the wish of the Patriarchs that their descendants should not be overcome by the bondage of Egypt nor perish in the Babylonian exile.

---

[1] Writers and poets have repeatedly described Rashi's impact on generations of Torah students, scholar and layman alike. In this context a reading of Shimshon Meltzer's ode to Rashi (*Ashira le-rashi*) is richly rewarding, in particular, p. 21 of his *Sefer Ha-shirot Veha-baladot*, Dvir, Tel Aviv 5713. There he weaves the Rashi we have quoted into a nostalgic description of the way the prince of Bible commentators was studied in the east-european *heder*.

SIMEON AND LEVI

שִׁמְעוֹן וְלֵוִי אַחִים
כְּלֵי חָמָס מְכֵרֹתֵיהֶם.
בְּסֹדָם אַל־תָּבֹא נַפְשִׁי
בִּקְהָלָם אַל־תֵּחַד כְּבֹדִי
כִּי בְאַפָּם הָרְגוּ אִישׁ
וּבִרְצֹנָם עִקְּרוּ־שׁוֹר.
אָרוּר אַפָּם כִּי עָז
וְעֶבְרָתָם כִּי קָשָׁתָה
אֲחַלְּקֵם בְּיַעֲקֹב
וַאֲפִיצֵם בְּיִשְׂרָאֵל.

Simeon and Levi are brethren;
Weapons of violence their kinship.
Let my soul not come in their council,
Unto their assembly let my glory not be united;
For in their anger they slew men,
And in their self-will they houghed oxen.
Cursed be their anger, for it was fierce,
And their wrath, for it was cruel;
I will divide them in Jacob,
And scatter them in Israel.   (49, 5–7)

Jacob took a very grave view of his sons' conduct. Many de-
cades after the massacre of Shechem, the Patriarch, on his
deathbed, severely reprimanded Simeon and Levi for their dread
deed, though all were now safely and comfortably settled in
Egypt. His indignation at the crime does not seem to have
diminished, with the passing of time. On the contrary, it seems

to have increased. What was Jacob's immediate reaction to the crime?

עֲכַרְתֶּם אֹתִי לְהַבְאִישֵׁנִי בְּיֹשֵׁב הָאָרֶץ
בַּכְּנַעֲנִי וּבַפְּרִזִּי
וַאֲנִי מְתֵי מִסְפָּר
וְנֶאֶסְפוּ עָלַי וְהִכּוּנִי
וְנִשְׁמַדְתִּי אֲנִי וּבֵיתִי.

Ye have troubled me, to make me odious unto the inhabitants of the land, even unto the Canaanites and Perizzites; and, I being few in number, they will gather themselves together against me and smite me; and I shall be destroyed, I and my house. (34, 30)

Jacob's first reaction was eminently practical. They had placed the whole family in danger, a minority surrounded by hostile tribes, far outnumbering them. But on his deathbed, no such consideration could exist. The House of Israel was secure, enjoying the protection of the Egyptian viceroy. His anger is now directed at the cruelty and injustice of their deed. Here is Ramban's explanation:[1]

Jacob implied that Simeon and Levi were brothers in deed and counsel. Jacob disapproved of their massacre of the Shechemites because, in so doing, they had committed violence against people who had done them no wrong but had, on the contrary, entered into a covenant with them and circumcised themselves. Perhaps they would sincerely acknowledge the true God and become part of the House of Abraham and of the souls they had gotten. The Patriarch was also disturbed at the defamation of the name of God that might ensue, that it might be thought, that the deed had been committed at his prompting, that a prophet of the Lord should be suspected of lending his hand to violence and pillage. This is the implication of the phrase: "Let my soul not come in their council"—disassociating himself from the deceit they practised, when they answered Shechem and Hamor with guile (34, 13). Similarly, he did not wish his glory to be united with their assembly, when they descended on the city to massacre its inhabitants. He therefore cursed their anger and wrath.

Two aspects of their deed angered Jacob—the *ḥillul hashem*, the desecration of the Divine name: "that a prophet of the Lord should be suspected of lending his hand to violence and pillage" and the iniquitousness of the deed itself. But the point may be made that Jacob's reaction ignored completely Simeon and Levi's own, publicly expressed motive: "Should one deal with our sister as with a harlot?" Did the Torah condemn out of hand any display of extreme zeal? Did Jacob condemn them just for the massacre of innocent people or did his denunciation include their killing of Shechem, the guilty one, without due process of law? Could not their deed be compared to that of Phinehas (Numbers 25, 7–8)? Here is the *Ha'amek Davar's* comment on the problem:

> Both Levi and Phinehas were prompted to an extreme act by the sight of immorality and endangered their lives in protest against it. Phinehas was praised and exalted for his action; Levi was rebuked by his father, and there are many parallels to this. This is the lesson taught us in the *Ethics of the Fathers*: "An unlearned man cannot be pious"—extreme exactitude and an unerring sense of judgement is required, before one may take the law into on's own hands, according to the time and place. The dictum applies to many matters in relation to rules of action, which are not plainly evident from the text of Scripture [2] (and therefore require painstaking study and a thorough knowledge of the sources of Judaism).

The time and place constitute the all-important considerations which clearly differentiate the deed of Phinehas from Levi's. In risking his life in order to strike down a prince of Israel Phinehas wished to shake the Jewish people out of their moral lethargy and put a stop to their immoral behaviour. Simeon and Levi's deed would only be seen in the light of an unjust massacre, by the surrounding nations and would accomplish no moral purpose. If this quality of zealousness is then so dangerous an asset, why did Jacob express his wish to scatter and disperse those endowed with it, among the rest of his sons? Here are two answers to this question:

Jacob here utters a truth which Aristotle has publicised in his *Ethics*. Anger and temper, though undesirable qualities may sometimes prove useful in arousing the heroic in man. Soldiers in battle are spurred to bravery and courage by anger and indignation. This idea is also expressed in the text (Isaiah 63, 5): "Mine own arm brought salvation unto Me, and My fury, it upheld Me". In other words, anger in extremes is detrimental, but in moderation, can be useful. Jacob had the same idea in mind. It was advisable that the qualities of anger and passion that had been concentrated in Simeon and Levi should be dispersed among all the tribes of Israel. All of them would share some of it. A little spread everywhere would prove useful, but if concentrated in one place, would be dangerous. (Akedat Yizḥak)

The dangers of extremism are particularly great at the height of a nation's power when a united and strong public can easily be influenced by the headstrong policies of two mighty tribes into an excessive display of zeal. But this is not the case when the nation is scattered and divided, in exile, suffering from persecution and reviled by others. Then the Jew, peddling his wares from house to house stands in need of that ingredient of zeal and passion, to be able to cherish his national self-respect and look down on his tormentors ... The Holy One blessed be He did his people a kindness by scattering the tribes of Simeon and Levi among the rest of the House of Israel, so that all its members should share some of that badly-needed courage and zeal and Jewish pride, even after the destruction of its state. (Hirsch)

The difference between the two foregoing explanations is this: The first one sees the danger in the qualities of zeal and hot-headedness being concentrated in too great an intensity and being only destructive. But in moderation, they were useful and, indeed, an essential ingredient of national life. The second sees the dangers of zeal being particularly great when the nation is free and strong, settled in its own land. But the qualities condemned by Jacob in Simeon and Levi were vital for the nation groaning under an alien yoke, giving it the courage and fortitude to withstand and outlive the oppressor.

Questions for Further Study

1. The phrase: "Simeon and Levi are brethren" is given yet another emphasis in Ramban:

    > It implies that they were full of brotherly feeling, since they were full of compassion for the plight of their sister. The text speaks favourably of them in that their zeal was inspired by brotherly love. Consequently they did not deserve a severe punishment. On the other hand, their crime was one which could not be passed over, since they had committed violence.

    What is the difference between Ramban's two explanations of the word: "brothers"?

2. Explain the meaning of the phrase we quoted from Ramban on page 543 which states: "and of the souls they had gotten" (cf.: Genesis 12, 5).

3. אפילו בשעת תוכחה לא קילל אלא את אפם וזהו שאמר בלעם (במדבר כג, ח): "מה אקוב לא קבה אל ?"

    > "Cursed be their anger, for it was fierce"—Even at a time of reproof he only cursed their anger. To this Balaam referred when he stated (Numbers 23, 8): "How shall I curse, whom God hath not cursed?"   (Rashi)

    What idea is contained in Rashi and what moral lesson may we extract from it?

4. Compare Moses' blessing to the tribe of Levi (Deuteronomy, 33, 8–11) with Jacob's blessing here of Simeon and Levi. What difference do you find and what do you think could be the reason for the difference?

---

1 Ramban's view of Simeon and Levi's conduct has been elaborated on in our *Studies* on "The Story of Dinah" on pp. 380ff.
2 The dangers of zealotry even when time and circumstance seems to call for it are expounded by the author of *Haamek Davar* in his com-

546

ment on Deut. 33, 8 *s.v. Ve-urekha* "Thy oracles to Thy pious ones":
"In the context of performing the commandments with extra piety,
the public display of devotion and religious faith calls for especial
caution. This was the force of Moses's blessing to the tribe of Levi
in his use of the words: *ve-urekha*, literally: "Thy light" expressing
the hope that their piety would be inspired by the sincerest of motives and illumined by the true light of the Torah and not mislead
them into committing acts ultimately repugnant to the Torah."

WAITING FOR THY SALVATION

The statement: "For Thy salvation I do wait, Lord" (49, 18) which stands between the blessing of Dan and Gad, has puzzled all the commentators. Jacobs speaks in the first person, only in his reprimanding of the first three of his sons ("my first-born", "my strength" "my soul" "my glory" "I shall divide them" "I shall scatter them"). This phenomenon reappears in the blessing of Joseph where the link between the paternal blesser and the son blessed is given special emphasis in the mention of the two names of the Patriarch—Jacob and Israel and the double allusion to "thy father", But the "I" of the blesser does not appear or is not even remotely alluded to in the blessing addressed to the other brothers. The blessings (or perhaps prophecies) are all recorded in the third person. For this reason our text appears to violate the framework of the whole. Let us see it in context:

דָּן יָדִין עַמּוֹ
כְּאַחַד שִׁבְטֵי יִשְׂרָאֵל.
יְהִי־דָן נָחָשׁ עֲלֵי־דֶרֶךְ
שְׁפִיפֹן עֲלֵי־אֹרַח
הַנֹּשֵׁךְ עִקְּבֵי־סוּס
וַיִּפֹּל רֹכְבוֹ אָחוֹר.
לִישׁוּעָתְךָ קִוִּיתִי יְיָ.
גָּד גְּדוּד יְגוּדֶנּוּ
וְהוּא יָגֻד עָקֵב.

Dan shall judge his people as one of the tribes of Israel. Dan shall be a serpent in the way, a horned snake in the path, that biteth the horse's heels so that his rider falleth backwards.

For Thy salvation do I wait O Lord.
Gad, a troop shall be upon him, but he shall troop upon
their head.
(49, 16–19)

Does our verse belong to Dan's blessing, constituting its conclusion or to God's, constituting its beginning? Most commentators take the first view, but they are divided over the question
of speaker. Rashi following the Sages regards these words as the
prayer destined to be offered up by Samson, Jacob citing it pro-
phetically.

"דן ידין עמו": ינקום נקמת עמו מפלשתים, כמו (דברים לב, לו): "כי ידין
ה' עמו". "כאחד שבטי ישראל": כל ישראל יהיו כאחד עמו ואת כולם ידין,
ועל שמשון ניבא נבואה זו.
"שפיפון": הוא נחש. ואומר אני שקרוי כך על שם שהוא נושף, כמו
(בראשית ג, טו): "ואתה תשופנו עקב".
"ויפל רוכבו אחור": שלא נגע בו. ודוגמתו מצאנו בשמשון (שופטים טז,
כט—ל): "וילפות שמשון את שני עמודי התוך אשר הבית נכון עליהם ויסמך
עליהם . . . ויט בכוח ויפל הבית על הסרנים ועל כל העם", ושעל הגג מתו.
"לישועתך קויתי ה'": נתנבא שינקרו פלשתים את עיניו וסופו לומר (שופטים
טז, כח): "זכרני נא וחזקני נא אך הפעם הזה האלהים".

"Dan shall judge his people"—avenge his people of the Philistines ... "as one of the tribes of Israel"—all the tribes of Israel", all Israel will be united with him and he will judge them
all—this message he prophesised concerning Samson.
  "... so that his rider falleth backward" whom it (i.e. the
snake), did not touch. A parallel is to be found in Samson
(Judges 16, 29) when he grasped hold of the pillars and those
on the roof died.
"For Thy salvation do I wait O Lord"—he prophesied that the
Philistines would pluck out his eyes and that he was destined
to say: "O Lord God remember me and strengthen me, only
this once O God..."

But according to other commentators, these words were not
Samson's but Jacob's who, just because he foresaw the exploits
of Samson was prompted to apply directly to God in his prayer
(notice that the name of God has not hitherto been mentioned
in the blessings!). Jacob's appeal to God, after being vouchsafed a vision of Samson's career may be explained in two

549

ways. Some regard Samson's cruel fate as that which prompted Jacob to shift from expectation of mortal salvation to that coming from the Lord.

> The text "a horned snake that biteth the horse's heels so that the rider falleth backwards" implies that the snake itself will of necessity be killed as well by the horse falling upon it after its hind leg has been bitten, the rider attacking it after he has been thrown from the smitten horse. Similarly, Samson's last exploit involved sacrificing his own life in dying with the Philistine whose death he himself had encompassed. Since a deliverance involving the death of the deliverer is no true salvation, the Lord is addressed with the words: "For Thy salvation do I hope O Lord", it being comparable to the text (Deut. 33, 29) "Happy art thou O Israel, who is like thee saved of the Lord". For those saved by the Lord are privileged to behold the presence of the living King.
>
> (Akedat Yiẓḥak)

Others regard Jacob's expression of the limitations of human capacity to save as prompted by a vision of Samson as the symbol of the end of an epoch.

Ramban observes:

> No other Israelite judge fell into the hands of the enemy like Samson, who was alluded to in the symbol of the snake, as the text bears witness: "And the Lord was with the judge and saved them from the hands of their enemies all the days of the judge" (Ju. 2, 18), and Samson was the last of the judges; for Samuel was a prophet and did no fighting for them. In his days the kings reigned. When the prophet saw that Samson's deliverance had come to an end, he said, "For Thy salvation do I hope O Lord" —not for the salvation of a snake, but in Thee is salvation and not the judge; for Thy salvation is an eternal one.

Accordingly, it was not Samson and his exploits that aroused Jacob to appeal to God and seek salvation for his people but, on the contrary, the end of the Samsonian epoch and that of the judges, as a whole, that prompted Jacob to seek his salvation from the Lord.

But the Pentateuchal Tosaphist gloss *Da'at Hazekenim* regards

Samson's very exploits as indicative of the limitations of man, even the mightiest. It was not just his tragic end, the moment of his fall that made Jacob realise that, but he appreciated it even during the height of his prowess:

> As soon as Jacob saw the might of Samson he felt it was not seemly to boast of it. So we find in the text that Samson boasted of his prowess with the jawbone of the ass and then "became very thirsty" (Ju. 15, 14–19) till he admitted and said to the Lord: "Thou hast given this great deliverance by the hand of Thy servant". He acknowledged that might comes from God alone. Similarly Dan's blessing runs: "Dan shall be a serpent in the way, a horned snake in the path". Notwithstanding, might and victory is the Lord's, as is written immediately afterwards: "For Thy salvation do I hope O Lord".

But many of our commentators do not regard the snake and horned snake as symbolising a specific individual but the whole tribe of Dan. In the forefront of this approach is Rashbam who, as customary, castigates those who do not share it, aiming his shafts particularly at his grandfather, Rashi whom, out of respect, he does not mention by name:

> The one who interpreted the text as applying to Samson did not grasp the profundity of the Scriptures in its plain sense. Did Jacob come to prophesy regarding one single individual who fell into the hands of the Philistines and had his eyes plucked out by them, meeting together with them an evil end? Far be it! But he referred to the tribe of Dan which was the rearguard of all the camps about whom Joshua wrote (Josh. 6, 9): "and the rearward went after the ark". Since it went behind all the standards, both under Moses and Joshua, and had to fight all nations, pursuing after them to harass the stragglers at the rear and avenge their depredations, for they were mighty men, Jacob states: "Dan shall judge his people", in other words, avenge his people, "all the tribes of Israel, as one, together". Cf. Deut. 32, 36–43: "For the Lord will judge His people" ("judge" in the sense of "avenge") or Ps. 110, 6: "He shall judge the peoples...". "His rider falleth" —his enemies shall fall before him. "For Thy salvation" O Dan "do I hope O Lord", in other words: I hope that the Lord will save thee and exalt thee over the nations."

Rabbi Abraham, Maimonides' son [1] shares this approach, though leaving the question of the reference to Samson or the tribe of Dan open.

> "The text implies that Dan adopted guerilla tactics, ambushes and not the open warfare of Judah who won in pitched battles as in David's challenge of Goliath. An allusion to Samson judging Israel (Ju. 16, 31) can be found in the reference to all the tribes of Israel. The text may be read "Dan shall judge his people and the tribes of Israel as one", referring to their acceptance of Samson's leadership, comparing his slaying of the Philistines to the bite of a serpent just as the bravery of David of the tribe of Judah was likened to a lion tearing its prey. How apt are these comparisons in this prophecy! David's prowess in battle, being open, is compared to a lion, whereas Samson's relying on cunning, taking them unawares, is compared to a serpent...
>
> The passage "For Thy salvation do I hope O Lord" is a prayer offered up on behalf of Samson that God should save him from the Philistines, after he had fallen into their clutches. The text indeed notes that he subsequently killed more at his death than during his lifetime. Since he compared them to a snake which can only elude its victim so long as it takes it unawares, so he prayed for the safety of the camp of Dan, or if the allusion is to Samson, for Samson, to save them from the danger they courted...

But there are some commentators, a small minority, who regard our text not as the conclusion to Dan's blessing but the beginning of Gad's. Luzzato's explanation along these lines is strange:

> When Jacob came to bless Gad he was prompted, as in the case of Dan, to employ a pun and exploit the association of the word Gad with its etymological meaning of "luck" (just as Dan means "judge"). But he immediately thought better of it, emphasising, on the contrary, that it was proper to trust in God alone and not in the stars. He therefore proclaimed: "For Thy salvation do I hope O Lord" and not in that of fortune. And then he immediately bethought himself of another association of the word *gad*, in the sense of "troop"...

But this explanation sounds forced. Benno Jacob cites a different interpretation but likewise linking our text with Gad's

blessing. Perhaps this invocation of the help of God was meant
in anticipation of Moses' appeal to the tribe of Gad to join their
brothers in conquering the Promised Land and fight alongside in
exchange for the inheritance on the east bank of the Jordan
that they so desired because of its fertility. It may be recalled
that the two and a half tribes did not mention the name of God
at all their proposal,[2] formulating a purely commercial *quid pro
quo* transaction. Moses in recapitulating their proposal subtly
reproved them for this omission by introducing the name of
heaven no less than six times ("if you will go armed *before the
Lord* and all the armed men shall pass over the Jordan *before
the Lord* ... and the land is conquered *before the Lord* ...).
Jacob links the patriarch's invocation of Divine salvation at the
beginning of Gad's blessing with Moses' words to the sons of
Gad and their implication that it was not their battles and
conquests and armed participation that would bring salvation,
but the Lord.

Accordingly, with all their differences of approach, all the
commentators share the view that the underlying message of
the text is the same. Jacob wished to place all the future visions
of his children's greatness and might, the rule and wisdom of
Judah, the cunning and prowess of Dan, the martial qualities
and courage of Gad, the wealth of Asher, in the perspective of
ultimate trust in God on whom all these achievements would
ultimately and exclusively depend.

The Sages distilled this message from Isaiah 45, 17: "Israel
will be saved by the Lord an everlasting salvation."

אמרה כנסת ישראל לפני הקב"ה: אין לי ישועה אלא בך ואין עיני מייחלות
אלא לך. אמר להם הקב"ה: "ישראל נ ו ש ע ב ה ' תשועת עולמים, לא
תבושו ולא תכלמו עד עולמי עד".

The assembly of Israel addressed the Holy One blessed be He:
I have no salvation but in Thee and my eyes are turned in expectation only to Thee. The Holy One blessed be He answered
them: Since that is so, I shall save thee, as it is stated: "Israel
is saved by the Lord an everlasting salvation, you shall not be
ashamed or confounded world without end."

(Yalkut Shimoni 2, 839)

553

Questions for Further Study

1. The text compares Dan to a serpent that goes alone and kills many,
    and not like other beasts that usually hunt in groups. Similarly
    Samson went alone and killed many of the enemies of Israel.
    To this Jacob referred in the words: "For Thy salvation do I
    hope O Lord", since such a salvation where one vanquishes many
    thousands can only be from God.   (Redak)

    Explain whether Redak's approach is identical with any
    of the views cited in our *Studies* or whether it follows its
    own specific viewpoint which has nothing in common with
    any expressed here.

2. "For Thy salvation do I hope, O Lord": Jacob was addressing
    Dan: O Dan! I hope for the Lord to save you and deliver you
    from your enemies. An alternative explanation: "For Thy salva-
    tion" that you yourself will perform, that you shall save Israel,
    as it is written: "He will begin to save Israel" (Judges 13, 5).
                                                           (Ḥizkuni)

    (a) What is the difference between the two explanations
        in their understanding of the word ישועתך "Thy sal-
        vation"?
    (b) In what way is the latter explanation different from
        all the others we have cited?

3. Why did Rashi (on p. 549) understand the word ידין in
    the sense of "avenge" rather than "judge"?

4. What is the difference between the Rashi and Ramban's
    interpretation of the verse? What prompted Jacob to utter
    these words at this juncture according to each of the above
    commentators?

5. What has the comment of Rambam's son (p. 552) in
    common with Rashbam's and where do they differ?

---

1 The Arabic commentary of Rambam's son, Abraham to Genesis and

Exodus was first published from an Oxford MS by Rabbi Suleiman David Sassoon (London 5718) annotated with Hebrew translation by Professor A.I. Weisenberg.

2 For an analysis of the debate between Moses and the two tribes and the difference between their respective proposals see "Studies in *Bamidbar* pp. 379ff.

WHAT IF JOSEPH HATES US

וַיִּרְאוּ אֲחֵי־יוֹסֵף כִּי־מֵת אֲבִיהֶם
וַיֹּאמְרוּ: לוּ יִשְׂטְמֵנוּ יוֹסֵף
וְהָשֵׁב יָשִׁיב לָנוּ אֵת כָּל־הָרָעָה אֲשֶׁר גָּמַלְנוּ אֹתוֹ

**When Joseph's brethren saw that their father was dead,
they said: It may be that Joseph will hate us, and will
fully requite us all the evil we did unto him.**   (50, 15)

This one verse raises a host of problems and questions. Jacob
had died, deeply mourned, laid to rest in his native land, after
a magnificent state funeral. "And Joseph went up to bury his
father; and with him went up all the servants of Pharaoh, the
elders of his house, and all the elders of the land of Egypt, and
all the host of Joseph and his brethren, and his father's house.
And there went up with him both chariots and horsemen; and
it was a very great company." It was a "grievous mourning";
eulogies were made and his sons bore the bier to the cave of
Machpelah, in accordance with his last wish. After all these
inner and outward trappings of woe, after "Joseph returned
into Egypt", many weeks after the Patriarch's death, the text
blandly informs us: "And when Joseph's brethren *saw* that their
father was dead..." Had they hitherto not seen it? It is obvious
that the text is here referring to an inward awareness of the
consequences of their father's death, rather than the physical
fact of his demise. They realised that all was not the same as
it had been, that certain things had changed:

"וַיִּרְאוּ אֲחֵי יוֹסֵף כִּי מֵת אֲבִיהֶם": מה "וַיִּרְאוּ"? הכירו במיתתו אצל יוסף,
שהיו רגילים לסעוד על שולחנו של יוסף והיה מקרבן בשביל כבוד אביו,
ומשמת יעקב לא קרבן.

"And when Joseph's brethren saw that their father was dead". What does the text mean by "saw"? They perceived the effects of his death on Joseph. They were used to ·dining with Joseph, the latter keeping on close terms with them out of respect for his father. As soon as Jacob died, he ceased to be on close terms with them. (Rashi)

Let us try to trace the source for Rashi's interpretation. Our Sages propounded various views on this text:

ר' לוי אמר: שלא זימנן לסעודה. אמר ר' תנחומא: הוא לא נתכוון אלא לשם שמים; אמר: לשעבר אבא מושיבני למעלה מיהודה שהוא מלך ולמעלה מראובן שהוא בכור, עכשיו אינו בדין שאשב למעלה מהם. והם לא אמרו כן, אלא: "לו ישטמנו יוסף".

R. Levi said: He (Joseph) no longer invited them to dine with him. Said R. Tanḥuma: He was inspired by the purest of motives (literally: "meant it for the sake of Heaven"). He said: Formerly, Father used to seat me higher than Judah who is king, and higher than Reuben who is the firstborn. Now it is not right that I should sit higher than them. But they understood matters differently and said: "It may be that Joseph will hate us . . ."
(Bereshit Rabbah 100, 8)

Rashi did not wish to echo Rabbi Tanḥuma's special pleading on behalf of Joseph, the unconvincing nature of which hardly allows us to exonerate him. Why, in any case, had Joseph any need to change the usual order of seating? Why didn't he sit with them, if he did not wish to continue the old seating arrangement instituted by his father? Rashi therefore preferred not to resort to this special pleading, but assumed that Joseph was in view of the circumstances behaving naturally. Now that his father had died, public affairs and the burden of state overshadowed family matters; each one repaired to his own business, the focal point of their family interest having disappeared.

A really competent commentator will endeavour to explain each point and passage in the light of the context, against the whole background of the story, its atmosphere and plot. The previous chapters depict Joseph, from the moment his father and brothers arrived in Egypt, as behaving as the ideal brother and son respecting his father, and using his power not to dominate but to serve the family interest. His speech of recognition (45, 4–13) is pervaded by a tone of forgiveness, of let bygones be bygones, as is his solicitude for his family's livehood ("And Joseph sustained his father and brothers and all this father's household with bread according to the want of their little ones" — 47, 12). We cannot detect the slightest hint of vengeance or of highhandedness. In what then did R. Levi base his assumption that Joseph began to become estranged and cold towards his brothers, from the moment their father died? For this reason, R. Isaac endeavoured to find another explanation of the phrase "when Joseph's brethren saw."

אמר ר' שמעון: בתורה בנביאים ובכתובים מצינו שאדם צריך לצאת ידי הבריות כדרך שהוא יוצא ידי המקום. מן התורה מניין? שנאמר (במדבר לב, כב): "והייתם נקיים מה' ומישראל"... וכן הוא אומר: "ויראו אחי יוסף כי מת אביהם", מה ראו? אמר ר' יצחק: ראו את יוסף כשחזר מלקבור אביו, הלך והציץ בתוך הבור, והוא לא נתכוון אלא לשם שמים. אמר: כמה נפלאות עשה לי הקב"ה שהצילני מן הבור הזה — והם לא ידעו מה היה בלבו ואמרו: "לו ישטמנו".

Said R. Simeon. In the Pentateuch, Prophets and Hagiographa we find exemplified the principle that man must satisfy the conscience of his fellows, just as he must satisfy God. Where in the Pentateuch?—as it is stated (Nu. 32, 22): "and ye shall be clear before the Lord and before Israel." It is likewise stated: "Joseph's brethren saw that their father was dead." What had they seen? Said R. Isaac: They saw Joseph on his way back from burying his father, go and peep into the pit (into which they had cast him), though he had been inspired by the purest of motives (literally: "meant it for the sake of Heaven.") He (Joseph) said: How many wonders did the Almighty perform for me when He delivered me from this pit! But they, not knowing what had gone through his mind, said: "It may be that Joseph will hate us..."   (Mishnat R. Eliezer, Torah Shelemah)

This Midrash contains an important message. Had Joseph conducted himself rightly? Bahya, the great medieval Jewish moralist dwells; in each of the "gates" of his *Duties of the Heart* on the importance of remembering, at all times and seasons, the bounty and kindnesses of our Creator. He has penetratingly described for us how man is reluctant to acknowledge his gratitude for the good fortune and happiness bestowed on him, by the source of all good.

> Many blindly ignore them (i.e. the kindnesses of God) out of their deep preoccupation with worldly pleasures and the material enjoyments and satisfactions they can derive therefrom. The more they achieve, the more they desire, the abundant benefits they have been granted receding in importance and the most bountiful gifts counting for little, till they imagine that only the good enjoyed by the other man is being withheld from them.
>
> (Sha'ar Habeḥina)

Baḥya frequently alludes to this weakness of man in taking his good fortune for granted, accepting it as "natural" or accidental, failing to acknowledge His Creator as the source of all his bounty. In the all-important debate between the intelligence and the soul in the gate of "The Service of God", Baḥya explains the reason for the lack of appreciation in man's approach to God.

> The second attribute consists of your failing to acknowledge the kindness of the Creator towards you, in granting you benefits, both open and unawares... and the third in not knowing yourself, imagining that you deserve the distinction of all these favours.

The prosperous and comfortable have always to be on their guard against the dangers of complacency and ingratitude. The Midrash illustrates this with reference to Joseph. He wanted to remind himself of the good fortune bestowed on him by the Almighty. He therefore turned aside from his path to have a look at the pit, in order to recall, during his period of greatness, the moments of despair and humiliation he had suffered, when he had been on the brink of death, had not the Almighty saved him. Though Joseph here did not conduct himself according to the pattern of the average man depicted by Baḥya, but behaved in an apparently ideal and model fashion, the Midrash nevertheless found fault with his action. He should have taken account of not only his own spiritual needs and duties towards

559

his Creator, but also of his brothers' feelings. When the latter
saw him standing over the ill-famed pit, they were seized with
dread: "It may be that Joseph will hate us . . ." Joseph did not
observe the Pentateuchal principle of "ye shall be clear before
God and man." But on hearing the message sent him by his
brothers who had been afraid or ashamed to speak to him face
to face, on being apprised of their request, and the parental testament they had fabricated, he wept. Why? The Midrash suggests
that it was because they had suspected him of bearing a grudge
and harbouring designs against them. When his brothers came
to see him in person, he answered them:

אַל־תִּירָאוּ, כִּי הֲתַחַת אֱלֹהִים אָנִי?

Fear not, for am I in God's stead?

His father Jacob had uttered these very same words, in another
context, and with another implication. The patriarch's "am
I in God's stead" had been condemned, whereas Joseph's was
lauded as a proof of his righteousness.

Jacob had shirked responsibility in these words, rejecting his
wife's Rachel's request to pray for her in time of trouble and
share her distress, on the grounds of man's incompetence and
his limitations in the matter concerned. He had adopted this
pose of humbleness and inadequacy in order to absolve himself
of all responsibility. Joseph, on the other hand, uttered this expression of inadequacy and self-abasement in order to save his
brothers' feelings and reassure them. It was not for him to judge
them; the judgement was God's.

The Midrash contrasts these two identical statements of "Am
I in God's stead" condemning one and lauding the other:

אמרה רחל ליעקב (בראשית ל, א—ב): "הבה לי בנים ואם מתה אנכי.
ויחר אף יעקב ברחל ויאמר: התחת אלהים אנכי". ורוח הקודש אומרת (איוב
טו, ב): "החכם יענה דעת רוח" — אמר יעקב לרחל: וכי אנטי־קיסר [משנה
לקיסר] של הקב"ה אני? אמר לו הקב"ה: חייך, בלשון שאמרת: "התחת
אלהים אני" בו בלשון בנה עומד ואומר לבניך": "התחת אלהים אנכי".

560

Said Rachel to Jacob (30, 1-2): "Give me children, or else I die. And Jacob's anger was kindled against Rachel; and he said: Am I in God's stead...?" Whereupon the Holy Spirit said: "Should a wise man make answer with windy knowledge?" Said Jacob to Rachel: Am I then the Holy One blessed be He's vice-regent? Said the Holy One blessed be He to him: By your life, her son will stand forth and utter the very same expression that you used: "Am I in God's stead?" (Tanḥuma)

Questions for Further Study

1. "Thy father did command before he died, saying: So shall ye say unto Joseph: Forgive, I pray thee now, the transgression of thy brethren, their sin, for that they did unto thee evil. And now, we pray thee, forgive the transgression of the servants of the God of thy father."

    (Gen. 50, 17)

    Rashi comments on the above passage that "they altered matters for the sake of peace, since Jacob had not so commanded, because he did not suspect Joseph's intentions." This view is shared by most commentators. The super-commentary *Divrei David* asks how indeed can we be so sure that Jacob did not so command, though it was not explicitly related in the text. Surely we can accept the testimony of the brethren! This commentary refers us to Ramban's observation in Leviticus 9, 2, on the text: "Take thee a bull-calf..."

    (a) Try to answer his question.

    (b) What resemblance to our case can be found in the text in Leviticus 9, 2?

2. In *Vayeshev*, in the description of Joseph's sufferings at the hands of his brethren we do not find that he actually wept. But during his period of greatness, in *Mikez*, we find him reported as weeping on a number of occasions:

"And he wept aloud" (45, 2); "And he fell upon his brother's neck and wept" (ibid. 14); "And he kissed all his brethren, and wept upon them" (ibid. 15). Explain in what way his weeping in our context (50, 17) resembles the foregoing ones.

TRUTH GIVES WAY TO PEACE

Is it permissible to deviate from the literal truth for the sake of peace? As a point of departure let us take two verses in our sidra which mark the end of the story of Joseph and his brethren begun in *Vayeshev*. In *Vayigash* we noted how harmony had once more returned to the house of Jacob, a spirit of pardon and reconciliation characterising Joseph's words to his brothers after he had made himself known to them. Yet what do we find after Jacob's death?

> **When the brothers of Joseph saw that their father was dead, they said,**
> **Peradventure Joseph will hate us and will fully requite us all the evil we did unto him.**
> **So they sent a message unto Joseph saying,**
> **Thy father did command before he died saying,**
> **So shall ye say unto Joseph,**
> **Forgive now I pray thee the transgression of thy brethren and their sin.** (50, 15–17)

A strange testament is this! At the beginning of the sidra we were told of Jacob's deathbed message. If he had wished to add this, why hadn't he done so? Is it conceivable that he would have entrusted the brothers with such a message and left Joseph out? According to Luzzato, Joseph immediately divined that his father had left no such message:

> He understood that the brothers had instructed the messenger what to say; otherwise Jacob would have told him himself. Joseph therefore wept at seeing the tragic state of his brothers, going in fear of their lives and forced to such shifts to stave off his vengeance.

Another objection may be raised against the authenticity of his testament: Did Jacob ever find out what the brothers had done to Joseph? The Torah affords us no clue that he ever found out. Had he ever found out, surely he would, in some way, have referred to it and reproved his sons even indirectly, just as he alluded to Reuben, Simeon and Levi's misconduct?

The *Pesikta Rabbati* is so convinced that Joseph never divulged his brother's meanness and cruelty to his father, that it uses this fact to explain another problem raised by the text: "one told Joseph, Behold thy father is sick" (48, 1):

> Behold all Joseph's praiseworthiness consisted of the great respect he paid his father, ye he did not visit him frequently! For were it not for the fact that others came to tell him, Father is sick, wouldn't he have known? The purpose of this is however to make known to you his righteousness, that he did not want to be alone with his father that he should not say to him, What did your brothers do to you and he (Jacob) would be prompted to curse them. For this reason he refrained from paying frequent visits to his father.

Accordingly, our Sages maintained that Jacob left no such message and it could never have even occurred to him. Rashi similarly comments:

> "אביך צוה": שינו בדבר מפני השלום, כי לא ציוה יעקב כן, שלא נחשד יוסף בעיניו.

> The brothers deviated from the truth for the sake of peace; for Jacob had given no such command, since Joseph was not suspect by him of committing any injury to them.

Ramban says as follows (on 45, 27):

> It seems to me that the plain meaning of the text is that Jacob was never told of the sale of Joseph by his brothers, but imagined that he got lost in the fields and was sold by his finders to Egypt. His brothers did not wish to divulge their misconduct, especially, for fear of his curse and anger. Joseph out of his good nature also did not wish to tell his father. That is why the text states that "they sent a message to Joseph, saying, thy father commanded

564

before his death saying, Forgive now I pray thee the transgressions of thy brethren". Had Jacob known all the time, they should have begged their father on his deathbed to command Joseph to forgive them and not violate his word. They would not then have had to endanger themselves and wouldn't have had to fabricate the message.

But neither of these commentators deal with the problem whether it is permissible to behave in this way. After the brothers had realised their guilt, if they still imagined that Joseph harboured any designs against them surely they were, obliged to accept any punishment he would mete out on them? This question is dealt with by our Sages in the Midrash:

ר' שמעון בן גמליאל אומר : גדול השלום, שאף השבטים דיברו דברים בדויים בשביל להטיל שלום בין יוסף לשבטים. הה"ד : "ויצוו אל יוסף לאמר : אביך צוה וכו'" — והיכן ציוה ? לא מצינו שציוה !

R. Shimon b. Gamliel said: Great is peace, for even the tribes uttered fabrications in order to promote peace between themselves and Joseph, as it is written: "And they sent a messenger unto Joseph saying, Thy father did command." For where did he command? We do not find that he so commanded.

(Bereshit Rabbah 100, 9)

This problem is one that forms part of a larger question of principle. Are there any situations which entitle one to depart from strict adherence to the truth or perhaps even demand it? What the Midrash discusses from the point of view of desirability or otherwise, the Talmud treats from the point of view of obligation and permissibility.

אמר ר' אילעא משום ר' אלעזר בר' שמעון : מותר לו לאדם לשנות בדבר שלום, שנאמר : "אביך צוה . . . כה תאמרו ליוסף אנא שא נא". ר' נתן אומר : מצוה ! [לא רק מותר לשנות מפני השלום, אלא מצוה], שנאמר (שמ"א טז, ב): "ויאמר שמואל : איך אלך ושמע שאול והרגני. ויאמר ה' : עגלת בקר תקח בידך ואמרת וכו'" (ר ש "י : הקב"ה ציוה לשנות).

Said R. Ila'a in the name of R. Eleazar b. R. Shimon: It is permissible for a man to deviate from the true facts in the interests of peace, as it said, "Thy father did command..." R. Nathan said: It is in the nature of an obligation (*miẓvah*) as it is stated: "And Samuel said, How can I go? if Saul hear it he will kill me. Whereupon the Lord said, Take a heifer with thee and say..." (the Holy One bade him deviate from the truth' — Rashi).

(Yevamot 65b)

The incident from which our Sages deduce our obligation to deviate from the truth is even more puzzling than our text. What is related in 1 Samuel 16 after God had withdrawn his support from Saul as king of Israel? Samuel was despatched to crown a new king:

And the Lord said unto Samuel, How long wilt thou mourn for Saul, seeing I have rejected him from being king over Israel? fill thy horn with oil and go, I will send thee to Jesse the Beth-lehemite; for I have provided Me a king among his sons. And Samuel said, How can I go? If Saul hear it he will kill me. Whereupon the Lord said, Take a heifer with thee and say, I am come to sacrifice to the Lord.

Now here we are not dealing with Jacob's terrified and anxious sons whose shift was prompted by their fear, but with the Lord Himself! Our commentators have noted this. Here is Abravanel's wording of the problem:

How could Samuel say this when he should have trusted in the mercies of God which are never ending? Moses never suggested that he was afraid of Pharaoh slaying him. God should have reproved Samuel for this. Why did He not say, "Fear not for I am with thee, and I have made thee for a fortress and pillar of iron" as He said to Jeremiah? Instead He suggested to Samuel a subterfuge: "Take a heifer with thee and say..." This was certainly inadequate.

We are not dealing here with Samuel's fear but with the subterfuge which God suggested to Samuel which involved deviating from the truth. Radak, however attempts to explain the answer of the Almighty by indicating that no deviation from the truth is involved, but on the contrary, extraordinary frankness:

> The Holy One blessed be He said, I told you to go quietly, yet you object saying, "How can I go? if Saul hear it, he will kill me." Now I tell you to go publicly and take a heifer to make a sacrifice on the day you anoint him king. This is what is implied by the text: "and called Jesse to the sacrifice". He said to him, Go publicly and see who will kill you! The Midraṣh similarly explains what the Almighty told (Exodus 17, 5) Moses to "pass through his people", after Móses had said to Him: "A little more and they will stone me." Said the Holy One blessed be He: Pass through this people and see who will stone you!

In other words, Abravanel misunderstood the text as did all other commentators, when they imagined the Divine message to imply any deviation from the truth or a subterfuge. On the contrary, He bade him do his mission publicly and not quietly. The latter explanation however does not fit in with the plain sense of the text. If the Divine message was meant as a rebuke to Samuel and not to placate him, it was his duty to anoint the son of Jesse publicly, since this was precisely what he was afraid of doing. Whereas the text states: Give your visit another aim; say you come on different business: say "I am come to sacrifice to the Lord". This is what Abravanel calls a "subterfuge".

We therefore prefer Baḥya's words in *Hovot Halevavot* ("Duties of the Heart") who does not wish to cover up the Almighty's instruction by deviating from the plain sense of the narrative, who does not wish to make allowances, as it were, for the conduct of God but learn rather from His ways:

> He who takes his own life forsakes the service of God and goes over to the enemy ... Consequently you find Samuel saying: "How can I go? if Saul hear he will kill me". This was not considered as displaying any lack of faith in God. The Divine answer indicated that his caution was praiseworthy, ordering him: "Take a heifer ..." Had this been a sign of lack of faith, the answer would have been: I kill and make alive or something similar, as He said to Moses: "Who maketh articulate the dumb ..." And if Samuel, in the perfection of his righteousness would not stretch a point and court the slightest danger,

even though it would have been at the behest of his Creator who said to him: "Fill thy horn with oil and go, I will send thee", how much more reprehensible would it be for anyone else to do such thing, except at the behest of God!

In other words, Bahya maintains that God really did deviate from the literal truth. This teaches us that truth is not an absolute value. But it sometimes must give way to other values more important, sometimes in the interests of peace and sometimes, as Bahya points out, for the sake of life itself.

Since Joseph's brothers realised their guilt and imagined that nothing less than death was their due for the crime they had committed, they felt their lives were in mortal danger. They therefore concocted the story of Jacob's testament to save their skins. Our Sages regarded their conduct as warranted on the principle that truth has sometimes to be subordinated to more important values.

Questions for Further Study

1. Compare the wording of Rashi with his source in *Bereshit Rabbah* and point out the variations giving reasons for the changes Rashi made.

2. Why did Ramban make his point only in *Vayigash*, instead of making it in our context? What difficulty did he wish to solve thereby?

3. Compare Rashi below (as well as the *Pesikta* and Ramban) with Rashi in our sidra: On 49, 6: "in their self-will they houghed (*'ikru*) oxen" Rashi comments: "they wished to uproot (*la-akor*) Joseph who is called (in Moses' blessing. Deut. 33, 17) 'a firstling bullock'." On 49, 9 "From the prey (*mi-teref*) thou (i.e. Judah) art gone up" he comments: "from that which I suspected you in respect of 'Joseph is surely torn to pieces (*tarof toraf*), a wild beast hath devoured him'" and this means Judah

who is compared to a lion. On the phrase "thou art gone up", Rashi comments: "you did disassociate yourself and said 'What profit...'" On 49, 23 "The archers have dealt bitterly with him"—i.e. his brothers; "and shot at him" (*va-robu*)—his brothers became antagonists (*anshei riv*) to him. Do not Rashi's comments here contradict his interpretation we cited of the text 50, 16: "thy father did command..."?

4. Abravanel comments as follows on the incident we quoted from Samuel:

> In my opinion Samuel's argument "how can I go..." was not truthful since Samuel had no desire to anoint another man in Saul's lifetime. It went ill with him that he personally should have to destroy the work of his hands. Therefore, in order to avoid going, he excused himself by saying, "how can I go" etc., though he knew that the Almighty would not forsake his pious ones and that Saul would not dare to harm a prophet of God, honouring and respecting Samuel more than his own father. How then could he kill him! But we must admit that it was Samuel's wish to avoid going. Now though God knows the thoughts of man, the prophets nevertheless often sought pretexts (cf. Moses: "How will Pharaoh hearken to me?" though he knew quite well that the counsel of the Lord shall be established, but he wished to avoid going and chose that pretext instead of having to say, I do not want to go).
>
> For this reason God replied to him here: "Take a heifer", an answer in keeping with his question, placating him with words, even though Samuel was aware that no harm would come to him seeing he was going on a Divine mission.

In what way does Abravanel's answer differ from those we have cited in our *Studies*? Do you find his answer plausible?

5. Cf.: with R. Nathan's words cited on pp. 565–6 the following:

> The school of R. Ishmael taught: Great is peace since for its sake God Himself misreported. For originally the text wrote

(Gen. 18, 12): "My master is old". At the end it is written (ibid. 18, 13): "and I am old".

Rashi, in his comment on the phrase "My lord is old", transmutes this into the following:

Sarah spoke in disrespectful terms. When God reported the matter to Abraham it is written: "Why did Sarah laugh ... and I am old?" He altered Sarah's actual words for the sake of peace.

Explain why R. Nathan did not cite this text from the Torah in support of the principle that it is one's duty to deviate from the truth in the interests of peace, choosing instead the verse from Samuel?

INDICES

BIOGRAPHICAL NOTES ON THE COMMENTATORS *

ABRAVANEL (or Abarbanel) Don Isaac, b. Lisbon 1437, d. Venice 1508. Spanish-Jewish Bible commentator, philosopher and statesman. He was Finance Minister to the kings of Portugal, Spain and Naples, the victim of court intrigues and suffered expulsion in 1492 with the rest of the exiles. During the course of his vicissitudes he penned monumental commentaries to the Bible, the Haggadah, Pirke *Avot and *Rambam's Guide. English biography *Don Isaac Abravanel* by Netanyahu (1968).

AGGADA literally "telling" referring to the ethical, imaginative and homiletical portions of Talmudic literature—the lore as opposed to *Halacha*—the law or legal-ritual part.

AKEDAT YITZHAK Philosophic commentary to the Pentateuch of Isaac Arama (1420–1494) Spanish Talmudist and exegete of Expulsion Period.

ALBO Yosef (14th-15th century) flourished in Saragossa, Spain and famous for his Jewish philosophic classic *Sefer Ha-Ikkarim* "The Book of Roots" in which he reduced the essential "roots" or principles of Judaism to three: Divine Existence, Providence and Revelation.

ALSHIKH Moshe b. Adrianopolis 1508, d. Damascus 16(?). Spent most of his life in Safed, Eretz Israel. Famous for his commentary to the Pentateuch which was a record of his popular Sabbath sermons.

ARAMA Isaac see Akedat Yitzhak.

ASHKENAZI Eliezer see *Ma'aseh Hashem*.

ASTRUC Anselm see Midreshei Torah.

---

* I have compiled the following items to give the reader some idea of the background of the various authorities cited by Prof. Leibowitz in her *Studies* and encourage a closer acquaintance with the Jewish heritage and its bearers. For further information readers are advised to consult the Encyclopedia Judaica and the bibliography given there and occasionally in the items here. An asterisk before a word indicates a cross-reference.   A. N.

AVOT see Mishnah.

AVOT DE RABBI NATHAN a Tannaitic amplification of *Avot, compiled
by R. Nathan, an older contemporary of Rabbi Judah Hanasi, the
editor of the Mishnah.

AVRAHAM BEN HARAMBAM only son of *Rambam and worthy successor
1186–1237. Succeeded his father to leadership of the Egyptian Jewish
community. Philosopher, moralist, rabbinic authority, Bible commentator and physician. Though his works reflect more pronounced mystical
leanings, basically they follow in the footsteps of his father. One
of his works an ethical treatise in Arabic has been translated into
English under the title *Highway to Perfection*, Rosenblatt, Columbia.
1927.

BAER Yitzhak (Fritz) (1888–). Jewish historian born Halberstadt. Professor of general medieval history at Hebrew University and head
of its history department. Among his best known works are the
History of the Jews in Christian Spain and *Yisrael Ba'Amim*.

BAHYA BEN ASHER flourished in Saragossa, Aragon in the 14th century.
A disciple of the Rashba (Shelomo b. Aderet), chiefly known for
his commentary to the Pentateuch. Not to be confused with Bahya
ibn Pakuda the author of *Hovot Halevavot*.

BAHYA ibn Pakuda see *Hovot Halevavot*.

BAMIDMAR RABBAH see Midrash

BAVA BATRA see Talmud.

BECHOR SHOR, French Jewish Talmudist of 12th century of Tosafist
school. Probably to be identified with Yosef of Orleans, a disciple of
Rabbenu Tam, Rashi's grandson. Fragments only of his commentary
have been published. Most is still in manuscript.

BE'ER YITZHAK supercommentary to Rashi, of Yitzhak (Ya'acov) Horowitz of Yaroslav (died 1864). First printed in Lemberg 1873 by
his daughter and grandson and little known till popularised by
Nehama Leibowitz and reprinted in Jerusalem by Kiryah Ne'emana
1967, with an introduction by Rabbi Yehuda Copperman principal
of Michlala College for Women, Jerusalem who describes it as
"the only real comprehensive supercommentary of Rashi exclusively'.

BENAMOZEGH Elijah ben Avraham (1822–1900). Rabbi of Leghorn, Italy
and professor of theology in its rabbinical seminary. He combined
modern and traditional scholarship in his commentary to the Torah:
Em Lamikra. He advocated a deeper appreciation of Kabbalah and
used his intellectual gifts to oppose the inroads of Reform.

574

BERAKHOT see Talmud.

BERESHIT RABBAH see Midrash.

BERTINORO, Ovadia ben Avraham. Born c. 1456 and died before 1516. Italian rabbi renowned for his classic commentary to the *Mishnah. Author of a supercommentary to Rashi, *Amar Nekei* (published 1810). Emigrated to Eretz Israel in 1488 and became leader of the Jerusalem community and was buried on the Mount of Olives.

BIUR (1780–83). The Hebrew commentary to the Pentateuch composed by Moses Mendelssohn (1729-1786) in collaboration ,with Solomon Dubnow, Naftali Herz Wessely and Aaron Yaroslav. It was printed together with Mendelssohn's translation of the Pentateuch into High German in Hebrew characters and formed part of his programme to "enlighten" his co-religionists and give Jewish tradition a new western look. Solomon Dubno (1738-1813) a Bible scholar and Hebrew poet and tutor to his son was responsible for the commentary to Genesis (excepting chapter 1) and a part of Exodus. A large volume of rabbinic opinion accused him of speeding the process of assimilation, a diagnosis that would seem to have been borne out by the rapid conversion of most of his followers and descendants to Christianity. It is possible, of course, that this would have happened in any case. The fact remains that the *Biur* proved a valuable addition to the corpus of traditional Jewish Bible commentary.

BUBER, Mordecai Martin (1878-1965). Born in Vienna and a graduate of Vienna, Zurich and Berlin universities, he combined involvement with the Zionist movement with a modern philosophic restatement of Judaism and close study of the Bible and Hassidic lore which he introduced to western sophisticated culture. He collaborated with Franz *Rosenzweig on a new German translation of the Bible which attempted to preserve all the nuances of the original. In 1938 he accepted the post of professor of the sociology of religion at the Hebrew University. His I-Thou philosophy of dialogue with its theological emphasis and total ignoring of practical Jewish observance found more favour with Christian than Jewish circles. Despite the fact that his views on contemporary Jewish issues found little acceptance among his co-religionists, his writings on Biblical texts are a mine of profound and inspiring comment. Most of his writings have appeared in Hebrew, German and English.

CASSUTO Umberto (1883-1951). Italian Jewish Bible commentator who came to Eretz Israel in 1939 and was professor of Bible at the Hebrew university. Renowned for his demolition of the documentary theories of Higher Criticism in his *The Documentary Hypothesis* that appeared in Italian, Hebrew and English and commentaries to Genesis (unfinished) and Exodus that appeared in both Hebrew and English.

DA'AT ZEKENIM MI'BA'ALEI HATOSAFOT A compendium of Torah commentary originating with the Tosafists (13th century), disciples of Rashi who received their name from the Tosafot or *addenda* incorporated in all editions of the Talmud, in the opposite column to Rashi's Talmud commentary. These addenda analysed Talmudic rulings and attempted to harmonise contradictions by establishing logical distinctions rather than accepting traditional explanations emanating from the Geonim—the post-Talmudic teachers who flourished in Babylon and exerted world-wide authority till their eclipse at the dawn of the medieval period. The *Da'at Zekenim* was first printed at Livorno in 1783, reprinted by Lewin-Epstein together with the commentary of *Bertinoro and *Riyva.

DARKEI AGGADA see Heinemann Yitzhak.

DEVARIM RABBAH see Midrash.

DIVREI DAVID (1689). Supercommentary to Rashi of David ben Samuel Halevi (1586-1667) Polish Talmudist known as the TaZ after the initials of his authoritative commentary to the *Shulhan Arukh, Yoreh Deah: Torei Zahav.*

DUBNOW Solomon see *Biur.*

EDUYOT see Mishnah.

EINHORN see *Maharzav.*

ELDAD Israel (Scheib) (1910–   ) Israeli journalist and educator. Editor of *Divrei Hayamim* (Chronicles) newspaper history of Jewish people. Came to Eretz Israel in 1940 from Poland and a leader of Lehi (Lohamei Herut Israel) underground fighters organisation. Co-founder of Eretz Israel Hashelema movement and author of *Hegyonot Hamikra* —contemporary sermons on the Bible.

EM LA'MIKRA see Benamozegh.

ERUVIN see Talmud.

EVEN SHEMUEL Judah (Kauffman) (1886–1976) Jewish educationalist, lexicographer and scholar. Born in the Ukraine, founder of Montreal Jewish teacher training college. Settled in Eretz Israel 1926 and produced for Dvir publishing house first modern comprehensive English-Hebrew dictionary. Renowned for his scholarly edition of Rambam's *Guide for the Perplexed* which includes vocalised text, introductions and comprehensive notes and commentary. (3 vols. 1936–1960).

GABIROL Ibn Solomon (1021-1058) Poet, philosopher of the Spanish Golden Age of Jewish history. Many of his poems are included in the prayer book including the famous song of praise to God *Keter Malchut* (The Crown of Sovereignty). Known to the gentile world as Avicebron, the author of *Fon Vitae*, a Latin translation of his philosophic classic *Mekor Hayim*.

GITTIN see Talmud.

GUR ARYEH. Supercommentary to Rashi of Judah Loew Ben Bezalel (1525-1609) usually known as Maharal of Prague. He was highly esteemed by gentile scholars and kings. This and his versatility—he was equally at home in the fields of Talmud, Kabbalah, mathematics and astronomy caused many legends to be woven round his person— in particular the famous story of the Golem. His works on Jewish ethics, philosophy and rabbinic law are regarded as classics and they have inspired many modern revivers of Jewish nationalism and religion. A selection from his works (Hebrew) under subject headings has been produced by the Israel writer, Abraham Kariv.

GUTTMANN Julius (Yitzhak) (1880-1950) authority on Jewish and general philosophy on which he lectured at Berlin and Breslau. From 1934 onward professor of Jewish philosophy at the Hebrew university. His major work: *The Philosophies of Judaism*, 1964 (English translation).

HA'AMEK DAVAR, commentary to the Pentateuch of Naftali Zvi Yehuda Berlin, known by the initials of his name as the Netziv (1817-1893). He was the principal of the famous Volozhin yeshiva succeeding his father-in-law Rabbi Yitzhak of Volozhin. He was an enthusiastic supporter of the Lovers of Zion movement and his sentiments find eloquent expression in his Torah commentary which are a record of lectures on the weekly portion delivered in the yeshiva.

HAKETAV VEHAKABBALAH (1839). One of the first comprehensive commentaries to the Pentateuch aimed at demonstrating how the Oral Tradition (Kabbalah) could be read into the written text (Haketav). Composed by Jacob Zvi Mecklenburg (1785-1865), Chief Rabbi of Konigsberg who appended a German translation of the Pentateuch based on his commentary.

HALLAH see Mishnah.

HAMIDRASH VEHAMA'ASEH, commentary on Genesis and Exodus by Yehezkel ben Hillel Arych Leb Lipschuetz (1862-1932), Lithuanian rabbi and scholar.

HARECHASIM LABIKE'A (1815) Torah commentary by 17th-18th century rabbi Judah Leib Spira, probably of Frankfurt-on-Main, printed together by *Heidenheim with his *Havanat Hamikra*.

HAZON HAMIKRA: Studies in the Haftarot by Issachar Jacobson—Israeli teacher and scholar. His studies in the Sidra, *Bina Bamikra*, have been translated into English under the title "Meditations on the Torah" by Rabbi Zeev Gotthold, and "Meditations on the Siddur" by Rabbi Aryeh Oschry.

HEFETZ see *Melekhet Mahshevet*.

HEIDENHEIM Zeev Wolf (1757–1832). Eminent Jewish scholar and Hebrew philologist born Heidenheim, died Rodelheim which became famous in the Jewish world for the *siddurim* and *mahzorim* printed by him, the master-editions of all modern Jewish prayer books. He wrote a commentary on Hebrew liturgical poetry and a supercommentary to Rashi called *Havanat Hamikra*.

HEINEMANN Yitzhak (1876–1957) Israel scholar and thinker born in Frankfurt, lecturer in Jewish and general philosophy, Berlin and Breslau. Settled in Jerusalem 1939. Specialist in Hellenistic and medieval philosophy. Notable works: *Ta'amei Hamitzvot* (2 vols.) surveying the reasons given for Jewish observances by Jewish thinkers down the ages and *Darkei Aggada*—a study of the rhetorical, literary and other conventions underlying the *Aggada in the light of Hellenistic parallels.

HIRSCH Shimshon Raphael (1808–1888) German-Jewish rabbinical leader and creator of Torah-im-Derech-Eretz synthesis by which he successfully withstood the inroads of Reform Judaism. He rebuilt orthodox Jewish life in Germany in the 19th century and in particular the community of which he became rabbi—Frankfurt-on-Main. The latter became the strongest bastion of modern orthodoxy in the western world, famous for its educational institutions from kindergarten onwards. They combined meticulous religious observance with involvement with contemporary culture. His ideas were promulgated in the *Nineteen Letters of Ben Uziel* and *Horeb* and his commentary to the Pentateuch in German, latterly translated into Hebrew and English (*Judaism Eternal, Timeless Torah* by Grunfeld).

HIRSCHENSON see *Nimukkei Rashi*.

HIZKUNI (Hazkuni) mid-thirteenth century commentary to the Pentateuch of Hezekiah ben Manoah. First printed in Venice 1524. Probably a member of the school of *Rashi.

HOFFMAN David Zvi (1843–1921) German-Jewish rabbinical authority and rector of Hildesheimer rabbinical seminary, Berlin. He was the first leading orthodox rabbi to rebut the claims of the Wellhausen school of Bible Criticism with the weapons of modern scholarship. In his commentary to Leviticus (1904) and Deuteronomy based on his lectures at the seminary delivered in the eighteen seventies, he shows an equal mastery of rabbinic sources and the documents and archaeological data cited by the Bible critics.

HOVOT HALEVAVOT "Duties of the Heart", Jewish ethical classic outlining the gates to moral perfection by Bahya Ibn Pakuda, Spanish-Jewish poet of the 11th century. Emphasising that the essence of Judaism lies in the commandments of the heart—the moral duties as did moralist writers before and after him, he wrote his classic to combat the preoccupation with ritual rather than ethical commandments. Has been translated into many languages. Cf. *Luzzato's *Messilat Yesharim.*

IBN EZRA Avraham Born in Toledo, Spain 1092. Renowned Bible commentator, astronomer, poet and grammarian. His extensive travels took him to England, France and North Africa. His chief fame rests on his Bible commentary in which his independent ideas aroused much controversy which has still not died down. His strict upholding of traditional rabbinic exegesis did not preclude him offering original interpretations or caustic comment on those that failed his exacting standards of grammatical analysis.

JACOB Benno (1862–1955) German-Jewish Bible scholar, graduate of Breslau seminary and disciple of Graetz. Chiefly known for his commentary to the Pentateuch in which he made use of keen critical analysis and modern scholarship in support of the traditional position.

KASPI Joseph Ibn (1278–1340) philosopher, Bible commentator, grammarian and traveller. Flourished in Provence. Ardent admirer of *Rambam and advocate of harmonisation of religion with reason. Prolific author (30 known works). The germs of political Zionism and a scientific approach can be found in his commentaries which included *Mishneh Kesef* on the Pentateuch printed as late as 1905.

KAUFMANN Yehezkel (1889–1964) Modern Jewish Bible scholar born in Ukraine and settled in Israel in 1929 where he occupied chair of Biblical Studies at the Hebrew University. Renowned for his *History of the Israelite Religion* and commentaries to *Joshua* and *Judges.*

KELI YAKAR commentary to the Torah of Ephraim Solomon ben Haim of Luntshitz (1550–1619), Rabbi of Lemberg and renowned preacher. His commentary which is largely homiletic in character is included in the popular poly-commentary edition of the Pentateuch *Rav Peninim* facing *Or Hahayim.*

579

KIDDUSHIN see Talmud.

KIMHI see Radak.

KOOK, Avraham Yitzhak Hakohen (1865-1935). First Chief Rabbi of Eretz Israel after Balfour Declaration and ardent supporter of modern return to Zion. He came to Eretz Israel in 1904 after attending Volozhin yeshiva and serving as rabbi in several Lithuanian communities. Henceforth he devoted himself to involving religious Jewry in the upbuilding of the Holy Land as the cardinal mitzva of Judaism of the time. This attitude, coupled with his original analysis of the positive motives of contemporary Jewish revolutionarism, led him to regard the socialist and secular halutzim with deep affection and respect, feelings which were reciprocated. His philosophy of religious nationhood outlined in poetic mystic language is still being interpreted and is regarded as particularly relevant today by Jewish thinkers of widely differing outlooks. Penned monumental works on the Talmud, rabbinic law and Jewish thought, as well as a commentary to the Siddur. His published letters are a rich source of valuable comment on Jewish problems and texts.

KROCHMAL Nachman (1785-1840). Popularly known as RaNaK, Polish Jewish philosopher and historian chiefly known for his *Morei Nevukhei Hazeman*, "Guide to the Perplexed of our Time," which became the text book of Jewish humanism in the 19th century.

KUZARI see Yehudah Halevi.

LEKAH TOV a *Midrash commentary to the Pentateuch and Five Scrolls compiled by Tobias b. Eliezer, a Balkans rabbinic scholar in the late 11th century. Also known as *Pesikta Zotarta*.

LEVUSH HA-ORA supercommentary to Rashi of Mordecai ben Avraham Jaffe (c. 1535-1612) known as the *Baal ha-levushim*, literally, the "author" or "owner" of the *levushim*—ten commentaries on the texts of Judaism including the Shulkhan Arukh—the religious codex, Kabbalah, philosophy and astronomy, all of which he regarded as an integral part of rabbinic studies. He was a disciple of Solomon Luria and Isserles and succeeded the Maharal (see *Gur Aryeh*) to the rabbinate of Prague, his birthplace.

LUZZATTO Moshe Hayyim (RaMHaL) (1707-1746): Moralist, Kabbalist and Hebrew poet. Combined, like most Italian-Jewish scholars deep rabbinic learning with secular attainments. As a result of his Messianic speculations and the heresy-hunting that followed the eclipse of the false Messiah, Shabbatai Zvi, he was a target of controversy.

But after his death his works were acclaimed as classics by all circles of Jewry, Hassidic, secular-nationalist and Yeshiva. His *Messilat Yesharim* "Pathway of the Upright" became with **Hovot Halevavot* the classic moralist-*mussar* textbook of the Lithuanian Yeshivot in which he outlined step-by-step the qualities to be mastered in order to attain moral perfection. His poetic dramas in Hebrew were regarded as the forerunner of modern Hebrew literature and his Kabbalistic commentaries and works the guidebooks for mystic Hassidic enthusiasts.

LUZZATTO Shemuel David (ShaDaL), Italian-Jewish scholar born Trieste 1800, professor of Jewish Studies at rabbinic seminary of Padua till his death in 1865. Precursor of modern Hebrew and Zionist renaissance. Noted for contribution to modern Jewish scholarship permeated with strong national and traditional overtones. He penned commentaries to the Pentateuch, Isaiah, Jeremiah, Ezekiel, Proverbs and Job, noted for their clarity, simplicity and literary approach. He was a romantic believing in the heart rather than mind, preferring **Yehuda Halevi* to **Rambam*. His versatile achievements included the writing of Hebrew poetry, a Hebrew grammar at age of 11, an Aramaic grammar translated into German, English and Hebrew, a popular treatise on the fundamentals of Judaism (English edition: *Foundations of the Torah*, N. H. Rosenbloom 1965) and the translation of the *Mahzor* into Italian.

MA'ASEH HASHEM (1583) Commentary to the Pentateuch of Eliezer ben Elijah Ashkenazi (1513–1586) rabbi and physician. Held positions in Egypt, Cyprus, Venice, Prague and Posen. Died in Cracow. Insisted on rational, independent approach in Bible commentary: "Let not opinions, however ancient and authoritative hinder our own research. Research and choose! You have been created for that. Reason has been given you from Heaven."

MA'AYAN GANIM Midrashic commentary to the Pentateuch compiled in 1196, anonymous. Cited by Kasher in **Torah Shelemah.*

MAHARSHA Shemuel Eliezer ben Yehuda Halevi Edels (1555–1631), author of foremost commentary to Talmud after Rashi and Tosafists; included in all Talmud editions. Analytic and critical, he explained many of the difficulties both in the legal and homiletical parts. He was born in Cracow and held position of rabbi in Chelm, Lublin and Ostrog.

MAHARZAV Zeev Wolf ben Israel Isaar, 19th century Russian rabbi and commentator to the **Midrash Rabbah*. His commentary was printed in the large Vilna Romm edition. He was born in Grodno, flourished in Vilna where he died in 1862.

MAKKOT see Talmud.

MALBIM initials of Meir Yehuda Leibush ben Yehiel Michal (1809–1880), Russian-Jewish rabbi chiefly noted for his commentary to the Pentateuch *Hatorah Vehamitzvah* in which he combined the Oral and Written texts and demonstrated the profound linguistic foundations of rabbinic exegesis. He strove to harmonise Genesis with the findings of 19th century science and waged war against the Reformers in the various prominent rabbinic positions he filled which included that of Bucharest, Rumania.

MECHILTA see Mishnah.

MEGILLAH see Talmud.

MELEKHET MAHSHEVET Pentateuch commentary (1710) of Italian Talmudist Moshe ben Gershon Hefetz (Gentili), born Trieste 1663 died Venice 1711.

MELTZER Shimshon (1909–) Hebrew poet born in Galicia, emigrated to Eretz Israel in 1933, edited Israeli childrens newspaper *Davar Liyeladim*. In his poems and ballads he has given nostalgic portrayals of Jewish life in the *shtetl* in previous centuries.

MENAHOT see Talmud.

MESHEKH HOKHMA Commentary to the Pentateuch (1927) of Meir Simha Hakohen, rabbi of Dvinsk (1843–1926) renowned as brilliant Talmudist and respected as compassionate rabbinic leader. Author of analytic commentary to *Rambam's Code of Jewish law: Or Sameach*. His Bible commentary displays profound insights, combining Talmudic erudition with a philosophic exposition of the fundamentals of Judaism.

MESSILAT YESHARIM see Luzzatto Moshe Hayyim.

MIDRASH "Exposition" — refers to homiletic and *Aggada material compiled on the Biblical text mainly in Eretz Israel from the 3rd to 10th centuries, largely a record of popular sermons delivered by the rabbis of the early centuries of the present era to comfort, entertain and instruct the general public. The major compilation of this genre is the *Midrash Rabbah* on the Pentateuch and the five *Meggilot* or Scrolls read in the synagogue: Shir Hashirim (Song of Songs), Ruth, Echah (Lamentations) Kohelet (Ecclesiastes), Esther. But there are literally hundreds of Midrash compilations, all of which preserved, in some measure or another the oldest homiletic and exegetic traditions of the Jewish people. Cf. also *Midrash Halacha* in the item: Mishnah.

MIDRASH HAGGADOL a collection of Midrashim on the Pentateuch compiled from ancient Tannaitic sources by David ben Amram Adani, a Yemenite scholar in the 13th century, the standard Midrash commentary of Yemenite Jewry circulating in manuscript but eventually published by European Jewish scholars in scientific editions within the last century and particularly in the last fifty years. It is the only authentic record of many dicta of the Tannaim and Talmudic sources, shedding light, for instance on those forming the basis of some of *Rambam's rulings in his code.

MIDRASH HAHEFETZ Midrash on the Pentateuch, Lamentations, Esther and the Haftarot compiled by Yemenite scholar and physician Yahya Zechariah ben Solomon during the years 1413-1430.

MIDRASH OR HAAFELAH Midrash compiled by rabbi Netanel ben Yeshayah of Yemen in the 14th century, cited from manuscript by Kasher in *Torah Shelemah.

MIDRASH SECHEL TOV Aggadic and Halakhic anthology on the weekly Sidra compiled by Menachem ben Solomon in 1139. The author's grammatical interests are prominent—he wrote one of the earliest Hebrew grammars, *Even Bohan* but only fragments of this as well as of his Midrash (that on Genesis and Exodus) are extant.

MIDRASH TADSHEI, MIDRASH TANHUMA, MIDRASH TANHUMA YASHAN see Midrash.

MIDRASH VAYOSHA late *Aggadic work on Song of Red Sea compiled at end of 11th century.

MIDRESHEI TORAH commentary to Pentateuch of Anselm, Solomon Astruc the martyr, composed after 1376. Hailing from Provence he was probably a victim of a Christian pogrom in Barcelona in 1391. Little is certain of his identity and biography. He liberally quotes Ramban, Ibn Ezra and other commentators preceding him and is especially cited by Abravanel and Sforno.

MISHNAH—"teaching"—the oral tradition, mainly of a legal and ritual nature, complementing the written Torah as codified by Rabbi Yehuda Hanasi (Rabbi) in Eretz Israel at the end of the second century. The Mishnah comprises six "Orders" or divisions and 63 tractates the following of which are cited in this book: *Hallah*—dealing with the laws governing the separating of the portion of dough for the priest; *Kiddushin*—the modes of betrothal and family law; *Eduyot*— a mnemonic listing of 100 Talmudic rules and 30 disputes where the School of Hillel adopted a more stringent ruling than the School of Shammai and *Avot*—a treasury of ethical dicta of the Mishnah teachers. The latter are known as *Tannaim*. They flourished during the latter half of the second Temple period till the end of the second century. Parallel collections of this material which amplify the Mishnah are called *Tosefta* and other uncollected dicta of this genre excluded by Rabbi from this Code are known as *Baraita* ("outside material"). The Oral Tradition that was not transmitted in code form like the above but was studied in the form of a verse by verse commentary to the text of the Pentateuch is known as *Midrash Halacha*. Two such commentaries referred to in this book are *Mechilta* on the book of Exodus and *Sifrei* on Numbers and Deuteronomy.

MISHNEH KESEF see Kaspi.

MIZRAHI Eliyahu (1440–1525) noted for his supercommentary to Rashi on the Pentateuch. A renowned Talmudist, mathematician and astronomer who, as chief rabbi of Turkey and friend of the Sultan at the time of the Spanish Expulsion, was able to extend valuable help to his exiled coreligionists.

NIDDAH see Talmud.

NIMMUKEI RASHI supercommentary to Rashi of Haim Hirschensohn (1857–1935). Eretz Israel rabbi and scholar who was born in Safed and lived in Jerusalem from 1864–1904. There he was one of the few orthodox rabbis who supported the revival of Hebrew under Eliezer ben Yehuda and edited a scholarly Hebrew journal *Hamisderona*. He subsequently became rabbi in New Jersey.

OR HAHAYYIM Pentateuch commentary of Hayyim Ibn Attar (1696–1743), outstanding Moroccan Jewish Kabbalist, Talmudist and leader of Moroccan Jewish resettlement in Eretz Israel. He established a Yeshiva in Jerusalem. He is chiefly noted for his Pentateuch commentary that combines Kabbalistic and Talmudic erudition. A collection of letters and documents relating to his emigration to Eretz Israel edited by Dr. Benjamin Klar has been published by Mossad Harav Kook Jerusalem under the title of *Rabbi Hayyim ben Attar*.

OTZAR HAMIDRASHIM (2 vols. 1915) anthology of *Midrash compiled by Yehuda David Eisenstein (1845–1956) Polish born encyclopedist and anthologist. Emigrated to the U.S. in 1872 and founded first Hebrew speaking society. Chiefly known for his Jewish encyclopedia in Hebrew *Otzar Yisrael*.

PANEAH RAZA commentary to Pentateuch first published 1607 of Isaac ben Yehuda Halevi of the Tosafist school. He lived at Sens probably second half of 13th century. He also wrote Tosafot to the Talmud known as *Ba'al Hatosafot Misens*.

PESAHIM see Talmud.

PESIKTA DERAV KAHANA, PESIKTA RABBATI see Midrash.

PESIKTA ZOTARTA see *Lekah Tov*.

PIRKE DERABI ELIEZER see Midrash.

RADAK initials of Rabbi David Kimhi (1160–1236). Most famous Bible commentator of his time. Flourished in Provence. His commentary became an inexhaustible source of inspiration for Bible commentators both Jewish and non-Jewish, and was reprinted alongside that of *Rashi and *Ibn Ezra.

RADAL initials of Rabbi David Luria (1798–1855). Lithuanian rabbi and scholar born in Mogilev. Regarded as leading rabbinic figure after the death of the Gaon of Vilna. Author of Talmudic glosses and notes and commentary to Midrash Rabbah included in printed Vilna Romm editions.

RAMBAM initials of Rabbi Moshe ben Maimon or Maimonides. Born Cordova Spain 1135. Died 1204 Fostat, Egypt. Renowned as greatest post-Talmudic authority on Judaism, author of master-code of Jewish law: *Mishneh Torah*, classic commentary on the Mishnah, controversial but widely-accepted philosophic handbook to Judaism—*Guide for the Perplexed*, compendium of 613 commandments of Judaism: *Sefer Hamitzvot*. In addition he penned authoritative responsa and three outstanding epistles—*Kiddush Hashem* on martyrdom, *Tehiyat Hametim* on the Doctrine of the Resurrection and *Petah Tikva* addressed to Yemenite Jewry on Messianic problems. Besides all this, he found time to be a world-famous authority on medicine, the Caliph's physician and leader of Egyptian Jewry.

RAMBAN initials of Rabbi Moshe Ben Nahman (1194–1270) Born in Gerona Spain, he became the next star on the Jewish firmament after the *Rambam, noted for his Talmudic and Bible commentaries, his championship of Judaism in a famous disputation with Christian bishops and the Jewish apostate Pablo Christiano in Barcelona in 1263, and his reestablishment of the Jewish community in Jerusalem just before his death there. His Bible commentary abounds with love of Eretz Israel which he regarded as the underlying sanction of every Jewish precept. He usually takes Rashi's explanation as the starting point for his discussion on the text in the course of which he expounds basic principles of Judaism, coloured by Kabalistic insights but basically adhering to the plain sense and guided by the insights of Oral Tradition. Rashi, Ibn Ezra and Rambam are all targets of his deeply respectful criticism in his search for truth. See *A Ramban Reader* by Aryeh Newman, World Zionist Organization, Torah Education and Culture, Jerusalem 1968 and *Ramban, his life and teachings*, Charles B. Chavel, Feldheim, New York, 1960.

RAN or RABBENU NISSIM ben Reuven Gerondi. Talmudic commentator, philosopher and physician flourished in 14th century Spain and author of *Derashot* or discourses on Judaism. Died in 1380.

RASHBAM initials of Rabbi Shemuel ben Meir (1080–1158) member of Tosafist school—grandson of Rashi renowned for his commentary to the Torah in which he insisted on not deviating from the plain sense —the *peshat*—in the interests of which he often took issue with his illustrious grandfather. He was also an author of commentaries of the Talmud which fill in the gaps left by Rashi in the printed editions.

RASHI initials of Rabbi Shelomo Yitzhaki—the prince of Jewish Bible commentators (1040–1105). Flourished in Troyes, France. No edition of the Jewish Bible or Talmud is complete without his commentary which with remarkable brevity and clarity has been the key that has unlocked these classics to every student and scholar since his time. His commentary to the Bible was the first Hebrew book to be printed in 1475.

RA'VAD initials of Rabbi Avraham ben David of Posquières (1125–1198). Outstanding French rabbinical authority chiefly noted for his *Hasagot* or "Strictures" on *Rambam's Code of Jewish Law.

REGGIO, Yitzhak Shemuel, YaSHaR (1784–1855), Italian rabbi versed in Talmud, Kabbalah and modern scholarship. Translator of Bible into Italian, accompanied by Hebrew commentary. His attempts at reconciliation of science and Judaism did not always meet with the approval of traditionalists. Author of *A Guide for the Religious Instruction of Jewish Youth* (London 1855).

RIYVA initials of Rabbi Yehuda ben Eliezer author of 14th century commentary to the Pentateuch of Tosafist school, flourished in Troyes, Rashi's birthplace. Usually printed together with *Da'at Zekenim.

ROSENZWEIG Franz (1886–1929) Jewish existentialist religious philosopher flourished in Germany but exerted influence throughout the Jewish world, particularly after his death. Noted for his collaboration with Martin *Buber on the translation of the Bible into German and his philosophical work *The Star of Redemption* (translated by Hallo, published by Holt Reinhardt Winston, 1971) synthesising Jewish observance and symbols into a contemporary philosophical framework. Came from an assimilated German Jewish home and almost embraced Christianity but out of intellectual conviction and in the process of intense Jewish studies gradually moved forward to an observant though not conventionally orthodox way of life.

ROSH HASHANAH see Talmud.

SA'ADIA Gaon born in Egypt 880, one of the last and most illustrious of the Gaonim—the post-Talmudic authorities of Judaism heading the academies of Babylonia which regulated the norms of Jewish life everywhere for a period of 500 years. With the help of his vast

586

erudition, philosophical insight, expertise in Hebrew grammar, Talmudic mastery and literary gifts, he waged a successful struggle against the Karaite heresy and other divisions that threatened the unity of Judaism. He wrote the accepted Arab translation of the Bible for Jews in Arab-speaking countries and Bible commentary, the first philosophic classic of Judaism *Emunot Vedeot* (Religion and Morals) characterised by a rationalist approach and a liturgical handbook: "Siddur".

SANHEDRIN see Talmud.

SAR-SHALOM HA'ADULAMI pen name of Simha Reuven Edelmann (1821–1892). Lithuanian Hebrew scholar, poet and grammarian. Born in Vilna, studied at Volozhin yeshiva. Author of *Hamesillot* (1875) comprising three parts (i) study of the Massora, (ii) commentary on several Psalms, (iii) exposition of difficult Aggadot in the Babylonian Talmud.

SECHEL TOV see Midrash Sechel Tov.

SFORNO Ovadiah ben Jacob (1475–1550). Italian-Jewish Bible commentator, Talmudist and physician. His commentary to the Pentateuch is included in the standard editions of *Mikraot Gedolot*.

SHEMOT RABBAH, SHIR HASHIRIM — RABBAH see Midrash.

SIFREI see Mishnah.

SOLOVEITCHIK Joseph Dov (1903–) spiritual leader of modern orthodox rabbinate in the U.S. combining profound Torah knowledge with modern philosophy. Since arrival in U.S. in 1932 from Lithuanian Torah milieu via Berlin university, rabbi of Boston where he established his own Jewish high school and Yeshiva. Professor of Jewish philosophy and Talmud at Yeshiva University and Isaac Elhanan Yeshiva respectively. Main written work a monumental essay on the Halachic personality: *Ish Hahalacha.*

SOTA see Talmud.

TA'ANIT see Talmud.

TALMUD (Bavli-Babylonian) commentary and discussion of the *Mishnah, containing both Halacha and *Aggada as expounded in the academies of Babylonia from second to end of fifth century and major source-book of Judaism. The Talmudic teachers were designated *Amoraim*. The Jerusalem (Yerushalmi) or Palestinian Talmud was finalised a century earlier. The following Tractates are referred to in this book: *Berakhot* dealing with the blessings or benedictions accompanying the Shema and uttered on various occasions; *Bava Batra* dealing with laws of property, inheritance and partnership; *Eruvin*, circumventions of the prohibition of carrying from one domain to another on the Sabbath; *Gittin* — divorce laws; *Ketubot* — marriage contracts; *Makkot* — the penalty of lashes, laws against false witnesses and cities of refuge; *Megillah* — on the feast of Purim and rules for reading the scroll of Esther; *Menahot* — the meal-offerings with a digression containing a major source for rulings on *tzizit*, *mezuzah* and *tefillin*; *Niddah* — on regulations governing a menstruant woman; *Pesachim* — Passover laws; *Rosh Hashana* — laws of the New Year Shofar and Jewish Calendar; *Sanhedrin* — judiciary and capital punishment including a large amount of *Aggada; Sota* — the laws of the adultress, priestly blessing, the king and making war and large amount of Aggada; *Ta'anit* — the statutory fasts; *Yevamot* — levirate marriage; *Yoma* — the Day of Atonement.

TANNA DEBE ELIYAHU see Midrash.

TORAH SHELEMAH monumental compendium of early rabbinic commentary to the Torah including citations from unpublished works, compiled by Rabbi Menahem Kasher and a team of scholars at the Torah Shelemah institute in Jerusalem and begun in 1926. 24 volumes have been published comprising the books of Genesis, Exodus and the first sidra of Leviticus. The Midrashim are printed beneath the Pentateuch text, Rashi's commentary and the Aramaic Targumim, accompanied by detailed explanatory notes and appendices by rabbi Kasher. An English edition (abridged) is being published of which seven volumes covering Genesis and the beginning of Exodus have so far appeared. Begun by the late Rabbi Hyman-Klein it is being continued by Rabbi Henry Freedman of Melbourne, Australia.

TORAH TEMIMAH commentary to the Pentateuch of Rabbi Baruch Epstein, Russian Talmudist (1860–1942) in which he appended to the written text his own selection of the main dicta of Oral Tradition culled from Talmudic literature, appending a commentary explaining their relevance. Like the *Malbim before him his aim was to demonstrate the intimate connection between Oral and Written Law. He was killed in the Nazi liquidation of the Pinsk Ghetto. His father R. Yehiel Michal Epstein was renowned for his compilation of the only modern complete code of Jewish law: *Arukh Hashulhan* — an essential reference book for determining Jewish religious law today.

TOSEFTA see Mishnah.

TZEDAH LADEREKH super-commentary on Rashi (1623–24) of Issachar Ber ben Israel-Lazer Parnas Eilenburg (1550–1623) born in Posen, disciple of Mordecai Jaffe (see Levush Ha-Ora). He was rabbi of Gorizia, Italy and subsequently elected rabbi of Safed but died on the way there.

URBACH Ephraim (1912–) Israeli educator and professor of rabbinics (Talmud and Midrash) at the Hebrew university noted for his monumental works on the Tosafists and Rabbinic thought respectively. Leader of the movement for Torah Judaism, which aims at synthesising traditional Judaism with the realities of Israeli life.

WEISS Meir, Hungarian rabbi and professor of Bible Studies at the Hebrew university. Author of (Hebrew) *The Bible and Modern Literary Theory*, 1962.

YALKUT SHIMONI Midrash collection compiled probably in the first part of 12th century by Rabbi Shimon Ashkenazi.

YEHUDAH HALEVI (c. 1080–1142?) Spanish-Jewish poet, philosopher and physician. Noted for his philosophic classic the *Kuzari* where he outlines his picture of a Zion and Hebrew-centred Judaism in the form of a dialogue between the king of the Khazars and the Jewish Sage summoned along with the representatives of Mohammedanism and Christianity to explain their respective religions to him. His overriding love of Zion was expressed in his poems or Zionides that have entered the liturgy recited on Tisha B'Av in mourning the Destruction of the Temple. His philosophy inspired Jewish nationalist ideologists in succeeding ages. According to tradition he met his death by the hooves of an Arab horseman at the Wailing Wall where he had come to pay pilgrimage at the last relic of the ancient Temple he had so poignantly ˙lamented.

YOMA see Talmud.

ZOHAR mystical commentary on the Pentateuch attributed to the *Mishnah teacher and recluse Rabbi Shimon b. Yohai, first publicised in 13th century Spain. The classic text book of Jewish mysticism or Kabbalah.

INDEX OF BIBLICAL AND RABBINIC SOURCES*

Words marked with * are found in footnotes. Words marked with ° are found in questions for further study

* Thanks are due to Rabbi Z. Mazabov who compiled the indices of Biblical and Rabbinic sources, commentators and authors and subjects.

590

592

13:21 — 508
14:19 — 508
16:4 — 192°
17:5 — 567
18:24 — 406
19:5 — 310°
20:17 — 192°
20:21 — 161
21:12–18 — 407
21:28 — 330*
22:7 — 55
23:21 — 163*
23:25 — 258
24:5 — 270°
24:17 — 36°
24:30 — 36°
29:26 — 266
31:7 — 267
31:13 — 188
32:14 — 269°
32:16 — 506*
32:21 — 506*
32:27–29 — 267, 268
33:5 — 57°
33:11 — 268
33:17 — 167
34:4 — 36°
34:9 — 488°
41:25–32 — 443

Leviticus
1:17 — 148
9:2 — 561°
9:23 — 160
11:29 — 231
14:7 — 150
18:3 — 219, 414
20:10 — 8°
22:27 — 281
22:28 — 281
22:32 — 202
25:23 — 527
25:42 — 527
25:55 — 527

26:42 — 89°
26:44 — 147
26:45 — 147
26:55 — 527

Numbers
12:1–2 — 341
12:9 — 341
15:39 — 33
16:12–14 — 341
16:28 — 482*
18:23–24 — 527
21 — 353
21:1 — 249*
21:3 — 406
21:34 — 359, 512°
22:6 — 8*
22:9 — 47
23:8 — 546°
23:23 — 354
24:6 — 349
25:7–8 — 544
32:1 — 129*
32:2–5 — 450*
32:20–28 — 442°
32:22 — 558

Deuteronomy
1:4 — 291*
2:7 — 360
2:28 — 212°
3:23 — 57°
4:4 — 297°
4:6–8 — 392
6:18 — 168
8:16 — 193°
10:8–9 — 528
11:7 — 403, 408
12:3 — 389
13:3 — 385
13:4 — 188
14:26 — 11
14:29 — 95
16:22 — 388

INDEX OF COMMENTATORS AND AUTHORS

Gur Aryeh — see Judah Loew b. Bezalel
Guttmann, Julius — "Dat Umada" — pp. 2, 3, 6
Ha'amek Davar — see Berlin
Ha-ketav Veha-kabbalah — see Mecklenburg
Ha-rechasim Labike'a — see Spira
Hazon Ha-mikra — see Jacobson
Heidenheim, Zeev Wolf — Gen. 27:43–45 — pp. 290°, 291°

Heinemann, Yitzhak — "Darkei Ha'aggadah" — pp. 26*, 39, 96, 138,
139, 152*, 338*, 379*, 508
Herder, Gottfried — Gen. 4 — p. 58*

Hirsch, Shimshon Raphael — Gen. 24:39 — p. 219; 24:14 — p. 249°;
24:46 — p. 249°; 33:4 — p. 375;
35:7 — pp. 389, 390; 46:27 — pp.
505°, 506°; 49:5 p. 545

Hirschensohn, Haim — "Nimukkei Rashi" — Gen. 3:3 — p. 25°
15:10 — 146
29:15 — 320
Hizkuni, Ben Manoah — Gen. 9:6 — p. 82

23:7 —	209
27:45 —	288
31:38 —	344°
37:28 —	401, 402, 405
46:3 —	501
49:18 —	554°

Horowitz, Yitzhak — "Be'er Yitzhak" — Gen. 46:29 — p. 504
Hovot Ha-levavot — see Ibn Pekudah
Ibn Attar, Haim — "Or Ha-hayyim" —

Gen.		Gen.	
3:1 —	29	31:39 — p.	344°
14:17 —	131	41:29 —	521
14:18 —	133	41:55 —	522
24:17–19 —	246	47:1 —	515

Ibn Ezra, Abraham — "Commentary to the Torah" —

Gen. 2:17 — p. 26°		Gen.	
4:23 —	57°, 58*	24:12 —	239
9:5 —	79, 80	37:15 —	399°
18:26 —	183	37:16 —	399°
22:1 —	189	40:8 —	450*
23:19 —	208	48:7 —	539
24:4 —	220°		

Moshe ben Maimon (Rambam) — "Mishneh Torah" —
Hilkhot Teshuva — pp. 9, 174, 268, 297°, 460
Hilkhot Rotzeah — p. 83*
Hilkhot Avodah Zarah — pp. 109, 110, 111, 297*, 224
Hilkhot Melakhim — p. 387*
"Moreh Nevukhim" — pp. 18, 26*, 83*, 188, 189, 294, 301°, 302°, 476, 497, 498
Introduction to chapter Helek — p. 96
Mikhtav leger tzedek — p. 216
Sefer Hamitzvot — p. 37*
Moshe ben Nahman (Ramban) —

608

SUBJECT INDEX

Abaye — 427

Abel — name as a symbol of vanity — 20; his intellectual superiority — 20; his conduct of life — 21.

Abner — 422

Abraham — his compassion — 61; his acknowledgmeñt of the one God and Creator — 110f; miracle wrought for him — 110; first revelation characterized by particularism and universalism — 111f; his spiritual withdrawal — 113; as dispenser of blessings — 114, 118; justification for election of — 117f; as observer of Torah — 118; early accomplishments omitted by Torah — 118f; spiritual world compared with that of Lot — 125f, 181; his faith compared with Melchizedek — 132ff; his use of the Tetragrammaton — 134; as partner of the Creator — 134; reasons for his fears as advanced by the Midrash — 136ff; his spiritual excellence — 152; his relationship to Sarah — 154; honoured by God's presence — 160; his hospitality — 162; motivation for Abraham's chosenness — 167f; his compassion — 181; his intercession on behalf of Sodom — 183; nature of his trial — 188ff; his inner struggles during trial — 194ff; his absolute freedom of choice — 202; as distinguished from martyrs of Israel — 202, 203; as prince — 209f; acceptance of humiliation — 210; reason for his prohibition against inter-marriage with Canaanites — 215ff; proselytization efforts amongst his family questioned — 215f; as the Ivri — 220; crowns God over heaven and earth — 229; his old age contrasted with David's — 250; his preoccupation with spreading the knowledge of God — 259.

Abravanel — his negative views towards civilization in the light of his experiences as statesman — 21f.

Achish — involves David in a dilemma — 362.

Ada and Zillah — 57.

Adam —as prototype of Mankind — 28; his offence — 54; his punishment — 34, 36; his remorse and conscience — 34f, 48; nature of his hiding place — 54f.

Adultery — 7f, 421.

Acha R. — 231, 354.

Ahiyah the Shilonite — 349.

Aibu R. — 308.

Akiba R. — his martyrdom — 202.

Alexandri R. 335.

Amida — 134.

Ammon and Moab — their crime — 132; Israel bidden not to fight against — 217.

Amaziah — 449.

Aner and Eshkol — 215.

Angels — 268, 276; as guardians of Jacob and his descendants — 300, 301; angel of Esau — 367f; as princes of the nations — 299, 368; conversation of angels with Joseph — 396.

Anger — of Jacob and Moses — 341; of the Almighty — 341; useful in moderation — 545.

Animals — as food for Noah's descendants — 76; reasons for dispensation to eat — 76f.

Antiochus — 149.

Antoninus — friendship with Judah Hanassi — 347, 348, 376.

Aphes R. — 348.

Aram Naharaim — inhabitants as idolators — 215; Jacob's journey to — 311.

Ark — reason for Divine command to build — 70, 71; Philistines take captive — 240, 241.

Avimelech — 260ff; recognizes God — 411.

Azariah R. — 116.

Babylon — 149, 511.

Balaam — 47, 242, 349.

Bathsheba — her report of Adonijah's rebellion — 251.

Beauty — attitude towards physical — 229.

Beersheba — 345.

Benjamin — 467.

Berachiah — 281.

Bethel — 268.

Bethlehem — 540.

Biblical literature — repetition in — 15; identity of expressions — 120; in contrast to Greek style of writing — 196ff; narrative artistry of — 464.

"Binding of Isaac" — as central theme of Judaism — 201; evaluations of act — 202ff; as a lesson for the elevation of mankind — 204, 205.

Blessing — of Isaac — 272f.; of Jacob — 268, 364f.; marriage as a — 11; of Jacob's adversaries — 370, 371; blessing of Jacob contrasted with that of Esau — 277; to Patriarchs — 112f.; of Abraham corresponding to fivefold abundance of light created on 1st day — 114.

Boaz — 167.

Brotherhood — dictated by self-interest — 419f.

Buildings — as a means of perpetuating oneself — 93, 103.

Haman — 274, 281, 282, 284.

Hamor — father of Shechem — 208, 381ff; suggested alliance of friendship with Jacob analysed — 381ff; intentions towards Dinah — 386.

Ham — 222.

Hammurabi Code — 154.

Hasmoneans — reasons for overthrow — 351.

Hate — nature of — 432.

Heathen nations — their future — 147.

Hebrew negative — 10f.

Hebrew slave — 420; humiliation of — 524.

Hebron — vale of — 394, 499; as a figurative expression for Abraham — 395.

Hezekiah — 47.

Hillul Hashem — 544.

Hineni (Heb.) — "Here-I-am" — as indicating a moral position — 197; as expression of humility and readiness — 434f, 477, 482.

Hittite Code — 213.

Hiyyah bar Abba — 370.

Hiyyah bar Hanina — 144.

Holocaust — 376.

Homer — 196.

Honour of parents — brother included in command — 358.

Hospitality — importance of — 161f; Abraham's example of — 162; takes precedence over spiritual enjoyment — 162; of Rebecca — 225.

Human initiative — in praise of — 360, 361, 372; precedes reliance on God — 363.

Huna R. — 309, 346, 354.

Hushim — son of Dan — 491.

Idolatry — early beginnings of — 97; growth of — 109ff; characteristics of — 204; as a symbol of mediator between man and God — 294, 295.

Inclination — good and evil — 18.

Individual — responsibility to society and the world — 175

Isaac — his special purpose — 166; accused by Avimelech — 261; his reasons for blessing Esau — 275ff; his incapability of understanding falsehood explained — 275, 276; nature of his blessings as conferred to Jacob and Esau — 277; designs against — 282.

Isaac R. — 95, 134, 336, 533, 558.

Ishbosheth — 422.

Ishmael R. — blesses the Almighty — 115; school of — 150, 569.

Ishmaelites — their part in the sale of Joseph to Egypt — 400, 401.

Israel — its eternity despite persecution — 146f, 147; its exile — 147, 369; loyalty to God — 147; future of enemies — 147; in the Messianic age — 147; vicissitudes of — 149; its prayers accepted by God

a prophetic figure — 447f; his conduct towards brothers explained — 457ff; puts brothers to test — 463ff; Joseph's brothers as true penitents — 467, 468; his Midrashic dialogue with Judah — 490ff; his efforts to ensure Israel's preservation through segregation — 516ff; his austerity programme — 520ff; accused of ignoring brothers after his father's death — 557.

Jonathan R. — 119, 308, 348.

Joshua of Sakhnin — 39

Judah — 147, 404; his address to Joseph analysed — 483ff; his resort to psychological and rhetorical devices — 483ff; Midrashic dialogue with Joseph — 490ff.

Judah ben Baba — his generation of persecution — 370.

Judah Hanassi — his display of diplomacy — 34, 348; his friendship with Antoninus — 347, 376.

Kazars — king of — 116.

Kibbutz Ein Hanetziv — 517.

Kindness — as most important of moral qualities — 229.

King of Shalem — 136.

King of Sodom — his cunning and wickedness — 131, 132.

Krilov — 349.

Koneh — (Heb.) — interpretation of — 133.

Laban — as heathen — 246f; his allusion of Esau's complaint — 267; his welcome of Eliezer and Jacob suspect — 318; places responsibility for his deeds elsewhere — 327.

Labour — Rabbinic attitude towards — 21f, 95; division of — 11.

La Fontaine — 349.

Land of Israel — as eternal possession — 149, 537f; bond of Jewish people with — 207f; pre-eminence of — 208; as source of Israel's preservation — 507.

Leah — deceives Jacob — 265; buried in Machpelah — 539.

Lema'an (Heb.). — explanation of connotation — 168, 188.

Lemech — nature of his transgression — 54ff, 57; his song — 54ff.

Levi bar Hama — 119.

Levi R. — 137, 282, 452, 557.

Life — as a gift of God — 81.

Lot — reasons for his accompanying Abraham — 121; his return from Egypt compared with original journey from Haran — 122; causes of his separation from Abraham — 124ff; symbolism of his separation — 176; prostitution of his daughters condemned by Rabbis — 176; mocked by sons-in-law — 177.

Love — nature of — 386.

Lovers of Zion — 517.

Majestic plural — 8, 326.

Man — special creation of — 1, 7; pre-eminence and uniqueness of —

Moses — rebuked for questioning God's ways — 211f; his choice — 117, 129.

Mt. Zion — 377.

Murder — its root causes — 39; prohibition after flood — 79ff; punishment of murderer — 81; justification for punishment — 81f; through an agent — 83; Abraham's fear that he had killed the innocent — 137f; Jacob's fear that he might do likewise — 356.

Naboth — 212.

Nachor and Bethuel — as idolators — 215.

Naomi — 167.

Naphtali — 491.

Nathan — his report of Adonijah's rebellion — 254.

Nathan R. — 378.

Nations — their rise and fall — 299.

Nebuchadnezzar — 498.

Nebuzaradan — 540.

Negev — 257.

Neilah prayer — 70.

New Moon — 145.

Nimrod — his subterfuges to gain ascendancy over his people — 92, 98; as the first monarch — 92f; as tyrant — 92.

Nineveh — repentence of — 310, 353.

Nishmat — 139.

No — 368.

Noachian laws — 84, 260, 263.

Noah — his righteousness as compared to Abraham's — 59ff, 181; in relation to his generation — 59f; limited in his horizons — 61; his inferior spiritual powers — 62; his descendants' domination over the animal kingdom — 76; protected by God — 73.

Og — 291; Moses' fear of — 353.

Ornan — 208.

Padan — 539

Pale of Settlement — 262.

Patriarchs — their experience repeated by descendants — 257f, 261, 262, 351, 372, 379, 508; their shortcomings not concealed by Sages — 331; title reserved for Abraham, Isaac, Jacob alone — 430.

Peace — 74, 378.

Pelotit — 173.

Pharaoh — his attempts to immortalize himself — 93; as prototype — 284, 357f, 368; analysis of dreams — 441; defers to God — 442; convinced of the truth of Joseph's interpretation — 451ff; unconvinced by that of magicians — 452, 453.

Philistines — their use of oracles — 240; reasons for stopping up wells of Abraham — 258ff.

621

sale of Joseph — 403, 405f; his repentance — 404, 409, 467.
Reward — 190, 191.
Righteous — no guarantee for righteous in this world — 354, 359.
Righteousness — as the "Way of the Lord" — 166; demanded of God by Abraham — 184, 186f.
Romans — slaves of — 413.
Sacrifice — attitudes towards — 41f, 148; as a symbol — 145; its merit — 144f; types of — 148; difference between true sacrifice and that of the idolator — 333.
Samson — 427; his tragic end envisioned by Jacob — 549ff.
Samuel — bidden to take precautions — 361; 415, 450.
Sanctification of God's name — 370.
Sarah — her righteous character — 154; Ramban's and Radak's condemnation of her behaviour towards Hagar — 156.
Satan — accosts Abraham — 195; significance of his dialogue with Abraham — 196; questions Abraham's chosenness — 201f, 203; admits to his faithfulness — 211.
Saul — 82.
Secluded life — not for righteous — 186.
Second Tithe — 16.
Seir — 375, 377, 378.
Sennacherib — 269, 281, 525.
Serpent — as seducer — 29ff; as symbol of evil inclination — 29ff; his wiles and insinuations — 32.
Seth — as realizing the true ideal — 21.
Sexual corruption — 69, 97f.
Shechem — 388, 398, 467.
Shem — 110.
Shema — 502.
Shimei b. Gera — 498.
Shimon b. Eliezer — 373, 375.
Shimon ben Gamliel — 285, 565.
Shimon b. Yohai — 36, 52.
Shimon b. Yosina — 303.
Shinar — 107.
Shushan — 271.
Sihon — 291.
Simeon and Levi — as men of zeal and courage — 545; their massacre of Shechem — 138, 380ff.
Simeon — 467.
Simon R. 64f, 97, 558.
Sin — futility of denying sin — 48, 49; its dangers and man's power to conquer it — 42, 43; of the generation of the flood — 69; of the generation of Babel — 93f; of idolatry, promiscuity and blood-

623

nature — 25; consequences of eating thereof — 25, 26, 34, 36.
Trial — nature and object of Abraham's — 188ff; ten trials of Abraham — 210.
Truth — speaks for itself — 427; deviating from the truth in the interests of peace — 563ff.
Tzitzit — 33, 87.
Universalism — 112.
Vav conversive — 134f; 320, 326.
Vegetarianism — as an ideal of the Torah — 77; as special command — 81.
Violence and robbery — as main reason for deluge — 69ff; as sin of Lot — 126; rabbinic attitude to — 129.
Vision of Abraham — 144f; symbolic interpretations of — 145, 146f, 148, 149f, 151.
Visiting the sick — God fulfills Mitzvah of — 159.
Vocal points — 373f.
Volozhin yeshiva — 376.
Vows — attitude of sages towards — 156f, 533; Jacob's vow — 306; Joseph's reluctance to make a vow in contrast to Eliezer's readiness — 532, 533.
War — Rabbinic attitude towards — 4f; causes of — 39; invention of sophisticated weapons of — 57, 76; Abraham's concern with the contingency of — 140; the Divine attitude to — 140f.
Water — importance of — 258.
Wells of Abraham — symbolic significance of — 259; as means of fertilization of desert — 260.
Wisdom — in antiquity — 448.
Woman — as helpmeet for man — 13; endowed with greater understanding — 15; having same purpose as man — 334; as childbearer — 334; frivolity of — 421.
World to Come — Abraham's fear that he would be deprived of — 137, 139.
Yada (Heb.) — Explanation of connotation — 167, 171.
Yannai R. — his experiences with the Romans — 372f.
Yehoshua R. — 452.
Yehuda R. — 61, 90, 181.
Yehuda ben Ami — 39.
Yohanan R. 69, 201, 493.
Yohanan ben Zakai — 349.
Yom Kippur — 145, 353.
Yose ben Zimra — 201, 202.
Yudan bar Simon — 208, 285.
Zealotry — of Simeon and Levi — 542ff; of Phineas — 544; useful in moderation — 545.
Zealots — actions criticised — 348f.
Zedekiah — 419.
Zelem (Heb.) — 2.
Zerubabel — 460.